S0-BFE-032

THE VICTORIA HISTORY
OF THE
COUNTIES OF ENGLAND

A HISTORY OF
MIDDLESEX

VOLUME X

THE VICTORIA HISTORY
OF THE
COUNTIES OF ENGLAND

EDITED BY C. R. J. CURRIE

THE UNIVERSITY OF LONDON

INSTITUTE OF

HISTORICAL RESEARCH

Oxford University Press, Walton Street, Oxford OX2 6DP
Oxford New York
Athens Auckland Bangkok Bombay
Calcutta Cape Town Dar es Salaam Delhi
Florence Hong Kong Istanbul Karachi
Kuala Lumpur Madras Madrid Melbourne
Mexico City Nairobi Paris Singapore
Taipei Tokyo Toronto

and associated companies in
Berlin Ibadan

Oxford is a trade mark of Oxford University Press

Published in the United States
by Oxford University Press Inc., New York

All rights reserved. No part of this publication may be reproduced,
stored in a retrieval system, or transmitted, in any form or by any means,
without the prior permission of Oxford University Press.
Within the UK, exceptions are allowed in respect of any fair dealing for the
purpose of research or private study, or criticism or review, as permitted
under the Copyright, Designs and Patents Act, 1988, or in the case of
reprographic reproduction in accordance with the terms of the licences
issued by the Copyright Licensing Agency. Enquiries concerning
reproduction outside these terms and in other countries should be
sent to the Rights Department, Oxford University Press,
at the address above

© University of London 1995

British Library Cataloguing in Publication Data
A catalogue record for this book is available
from the British Library

ISBN 0 19 722782 1

Typeset at the University of London Computer Centre
Printed by H Charlesworth & Co Ltd
Huddersfield, England

INSCRIBED TO THE

MEMORY OF HER LATE MAJESTY

QUEEN VICTORIA

WHO GRACIOUSLY GAVE THE TITLE TO

AND ACCEPTED THE DEDICATION

OF THIS HISTORY

A HISTORY OF THE COUNTY OF
MIDDLESEX

EDITED BY T. F. T. BAKER

VOLUME X

HACKNEY PARISH

PUBLISHED FOR

THE INSTITUTE OF HISTORICAL RESEARCH

BY

OXFORD UNIVERSITY PRESS

1995

CONTENTS OF VOLUME TEN

LIST OF ILLUSTRATIONS

For permission to reproduce material in their possession, thanks are rendered to: City of London, Guildhall Library; the Greater London Record Office (Photograph Collection and Print Collection); London Borough of Hackney, Hackney Archives Department (H.A.D.); the Museum of London; the National Monuments Record (N.M.R.) of the Royal Commission on Historical Monuments (England). The coats of arms were drawn by Pamela Studd.

Plates between pages 90 and 91

LIST OF ILLUSTRATIONS

LIST OF ILLUSTRATIONS

LIST OF MAPS

The maps on pages 1, 2, 6, 12, and 76 were drawn by K. J. Wass of the Department of Geography, University College, London, from drafts prepared by T. F. T. Baker

EDITORIAL NOTE

The present volume is the third to have been compiled for the Committee formed in 1979 to complete the Middlesex History.

The Committee was at first financed according to their rateable value by the seven London Boroughs whose areas make up what may be called inner Middlesex and, until its abolition in 1986, by the Greater London Council. The Local Government Finance Act, 1988, abolished rates from 1990. A consequent move towards payments of equal sevenths for 1990–1 was assisted by a compromise formula for the poorer boroughs and by an extra sum from Westminster. For 1991–2, however, equal shares were not fully paid by two boroughs and for 1992–3 two more made no payment; for 1993–4 one default was partly offset by contributions from Bethnal Green and Stepney neighbourhood councils. Increased support from two boroughs, and generous donations from charities and individuals, have enabled work to continue at a reduced pace. Contributors since 1990–1 include the Corporation of London, the Marc Fitch Fund, the British Academy, the Pilgrim Trust, the Goldsmiths' Company, the Mercers' Company, Camden History Society, and the late Mr. S. E. Piesse, as well as others giving privately. All are warmly thanked for their help.

The University of London gratefully acknowledges the help of the Middlesex V.C.H. Committee, which has continued under the chairmanship of Dr. David Avery, and the generosity of the London Boroughs of Westminster and of Kensington and Chelsea, which have raised their payments, of Islington, which has maintained its full contribution, and of Hackney.

As a result of the reductions in funding the County Editor (Mr. T.F.T. Baker) and the Assistant Editor (Miss D.K. Bolton) retired early in 1992 and were re-employed part-time, while the other Assistant Editor (Dr. P.E.C. Croot) was temporarily seconded elsewhere. She has since continued as full-time Assistant Editor.

The structure and aims of the Victoria History as a whole are set out in the *General Introduction* (1970). The contents of the first seven volumes of the Middlesex History are listed and indexed in outline in a booklet, *The Middlesex Victoria County History Council, 1955–84*, which also describes the work of the precursor of the present Middlesex Victoria County History Committee.

Those who have provided information for the volume or commented on parts of the text are named in the footnotes, and they are sincerely thanked for their help. Particular mention may be made here of the valuable contributions of Mr. R. M. Robbins, C.B.E., who helped with the section on communications, and of Isobel Watson and Mr. D. Mander, who separately read the whole text of the volume.

MIDDLESEX
VICTORIA COUNTY HISTORY
COMMITTEE

As at 31 December 1994

Chairman

DAVID AVERY, ESQ

Representatives of the following London Boroughs

Hackney   Islington
Kensington and Chelsea   Westminster

Representatives of

The Greater London Record Office
The London and Middlesex Archaeological Society
Institute of Historical Research

Co-opted Members

MISS HERMIONE HOBHOUSE, M.B.E.

Hon. Secretary: C. J. KOSTER, ESQ.

Hon. Treasurer: K. A. BAILEY, ESQ.

CLASSES OF DOCUMENTS
IN THE PUBLIC RECORD OFFICE

USED IN THIS VOLUME

WITH THEIR CLASS NUMBERS

Chancery

	Proceedings	
C 1	Early	
C 5	Six Clerks Series, Bridges	
C 7		Hamilton
C 8		Mitford
C 54	Close Rolls	
C 78	Decree Rolls	

Court of Common Pleas
    CP 25(1)   Feet of Fines, Series I
    CP 25(2)   Series II

Exchequer, King's Remembrancer
    E 179   Subsidy Rolls, etc.

Ministry of Education
    ED 4   Transfer Files, London
    ED 7   Public Elementary Schools, Pre-
                  liminary Statements
    ED 14   London General Files

Registry of Friendly Societies
    FS 2   Indexes to Rules and Amend-
                  ments, Series I

Home Office
    HO 129   Ecclesiastical Returns

Justices Itinerant, Assize and Gaol Delivery
      Justices, etc
    JUST 3   Gaol Delivery Rolls

Ministry of Agriculture, Fisheries, and Food
    MAF 68   Agricultural Returns: Parish
                  Summaries

Prerogative Court of Canterbury
    PROB 11   Registered Copies of Wills proved
                    in P.C.C.

Privy Council Office
    PC 2   Registers

Special Collections
    SC 2   Court Rolls
    SC 6   Ministers' and Receivers' Ac-
                  counts

Court of Star Chamber
    STAC 2   Proceedings, Hen. VIII
    STAC 7   Eliz. I

Court of Wards and Liveries
    WARD 5   Feodaries' Surveys

SELECT LIST OF
CLASSES OF DOCUMENTS IN THE
GREATER LONDON RECORD OFFICE
USED IN THIS VOLUME
WITH THEIR CLASS NUMBERS

Deposited Records

Acc. 1063	Monro family
Acc. 1876	London Charterhouse
AR/CB	London County Council Architect's Department, Council Buildings, records
AR/TP	London County Council Architect's Department, Town Planning, records
E/BVR	De Beauvoir Estate, records
EO/PS	London County Council Education Officer's Department, records
Ha/BG	Hackney Board of Guardians, records
H1/ST	St. Thomas's Hospital, records
M79/G	Hackney Manorial Records, Grumbolds
M79/KH	Hackney Manorial Records, Kingshold
M79/LH	Hackney Manorial Records, Lordshold
M79/TA	Hackney Manorial Records, Tyssen-Amherst Estate
M93	Stepney and Hackney Manorial Records
MAB	Metropolitan Asylums Board, records
MBW	Metropolitan Board of Works, records
MC/R	Clerk of the Peace, Registers
MR/B/C	District Surveyors' Certificates
MR/LV	Licensed Victuallers' Lists
MR/TH	Hearth Tax Assessments
P79	Parish Records, Hackney
SBL	School Board for London, records

NOTE ON ABBREVIATIONS

Among the abbreviations and short titles used the following may require elucidation, in addition to those noted in the Victoria History's *Handbook for Editors and Authors (1970)*:

Archit. of Lond.	E. Jones and C. Woodward, *A Guide to the Architecture of London* (1983)
B.L.	British Library (used in references to documents transferred from the British Museum)
Bacon, *Atlas of Lond.* (1910)	*New Large-Scale Atlas of London and Suburbs*, ed. G. W. Bacon (1910)
Bagust, 'Hackney'	Florence Bagust, 15 vols. of notes and cuttings (*c.* 1913–29) in H.A.D. (D/F/BAG) and other notes in H.A.D.
Beaven, *Aldermen*	A. Beaven, *The Aldermen of the City of London temp. Henry III to 1912* (2 vols. 1908–13)
Booth, *Life and Labour*	C. Booth, *Life and Labour of the People in London* (17 vols. revised edn. 1902–3). Survey begun 1886
Booth's Map (1889)	*Charles Booth's Descriptive Map of London Poverty, 1889* (London Topographical Society 1984)
Calamy Revised	*Calamy Revised*, ed. A. G. Matthews (1934)
Cal. Mdx. Sess. Bks.	Calendar of Sessions Books, 1638–1752, at G.L.R.O.
Clarke, *Hackney*	B. Clarke, *Glimpses of Ancient Hackney and Stoke Newington*, intro. D. Mander (1986)
Clarke, *Lond. Chs.*	B. F. L. Clarke, *Parish Churches of London* (1966)
Colvin, *Brit. Architects*	H. Colvin, *Biographical Dictionary of British Architects, 1600–1840* (1978)
Cruchley's New Plan (1829)	[G. F.] *Cruchley's New Plan of London and Its Environs* (1829)
Freshfield, *Communion Plate*	E. Freshfield, *Communion Plate of the Parish Churches in the County of London* (1895)
Ft. of F. Lond. & Mdx.	*Calendar to the Feet of Fines for London and Middlesex*, ed. W. J. Hardy and W. Page (2 vols. 1892–3)
G.L.C.	Greater London Council
G.L.R.O.	Greater London Record Office. Contains the collection of the former Middlesex Record Office (M.R.O.)
Green's Hackney Dir	*R. Green & Co.'s Hackney and North-East London Directory* (1869–70)
Guildhall MSS.	City of London, Guildhall Library. Contains registers of wills of the commissary court of London (London division) (MS. 9171), bishops' registers (MS. 9531), diocesan administrative records (MSS. 9532–9560), and registers of nonconformist meeting houses (MS. 9580)
Gunnis, *Sculptors*	R. Gunnis, *Dictionary of British Sculptors, 1660–1851* (1951)
H.A.D.	London Borough of Hackney, Hackney Archives Department
H.B.M.C. Lond.	Historic Buildings and Monuments Commission, London Division
Hackney and Stoke Newington Past	I. Watson, *Hackney and Stoke Newington Past* (1990)
Hackney Camera	*A Hackney Camera, 1883–1918* (Hackney Workers Educational Association and Hackney Libraries, 1974)
Hackney Dir.	*Directory of Hackney*, pub. Caleb Turner (1845 and later edns.)
Hackney Photos. i	D. Mander, *The London Borough of Hackney in Old Photographs, before 1914* (1989)
Hackney Photos. ii	D. Mander and J. Golden, *The London Borough of Hackney in Old Photographs, 1890–1960* (1991)
Hennessy, *Novum Rep.*	G. Hennessy, *Novum Repertorium Ecclesiasticum Parochiale Londinense* (1894)
Hist. Lond. Transport	T. C. Barker and M. Robbins, *History of London Transport* (2 vols. 1975)
Hist. Mon. Com. E. Lond.	Royal Commission on Historical Monuments of England, *Inventory of the Historical Monuments in London*, v, *East London* (H.M.S.O. 1930)

NOTE ON ABBREVIATIONS

Insurance Plans	Insurance plans of London, mostly 40 ft. to 1 in., pub. by Chas. E. Goad Ltd. Plans and revisions from 1891 to 1961 for parts of Hackney in H.A.D.
L.B.	London Borough
L.C.C.	London County Council
L.C.C. *Lond. Statistics*	L.C.C. *London Statistics* (26 vols. 1905–6 to 1936–8, beginning with vol. xvi). Followed by ibid. new series (2 vols. 1945–54 and 1947–56) and by further new series from 1957
L.C.C. *Names of Streets*	L.C.C. *List of the Streets and Places within the County of London* (1901 and later edns.)
List of Bldgs.	Department of the Environment, *21st List of Buildings of Historic Interest* (1975 and amendments to 1991)
Lost Hackney	E. Robinson, *Lost Hackney* (Hackney Society 1989)
Lysons, *Environs*	D. Lysons, *The Environs of London* (4 vols. 1792–6 and Supplement 1811)
M.B.	Metropolitan Borough
M.B.W.	Metropolitan Board of Works
M.L.R.	Middlesex Land Registry. The enrolments, indexes, and registers are at G.L.R.O.
Mackeson's Guide	C. Mackeson, *A Guide to the Churches of London and Its Suburbs* (1866 and later edns.)
Mdx. County Rec.	*Middlesex County Records* [1550–1688], ed. J. C. Jeaffreson (4 vols. 1886–92)
Mdx. County Rec. Sess. Bks. 1689–1709	*Middlesex County Records, Calendar of the Sessions Books 1689–1709*, ed. W. J. Hardy (1905)
Mdx. Sess. Rec.	*Calendar to the Sessions Records* [1612–18], ed. W. le Hardy (4 vols. 1935–41)
Middleton, *View*	J. Middleton, *View of the Agriculture of Middlesex* (1798)
Mudie-Smith, *Rel. Life*	R. Mudie-Smith, *The Religious Life of London* (1904). Census taken 1903
N.M.R.	Royal Commission on Historical Monuments of England, National Monuments Record
New Lond. Life and Labour	H. Llewellyn Smith and others, *New Survey of London Life and Labour* (9 vols. 1930–5). Survey undertaken 1928
Newcourt, *Rep.*	R. Newcourt, *Repertorium Ecclesiasticum Parochiale Londinense* (2 vols. 1708–10)
Norden, *Spec. Brit.*	J. Norden, *Speculum Britanniae: Middlesex* (facsimile edn. 1971)
Old O.S. Map	Old Ordnance Survey Maps: the Godfrey edition (from 1983) (reduced facsimile reproductions of 1: 2,500 maps c. 1866–1914)
P.N. Mdx. (E.P.N.S.)	*Place-Names of Middlesex* (English Place-Name Society, vol. xviii, 1942)
Par. mins.	Minute book of Hackney parish meetings (1762–1824 in G.L.R.O.; 1824–35 in H.A.D.)
Pevsner, *Lond.* ii	N. Pevsner, *Buildings of England: London except the Cities of London and Westminster* (1952)
Rep. on Bridges in Mdx.	*Report of the Committee of Magistrates Appointed to make Enquiry respecting the Public Bridges in the County of Middlesex* (1826). Copy at G.L.R.O.
Rep. Com. Eccl. Revenues	*Report of the Commissioners Appointed to Inquire into the Ecclesiastical Revenues of England and Wales* [67], H.C. (1835), xxii
Rep. Cttee. on Returns by Overseers, 1776	*Report of the Select Committee on Returns by Overseers of the Poor, 1776* H.C., 1st ser. ix
Robinson, *Hackney*	W. Robinson, *The History and Antiquities of the Parish of Hackney* (2 vols. 1842–3)
Rocque, *Map of Lond.* (1741–5)	J. Rocque, *Exact survey of the cities of London, Westminster, and the borough of Southwark, and the country near ten miles around* (1746, facsimile edn. 1971)
Root's Map (1741)	R. Root, 'A Plan of Hackney Church and Churchyard' (1741) in H.A.D.
S.J.C.F.	Sir John Cass Foundation
Stanford, *Map of Lond.* (1862–5)	*Stanford's Library Map of London and Its Suburbs* (1862 edn. with additions to 1865)
Starling's Map (1831)	T. Starling, *Plan of the Parish of Hackney* (1831, H.A.D. facsimile edn. 1985)

Stow, *Survey* (1720)	J. Stow, *Survey of London*, ed. J. Strype, 2 vols. (1720)
T.L.M.A.S.	Transactions of the London and Middlesex Archaeological Society (1856 to date). Consecutive numbers are used for the whole series, although vols. vii–xvii (1905–54) appeared as N.S. i–xi
Terrier	*The Terrier* (*The Hackney Terrier* from 1991). Nos. 1–9 (1985–7) newsletter of H.A.D.; nos. 10 to date newsletter of Friends of Hackney Archives
Thomas, 'Hackney'	J. Thomas, 'History and Antiquities of Hackney' (H.A.D., TS. from MS. of 1832)
Tower to Tower Block	*From Tower to Tower Block: the Buildings of Hackney* (Hackney Society 1980)
Vestry mins.	Minutes of Hackney vestry in G.L.R.O. (1613–1771, 1807–83) and H.A.D. (1771–1807 and transcripts in Tyssen collection 1581–1771)
Walford, *Lond.*	E. Walford, *Old and New London*, v (*c.* 1878)
Walker Revised	*Walker Revised*, ed. A. G. Matthews (1948)
Watson, *Gentlemen*	I. Watson, *Gentlemen in the Building Line. The Development of South Hackney* (1989)

OSSULSTONE HUNDRED

(*continued*)

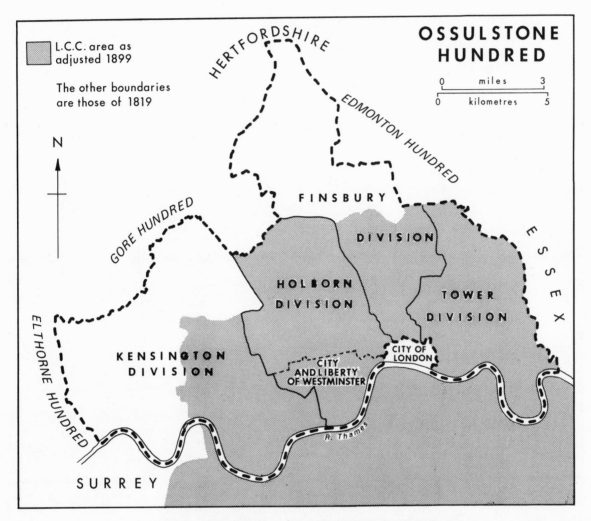

TOWER DIVISION
HACKNEY

HACKNEY,[1] a favourite residence of wealthy Londoners from the Middle Ages until the 19th century, was the largest Middlesex parish to be included in the county of London in 1889. Near the south-western corner, the bridge bearing Kingsland Road across the Regent's canal was *c*. 1.8 km. north of the bar of London at Bishopsgate. From the bridge the road, a section of Ermine Street and under various names, led almost due north for 3.8 km. to enter Tottenham at Stamford Hill. For part of its length, as Stoke Newington Road and High Street, it formed Hackney's western boundary, whence the parish stretched eastward for *c*. 3.6 km. to Temple Mills on the river Lea. Besides Hackney village, the parish included part of Kingsland, Dalston, Shacklewell, Stamford Hill, Upper and Lower

---

[1] The article was written in 1989–92. Para. based on *Starling's Map* (1831); O.S. Maps 1/2,500, Lond. V, VI, X, XI, XVIII, XIX, XXVII, XXVIII (1870–6 edn.); ibid. 1/10,000, TQ 38 NW., NE., SW., SE. (1982–8 edn.).

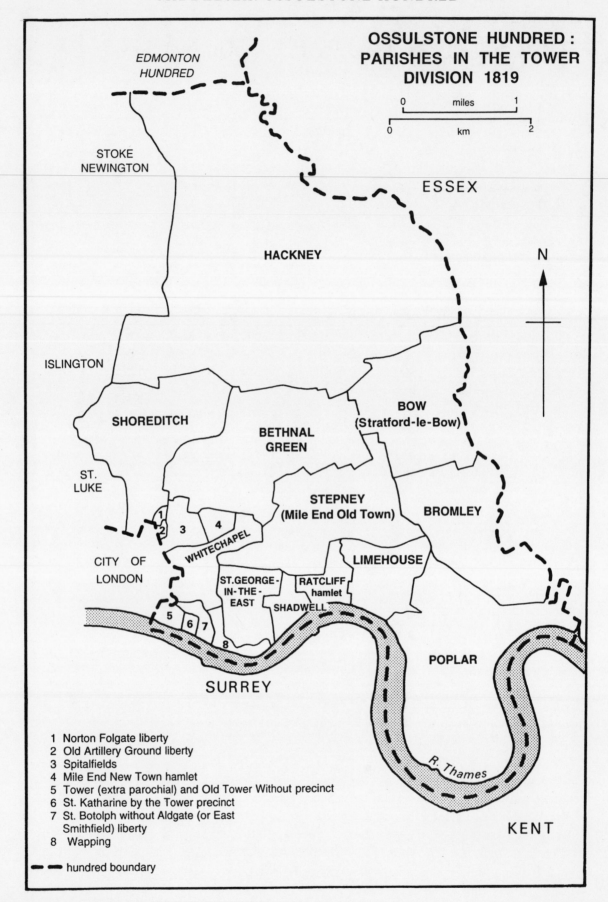

**OSSULSTONE HUNDRED :
PARISHES IN THE TOWER
DIVISION 1819**

EDMONTON
HUNDRED

ESSEX

STOKE
NEWINGTON

HACKNEY

N

ISLINGTON

BOW
(Stratford-le-Bow)

SHOREDITCH

BETHNAL
GREEN

ST.
LUKE

STEPNEY
(Mile End Old Town)

BROMLEY

1
2
3
4

WHITECHAPEL

CITY OF
LONDON

LIMEHOUSE

ST.GEORGE-
IN-THE-
EAST

RATCLIFF
hamlet

SHADWELL

5 6 7
8

POPLAR

SURREY

R. Thames

KENT

1 Norton Folgate liberty
2 Old Artillery Ground liberty
3 Spitalfields
4 Mile End New Town hamlet
5 Tower (extra parochial) and Old Tower Without precinct
6 St. Katharine by the Tower precinct
7 St. Botolph without Aldgate (or East
   Smithfield) liberty
8 Wapping

━ ━ ━ hundred boundary

Clapton, Homerton, Hackney Wick, and part of Stoke Newington village along the high road.

The area of the parish was estimated with some accuracy at *c.* 3,300 a. in 1765 and 1831.[2] A south-westerly projection beyond Kingsland Road had sometimes been described as in the northern part of Hoxton, a manor of Shoreditch, before Hackney and Shoreditch reached agreement in 1697. After building had obscured the field lines, it was confirmed in 1843 that the boundary followed Branch Place and De Beauvoir Crescent across the canal; its course farther east was also established.[3] Other boundary disputes had arisen with Islington in 1655, 1660, and 1666–7, the last leading to a lawsuit about grazing rights behind Kingsland chapel,[4] with Bethnal Green in 1732 and again in 1779, when a perambulation was ordered, with Bow in 1806, and with Stoke Newington in 1822.[5] In 1690 the bounds had not been perambulated for five years.[6] Although most of the eastern boundary followed the original course of the Lea, *c.* 65 a. beyond the river lay in Hackney: in the extreme north-east opposite the foot of Spring Hill, at Lea bridge, and at Temple Mills where the boundary was a mill stream, presumably of medieval origin and later a waterworks river.[7]

Under the Metropolis Management Act, 1855, Hackney became a civil metropolitan parish within the area of the M.B.W. Under the London Government Act, 1899, it became a metropolitan borough of 3,288 a. (1,330.7 ha.),[8] whereupon the boundaries with boroughs to the west and south were adjusted. The main changes were that Hackney gained houses along the east side of Bethune Road from Stoke Newington and the south side of Ball's Pond Road from Islington, that it surrendered the west side of Southgate Road to Islington, that the Shoreditch boundary was rationalized to run along the canal south of De Beauvoir Town and farther east to follow Albion Road (from 1939 Albion Drive) and Brougham Road, and that the straight boundary with Bethnal Green was made to follow the curve of Gore Road.[9] A further change was the transfer to Tottenham from 1908 of houses on the south side of Bailey's Lane (later Craven Park Road) in exchange for some on the north side of Vartry Road.[10] From 1965 the metropolitan borough became part of the London Borough of Hackney, along with Stoke Newington and Shoreditch.[11]

Alluvium lies along the Lea and beneath Hackney marsh. It is bordered on the west by a narrow strip of London Clay, which broadens out along the Tottenham boundary, covering the north- western tip of the parish and extending south in a shorter strip beneath the G.E.R.'s Enfield branch line to a little beyond Hackney Downs. Brickearth lies beneath Stamford Hill and Clapton common, between the tongues of clay, and farther south intrudes from the west beneath Stoke Newington High Street. The centre and the south-western part of the parish lie on Taplow Gravel, stretching from Lower Clapton and Hackney village along Mare Street and Kingsland Road. Victoria Park and the area around Well Street common are on flood-plain gravel.[12]

The land rises westward from the Lea, most steeply towards the north-west to

[2] Robinson, *Hackney*, i. 6; *Census*, 1831.
[3] Robinson, *Hackney*, i. 164–7; vestry mins. 6 Feb. 1697; H.A.D., P/J/P/70.
[4] Vestry mins. 19 Aug. 1655, 27 May 1660, 28 Oct. 1666, 20 Jan., 20 May 1667.
[5] Vestry mins. 13 May 1732, 6 Jan. 1806; par. mins. 29 Mar., 2 June 1779; 1 Feb. 1822.
[6] Vestry mins. 25 May 1690.
[7] Robinson, *Hackney*, i. 5; Old O.S. Maps Lond. 21, 31–2, 42 (1868 and later edns.).

[8] *Census*, 1901; below, local govt. (local govt. after 1837).
[9] H.A.D., J/V/C/2 (changes on O.S. Maps); *V.C.H. Mdx.* viii. 2, 139. Except where otherwise stated, modern changes of street names are from L.C.C. *Names of Streets* (1901 or later edns.).
[10] *Rep. of L.C.C.* (1906–7), 246; ibid. (1907–8), 263–4.
[11] Below, local govt. (local govt. after 1837).
[12] Geol. Surv. Map 1", drift, sheet 256 (1951 edn.); K. G. T. McDonnell, *Medieval Lond. Suburbs* (1978), 2, 11.

reach more than 30 m. above sea level around the top of Clapton common and Stamford Hill. The highest point on the road from London is at 33 m. near Portland Avenue. Thence the road falls steeply towards Tottenham, to 20 m. just beyond the boundary, but more gradually towards the south, to below 25 m. at Stoke Newington station, rising slightly along Stoke Newington Road but dipping to remain at below 20 m. south of Dalston junction. Upper Clapton is mainly above 25 m. and Lower Clapton, like Shacklewell, above 20 m. Hackney Downs lies at 20 m. but to the south and east most of the parish, drained by Hackney brook and minor streams through the gravel towards the Lea, is lower. Victoria Park lies below 15 m. and part of Hackney Wick below 10 m. There the almost imperceptible slope to the river contrasts with the abrupt descent farther north, from Upper Clapton: steep roads fall from nearly 25 m. to less than 10 m. at High Hill ferry and from more than 25 m. at the longer Spring Hill.[13]

The parish was crossed by Hackney brook.[14] In Hackney its upper stretch, described as Dalston brook in 1745[15] and 'the old brook' by 1831, ran along the north side of Stoke Newington common before turning southward to skirt the western side of Hackney Downs and then south-eastward across Dalston Lane to cross Mare Street a few yards south of Bohemia Place. Above Mare Street, immediately south of a garden behind the Mermaid, Hackney brook was joined by Pigwell or Pitwell brook, which flowed from Kingsland green and followed part of the line of the modern Graham Road.[16] From Mare Street Hackney brook runs north of Morning Lane, giving its name to the curving eastern section once called Water Lane, and the line of Wick Road to Hackney Wick, whence it passed southward to White Post Lane in Bow and so to the Hackney cut and the Lea. The well drained gravel of southern Hackney gave rise to unnamed streamlets, sometimes marked as common sewers and perhaps including a tributary of the brook along the line of Well Street. The long stretches of Hackney brook which remained open in 1857,[17] north-west and east of Hackney village, had been covered by the M.B.W. by 1861.[18]

As a much visited resort, Hackney in the 18th century was thought to have given rise to the term 'Hackney horse' and so to the Hackney coaches or chairs which plied for hire.[19] The place-name, however, was of pre-Conquest origin and unconnected with the occupation of hackneyman, recorded in 1308,[20] and the French horse called a *haquenée*.[21]

COMMUNICATIONS

Ermine Street,[22] the main artery from Roman London to Lincoln and the north, kept to the west side of the parish to avoid flooding from the Lea.[23] A Roman way to Great Dunmow (Essex) crossed the Lea and the later line of the Lea's Hackney cut near Pond Lane bridge. Its course, near which a sarcophagus was found at Lower Clapton,[24] presumably led north-eastward through Hackney from the Roman road through Bethnal Green, which ran by Old Ford to Colchester.

The section of Ermine Street through Hackney was a major road in the Middle Ages.[25] Triennial grants of pavage for repairing the highway between Hackney and Tottenham were made by the Crown in 1365, 1369, and 1373.[26] Before it

[13] O.S. Maps 1/10,000, TQ 38 NW., NE., SW., SE. (1982–8 edn.).
[14] Para. based on N. J. Barton, *Lost Rivers of Lond.* (1962), 48; H.A.D., V 15 (plan c. 1825); *Starling's Map* (1831).
[15] Rocque, *Map of Lond.* (1741–5), sheet 5.
[16] H.A.D., V 7; ibid. M 3513; below, plate 9.
[17] Ibid.; G. Grocott, *Hackney Fifty Years Ago* (1915), 8–9; *Metropolitan Drainage*, H.C. 233, p. 181 (1857 Sess. 2), xxxvi.
[18] Stanford, *Map of Lond.* (1862–5 edn.), sheets 3, 8; *Rep. of*

M.B.W. 1861, H.C. 11, p. 391 (1862), xlvii; below, pub. svces.
[19] W. Maitland, *Hist. Lond.* ii (1756), 1365–6; *Lond. and Its Environs Described*, iii (1761), 122.
[20] *Memorials of Lond.* ed. H. T. Riley (1868), 63; *Oxford Eng. Dict.* (1989), vi. 1003.
[21] *P.N. Mdx.* (E.P.N.S.), 105; Robinson, *Hackney*, i. 2.
[22] Para. based on I. D. Margary, *Rom. Rds. in Britain* (1967), 55–7, 194–5, 250.
[23] M. Rose, *East End of Lond.* (1951), 3–4.
[24] *V.C.H. Mdx.* i. 70.   [25] Ibid. v. 309.
[26] *Cal. Pat.* 1364–7, 183; 1367–70, 217; 1370–4, 336.

was turnpiked,[27] many private bequests were also made to maintain the high road,[28] which Defoe called 'the great north road'.[29] The southernmost section, to Kingsland green, was known by 1745 as Kingsland Road.[30] By the 1860s the northerly stretches to Stamford Hill had acquired their modern names, Kingsland High Street, Stoke Newington Road, and Stoke Newington High Street.[31]

Another main route led north[32] from Cambridge Heath along Mare Street, perhaps so called from the boundary (Middle English *mere*) with Stepney (later Bethnal Green) or from the existence of many ponds.[33] The northern end, roughly from the modern Reading Lane to where it divided into Dalston Lane and the road to Lower Clapton, formed the main street of Hackney village and was known as Church Street until 1868.[34] From Lower Clapton the route continued northward as Clapton Street and Hackney Lane along the line of Upper Clapton Road and Clapton Common to reach Stamford Hill. The lane from Dalston to Hackney was mentioned in 1553;[35] Clapton Street occurred in 1378 and 1581[36] and as the 'back road' from Stamford Hill to Hackney in 1722.[37] Roughly parallel with the southern stretch of Mare Street, a way known as Church Path in 1745 led northward from Shoreditch across London Fields, curving into Mare Street at the modern junction with Sylvester Road.[38]

From west to east across the parish the north–south routes were linked in 1745 by a track from Kingsland, part of it marked as Willow Walk south of the stream in 1831, by Dalston Lane, by a 'crossway' to Lower Clapton, roughly on the line of Downs Park Road, by a track to the north across Hackney Downs, and by a road from Stoke Newington common to Upper Clapton, called Dows (by 1831 Kates) Lane (later Northwold Road). Dalston Lane and the crossway were described in 1825 as the South and North Cross roads from Kingsland to Lower Clapton.[39] From Mare Street north-east towards Homerton ran Well Street, which had given its name to a field by 1443;[40] its course continued as Water Lane, later the east end of Money or Morning Lane, which linked Homerton and Church Street. A branch from Well Street led south-east to Grove Street, a hamlet around the modern Lauriston Road, and into Bethnal Green.

Roads towards the Lea in 1745 included one running north-east from Grove Street to Hackney Wick, called Grove Street Lane in 1831 and later built up as Victoria Park Road. Slightly to the north a route later marked by Cassland Road existed only as a track. Another route, called Wick Lane in 1831, ran south-south-eastward from the end of Homerton's high street, along the line of the modern Kenworthy Road. From Hackney Wick the lane headed north-eastward across the marsh along the line of Eastway and met a more direct route from Homerton, the modern Homerton Road, at Temple Mills bridge. Marsh Lane ran from Lower Clapton to the marsh, but not to the Lea; by 1831 it was called Pond Lane and from 1887 Millfields Road.[41] Mill Field Lane was recorded in 1582[42] and as Mill Lane in 1443.[43] It linked Clapton with Jeremy's ferry, and became Lea Bridge Road in 1745, when the bridge was built.[44] From Upper Clapton forerunners of Mount Pleasant Lane and Springfield ran towards Morris's (later High Hill) ferry. A road on the line of Spring Hill led to a bridge by 1831.

The Stamford Hill turnpike trust,[45] for the main road north from Shoreditch to Enfield, was established by an Act of 1713, with tollgates at Kingsland and the top of Stamford Hill.[46] A weighing machine was installed at Stamford Hill under an Act of 1751 and was replaced in 1766.[47] Both tollhouses stood on the west side of the road, the one at Kingsland being immediately south of the chapel with views along Ball's Pond Road and Dalston Lane.[48]

Hackney turnpike trust was established by an Act of 1738[49] for the roads from Shoreditch church (Hackney Road) and Mile End (Cambridge Heath Road), which met on the boundary at Cambridge Heath and led north through Hackney and Clapton to Stamford Hill.[50] Clapton gate was erected at the junction of Upper Clapton and Lea Bridge roads, probably on the opening of Lea Bridge Road in 1758. Dalston Lane, apparently incorporated by the trust after 1799, had a gate by 1770[51] and a new gate from 1814 to 1823 near Queen's (from 1939 Queensbridge) Road; the gate was re-erected in 1839 and moved to Navarino Road in 1858, when side-bars accompanied the building up of neighbouring streets. Other tollgates of the trust, in Bethnal Green and Shoreditch, were sometimes loosely referred to as 'Hackney gate'.

A third turnpike trust, for Lea bridge and its

27 Below.
28 e.g. *Cal. of Wills in Ct. of Husting*, ii (2), 674.
29 D. Defoe, *Jnl. of the Plague Year* (Falcon Press 1950), 144.   30 Rocque, *Map of Lond.* (1741–5), sheet 6.
31 Stanford, *Map of Lond.* (1862–5 edn.), sheets 3, 7. 'High road' is used below for the entire stretch of the route in Hackney.
32 Three paras. based on Rocque, *Map of Lond.* (1741–5), sheets 3–6; *Starling's Map* (1831).
33 *P.N. Mdx.* (E.P.N.S.), 106–7, 202.
34 Clarke, *Hackney*, 303; M.B.W. *Return of Alterations in Street Nomenclature since 1856* (1882), 92. Rocque misleadingly marked Church Street as extending south of Reading Lane to the Triangle beyond Well Street.
35 G.L.R.O., M 79/LH/85.
36 Guildhall MS. 9171/1, f. 56v.; B.L. Eg. Ch. 2080.
37 Defoe, *Jnl. of Plague Year*, 144.
38 Clarke, *Hackney*, 14–16.

39 *Rep. on Bridges in Mdx.* 116.
40 *P.N. Mdx.* (E.P.N.S.), 108.
41 L.C.C. *Names of Streets* (1901), 345.
42 B.L. Eg. Ch. 2081.
43 *P.N. Mdx.* (E.P.N.S.), 107.   44 Below.
45 Four paras. based on M. Searle, *Turnpikes and Toll-Bars* (1930), i. 183–4, 191, 228–9, 259, and illus.; ii. 668, 691–2; J. L. Dailey, 'Turnpikes and Turnpike Rds. in Hackney' (TS. 1981 in H.A.D.).
46 12 Anne, c. 19. Trust's rate bks. in H.A.D., P/J/T/11–30.
47 24 Geo. II, c. 43; D. Pam, *Hist. Enfield to 1837* (1990), 299–300.
48 Grocott, *Hackney*, 56, 60; below, list of churches.
49 11 Geo. II, c. 29; H.A.D., P/J/T/1, ff. 66, 163. Min. bks. in H.A.D., P/J/T/1–5.
50 H.A.D., plan of Hackney turnpike rd. by W. H. Ashpitel (1799).   51 Ibid.; Pam, *Enfield*, 302.

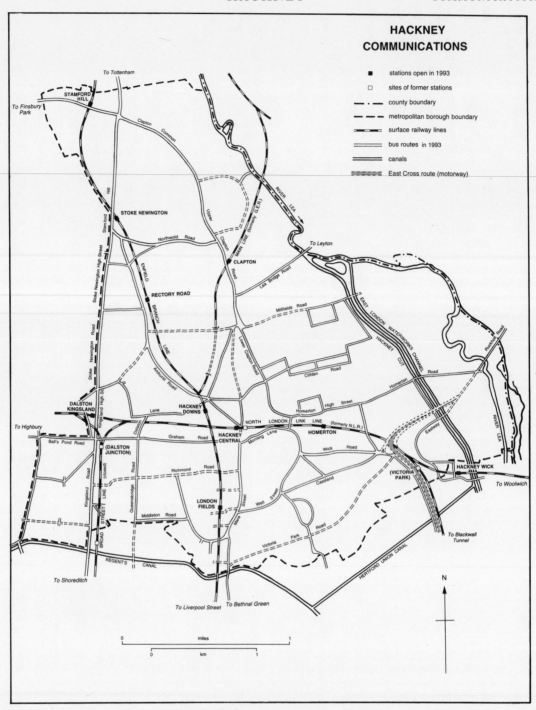

**HACKNEY
COMMUNICATIONS**

- ■ stations open in 1993
- □ sites of former stations
- –·– county boundary
- – – metropolitan borough boundary
- surface railway lines
- bus routes in 1993
- canals
- East Cross route (motorway)

new road, was set up in 1757.[52] Its only tollhouse stood on the west side of the river, where new gates were installed on the rebuilding of the bridge in 1820–1.

The Stamford Hill and Hackney trusts were superseded by the commissioners for the metropolitan turnpike roads in 1826.[53] By the 1850s the opening of new side streets had led to widespread evasion of tolls, and to travellers' complaints of delay had been added a charge that tolls were preventing the building of wharves along the Lea.[54] Clapton gate was abolished in

1856 and all the commissioners' roads, with part of Lea Bridge Road, were transferred to Hackney board of works in 1863.[55] Public barriers were then removed, the Stamford Hill gate being reinstalled until 1872 in Tottenham. Since the Essex section of Lea Bridge Road retained its own trustees, their tollhouse in Hackney also remained in use until 1872.[56] A private tollgate at Temple Mills,[57] conveyed with the mills by 1772,[58] existed until 1911.

The road pattern changed little between the 1740s and the 1830s:[59] Cassland Road, which

52   30 Geo. II, c. 59; below.
53   7 Geo. IV, c. 142 (Local and Personal).
54   *The Times*, 21 July 1856, 6e.
55   26 & 27 Vic. c. 78.

56   Ibid. 3rd schedule; *Hackney Photos*. i. 47.
57   H.A.D., M 3652 (plan).   58   Ibid. M 1422–3.
59   Para. based on Stanford, *Map of Lond.* (1862–5 edn.), sheets 3, 4, 7, and 8.

was to contain Hackney Terrace, was constructed from 1786[60] and a start was later made on Richmond Road, which was to reach Mare Street from Kingsland Road. By 1865 south-western Hackney was covered by streets almost in a grid, the longest being Richmond Road and the north–south Queensbridge Road. Development elsewhere took place more slowly, although Wick Road existed, as did the long streets already called Amhurst, Rectory, Downs Park, and Downs roads. Most other new roads, then and later, were the result of infilling. The network was complete by 1900 and thereafter was modified mainly by road widening, notably in Mare Street from 1901,[61] and by clearance for housing estates. A motorway, the East Cross route to Blackwall tunnel, was completed in 1979 across the end of Wick Road and south alongside the railway, separating the eastern and western parts of Hackney Wick.[62]

A third major north–south line of communication was the Lea.[63] In the 1770s, under an Act of 1767, the River Lee trustees made the straighter Hackney cut or New cut farther west,[64] from Lea bridge through the marsh and passing east of Hackney Wick.[65] A parallel channel was made by the East London Waterworks Co. under an Act of 1829.[66] Immediately southeast of Spring Hill a loop in the river around Horse Shoe point so hindered navigation that the neck of land was severed, forming an island, c. 1890.[67] The Regent's canal was authorized in 1812, to link the Paddington branch of the Grand Junction canal with the docks at Limehouse. Running near the southern boundary of Hackney west of Kingsland Road and again on either side of Cambridge Heath Road, it was opened throughout in 1820.[68]

Bridges were required for Hackney brook, which could flood to a width of 70 ft. at Homerton, at Hackney village, and as far upstream as Stoke Newington High Street.[69] Stamford, originally Sanford, Hill took its name from a sandy ford, almost certainly of the main north road across the brook.[70] Probably it was there that a bridge had been destroyed and rebuilt by 1255.[71] The crossing came to be known as Newington bridge, in 1825 a two-arched brick structure which had been built by the turnpike trustees and was maintained by the county.[72] Kingsland Road bridge over the Regent's canal was the responsibility of the Regent's Canal Co.[73]

Kates Lane crossed Hackney brook[74] in 1825 by a ford and a footbridge, which the parish replaced with a brick bridge c. 1841. A ford and footbridge carried the North Cross road from Kingsland to Lower Clapton. Dalston Lane bridge over Hackney brook needed repair in 1722.[75] The Hackney turnpike trust rebuilt it as a triple-arched brick bridge which in 1825 often impeded the stream and caused water to flow across Church Street; that bridge was rebuilt as a single arch in the 1830s. Hackney bridge, to be repaired in 1543,[76] was presumably the Church Street (later Hackney) bridge which was to be railed in 1657 and which needed repair in 1703; its upkeep[77] was accepted by the parish in 1716 and it was rebuilt in brick with three arches, by public subscription, in 1799. Blew (later Homerton Street) bridge was built by the parish to link Homerton with Morning Lane across Hackney brook; it was often repaired from 1657[78] and comprised two brick arches after work in 1821. A path from the churchyard to Morning Lane crossed the brook by a footbridge of 1827. At Hackney Wick the road from Homerton to Old Ford crossed the brook by a single-arched brick bridge, repaired by the parish in 1821. Another bridge was built by the parish near the silk mills in 1830.

Until c. 1758 the Lea was bridged in Hackney only at Temple Mills, where the converging roads from Homerton and Hackney Wick led to Stratford and Leyton. Temple Mills bridge was later occasionally called White bridge, to distinguish it from one closer to the mills, which were east of the old river on the mill stream.[79] Lock bridge, mentioned with Temple Mills bridge in 1578, may have been a third bridge immediately east of the mills; responsibility for repairs was uncertain in 1589.[80] Temple Mills alias Marsh Street bridge was ruinous in 1512, when William Tey was ordered to repair it.[81] Money for repairs, to be collected by the county, was advanced by the parish in 1633.[82] More work was needed in 1671 and again in 1689, when half of the cost was to be paid by the lord of Lordshold manor, a quarter by the lord of Kingshold, and the rest by occupiers of contiguous lands, including the mills.[83] The parish clerk laid responsibility for maintenance on the county in 1802 but the parish was indicted for failure to repair in 1824.[84] The trustees of the River Lee Navigation had provided a timber bridge but were not responsible for its upkeep in 1842.[85]

60 I. Watson, *Gentlemen in the Bldg. Line* (1989), 28–9.
61 L.C.C. *Ann. Rep.* (1900–1), 105–6; ibid. (1908–9), 156.
62 *P.O. Dir. Lond.* (1977, 1979); *Hackney Gaz.* 13 Mar. 1979, 29.
63 Para. based on Rocque, *Map of Lond.* (1741–5), sheets 3–5; *Starling's Map* (1831); Old. O.S. Maps Lond.
64 7 Geo. III, c. 51; *2nd Rep. Com. on Pollution of Rivers* [3835], p. 26, H.C. (1867), xxxiii. The spelling 'Lee', used in Acts of Parliament, was adopted by the trustees and the later Lee Conservancy Bd., although 'Lea' has remained the normal spelling.
65 H.A.D., M 3605 (plan of cut and proposed cut).
66 10 Geo. IV, c. 117 (Local and Personal); below, pub. svces.
67 Grocott, *Hackney*, 66; *Hackney Photos.* i. 126.
68 E. C. R. Hadfield, *Canals of E. Midlands* (1970), 128–31.
69 Barton, *Lost Rivers*, 48.
70 Ibid. 62 and *T.L.M.A.S.* xvi. 171, correcting statement that the ford was across the Lea, as in *P.N. Mdx.*

(E.P.N.S.), 107.
71 McDonnell, *Medieval Lond. Suburbs*, 71.
72 *Rep. on Bridges in Mdx.* 142.   73 Ibid. 127, 134.
74 Para. based on ibid. 115–18; Robinson, *Hackney*, i. 22–24.   75 Vestry mins. 20 July 1722.
76 *L. & P. Hen VIII*, xviii (2), p. 124; xix (1), p. 243.
77 Vestry mins. 24 Aug. 1657; 3 June 1703; 30 June 1716.
78 e.g. vestry mins. 24 Aug. 1657; 20 Apr., 3 Aug. 1691; 3 June 1703.
79 e.g. Stanford, *Map of Lond.* (1862–5 edn.), sheet 4; *Bacon's Atlas of Lond.* (1910), sheet 40.
80 S.J.C.F., 'Note on Meadows in Hackney, 1578'; *Acts of P.C.* 1588–9, 301.
81 B.L. Cott. MS. Nero E. vi, f. 64.
82 Vestry mins. 7 July 1633; 24 May 1635.
83 G.L.R.O., M79/LH/41.
84 Par. mins. 22 Sept. 1802; 22 Sept. 1821; G.L.R.O., MJ/SPB/154–63.
85 Robinson, *Hackney*, i. 20.

In 1671 the manor court fined one man for installing a ferry over the Lea without licence and another for removing Lock bridge ferry, presumably at Temple Mills.[86] Ferries in 1745 were, from south to north, Tyler's leading to the isolated White House between the Lea and the mill stream,[87] Jeremy's at the end of Mill Field Lane, Smith's by a building (then or later the Jolly Anglers) a little farther north, and Morris's (later High Hill).[88] Jeremy's ferry was so called by 1709.[89] Other names may have commemorated different owners or ferrymen rather than additional crossing points: Frazier's or Brasier's ferry was recorded in the 1750s, Collins's, in place of Tyler's, c. 1767, and Hillier's in 1773.[90]

The Lea Bridge Turnpike Road Act of 1757 provided for a bridge at Jeremy's ferry, with tolls to improve the approach road both in Clapton (Mill Field Lane) and in Essex.[91] A permanent bridge, presumably preceded by a temporary one, was built only in 1772, of timber,[92] and replaced by an iron one in 1820–1. It became a county bridge in 1870[93] and was again rebuilt in 1896–7, with contributions from Essex, the Lee Conservancy Board, and the Lea Bridge, Leyton & Walthamstow Tramways Co.[94]

The River Lee trustees provided ways over the Hackney cut. In 1803 they objected to repairing a bridge at the end of Cow or Pond Lane (later Millfields Road).[95] In 1825 they also maintained Wick (in 1842 Wick Lane) bridge and Homerton (in 1842 Marshgate) bridge, forerunners of the modern bridges bearing Eastway and Homerton Road. By 1842 they had a crossing to the new engine house at Lea bridge, south of the main road bridge, and Bricklock bridge for a lock house south of Cow bridge. All their bridges save that to the engine house had been extended to the east by one arch, to the design of Thomas Wickstead, to cross the East London Waterworks Co.'s channel. North of Lea bridge the trustees had High bridge, a wooden footbridge at the foot of Spring Hill, which was taken over by Hackney district board.[96] The High Hill ferry remained in use after the nearby railway viaduct had been built. Horse Shoe footbridge, midway between the ferry and High bridge, by 1894 led to the new island.[97]

A coach ran daily from Bishopsgate to Hackney in 1740, when Kingsland and other places along the great north road were presumably served by coaches which left Bishopsgate two or three times a day for Tottenham.[98] By 1760 Stoke Newington coaches also used that road.[99] Hackney had a half-hourly service in 1780, when fares for hire from West End theatres to Hackney church were also quoted and four coaches a day went to Clapton. By 1795 Clapton had an hourly service and Kingsland, Homerton, and Stamford Hill apparently enjoyed their own services, besides those which passed through or nearby.[1] By 1817 Hackney was served hourly from Bishopsgate and every quarter of an hour from the Royal Exchange.[2] In 1825 twelve short-stage coaches, making 44 return journeys a day, terminated at Clapton, seven at Hackney, five at Homerton, and two at Stamford Hill.[3] An unpunctual journey to the first Swan, half way along Clapton Common, was described by Dickens in his first published work.[4] Services ran from the City, the Strand, and Oxford Street in the 1830s.[5]

An omnibus from the City ran to Stoke Newington in 1830.[6] Omnibuses licensed in 1838–9 included seven to Hackney, another seven to Clapton or Clapton gate, one to Dalston, and one to Kingsland. The licensees included J. Kerrison and J. Barber,[7] who in 1849 were among the leading operators, with departures hourly from Upper Clapton and quarter-hourly from Church Street respectively. Among other services in 1849 were those of Bryan, with 17 departures from Upper Clapton, and Parker, whose omnibus ran from Homerton through London to Kennington.[8] Fifty-two vehicles were bought from local operators early in 1856 by the new Compagnie Générale des Omnibus de Londres, reconstituted in 1858 as the London General Omnibus Co. (L.G.O.C.),[9] then or soon the main provider in Hackney.[10] Horse buses were also supplied by the Kingsland Association from 1875 or earlier and by the Camden Town Association from 1895; both groups had been absorbed into the L.G.O.C. by 1901.[11]

Tramways were authorized in 1871[12] and inaugurated in 1872 by the North Metropolitan Tramways Co., whose line from Moorgate along Kingsland and Stoke Newington roads to Stamford Hill was met at Dalston by one from Aldersgate through Islington by way of Essex and Ball's Pond roads. The company's line from Bishopsgate by way of Haggerston to Mare Street and Lower Clapton was opened in 1873 and extended to Clapton common in 1875. Its lines from Dalston to Mare Street along Dalston Lane and Graham Road and from Bethnal

86 G.L.R.O., M79/LH/41.
87 *Hackney Photos.* i. 128.
88 Rocque, *Map of Lond.* (1741–5), sheets 4–5.
89 G.L.R.O., M79/LH/122/1.
90 H.A.D., 900.2, pp. 13, 15–17, 22; ibid. M 3605.
91 30 Geo. II, c. 59.
92 *Rep. on Bridges in Mdx.* 115.
93 Below, plate 7; 33 & 34 Vic. c. 73; 51 & 52 Vic. c. 41.
94 L.C.C. *Ann. Rep.* (1896), 16; W. G. S. Tonkin, *Lea Bridge Turnpike and the Wragg Stage Coaches* (Walthamstow Antiq. Soc. 1974), 12–14, 21, and illus.
95 Vestry mins. 17 Oct. 1803.
96 *Rep. on Bridges in Mdx.* 115; *Starling's Map* (1831); Robinson, *Hackney*, i. 20–1; Hackney bd. of wks. *Ann. Rep.* (1894), 15.
97 Old O.S. Map Lond. 21 (1868, 1894); cf. *Hackney Photos.* i. 126.

98 *Complete Guide to Lond.* (1740, 1755).
99 *V.C.H. Mdx.* viii. 142.
1 *Lond. Dir.* (1780, 1795).
2 *Cary's New Itinerary* (1817).
3 *Hist. Lond. Transport,* i. 392.
4 Pub. in *Monthly Mag.* Dec. 1833 but retitled for *Sketches by Boz* (1836).
5 *P.O. Dir. Lond.* (1830, 1836, 1840).
6 Ibid. (1836).
7 *Hist. Lond. Transport,* i. 395, 397.
8 *Hackney Dir.* (1849).
9 V. Sommerfield, *Lond.'s Buses* (1933), 20. Several vendors named in *Hist. Lond. Transport,* i. 404–5, 410.
10 *Dickens's Dict. Lond.* (1880).
11 A. W. McCall, *Kingsland Rd.* (Omnibus Soc. 1958), 4.
12 Para. based on *Hist. Lond. Transport,* i. 185, 259 (maps). Tramcars' colours are in *Dickens's Dict. Lond.* (1880).

Green, across Victoria Park to Lauriston Road and the west end of Cassland Road, followed in 1879. A depot in Portland Avenue, Stamford Hill, was acquired in 1873.[13] The Lea Bridge, Leyton, and Walthamstow Tramways Co. opened part of a projected line from Clapton to Woodford, but only on the Essex side of the river, in 1883; a second company of the same name extended the Essex line, which later passed to Leyton U.D.C., and in 1892 opened the stretch from Clapton to Lea bridge, which at first was not connected to the North Metropolitan system.[14] The North Metropolitan again extended its Clapton route, from the Swan to Stamford Hill, in 1902.[15] The company's lease was surrendered in 1906 to the L.C.C.[16]

Electrification of the horse-tram routes began in 1907 along Kingsland Road to Stamford Hill. The line from Clapton to Lea bridge was electrified in 1908, the one along Mare Street and through Clapton to Stamford Hill in 1909, and the link between Dalston and Hackney in 1913. The line across Victoria Park to South Hackney followed in 1921, with a new link along Well Street between Mare Street and Cassland Road.[17] A long-projected service along Amhurst Park, linking Hackney and Clapton with Finsbury park and Camden Town, was started in 1924.[18]

The London Passenger Transport Board (L.P.T.B.), which took over trams and buses in 1933,[19] converted Hackney's tram routes to trolleybus operation in 1939. London Transport still operated four weekday trolleybus services through Hackney in 1960[20] but all had given way to motorbuses by 1962.[21]

Meanwhile the Motor Bus Co., soon absorbed by the Vanguard Co., had briefly introduced a service to the Swan, Clapton, by way of Stamford Hill in 1906. Motorbuses were also operated in 1906 by the London Standard Motor Omnibus Co. and, more successfully, by the Great Eastern London Motor Omnibus Co. and the Road Car Co. The Vanguard and Road Car cos. merged with the L.G.O.C. in 1908[22] and motorbuses had replaced all the L.G.O.C.'s horse buses by 1911.[23]

Motorbuses ran along all the tram routes in 1913 and along several additional routes: Stamford and Englefield roads, Dalston Lane, the west part of Victoria Park Road, Well Street and Cassland Road to Hackney Wick, Pembury and Cricketfield roads, Median and Dunlace roads to Glyn Road, Northwold Road, and Amhurst

Park.[24] Among short lived independent operators in the 1920s were the Primrose Omnibus Co. in 1922 and later the Aro, Havelock Motors, and Fallowfield & Knight, all three of which passed in 1927 to the London Public Omnibus Co., itself absorbed by the L.G.O.C. in 1929.[25] Changes made by 1930 included a route from Dalston Lane by way of Queen's and Albion roads to London Fields and Mare Street, additional routes to Hackney Wick along Morning Lane and Wick Road (and thence to Gainsborough Road and Eastway) and along Homerton High Street and Sidney Road, and from Stoke Newington Road along Amhurst Road to the junction of Dalston Lane with Pembury Road.[26] Similar services were provided by London Transport in 1962,[27] and, slightly extended to serve housing estates, in the 1980s.[28] Private operators reappeared in 1990, when the Kentish Bus Co. was awarded three of the nine routes put out to tender within Hackney L.B.[29]

Stables and car sheds of the North Metropolitan Tramways Co. in Bohemia Place and Portland Avenue were transferred to the Metropolitan Tramway & Omnibus Co. in 1894.[30] The depot in Bohemia Place, opened in 1882, was rebuilt in 1909 for electric trams,[31] and, with one in Rookwood Road opened in 1907, was converted for trolleybuses by the L.P.T.B. The first, later known as London Transport's Clapton bus garage, was closed in 1987 and reopened as Hackney garage in 1989; the second survived as Stamford Hill garage.[32] A depot of the Lea Bridge, Leyton, & Walthamstow Tramways Co., immediately south of the junction of Lea Bridge and Upper and Lower Clapton roads, was disused in 1967 and demolished thereafter.[33] The L.G.O.C. had garages in Shrubland Road (Dalston garage) from 1908 and Well Street (Hackney garage) from 1911. Both were replaced when in 1981 London Transport opened a new central garage, its first for 25 years, and holding 170 vehicles, in Ash Grove, where the L.G.O.C. had had a depot in 1892.[34]

The East & West India Docks & Birmingham Junction Railway was authorized in 1846 primarily for the conveyance of goods for the London & North Western Railway (L.N.W.R.) from Camden Town to Blackwall by way of Islington, Hackney, and Bow.[35] Land was acquired in 1847[36] but construction was slow; in 1850, before the line had reached the docks, a passenger service ran every 15 minutes by the circuitous route from Islington to Fenchurch

13 H.A.D., D/F/AMH/555, p. 21.
14 *Hist. Lond. Transport*, i. 267; L.C.C. *Ann. Rep.* (1906–7), 144.   15 H.A.D., D/F/BAG/1, p. 18.
16 *Hist. Lond. Transport*, ii. 94.
17 Ibid. ii. 101 (map); L.C.C. *Municipal Map of Lond.* (1930).
18 H.A.D., D/F/BAG/1, p. 21; 14, pp. 74–5.
19 23 & 24 Geo. V, c. 14.
20 Hackney, *Official Guide* [1960].
21 *Hist. Lond. Transport*, ii. 351.
22 McCall, *Kingsland Rd.* 4–5; H.A.D., D/F/BAG/1, pp. 20–1.   23 *Hist. Lond. Transport*, ii. 168.
24 Ibid. ii. 231 (map); L.C.C. *Municipal Map of Lond.* (1913).
25 McCall, *Kingsland Rd.* 7, 9; *Hist. Lond. Transport*, ii. 229, 428, 444, 459.
26 L.C.C. *Municipal Map of Lond.* (1930).

27 *Hist. Lond. Transport*, ii. 231 (map).
28 London Regional Transport and Hackney Public Transport Action Cttee. route maps.
29 *Hackney Echo*, 11 Oct. 1989, p. 1.
30 'Rodinglea', *Tramways of E. Lond.* (1967), 226.
31 'Kennington', *L.C.C. Tramways Handbk.* (1974), 66–7; inf. from pub. relations administrator, Lond. Buses Ltd.
32 D. W. Willoughby and E. R. Oakley, *Lond. Transport Tramways Handbk.* (1972), 98; inf. from Lond. Buses Ltd.
33 *Tramways of E. Lond.* 52 (illus.).
34 *Kelly's Dir. Hackney* (1892–3); O. Green and J. Reed, *Lond. Transport Golden Jubilee Bk.* (1983), 186; *Hackney Gaz.* 25 Sept. 1973, 7; 20 Apr. 1979, 48; 13 Feb. 1981, 13; 28 Apr. 1981, 5; inf. from Lond. Buses Ltd.
35 Para. based on M. Robbins, *N. Lond. Rly.* (1974), 1–2, 12, 15–16; *Hist. Lond. Transport*, i. 47, 51–2, 137.
36 G.L.R.O., M79/KH/12, pp. 242, 244–6, 257, 299, 304.

Street, with stations called Kingsland, Hackney, and from 1856 Victoria Park (Hackney Wick). The company, renamed the North London Railway (N.L.R.) in 1853, came to be dominated by the L.N.W.R., which took over its working in 1909 and formally absorbed it in 1922, itself becoming part of the L.M.S. in 1923. From 1854 Victoria Park was linked by the Eastern Counties Railway with Stratford and the main line of that company, from 1862 the Great Eastern Railway (G.E.R.), to Cambridge, Ipswich, and Norwich.

In 1865 the N.L.R. provided a shorter link with the City. From Broad Street the line, built at great expense through crowded Shoreditch, ran close to the east side of Kingsland Road to Dalston Junction station, whence the tracks branched north-east and north-west to join the older line through Hackney. Kingsland station, directly north of Dalston Junction, was closed. Later improvements by the N.L.R. included the resiting of Victoria Park (Hackney Wick) station in 1866, the opening of Homerton station in 1868, and the removal of Hackney station from the east to the west side of Mare Street in 1870. The stretch from Broad Street to Dalston did much to open the northern suburbs to commuters; workmen's fares were available and it soon had one of London's heaviest traffic flows, with 322 trains terminating on weekdays at Broad Street in 1903.[37]

A northward branch from the G.E.R.'s main line at Bethnal Green, itself to be extended from Shoreditch to a new terminus at Liverpool Street, was authorized in 1864. The branch was opened in 1872, with stations at London Fields and Hackney Downs Junction (later known simply as Hackney Downs), where it divided. The north-westerly or Enfield branch ran to join an existing line at Edmonton, with stations at Rectory Road, Stoke Newington, and Stamford Hill. The north-easterly branch curved across the Lea to Walthamstow, connecting with the main Cambridge line, and in 1873 to Chingford, through a tunnel under Hackney Downs and a station at Clapton. Trains for Cambridge were later diverted from Stratford to the Hackney Downs route, which became part of the L.N.E.R. in 1923.[38]

The stretch of the original N.L.R. line between Dalston eastern and western junctions was used only intermittently until 1914 for passenger traffic after the closure of Kingsland station; it continued to be used for goods. Passenger services to the east ceased in 1944 with the closure of Hackney and Homerton stations, which had been preceded by closures at Victoria Park in 1942 and 1943.[39] On the Enfield branch line Stoke Newington station was rebuilt as a plain glass and steel box in 1975;[40] Rectory Road station was also rebuilt, in brick. New stations called Hackney Central and Hackney Wick (a resiting of Victoria Park) were opened in 1980 as part of the North London Link line, revived by British Rail with help from the G.L.C.[41] The entire line from North Woolwich to Richmond was reopened for electric trains in 1985, with stations at Hackney Wick, Homerton, Hackney Central, and Dalston Kingsland;[42] a south–west curve at Graham Road, by which trains from Richmond could reach Liverpool Street, was also opened in 1985 but later closed. The Broad Street line and Dalston Junction station were closed in 1986 and the track was taken up,[43] although the route had not been built upon in 1990.

No Underground railways served Hackney M.B., despite its size. Two lines from the City were projected in 1901, the North East London to Stoke Newington and the City & North East Suburban by way of Victoria Park to Walthamstow, but both failed in Parliament in 1902.[44] The nearest Underground stations were at Essex Road and Highbury, to the west,[45] from 1904 and at the Victoria line's Seven Sisters, to the north, from 1968.[46]

SETTLEMENT AND BUILDING

SETTLEMENT AND BUILDING TO *c.* 1800. Roman finds,[47] unexplained by structural remains, have included coins in an urn at Temple Mills, stone coffins at Upper Clapton, and a marble sarcophagus at Lower Clapton. The Temple Mills hoard, with articles of a later date, may indicate merely a crossing of the Lea and the Clapton burials a possible line of the road from Ermine Street to Great Dunmow.

Well watered gravels attracted Anglo-Saxon settlers.[48] Hackney, although first recorded only in 1198, probably commemorates Haca's *ey* or raised ground in marshland. The Old English *tun* or farm in Clapton, Dalston, and Homerton, the *wic* or dairy farm in Hackney Wick, and the Middle English *mere* or boundary in Mare Street also suggest early settlement.[49] A 6th-century battle has been associated with Hackney, apparently on no stronger grounds than that it took place by a river near London.[50] Physical remains of traffic along the Lea were a clinker-built boat of uncertain date, *c.* 6 m. long,[51] from north of

37 Robbins, *N. Lond. Rly.* 3, 7–8, 12, 15, 29; J. T. Coppock and H. C. Prince, *Gtr. Lond.* (1964), 62, 64, 69, 129; *Hist. Lond. Transport*, ii. 418.
38 *Hist. Lond. Transport*, i. 133, 349; C. J. Allen, *Gt. Eastern Rly.* (1955), 58, 199.
39 Robbins, *N. Lond. Rly.* 16; J. E. Connor and B. L. Halford, *Forgotten Stations of Gtr. Lond.* (1978), 39–40, 43–4.
40 *Tower to Tower Block*, no. 53.
41 *Hackney Gaz.* 13 May 1980, 3; 13 June 1980, 15.
42 *London's Missing Link* (Brit. Rail and G.L.C. pamphlet, 1985).
43 Inf. from Mr. R. M. Robbins and Mr. P. S. Hadley;

Rly. Mag. Sept. 1986, 580.
44 *Hist. Lond. Transport*, ii. 65, 77–8, 80, 83–4.
45 Hackney, *Official Guide* [1920]; *V.C.H. Mdx.* viii. 7.
46 A. E. Bennett and H. V. Borley, *Lond. Transport Rlys.* (1963), 15–16; *V.C.H. Mdx.* v. 313.
47 Para. based on Hist. Mon. Com. *Rom. Lond.* 56, 164, 173, and pl. 67; *V.C.H. Mdx.* i. 70–1. Fuller details in *Gent. Mag.* liii (2), 899; ibid. clxvii. 793; Robinson, *Hackney*, i. 30; Clarke, *Hackney*, 6, 8; *T.L.M.A.S.* iii. 192–4.
48 McDonnell, *Medieval Lond. Suburbs*, 5, 10.
49 *P.N. Mdx.* (E.P.N.S.), 105–7.
50 Thomas, 'Hackney', 84, 328–33.
51 Robinson, *Hackney*, i. 24.

Temple Mills, and an oak dugout of *c.* 950, originally 3.73 m., from Springfield park.[52] Before the Conquest most of the later parish formed part of the bishop of London's large manor of Stepney.[53]

Presumably most of the medieval people described as of Hackney came from the centrally placed village, which had a church by 1275.[54] Settlements were recorded at Dalston in the 13th century, Clapton, Homerton, and Kingsland in the 14th, and Shacklewell in the 15th, but only Homerton in 1605 was more populous than Mare Street and Church Street.[55]

Robert of Hackney (de Hakeney) was among Londoners trading with Lucca in 1275[56] and William of Hackney, recorded from 1297 to 1312,[57] and Richard of Hackney, alderman, recorded from 1297 or 1312 to 1343, were leading wool merchants.[58] Richard's son Niel received lands in Stepney and Hackney in 1349.[59] Their surname was shared by many late 13th- and 14th-century citizens,[60] among whom Osbert in 1293–4 and Robert and Simon of Hackney in 1320 also dealt in wool.[61] Other Londoners with land in Hackney included Ralph Crepyn, the first common clerk and in 1280 an alderman,[62] John Duckett or Duket, perhaps son of the goldsmith Laurence Duckett murdered by Crepyn's followers in 1284,[63] Thomas of Aldgate, a tailor, in 1291, and John de la Bataille, a cordwainer, in 1332.[64] Theirs were among the early acquisitions by rich citizens, continued by the Shoreditch family in the 14th century and establishing a practice which lasted until the early 19th.

In the Middle Ages the creation of the Templars' (later the Hospitallers') sub-manor and others produced houses and farms, as in southern Hackney for the Shoreditches,[65] and in Clapton on the site of Brooke House.[66] Little other building was recorded, although the custom of gavelkind, by dividing copyholds,[67] probably led to crowded development in the main settlements. Building speculation was indicated by Elizabeth Graunger's claim that her husband Thomas (d. 1510), a London alderman, had incurred great expense in putting up new houses on the site, later estimated at 3 a., of a copyhold cottage and garden.[68]

Merchants, who made many gifts to the church, were not alone in favouring Hackney up to the 17th century.[69] Aristocrats, most numerous in the 16th and early 17th centuries, were preceded by office-holders such as Sir John Elrington (d. 1482–3), William Worsley (d. 1499), Sir Reginald Bray (d. 1503), Sir John Heron (d. 1522), and Christopher Urswick (d. 1522). Residents included the earl of Northumberland (d. 1537), James I's grandmother the countess of Lennox (d. 1578), Lady Latimer (d. 1583), the Chancellor of the Exchequer Sir Walter Mildmay at his death in 1589, Lord Vaux of Harrowden (d. 1595), Lord Hunsdon (d. 1596), the earl of Oxford (d. 1604), and Lord Zouche (d. 1625), although not the Wentworths who acquired the bishop's manor at the Reformation. Many lived at the King's Place, later Brooke House, where visits were paid by Henry VIII, Princess (later Queen) Mary, and Elizabeth I. Among lord mayors of London were Sir William Bowyer (d. 1544), Sir Rowland Hayward (d. 1592), and Sir Thomas (d. 1570) and Sir Henry Rowe (d. 1612). Four titled parishioners and one hundred others, listed as citizens of London, paid under a county assessment in 1602.[70] Londoners were the main local benefactors[71] and gained still more prominence during the 17th century. By the 1660s the nobility were represented only by the Brooke family, perhaps because the growing role of Whitehall and Westminster had made the districts west of London more attractive.

Large rambling houses of the 16th century, often on medieval sites, were noted by antiquaries as a feature of Hackney.[72] Widely scattered, they included those associated with the manors of Wick, Shoreditch Place, Shacklewell, and Balmes, beside the Black and White House near the church, the Plough range and Sutton House in Homerton, and the house later rebuilt by the Norris family. Brooke House, eventually survived only by Sutton House, was probably always the grandest of the old seats.[73] Wholesome air was an obvious attraction: in 1537 the earl of Northumberland hoped to regain his health at Clapton and Sir Ralph Sadler said that the plague in London had not affected Hackney.[74]

The parish was comparatively populous, with 156 people assessed for subsidy in 1524, including a few in Stoke Newington,[75] and 600 communicants in 1548.[76] Church rates were sought from 195 landholders in six districts in 1605, when 29 non-residents were also approached.

52 *Hackney Echo*, 15 Oct. 1987, 1b; *Terrier*, Summer 1988; *Internat. Jnl. of Nautical Archaeol.* xviii (2), 89–111; inf. from Hackney mus.   53 Below, manors (Hackney).
54 Below, parish church.
55 *P.N. Mdx.* (E.P.N.S.), xviii. 105–7; below.
56 *Cal. Close, 1272–9,* 123.
57 G. A. Williams, *Medieval Lond. from Commune to Capital* (1963), 115–16, 151; *Cal. Close, 1296–1302,* 35, 112.
58 Williams, *Medieval Lond.* 115–16, 151; *Cal. Pat. 1292–1300,* 300; 1334–8, 6, 384, 480, 516, 572–3; *Cal. Close, 1318–23,* 235, 611; 1330–3 sqq., *passim.*
59 *Cal. of Wills in Ct. of Husting,* i. 468; *Cal. Close, 1349–54,* 146.
60 *Cal. of Letter Bks. of City of Lond., A to H* (1899–1907), *passim.*
61 *Cal. of Wills in Ct. of Husting,* i. 113; *Cal. Close, 1318–23,* 261.
62 Williams, *Medieval Lond.* 95, 103–4; *Cal. Inq. Misc.* i, p. 390.
63 Stow, *Survey* (1720), i, app. 122–3; Williams, *Medieval Lond.* 254; *V.C.H. Mdx.* v. 329.
64 *Cal. of Wills in Ct. of Husting,* i. 100, 372.
65 Below, manors (Shoreditch Pl.).
66 Ibid. (Brooke Ho.).
67 Below, econ. hist. (agric.).
68 P.R.O., PROB 11/16, f. 269; ibid. C 1/314/8; C 1/465/31.
69 Below, parish church. Rest of para. based on sections below.
70 H.A.D., D/F/TYS/1, pp. 45–7.
71 Below, charities.
72 e.g. Stow, *Survey* (1720), ii, app. 122.
73 Below, Clapton; Homerton; manors.
74 *L. & P. Hen. VIII,* xii (1), p. 557; xii (2), p. 479.
75 P.R.O., E 179/141/116. Stoke Newington's assessment was less than 5 per cent of Hackney's in 1546: ibid. E 179/141/138.
76 *Lond. and Mdx. Chantry Certificates, 1548,* 68.

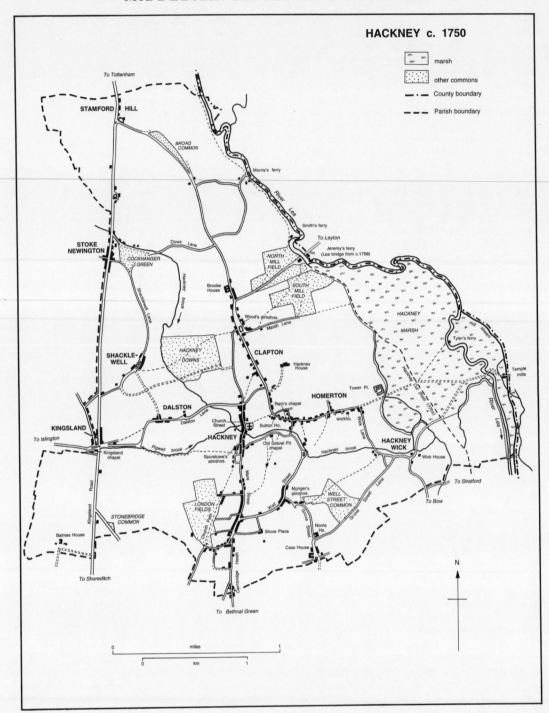

HACKNEY c. 1750

marsh
other commons
County boundary
Parish boundary

Homerton was assessed for 49 names, Church Street for 34, Mare Street for 23, Well Street and Grove Street together for 24, Clapton for 32, and 'Newington', Shacklewell, Kingsland, and Dalston together for 33.[77] If landholders' numbers indicated the distribution of the population as a whole, most people lived in the central north–south section of the parish, along Mare and Church streets, their offshoots in the south, or in Homerton and Clapton rather than along the high road.

Hackney's contribution to a county assessment was exceeded only by those for Harrow and

Stepney in 1614; a reduced contribution in 1636 was probably due to the proximity of the plague.[78] Alarm at immigration by the poor led in 1618 to a temporary ban on the division of cottages or the building of new ones.[79] The number of householders was estimated to have reached 324 by 1640.[80] In 1664 there were 305 houses chargeable for hearth tax and 83 exempt. Of the chargeable houses, c. 278 were occupied and 27 empty: Homerton was assessed for a total of 71, Mare Street for 55, Church Street for 45, Grove Street and Well Street for 32, and Clapton, Dalston, Kingsland, Shacklewell, and

77 H.A.D., D/F/TYS/1, pp. 63–71.
78 Mdx. County Rec. ii. 104; iii. 63.
79 Vestry mins. 31 July 1614; 1618.
80 Lysons, Environs. ii. 481–2.

Newington together for 102.[81] In 1672, when assessments were by 11 districts, the total of all houses was 462.[82]

Prominent merchants were so numerous that an unusual system of government prevailed from 1613, whereby a select vestry coexisted for over 200 years with a wider body of parishioners.[83] Some merchants retired and others merely resorted to Hackney, which from 1636 was included in the area of London's bills of mortality.[84] Nearly all those assessed for ship money in Hackney in 1639 were citizens; very little could be collected after occupants had closed their houses and moved to London.[85] Business interests presumably explained why so many men paid fines rather than serve as parish or manorial officers: in 1682 a headborough was excused after claiming that he worked in London and had hired a house in Hackney only for his children.[86] Accessibility and a reputation for clean air had given rise from the mid 17th century to schools, at first notably for young ladies.[87] Nonconformist academies followed, as dissenters sought protection under patrons from the city.[88] The patrons were often interrelated: some were Turkey merchants and many held civic office. Active parishioners included Sir Thomas Vyner (d. 1665), Sir Robert Dycer (d. 1667), and Sir Francis Bickley (d. 1670), all parliamentarians who had received baronetcies at the Restoration, Sir Thomas Player (d. 1672), and Sir Stephen White (d. 1678).[89] The predominance of such citizens was symbolized by the passing of the manors from the royalist Wentworths through a succession of Londoners to the naturalized Francis Tyssen (d. 1699).[90]

Among tributes to Hackney was that of Pepys, whose claim in 1666 to grow more in love with it every day[91] perhaps applied to the village rather than the parish, although he later ventured to Clapton, to Balmes in the south-west, and to the marshes.[92] John Strype, a resident, noted a healthy town when adding Hackney to Stow's description of London.[93] Defoe in the 1720s considered the 'long divided town of Hackney'[94] to consist of 12 separate hamlets, all increased and some more than trebled in size over the past few years. Nowhere joined to London, the parish was 'in some respects to be called a part of it', having so many rich citizens that it contained nearly a hundred coaches.[95] Dudley Ryder, when a law student in 1715–16, found little commercial entertainment but many neighbours enjoying a modest social life as self-

sufficient as that of any small town in rural Middlesex or Surrey.[96]

The 18th century brought more rich newcomers, including Huguenots and Jews.[97] Some moved further afield but, like the Tyssens and the Ryders, retained their local property. Recognized as having long been deserted by the nobility, Hackney was declared in 1756 to excel all other villages in the kingdom and probably in the world in the opulence of its inhabitants.[98] Recent parishioners had included the philanthropist Sir John Cass (d. 1718), the chief founder of the new East India Co. Sir Gilbert Heathcote (d. 1733), reputedly England's wealthiest commoner, the speculator John Ward (d. 1755), and the Bank of England's governor Stamp Brooksbank (d. 1756) at Hackney House.[99] As before, many of the richest had common interests, notably as Bank or East India Co. directors. Much of Hackney, 'that Arcadia beyond Moorfields' for both the prosperous shopkeeper and the knight,[1] resembled Stoke Newington, with which it shared members of the influential Gould and Cooke families.[2] Seats were built or rebuilt, sometimes in landscaped grounds; where older houses were converted into schools or asylums, they continued to cater for the well-to-do.[3]

More people in the mid 18th century still lived in the centre than along the high road to the west. The poor-rate assessment listed 448 householders, besides 25 living elsewhere, in 1720 and 658, besides 15 outsiders, in 1735. Numbers for Mare Street rose from 111 to 140, for Church Street from 83 to 149, for Homerton from 104 to 155, and for Clapton from 71 to 100, while the total for the other six districts rose from only 79 to 114.[4] A similar distribution, apparent in 1745,[5] persisted in 1761, when 976 residents were listed: 199 were in Mare Street, 174 in Church Street, 213 in Homerton, and 157 in Clapton, although the number in Newington had also increased, to 91. There were over 1,150 ratepayers by 1779, when Mare Street and Church Street had scarcely grown since 1761 and when the largest increase had been in Kingsland.[6]

Continued growth caused concern over the inadequacy of the old church and burial ground.[7] The number of houses was 983 in 1756, 1,212 in 1779, and more than 1,500 in 1789[8] shortly before a dispersal of the church's monuments which had attested the parishioners' wealth over three centuries.[9] With meadows along the Lea

---

[81] G.L.R.O., MR/TH/4, mm. 1–4d. Occupied and empty hos. were returned separately except for the northernmost dist.   [82] Ibid. MR/TH/34.
[83] Below, local govt. (par. govt.).
[84] F. P. Wilson, *Plague in Shakespeare's Lond.* (1927), 195.   [85] *Cal. S.P. Dom.* 1639–40, 120.
[86] Cal. Mdx. Sess. Bks. vi. 139.
[87] Below, educ. (private schs.).
[88] Below, prot. nonconf.
[89] Vestry mins. *passim*; below, local govt. (par. govt.).
[90] Below, manors.
[91] *Diary of Sam. Pepys*, ed. R. Latham, vii. 181.
[92] Ibid. v. 181–2; ix. 197, 546.
[93] Stow, *Survey* (1720), ii, app. p. 122.
[94] Defoe, *Jnl. of Plague Year*, 144.
[95] Idem, *Tour through Gt. Britain* (1971), 337.
[96] A. Palmer, *East End* (1989), 13; *Diary of Dudley Ryder*,

ed. W. Matthews (1939), *passim*. Transcriptions of later diaries, 1744–58, are in Harrowby MSS. Trust, Sandon Hall, vol. 430.   [97] Cf. below, manors.
[98] Maitland, *Hist. Lond.* ii. 1366.
[99] *Diary of Dudley Ryder*, ed. Matthews, 14; *D.N.B.*; below, Clapton;
[1] *Diary of Dudley Ryder*, ed. Matthews, 4, 17.
[2] *V.C.H. Mdx.* viii. 183.
[3] Below, pub. svces.; educ. (private schs.).
[4] H.A.D., P/J/P/76; ibid. P/J/P/91/ Nos. are for all names, whether or not a rate was paid.
[5] Rocque, *Map of Lond.* (1741–5), sheets 5, 6.
[6] H.A.D., P/J/P/121.   [7] Below, parish church.
[8] Lysons, *Environs*, ii. 482, based on par. mins. 23 Mar. 1789.
[9] Below, parish church. For early memorials, from 1399, Stow, *Survey* (1720), ii, app. 124–9.

and elsewhere interspersed in the arable, Hackney in the 1790s was noted for its cowkeepers and as a supplier of hay to London. Although brickfields, nurseries, and market gardens had long been worked,[10] they together accounted for barely a tenth of the parish c. 1806. Two-thirds was still farmland, of which 1,570 a., including the marsh, were under grass.[11]

Prominent early residents[12] not mentioned elsewhere included the ambassador Sir Jerome Bowes (d. 1616), who was buried at Hackney, the royalist divine Lionel Gatford (d. 1665) and the Cromwellian major-general John Desborough (d. 1680), both of whom retired there, the Jacobite conspirator Sir John Friend (d. 1696), and the scientist and royal clockmaker John Ellicot (d. 1772). Those born in the parish included the scholar Christopher Wase (d. 1690), the medical writer Peirce Dod (d. 1754), the serjeant-at-law Edward Leeds (d. 1758), the architect James Savage (d. 1852),[13] and the zoologist Edward Turner Bennett (d. 1836). The landscape painter John Varley (d. 1842) and his brothers Cornelius (d. 1878) and William (d. 1856) were said to have been born at the Blue Posts (formerly the Templars' house)[14] after their father had converted it to private use,[15] although the building was still an inn in 1785.[16]

BUILDING AFTER c. 1800. Despite the closeness of Church Street to Lower Clapton and Homerton, the villages were still distinct in 1801, when there were 2,050 inhabited houses. By 1831 the number had doubled and the villages were merging along the old roads. Infilling with new roads started in the 1820s at De Beauvoir Town, slackened a little in the 1830s, and thereafter gathered pace.[17]

The late 18th century had seen only isolated instances of speculative building, notably Sanford's cottages and Hackney Terrace.[18] More widespread changes depended on the major landowners, most of them absentees. An Act of 1796 for the sale of William Parker Hamond's estate had assisted the extension of Hackney village[19] but neither that nor an Act of 1808 for Nathaniel Lee Acton[20] led to more than building along existing roads; brickearth could be dug from the land behind, which was to be left fit for a return to agriculture.[21]

Systematic development was pioneered by the Rhodes family, whose members were not established landowners but enterprising lessees. They were active in several parishes[22] and acquired

land on both sides of the Regent's canal, whose construction itself stimulated the spread of building from London's east end. In a Bill of 1823 the Rhodeses proposed the erection of a new town which, to the alarm of both Hackney and Shoreditch, would be rated as a separate district.[23] Although their first activity was halted, work at De Beauvoir Town was resumed in the 1830s for their landlord. Meanwhile Thomas and William Rhodes began to build east of Kingsland Road, largely in cooperation with Acton's heir Sir William Middleton.[24] 'Vast changes' had taken place across southern Hackney by 1843, where plots straddled a parish boundary which in 1803 had been clearly shown by field lines.[25]

Building accelerated, until Hackney had 9,027 inhabited houses by 1851, 12,352 by 1861, and 17,791 by 1871.[26] Landowners' cooperation was most visible east of Kingsland Road, between the boundary and Dalston, where long avenues formed a rough grid pattern.[27] Agreements were also made for tracts east of Mare Street, where the opening of Victoria Park in 1845 encouraged St. Thomas's hospital to progress to wholesale development, in conjunction with the Cass foundation and the Norris family.[28] Speculators appeared, in emulation of the Rhodeses: among them was the native John Musgrove and outsiders such as William Bradshaw and the partners Wilkinson and Matthews. They bought land piecemeal and tended to build to a lower standard than did contractors on the older estates. Southern Hackney, from the boundary to Dalston, Hackney village, and Homerton, had been almost entirely built up by 1870.[29] Clapton had also grown, forming with Hackney and Dalston 'one of the handsomest suburbs of London' in 1862.[30]

Cheaper housing transformed the social character of most of Hackney. Demolition was often deplored, as in 1832; it was blamed on a 'shopocracy' c. 1875.[31] From 1847 railways both took the grounds of old houses and created barriers across short streets which soon became slums. The vestry in 1864 vainly opposed all further railway schemes, fearing in particular for Hackney Downs.[32] Meanwhile industry made increasing use of the waterways. Factories, at Hackney Wick and Homerton, and the establishment of institutions for the poor, were causing the better off to move and opening the way for crowded terraces at Lower Clapton.

The 1860s and 1870s saw building across the centre of the parish, on estates such as the Massies' at Dalston, the Powells' at Clapton, and the Glyns' at Homerton. The large Tyssen-Amhurst holdings[33]

10 T. Milne, Land Use Map of Lond. (1800) (Lond. Topog. Soc. 1975–6). 11 Lysons, Environs, Suppl. 163.
12 Para. based on D.N.B.
13 Colvin, Brit. Architects, 719–20.
14 Below, manors (Kingshold).
15 A. T. Story, John Holmes and John Varley (1894), 262; A. Bury, John Varley of the 'Old Society' (1846), 16.
16 G.L.R.O., MR/LV9/136.
17 Census, 1801–31; Starling's Map (1831); below, De Beauvoir Town.
18 Below, Newington; Well Street.
19 36 Geo. III, c. 83 (Priv. Act); below, Hackney village.
20 48 Geo. III, c. 123 (Local and Personal); below, manors (Hickmans).
21 Below, econ. hist. (ind).
22 V.C.H. Mdx. viii. 62, 191.

23 Below, De Beauvoir Town; below, manors (Lamb Farm); H.A.D., 346.3351.
24 Below, De Beauvoir Town; below, manors (Lamb Farm; Hickmans). 25 H.A.D., P/J/P/70.
26 Census, 1841–71.
27 Old O.S. Map Lond. 40 (1870); below, Dalston.
28 Old O.S. Map Lond. 41 (1870); Watson, Gentlemen, passim.
29 Old O.S. Maps Lond. 40–1 (1870); Stanford, Map of Lond. (1862–5 edn.), sheets 7, 8.
30 G. R. Emerson, London: How the Great City Grew (1862), 281.
31 Thomas, 'Hackney', 2; H.A.D., H/LD 7/4.
32 H.A.D., J/V/2, pp. 123, 127.
33 Hereafter referred to as the Tyssen estate. For the family's changes of name, below, manors (Lordshold).

were also developed, with sales of commercial premises, notably along the high road,[34] and the laying out of long residential roads around Hackney Downs and to the north. The Downs and other threatened common lands were preserved from 1872 and the marsh from 1893,[35] when other available land in southern Hackney had been filled. Inhabited houses numbered 23,934 in 1881 and 28,422 in 1891,[36] by which time roads had been planned over most of the north part, on both sides of Stamford Hill. Spacious private grounds survived only between Clapton common and the Lea,[37] where the creation of Springfield park in 1905 was followed by the spread of housing to the north.

Change continued, under pressure from London's east end. As public transport enabled clerks and artisans to move in, the old main roads grew noisier, large houses were converted or subdivided, and the better-off retreated northward. In the 1880s most of Hackney was middle- or lower middle-class[38] but many led 'pinched' lives and in 1897–8 the parish was seen to have been growing poorer over half a century. The trend had been uneven, as London businessmen remained in Upper Clapton and more had moved to Stamford Hill. Poverty existed mainly east of Mare Street and Clapton Road, but had also spread north across the canal to London Fields. The poor combined footwear makers from Bethnal Green with Hackney's indigenous poor off Homerton's high street and those drawn by low rents to Hackney Wick; while there had been some improvement in behaviour at Homerton, cheap housing was creating 'a dismal but not a rowdy district' near South Mill field at Lower Clapton.[39] The social decline of the neighbourhood was perhaps modified by the scattered building of private blocks of flats from the 1890s but it was to continue in nearly all parts, assisted by laxly controlled conversions in residential streets and the provision of council housing.

Hackney had been covered by the Metropolitan Building Act, 1844, which lack of inspection made relatively ineffective, and with Chelsea had led the enforcement of the Sanitary Act, 1866, against landlords.[40] The death rate then compared favourably with London's average.[41] While riverside cottages and some alleys remained unhealthy until their clearance after the First World War, the main patches of poverty c. 1890 were relatively small, around the factories at London Fields, Homerton, and Hackney Wick. In 1902 only 23.1 per cent of Hackney's population was in total poverty, little more than half the proportion in Bethnal Green.[42] Comparatively favourable statistics, however, hid differences between the northern and southern

halves of the new metropolitan borough, whose overall population density was kept low by the existence of the commons and Hackney marsh. Overcrowding grew worse between 1901 and 1911, partly as a result of Jewish immigration, and made necessary the municipal estates which were to produce a predominantly working-class suburb.

The parish was noted throughout the 19th century for its many charitable institutions, either national or connected with London.[43] The general provision of model dwellings, a philanthropic cause from the 1840s, followed only after the south part had been built up and in the wake of schemes for the middle class, such as those of the St. Pancras, Marylebone and Paddington Freehold Land Society or the Suburban Villa and Village Association in the 1850s.[44] Housing in Chapel Road was leased to the London Labourers' Dwellings Co. in 1866 and land at Baker's Hill to the London Labourers' Association in 1878.[45] Seeking cheaper land in the suburbs, the Metropolitan Association for Improving the Dwellings of the Industrious Classes built artisans' flats at Gibson Gardens in 1880.[46] The Four Per Cent Industrial Dwellings Co. (in 1951 renamed the Industrial Dwellings Society) similarly looked farther afield; originally for rehousing Jews in the East End, it had flats in Stoke Newington from 1903 and opened Hackney's Navarino Mansions in 1905.[47]

Public provision, prompted by slum clearance, was first made by the L.C.C., whose Darcy and Valette Buildings, opened in 1904 and 1905, together contained 120 dwellings. It was resumed in 1928–30 with the Shore estate, followed from 1931 by work at Stamford Hill, and by 1938 on five other estates, the largest being Northwold.[48] Meanwhile Hackney council in 1925 had started to build 48 maisonettes in Fletching Road; they were followed in 1930 by 92 in Southwold Road, by a few conversions of older houses, and by estates of which the largest were Powell House and Banister House. By 1939 Hackney owned 13 estates, mostly smaller than the L.C.C.'s, and hoped soon to have met all reasonable housing demands.[49] Between the World Wars 5,189 dwellings of all types were provided by the L.C.C. and 2,780 by the borough.[50]

Hackney between the wars was chiefly a dormitory: 53 per cent of the working residents travelled to the City or neighbouring boroughs in 1921. Only one person in five, mostly in Upper Clapton or Stamford Hill, was middle-class c. 1930, when both birth and death rates were about the average for an east London borough. Overcrowding in the south part was 'not pronounced',[51] perhaps because of rehousing and

34 H.A.D., D/F/AMH/555, pp. 4–5, 8.
35 Below, pub. svces.   36 Census, 1881–91.
37 Stanford, Map of Lond. (1891 edn.), sheets 3–4, 7–8.
38 Booth's Map (1889), NE.
39 Booth, Life and Labour, iii (1), 73–9.
40 J. N. Tarn, Five Per Cent Philanthropy (1973), 114–15, 124–5; A. S. Wohl, The Eternal Slum (1977), 18, 122.
41 F. H. W. Sheppard, Lond. 1808–70: the Infernal Wen (1971), 17.
42 Wohl, Eternal Slum, 301, 312.
43 e.g. Emerson, Lond. 280; E. Walford, Old and New

Lond. v. 514; below, social.   44 Below, Well Street.
45 G.L.R.O., M79/TA/20; H.A.D., D/F/AMH/555, p. 24.   46 Below, Newington.
47 H. Pearman, Excellent Accommodation (1985), 83, passim; V.C.H. Mdx. viii. 170.
48 L.C.C. Lond. Statistics, xli. 144–53.
49 H.A.D., D/F/BAG/1, pp. 108–9; ibid. D/F/BAG/8, pp. 58–9; Hackney, Official Guide [1938, 1960].
50 L.C.C. Lond. Statistics, N.S. ii. 162.
51 New Lond. Life and Labour, iii (1), 142–3, 220, 242, 361–2; Census, 1921.

 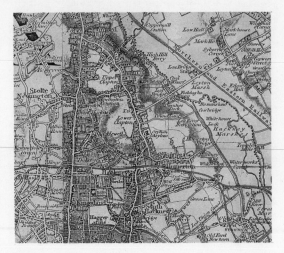

1805   1864

HACKNEY: EVOLUTION OF SETTLEMENT, 1805-1904
(scale 1 in. to 1 mile)

because of the falling population, itself attributed to a continued displacement of houses by
factories and workshops.[52] The 1930s, with their
widespread council building, brought more
housing by charities, notably the Samuel Lewis
trust, already active in Dalston, the Guinness
trust, and the Four Per Cent Industrial Dwellings Co.[53] Bethnal Green and East London
housing association was a builder in Devonshire
Road in 1931[54] and Shoreditch housing association bought property in Loddiges Road in
1937.[55] In general plans by the L.C.C. to control
the spread of commercial and industrial zones
were too weak for the borough council but
alarming to landowners.[56] The Cass trustees
wanted their estate to be 'residential' rather than
'special residential', in order to build flats, and
opposed any reduction in the housing density.[57]
The Tyssen trustees, finding many large houses
in less demand, in 1932 felt justified in letting
for 'trade purposes of a more or less private
character', notably dressmaking.[58]

Widespread damage in the Second World
War[59] led to more municipal building. Post-war
activity accounted for 4,891 new dwellings in
1957, of which the borough provided 2,816, the
L.C.C. 1,772 and a further 33 in conjunction
with housing associations, and private builders
270.[60] In 1967 the borough owned a total of
17,063 permanent dwellings and the G.L.C.

12,475; in addition there were nearly 5,000
temporary dwellings.[61] Hackney had complained
in the war about plans by the L.C.C. for tower
blocks, since it had more than enough buildings
of five or six floors.[62] Lack of space nonetheless
led to high-rise construction, of which eleven-
and fifteen-storeyed examples were quoted in
1960; towers of up to twenty-one storeys followed.[63] Transfers from the G.L.C. to the
London Borough were first proposed in 1969.[64]

The new London Borough had a reduced
waiting list of 10,000 persons in 1973 and a stock
of 41,000 dwellings in 1992.[65] The decay of older
blocks and fears for the safety of towers built in
the 1960s led to demolition and extensive renovation in the 1980s.[66] The previous 20 years had
seen an increase in council housing and, to a
lesser extent, in owner occupancy, at the expense
of private rented accommodation.[67] Building and
conversion were also being undertaken, with
government help through the Housing Corporation, by housing trusts. Newlon and Circle
Thirty Three housing trusts, both founded in
1968 and concerned chiefly with north-east London, were active in 1992.[68] When the Salvation
Army's Mothers' hospital closed, it was Newlon
trust which redeveloped much of the site as
Mothers' Square.[69] Private building, restricted
in the 1970s to modest infilling, also gathered
pace.[70]

52 New Lond. Life and Labour, iii (1), 361; Hackney M.B.
Rep. on San. Condition (1928), 116-20.
53 Below, Dalston; Stamford Hill.
54 Tower To Tower Block, no. 46.
55 G.L.R.O., H1/ST/E65/C/14/2/1-2.
56 Ibid. AR/TP/2/143.
57 Ibid. AR/TP/2/386.
58 Ibid. AR/TP/2/419.
59 Hackney Photos. ii. 145-59.
60 L.C.C. Lond. Statistics, N.S. iii. 110.
61 Ann. Abstract of Gtr. Lond. Statistics, ii. 161-3.
62 G.L.R.O., AR/TP/2/143.

63 Hackney, Official Guide [1960, 1961]; below, Hackney
Wick.
64 Stoke Newington and Hackney Observer, 24 Jan. 1969, 20.
65 Hackney, Official Guide [1973]; inf. from Hackney
L.B., dir. of housing.
66 e.g. Trowbridge est.; below, Hackney Wick.
67 Hackney Boro. Plan. (1982).
68 Inf. from group dir., Newlon Housing Trust, and manager, Circle Thirty Three Housing Trust Ltd., east area office.
69 Inf. from Newlon Housing Trust; below, Clapton;
pub. svces.
70 Hackney Boro. Plan (1982); below, Clapton.

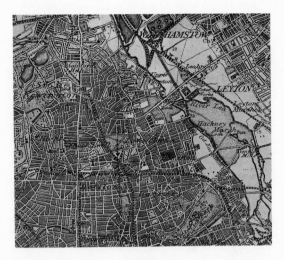

1904

In 1981 Hackney L.B.'s highest concentrations of council housing and of owner occupiers were outside the former parish, respectively in Shoreditch and Stoke Newington.[71] The widest variations, however, existed in the 15 wards[72] which covered the former Hackney metropolitan borough. King's Park, stretching from Homerton Road to Lea bridge, had 94.9 per cent of its households in council housing; Queensbridge had the next highest, 77.1 per cent, another six wards had over half, and Homerton had the lowest, 24.2. Homerton included much of the older Clapton Park and had the highest percentage of owner occupiers, 42.7; a further 23.9 per cent of its households was in private rented accommodation, which category accounted for as many as 29.7 per cent in Northfield west of Stamford Hill. Housing associations accounted for more than 17.5 per cent only in Westdown, around Kingsland High Street and Colvestone Crescent, where ownership was relatively evenly distributed between the council with 27.3 per cent, housing associations with 26.3, private landlords with 29.1, and occupiers with 15.6. Owner occupancy was not everywhere a sign of prosperity; many owners were immigrants, who lacked the residential qualifications for council housing and had difficulty in carrying out repairs.[73]

Ethnic minorities increased, while the population fell. Jews, the most clearly differentiated newcomers in the late 19th century, tended to move northward and after 1945, with orthodox reinforcements, were most prominent around Stamford Hill.[74] From the 1950s immigrants

came mainly from the new Commonwealth: by 1972 children of West Indian origin were numerous at St. John of Jerusalem's primary school and Afro-Caribbean boys were replacing Jews at Hackney Downs.[75] The trend continued during the 1970s, the largest new group being of Caribbean and the second largest of Mediterranean origins. Statistics showing that Hackney had, after Brent and Haringey, London's highest percentage of heads of households from the New Commonwealth or Pakistan include Stoke Newington and Shoreditch. The wards with more than 35 per cent, however, were Hackney's central ones from Lea bridge to the southern end of Stoke Newington. In 1981 more than half of the people in immigrant households were aged under 30.[76]

Industrial decline, most noticeable in the departure of large firms, continued as elsewhere in inner London. Interviews with Hackney families in 1979 revealed 32 per cent to be in poverty, apparently the highest percentage shown in any study; in 1983 there was little difference in the living conditions of natives and immigrants. Local government reorganization was resented, for having created an impersonal authority, which had deprived residents of their sense of neighbourhood. As early as 1972 economies had removed the caretakers from most housing estates; vandalism and neglect had worsened.[77] Complaints continued through the 1980s,[78] as improvements were balanced by the need for further savings: Clapton's Lea View flats, whose renovation brought a royal visit in 1986, were again poorly maintained in 1991.[79] Few tower blocks could be replaced; some were strengthened and some in 1992 stood empty while neighbouring low-rise homes were retained.[80]

A contradictory trend was the building or refurbishment of houses for the middle class. Gentrification came comparatively late, since Hackney lacked the squares of southern Islington,[81] while all parts had large council estates; it also suffered from traffic congestion and the absence of Underground stations.[82] By 1982, however, the national press was drawing attention to desirable terraces, in 1985 professional people were moving in from more expensive suburbs, and in 1987 much of Hackney was seen as a friendlier alternative to Islington; Victoria Park, De Beauvoir Town, Lower Clapton, and some avenues near London Fields proved particularly popular.[83] Few new sites were available, except on the old fringe of building near the marsh or the Lea, but much restoration continued after the end of the property boom. Patches of desirable housing in conservation areas and extensive public spaces attracted residents.

In 1992 a local task force, funded by the

71 Para. based on E. Howes, '1981 Census for Hackney: Ward Profiles'; ibid. 'Ward Rankings' (Research and Intelligence Section, Hackney L.B. (1983), in H.A.D.).
72 Incl. De Beauvoir ward, extending into Shoreditch.
73 Hackney Boro. Plan (1982).
74 Below, Stamford Hill; Clapton; Judaism.
75 Nat. Soc. files; G. Alderman, Hist. Hackney Downs Sch. (1972), 79.
76 D. Mullins, 'Race and the 1981 Census' (Research and Intelligence Section, Hackney L.B. (1983), in H.A.D.), 8–10, 12.

77 Ibid. 13; A. Palmer, East End (1989), 164.
78 e.g. Hackney Echo, 26 Oct. 1988, 7; Hackney Gaz. 16 Mar. 1990, 2.
79 Hackney Herald, June 1986, 7; Daily Telegraph, 4 Oct. 1991, 28.
80 Hackney Echo, 7 Oct. 1987, 1; below, Hackney Wick; Well Street.   81 V.C.H. Mdx. viii. 13, 28.
82 Hackney Boro. Plan (1982); above, communications.
83 Standard, 27 Sept. 1982, 21; The Times, 5 June 1985, 26; Observer, 19 Apr. 1987, 55.

Department of the Environment, was set up to identify needs as part of a programme to revive the economies of the poorest urban areas. Proximity to the City of London, many and varied small businesses, and cultural diversity combined with communal cooperation were seen as Hackney's chief strengths. The council successfully sought funds under the City Challenge scheme, with proposals for development centred on the high road through Shoreditch and Kingsland as far as the railway in Dalston, to form the Dalston City Corridor.[84]

The population[85] rose from 12,730 in 1801 to 16,771 in 1811, 22,494 in 1821, 31,047 in 1831, and 37,771 in 1841. Steeper rises followed, to 53,589 in 1851, 76,687 in 1861,[86] 115,110 in 1871, and 163,681 after the decade of fastest growth in 1881. Further increases brought it to 198,606 in 1891, 219,272 in 1901, and a peak of 222,533 in 1911. From 222,142 in 1921 it fell to 215,333 in 1931, to 171,342 in 1951, and 164,766 in 1961, the density falling over those 40 years from 68 to 50 persons to an acre. The trend continued after Hackney joined Shoreditch and Stoke Newington, whose total population of 257,522 in 1961 had fallen to give the L.B. 220,279 by 1971 and 180,434 by 1981. In the former Hackney M.B. the fall in the 1970s was 28 per cent in Queensbridge and over 20 per cent in five other wards; it was over 10 per cent elsewhere except in Eastdown, around Hackney Downs, where the rise was 14.4 per cent, and King's Park, where new housing produced a rise of more than 55 per cent.[87]

HACKNEY VILLAGE originally lay along Church Street, whose course bent slightly where it crossed Hackney brook. Church Street since 1868 has formed the northernmost stretch of Mare Street from Hackney Grove, in front of the modern town hall, to the junction with Dalston Lane and Lower Clapton Road.[88] The change of name recognized that building had come to line the whole of Mare Street, leading some writers to include all of Mare Street in descriptions of the village.[89] The area treated below, however, is limited to Church Street and its offshoots, a separate administrative division in the 17th and 18th centuries.[90]

The medieval village, called the vill or township of Hackney from the 14th century,[91] included the church by the 13th century,[92] the vicar's house acquired c. 1345,[93] and cottages in Church Street near the rectory house in 1486;[94] a brotherhood of Church Street existed in 1428.[95] In 1991 only the church tower survived, perhaps rebuilt by the rector Christopher Urswick (d. 1522), who was also credited with building Church House immediately to the west, where parish meetings took place by 1547.[96] A gap in the street front thereafter remained on either side of Church House where the churchyard bordered the road.[97]

Other large buildings by the early 17th century included the so-called Templars' house opposite Dalston Lane,[98] marking the northern end of the village, and the Black and White House. In 1741, when used by the free school, Church House was of brick, tall chimneyed and much altered, with the stocks in front and lychgates to the north and south. The walled churchyard was overlooked on the north by the Vicarage and on the south by a range including the Black and White House and, nearer the road, a building rented for the charity school.[99] The Black and White House, said to date from 1578, contained the arms of an unknown merchant and, among others in stained glass, those of Frederick V, count palatine and king of Bohemia. It was bought with 18 a. of Church field by the lord mayor Sir Thomas Vyner (d. 1665), who apparently altered it and occupied the second largest house in Church Street in 1664.[1] House and land were divided in 1683 between the cousins Elizabeth Marchant, Edith Lambert, and Elizabeth Tombs, all living in Gloucestershire, whose heirs sold their portions to the Ryders.[2] The house held a school in 1765 and was sold in 1796, to make way for Bohemia Place.[3]

A few other seats were set back from the street front: Spurstowe's house to the west,[4] Robert Perwich's, unidentified but largest of all in 1664,[5] and that of the Marsh family, Cambridgeshire landowners who also held Darkes in South Mimms.[6] Sir Thomas Marsh (d. 1677), who was said to have owned the White House perhaps at the north-east end of Baxter's Court,[7] was in 1678 admitted in remainder to a chief house on the west side of Church Street, which had been held by Thomas Marsh (d. 1657).[8] Sir Thomas's chief house, with land stretching south behind Mare Street to Shoreditch Place, passed to his son Edward (d. 1701), who left it to his wife Grace and her son by an earlier marriage, William Parker.[9]

[84] Hackney Echo, 29 Apr. 1992; Task Force Hackney, Autumn 1992.   [85] Para. based on Census, 1801–1831.
[86] Nos. for 1851 and 1861 are for the superintendent registrar's dist., coinciding with Hackney poor-law union, less those for Stoke Newington.
[87] Howes, '1981 Census: Ward Profiles'.
[88] L.C.C. Names Of Streets (1901), 330.
[89] e.g. Defoe, Jnl. of Plague Year, 144. Rocque applied 'Church Street' to most of Mare Street: Map of Lond. (1745–6), sheet 6; below.
[90] Below, local govt. (par. govt.).
[91] e.g. Feud. Aids, iii. 374; Cal. Pat. 1345–8, 214; ibid. 1354–8, 283.   [92] Below, parish church.
[93] Cal. Pat. 1343–5, 471.
[94] H.A.D. D/F/TYS/40.
[95] Guildhall MS. 9171/3, f. 211r.
[96] Robinson, Hackney, i. 91; Lost Hackney, 31–2; below, local govt. (par. govt.).   [97] e.g. Starling's Map (1831).

[98] Below, manors (Kingshold); plate 14.
[99] R. Root, 'Plan of Hackney churchyard' (1741) on back of Lost Hackney (H.A.D., V 239; copy in Bethnal Green Mus. of Childhood).
[1] Lysons, Environs, ii. 459–60; Robinson, Hackney, i. 95–7; G.L.R.O., MR/TH/4, m. 2; below, manors (Kingshold). Another 'Black and White Ho.' was at London Fields: below, Mare Street.
[2] H.A.D., M 88 sqq.; below, manors (Ryder).
[3] H.A.D., M 158 (b); Clarke, Hackney, 57.
[4] Below, manors (Spurstowe's ho.).
[5] G.L.R.O., MR/TH/4, m. 2; below, educ. (private schs.).
[6] V.C.H. Cambs. vi. 106; V.C.H. Mdx. v. 287.
[7] Vestry mins. 27 Mar. 1722; Clarke, Hackney, 46; H.A.D., P 9075.
[8] G.L.R.O., M79/KH/1, pp. 80–1, 106–8.
[9] Ibid. 3, p. 22.

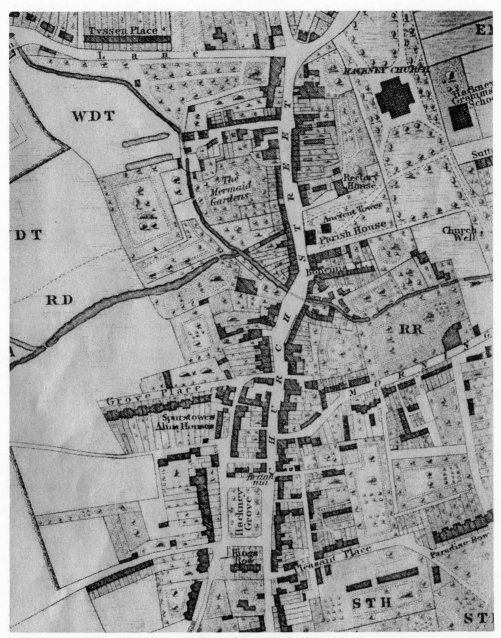

HACKNEY VILLAGE *c.* 1830

Most houses were much smaller, on frag-mented copyholds, and were repeatedly rebuilt. Six tenements were held in 1653 by Ralph Macro, a saddler of London, presumably on land north of the Vicarage and held by his son and namesake, a physician, in the 1690s.[10] Church Street, although populous, paid less rates in 1605 than the five other divisions of the parish[11] and in 1735 barely half as much as Mare Street and less than Homerton or Clapton.[12] It contained only 4 of Hackney's 36 select vestrymen in 1729, one of them the vicar and another the bankrupt John Ward.[13] Its slower rise in population after 1735, with no increase between 1761 and 1779, indicated a shortage of space.[14]

A map of 1724 shows in stylized form unbro-ken lines of building on both sides of Church Street except by the churchyard, above and below the brook.[15] A site conveyed with the Black and White House in 1765 had been com-mercially developed, to include a collarmaker's shop, a carpenter's shop and yard, a cheesemon-ger's house on Church field, and an apothecary's in a recently divided house next to the church-yard.[16] Similarly a site on the west side conveyed in 1766 included the Mermaid inn, a path called Sweet Briar Walk and houses in Buck House or Buck Horse Lane to the north, and a space to the south between the inn and an apothecary's; by 1777 the walk had disappeared and the space

10 H.A.D., D/F/TYS/40, pp. 199, 201.
11 Ibid. D/F/TYS/1, pp. 63–9.   12 Ibid. P/J/P/91.
13 Vestry mins. 23 Aug. 1729.
14 H.A.D., P/J/P/76, 91, 121, 150; above, settlement and building.   15 H.A.D., M 3513.
16 Ibid. M 158 (b).

to the south had been filled, when the Mermaid was leased with a cheesemonger's, a pastry cook's, a combmaker's, and a carpenter's.[17] An unusual later survival, with alterations, was the King's Head, gabled and perhaps of 16th-century origin, which was not rebuilt until 1878.[18]

At the northern end of the village John Ward (d. 1755) built himself a large house before his expulsion from the House of Commons in 1726 for forgery.[19] In 1711 he had taken a lease of copyholds of Grumbolds, later including a former bowling green.[20] The plain red-brick house had a central block flanked by two- and three-storeyed wings, of which one rose straight from the road at the corner of Dalston Lane. It was divided among genteel tenants in the early 19th century and had made way for houses and shops by 1848, although the name Ward's Corner survived in 1870.[21]

In the 1740s Hackney village remained essentially a single street, with some large gardens behind: on the west side those of Ward's house stretched back to Hackney brook,[22] as did those of the Mermaid and the adjoining grounds of Spurstowe's house. The last were landscaped by Sir John Silvester, who from the 1760s began the village's westward expansion near Spurstowe's almshouses, which for a century had stood alone in a stretch of Church Path which was to become Grove Passage (in 1907 part of Hackney Grove and from 1937 Sylvester Path). Besides establishing a coffee house in the street, Silvester built five houses in Sylvester Row (later extended as Grove Place and from 1883 Sylvester Road). Richard Dann, who bought most of Silvester's estate, in 1792 leased to George Scott land on which a terrace of twelve houses projected into the fields north of the almshouses.[23]

Building soon spread farther south along the west side of Church Path, forming a line known as the Grove or Hackney Grove.[24] It followed the breakup of the estate which had passed from William Parker (d. 1728) to his son William (d. 1776) of Haling (Surr.) and then to his daughters Grace Parker (d. 1781) and Elizabeth Hamond (d. 1789).[25] An Act of 1796 authorized the sale of the Hackney property of Elizabeth's son William Parker Hamond (d. 1812),[26] who as early as 1791 had leased Gravel Pit and Pitwell fields, behind the Grove, to James Potts.[27] From 1798 local purchasers from W. P. Hamond's trustees included Potts, Arthur Windus, David Whitaker, and the elder Richard Dann.[28] Coach

houses for the Grove were provided in Willow Walk as Potts Mews (later Grove Mews and finally part of Wilton Way).[29] Land between Church Path and Church Street was left partly as an open space, newly railed in by Potts in 1806[30] and itself called Hackney Grove in 1831. King's Row was built along its southern side and extended westward by a humbler terrace called Grove Lane (previously Cut Throat Lane[31] and from 1913 Reading Lane). With a few houses farther south in Church Path (later the north end of Martello Street), they formed the south-western corner of the village in 1831.

The south-eastern corner had dense building along the street, in its offshoots Baxter's Court and Jerusalem Square, with small houses from c. 1700,[32] and Pleasant Place (from 1878 the west end of Paragon Road), and behind in Jerusalem Passage.[33] Some of it came to be part of the scattered property of John Musgrove (later lord mayor of London and a baronet), a local auctioneer's son whose purchases included in 1828 houses from David Whitaker's executors, besides 7 houses and shops mostly facing the Grove.[34] Farther east there were two new fourth-rate houses in Morning Lane in 1807[35] but south of the lane there was only scattered housing until a lease by St. Thomas's hospital in 1809 to Robert Collins led to the building of the Paragon (later Paragon Terrace and the east end of Paragon Road).[36] After Collins's bankruptcy his partner John Scott, an attorney, began to build on the west side of Chatham Place c. 1815 and was leased land on both sides in 1820.[37] By 1831 terraces also formed Paradise Row immediately west of the Paragon and stretched along the west side of Chatham Place to Morning Lane, which had building on its south side and near Church Street on both sides. Homerton Terrace, Retreat Place, and neighbouring streets east of Chatham Place, also on the hospital's land, were considered in 1821 to be an extension of Homerton.[38]

The northern half of the village remained more confined: on the west by the gardens of Ward's house, the Mermaid, and Spurstowe's house, on the east by grounds around the church after its rebuilding farther from the street in the 1790s, and on both sides by Hackney brook.[39] Improvements were secured by the Tyssens, as in 1800 when John Musgrove the elder, carpenter, was to replace stabling with houses on the north side of Buck House Lane.[40] In 1812 a watchmaker was permitted to continue in his house north of the Mermaid on a repairing lease and Musgrove

17 Ibid. M 523; M 529.
18 Hackney Photos. i. 14; H.A.D., 'Our Local Sketches', first ser., p.60; LBH 7/5/406.
19 Hist. Parl., Commons, 1715–54, ii. 519.
20 H.A.D., M 736; M 763.
21 Robinson, Hackney, i. 122–4; below, plate 17; Clarke, Hackney, 118–19; Hackney Dir. (1847, 1849); Old O.S. Map Lond. 41 (1870).
22 Rocque, Map of Lond. (1741–5), sheets 5–6.
23 Below, manors (Spurstowe's ho.); G.L.R.O., M 79/KH/6, p. 293; ibid. 10, p. 230.
24 Para. based on Starling's Map (1831); Old O.S. Maps Lond. 40–1 (1870).
25 V.C.H. Cambs. vi. 106–7. Parkers' successive admissions in G.L.R.O., M 79/KH/3–6.
26 36 Geo. III, c. 83 (Priv. Act).
27 G.L.R.O., M79/KH/7, p. 43; H.A.D., V 2/3.

28 G.L.R.O., M79/KH/7, pp. 5–13, 23–4, 32–8, 43–4, 50, 58, 163, 186 sqq.
29 Ibid. 10, p. 301.
30 Vestry mins. 6 Jan. 1806.
31 G.L.R.O., M79/KH/9, p. 230; M79/LH/41, s.v. Whitaker.
32 Lost Hackney, 13.
33 Para. based on Starling's Map (1831).
34 G.L.R.O., M79/KH/8, pp. 268–73; H.A.D. M 4232/13/8, lots 2–10.
35 G.L.R.O., MR/B/C. 1807/565.
36 H.B.M.C. Lond., HAC 8; M.L.R. 1812/4/701; below, this section.
37 M.L.R. 1816/2/348; 1821/5/730.
38 H.A.D., P/J/CW/124, pp. 41 sqq.
39 Starling's Map (1831); below, parish church.
40 H.A.D., M 540.

was to build one or more third-rate houses at the south corner of Buck House Lane; shops at the north corner were conveyed on a repairing lease in 1828.[41]

Apart from yards, the only offshoots from Church Street north of Hackney brook in 1831 were Coldbath (formerly Buck House) Lane, which ended at the brook, the houses on the south side of the old churchyard, and Bohemia Place,[42] all in the 1820s inhabited by people in trades or crafts. Church Street itself was mainly commercial. So too, south of the brook, were Grove Lane, much of the Grove, Pleasant Place, Jerusalem Square and Place, and Morning Lane. Gentry, professional people, and prosperous merchants lived mainly in the newer houses, notably in Grove Place, the south end of the Grove and King's Row, and Chatham Place.[43]

Eastward development continued after 1836, when Samuel Fox bought houses in Pleasant Row and Paradise Place, with land stretching north to Morning Lane, where many cottages formed crowded courtyards such as Buck's Buildings, with 19 dwellings, or Jackson's Buildings.[44] The houses which he built, praised in the 1890s for their durability,[45] included a terrace called Albion (from 1877 Stockmar) Road, parallel with a private road known as Fox's Lane.[46]

From 1850, when the first railway station was opened, improved communications both changed the village and destroyed its surrounding countryside.[47] Overshadowed by an iron railway bridge, Church Street took on an urban appearance which was reinforced by the culverting of the brook in 1859–60 and by the opening of tramways in 1872 along what had become no more than one end of Mare Street. To benefit London as a whole, the M.B.W. paid for road-widening between 1877 and 1879, when frontages of c. 250 ft. were set back from the west side north of the resited station.[48] An ornate town hall superseding the one at Church House was built on the former green called the Grove from 1866, a major junction was created by the construction of Amhurst Road East, and a tram depot was opened at the end of Bohemia Place in 1882. Part of the village was still thought to look old fashioned, although perhaps only in contrast to the avenues around, where many of the better off retreated as traffic along the main street increased.[49] Additions to the town hall[50] emphasized the urban character, along with the opening of the Hackney Empire music hall in 1901 and the L.C.C.'s long delayed widening of the road south of the railway, approved in 1899 and completed by 1906.[51] The crowded courts between Morning Lane and Paragon Road made

way for a block backed by Valette Street. It replaced Jerusalem Passage and Square, where St. Thomas's hospital sold property in 1902. Some 500 people were resettled, mostly in Valette Buildings (1904), among the L.C.C.'s first flats in Hackney.[52]

Amhurst Road East by 1865 had semidetached villas along part of its northern side;[53] land on the south was being dug for bricks and by 1870 was covered by terraces in Manor Place, Spurstowe Road, and Aspland Grove. Coldbath Lane was extended west as Kenmure Road and the Mermaid's gardens made way for Brett Road, both named in 1874. South of the railway Grove Place, Grove Mews, and Grove Lane in 1865 still led to market gardens between them and the housing which was spreading from Dalston. Following the opening of the G.E.R.'s branch line in 1872, however, the land west of Mare Street was filled with terraces, as in Graham, Penpoll, and Casterton roads, the last two named in 1878 and 1879.

East of Mare Street, space around the church was preserved as public gardens. North of the railway, the only major changes were the resiting of the station and the building of the tram depot.[54] Between the railway and Morning Lane watercress beds survived the culverting of Hackney brook until replaced by cramped terraces in Chalgrove Road, named from 1875, and south of Morning Lane an orchard made way for Trelawney Road, named from 1871. Between 1900 and 1905 St. Thomas's hospital leased the gardens of superior houses in the Paragon and the west side of Chatham Place, with land behind, to Henry William Rowlandson and Hervey Rowlandson. Large factories, mainly for clothing or furniture, were soon built in Belsham Street, named from 1902, and in Chatham Place.[55]

Shops had spread along the east ends of Amhurst Road and the uncompleted Graham Road by 1880, when there were many more in Morning Lane.[56] Blocks of private flats included the Improved Industrial Dwellings Co.'s Quested Buildings (later Court), begun in Brett Road in 1878, and Graham Mansions, displacing shops east of Penpoll Road, by 1900.[57] Residents of Mare Street were in 1889 classified as well-to-do, as were those of Amhurst, Spurstowe, and Graham roads and some of Sylvester Road and Chatham Place. Those of most other roads were moderately comfortable. The poor lived in Grove Mews and east of Mare Street in Bohemia Place and courts south of Morning Lane; chronic poverty was observed in Chalgrove Road, in a narrow lane which was the forerunner of Belsham Street, and around Jerusalem Passage.[58]

41 Ibid. M 553–4; M 700.
42 Starling's Map (1831).
43 H.A.D., P/J/CW/124, pp. 89–120.
44 G.L.R.O., M 79/KH/9, pp. 532–5.
45 Clarke, Hackney, 47–8.
46 Old O.S. Map Lond. 41 (1870).
47 Para. based on Hackney Photos. i. 6, 9–22; above, communications.
48 L.C.C. Ann. Rep. (1899–1900), 88; P. J. Edwards, Hist. Lond. Street Improvements, 1855–97 (1898), plan xxiii.
49 Walford, Lond. v. 512; Suburban Homes of Lond., Residential Guide (1881), 197–8.
50 Below, local govt. (local govt. after 1837).

51 L.C.C. Ann. Rep. (1899–1900), 88–9; (1900–1), map facing p. 105; (1905–6), 172.
52 Ibid. (1907–8), 41; G.L.R.O., H1/ST/E65/C/11/1; Hackney Photos. ii. 96.
53 Two paras. based on Stanford, Map of Lond. (1862–5 and 1891 edns.), sheet 7; Old O.S. Maps Lond. 40, 41 (1870, 1913).
54 Below, pub. svces.; above, communications.
55 G.L.R.O., H1/ST/E65/C/5/5/2–3, 5, 7–9; Hackney M.B. Rep. on San. Condition (1928), p. 119.
56 P.O. Dir. Lond. Suburban North (1880, 1888).
57 H.A.D., LBH/7/5/23/183; Kelly's Dir. Hackney (1890, 1900–1).   58 Booth's Map (1889), NE.

Development from *c.* 1900 consisted largely of the rebuilding of commercial premises.[59] Imposing additions to Mare Street included the central library (1908), the Salvation Army's offices (1911) and the Methodists' central hall (1925).[60] Sylvester House provided flats immediately south of Graham Mansions by 1913 and a large post office and telephone exchange had replaced a Brethren's chapel in Paragon Road by 1930. A new town hall (1934–6) was built on the west side of Hackney Grove, with Hillman Street behind, the old site becoming a public garden.[61] Houses overlooking the churchyard and a parallel range along the south side of Bohemia Place were to be cleared in 1937[62] and probably had gone before the site was bombed in 1941. The same air-raid destroyed Chalgrove Road, later used for prefabricated housing and afterwards for a car park, and necessitated the rebuilding of shops south of the old church tower.[63] The remaining slums off Morning Lane made way *c.* 1960 for the L.C.C.'s Trelawney estate,[64] on the site of Trelawney and Stockmar roads and Fox's Lane, while Aspland Grove and Spurstowe Road made way for the Aspland estate and Marcon Court. In Sylvester Path a warehouse replaced Spurstowe's almshouses.[65] Changes behind the town hall included rebuilding for the council's technical services department, the replacement of Casterton Road by a sports centre opened in 1979,[66] and the conversion of a factory next to Sylvester House into flats called the Colonnades.

Open space around the church stretches northward into Clapton Square, dividing the shops of Mare Street from those which continue northeast, with other buildings, along Lower Clapton Road. It lies within a conservation area which extends beyond Church Well Path, the east side of the space, to Sutton Place in Homerton and west to Mare Street,[67] where the first town hall, the refaced successor of Church House, stands alone, flanked by gardens and partly screening the old church tower and the churchyard with its established trees.[68]

The adjacent stretch of Mare Street, known locally as the 'Narrow Way',[69] has a slight curve despite its improvement in the 1870s. Many shops occupy the ground floors of three- or four-storeyed stock brick houses of the early 19th century. The curve, the irregular rooflines, and glimpses of the churchyard combine with iron posts and lamps installed *c.* 1990 to suggest the survival of a village street, an appearance strengthened by widening of the pavements and restriction to one-way traffic. Apart from the old town hall and the so-called Manor House,[70] the

most notable buildings are those of the early to mid 19th century which replaced the 'Templars' house' at the corner of Lower Clapton Road. As nos. 406–22 (even) Mare Street, they form a three-storeyed convex crescent of brick, with stuccoed pilasters dividing the houses; part of the Crown inn (no. 418) and modern shops project from the ground floors.[71]

West of Mare Street between the railway and Dalston Lane are modest late 19th-century terraces in Kenmure Road and a small block of flats by E. D. Mills, praised in 1952 for its modernity.[72] In Brett Road the late 19th-century five-storeyed block of 40 flats at Quested Court has Tuscan pillared porticos. South-west of Amhurst Road the yellow-brick Aspland estate and Marcon Court have no building taller than seven storeys.

South of the railway a wider stretch of Mare Street carries more traffic. The only open space is where the civic garden with its low walls, lamp piers, and bronze lanterns, forms a group of the 1930s with the town hall.[73] The refurbished Hackney Empire and, opposite, a block mainly of public buildings centred on the former Methodist central hall,[74] contribute to a wholly urban scene.

Notable buildings survive off Mare Street only in isolation. No. 4 Sylvester Path, a small two-storeyed house of the 18th century but partly refaced in the early 19th, retains original panelling.[75] No. 33 Hackney Grove is half of a pair and early 19th-century, of stock brick with two storeys, attic, and basement, and has a wooden Doric porch. It stands at the corner of Reading Lane, whence the remains of Hackney Grove lead south as a back way past nos. 25 and 27, an early 19th-century pair of three storeys and basement, where no. 27 is boarded up.[76]

Nos. 71 to 83 (odd) Paragon Road were erected under the lease of 1809 to Robert Collins[77] in which an unusual reference to building specifications indicated that a high standard was required. A row of eight houses was occupied by 1813, when Collins's interest had passed to John Scott. Seven survivors were bought *c.* 1979 by Newlon housing trust, which restored them as three and a half linked pairs. The houses have three storeys and two bays, of stock brick stuccoed on the ground floor, and are linked by single-storeyed Doric colonnades enclosing the front doors. They are Hackney's earliest example of a type which became widespread, as in Chatham Place and Clapton Square, and older than the many examples on the Lloyd Baker estate in Finsbury, where the links are two-storeyed. Visually the row is all the more remarkable for lying in the shadow of the fifteen-storeyed towers of the Trelawney estate.[78]

59 Para. based on *Kelly's Dir. Hackney* (1910 and later edns.); *P.O. Dir. Lond.* (1927 and later edns.).
60 Below, pub. svces.; prot. nonconf.
61 Below, local govt. (local govt. after 1837).
62 H.A.D., H/PD/3/4; *Hackney Photos.* ii. 91.
63 *Hackney Photos.* i. 6; ii. 153.
64 Hackney, *Official Guide* [1960], 63.
65 *Lost Hackney*, 50; below, charities.
66 Below, social.
67 H.A.D., Conservation Areas file.
68 Below, local govt. (local govt. after 1837); pub. svces.;

parish church.
69 *Hackney Photos.* i. 9.
70 Below, local govt. (local govt. after 1837); manors (Lordshold).
71 Below, manors (Kingshold); *Hackney Photos.* i. 17; *List of Bldgs.* (1975).
72 Pevsner, *Lond.* ii. 168; *Architectural Rev.* cvi. 235.
73 *List of Bldgs.* (1991).
74 Below, local govt. (local govt. after 1837); prot. nonconf.
75 *List of Bldgs.* (1985).   76 Ibid. (1975).
77 M.L.R. 1812/4/701.
78 H.B.M.C. Lond., HAC 8; below, plate 31.

MARE STREET AND LONDON FIELDS.

There may have been a settlement on the boundary at Cambridge Heath to give its name to Mare Street, the way to Hackney village from Bethnal Green.[79] Cambridge Heath was common pasture in 1275 and adjoined London Field, which was recorded from 1540, at first in the singular, and was perhaps named from its position at the London end of Hackney's busiest local road.[80] This section treats the modern Mare Street as far north as Hackney Grove, including the stretch south of the Triangle, which until 1868 was called Cambridge Heath.[81] It also includes London Fields, both the open space and the built-up land east and south of it.

Mare Street was a distinct settlement in 1593.[82] By that date it may have included the Flying Horse inn, said to have been a staging post perhaps because of its 18th-century name, the Nag's Head, and the Horse and Groom, since all three were timber built. The first two stood at the corners of Flying Horse Yard and London Lane, both leading from Mare Street to London Fields.[83] Farther south a way to the fields, the 19th-century Mutton Lane (later West, from 1911 Westgate, Street), was described in the 17th century as Sheep Lane, which name was later applied to a route south from Mutton Lane parallel with Mare Street.[84]

In 1605 Mare Street had 23 residents who contributed to repair of the church. The highest payers included Mr. Huggins, presumably Edmund Huggins recorded in 1602, William Bird, Thomas Catcher, recorded as a moneyer in 1602, and Mr. De Quester, probably James De Quester, a foreign merchant; all were citizens of London.[85] Another William Bird, a merchant with Spanish connexions, had a house in Mare Street in 1695.[86] Some property of George Clarke was occupied in 1657 by Robert Neighbours, a blacksmith, who was allowed to build on waste in Mare Street near the sign of the Magpie, adjoining St. Thomas's hospital's land.[87] Forty-nine houses owed hearth tax in 1664, the largest being those of Clarke and of the City chamberlain Sir Thomas Player at 14 hearths, and 6 stood empty;[88] 78 were assessed in 1672.[89]

The ownership and occupation of holdings between Mare Street and London Fields had already begun to be reorganized. Dr. William Parker and his wife Elizabeth were licensed to pull down an old building in 1667 and 1675, and occupied a new house in 1685, formed from two out of four tenements on ½ a. in the north angle of Sheep Lane (later Westgate Street).[90] The site abutted north and west on other land of Parker, who also held two tenements formed out of one in Mare Street, acquired in 1672 from James Debutt, and two houses in Sheep Lane, one of them the Shoulder of Mutton.[91] All passed to the son of William Parker and his heirs.[92]

James Debutt, presumably as heir to Giles Debutt who had been made a vestryman in 1627,[93] occupied part of a neighbouring copyhold of Kingshold in 1666 and settled it on his son-in-law Richard Bristow, grocer of London, in 1672.[94] Bristow acquired a Lordshold copyhold with 5 a. in London Fields in 1695 and bought the freeholds of five Kingshold houses in Mare Street, with three tenements behind them; they included Debutt's house, which had been assessed at 10 hearths, and Lady Player's late residence.[95] His widow Elizabeth Bristow, with William Parker and Joseph Thompson, was one of the chief landholders in London Fields in 1719.[96] By will dated 1722 she left her Lordshold copyhold, the former 'Black and White House, now called the madhouse', with land in Mare Street adjoining Sheep Lane, to her son John, of the Grove, in Ellesborough (Bucks.),[97] whose nephew Richard Bristow in 1769 left them for sale to Richard Heron.[98]

East of Mare Street building was carried out by Thomas Tryon, a merchant and from 1692 a copyholder, who bought more land in 1696. By will dated 1703 he left several houses to his daughter Elizabeth, wife of Richard Wilkinson, and five to his daughter Rebecca, wife of John Owen.[99] Thomas Tryon Owen and his brother John Owen in 1728 held ten houses, presumably where Tryon's Place marked the narrow end of a track leading to Shore Place.[1]

Near Hackney village, south of the modern corner of Darnley Road, stood a three-storeyed gable-ended house reputedly built c. 1590.[2] It was granted in 1658 with nearly 4 a. of pasture called Barber's Barn to John Jones, who held adjoining premises and presumably leased it to the regicide Col. John Okey (d. 1662).[3] The house, formerly Barber's Barn, was occupied with 1½ a. by Katharine Clarke, widow, in 1715, when John Bird mortgaged it to his fellow citizen of London, the grocer John Iveson.[4] It later passed to the nurseryman Conrad Loddiges, who replaced it with his own house and Loddiges Terrace. Residents in the terrace were to include the line engraver George Cooke (d. 1834), who worked for Loddiges, and his son Edward Cooke (d. 1880), the marine painter.[5]

79 P.N. Mdx. (E.P.N.S.), 107; above, communications.
80 P.N. Mdx. (E.P.N.S.), 83, 106.
81 L.C.C. Names of Streets (1901), 83, 330. The modern Cambridge Heath Rd. is in Bethnal Green.
82 Norden, Spec. Brit., map of Mdx.; cf. Ogilby, Map of Mdx. [c. 1672].
83 Clarke, Hackney, 23, 31, 33, 289 n., 290 n.
84 G.L.R.O., M79/KH/2, p. 21; Starling's Map (1831).
85 H.A.D., D/F/TYS/1, pp. 45–6, 64.
86 P.R.O., PROB 11/444.
87 G.L.R.O., M93/2, p. 56; Trade Tokens, ed. Williamson, ii. 817.
88 G.L.R.O. MR/TH/4, mm. 1d.–2; D.N.B.
89 Ibid. MR/TH/34; Ogilby, Map of Mdx. [c. 1672].
90 G.L.R.O., M79/KH/1, pp. 12, 74; M79/KH/2, p. 21.
91 Ibid. M79/KH/3, pp. 58–60.
92 Above, Hackney village.
93 Vestry mins. 4 Oct. 1627.
94 G.L.R.O., M79/KH/1, pp. 2b, 51b.
95 Ibid. M79/LH/47, 7 Dec. 1695; M79/KH/9, pp. 321–5; MR/TH/34.
96 Ibid. M79/LH/49, 3 Apr. 1719.
97 Ibid. M79/LH/49, 10 Apr. 1724; cf. V.C.H. Bucks. ii. 335.   98 G.L.R.O., M79/LH/15, pp. 100, 125.
99 Ibid. M79/LH/47, 8 Apr. 1696; M79/LH/48, 21 Apr. 1704.
1 Ibid. M79/LH/50, 16 Apr. 1728, 30 Apr. 1736; Watson, Gentlemen, 18.
2 Robinson, Hackney, i. 88; Hackney and Stoke Newington Past, 135; H.A.D., 900.2; below, plate 13.
3 G.L.R.O., M79/KH/9, p. 293; D.N.B.
4 M.L.R. 1715/3/109–10.
5 Robinson, Hackney, i. 89–90; Terrier, Winter 1991/2; D.N.B.; below, econ. hist. (mkt. gdns).

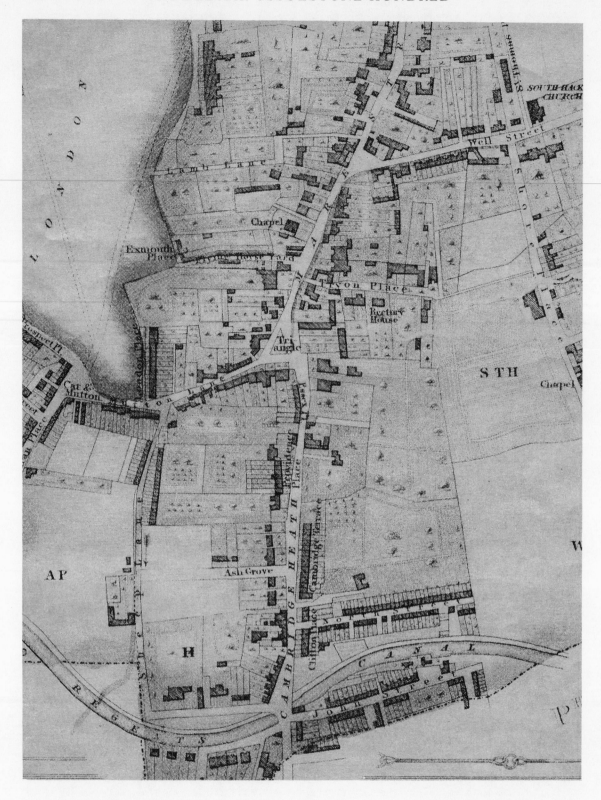

THE SOUTH END OF MARE STREET *c.* 1830

A Haggerston brickmaker, John Waxham, in 1713 mortgaged land in Tower Street fronting London Fields, where a house had been built and others were planned.[6] That Tower Street was probably not the later Tower (from 1938 Martello) Street, at the end of London Lane along part of the line of Church Path, but rather the later Lamb Lane, said to commemorate the owner of a large house of *c.* 1720 at the corner of Mare Street;[7] nearby pasture was bordered on

6 M.L.R. 1713/4/95.
7 [W. A. South], *Letter to J– C–, being an Epitome of the*   *Case of Mrs. Piggott* (1836), 6 (in H.A.D.); *D.N.B.* s.v. Barker, John; Clarke, *Hackney,* 26.

the south-west by Sheep Lane.[8] Jacob Alvares had moved to the neighbourhood by 1717 and held 7 copyhold houses, some having been divided, by 1730.[9]

Mare Street was the most populous district of the parish in 1720, with 111 ratepayers, and contained 9 of the 36 select vestrymen in 1729.[10] More built-up than the high road through Kingsland, it had 19 licensed inns by 1723, including the Shoulder of Mutton where Church Path reached the south end of London Fields and the Red Lion at Cambridge Heath; three inns were called the Swan, two the Cock, and two the Ship.[11] Ratepayers numbered 140 in 1735 and 199 by 1761 but had barely increased by 1779, when Mare Street was overtaken in numbers by Homerton and rivalled by Clapton.[12] The traveller Celia Fiennes died at a house in Mare Street near Well Street in 1741.[13]

In 1745 buildings lined both sides of Mare Street between Mutton Lane and London Lane, leading respectively to the south and north ends of London Fields. They were probably densest at the junction with Well Street and did not extend far down that road or any side road except Mutton and London lanes, although at the end of London Lane they lined part of London Fields. Houses were not yet continuous along Mare Street: there were breaks between Bethnal Green and the houses at Cambridge Heath, between those houses and Mutton Lane, where the road widened beside a pond at what was later called the Triangle, and between London Lane and Church Street.[14]

The most impressive 18th-century development was on the east side of Mare Street. St. Thomas's hospital followed its decision to build on the site of Shore Place[15] with a lease in 1769 under which Robert Collins laid out St. Thomas's Square in 1771–2. A Congregational chapel was opened on the south side in 1772 and served by distinguished ministers. Richard Price (d. 1791), of the Old Gravel Pit meeting, moved to no. 2 in 1786.[16]

Farther north the hospital allowed small-scale development east of Mare Street under a lease of 1780 to Joseph Spackman, whose Spackman's Buildings until 1868 marked the beginning of Hackney village.[17] Building also began to spread along the north side of Well Street as far as Shore Place, with a short terrace of 1785 and a slightly earlier pair. The first terrace in St. Thomas's Place, a narrow way between the square and Well Street, was built by Thomas Pearson between 1805 and 1807. Denmark Place was built on the south side of Well Street in 1810.[18]

Farther south the village around the Triangle

became linked with Cambridge Heath. In 1789 Benjamin Bond Hopkins leased land stretching east for c. 300 yd. to Giles Wells, a market gardener of Bethnal Green, and the Mare Street frontage was subleased to James Benson, who in the 1790s built a terrace called Cambridge Row (later part of the neighbouring Cambridge Terrace and from 1868 nos. 30 to 56 (even) Mare Street).[19] Close to the parish boundary John (from 1871 Vyner) Street ran eastward by 1811,[20] before the Regent's canal cut it off from land to the north, where similarly cramped houses were built on former Hopkins land in North (from 1938 Northiam) Street.[21]

South of London Fields the Cat and Mutton (formerly the Shoulder of Mutton) in 1790 marked the end of a row of building along the south side of Mutton Lane on land of William Parker Hamond, whose Shoulder of Mutton field lay to the west.[22] Garden ground south of the row, bounded east by Sheep Lane, was sold to Thomas Pearson in 1799, with 1 a. north of Mutton Lane. Neighbouring pieces included 11 houses newly built by George Plumridge, sold in 1798 to Peter Pearse, and adjoining land sold in 1800 to James Potts, a purchaser of Hamond's lands near the Grove,[23] who was bankrupt by 1817.[24] Duncan Place on the line of Church Path (from 1881 part of the Broadway, in 1937 renamed Broadway Market), had been named by 1811. So too had London Place (later part of London Fields East Side) leading north from Mutton Lane.[25] Isaac Alvares built a house for his mistress Mrs. Jenkins in Tower Street (soon renamed Lamb Lane) in 1810 and his own residence had made way for several buildings in Mare Street by 1812.[26] Flying Horse Yard (in 1821 called Exmouth Place) and Lamb Lane, although not wholly built up, housed tradesmen and workmen in 1821.[27]

In 1831 buildings formed almost a continuous ribbon from Cambridge Heath to Hackney village. Houses in Mare Street north of St. Thomas's Square were compared favourably with those farther south, many of which presumably were older, and with shops north of the Grove.[28] Towards Grove Street further growth waited on plans for the Cass and St. Thomas's hospital estates: behind Cambridge Row, Giles Wells's widow Mary held garden ground where Victoria Park Road could not be constructed until the lease expired in 1850.[29] Towards London Fields there was some cramped building in Sheep Lane and more on Shoulder of Mutton field in George and John streets (later Hamburg and Bremen, from 1918 Croston and Dericote, streets). South-west of the Fields a start made

8 M.L.R. 1715/3/52–3.
9 G.L.R.O., M79/LH/50, 12 Aug. 1730; below, manors (Alvares).
10 H.A.D., P/J/P/76; vestry mins. 23 Aug. 1729.
11 G.L.R.O., MR/LV3/16, 107.
12 H.A.D., P/J/P/91, 121, 150.
13 Illustrated Journeys of Celia Fiennes, ed. C. Morris (1982), 13, 15, 24; H.A.D., P/J/LT/6, p. 17; inf. from H.A.D.   14 Rocque, Map of Lond. (1741–5), sheet 6.
15 Below, Well Street.
16 Watson, Gentlemen, 24; Lost Hackney, 14; below, prot. nonconf. (Congs.).
17 Watson, Gentlemen, 27, 132; Hackney Dir. (1849).

18 Watson, Gentlemen, 24, 27, 52, 72.
19 H.B.M.C. Lond., HAC 12; Pevsner, Lond. ii. 173.
20 H.A.D., P/J/Misc/II/1.
21 Watson, Gentlemen, 52.   22 H.A.D., V 2.
23 G.L.R.O., M79/KH/7, pp. 47, 53, 82; above, Hackney village.   24 G.L.R.O., M79/KH/8, p. 46.
25 H.A.D., P/J/Misc/II/1.
26 G.L.R.O., M79/LH/27, p. 98; below, manors (Alvares); Case of Mrs. Piggott, 6.
27 H.A.D., P/J/CW/124, p. 61.
28 Thomas, 'Hackney', 2. Rest of para. based on Starling's Map (1831).
29 H.B.M.C. Lond., HAC 12.

on Lansdowne Place in Lansdowne Road (from 1938 Lansdowne Drive) preceded the exploitation of adjoining land in Dalston.[30] The eastern edge of London Fields was built up only with London Place, a few houses in Exmouth Place (shown at the end of Flying Horse Yard), and near the ends of Lamb Lane and London Lane. Arnold House faced London Fields opposite the buildings south of London Lane; it had been leased in 1825 from William Thompson Corbett (d. 1832) of Elsham (Lincs.) and probably in 1802 from Thomas Corbett (d. 1808), whose wife had inherited land of Joseph Thompson.[31] Between the Fields and Mare Street the land was mainly occupied by outbuildings and gardens; they included those of Dr. Warburton's house, once William Parker's, Pembroke House, and the Corbetts' London House in London Lane, all three being asylums.[32]

The junction at the Triangle was so busy in 1827 that all the verges were to be cut back to widen Mutton Lane and a footpath along Mare Street; the central plot was to be fenced as an ornamental space.[33] Infilling began towards London Fields, where dense building around Helmsley Street, reaching the Fields at Helmsley Terrace, by 1852 represented the development of the Alvares estate for George Jenkins.[34] Warburton Road, parallel with Flying Horse Yard, replaced Dr. Warburton's asylum and its long garden; William Frederick Tuck planned to build at least 20 houses in 1847 and Warburton Place along Mare Street in 1848.[35] More small houses formed Warburton Square, which was separated from London Fields by Pacifico's almshouses of c. 1851 and a chapel of c. 1863, both built on land sold by the Brandon family to William Bull in 1846.[36] Thomas George Corbett made a building lease for the west side of Tower (later Martello) Street in 1856.[37] St. Michael and All Angels' church was built in 1864 at the west end of Lamb Lane, while Pembroke House, with Melbourne House and West Lodge to the north, survived at the east end.[38]

New houses behind the east frontages of Mare Street were chiefly the work of builders active around Well Street. Marmaduke Matthews, of Cambridge Lodge south of the Triangle, in 1856 built a large pair called Cambridge Lodge Villas farther back, blocking plans by the St. Pancras land society to reach the main road.[39] Tryon's Place was extended to the east in the 1840s by

H. D. Hacon as Tryon's Terrace, the whole length being named Tudor Road by 1865.[40] Avenues were planned north and east of St. Thomas's Square in 1853, in expectation of the closure of Loddiges's nursery.[41]

London Fields only narrowly escaped development. Agents of the landholders were denying access to all but Church Path in 1860[42] and presumably united to advertise for builders in 1862. The offer did not include a square plot of nearly 4 a. in the north-west, formerly of Mrs. Hamond and later of William Rhodes and still nursery ground in 1862. Covered with the houses south of Wilman Grove by 1870, it was where a west London surveyor called George Clarkson was building quickly c. 1867, when his title was disputed by preservationists.[43] Supporters of building pointed to the neglected state of London Fields but were frustrated by concern to save a large space so close to the City.[44] The district's only other public spaces were the garden of St. Thomas's Square and disused graveyards south of the Congregational chapel and along the east side of St. Thomas's Place.[45]

South-west of the Triangle, towards the Regent's canal, conditions were cramped. A few private grounds survived between the Cambridge Heath houses and Sheep Lane in 1865 but most made way for the G.E.R.'s line opened in 1872.[46] The raised railway, whose arches were to attract workshops, cut north between Mare Street and London Fields, with a station in Grosvenor (from 1878 Mentmore) Terrace, and added to the industrial character of an area said in 1870 to be very poor.[47] The G.E.R.'s purchase of Pembroke House[48] led to infilling south of Lamb Lane, where Sidworth Street was named in 1872 and Bayford Street in 1873. Crowded housing also filled Fortescue Avenue and other roads to the north, where Grosvenor Terrace like Sidworth Street faced the railway and where Ellingfort Road was named in 1878 and Gransden Avenue in 1880.[49] Small businesses by 1872 were numerous in London Place and by 1888 had spread farther along the frontage to London Fields.[50]

The main street, with tramways from 1873,[51] attracted purpose-built institutions, including chapels, Morley hall at the Triangle in 1879, and Lady Holles's sch. midway between Well Street and St. Thomas's Square in 1882.[52] Other bodies, notably the Elizabeth Fry refuge and later, at Cambridge Lodge Villas, St. Joseph's hos-

30 Below, Dalston.
31 H.A.D., M 4404/1, 6; M.L.R. 1803/1/404–5; cf. G.L.R.O., M79/LH/49, 3 Apr. 1719; Burke, Land. Gent. (1846), i. 264.   32 Below, pub. svces.
33 G.L.R.O., M79/LH/22, pp. 250–1.
34 Ibid. M79/LH/27, p. 100; below, manors (Alvares).
35 G.L.R.O., M79/KH/12, pp. 83, 86–9, 119–24.
36 Old O.S. Map Lond. 40 (1870); below, social; prot. nonconf. (Meth.); manors (Alvares).
37 H.A.D., M 4404/2/1–3.
38 Old O.S. Map Lond. 40 (1870); below, list of churches; pub. svces.
39 Watson, Gentlemen, 79; below, Grove Street and Well Street.
40 Watson, Gentlemen, 52; Stanford, Map of Lond. (1862–5 edn.), sheet 7.
41 Below, Grove Street and Well Street.
42 H.A.D., J/V/1, pp. 354–5.

43 Ibid. H/LD 7/4; ibid. V 2/6; ibid. M 4404/3/1–7; M 4404/10; Starling's Map (1831); Old O.S. Map Lond. 40 (1870).
44 H.A.D., H/LD 7/4; M.B.W. Mins. of Procs. (1866), pp. 358, 894; J. J. Sexby, Municipal Pks. of Lond. (1898), 351–2; below, pub. svces.
45 Below, pub. svces.
46 Stanford, Map of Lond. (1862–5 edn.), sheet 7; above, communications. The frontage of the former British Penitent Female refuge, opened c. 1845 in Cambridge Heath, survived in 1994: inf. from Isobel Watson.
47 Below, econ. hist. (ind.); Nat. Soc. files.
48 Below, pub. svces.
49 Stanford, Map of Lond. (1891 edn.), sheet 7.
50 e.g. Helmsley Terr.: Hackney Dir. (1892); Kelly's Dir. Hackney (1888).   51 Above, communications.
52 Below, prot. nonconf. (Baptists, Congs., Cath. Apost.); educ. (private schs.); Hackney Photos. ii. 22.

pice, took over existing houses.[53] The sanitary chemist Charles Meymott Tidy (d. 1892), a local doctor's son, lived in 1870 at Cambridge Heath.[54] Three schools were built around London Fields between 1873 and 1898.[55]

Well-to-do residents still lived along Mare Street in the 1880s, with some who were 'fairly comfortable' south of Well Street and with a few immediately south of Hackney Grove. Around London Fields the well-to-do along the north side were separated from the fairly comfortable in Lansdowne Road and the Broadway by mixed households along the east side and by the poor along the west side south of Wilman Grove. Many streets near the railway were also mixed, including Lamb Lane and Helmsley Street; Exmouth Place, Warburton Road and Square, and Helmsley Place were poor. South of London Fields, Ash Grove was mixed but Ada Street and its parallels on the opposite side of Sheep Lane were poor, as were Hamburg and Bremen streets west of Lansdowne Road. Duncan Street, Road, and Square were very poor.[56]

Widening of Mare street was sought in 1885 but it was not until 1899 that the L.C.C. agreed to improve the whole length from the Triangle to Hackney village.[57] The forecourts of several large houses on both sides south of Hackney Grove, including Spackman's Buildings, were compulsorily purchased in 1902 for work that was finished by 1906.[58] Building was planned in the gardens of nos. 263-9 (odd), at the corner of Richmond Road, in 1903.[59] Many factories were built behind, on the east side notably off Tudor Road and Well Street, including a bus garage of 1911, and near the end of Darnley Road. On the west side they faced the street, displacing old houses over shops south of London Lane. Near the railway they included Silesia Buildings, named in 1906, off Gransden Avenue. Demolition had taken place south of Lady Holles's school by 1905 and more was awaited south of the Triangle c. 1912.[60] The L.C.C. in 1904 opened Darcy Buildings (later House), 40 dwellings and one of the first of its blocks in Hackney, on the site of Pacifico's almshouses.[61]

After the First World War the area grew more industrial. Conversions of houses into workshops were reported in 1928, notably in Tudor Road and Mentmore Terrace, as were new factories in Mare Street and around Tower Street and Ash Grove.[62] Large houses also made way for flats over shops, as at nos. 206 and 208 Mare Street, on the corner of Devonshire Road, in 1925 and at Richmond Court (no. 257) by 1937.[63] The timber-framed no. 149 Mare Street, once the Flying Horse, and two houses north of

Tudor Road, probably the last remnants of Tryon's Place, were in poor condition by 1930.[64] The closure of Cambridge Heath Congregational church in 1936 later provided more space for St. Joseph's hospice.[65]

Slum clearance was chiefly around London Fields. In 1935 more than half of the inhabitants of 75 houses around Duncan Square had been rehoused by the L.C.C., presumably in part of its massive Duncan (from 1974 Alden) House.[66] Warburton Square had been newly cleared of 156 houses in 1935 and most of its inhabitants resettled, presumably in Warburton House next to Darcy House, by 1938.[67] Hackney M.B. planned to clear most of Essex Street, south of the Triangle, in 1936.[68]

Victims of bomb damage included churches, the north-west corner of St. Thomas's Square, Georgian houses (nos. 107-9) at the Triangle, and Mentmore Terrace.[69] The entire northern and eastern sides of St. Thomas's Square were compulsorily purchased in 1952 and later demolished,[70] the northern making way for Pitcairn House of 1961-3, designed by Eric Lyons as part of the L.C.C.'s Frampton Park estate.[71] The garden on the east side of St. Thomas's Place was incorporated into the estate, whereas the older houses on the west side were bought in 1963 by Hackney M.B.[72] In Mare Street piecemeal rebuilding was most obvious towards the south end, with extensions for the Cordwainers' college at the former Lady Holles's school and for St. Joseph's hospice.[73] The site around the bombed nos. 107-9 was taken for Netil House, partly occupied by Hackney technical college.[74]

South of London Fields large new buildings included flats at Broadway House from 1951 in Jackman (formerly Goring) Street and the 17-storeyed Welshpool House from 1965 in Welshpool Street.[75] In 1975 Hackney L.B. approved the G.L.C.'s proposals to rehabilitate Broadway Market and the streets to the west; London Transport's depot in Ash Grove had been planned and smaller industries were to be regrouped.[76] In Ada Street a long eight-storeyed block in 1992 was being prepared for use as workshops.

In 1993 Mare Street was a nondescript mixture of low-rise factories, shops, and institutional buildings, the tallest being Pitcairn House. At the south end new factories around Ash Grove faced the junction of Northiam Street and Victoria Park road, whence new houses stretched eastward, with an empty site to the north. The last reminder of early 19th-century Cambridge Heath, a row listed in 1975 as nos. 12-20 (even) Mare Street,[77] had been acquired by the Spital-

53 Below, misc. institutions; Rom. Cathm.
54 *D.N.B.*; *Medical Reg.* (1870, 1873).
55 Below, educ. (pub. schs.).
56 *Booth's Map* (1889), NE.
57 L.C.C. *Ann. Rep.* (1899-1900), 88-9; (1900-1), 105-6.
58 Ibid. (1905-6), 172; G.L.R.O., H1/ST/E65/C/11/1.
59 G.L.R.O., H1/ST/E65/C/5/5/4.
60 Old O.S. Map Lond. 40, 41 (1913); *Hackney Photos.* i. 24, 26, 30.   61 L.C.C. *Lond. Statistics*, xli. 144-5.
62 Hackney M.B. *Rep. on San. Condition* (1928), 118.
63 G.L.R.O., H1/ST/E65/C/15/6/1; *P.O. Dir. Lond.* (1936, 1937).   64 Hist. Mon. Com. *E. Lond.* 47.
65 Below, Rom. Cathm.; prot. nonconf. (Congs.).
66 L.C.C. *Lond. Statistics*. xxxix. 134; *P.O. Dir. Lond.*

(1974); *Hackney Photos.* ii. 91.
67 L.C.C. *Lond. Statistics*, xxxix. 135; xli. 138.
68 H.A.D., H/PD/3/4.
69 *Hackney Photos.* ii. 30, 149-50, 154.
70 *Lost Hackney*, 14-16; G.L.R.O., H1/ST/E65/C/21/3.
71 Nairn, *Modern Bldgs. in Lond.* 31; below, Grove Street and Well Street.
72 H.A.D., 'Pks. and Open Spaces', 58; G.L.R.O., H1/ST/E65/C/20/1.
73 Below, educ. (tech.); Rom. Cathm.
74 *P.O. Dir. Lond.* (1975); below, educ. (tech.).
75 *P.O. Dir. Lond.* (1950, 1951, 1964, 1965).
76 H.A.D., Statutory Lists file.
77 *List of Bldgs.* (1975).

fields trust from the Crown Estate and awaited restoration.[78] Nos. 24–28, dated 1811 and similarly listed as a terrace of three storeys over a basement, had already gone. So too had James Benson's nos. 30–56 and, at St. Thomas's Square, a pedimented archway which had probably been its carriage entrance.[79] At the south-east corner of London Fields, the Ann Tayler centre had been built on the site of London Place.

Shops in Mare Street were mainly around the Triangle, which was adorned by a single tree, and the junction with Well Street. Broadway Market, much of it still awaiting refurbishment, retained most of the 60-odd shops noted in 1975.[80] Near the railway the new Bayford industrial centre had replaced terraces east of Sidworth Street. London Fields industrial area around London Lane appeared run down: nearly all the railway arches had been blocked up, many Victorian houses stood derelict or had made way for yards, and much factory space was unused. Victorian terraces were mixed with more prosperous industry in Ellingfort and Richmond roads.

The sole representative of Mare Street's early 18th-century gentlemen's residences is no. 195 (the New Lansdowne club).[81] It has five bays, of three storeys over a basement, with steps to a Doric doorcase; brown and red brickwork has been renewed, in the original style, on the upper storeys at the front.[82] Of the 18th century with alterations, and of three storeys over a basement, are nos. 224–32 (even); the first, at the corner of Darnley Road, has a bow front and was no. 1 Spackman's Buildings, the residence from 1850 to 1863 of the local historian Benjamin Clarke.[83] The early 19th-century houses of Loddiges Terrace can be seen to the south, behind the projecting shop fronts of nos. 210–218. Immediately south of the Cordwainers' college, seven early 19th-century cottages survive unexpectedly in the cul-de-sac Pemberton Place. A three-storeyed terrace, mostly over basements, forms nos. 1–24 St. Thomas's Place, where the southernmost eight houses were built by Thomas Pearson in 1807.[84]

London Fields is a flat utilitarian open space, with some mature plane trees. The former Helmsley Terrace, two- and three-storeyed over basements, survives from the early 19th century as part of London Fields East Side. Broadway Market has two-storeyed early 19th-century houses, of which nos. 75–81 (odd) are at the north-west end; the group is in poor condition and no. 77, a 'perfectly preserved contemporary small shop' in 1975, stands empty. To the west,

Dericote Street has refurbished early 19th-century linked pairs of two storeys over basements, nos. 4–18 and 5–23; they form a T-junction with the similar nos. 1–4 and 6–15 Croston Street, where others are being built in the same style.

DALSTON AND KINGSLAND ROAD. Dalston, in 1294 Derleston, probably derived from Deorlaf's tun or farm.[85] A small hamlet half way along Dalston Lane in the mid 18th century,[86] it came to denote the built-up area east of the high road.[87] The area under discussion extends west from London Fields and the edge of Hackney village to Kingsland Road and Kingsland green, where the parish boundary diverged from the road,[88] and north from the Shoreditch boundary across Dalston Lane to Downs Park Road. Dalston Lane, the only road from Kingsland to Hackney village until the 19th century, was not described as a street. The stretch nearest Kingsland Road was an easterly continuation of Ball's Pond Road and had strips of waste, largely built upon by 1831,[89] which were later sometimes called Dalston green.[90] Dalston hamlet lay east of the dog-leg which the lane followed presumably to keep its distance from the broadening Pigwell brook before crossing Hackney brook at Dalston bridge.[91] For assessments in the 16th and 17th centuries the hamlet was normally included with Newington, Shacklewell, and Kingsland, all four of them together about as populous as Hackney village (Church Street) in 1605.[92] Dalston had 23 householders assessed for hearth tax and Kingsland 28 in 1672.[93]

A house at Kingsland belonged to Alderman John Brown (d. 1532), serjeant painter to Henry VIII.[94] Dalston's largest houses in 1664 were those of Sir Francis Bickley and Alderman Thomas Blackall. By 1672 Bickley had sold to Sir Stephen White[95] and a third seat was held by Jacob Willis. Kingsland had the leper hospital south of the green.[96] Five buildings on the east side of the road included an inn in 1660.[97]

The 18th century brought faster growth to the high road settlement than to Dalston. There were at least five inns at Kingsland by 1724 but only two at Dalston,[98] where in 1733 an applicant for a third licence was refused.[99] Kingsland's ratepayers numbered 8 in 1720, 11 in 1735, 47 in 1761, and c. 120 in 1779, while Dalston's numbered 17 in 1720 and 1735, 18 in 1761, and 26 in 1779.[1]

Dalston in 1745 was a group of buildings mostly on the north side of Dalston Lane, at the turning of a way towards Shacklewell called Love Lane in 1831 (later Norfolk and from 1938

78 Inf. from H.A.D.
79 List of Bldgs (1975)
80 H.A.D., Statutory Lists file.
81 Two paras. based on List of Bldgs. (1975).
82 Hist. Mon. Com. E. Lond. 47; Pevsner, Lond. ii. 173.
83 Clarke, Hackney, pp. xv, 290 n.
84 Datestone.
85 P.N. Mdx. (E.P.N.S.), 106.
86 Rocque, Map of Lond. (1741–5), sheet 5.
87 Old O.S. Maps Lond. 40 (1870, 1913).
88 Kingsland green is partly treated under Islington: V.C.H. Mdx. viii. 41–2.

89 Starling's Map (1831).
90 Clarke, Hackney, 241.
91 Starling's Map (1831).
92 H.A.D., D/F/TYS/1, p. 69.
93 G.L.R.O., MR/TH/34.
94 D.N.B.
95 G.L.R.O., MR/TH/4, m. 4; below, manors (Graham Ho.).
96 G.L.R.O., MR/TH/34.
97 P.R.O., C 54/4038/13.
98 G.L.R.O., MR/LV4/3.
99 Ibid. P79/JN1/214, p. 72.
1 H.A.D., P/J/P/76, 91, 121, 150.

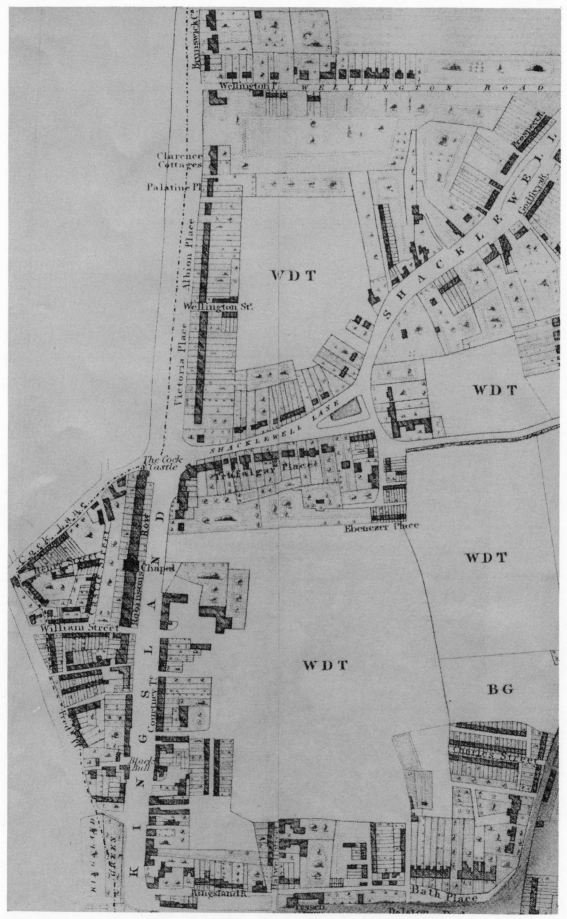

KINGSLAND HIGH STREET AND SHACKLEWELL c. 1830

Cecilia Road); a few stood opposite the junction, while the Red Cow was on the north side nearer the bridge.[2]

At Kingsland development in 1745 was confined to the high road, on the west side to Kingsland hospital and buildings west and north of the green and on the east to a short stretch north of the junction with Dalston Lane, which was to become the high street. The Three Tuns, forerunner of the Tyssen Arms, stood alone a short way along the lane and perhaps two houses bordered the high road towards Shoreditch. In 1765 the chief buildings apart from the hospital and the inns were the farmhouses of John Bartmaker and John Bellis. A strip of water on the east side of the rectangular green was presumably a channelled part of Pigwell brook; three new houses had been built to the north, beyond the Black Bull.[3] By c. 1785 houses had spread to include north of the green a row of 15 and a further row of 41, leased to William Robinson and ending in the Cock and Castle. The east side of the road was more open but included 11 houses, probably Conduit Terrace, built on a cow-layer. Towards Shoreditch 21 houses north of Haggerston Road were leased to Peter Upsdell and included the Swan.[4]

Dalston village had spread very little by 1796, when most of it belonged to the Grahams. To the north their holding stretched along Love Lane to a path which became Downs Park Road. Southward the Grahams' land reached Pigwell brook, with lands of the Tyssens, Spurstowe's charity, the Danns, and the Actons to the east and south-east and of the Rhodes family's Lamb farm to the south and south-west.[5] Dalston c. 1800 was known for its nurseries, especially the Smiths' on the south side of Dalston Lane.[6]

Large-scale development began at the west end of Dalston Lane, along the high road, and in roads projected across Lamb farm. Robert Sheldrick of Warwick Place, Kingsland Road, was building on the Rhodeses' land on the south side of Dalston Lane in 1807;[7] Dalston Terrace had new houses by Sheldrick, then of Kingsland Place, in 1813 and 1816.[8] The terrace, like Kingsland Row and Bath Place on the north side, housed mainly merchants and professional people in 1821, when the poor lived in short side streets to the north, including Charles Street, the most crowded, and Hartwell Street, named after a resident cow-keeper. A start had also been made on Roseberry Place and Mayfield Street (from 1876 Mayfield Road and from 1948 Beechwood Road), to the south. In 1821 the population of Dalston, embracing Dalston Lane and its offshoots, was 1,366.[9]

By 1831 building lined Dalston Lane eastward to the hamlet,[10] itself extended almost to Hackney brook by Navarino Terrace on the south side and Dalston Rise (until 1875 also the name of a section of the lane) on the north. Parallel with Mayfield Street, where Sheldrick was a builder,[11] Woodland and Holly streets and Park Place (later Park and from 1877 Parkholme Road) had been started by 1825, as had Forest Road.[12] Farther south Richmond Road had been projected past Lansdowne Place (later Lansdowne Road and from 1939 Lansdowne Drive) as far as London Fields, through market gardens leased to Thomas and William Rhodes. There was no building between Dalston Lane and Shacklewell, except along the high road, and very little between Pigwell brook and the Shoreditch boundary, although offshoots of Church Street and Mare Street threatened encroachment from the east.[13]

In Kingsland Road Joseph Jackson had built three houses by 1802 and Joshua Jackson was building in 1815.[14] The green was to be reduced on its south side and to be given an ornamental railing in 1807[15] and brickearth had been exploited by the Tyssens for building north of the junction with Dalston Lane by 1814.[16] Terraces in 1821 included Robinson's Row with several shops north of the Black Bull, the middle-class Kingsland Place a little south of Dalston Lane, and Kingsland Crescent from Haggerston Road to the boundary. The most crowded area was one of poor streets between the green and Cock and Castle Lane (later Castle Street, from 1913 Crossway), which helped to raise the population to 4,241. In Providence Row, behind Providence Place which adjoined Robinson's Row, a cramped terrace was leased in 1824.[17] By 1831, when part of De Beauvoir Town's frontage to Kingsland Road had yet to be built, houses lined all the east side of the road; they included Prospect Terrace, apparently containing Upsdell's Row on land belonging to Stoke Newington rectory.[18]

The roads planned for Lamb farm were extended and multiplied to form a rough grid which by 1870 covered all the land south of Pigwell brook. Many were more than ½ mile long, although London Fields and the N.L.R. and G.E.R. lines impeded direct links between Kingsland and Mare Street.[19] William and Thomas Rhodes from 1833 made many leases for c. 70 years of houses in Richmond Place, Queen's (from 1939 Queensbridge) Road, Forest Road, which included Forest Row, and Holly Street.[20] Leases for c. 90 years for more houses in Grange (from 1873 Lenthall) and Queen's roads, including Richmond Terrace and Richmond Villas, and in Shrubland Grove (later Mapledene Road) followed in 1839–40. Lessees included the builders John William Rowe of

2 Rocque, *Map of Lond.* (1741–5), sheets 5, 6.
3 Ibid.; H.A.D., V 19.
4 H.A.D., D/F/TYS/66.
5 Ibid. V 14; V 70; below, manors (Graham Ho.; Lamb Farm).
6 Foot, *Agric. of Mdx.* 16; below, econ. (mkt. gdns.).
7 M.L.R. 1807/5/281.
8 Ibid. 1814/1/95; 1816/5/264, 555.
9 H.A.D., P/J/CW/124, pp. 122–34.
10 Para. based on *Starling's Map* (1831).
11 Leased from 1819: M.L.R. 1825/10/607.
12 Ibid. 1823/1/270; 1825/6/683; 1825/10/256, 372, 606.
13 Above, Hackney village.
14 M.L.R. 1803/4/337; 1815/5/269.
15 G.L.R.O., M79/LH/20, pp. 9–10.
16 H.A.D., M 557.
17 Ibid. P/J/CW/124, pp. 135–59; M.L.R. 1824/11/313.
18 *Starling's Map* (1831); G.L.R.O., M79/LH/23, pp. 29–30; *V.C.H. Mdx.* viii. 205.
19 Old O.S. Map Lond. 40 (1870).
20 e.g. M.L.R. 1838/2/603, 757; 1838/5/389–90; 1839/8/393.

Ball's Pond, Richard Liscombe of Haggerston, and Louis England,[21] an Islington timber merchant who often subleased to smaller builders.[22] St. Philip's, the district's first church, was on land given by William Rhodes.[23] East of the high road, villas were to be built facing Stonebridge common in 1845 on the rector of Stoke Newington's land, which was also taken for Blomfield (from 1877 Welbury) Street.[24]

Meanwhile Sir William Middleton, heir to the Actons, was building in Shoreditch.[25] One of his fields extended into Hackney east of Stonebridge common and he may have bought land from William Rhodes farther north, where Shrubland Road was built; Queen's Road, partly through Rhodes's land, was apparently designed by Sir William's surveyor George Pownall as a carriage way from his property near the Regent's canal through more spacious streets, commemorating the Middleton family, around Albion Square. Exchanges of lands took place with Rhodes in 1843 and 1845.

Middleton's development in Hackney began under an agreement of 1840 with Islip Odell, from Upper Clapton, for the land immediately east of Stonebridge common. The Middleton Arms was followed by houses in Middleton Road, leased in 1842.[26] Odell, a brickmaker who promoted development by others, settled until 1862 at Shrubland Cottage in Queen's Road, where Hemblington Cottages had been built by 1843.[27] Presumably Pownall was responsible for the layout of Albion Square, where many of the houses had been built by 1844.[28]

The development of Middleton's outlying land north and east of London Fields involved his buying part of Pitwell field behind Hackney Grove from the Danns' estate in 1838[29] and agreements with St. Thomas's hospital in 1843, for extending Richmond Road eastward to Mare Street, and with Spurstowe's charity. The land in Pitwell field was leased in 1847 to James Kent Vote[30] but remained open until most was taken for the G.E.R. line. Vote, who had built cheap housing for Middleton in Haggerston, in 1852 was to be leased further parcels near London Lane behind Mare Street. There was building on Spurstowe's charity land in Navarino Road in 1860 and in the new Graham Road 'at Pitwell' in 1861.[31] Nearby the Rhodes estate continued its development eastward: in St. Philip's Road, Forest Road East, Lavender Grove East, Lansdowne Road (later Drive), and Albert Road East (later part of Middleton Road) in 1861,[32]

and also in Wilton, Salisbury, and Greenwood roads in 1863.[33] Houses linked Dalston with the south end of Hackney village, lining both sides of Richmond Road, by 1865. Wilton and Graham roads did not yet run for their full length to the north, where Wilmot (later Greenwood) and Alma (later part of Navarino) roads had been planned across market gardens stretching to the N.L.R. line.[34]

While building spread to the south, the middle section of Dalston Lane attracted charitable institutions: at the east end a school of industry in 1803 and among the houses along the middle section an orphans' asylum in 1832, succeeded by the German hospital in 1845, and a girls' refuge at Manor House in 1849.[35] The middle and eastern sections of the lane were largely cut off from the south by the N.L.R. branch line but were linked more directly with the high road by Ridley Road. The land at the western end came to be largely industrial after the opening of Dalston Junction and its diverging railway lines in 1865.[36]

Around the grounds of the German hospital, resited south of the railway, and of Dalston Refuge, building proceeded quickly for the Massies, heirs to the Graham estate. In 1853 they had planned the lines of Graham Road from its western end and of Albion Grove (from 1877 Stannard Road), Alma (from 1877 Ritson) and Massie roads, and the western half of Fassett Square, although none had yet been named[37] and the last two were not finished until the late 1860s.[38] Houses were leased in Dalston Lane by 1855 and in Graham and Massie roads by 1860.[39] Farther north land on both sides of Love Lane was to be leased in 1862.[40] Much of it was taken by William Hodson, a builder resident at Graham House and responsible for part of Fassett Square. He and the Massies subleased to Cornelius Margetts, Silas Honeywill, and other builders who were active in Norfolk Road in 1863 and also in Church (from 1865 Sandringham) Road by 1864.[41]

Dalston in 1849 was described as a recently increased suburban village, with some handsome old houses.[42] Dalston Lane had a few shops near the Compasses at the corner of Love Lane but most were at the west end, where they had spread from the high road.[43] By 1859 both Dalston and Shacklewell were as populous as Kingsland, although more respectable.[44] East of the Graham estate building continued in the 1850s and 1860s between Graham Road and

21 e.g. ibid. l839/5/326, 726–32.
22 Ibid. 1839/8/314, 584, 586; *V.C.H. Mdx.* viii. 25–6.
23 Below, list of churches.
24 G.L.R.O., M79/LH/25, pp. 149–51; ibid. 28, pp. 213–15.
25 Three paras. based on inf. from Isobel Watson.
26 M.L.R. 1842/7/949–51.
27 Ibid. 1843/8/82.
28 H.B.M.C. Lond., HAC 22.
29 G.L.R.O., M79/KH/10, p. 296.
30 Ibid. 12, p. 67.
31 M.L.R. 1860/16/819; 1861/17/164, 569.
32 Ibid. 1861/17/7, 184, 439, 601, 860, 1217, 1353; 1862/2/453–4, 583–8.
33 Ibid. 1863/20/412, 516; 1863/21/246; 1863/20/349–57, 412–13; 1863/22/337–8; 1863/22/338, 702–8.
34 Stanford, *Map of Lond.* (1862–5 edn.), sheet 7.

35 Below, educ. (pub. schs.); social; pub. svces.; manors (Graham Ho.).
36 Above, communications; Stanford, *Map of Lond.* (1862–5 edn.), sheet 7.
37 G.L.R.O., M79/LH/27, pp. 220, 227.
38 Stanford, *Map of Lond.* (1862–5 edn.), sheet 7; M. Hunter, *Victorian Villas of Hackney* (Hackney Soc. 1981), 24–5.
39 G.L.R.O., M79/LH/28, pp. 72–4; ibid. 29, pp. 163–5, 186–91, 217–20, 234–5, 244–5, 257, 279–82, 399, 400–3; M.L.R. 1860/16/719–20.
40 G.L.R.O., M79/LH/29, pp. 421, 427–8.
41 M.L.R. 1863/20/418; 1863/22/188–9, 1267–9, 1343; 1864/9/1012–13, 1018–19; 1864/11/51–2, 950–3.
42 Lewis, *Topog. Dict. Eng.* (1849), iv. 4.
43 *Hackney Dir.* (1849).
44 *Ragged Sch. Union Mag.* xi. 77.

Dalston Lane over the Middleton, Spurstowe's charity, and Tyssen estates.[45] By 1870 houses along Dalston Lane and Amhurst Road East joined Dalston to Hackney village, although similar links farther south along Wilton and Graham roads, including a tramway, awaited the completion of the G.E.R. line. Amhurst Road, whose Dalston end in 1845 had been only a projection south of Downs Park Road, was built up; so too were Pembury Road, from its junction with Amhurst Road at Dalston Lane, and Pembury Grove.[46] In Downs Park Road land had still to be taken by the Grocers' Co. for the later Hackney Downs school, opened in 1878.[47] Only a few short roads remained for building: Cottrill Road, Spurstowe Terrace, and Sigdon and Bodney roads in the east, and Alvington Crescent and parts of Colvestone Crescent in the northwest. All those sites had been filled by 1891.[48]

Kingsland Road by 1865 denoted the high road as far north as Dalston Lane, while High Street (from 1869 Kingsland High Street) was the stretch between Dalston and Shacklewell lanes.[49] High Street, except where a few houses on the west side overlooked the green, was wholly commercial by 1849.[50] Premises there were sold by the Tyssens before and after the arrival of trams in 1872. Sales began with those of 8 houses and 2 shops on the east side and of the Black Bull and 5 shops on the west side in 1869;[51] they continued in the 1870s and 1880s,[52] when more sporadic sales took place in nearby residential roads, including Ridley Road in 1872 and Sandringham Road in 1877.[53] The remains of Kingsland green were about to be built on, despite local protests, in 1882.[54]

Most of the streets c. 1890 contained a mixture of people who were well-to-do or fairly comfortable. The most solidly prosperous areas were Queen's Road, Parkholme Road, parts of Richmond, Forest, and Graham roads and Kingsland High Street, the east end of Dalston Lane, and Downs Park and Amhurst roads. Poor streets formed a small block south of Wilman Grove in an angle of London Fields and also existed behind both High Street frontages and by the railway at the west end of Dalston Lane, where Tyssen Street, soon to be lined by factories, housed the very poor. Frederick Terrace (from 1938 Place), between Kingsland Terrace and the N.L.R. branch line, also held the very poor.[55] An outward movement from London by the better off was said to have been partially checked at Dalston, which possessed few public houses and to which some families had returned after finding working-class newcomers in remoter suburbs. St. Philip's church catered for the

middle class but Holy Trinity, in Woodland Street and nearer Dalston junction, was in a poorer district.[56] St. Mark's parish was claimed in 1894 to be growing rapidly poorer, with few houses still occupied by a single family.[57]

The 20th century brought little change until the Second World War. Houses at the corner of Dalston Lane and Navarino Road made way for Navarino Mansions, 300 flats completed in 1905 by the Four Per Cent Industrial Dwellings Co. for Jews from London's east end.[58] Dalston Lane lost its last spaces with the replacement of the girls' refuge by the five-storeyed Samuel Lewis Trust Dwellings in 1924[59] and further building for the German hospital.[60] Kingsland High Street underwent such normal commercial changes as the provision of cinemas[61] and the refronting of shops.[62] The slums of Frederick Place were planned for clearance in 1937.[63] On the border with Lower Clapton the L.C.C. compulsorily purchased c. 20 a. for its Pembury estate, a small part of which was opened in 1938.[64]

Bombing made room for Hackney M.B.'s first estates in Dalston. Mayfield Close was opened off Forest Road in 1948[65] and followed by Holly Street estate to the south before 1961, and Rhodes to the north.[66] Buildings were of five storeys or less, until Cedar Court and three other twenty-storeyed towers were built by 1975 along Queensbridge Road south of Richmond Road. Almost half of south Dalston's grid of Victorian streets, from Middleton Road along the west side of Queensbridge Road to Dalston Lane, was removed including Woodland Street, the north end of Holly Street, and the west ends of Lenthall and Mapledene roads. Farther east Hackney's Mapledene and Wilton estates had been built by 1961, followed by the L.C.C.'s Morland and Fields estates, by Wayman Court with a sixteen-storeyed tower by 1975, and Blackstone estate. The avenues immediately east of Queensbridge Road were relatively unaffected, as was the neighbourhood of Albion Square, designated a conservation area in 1975.[67] In north Dalston the terraces south of Downs Park Road between Abersham and Ferncliff roads made way for the low-rise Mountford estate. Pembury estate was extended southward by the G.L.C. to Dalston Lane, where building continued in 1987.

Parts of Dalston Lane and the high road looked neglected after the replacement of 19th-century buildings and the closures of cinemas, some factories, and, in the 1980s, of the German hospital and Dalston Junction station.[68] In particular the northern end of Kingsland Road,

45 Rest of para. based on Old O.S. Map Lond. 40 (1870).
46 H.A.D., M 725.
47 Below, educ. (pub. schs.).
48 Stanford, *Map of Lond.* (1891 edn.), sheet 7.
49 Ibid. (1862–5 edn.), sheet 7.
50 *Hackney Dir.* (1849).
51 H.A.D., D/F/AMH/555, pp. 8–9.
52 Ibid. *passim.*   53 Ibid. pp. 5–6, *passim.*
54 H.A.D., H/LD 7/4; Hackney bd. of wks. *Ann. Rep.* (1880–1), 10.
55 *Booth's Map* (1889), NE.
56 Booth, *Life and Labour*, iii (1), 79, 93.
57 Nat. Soc. files.

58 Pearman, *Excellent Accn.* 81–5.
59 Inf. from senior housing officer, Sam. Lewis Trust; below, manors (Graham Ho.).
60 Below, pub. svces.   61 Below, social.
62 *Hackney Photos.* ii. 36.   63 H.A.D., H/PD/3/4.
64 L.C.C. *Lond. Statistics*, xli. 152–3.
65 *Hackney Photos.* ii. 99.
66 Rest of para. based on Hackney, *Official Guide* [1961]; *P.O. Dir. Lond.* (1964 and later edns.); O.S. Map 1/10,000, TQ 38 SW. (1979 edn.).
67 H.A.D., Conservation Areas file.
68 Above, communications; below, social; econ. (ind.); pub. svces.

backed by a disused railway cutting, suffered the destruction after 1975 of Kingsland Place and neighbouring houses;[69] the shops which had occupied their ground floors were replaced by single-storeyed buildings southward to Forest Road. The cramped streets west of Kingsland High Street and south of Crossway contained some derelict property and sites cleared for car parks in 1991. The opening of Dalston Cross shopping centre on the east side,[70] on the site of Abbott Street and railway sidings, was intended to regenerate the district.

Dalston, like much of Hackney, is a patchwork of Victorian housing and council estates. It lacks impressive public buildings and open spaces, although it adjoins London Fields, and its busiest roads are the peripheral high road and Dalston Lane, around whose junction is the commercial centre. Nonetheless Kingsland High Street has a variety of shops to rival Mare Street and supplemented by a market in Ridley Road.

Dalston Lane, in addition to the listed buildings of the German hospital, has a few reminders of the roadside village, mostly of stock brick.[71] On the north side no. 57 is a three-storeyed L-planned house, built c. 1800 like the former Graham House at no. 113.[72] On the south nos. 128–46, called Dalston Place in 1831, form a refurbished row of plain houses, of three storeys over basements and with the ground storeys rendered.[73] No. 160, Marlow House, has three storeys, attic, and basement, and is early 18th-century, with a late 18th-century doorcase in an extension. Nos. 162–8 (even) form a group: no. 164, with its original red brick, is one of an 18th-century pair with three storeys, attics, and basements, and no. 166 is a two-storeyed stuccoed villa of the early 19th century. Nos. 212–226, refurbished and with grass in front, are four early or mid 19th-century pairs; the middle two have Ionic porticos and are of two storeys, attics, and basements, the others are of three storeys and basements. Navarino Mansions, boldly planned and detailed in the Arts and Crafts style, is the culminating work of the Four Per Cent Co.'s architect Nathan Joseph.[74]

The east side of Kingsland Road retains nothing noteworthy north of Haggerston Road, where nos. 358 and 360 may have formed the end of Kingsland Crescent before the demolition of intervening houses. Nos. 318–46 (even) survive to the south as a mistreated relic of most of the long shallow crescent depicted in 1852.[75] Each house has three bays and is of three storeys, attic in a mansard roof, and basement. Conversions for use as workshops, often clothiers', or offices have involved changes to most features, although former elegance is recalled by the refurbishment of no. 338.

South Dalston is rich in housing from the 1840s and 1850s, built sometimes in terraces but usually as semidetached villas, 'simple brick boxes with mass produced embellishments'.[76] The best known examples are the pairs and short terrace, each of two or three storeys and basement, around the rectangular garden at Albion Square, where only the narrow west side is empty after the demolition of the former Albion hall. The 30 houses were once ascribed to J. C. Loudon as an example of his transition from late Classical to Italianate;[77] their architect is not known,[78] although George Pownall presumably controlled the plans. The houses on the south side form a group with nos. 8–16 Albion Drive (until 1939 Albion Road), where nos. 15–21 (odd), 25, and 27 make a further group.

Queensbridge Road's east side contains no. 200, incorporating no. 202, an altered Italianate villa, next to Hope Cottages at nos. 204–6, dated 1844, both 'especially pretty'[79] and forming a group with no. 212. Terraces farther north include nos. 276–302 and 304–14 (even), with friezes and mansard roofs with dormers, forming a group with no. 332, and nos. 364–72, forming a neglected group with two pairs beyond. Lansdowne Drive's west side contains a long uniform early or mid 19th-century terrace at nos. 178–86. At the north corner of Croston (formerly George) Street no. 170, perhaps with an 18th-century core, was derelict in 1992. Mapledene Road's north side has a terrace at nos. 53–59 which forms a group with early or mid 19th-century pairs at nos. 61–71. Of similar date are linked pairs at nos. 131–41 (odd) Richmond Road and villas at nos. 1, 3, and 7–13 (odd) Parkholme Road.

Many unlisted terraces around Colvestone Crescent are notable for their embellishments, some taken from pattern books but others showing that in north Dalston 'builders reached a climax of ingenuity' in the early 1860s.[80]

DE BEAUVOIR TOWN is taken to be the south-west corner of Hackney parish from Kingsland Road west to Southgate Road and from the Regent's canal north almost to Ball's Pond Road.[81] It embraces the Hackney estate of the de Beauvoir family, lords of Balmes, whose land extended farther south into Shoreditch, and excludes Ball's Pond Road, which was built up as part of Islington.[82] Balmes House and the northern part of the estate were sometimes said to be in Kingsland.[83]

Development was stimulated by the cutting of the Regent's canal south of Balmes House,[84] by which time the house was an asylum and much of its land had been leased to the Rhodes family. William Rhodes (d. 1843) secured in 1821 a building lease from Peter de Beauvoir which was

69 List of Bldgs. (1975).
70 Below, econ. (ind).
71 Rest of section based on List of Bldgs. (1975).
72 Below, manors (Graham Ho.).
73 Starling's Map (1831).
74 Pearman, Excellent Accn. 84; Tower to Tower Block, no. 45.   75 Below, plate 8.
76 Archit. of Lond. 67.
77 Pevsner, Lond. ii. 169; Archit. of Lond. 67.

78 The architect was probably not Islip Odell, as in H.B.M.C. Lond., HAC 22.
79 Pevsner, Lond. ii. 169; Hunter, Victorian Villas, 30.
80 Hunter, Victorian Villas, 43, 46–7.
81 Cf. Starling's Map (1831).
82 Below, manors (Balmes); V.C.H. Mdx. viii. 42.
83 G.L.R.O., MR/TH/34; Old O.S. Map Lond. 40 (1870).
84 Three paras. based on H.B.M.C. Lond., HAC 2A.

to lead to lawsuits[85] and unusually made no stipulations about the buildings; it covered all 150 a., said in 1834 to have been the largest single amount conveyed to a speculative builder in London.

Rhodes planned a grid pattern, with four squares on diagonal streets intersecting at an octagon. His paving and lighting Bill of 1823[86] was abandoned, however, and development was piecemeal and mainly along the fringe, where modest buildings could most easily find tenants: by the canal, along or off Kingsland Road,[87] and in Tottenham Road. A few subleases were made by Rhodes from 1822 and more from 1823,[88] when Richard Benyon de Beauvoir stopped all activity through an injunction. Rhodes was soon allowed to resume work on Kingsland basin but apparently he started no new building before control of all development passed to de Beauvoir in 1834. Subleases were still made by Rhodes, as of houses in Kingsland Road in 1824, in Enfield Road in 1826, and in Tottenham Road in 1825 and 1828.[89]

Most of the land between Kingsland and Hertford roads had been built on by 1834, except immediately north of Englefield Road. To the west there was new building only by the canal, at the corners of Hertford and Downham roads, perhaps on the eastern side of the later De Beauvoir Square (nos. 1–16 Park Place), and part of Tottenham Road. Balmes House survived between Downham Road and the canal, although threatened by the lines of Whitmore and Frederick (later De Beauvoir) roads.[90] For the land thereafter leased by R. B. de Beauvoir a more spacious layout was devised, with terraces mainly in short blocks and many semidetached villas; of the projected squares only the southeastern was retained, as De Beauvoir Square, although the diagonals partly survived in Enfield, Stamford, and Ardleigh roads.[91] Progress was hastened by the proximity of depots in Kingsland basin and by loans from the estate to individual builders.[92] In the 1840s subleases were made for most of the remaining houses. Presumably most builders followed their own designs, although the remaining three sides of De Beauvoir Square, begun in 1838 with Thomas Smith as the chief builder, may have been by W. C. Lockner, architect of St. Peter's church.[93]

The estate was intended to be almost wholly residential, except around the basin and at the south-west corner, where a factory leased from 1823 was apparently the forerunner of that of Thomas Briggs the tentmakers.[94] Public houses were permitted, the Duke of York in Downham Road being leased to a brewing company as early as 1822, and shops were leased in Southgate Road from 1843.[95] Kingsland Road's west side

was commercial south of Downham Road and north of Beauvoir Terrace by 1849. Away from the high road nearly all the shops were in Southgate, Hertford, and Downham roads, as were the 7 public houses then and the 8 in 1869.[96]

Small areas were taken for a Roman Catholic church and school of 1855 in Tottenham Grove (from 1864 part of Tottenham Road) and for a fire station in St. Peter's Road (from 1936 St. Peter's Way), larger areas for Tottenham Road board school (1874), the Metropolitan hospital (1886), Enfield Road board school (1894), and Kingsland fire station (1895).[97] Such inroads perhaps affected the neighbourhood less than scattered and often partial conversions of houses into business premises.

Residents c. 1890 were well-to-do in Kingsland and Southgate roads and, with the fairly comfortable, in most other streets. They were merely comfortable in Tottenham Road and poorer in the lanes to the north and in Derby (from 1909 Lockner) Road, where a terrace was sandwiched between Kingsland Road and De Beauvoir Square, and in Hertford Road close to the basin. The very poor lived at the east end of De Beauvoir Crescent by the canal.[98] Workshops, many of them for wood products, existed around the fringes, notably in Derby Road and in De Beauvoir Crescent and other streets between Downham Road and the canal, besides a few in Englefield Road and the north part of De Beauvoir Road. At the heart of the estate was a small group that was to fill the east side of De Beauvoir Road from Church (from 1937 Northchurch) Road to Englefield Road; it originated in the long back gardens of houses in Mortimer Road and in 1902 it included a builder's merchant, a picture-frame maker, and a wheelwright. Tottenham Road had shops but those in Southgate Road were confined to the south end and those in Downham Road were mainly at the east end. North of Downham Road only a few houses were said to consist of apartments, in contrast to many where roads continued into Islington.[99]

Because of Kingsland basin the agents of the estate in 1937 asked for the south-east corner between Downham and Hertford roads to be zoned for general industrial rather than business purposes. Zoning for industry, soon recommended for all the area south of Downham Road, distinguished it from the north side of that road, which was already zoned for business and acted as a buffer for the mainly residential streets beyond. In 1938 De Beauvoir Crescent was suggested as another business zone to protect housing to the north. In 1951 the agents claimed that the area east of Hertford Road was suitable for light industry and asked for Southgate Road,

85 Below, manors (Balmes). 86 H.A.D., 346.3351.
87 M.L.R. 1822/10/433; 1823/1/473; 1824/5/414–15.
88 G.L.R.O., E/BVR/29–193 (rentals 1830–1950).
89 M.L.R. 1824/5/594; 1825/6/536–7; 1825/10/465–6;1828/6/535; 1838/3/336.
90 G.L.R.O., E/BVR/423. 91 Ibid. E/BVR/424.
92 e.g. in 1847: ibid. E/BVR/46, pp. 30, 38–42, 44.
93 Below, churches. No evidence found for attribution of square to Roumieu & Gough, as in Pevsner, Lond. ii. 169.
94 Old O.S. Map Lond. 40 (1870); G.L.R.O., E/BVR/46, p. 6; Insurance plan 392 (1891).
95 G.L.R.O., E/BVR/46, pp. 9, 23–4.
96 Hackney Dir. (1849); Green's Hackney Dir. (1869–70).
97 Old O.S. Map Lond. 40 (1913); below, pub. svces.; below, educ. (pub. schs).
98 Booth's Map (1889), NE.
99 Old O.S. Maps Lond. 40 (1870, 1913); P.O. Dir. Lond. (1902).

always partly commercial, to be scheduled for business. The L.C.C., however, retained both areas as residential.[1]

Continued erosion of the residential area was eventually followed by the better preservation of its centre.[2] Part of the northern segment of De Beauvoir Town, between Buckingham and Tottenham roads, was rebuilt in the early 1960s as Hackney M.B.'s Kingsgate estate. A larger area, west of the canal basin, containing many small factories, made way c. 1969 for the De Beauvoir Town council estate,[3] which included a library and shops. De Beauvoir Square lost its oldest (east) side to the Lockner Road estate.[4] The De Beauvoir Town association was formed in 1968, however,[5] and the rest of the square with the area bounded by Englefield, Northchurch, Southgate, Hertford, and Stamford roads in 1969 became a conservation area, later extended southward.[6] In 1988 the social problems of the De Beauvoir Town council estate produced complaints of a 'high-rise hell', whereas most of the 19th-century houses had been restored and some of their roads closed to through traffic to create a middle-class enclave.[7]

The Kingsland Road frontage has no survivals from the mid 19th century except north of Englefield Road, where two long terraces, separated by the rebuilt Prince of Wales public house, contrast with the assorted buildings on the east side of the high road. Both terraces have three storeys over basements and are of stock brick, the ground storeys rusticated and rendered. The south range, nos. 419–45 (odd), is complete except at the ends and retains part of a balcony for its central portion. The north one, nos. 457–77, built by Charles Henry Moore of Islington c. 1841,[8] bears a label on its parapet inscribed Beauvoir Terrace.

Behind the frontage the area south of Downham Road contains 19th-century industrial premises around the basin and, in the south-west corner, Briggs's red- and yellow-brick factory, in multi-occupation, besides newer works to the north. Between the two industrial sites the dark brown-brick and concrete buildings of the housing estate include towers of 18 storeys in De Beauvoir Road.

Refurbishment continued in 1992 north of Downham Road, in an area of stock-brick houses, semidetached or in short terraces and usually of two storeys over a basement.[9] Infilling has been mainly with flats or maisonettes built to the existing scale. Purpose-built works, used by signmakers and clothing firms, intrusively survive around the junction of De Beauvoir and Englefield roads. Perhaps the most striking loss has been the east side of De Beauvoir Square.

Rhodes's modest houses are represented only at the west end of Tottenham Road. Most houses are later and have classical details. Hertford Road contains Benyon Cottages, nos. 97–107 (odd), a symmetrical group of three pairs dated 1839, and De Beauvoir Road has five pairs, nos. 87–105 (odd), of about that date. Northchurch Road, elegant and little changed, has many semidetached villas, including nos. 40–46, 48 and 50, 52 and 54, 1–15, and 17 and 19; nos. 21–27 form a symmetrical composition of four houses and nos. 29–35 a near symmetrical terrace. Southgate Road, at nos. 110–16, has three-storeyed terraces with pillared porches, as at nos. 110–16 north of Ufton Grove. All those houses combine with their neighbours to form groups of architectural interest.

A transition from classical to Tudor and Jacobean styles, visible in nos. 387–401 Kingsland Road before the building of the Lockner Road estate,[10] can be seen in and around De Beauvoir Square. The north, west, and south sides of the square consist of pairs, mostly of two bays, in stock brick with stone dressings; all have high pitched roofs and two storeys over basements, with attics under shaped gable-ends. Features include a few clusters of diagonal chimneys and several windows with lozenge glazing. The north side of the square (1839) is a near symmetrical composition of five pairs. The four pairs surviving on the west side and the five on the south are later and more uniform. The group which they compose around the railed circular garden is completed at the north-west corner by modern flats disguised to match their neighbours and to the south-west by St. Peter's church and its former Vicarage, no. 85 Mortimer Road. Opposite the church is no. 10 Northchurch Terrace, altered but also Jacobean.

SHACKLEWELL originated in a settlement along Shacklewell Lane, a loop east of the high road between Dalston and Stoke Newington common.[11] In the 19th century the northern part of the loop was built up as Rectory Road, whereupon Shacklewell came to denote the district stretching eastward from Stoke Newington Road to where Hackney brook skirted Hackney Downs and northward to include the common.[12] Shacklewell and Newington, however, were by tradition separate localities and the area described here is confined to that around the surviving Shacklewell Lane, stretching from Downs Park Road only to the north end of Amhurst Road between the high road and Hackney Downs.

Despite its Old English name,[13] Shacklewell was not recorded until 1490 when Thomas Cornish, a London saddler, had a tenant there.[14] Presumably its quiet but accessible position off the high road and the presence of a spring or well had made the hamlet attractive to citizens.

1 G.L.R.O., AR/TP/2/33.
2 Para. based on *P.O. Dir. Lond.* (1952 and later edns.).
3 *Hackney Photos.* ii. 21.
4 Ibid. 102.
5 H.B.M.C. Lond., HAC 2A.
6 *Stoke Newington & Hackney Observer*, 21 Feb. 1969, 3a; H.A.D., Conservation Areas file.
7 *Hackney Echo*, 26 Oct. 1988, 7; H.A.D., Bldgs. file.
8 M.L.R. 1842/3/43.
9 Rest of subsection based on H.B.M.C. Lond., HAC 2A; *List of Bldgs.* (1975).
10 Pevsner, *Lond.* ii. 169; below, plate 30.
11 Rocque, *Map of Lond.* (1741–5), sheet 5; *Starling's Map* (1831). 12 Clarke, *Hackney*, 247.
13 *P.N.Mdx.* (E.P.N.S.), 107.
14 P.R.O., PROB 11/8 (P.C.C. 40 Milles).

Richard (d. 1504), son of Richard Cornish, also a Londoner, left lands in Hertfordshire and at Shacklewell.[15] Sir John Heron (d. 1522), perhaps the richest man in Hackney, had an estate extending into neighbouring parishes and centred on his seat at Shacklewell,[16] where his reputed manor included the holdings of five tenants in 1540.[17] Most if not all of Shacklewell was copyhold, part of a larger estate held in turn by the Herons, the Rowes, and the Tyssens.[18]

Shacklewell, normally assessed with Kingsland, Dalston, and Newington, had only 14 householders listed for hearth tax in 1672, when by far the largest house was the Rowes'.[19] The number of ratepayers rose from 11 in 1720 to 16 in 1735, 29 in 1761, and 47 in 1779.[20] Samuel Tyssen was Shacklewell's one select vestryman in 1729.[21] Its one inn in 1725 and 1750 was the Cock,[22] south-west of the village at the junction of Shacklewell Lane and the high road.[23] The Green Man at Shacklewell green was licensed by 1760.[24]

The village grew up along both sides of Shacklewell Lane c. ¼ mile east of the high road, where a strip of waste formed the green.[25] From the high road to the green the lane was known as the Crossway in 1701, when a watch house was to be built beside it, and in 1745. Waste which had been dug for gravel[26] apparently adjoined a plot at the north end of Shacklewell green which was leased in 1706 to William Francies, a merchant tailor, who built two brick houses and paid rent to the Tyssens 'in the hall of the mansion house at Shacklewell'.[27] The mansion with c. 3 a. was leased in 1741 to Richard Tillesley, a Shoreditch carpenter, who had pulled down part by 1743, when he mortgaged new houses to Charles Everard, a Clerkenwell brewer.[28] Everard was leased 12 new houses on the site in 1762.[29] He held most of the property on the north-west side of the lane by 1765, including part of the old manor house and at the north end of the village a house which before 1766 had been the poorhouse of St. Bride's parish, Fleet Street.[30] The Cock remained the only building at the south-west end of Shacklewell Lane. Shacklewell ponds filled part of the verge where the lane curved north towards the village, in the angle between the lane and the track to Hackney Downs (later Downs Park Road).[31]

On the south side of the green Doggett's dairy of 1770 partly survived in a wall adjoining the 19th-century Grove House. John Godfrey by 1785 had houses east of the corner with Love Lane (later Norfolk Road), where the end house of Godfrey's Row was dated 1799. Prospect Row, with pedimented doorcases, stood on the north side of Shacklewell Lane immediately north of the green by 1785.[32] The Revd. John Hindle, presumably the biblical scholar, was authorized to do some building in 1787[33] and a new house had been built next to two cottages on the south side of the lane in 1802.[34] The vicar hoped to provide a chapel at Shacklewell in 1807,[35] when the village was spreading towards the high road. In 1804 John Carruthers held five houses fronting Shacklewell Lane near the ponds and was to dig brickearth for neighbouring houses of the third or fourth class.[36] In 1811 six or more fourth-class houses were to be built almost opposite by John Hindle of Kingsland Crescent; he had secured an adjoining part of Cock and Castle field, which stretched to the high road. Thomas Greenwood was to replace four decayed houses in the village with one or more of the third class.[37] Two more third-class houses had been built by 1814,[38] when Hindle acquired land near Hackney Downs.[39]

Gentlemen lived along both sides of Shacklewell Lane between the high road and the green, with several tradesmen in the middle section, in 1821. Trafalgar Place at the west end had a mixed population, with cramped terraces in Ebenezer Place, a cul-de-sac to the south.[40] Old buildings west of the manor house were to make way for six fourth-class houses in 1824.[41] The composer Vincent Novello (d. 1861) moved in 1823 to Shacklewell green, reputedly to Milton House at the north-east end, but soon left lest his children's education should suffer from the village's seclusion.[42] George Thomas Landmann (d. 1854), an engineer in the Peninsular War, spent his later years at no. 2 Trafalgar Place.[43]

Meanwhile the high road north of Dalston Lane was built up with terraces, as was much of the Stoke Newington side by 1810.[44] A building plot with a 100-ft. frontage and c. 25 a. stretching to Shacklewell Lane were leased in 1806 to Thomas and William Rhodes.[45] In 1817 they obtained a 350-ft. frontage, with brickearth behind,[46] and in 1818 they were leasing new houses in Prospect Terrace close to the site acquired for West Hackney church.[47] An offshoot from the high road, called Wellington Place, had eight gentleman's residences by

15 Ibid. PROB 11/14 (P.C.C. 10 Holgrave).
16 Below, manors (Shacklewell).
17 B.L. Add. MS. 35824, f. 28b.
18 Below, manors.
19 G.L.R.O., MR/TH/4, m. 3d.; MR/TH/34.
20 H.A.D., P/J/P/76, 91, 121, 150.
21 Vestry mins. 23 Aug. 1729.
22 G.L.R.O., MR/LV4/15; MR/LV6/79. By c. 1785 the Old Cock: H.A.D., D/F/TYS/66.
23 H.A.D., V 19.
24 G.L.R.O., MR/LV7/49.
25 Ibid. M79/LH/48, 25 Apr. 1701; Rocque, Map of Lond. (1741–5), sheet 5.
26 G.L.R.O., M79/LH/48, 18 Apr. 1707.
27 Ibid. M79/LH/126/14.
28 M.L.R. 1743/3/256, 349.   29 H.A.D., M 517.
30 Ibid. V 19; ibid. M 516; Hackney Photos. ii. 38.
31 H.A.D., V 19.

32 Starling's Map (1831); Hackney Photos. ii. 38; H.A.D., M 3230, pp. 91, 116; ibid. D/F/TYS/66.
33 H.A.D., M 532; D.N.B.
34 M.L.R. 1803/4/198.
35 Vestry mins. 31 Mar. 1807.
36 H.A.D., M 544.   37 Ibid. M 551–2.
38 G.L.R.O., MR/B/C. 1814/84.
39 Ibid. M79/127/10.
40 H.A.D., P/J/CW/124, pp. 146–9, 183–4; Starling's Map (1831).
41 H.A.D., M 753 (1).
42 D.N.B.; M. Cowden Clarke, Life of Vincent Novello [1864], 24–5; Clarke, Hackney, 250.
43 Hackney Dir (1849); D.N.B.
44 V.C.H. Mdx. viii. 169.
45 M.L.R. 1807/1/435–6.
46 Ibid. 1817/4/19; 1863/21/822.
47 Ibid. 1818/5/350–3.

1821;[48] it had been extended due east as Wellington Road (from 1939 Shacklewell Road) to meet Shacklewell Lane north of the green by 1831. To the south Wellington Street formed a short cul-de-sac, later also extended to Shacklewell Lane (and from 1886 called Arcola Street, after Napoleon's victory). To the north Brunswick Grove (later the west end of Farleigh Road) also formed a cul-de-sac, leading to cottages in Caroline Place. From Shacklewell village another cul-de-sac thrust northward, as Shacklewell Row. There were no other houses behind those along the high road and Shacklewell Lane.[49]

Infilling advanced with a building lease of 1837 for John Ross's nursery along the south side of Wellington Road,[50] which had led to the building up of much of that road and Somerford Grove by 1849 and of the whole by 1865.[51] Buildings or their gardens filled all the land between the high road and Shacklewell Lane south of Wellington Road in 1865, when crowded terraces formed Hindle, Middle, and John (later Dunn) streets west of Shacklewell Row. Meanwhile the slightly superior Foskett Terrace was built on the south-east side of Shacklewell Lane in 1866;[52] it replaced Shacklewell ponds, although some waste survived to be known locally as 'the small green'.[53] More terraces were later built between the high road and Shacklewell green, behind the manor house and its neighbours, where Seal and Perch streets were named from 1881.

Farther east villas were built in the mid 1860s in Downs Park and Norfolk (later Cecilia) roads and also along the central section of Amhurst Road,[54] where they had been preceded by the modest Amhurst Terrace along a footway to Hackney Downs[55] and where the villas' long gardens were cut off from the downs c. 1872 by the G.E.R.'s Enfield line. Market gardens survived north of Wellington Road in 1865. Only a few houses stood in Farleigh Road and in the northernmost section of Amhurst Road by 1868; Foulden Road, between them, was no more than a name. All the sites had been filled by 1891.[56]

Mid 19th-century Shacklewell was largely residential, served by a few shops in Shacklewell Lane, some of them facing the green, and more in Wellington Road. Stoke Newington Road, similarly, was less commercial than the high streets of Kingsland and Stoke Newington.[57] Industrialization, presaged by Eyre & Spottiswoode's works at the corner of Shacklewell Lane and Downs Park Road,[58] accompanied the building of terraces around Hindle Street and south

of Arcola Street. A board school of 1876 displaced some houses,[59] local poverty induced Merchant Taylors' school to open a mission in Shacklewell Row in 1890, and factories, including a saw mill and an extension of the printing works, came to fill most of the nursery land behind the houses on the site bounded by Shacklewell Lane and Norfolk and Downs Park roads. A successor to the manor house was replaced by shops built c. 1880 by John Grover of New North Road, Islington.[60] Redevelopment in Stoke Newington Road involved the demolition of Prospect Terrace and the provision of shops at the corner of Amhurst Road c. 1878.[61] Institutions included the German orphanage, moved from Dalston, the North London magistrates' court in Stoke Newington Road, and a new synagogue for Stoke Newington near the west end of Shacklewell Lane.[62]

The synagogue, said to dwarf its surroundings, and new factories were criticized in 1903 by a resident who claimed to have witnessed over 25 years the village's absorption into London. The green, in public ownership since 1883, had recently been improved,[63] although at its north-east end it was planned to replace Acorn Cottage by two houses with workshops behind in 1896. Nearby it was planned that Milton House, latterly an academy, should make way for nine houses with workshops behind under a lease of 1906 to Frederick William Castle; a two-storeyed red-brick row ambitiously called Milton House Mansions was finished in 1907 and Milton works in 1908.[64] The streets south-east of Shacklewell green remained slightly better than those on the west side, whose poverty contrasted with the neatness of tree-lined Wellington Road and the spaciousness of Amhurst Road.[65]

Shacklewell was still mainly residential in 1928. Industry was spreading around Shacklewell Lane, in converted houses or their grounds, and a few workshops, chiefly for clothing, existed around Wellington Road;[66] Simpsons' large factory was built in Stoke Newington Road in 1929.[67] To the east villas in Amhurst Road near Downs Park Road made way c. 1934 for 320 flats in eight five-storeyed red-brick neo-Georgian blocks built by the Samuel Lewis housing trust.[68] East of Amhurst Road more villas, with gardens stretching to the railway, made way for the 320 flats of the Four Per Cent Industrial Dwellings Co.'s Evelyn Court; its five-storeyed blocks, designed by Charles Joseph and an early example of the use of pre-stressed concrete, were opened in 1934.[69] An adjoining 3½ a. to the south were compulsorily purchased by the L.C.C.,

48 H.A.D., P/J/CW/124, p. 181.
49 Starling's Map (1831).
50 H.A.D., M 718.
51 Hackney Dir. (1849). Rest of para. and following para. based on Stanford, Map of Lond. (1862–5 edn.), sheet 3; Old O.S. Map Lond. 30 (1868).   52 Datestone.
53 H.A.D., M 3230 [scrapbk. hist. by A. J. Hooper], p. 154.
54 Hos. leased from 1866 and 1867: G.L.R.O., M79/TA/20.
55 H.A.D., M 3230, pp. 23, 52.
56 Stanford, Map of Lond. (1891 edn.), sheet 5.
57 P.O. Dir. Six Home Counties (1845); Hackney Dir. (1849, 1869).   58 Below, econ. hist. (ind.).
59 Below, educ. (pub. schs.: Dalston county).

60 H.A.D., M 3230, p. 96; ibid. LBH 7/5/26/89; P.O. Dir. Lond. (1879).
61 G.L.R.O., M79/TA/22, p. 57.
62 Old O.S. Maps Lond. 30 (1868, 1894); ibid. 40 (1870, 1914); Kelly's Dir. Stoke Newington (1891); below, misc. institutions; manors (Shacklewell); Judaism.
63 H.A.D., M 3230, pp. 12, 44; below, pub. svces.
64 G.L.R.O., M79/TA/22–3; H.A.D., M 3230, pp. 109–110, 114.
65 W. Besant, Lond. North of Thames (1911), 571–2.
66 Hackney M.B. Rep. on San. Condition (1928), 117, 119.
67 Below, econ. hist. (ind.).
68 P.O. Dir. Lond. (1934).
69 Pearman, Excellent Accn. 93–4; below, plate 33.

which in 1936 opened the Downs estate, 204 dwellings also in five-storeyed blocks.[70] Hackney M.B. in 1936 replaced Prospect Row with the three six-storeyed blocks of Shacklewell House and by 1939 had replaced Hindle and Middle streets with 197 flats in five-storeyed ranges called Hindle House.[71]

Further changes accompanied rebuilding after the Second World War. The west end of Shacklewell (formerly Wellington) Road and 9 a. stretching to Farleigh Road were taken for Hackney's Somerford estate, the first part of which was opened in 1949; ultimately with 150 dwellings, it consisted of one- to three-storeyed buildings with interconnected squares, designed by Frederick Gibberd as a compromise between the L.C.C.'s 'cottage' estates and high density flats.[72] Immediately to the south Shacklewell primary school filled part of the site of Hindle street board school from 1951[73] and to the east the low-rise Shacklewell Road estate was built. Individual blocks of flats included Leigh House in Farleigh Road, Norfolk House in Cecilia Road c. 1957, Hurst Lodge in Farleigh Road by 1975, and, later, the Samuel Lewis trust's Charles Utton Court in Amhurst Road.[74]

In 1950 the Tyssen estate accepted that its property south of Arcola Street should be scheduled for light industry but asked the L.C.C. to retain shops at the corners of Shacklewell green and Cecilia Road.[75] Much small-scale industry survived in 1991, although at the south end of the green it had made way c. 1937 for Dalston county school,[76] which, as Kingsland school, came to occupy most of the land to the south. By 1991 the former printing works to the west, which had passed to the London Electricity Board, had been superseded by the yellow-brick Independent Place, advertised as offices and studios. Some clearance had taken place at the west end of Shacklewell lane, where the synagogue's conversion into a mosque was a sign of Turkish Cypriot immigration already apparent in the ownership of workshops and small factories, especially for clothing or for motor repairs, and of restaurants and shops.

Shacklewell is a mixture of council housing, late Victorian terraces, and industry, where the most notable building is St. Barnabas's church,[77] almost hidden off Shacklewell Row. The Amhurst Arms, at the corner of Amhurst Terrace, is mid 19th-century, stuccoed and with pilasters of different orders.[78] Shacklewell green, a strip of grass with railings and tall plane trees, serves as a traffic island. Its north-west side is still faced by two- and three-storeyed 19th-century houses, several containing empty shops. The 'small green' also forms an island, where some 19th-

century houses on the north side have been renovated; Foskett Terrace and a few shops are on the south side. Shacklewell Lane, with its reminders of the village, has been superseded as the commercial centre by Stoke Newington Road. Shops make that stretch of the high road virtually a continuation of the high streets of Kingsland and Stoke Newington; the magistrates' court and Simpsons' former factory remain prominent on the Hackney side, although to the north the building line has been set back for the Somerford estate. Least altered is the north part of Shacklewell, where stock-brick terraces line Farleigh and Foulden roads; the second is the more uniform, with long two-storeyed ranges regularly interspersed with three-storeyed houses. Off Shacklewell green a distinctive and partly pedestrianized enclave is formed by Perch, April, and Seal streets, whose modest yellow-brick terraces built by John Grover[79] have terracotta plaques dated from 1881 to 1886.

NEWINGTON AND STAMFORD HILL

consisted of those parts of Hackney which lay along the high road north of Shacklewell, on the east side of what became Stoke Newington High Street and on both sides where the road ascended from Hackney brook. Until the 19th century the area was called simply Newington and was grouped for assessments with Shacklewell, Kingsland, and Dalston.[80] Both Newington[81] and Sanford or Saundfordhill, probably named from the ford across the brook, were recorded in the 13th century; the spelling Stamford Hill is found from 1675.[82]

Although land at Stamford Hill was to be sold under a Londoner's will of 1394,[83] early building along the high road seems all to have been at the junction with Stoke Newington's Church Street. There were tradesmen and two inns on the west side of the high road in 1570, a wine tavern at Stamford Hill in 1600,[84] and buildings on the Hackney side of the high road, forming Newington Street, in the 1670s.[85] In Newington 23 houses were assessed in 1672, all of 5 hearths or less.[86] No select vestryman lived in Newington in 1729.[87] It nonetheless grew faster than other settlements along or near the high road in the mid 18th century: 16 residents paid poor rates in 1720, 35 in 1735, and 91 by 1761.[88]

East of the high road Hackney brook skirted the north side of Cockhanger green before turning south towards Hackney Downs. The green, later Stoke Newington common, apparently stretched almost to the high road before the inclosures of strips of waste, such as those authorized in 1711, which included a cottage and workshop, and in

70 Hackney, *Official Guide* [1938]; L.C.C. *Lond. Statistics*, xli, 150–1.
71 *Hackney Photos.* ii. 38; Hackney, *Official Guide* [1938; 1961].
72 *Archit. Rev.* cvi. 144–52; Pevsner, *Lond.* ii. 169; Hackney, *Official Guide* [1961].
73 Below, educ. (pub. schs.).
74 *P.O. Dir. Lond.* (1956 and later edns.).
75 G.L.R.O., AR/TP/2/419.
76 Below, educ. (pub. schs.).
77 Below, churches.
78 *List of Bldgs.* (1975).
79 H.A.D., LBH 7/5/26/89, 112.
80 e.g. H.A.D., D/F/TYS/1, p. 69.
81 *V.C.H. Mdx.* viii. 143.
82 Above, communications.
83 Guildhall MS. 9171, f. 302r.
84 *V.C.H. Mdx.* viii. 168, 172–3; Lysons, *Environs*, iii. 296.
85 Ogilby, *Map of Mdx.* [c. 1672].
86 G.L.R.O., MR/TH/34.
87 Vestry mins. 23 Aug. 1729.
88 H.A.D., P/J/P/76, 91, 121.

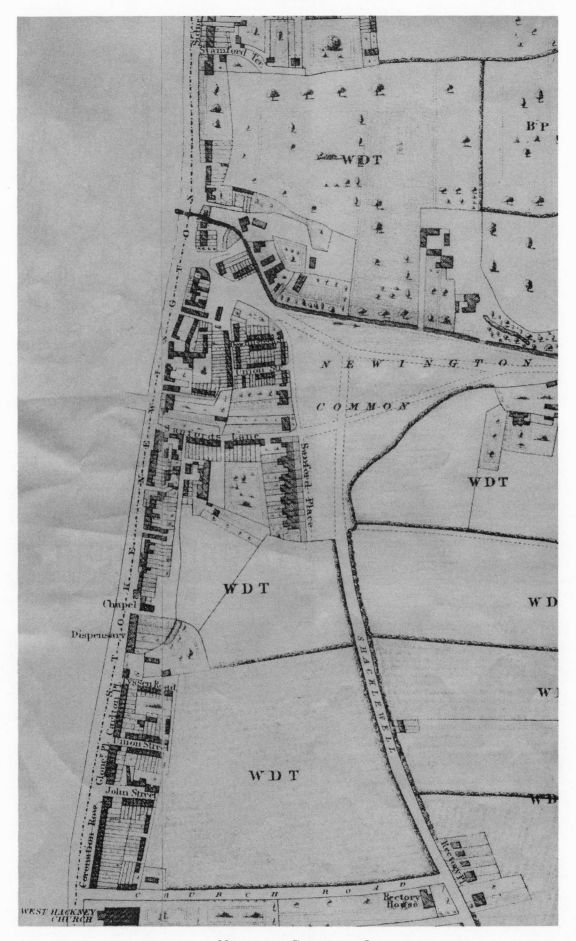

NEWINGTON COMMON *c.* 1830

1715, which lay near the Three Blackbirds inn.[89] On Stamford Hill the presence of brickearth may have led Francis Tyssen to lease 21 a. to the brickmaker Ralph Harwood in 1694.[90] Roadside waste was leased in 1706, when no building was to take place close to a particular existing house.[91] One of several strips at Stamford Hill included a cottage, beside a length of nearly 150 ft.[92] subleased in 1721 to a Hoxton brickmaker.[93]

While building spread along the high road as an extension of Stoke Newington village, it also grew up at the top of Stamford Hill. A little to the north of the junction with the way across Clapton common, a tollgate was set up under the turnpike trust of 1713.[94] Gentleman's houses, not yet occupied, existed in 1740 on the east side of the high road,[95] where the Turnpike inn was named by 1750.[96] A gibbet at Stamford Hill displayed the remains of criminals executed at Tyburn in the 1740s; gibbet field in 1765 lay south of the road from Clapton common, behind Cedar House.[97]

By 1745 buildings lined both sides of the high road above and below the junction with Church Street.[98] On the east side they included the Coach and Horses and the Black Bull, both licensed by 1723.[99] Nearly opposite the junction a narrow way (later Sanford Lane) led to Cockhanger green, where the triangular common had been reduced almost to its modern dimensions. North of the lane another way to the common contained almshouses built by Thomas Cooke under a lease of 1740.[1] At least four houses stood north of the brook and the common. To the south-east there were only fields. The east side of the road up Stamford Hill had buildings between Stamford bridge at the foot and a point almost half way to the approach from Clapton common; they included the Bird Cage, licensed by 1732,[2] near a horseshoe-shaped pond. The west side had a solitary building almost half way up the slope, called Panter's Farm in 1765. Since both the Bird Cage near the foot and the Turnpike inn at the summit were described as in Stamford Hill,[3] it seems that Newington contained only the houses south of the brook.

Stamford Hill's elevation made it increasingly desirable. Cedar House, three-storeyed and with a portico, was built on the south corner of the road from Clapton common,[4] perhaps under a lease of 1760 to the brickmaker Thomas Upsdell.[5] Land nearby was leased in 1766; it abutted four new houses, one of them presumably

Cedar House and another Warwick House.[6] They stood alone c. 1785, when the Turnpike marked the end of the more northerly group, which contained two large houses and five smaller ones.[7]

Dense development took place in and east of Stoke Newington High Street. By 1765 the Hackney side had shops for a carpenter, a blacksmith, and a wheelwright, 15 tenements in Webb's Yard opposite Church Street, and an inn beyond the brook, the Weaver's Arms, licensed by 1750. Behind the frontage a bowling green, leased to William Webb, bordered part of the common.[8] To the south Henry Sanford, the brewer,[9] in 1775 took on lease land along Sanford Lane, where he may already have had a brewhouse. He built, out of his own resources, 29 small houses forming Sanford Terrace and Place, which were to be sold under his will of 1795.[10]

Building continued at Newington: five other houses stood near the Bird Cage by c. 1785, four being north and one south of the pond.[11] Inclosures in 1793 included strips nearby[12] and beside Newington common, where the width of the brook was to be a uniform 10 ft.;[13] the pond was drained. More building leases for the east side of Stamford Hill were made in 1806, some of which were soon assigned to John Hindle.[14] The Rhodes family took leases of c. 25 a. between the high road and the north end of Shacklewell Lane (later Rectory Road) in 1806; Thomas and William Rhodes leased individual houses in the high road in 1817.[15] From c. 1821[16] the south end of Stoke Newington High Street was marked by West Hackney church,[17] whence Church Road (later the west end of Evering Road and Manse Road) led through fields to its Rectory and Shacklewell Lane. Coronation Row and other terraces lined the high street, past the culs-de-sac of John and Union streets (later roads, respectively renamed Batley Road in 1909 and Hollar Road in 1937) and Tyssen Road. Sanford Lane, housing mainly tradesmen and labourers in 1821, led to the superior Sanford Place, which had some Jewish occupants;[18] crowded alleys and courts included Lawrence's Buildings south of the lane and Bowling Green Street with its offshoots to the north. More buildings clustered around the road leading to the north side of the common, where there were several gardeners. The east side of the street remained commercial beyond Stamford or Newington bridge to the

[89] G.L.R.O., M79/LH/49, 6 Apr. 1711, 21 Apr. 1715; ibid. M79/LH/126/12, 28 Sept. 1711; ibid. M79/LH/126/15, 6 June 1715.
[90] H.A.D., M 508; below, econ. hist. (ind).
[91] G.L.R.O., M79/LH/48, 28 Mar. 1706.
[92] Ibid. M79/LH/49, 6, 26 Apr. 1717; M79/LH/126/16, 28 Sept. 1717; M79/LH/126/17, 28 Oct. 1717.
[93] Ibid. M79/LH/126/19, 7 Sept. 1721.
[94] Above, communications.
[95] H.B.M.C. Lond., HAC 54.
[96] G.L.R.O., MR/LV6/79.
[97] H.A.D., H/LD7/3; ibid. D/F/BAG/2, pp. 7–9; below, this section.
[98] Two paras. based on Rocque, Map of Lond. (1741–5), sheet 5. [99] G.L.R.O., MR/LV3/107, 116.
[1] Below, charities.
[2] G.L.R.O., P79/JN1/214, p. 45. Perhaps in 1725 the Bird in Hand: ibid. MR/LV4/15.

[3] Ibid. MR/LV passim.
[4] Hackney Photos. i. 117.
[5] H.A.D., M 515; ibid. D/F/TYS/65.
[6] Ibid. M 524; ibid. D/F/BAG/14, p. 53; ibid. D/F/TYS/66.
[7] Ibid. D/F/TYS/66.
[8] Ibid. D/F/TYS/65; G.L.R.O., MR/LV6/79.
[9] P. Mathias, Brewing Ind. in Eng. 1700–1830 (1959), 12. [10] H.B.M.C. Lond., HAC 14.
[11] H.A.D., D/F/TYS/65; ibid. 66.
[12] G.L.R.O., M79/LH/17, p. 338.
[13] Ibid. 17, p. 338; 18, p. 226; M.L.R. 1803/7/766.
[14] M.L.R. 1806/1/355–6; 1807/1/110–12.
[15] Ibid. 1807/1/435–6; 1818/3/63, 276.
[16] Para. based on Cruchley's New Plan (1829); Starling's Map (1831); H.A.D., P/J/CW/124.
[17] Below, list of churches.
[18] H.B.M.C. Lond., HAC 14.

Bird Cage, behind which *c.* 70 labourers or trades people were living by 1821.

The Bird Cage in 1829[19] stood on the north corner of a built-up road called Birdcage Walk (later Chapel and from 1905 Windus Road), which continued as a footpath through fields to join the new Hill (from 1893 Oldhill) Street from Clapton. Higher up, Grove Lane (from 1938 Lampard Grove) and Grove Road or Place (from 1890 Lynmouth Road) also headed east to the bottom of Hill Street. No other offshoots, except a path along the line of Portland Avenue, led eastward below the junction with Upper Clapton Road leading from Clapton common. Both sides of the hill were lined with substantial houses. No ways led west, except to outbuildings in the long rear gardens. Houses at the top of Stamford Hill on the west side had grounds extending along the road; the only untouched sites were on the east side, where a reservoir was soon to be built on a field later bordered by Portland Avenue[20] and where Leg of Mutton pond filled the north angle with Upper Clapton Road.[21] A few tradespeople lived beyond the summit near the Turnpike and at the end of Bell's (later Bailey's) Lane, which led along the Tottenham boundary towards the Lea.[22]

Stamford Hill had many large and spacious houses; its name was borrowed for St. Thomas's church, known as Stamford Hill chapel,[23] and Stamford Grove East and West in neighbouring Clapton.[24] Eminent Jews had lived at Stamford Hill since the time of Moses Vita Montefiore (d. 1789). The richest were leaving by *c.* 1840, perhaps because of increasing road traffic or because they could live farther afield.[25] In 1850, however, four seats won praise for their landscaped grounds; they included Lion House, with 20 a. west of the summit, and Craven Lodge.[26]

Craven Lodge stood near the Stamford Hill end of the estate of John Craven (d. 1836), who inclosed waste around Leg of Mutton pond in 1806[27] and was leased land on the south side of Upper Clapton Road in 1818.[28] His land stretched north to Bell's or Bailey's Lane (later Craven Park Road) and eastward to the Lea, where his son Arthur in 1846 bought land from Samuel Tyssen's executors.[29] Arthur Craven was followed by the philanthropist Samuel Morley (1809–86), after whose departure in 1870 Craven Lodge was left empty, while most of the 70-a. estate was probably sold piecemeal by Reuben Button. The early 19th-century house, of two storeys and five bays, stood behind the modern nos. 130–8 Clapton Common; it was demolished in 1904[30] save for a round tower which survived beneath ivy in 1992.[31]

Building between *c.* 1830 and 1870[32] was restricted chiefly to business premises along the high street and a little way up the east side of Stamford Hill[33] and to large houses farther north. Short streets filled the space between Stoke Newington High Street and the common, where a British school of 1838 and a Methodist chapel of 1861 were built near the almshouses.[34] In 1868 the common was otherwise bordered by fields and the grounds of Baden Farm and Thornbury Park to the north and of Elm Lodge to the south-east. The first two stood on *c.* 18 a. acquired in 1791 from Reston Gamage, son of Abraham Gamage, by Baden Powell; they were conveyed to Maria Powell in 1830 and mortgaged to W. G. T. Tyssen-Amhurst in 1862.[35] Housing did not yet extend from Clapton, although it was advancing along Brooke Street (from 1878 Northwold Road) and Fountayne Road had been planned. Stamford Terrace (from 1907 Belfast Road) led east to a brewery.

Land east of the high street and Stoke Newington common and on each side of Stamford Hill was made more valuable from 1872 by the opening of tramways and of the G.E.R.'s Enfield branch, with Stoke Newington station replacing Ibston Lodge near the foot of the hill and Stamford Hill station west of the summit.[36] The Tyssen estate accordingly made leases under which much of the high road frontage was rebuilt and terraced avenues were laid out around the open sides of the common,[37] itself bisected by the railway but preserved as an open space.[38]

Redevelopment continued along the high road, as in Shacklewell. Demolitions were planned to make way for shops between Tyssen Road and Union Street in 1882, in the high road and Tyssen Road in 1883, and between Union Street and Church Road in 1884, with houses in the new Leswin Street to the east.[39] In Stamford Hill shops and a public house were to be built near the railway station in 1877 and south of Grove Lane in 1889; workshops were permitted at the rear in 1888 and 1893.[40] Where Northwold Road met the high street, land was leased in 1879 for the artisans' flats called Gibson Buildings (later Gardens),[41] behind a site where the almshouses were reopened in 1889 after the school's enlargement.[42]

East of the high street and the common, long avenues were built towards Clapton. The chief were Evering and Brooke roads, Northwold Road (a renaming of Brooke Street) skirting the common, and, from the foot of Stamford Hill, Cazenove Road. Those and others were linked by many north–south roads parallel with Rectory

19 Para. based on *Cruchley's New Plan* (1829); *Starling's Map* (1831).   20 Below, pub. svces.
21 Clarke, *Hackney*, 223.
22 H.A.D., P/J/CW/124, p. 161.
23 Par. mins. 31 May, 7 June 1779.
24 *Cruchley's New Plan* (1829); *Starling's Map* (1831); below, Clapton.   25 Below, Judaism.
26 W. Keane, *Beauties of Mdx.* (1850), 71–2, 249–50.
27 G.L.R.O., M79/LH/19, p. 267; ibid. M79/LH/27, pp. 180–1.
28 M.L.R. 1818/3/685. Rest of para. based on H.A.D., D/F/BAG/1, pp. 33–44.
29 G.L.R.O., M79/LH/25, pp. 127–9, 322–4.
30 Clarke, *Hackney*, 223, 300 n.; *Hackney Photos.* ii. 18.

31 Listed as a folly: *List of Bldgs.* (1975). An ivy-clad 'chimney' abutted the conservatory in 1850: Keane, *Beauties of Mdx.* 250.
32 Para. based on Stanford, *Map of Lond.* (1862–5 edn.), sheet 5; Old O.S. Maps Lond. 21, 30 (1868).
33 *Hackney Dir.* (1849).
34 Below, prot. nonconf.; educ. (pub. schs.).
35 G.L.R.O., M79/LH/18, pp. 150–3, 205; H.A.D., M 4037/3/1–3, 5–6.   36 Above, communications.
37 G.L.R.O., M79/TA/22.   38 Below, pub. svces.
39 G.L.R.O., M79/TA/22, pp. 127, 154, 175, 191.
40 Ibid. pp. 35, 250–1, 291.
41 Ibid. p. 76; below, this section.
42 Below, charities.

Road (a renaming of the north end of Shacklewell Lane) and, farther north, with Fountayne Road.[43] Among builders granted leases were William Redmond for 26 houses in Rectory Road in 1876, Charles Baker for 15 in Maury Road and John Ware for 35 in Bayston and Darville roads in 1877, Charles Weeks for 48 in Cazenove Road in 1878, S. J. and W. J. Tucker for 39 in Reighton Road in 1880, and William Mattocks Dabbs for 68 in Kyverdale Road and 12 in Alkham Road in 1881.[44] Edward Withers was to build 45 houses in Benthal and Evering roads in 1877, 42 in Norcott Road in 1880, 77 in Brooke and Narford roads in 1882, and 50 in Alconbury Road in 1883.[45] Perhaps the biggest builder was William Osment, responsible for 21 houses in Evering Road in 1877, 46 in Fountayne Road in 1878, and 15 there, with 43 in Osbaldeston Road, in 1879.[46] By 1894 the isolated houses overlooking the common had gone and the last sites, in Geldeston and Durlston roads, were about to be filled with 116 houses by Osment.[47] Away from the high road there were only a few shops; in 1879 two were permitted at one end of Fountayne Road, where St. Michael's church (1884–5) was also built on the Tyssens' land.[48]

Terraces also spread northward across the slope in the triangle formed by Stamford Hill and Cazenove and Upper Clapton roads. William Osment was to build along Osbaldeston Road as far as Clapton in 1882, in Forburg Road in 1888, and in Chardmore Road, where 10 shops were permitted, in 1890.[49] The grounds behind Stamford Hill's villas in 1894 prevented building closer than Darenth Road, which had shops at its south end and where both Osment and Dabbs had been active in 1883–4.[50] The Congregational church of 1871 at the corner of Portland Avenue remained the only intrusion in the line of villas as far as Upper Clapton Road.[51] Not until 1905 could Osment start building on some of their gardens in Leweston Place.[52] Shops built by James Edmondson were permitted at the corner of Clapton Common (a renaming of part of Upper Clapton Road) in 1909 and, with houses, were to replace some adjacent Stamford Hill villas in 1911.[52] North of the corner the immediate surroundings of Craven Lodge remained empty in 1894, although the old Turnpike tavern had made way c. 1870 for Ravensdale Road. Semidetached houses were built in Ravensdale Road and cramped rows in Olinda Road and Bailey's Lane.[53]

The land behind the west frontage of Stamford Hill, divided by the G.E.R. line, was similarly built up. Thomas James, who also built shops

in the high road, was to provide substantial houses in Amhurst Park (sometimes called Amhurst Park Road) and the parallel Vartry Road in Tottenham from 1882 and 50 smaller houses in Bergholt Crescent and Cranwich Road in 1886.[54] Builders included W. J. and F. Collins in West Bank and in Dunsmure Road, which was to have shops, from 1884,[55] William Garside in Dunsmure Road from 1885, William Osment around Linthorpe Road from 1891,[56] and Withers and Dabbs.[57] Several houses, notably in Amhurst Park, were subleased to or built by Charles, Horace, or Chester Cheston, of the manorial steward's family.[58] By 1894 all the modern avenues existed except south of Dunsmure Road and between that road and Linthorpe Road, where gardens survived behind the older villas. New houses faced the hill higher up, together with the Skinners' girls' school of 1890.[59]

The most crowded area, north of Sanford Lane, benefited under leases from 1896 to Stoke Newington Improved Dwellings Syndicate, which was to provide houses over shops, workshops, and 14 three-storeyed blocks for artisans in and around the newly named Garnham Street.[60] Away from the high street the long tidy avenues near Stoke Newington common were c. 1910 considered superior to the roads of Shacklewell. 'Good middle-class' shops virtually continued the high street up Stamford Hill to Grove Lane, beyond which stretched villas in their gardens. Unremarkable terraces, mainly of red brick, filled most of the space behind both frontages.[61] The hill's last offshoot, Holmleigh (originally Homeleigh) Road, was so named from 1903. Two four-storeyed blocks of large flats, Stamford Hill Mansions, were built c. 1905–6 on the corners with Stamford Hill, with less imposing flats called Carlton Mansions in Holmleigh Road itself. On the summit Cedar House was demolished in 1908 and shopping parades created a new centre, at the crossroads formed by Amhurst Park and Clapton Common.[62]

In the period 1918–39, while Stoke Newington High Street acquired branches of national stores, the most striking changes took place along Stamford Hill. No. 122, north of Portland Avenue, made way for Portland Mansions in 1930–1.[63] South of Portland Avenue 11½ a. were bought for the L.C.C.'s Stamford Hill estate, for 516 flats in four- to six-storeyed blocks built in 1931–2 and from 1936.[64] Opposite its south end similar neo-Georgian blocks had been built by Charles Joseph for the Guinness trust in 1933–4.[65] A commercial garage stood immediately to the north, as from 1930 did Grey Green Coaches'

43 Old O.S. Map Lond. 30 (1868, 1894).
44 G.L.R.O., M79/TA/22, pp. 1, 9, 27, 38, 79, 113.
45 Ibid. pp. 3, 85, 121, 162.   46 Ibid. pp. 7, 41, 70.
47 Ibid. p. 309; Old O.S. Map Lond. 30 (1894).
48 G.L.R.O., M79/TA/22, p. 70.
49 Ibid. pp. 130, 253, 263.
50 Ibid. pp. 166, 185; Old O.S. Map Lond. 21 (1894).
51 Below, prot. nonconf. (Congs.).
52 G.L.R.O., M79/TA/23, pp. 7, 29, 35.
53 Old O.S. Map Lond. 21 (1894); H.B.M.C. Lond., HAC 54.   54 G.L.R.O., M79/TA/22, pp. 96, 117, 151, 226.
55 Ibid. p. 196; Victorian Villas of Hackney, 48, 68.
56 G.L.R.O., M79/TA/22, pp. 203, 271.
57 Ibid. pp. 232, 235, 256; H.B.M.C. Lond., HAC 16.

58 G.L.R.O., M79/TA/22, pp. 117, 351; M79/TA/20 (leases 1875–98).
59 Old O.S. Map 21 (1894); below, educ. (private schs.).
60 G.L.R.O., M79/TA/20 (leases 1898–9); M79/TA/22, p. 317.
61 Besant, Lond. North of Thames. 550; Bacon, Atlas of Lond (1910), sheet 33.
62 P.O. Dir. Lond. County Suburbs (1905, 1906, and later edns.); Hackney Photos. i. 117.
63 P.O. Dir. Lond. County Suburbs (1930, 1931).
64 Hackney, Official Guide [1938]; L.C.C. Lond. Statistics, xli. 152–3.
65 Pearman, Excellent Accn. 93. Rest of para. based on P.O. Dir. Lond. (1934 and later edns.).

station farther south.[66] The shopping centre at the summit assumed a more modern appearance with the opening of the Regent (later Odeon) cinema and an adjoining parade.[67] Flats at Regent Court (over shops) and Stamford Lodge were built in Amhurst Park, as was Cambridge Court in 1938–9 beyond the railway station. Meanwhile Jewish immigration, stimulated from the 1920s, led to the conversion of many houses into institutions[68] or to their use by professional men, especially doctors and dentists.

Piecemeal changes continued after 1945, involving the closure or enlargement of institutions and the provision of more flats.[69] Beyond the crossroads, where Stamford Hill dipped towards Tottenham, the four-storeyed ranges of the L.C.C.'s Hillside estate had been built by 1951. Much of Amhurst Park west of the station was rebuilt, with four- and five-storeyed flats by the Samuel Lewis trust, in scale with Cambridge Court, in 1953–4 and, between them, the L.C.C.'s six- and eleven-storeyed blocks of Joseph Court in 1962–3. Goodrich House was built farther west in 1964–5 and Stanton Court in 1979–80.

Jewish investment was most visible in Lubavitch House at the top of Stamford Hill, designed by David Stern and opened in two stages in 1968 and 1974.[70] Farther down, the road lost its chief landmark when the Congregational church made way for a library in 1966. Montefiore Court replaced the former Jewish school at no. 69 with flats between those of Stamford Hill Mansions and the Guinness trust in 1973–4. At the foot of the hill, Ockway House provided offices from 1964 and housed Hackney's directorate of education in 1992.

East of Stoke Newington High Street, the Tyssen estate in 1950 failed to obtain a change of zoning from residential to commercial for part of the most crowded area, between Northwold Road and Garnham Street and in Lawrence's Buildings.[71] Neighbouring streets, however, were cleared in the 1970s for Hackney's Smalley Road estate, low-rise and in keeping with Sanford Terrace to the east, renovated in 1974–5.[72] Houses along much of the north side of the common made way for Alkham Road's high-rise George Downing estate in 1965–6 and for Kyverdale Road's more modest Keates estate in 1971–2.

In the 1980s development included Safeways Stores' replacement of Stamford Hill Odeon by a red-brick supermarket and its provision at the foot of Stamford Hill of premises whose classical features were faintly imitated in those of the adjoining Currie Motors; a striking furniture showroom for M.F.I. was built almost opposite between Lynmouth Road and Lampard Grove.

The area remains commercial along Stoke Newington High Street, up the lower slope of Stamford Hill, and around its summit. The high street admits only north-bound traffic between Evering and Cazenove roads, but Stamford Hill is wider and, except by Montefiore Court, tree-lined. Multiple traffic lights and broad pavements create a busy but spacious crossroads at the top. An ornate three-storeyed shopping parade around the south-east corner contrasts with more recent buildings and is similar to rows of 1911–12 at Golders Green,[73] to which the resemblance is strengthened by many Jewish food shops.

The only survival of 18th-century settlement near the turnpike is the stock- and red-brick building of c. 1740 at nos. 266–8 Stamford Hill. Set back, and of three storeys and five bays, it has been divided and extended by shop fronts on the ground floor; brickwork appended to the north flank wall survives from the old Turnpike tavern, itself commemorated in a Victorian inn.[74] Stately mid 19th-century villas are represented by nos. 122, 124 (a youth club), and 126 Stamford Hill, each of two or three storeys over a basement and of a different coloured brick. A large late 18th-century pair of three storeys, attics under a mansard roof, and basements survives alone at nos. 51 and 53.[75]

Most of the streets behind the high road contain late Victorian or Edwardian terraces of stock or red brick, which have been dismissed, with slight exaggeration, as identical.[76] In the north-west part no. 50 Durley Road bears a plaque to Sir Ebenezer Howard (d. 1928), originator of the garden city movement.[77] Infilling or rebuilding away from the main roads has mainly been modest in scale, as in the flats of Beechwood Lodge and the additions to Orion hall in East Bank. Dunsmure Road retains its late 19th-century ranges of shops. To the south-east Stoke Newington common is well provided with plane trees[78] but marred by a railway cutting, a starting point for buses, and the shadow of a twelve-storeyed tower of the George Downing estate.

The west side of the common has 13 stock-brick houses, nos. 9–21 Sanford Terrace, no. 21 being built in 1788 as no. 1 Sanford Place. All were finished within two years, the earliest being nos. 18–21, which are of two storeys with attics and basements, whereas the others have three storeys and basements. Details, including fanlights and recessed doors between fluted pilasters, recall Henry Sanford's concern for uniformity and embellishment: he did not resort to speculative builders.[79] The row is extended by modern town houses built in imitation, Sanford Walk to the north and nos. 1–7 Sanford Terrace to the south.

Near its junction with the high street, Northwold Road is dignified by gates guarding the entrance to Gibson Gardens and by West Hackney almshouses.[80] Gibson Gardens, four-storeyed red- and yellow-brick ranges designed by Davis & Emanuel and dated 1880, represent one of the

66 *Hackney Photos.* ii. 118.
67 H.A.D., D/HE 66/9; below, social.
68 Below, Judaism; educ. (private schs.).
69 Three paras. based on *P.O. Dir. Lond.* (1950 and later edns.).
70 Inf. from dir. of educ., Lubavitch Foundation.
71 G.L.R.O., AR/TP/2/419.
72 H.A.D., 'Pks. and Open Spaces' (Hackney Soc. 1980),

41; *Tower to Tower Block*, no. 12.
73 *V.C.H. Mdx.* v. 14.   74 H.B.M.C. Lond., HAC 54.
75 *List of Bldgs.* (1975).
76 Besant, *Lond. North of Thames*, 572.   77 *D.N.B.*
78 'Pks. and Open Spaces' (Hackney Soc.), 41.
79 H.B.M.C. Lond., HAC 14; *List of Bldgs.* (1975).
80 Below, charities.

last schemes of the Metropolitan Association for Improving the Dwellings of the Industrious Classes.[81]

CLAPTON, so spelt in 1593,[82] was from 1339 until the 18th century normally rendered as Clopton, the 'farm on the hill'. The Old English *clop*, 'lump' or 'hill', presumably denoted the high ground which rises from the Lea.[83] Later to cover the north-eastern quarter of the parish, Clapton grew up along the way which in 1745 was called Hackney Lane, part of which ran through the waste of Broad (later Clapton) common. In the 19th century building spread to meet streets east of the high road and north of Homerton. The area treated below includes Hackney Downs and, towards the Lea, the terraces north of Clifden Road. Manorial courts from c. 1800 distinguished the parts north and south of Lea Bridge Road as Upper and Lower Clapton, and those names soon passed into general use.[84] Hackney Lane came to be known as Lower and Upper Clapton roads, until in the late 19th century the stretch through the common to Stamford Hill was named Clapton Common.[85]

Clapton Street, on a local route still in the 1720s a 'back road',[86] was recorded in 1378 and a high street in 1447.[87] In 1605 Clapton's 32 contributors to church rates compared with 34 for Church Street and 49 for Homerton.[88] Clapton in 1664 was assessed for hearth tax with districts farther west; in 1672 it was assessed on 74 houses, a number exceeded only by 78 for Mare Street and 113 for Homerton.[89]

Brooke House, formerly a royal seat called King's Place,[90] was centrally placed, on the later border between Upper and Lower Clapton. Early growth was probably densest along Lower Clapton Road. The 17th-century Flower de Luce[91] has not been identified; the White Hart, rebuilt in the 19th century, was one of four inns licensed in 1722.[92]

Other buildings in Lower Clapton Road included Wood's almshouses east of where the road widened by a pond, the Wood family's 16th- or 17th-century house, later the Powells' Clapton House, to the north, and the school which became Newcome's to the south.[93] On the west side a house with 1½ a. was conveyed in 1714 by John Coram, lately a timber merchant

of London, to Markham Eeles, who in 1715 was licensed to inclose roadside waste.[94] It was probably rebuilt as a five-bayed house by Eeles, a china merchant from whom it was nicknamed Piss Pot Hall, and as no. 179 Lower Clapton Road was to become the British Asylum for Deaf and Dumb Females.[95] Near the modern junction of Rowhill Road a gabled house apparently of c. 1600 was acquired with c. 4 a. in 1715 by Samuel and Bucknall Howard, merchants who conveyed it in 1727 to John Howard, a London upholsterer; it was the birthplace of his son John (d. 1790), the philanthropist.[96] Another large and apparently early 18th-century house stood in the south angle of a way from Clapton field (later Clapton Passage).[97] Sir Matthew Holworthy had a house with 14 hearths in 1672 which in 1713 was described as in Clapton Street.[98] Brooke House ceased to be an aristocratic seat in 1677[99] but at the south-eastern end of the village another rich citizen's residence was rebuilt in 1728 as Hackney House, the grandest of its kind in Clapton.[1]

Growth continued in the 18th century. Seventy-one residents of Clapton paid poor rates in 1720, 100 in 1735, 157 in 1761, and c. 200 in 1779.[2] Seven of the parish's 36 select vestrymen lived there in 1729 and eight in 1740.[3] The turnpiking of the road from Hackney to Stamford Hill may have drawn residents to Upper Clapton after 1738 and the construction of Lea Bridge Road brought more traffic to Lower Clapton from 1758.[4]

In 1745 buildings fronted most of Lower Clapton Road from its right-angle bend northward to a little way beyond Brooke House.[5] They did not extend along lanes leading east or west, nor along Back Lane (a forerunner of Clarence Road), a short cut from Church Street to the heart of Clapton village by the pond. The stretch which came to be Upper Clapton Road ran through fields, past buildings at the junction with the later Mount Pleasant Lane and a forerunner of Spring or Spring Hill House[6] and across Broad common to the turnpike at Stamford Hill. Isolated houses stood near the ferries: Jeremy's, Smith's, and Morris's,[7] of which Morris's had an inn by c. 1725.[8]

Behind the main road frontage the only substantial building in 1745 was Hackney House.[9] It was put up for Stamp Brooksbank, M.P. (d. 1756), governor of the Bank of England, whose father Joseph (d. 1726), a London haberdasher,

81 H.B.M.C. Lond., HAC 30; below, plate 32.
82 Norden, *Spec. Brit.* 17.
83 *P.N. Mdx.* (E.P.N.S.), 105; J. Bosworth and T. N. Toller, *A.-S. Dict., Enlarged Addenda* (1972).
84 G.L.R.O., M79/LH/18, p. 279; H.A.D., D/F/BAG/1, p. 10; *Starling's Map* (1831).
85 Stanford, *Map of Lond.* (1862–5 edn.), sheet 3; *Kelly's Dir. Highbury* (1884–5).
86 Above, communications.
87 Guildhall MS. 9171/1, f. 56v.; *Cal. Pat.* 1441–7, 483.
88 H.A.D., D/F/TYS/1.
89 G.L.R.O., MR/TH/4, m. 3; MR/TH/34.
90 Below, manors.
91 *Trade Tokens in 17th Cent.* ed. G. C. Williamson, ii (1891), 815.
92 G.L.R.O., MR/LV3/116; MR/LV4/3.
93 Below, charities; manors (Clapton Ho.); educ. (private schs.).
94 G.L.R.O., M79/LH/49, 2 Apr. 1714, 21 Apr. 1715.

95 Clarke, *Hackney*, 194, 299 n.; *Hackney Photos*. ii. 40–1; below, pub. svces.
96 G.L.R.O., M79/LH/50, 7 Apr. 1727, 12 Apr. 1743; J. Baldwin Brown, *Memoirs of John Howard* (1818), 3; Clarke, *Hackney*, 193; *Lost Hackney*, 40, and illus.; *D.N.B.*
97 Rocque, *Map of Lond.* (1741–5), sheet 5; below, this section. 98 G.L.R.O., MR/TH/34; M.L.R. 1713/5/19.
99 *Survey of Lond.* xxviii (1960), p. v.
1 Colvin, *Brit. Architects*, 185; below, this section.
2 H.A.D., P/J/P/76, 91, 121, 150.
3 Vestry mins. 23 Aug. 1729, Easter 1740.
4 Above, communications.
5 Para. based on Rocque, *Map of Lond.* (1741–5), sheet 5. 6 *Hackney Photos*. ii. 17.
7 Above, communications.
8 G.L.R.O., MR/LV4/15.
9 Rocque, *Map of Lond.* (1741–5), sheet 5. Rest of para. based on Robinson, *Hackney*, i. 117–20, map; *Lost Hackney*, 44–5, illus.; H.A.D., D/F/BAG/9, pp. 2–11.

HIGH STREET, HOMERTON, *c.* 1830

had lived in Clapton or Homerton in 1712.[10] The house, apparently finished by 1732, was designed with a plain façade by Colen Campbell; it was approached along the line of Tresham Avenue (in 1992 marked by Tresham Walk on the Jack Dunning estate) and commanded a vista, with ornamental waters, south to Homerton Row.[11] The estate, mainly freehold, in 1775 stretched to the Hackney cut, in part bordering Pond Lane (from 1887 Millfields Road), and contained c. 122 a., besides c. 97 a. in the marsh.[12] It was sold by Brooksbank's heirs to John Hopkins of Hornchurch (Essex) (d. 1772)[13] and by Hopkins's son-in-law Benjamin Bond Hopkins to Samuel Stratton, who sold most of it to Thomas Hubbard. A large part along Pond Lane was bought by Christopher Alderson and the house itself in 1786 for the dissenters' Hackney or New College. An east wing was added in 1788 by John Howard's friend William Blackburn[14] and a west wing in 1789, but demolition followed the college's closure in 1796. College House, put up nearby for the resident tutor Abraham Rees (d. 1825),[15] the cyclopaedist, survived until c. 1883-4.[16]

The destruction of Hackney House may not have been followed by the rebuilding of some substantial roadside villas[17] known as the Five Houses, a name also applied to that part of Lower Clapton and to the last surviving house.[18] In 1799 they stood back between the later junctions with Tresham Avenue and Powerscroft Road. Occupants included Christopher Alderson (d. 1810) and his great-nephew Christopher Alderson Lloyd (d. 1845), who took the surname Alderson, and Thomas Boddington, a purchaser of much of the college's land.[19] Reputedly the houses were built out of materials from the mansion, but Boddington had acquired a large residence with 4 a. in 1785.[20] The middle house passed to his son Benjamin and in 1822 was sold to William Amory, who rebuilt it as the Hall, of five bays and with a central Ionic pediment, which he sold in 1830 to John Berger.[21] East of the Hall stood the castellated Priory, probably contemporary with the Five Houses, which was approached from a lodge at the north end of Brooksby's Walk in Homerton.[22]

Development of the Tyssens' lands north of Hackney village led in 1816 to the laying out of Clapton Square. In 1817 residents on its west side included the manorial steward Thomas Tebbutt,[23] and in 1821, when building was still in progress, 15 householders included the sur-

veyor William Hurst Ashpitel (d. 1852) in a detached villa at the north-east corner near Clapton Passage. Clapton Place, facing the main road east of the square, had 17 householders in 1821, including Joshua Watson.[24] Smaller houses called Down Terrace, some occupied by tradespeople, lined part of Back Lane (later Clarence Road) by 1821. Hackney Church of England grammar school of 1829 stood alone, opposite them, in 1831, when houses around the square, almost opposite in Portland Place, Lower Clapton Road, and in Clarence Place linked Lower Clapton with Hackney village.[25]

Immediately north of the Five Houses, Newcome's school made way for the impressive London Orphan Asylum, opened in 1825.[26] To the north detached houses in 1831 stretched past the entrance to Laura Place as far as Pond Lane, beyond which denser building including St. James's Terrace faced Clapton pond and continued past Clapton House and Lea Bridge Road. Most building was on the Powells' land, as was that on the west side of the main road as far north as the Brooke House estate,[27] where a terrace called Brooke House Row had been occupied from 1760.[28] Farther south houses on the west side were built on land leased in 1822 and 1823 to John Maitland; they included seven which he sold in 1827 as Maitland Place.[29]

Meanwhile building had slowly spread towards the desirable heights of Stamford Hill. Beecholme House, opposite Brooke House, may have been the family home of Maj. John André (d. 1780), who was executed in the American War of Independence.[30] Beyond Kates Lane the Tyssens' land south-west of the road through the common was still open in 1765, although three isolated rows had been built between the modern Oldhill Street and Portland Avenue.[31] They stood on fields of Thomas Webbe, who in 1742 had succeeded his grandfather John Webbe and whose family had held land since 1664 or earlier.[32]

Planned development in Upper Clapton began on Webbe's 24 a.,[33] where by 1774 Oldhill Street (then Chapel and Hill streets) had rows of 4 and 10 cottages. A proprietary chapel (later St. Thomas's church)[34] stood in the street's north angle with the main road, separated by building land from 11 houses in Clapton Terrace, behind which were mews and a brickfield. In the south angle the King's Arms, apparently short lived, adjoined four houses; to the south-east were the driveway to a house which served as an academy, in the 19th century called Avenue House, and a

[10] Hist. Parl., Commons, 1715-54, i. 495; M.L.R. 1712/1/98; 1713/3/28.
[11] H.A.D., V 23; below, plate 18.
[12] H.A.D., V 31.
[13] G.L.R.O., M79/LH/13, pp. 300, 317; Hist. Parl., Commons, 1754-90, 101; V.C.H. Essex, vii. 33, 38.
[14] Colvin, Brit. Architects, 113.
[15] D.N.B.
[16] H.A.D., M 3551.
[17] Rocque, Map of Lond. (1741-5), sheet 5.
[18] H.A.D., AP 258; Clarke, Hackney, 126, 292 n.
[19] H.A.D., D/F/BAG/9, pp. 10, 14; G.L.R.O., Acc. 237/1.
[20] M.L.R. 1785/2/416-17.
[21] Ibid. 1863/22/576; H.A.D., V 20.
[22] Ibid.; G.L.R.O., M79/LH/24, pp. 41-2; H.A.D., D/F/BAG/9, pp. 15, 23; Starling's Map (1831).
[23] Hackney Photos. ii. 34; M.L.R. 1818/3/272-3.

[24] H.A.D., P/J/CW/124, pp. 2-3; Colvin, Brit. Architects, 71; Clarke, Hackney, 124, 292 n., 293 n.; E. Lond. Record, vi. 33-4; Hackney Photos. i. 32. Watson did not live in Jos. Priestley's former house, as in Clarke: inf. from H.A.D.
[25] H.A.D., P/J/CW/124, pp. 1-2; Thomas, 'Hackney', 7; Starling's Map (1831); below, educ. (private schs.).
[26] Below, social; educ. (private schs.).
[27] Starling's Map (1831).
[28] Survey of Lond. xxviii. 80-1.
[29] H.A.D., D/F/BAG/8, p. 70; G.L.R.O., M79/LH/22, pp. 169-70; below, this section.
[30] Clarke, Hackney, 74, 291 n.; D.N.B.
[31] H.A.D., D/F/TYS/65.
[32] G.L.R.O., M79/LH/41, passim; M79/LH/16, p. 192.
[33] Para. based on H.A.D., V 6.
[34] Below, list of churches.

terrace of four more by the main road. In contrast the Tyssens' land remained empty, save for the White Swan (later the Swan) near the north end of Clapton Terrace, in 1785.[35]

Below the common, part of Upper Clapton early in the 19th century became as urban as Lower Clapton. It was most crowded near the junction with Lea Bridge Road and along Kates Lane and in short streets built after 1790 on Conduit field in the lane's northern angle with the main road.[36] Over 70 labourers' families lived in Kates Lane in 1821, when construction was in progress.[37] Complaints were made about drinking, Sunday shopping, and gambling in the brickfields there in 1827.[38]

By 1831 the north end of Upper Clapton was a genteel area.[39] Many houses were detached, such as those north and south of Warwick Road, although terraces faced both sides of the common. They included Summit Place north of the Swan and, opposite, the long four-storeyed Buccleuch Terrace of c. 1825,[40] with Buccleuch Cottages on the slope behind; the villas later represented by Stainforth House and the Woodlands lay to the north and Cintra House and the pair forming Bellevue and Surrey House to the south next to Spring Hill, while West Springfield and Cedar Lodge lay in the southern angle of Spring Hill with the main road. A gap, soon to accommodate Champion Place,[41] stretched farther south almost to the corner of Spring Place (later Springfield). Terraces in such a setting were criticized in 1832 as 'formal, united, and destitute of all allusion to country pursuits'.[42] The connoisseur James Wadmore (d. 1853) lived on the west side of Upper Clapton Road.[43]

Lines of building did not reach far from the main road except along Kates Lane, almost to Newington common, and behind the proprietary chapel past Stamford Grove East and West to where Hill Street joined Grove Place (later Lynmouth Road) from Stamford Hill. A few detached villas lay along part of the south side of Spring Place. Individual seats included the first Summit House north-west of Summit Place, with its garden bordering the north side of a lane which became Portland Avenue;[44] a field to the west and the grounds of Craven Lodge to the north[45] still separated the houses around Clapton common from those on Stamford Hill. East of the common were the residences later known as Spring Hill House, south of Spring Hill, Springfield House, north of Spring Place,[46] and Springfield Cottage, in the angle between Spring Place and Mount Pleasant Lane or Big Hill.[47]

Riverside settlements grew up at Lea bridge, High Hill ferry, and the high bridge at the foot of Spring Hill.[48] Lea bridge had 21 householders in 1821 and Lea Road, presumably Lea Bridge Road, had 22, all tradesmen or labourers.[49] The Jolly Anglers at Middlesex wharf, on the site of Smith's ferry, and a dock to the north may have been included in those numbers. High Hill ferry was reached circuitously by Mount Pleasant Lane, part of which had 19 working-class households, or more directly by Spring Place; as Hilly ferry it had 44 householders in 1821, several of them dyers.[50] At the foot of Spring Hill Thomas Webbe had owned c. 39 a. in 1774, including Horseshoe Point and islands to the north, a tileyard, a calico printer's, and three wharves on a creek later called Giles's dock.[51] Premises adjoining the dock were leased by John Webbe Weston to a varnish maker in 1806.[52] Tile kilns in Spring Lane near the head of the dock were presumably those where 34 householders dwelt in 1821.[53]

In 1865 building along Lower and Upper Clapton roads, almost continuous to the north-west end of Clapton common, was still separate from that along the high road or by the Lea.[54] In Lower Clapton, Laura Place formed a 're-spectable row' north of the orphan asylum by 1842.[55] Opposite Clapton House the Revd. T. B. Powell gave a cottage and land called the strawberry garden as a site for St. James's church in 1840.[56] To the south a large house with grounds stretching back to Love (later Downs) Lane was for sale in 1861 and taken for Powell and Heyworth roads.[57] The south-eastern end of Lower Clapton was affected by the growth of Homerton, in particular by the proximity of the East London union's institution and the projected Eastern fever hospital.[58] The Hall and the Priory were for sale in 1860 and were bought in 1863 by the Cannock Chase & Ogley Land Co. and then by the London & Suburban Land & Building Co., which in 1866 also bought the Alderson estate.[59]

Hackney Downs, previously amid fields, by 1865 was edged north by Downs Road, border-ing the Powells' land offered for sale in 1861,[60] and south by Downs Park Road, in both of which building had started. A few middle-class rows already led northward from Hackney Downs, along London Road (later Clapton Way), and Avenue (later Midhurst), Oak Field, and Nightingale roads to the planned line of Kenninghall Road. Farther north a cartway behind Brooke House was still called World's End; by 1868 it was the east end of Brooke Road,

35 G.L.R.O., MR/LV9/136; H.A.D., D/F/TYS/66.
36 H.A.D., V 2/4.
37 Ibid. P/J/CW/124, pp. 8–11.
38 Vestry mins. 17 Apr. 1827.
39 Two paras. based on *Starling's Map* (1831).
40 *Hackney Photos.* i. 117.
41 H.A.D., D/F/BAG/1, pp. 70–101.
42 Thomas, 'Hackney', 11.
43 *Hackney Dir.* (1849); *D.N.B.*
44 H.A.D., D/F/BAG/2, p. 15.
45 Above, Stamford Hill.
46 Old O.S. Map Lond. 21 (1868).
47 Ibid. Lond. 22 (1894); *Hackney Photos.* i. 122.
48 Para. based on Rocque, *Map of Lond.* (1741–5), sheet 5; *Starling's Map* (1831).

49 H.A.D., P/J/CW/124, pp. 21–2.
50 Ibid. pp. 15–17.   51 H.A.D., V 6.
52 M.L.R. 1807/1/50.
53 H.A.D., P/J/CW/124, pp. 14–15; *Cruchley's New Plan* (1829); below, plate 38.
54 Two paras. based on Stanford, *Map of Lond.* (1862–5 edn.), sheet 3.
55 Robinson, *Hackney*, i. 131.
56 Ibid. ii. 217; below, list of churches.
57 Hunter, *Victorian Villas of Hackney*, 20–1.
58 Below, pub. svces.
59 M.L.R. 1863/22/576–7, 1081–3; H.A.D., V 20; ibid. D/F/BAG/9, pp. 12, 20; G.L.R.O., Acc. 256/9–10; Acc. 237/1.
60 Hunter, *Victorian Villas of Hackney*, 20.

which continued as a footpath between brick-fields to Stoke Newington common.[61] Upper Clapton remained much more open, although villas lined Warwick Road to where Mount Pleasant Lane approached the steep streets south of High Hill ferry.

Lower Clapton spread quickly as the London & Suburban Land Co. laid out Chatsworth Road along a field path from Brooksby's Walk to Pond Lane, filling the space between that and Lower Clapton Road with the western ends of Clifden, Glenarm, and neighbouring roads between c. 1867 and 1870. Farther east 61 a. were leased to a market gardener for 5¾ years in 1867, before they too were taken for the east part of the company's Clapton Park estate.[62] Plots in Elder-field Road were conveyed to Edward Withers for its Clapton Park No. 2 estate in 1872-3.[63] On the main road the Aldersons' house made way for the striking Round Chapel, founded in 1869 to meet recent 'enormous immigration'.[64]

Growth was stimulated by the opening of Clapton railway station in 1872, followed closely by the arrival of tramways at Lower Clapton and their extension in 1875 to Clapton common.[65] The spread of building, however, was limited by public control of the Mill fields, Hackney Downs, and Clapton common from 1872.[66]

The main road below the station became more urban. By 1880 there were many shops at its southern end, including a new range called Clapton Pavement,[67] and at the junction with Lea Bridge Road, which from 1892 carried trams, and south of Kenninghall Road.[68] Clearance north of the almshouses made way for Newick Road and St. James's Villas c. 1890; to the south, part of St. James's Terrace similarly made way for Mildenhall Road.[69] Between Laura Place and Pond Lane the Powell estate offered Durham House and nearby houses for sale in 1882, with nursery land in Pond Lane; Cromwell Lodge soon made way for Atherden Road.[70] Farther south the last of the Five Houses was superseded c. 1884 by Lesbia Road.[71] Shops open in Clarence Road by 1880, the municipal baths or King's hall of 1897, a skating rink (later Clapton Rink cinema), and the Salvation Army's Mothers' hospital of 1913 signalled the extension of central Hackney into Lower Clapton.[72] Purpose-built flats first appeared as Cavendish Mansions and St. John's Mansions, at the north-east corner of Clapton Square, in 1899-1901. In the main road Northumberland Mansions were opened south of Laura Place c.

1904, by which date St. Andrew's Mansions stood on the west side and Kinnoul and Rowhill Mansions, built by W. Andrews of Wood Green, in Rowhill Road.[73]

East of Lower Clapton Road, Chatsworth Road had shops from the beginning and many more by 1880.[74] Modest terraces reached the Hackney cut south of Millfields Road by 1894, although Mildenhall Road and parallel roads to the north extended only to the modern line of Cornthwaite Road.[75] Farther north James Stone and William Cooke had contracted for very small houses or maisonettes in Southwold Road in 1885 but G. R. Woodruff did not begin building in Gunton Road until 1894.[76] To the west shops by 1880 were mainly at the north end of Rendlesham Road, in Upper Clapton Road from Kenninghall Road northward to Rossington Street, in Northwold Road, and, serving Clapton common, in Hill Street.[77] Almost all the land between Hackney Downs and Clapton common was filled with terraces, mostly on the Tyssen estate in continuation of development around Stoke Newington common and Stamford Hill. Thomas James was to build in Ickburgh Road in 1883 and William Osment in Chardmore Road in 1890.[78]

Clapton common in 1894 was still separated by private grounds from the summit of Stamford Hill and, to the north-east, from the Lea.[79] Building, however, covered almost all the land to the south-west and had started on the Craven Lodge estate: Olinda Road was wholly and Castlewood Road partly built up, and Egerton, Rookwood, and neighbouring roads had been planned. Riverside settlement at Lea bridge and Lea dock had been restricted by the Mill fields. At High Hill ferry houses had spread higher up the slope since 1865 and the old village c. 1890 survived in a 'veritable Alsatia' where the workforce depended largely on summer pleasure-seekers.[80] Although premises were often flooded,[81] visitors delighted in the pastoral scene: poplars border-ing the Essex reservoirs evoked comparisons with Lombardy, while the heights of Clapton offered a view as fine as that from Richmond hill.[82]

Building approached its modern limits with additions to Clapton Park south of Redwald Road towards Homerton c. 1900,[83] when Meeson Street was named. They were followed by the construction of an electricity station and its appendages in Millfields Road and by expan-sion between Clapton common and the Lea north and south of Springfield park.[84] Infilling

61 Clarke, *Hackney*, 213; Old O.S. Map Lond. 30 (1868).
62 H.A.D., D/F/BAG/9, p. 20; Clarke, *Hackney*, 293 n.
63 G.L.R.O., Acc. 256/9-10.
64 H.A.D., D/F/BAG/9, p. 11; *Hackney & Kingsland Gaz.* 17 July 1869, p. 4; below, prot. nonconf. (Congs.).
65 Above, communications.
66 Below, pub. svces.
67 *P.O. Dir. Lond. County Suburbs, North* (1880); datestone.
68 *P.O. Dir. Lond. County Suburbs, North* (1880); above, communications.
69 *Hackney Photos.* i. 41-2.
70 H.A.D., M 3848; ibid. D/F/BAG/8, pp. 74-8, 81; *Hackney Photos.* i. 39.
71 Clarke, *Hackney*, 107, 126; *Hackney Photos.* i. 36-7.
72 *P.O. Dir. Lond. County Suburbs, North* (1880); below, social; pub. svces.

73 *Hackney Photos.* i. 34; H.A.D., H/LD 7/16; ibid. D/F/BAG/8, p. 70; ibid. LBH 7/5/43/135, 44/1,7,19-20; *P.O. Dir. Lond. County Suburbs* (1905).
74 *Hackney Dir.* (1872); *P.O. Dir. Lond. County Suburbs, North* (1880). 75 Old O.S. Map Lond. 31 (1894).
76 G.L.R.O., M79/TA/22, pp. 212, 214, 313.
77 *P.O. Dir. Lond. County Suburbs, North* (1880).
78 Old O.S. Map Lond. 21 (1894); G.L.R.O., M79/TA/22, pp. 159, 263.
79 Para. based on Old O.S. Maps Lond. 21-2, 31 (1894).
80 Stanford, *Map of Lond.* (1862-5 edn.), sheet 3; Booth, *Life and Labour*, iii (1), 153; below, social.
81 *Hackney Photos.* i. 124, 130.
82 Clarke, *Hackney*, 223; *Hackney Photos.* ii. 2.
83 Para. based on Bacon, *Atlas of Lond.* (1910), sheets 33, 40; Old O.S. Map Lond. 31 (1913).
84 Below, pub. svces.

included Knightland Road off Mount Pleasant Lane, where G.R. Woodruff was leased sites in 1904.[85] Springfield park, opened in 1905, was created out of the grounds of Spring Hill House, the Chestnuts in Spring Lane (both demolished), and Springfield House.[86] Some building followed the demolition of Summit House in 1902[87] but much of the Craven Lodge estate was still undeveloped in 1910.[88] Flats called Stamford Mansions and Stamford Grove Mansions were built at the ends of Stamford Grove East and West c. 1904.[89]

Clapton common remained select into the 20th century. From Buccleuch Terrace members of the Neilson family, West India merchants previously at Summit House, walked to the City until the 1880s. Stainforth House was given in 1879 by Richard Foster, a church benefactor, to William Walsham How (d. 1897), suffragan bishop for London's east end and styled bishop of Bedford, who also acquired the Woodlands as a boys' home.[90] How's successor was followed at Stainforth House by Frederick Janson Hanbury, of the chemists Allen & Hanbury, who made a large collection of plants. Although the slope behind was acquired for Ashtead and Lingwood roads, Stainforth House was saved on its purchase in 1909 by C. H. Turner, bishop of Islington, who lived there until 1923 while his son lived at the Woodlands.[91] About 1908 a novel portrayed the area as a 'far northern suburb overhanging the Lea', where merchants' grave old houses surrounded a sleepy common.[92] An attempt by the Elizabeth Fry refuge to buy no. 22 Clapton Common was treated in 1912 as a threat to high-class property values.[93]

The far northern and eastern fringes of Clapton were less exclusive. At Lea bridge some unhealthy houses in Middlesex wharf were demolished in 1912, as were others at High Hill ferry by 1915.[94] Piecemeal development east of Stamford Hill was served by Craven Park board school, in 1911 isolated with a 'particularly hideous row of houses', which ran out at the crest of a slope marking the edge of London and seeming like the edge of the world.[95]

Between 1918 and 1939 scattered premises were adapted for industry. In 1928 most were towards the Lea, but Upper Clapton Road and Clapton common had 25 houses partly used as clothing workshops, 11 of them recently converted.[96] Conversions were also made in Clapton Square.[97] In 1933 large houses on the east side

of Rectory Road were rescheduled for light industry after the Tyssen estate had warned that restriction to residential use would lead to multi-occupation. Similar rescheduling of houses in Upper Clapton Road near Warwick Road was refused, despite a claim that they could be let far more profitably for business than for private use.[98]

Commercial development included Hackney's electricity showrooms in Lower Clapton Road from 1925[99] and the conversion of a football stadium for greyhound racing.[1] Houses of the 18th and early 19th century near Clapton pond were demolished, including the end of St. James's Terrace with Bow House at the entrance to Mildenhall and Millfields roads in 1930 and the pedimented Sion House, the terrace incorporating Byland House,[2] and the Deaf and Dumb asylum in 1933.[3] Durham House, partly used as shops, survived a little longer.[4] A foretaste of change in Upper Clapton was the demolition of the northernmost house of Buccleuch Terrace in 1932.[5] Buildings of the late 1930s included Beaumont Court, with flats over shops, near Clapton station.[6]

Extensive rehousing by Hackney M.B. began in 1925 near the Mill fields, with 48 maisonettes in Fletching Road. By 1928 a further 79 houses were ready west of Casimir Road and 69 maisonettes on the borders of Clapton Park and Homerton around Daubeney Road. Work had started on 100 flats in Southwold Road, on maisonettes south of Mount Pleasant Hill, and, for the first time west of the main road, on Newcome House in Powell Road. St. James's Vicarage, no. 58 Kenninghall Road, was being subdivided.[7] The five-storeyed blocks of Powell House, replacing the Deaf and Dumb asylum and its neighbours, contained 198 flats opened in 1934.[8]

The east end of Northwold Road, with early 19th-century cottages built on Conduit field, was declared unhealthy in 1929.[9] The L.C.C. acquired 7¼ a., naming Woolmer House in Upper Clapton Road in 1934 and others in 1936. It also opened Charnwood House and Ettrick House in 1937, before renaming Caroline Street as Charnwood Street and Conduit Street as Rossendale Street. With 459 flats, Northwold in 1938 was the L.C.C.'s largest estate in the borough.[10] Hackney M.B. contributed 26 flats in Woodfield House, Rossington Street.[11]

Mount Pleasant Lane was recalled as deteriorating in the 1930s, when its upper end was the

85 G.L.R.O., M79/TA/22, p. 379.
86 Below, pub. svces.
87 H.A.D., D/F/BAG/2, pp. 15, 18. Chester Cheston had moved from the first to a second Summit Ho., in Stamford Hill: ibid.
88 Bacon, *Atlas of Lond.* (1910), sheet 33.
89 *P.O. Dir. Lond. Suburban, North* (1903); *P.O. Dir. Lond. County Suburbs* (1905).
90 H.A.D., D/F/BAG/1, p. 87; *D.N.B.*; below, misc. institutions.
91 H.A.D., D/F/BAG/1, pp. 72–3, 76, 84; *Hackney Photos.* i. 123.
92 H.A.D., D/F/BAG/1, p. 4; P. Gibbon, *Salvator* (1908), 115.
93 H.A.D., H/LD 7/24, p. 170.
94 Hackney M.B. *Rep. on San. Condition* (1912), 67, 70; *Hackney Photos.* i. 127.
95 Besant, *Lond. North of Thames*, 550.

96 Hackney M.B. *Rep. on San. Condition* (1928), 117, 119.   97 *P.O. Dir. Lond.* (1934).
98 G.L.R.O., AR/TP/2/419.
99 Hackney, *Official Guide* [1925].
1 Below, social.   2 *Hackney Photos.* i. 40–1, 158.
3 Ibid. ii. 40–1; *Lost Hackney*, 41–3.
4 *Hackney Photos.* i. 39.
5 H.A.D., D/F/BAG/1, p. 92.
6 *P.O. Dir. Lond.* (1942).
7 H.A.D., D/F/BAG/8, p. 59; Hackney M.B. *Rep. on San. Condition* (1928), 18; Hackney, *Official Guide* [1938].
8 Ibid.; *Hackney Photos.* ii. 100.
9 H.A.D., V 2/4; Hackney M.B. *Rep. on San. Condition* (1929), 25; *Hackney Photos.* ii. 89.
10 L.C.C. *Names of Streets* (1955), 157, 644, 827, *passim*; L.C.C. *Lond. Statistics*, xli. 152–3; *Hackney Photos.* ii. 94.
11 Hackney, *Official Guide* [1938]; H.A.D., D/F/BAG/1, p. 108.

better.[12] Flooding in 1928 affected 78 houses and in 1930 caused Middlesex wharf and High Hill ferry to be designated for clearance.[13] On 4 a. divided by Harrington Hill the L.C.C. built five-storeyed blocks, on its High Hill estate; Ferry House and Lea House were named in 1937 and Harrington House in 1938.[14] A little to the west, houses in Warwick Road (from 1938 Warwick Grove) and Springfield made way *c.* 1939 for the five-storeyed brown-brick ranges of Wren's Park House and Lea View House, 'uncommonly well designed' by Messrs. Joseph, and for a start on the estate called Wigan House.[15]

Farther north, Hackney M.B. built 120 flats on the site of nos. 124–8 (even) Cazenove Road in 1937–8. Inroads around Clapton common began with the opening of 65 flats in Fawcett House on the site of nos. 20 and 22 in 1937, when the relatively high cost of land had led to the building of blocks rather than cottage dwellings.[16] Large old houses had become less desirable: the nearby Buccleuch Terrace was badly maintained and mostly split into flats.[17] Cottages off Oldhill Street were condemned in 1937[18] and part of Stamford Grove East was cleared for Oldhill Street (later Tyssen) primary school.[19] Private flats at Rookwood Court were built at the north end of the common *c.* 1936.[20]

War damage robbed Clapton of Brooke House and neighbouring shops, which made way for a school, and of what remained on the east side of Clapton Square.[21] Piecemeal changes continued on and near the main road, including the building by 1981 of offices for Hackney's social services department in Clapton Square and later of a health centre at the corner of the low-rise Jack Dunning estate in place of Lesbia Road.[22] In the bomb-damaged Linscott Road the former Orphan Asylum was partly demolished after its abandonment in 1970 by the Salvation Army for a new hall at the corner of Laura Place.[23] Early 19th-century villas on the north side of Laura Place were demolished in 1975–6.[24] Closure of the Mothers' hospital in 1986 brought refurbishment at Maitland Place and rebuilding as houses and flats in Mothers' Square behind.[25] Shops at the junction with Lea Bridge Road were cleared in the early 1970s for a roundabout.[26]

Much municipal housing was built in relatively spacious Upper Clapton.[27] Buccleuch Terrace was demolished and Buccleuch House, a six-storeyed range for single women, opened in 1951.[28] On or near the same side of the common

there was more building on Hackney's Fawcett and Wigan House estates and, by 1958, on the new Webb estate and at the end of the common, where one block of Tower Court was nine-storeyed. On the west side the Summit estate had been built by 1957, Broad Common estate by 1960, and, nearer Stamford Hill, the Gardens by 1961. In Ravensdale Road, Priestley Close had been built by 1958.

Building east of the main road included the Chatsworth estate, additions to Wren's Park House, Keir Hardie estate in Springfield, and Pond Farm in Millfields Road, all of the 1950s, Beecholme in Prout Road by 1961, and the Mount at the corner of Southwold Road by 1962. The L.C.C.'s Nye Bevan estate, including a 12-storeyed tower, had been built between Glyn Road and Pedro Street by 1964 and many more low-rise flats to the south by 1975. The east end of Rushmore Road was taken for a shopping precinct, which also served the 19-storeyed Willington Court and its neighbours of *c.* 1970. The low-rise yellow-brick Millfields estate replaced Clapton stadium *c.* 1980.

On the west side of the main road Hendale House was open by 1954 and Hackney M.B. had built many flats, as in Narford, Kenninghall, Evering, Brooke, and Maury roads, by 1961. Schemes included the Ickburgh estate of the 1950s and the sixteen-storeyed Gooch House by 1964. The G.L.C. built its large Nightingale estate, replacing roads leading north from Hackney Downs with towers of up to 21 storeys, between 1967 and 1972.[29] The Dachtler estate, behind Clapton Terrace and named after a vicar of St. Thomas's, was built *c.* 1979.

Powell House and Lea View House were described as slums by 1980. The first was demolished but the second had been renovated by 1986.[30] Wren's Park House was also renovated; work on the Fawcett estate was in progress in 1987[31] but unfinished in 1992. The 19-storeyed Norbury and Ambergate courts, in Mandeville Street and Daubeney Road, were demolished in 1993.[32] Declining municipal development in the 1970s was balanced by increased private activity in both Lower and Upper Clapton. Most work consisted of refurbishment, but by 1985 a national firm was building middle-class houses at Baker's Hill.[33] At Hackney's north-eastern extremity a private road called Watermint Quay was laid out from Craven Walk to the Lea and opened, with terraces by Kentish Homes, in 1988.[34]

[12] D. Jameson, *Touched by Angels* (1988), 39–40, 54.
[13] Hackney M.B. *Rep. on San. Condition* (1928), 99–100; ibid. (1930), 18.
[14] L.C.C. *Names of Streets* (1955), 291, 361, 449; Hackney, *Official Guide* [1938]; *Hackney Photos.* ii. 90.
[15] *P.O. Dir. Lond.* (1942); Pevsner, *Lond.* ii. 170; Hackney, *Official Guide* [1961]. Wren's Park had been a house on the east side of Mount Pleasant Lane: *Starling's Map* (1831).
[16] Hackney, *Official Guide* [1938]; H.A.D., D/F/BAG/1, pp. 108–9.   [17] H.A.D., D/F/BAG/1, p. 92.
[18] Ibid. H/PD/3/4.   [19] Below, educ. (pub. schs.).
[20] *P.O. Dir. Lond.* (1935, 1937).
[21] *Hackney Photos.* i. 118; ibid. ii. 151; *Lost Hackney*, 19, 28; below, educ. (pub. schs.).
[22] *P.O. Dir. Lond.* (1980, 1981); *Lost Hackney*, 18; *Hackney Photos.* i. 35.
[23] *Hackney Photos.* ii. 152; below, prot. nonconf.

[24] *List. of Bldgs.* (1975).
[25] Below, this section; pub. svces.
[26] *Hackney Photos.* i. 46.
[27] Pevsner, *Lond.* ii. 170.
[28] *Hackney Photos.* i. 117; Hackney, *Official Guide* [1961]; H.A.D., H/LD 7/39. Three paras. based on Hackney, *Official Guide* (1960 and later edns.) and *P.O. Dir. Lond.* (1952 and later edns.).
[29] *Hackney Gaz.* 16 Mar. 1990, 2; G.L.C. Housing Dept. *Ann. Rep.* (1971–2), 12.
[30] *Hackney Gaz.* 13 Mar. 1979, 1; *Hackney Photos.* ii. 100; *Hackney Herald*, June 1986, 7.
[31] Advert. on site.
[32] *Hackney Gaz.* 15 Oct. 1993, 10–11; *The Times*, 11 Oct. 1993, 7e.
[33] *The Times*, 5 July 1985, 26.
[34] Datestone.

Clapton's main artery in part serves as a continuation of Mare Street, with shops that have led Lower Clapton to be described as the 'hub of Hackney'.[35] In Upper Clapton they give way to housing estates, some of them nearer the shops of Stamford Hill. Clapton Square conservation area, designated in 1969, extends southward into Hackney village and Homerton.[36]

The garden of Clapton Square retains its original wall and railings.[37] No. 17 Lower Clapton Road is early 19th-century and rendered; demolitions have separated it from stock-brick houses of a similar date in Clapton Square. On the west side nos. 8 and 9 have four storeys and basements and have been converted as flats, and nos. 10–13 form a terrace of three storeys, attics, and basements. Nos. 14–19 are three linked pairs, taller and slightly later. On the north side the larger no. 20 is distinguished by pilasters above its stuccoed ground floor and nos. 21–24 are a detached house and terrace of three storeys, attics, and basements. They form a group with the partly rebuilt terrace nos. 1–7 Clarence Place and with no. 8, which is said to have been the coachhouse of no. 20 Clapton Square.

Lower Clapton Road has a few early 19th-century town houses, as offices, among its shops. Two pairs, of multicoloured stock brick with stucco details, stand back between the police station and the Art-Deco electricity showroom; no. 6 and no. 8 (Hackney urban studies centre) have three storeys, attics, and basements, nos. 10–12 have no attics, and all save no. 10 retain their Doric porches. Together with nos. 26–28, a large three-storeyed pair with similar porches, they are all that remains of Portland Place. Farther north the health centre lowers the line of buildings, continuing past the tree-shaded Round Chapel and Linscott Road, which affords a view of the truncated shell of the Orphan Asylum resembling a majestic stage set. Opposite, the three-storeyed no. 143 is late 18th-century and under repair in 1992. Also being restored were nos. 145 to 153 (odd), large pairs of three storeys and basements, with later stuccoed linking sections. Together with a slightly later grey-brick block to the north, they constituted Maitland Place and served until 1986 as the front buildings of the Mothers' hospital. Behind lies Mothers' Square, laid out with semicircular ends, where the three-storeyed blocks designed by Hunt Thompson Associates combine neo-Georgian and Palladian features. A large early 19th-century house of three-storeys and basement, with an Ionic porch, formerly the Salvation Army's Crossways, survives at no. 13 Laura Place.[38]

A conservation area includes Clapton pond and its ornamental garden where the road widens, Wood's almshouses, Clapton's oldest buildings, and St. James's church.[39] The almshouses form a group with the only reminders nearby of early 19th-century elegance: Pond House at no. 162, with its stable building, and nos. 158–160, left from St. James's Terrace. Pond House is a stuccoed villa of c. 1800, of two storeys, attic, and basement, with a semicircular Doric porch; nos. 158–160 are stock-brick, of four storeys and basements.[40]

Upper Clapton Road retains few notable buildings. The main road, although its northern stretch is less commercial than Lower Clapton Road, has none. Clapton common, where the road curves through grass partly lined with mature trees, is overlooked chiefly by housing estates. A conservation area embraces the common and buildings along part of its south side, where St. Thomas's church stands at the end of Clapton Terrace, renamed as nos. 37–69 (odd) Clapton Common, a red- and brown-brick row of c. 1790; the houses are three- or four- storeyed with basements, some with pedimented doorcases and two with pillared porches.[41] To the north, the Swan is a solitary mid 19th-century survival, refronted in 1993. Behind St. Thomas's church the early 19th-century Grove House, of two storeys and basement, and its wing called Grove Cottage, stand derelict in Stamford Grove East. Three pairs and a half, of two storeys and basement, form an early 19th-century group in Stamford Grove West. Springfield House, spared on the creation of Springfield park, is a five-bayed stuccoed villa with a Tuscan porch.[42]

Many buildings house Jewish institutions, as at Stamford Hill. On the north side of Clapton common they include the former Deaf and Dumb asylum at no. 26,[43] Stainforth House, and Woodland Mansions at no. 98. Although they are not advertised, their patrons, like those of Jewish shops in Oldhill Street, dress distinctively, giving north-western Clapton a special character.

HOMERTON AND HACKNEY WICK. Homerton was recorded from 1343, often as Humberton, and recalled the farm of a woman named Hunburh.[44] A hamlet (*hamella*) by 1363,[45] it grew up north of Hackney brook along an easterly route from Hackney village and Lower Clapton. From what became the east end of the high street (from 1935 styled Homerton High Street), one way continued east across the meadows to the 13th-century Temple Mills and another led south across the brook as Wick Lane (part of it later Sidney, then Kenworthy, Road) to the Templars' manor of Wick.[46] The area treated here stretches from Chatham Place to the Lea and from the line of Clifden Road southward to Wick Road and the streets immediately south of Retreat Place.

Homerton was the most populous of the parish's

35 *Observer*, 19 Apr. 1987, 55.
36 H.A.D., Conservation Areas file.
37 Rest of subsection based in *List of Bldgs.* (1975).
38 *Daily Telegraph*, 30 Nov. 1988, 37; below, pub. svces.; plate 29.
39 H.A.D., Conservation Areas file.
40 *Hackney Photos.* i. 41; below, plate 28.

41 H.A.D., Conservation Areas file; Pevsner, *Lond.* ii. 170; *Tower to Tower Block*, no. 10.
42 Pevsner, *Lond.* ii. 170.
43 Local inf.; below, pub. svces.
44 *P.N. Mdx.* (E.P.N.S.), 106.
45 *Cal. Inq. Misc.* iii, p. 190.
46 Below, econ. hist. (mills); manors (Wick).

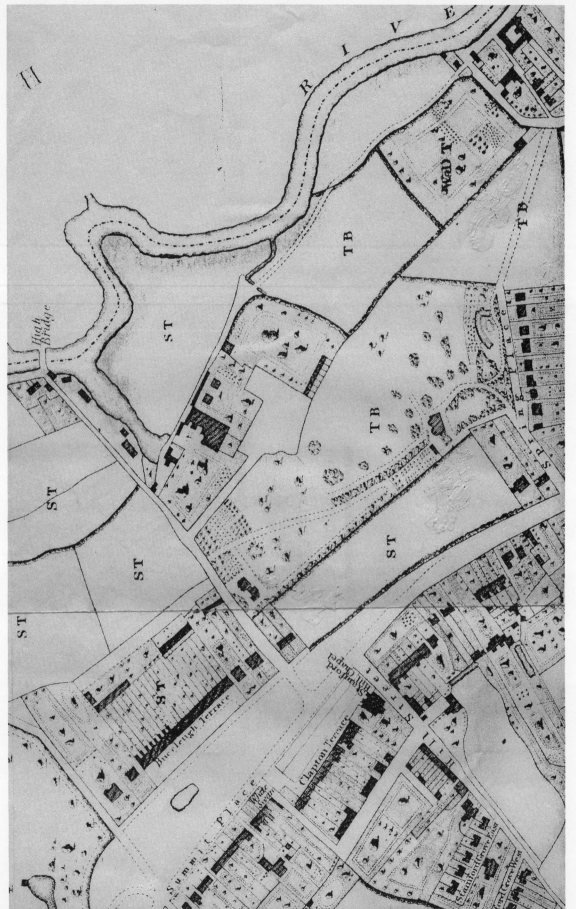

CLAPTON COMMON c. 1830

six divisions in 1605, with 49 contributors to church rates.[47] By 1655 headboroughs were appointed for both Upper and Lower Homerton,[48] and the subdivision was retained for manorial but not for parish government until 1808.[49] Upper Homerton was the small area around the modern Urswick Road.[50] It may therefore have been only a part of Great Homerton, recorded as having almost the same number of houses as Little Homerton in 1672.[51] Benedict Haynes, the holder of Wick manor, in 1605 was assessed under Grove Street[52] but by 1664 the holder was listed as in Homerton.[53]

Rich Londoners, numerous in Homerton by c. 1600, had settled much earlier along what by 1551 was called Humberton Street.[54] An undated timber-framed range, of two storeys beneath its gables, lined the north side from the later Plough Lane to John (from 1909 Banister) Street, opposite a way to where by the 17th century Blew bridge crossed Hackney brook. The range's prominence on maps and the apparent existence of a courtyard behind gave rise to a theory that it had been a manorial seat. More probably it was a royal official's or citizen's retreat before it was divided to include the Plough and several shops, all demolished piecemeal in the 1880s.[55] Farther east the street extended before 1565 to a large house at the corner of a lane which became Glyn Road. Beyond, at the foot of Marsh Hill, the 17th-century Tower Place may have been medieval, since it was later depicted with a moat.[56]

The west end of the street was separated from the north end of Hackney village only by the rectory manor's Church field, through which a path (later Sutton Place) led to the churchyard.[57] Alfordscroft, 5½ a. between the path and Hackney brook, was conveyed in 1488 by John Broke to his mother's kin William and Margaret Berytell, who conveyed it in 1499 to Thomas Marshall, fishmonger of London, together with the Tanhouse in the south angle of the path and the street. The estate passed in 1508 to William Botry, a mercer, with another house next to the Tanhouse, in 1511 to Sir John Heron, who acquired the rest of Church field, and in 1538 to the diplomatist Sir Ralph Sadler (d. 1587). In 1551 Sadler sold the land, including two houses and a cottage, to John Machell the elder (d. 1558), an alderman of London and once thought to have been the builder of Sutton House. That house in reality was built for Sadler[58] and named after Thomas Sutton (d. 1611), founder of the

London Charterhouse and reputedly England's richest commoner.[59] Sutton probably lived on the adjacent Tanhouse plot, which the Charterhouse received on his death and retained until the 20th century. Machell's estate passed to Sir James Deane (d. 1608), then to Olive Clarke, and in 1688 from her grandson John Clarke to Sir George Vyner. The house was divided c. 1752: in the 19th century the west half was a boys' and then a girls' school and the east half the home of the vestry clerk Charles Horton Pulley.[60] The building was bought c. 1890 by the rector, who adapted it as St. John's Institute for young men, and in 1938 by the National Trust. Having stood empty from 1982, proposals for its conversion into flats in 1988 led to the formation of the Sutton House society, which ensured its conservation.[61]

Nearby, although unidentified, was a freehold house, 'upon the corner of Humberton Street', apparently conveyed in 1595 with property which had been Robert Burgane's to Edward, Lord Zouche (d. 1625).[62] Zouche cultivated a physic garden, acquired other plots, and was Homerton's most distinguished householder in 1602[63] but, despite tradition,[64] was not buried in the parish church.[65] His seat was probably conveyed in 1620 by Paul Ambrose Croke to the Master of the Rolls Sir Julius Caesar (d. 1636), a native of Tottenham but resident at Hackney in 1634.[66]

Other householders in 1605[67] were Lord Rich (later earl of Warwick, d. 1619), Lord Cromwell (d. 1607), and Sir John Peyton (d. 1630), governor of Jersey,[68] who like Zouche were perhaps only occasional residents since they did not contribute to repair of the church. Payments were made by Sir Thomas Leighton, governor of Guernsey, whose son married Zouche's daughter,[69] Sir James Deane, Sir Edward Holmeden, and Roger Clarke, aldermen,[70] Sir Marmaduke Wyvell (later a baronet),[71] and Sir William Hynde.

Homerton's 57 chargeable houses in 1664 included Sarah Freeman's with 22 hearths and Henry Clobery's at Hackney Wick.[72] In 1672 Great Homerton had 55 houses and Little Homerton 58, together almost a quarter of all those in Hackney. Prominent residents included John Forth, alderman of London, who was charged on 23 hearths in 1672 and sold Lordshold manor in part to (Sir) Thomas Cooke (d. 1695).[73] Cooke possessed large gardens where expensive improvements were planned in 1691 and which included greenhouses, 2 a. stocked with rabbits,

47 H.A.D., D/F/TYS/1.
48 G.L.R.O., M/93/1, f. 61.
49 Ibid. M79/LH/20, p. 22.
50 Ibid. M79/LH/48, 28 Mar. 1706; Clarke, *Hackney*, 131; inf. from H.A.D.   51 G.L.R.O., MR/TH/34.
52 H.A.D., D/F/TYS/1; below, manors (Wick).
53 G.L.R.O., MR/TH/4, m.1.
54 H.A.D., M 820.
55 Clarke, *Hackney*, 144, 294 n.; *Hackney Photos.* i. 57–8; Rocque, *Map of Lond.* (1741–5), sheet 6; *Starling's Map* (1831); below, plate 4.
56 Below, manors (Tower Place).
57 Para. based on Nat. Trust and Sutton Ho. Soc., *Sutton Ho., Hist. and Guide* (1988), *passim*; H.A.D., D/F/TYS/40.
58 *List of Bldgs.* (1990).
59 *D.N.B.*
60 Clarke, *Hackney*, 135.

61 *Terrier*, Mar. 1987, Spring 1988, Winter 1990; for Sutton Ho., below, this section.
62 B.L. Eg. Ch. 1423 (partly destroyed).
63 H.A.D., D/F/TYS/1, p. 4; D/F/TYS/40; below, econ. hist. (mkt. gdns.).
64 *D.N.B.*
65 *Complete Peerage*, xii (2), 951.
66 B.L. Eg. Ch. 1423; *D.N.B.*; *V.C.H. Mdx.* vi. 108; *Mdx. Pedigrees* (Harl. Soc. lxv), 95.
67 Para. based on H.A.D., D/F/TYS/1, p. 66.
68 *D.N.B.*
69 *Hist. Parl., Commons*, ii. 1558–1603, 459; *Complete Peerage*, xii (2), 953.
70 Beaven, *Aldermen*, ii. 49, 64.
71 *Hist. Parl., Commons*, 1558–1603, iii. 677.
72 G.L.R.O., MR/TH/64, m. 1; below, manors (Wick).
73 G.L.R.O., MR/TH/34; below, manors (Lordshold).

and ponds supplied by pipes.[74] The precise site of his 'great house', with an access road running north from the west end of the high street,[75] and the extent of its grounds are unknown. Apparently not a manorial seat, part of the property was bought in 1704 by Richard Ryder (d. 1733), including the later Upton House in Urswick Road, and other houses perhaps in Alderman's Walk (later Homerton Row). Ryder soon made building leases for three plots north of his own house. His family had also built immediately south of the residence by 1717 and was probably responsible for most nearby development north of the high street.[76]

Homerton had 104 residents who paid poor rates in 1720 and soon had more than any other parochial division, with 155 by 1735 and 213 by 1761, although only 220 in 1779.[77] There were at least eight taverns in 1725, apart from the White Hart at Temple Mills; they included the Plough, a disorderly house in 1734, the Coach and Horses, perhaps the best appointed since courts baron were held there in the 1750s, and the Greyhound at Marsh gate, the eastern end of the village.[78] Nine of Hackney's 36 select vestrymen lived at Homerton in 1729 and 7 in 1740.[79]

In Ram's chapel of 1723 Homerton possessed the parish's first place of Anglican worship to be built after the parish church.[80] Stephen Ram (d. 1746), a goldsmith, was a manorial constable in 1718 and later an active vestryman.[81] His chapel was built on a copyhold west of the Plough, which he acquired in 1722 as one of a succession of Londoners, including Charles Booth, a salter, admitted in 1702; by 1704 it contained a new house with 2 a., another house, and four cottages.[82] The estate passed to Ram's brother Andrew, to Andrew's widow Eleanor, and to John Hopkins, owner of Hackney House.[83] The chapel had its own trustees from 1775 and later gave rise to a school; building obscured the identity of Ram's own residence, which may have been at the corner of Plough Lane and Homerton Row.[84]

Edward Brooksby in 1725 bought from John Smith of Hammersmith other property which had been held by Charles Booth. Some of it lay farther east on the north side of the high street, where Booth had acquired lands formerly of Richard Cheney, whose residence had contained 14 hearths in 1664 and 1672. The estate inherited in 1753 by Edward's cousin William Brooksby, a London haberdasher, included four houses in the street,[85] part of property which he left to his

widow Mary and then to Susannah Frames, who in 1805 was admitted with her husband John Musgrove.[86] Edward also left several houses in Brooksby's Walk, with scattered parcels, to William Frames.[87] More property, separated in 1706 from some which had passed to Booth, was conveyed by F. J. Tyssen's trustees to William Pratt, a brickmaker, in 1743, when it included eight houses.[88] Pratt acquired many more sites in or near the high street in the 1740s and 1750s,[89] all of which passed by will dated 1759 to his wife Jane and on her death by 1772 to their six children.[90]

In 1745 building was confined mainly to the high street,[91] although at the west end it stretched along Plough Lane to Homerton Row and south along Bridge Street to Money or Morning Lane. The lane led west past the solitary Old Gravel Pit chapel of 1715-16[92] to Hackney village and south-east beside the brook, where it was called Water Lane, to Well Street and so to the London end of Mare Street. By 1697 Bowling Green House had been built south of Morning Lane, from which it was reached by converging ways along the lines of Chatham Place and Meeting House path; it was rebuilt c. 1762 and later called Grove House.[93] From the high street Shepherd's Lane also led to the brook and had a barn and cottages, three of them new when claimed by Pratt in 1743.[94] A brewery, presumably by the brook, was owned in 1724 by Thomas Prior and Thomas Marsh, whose property when sold in 1731 included a lease of the White Hart at Clapton.[95] The south end of Brooksby's Walk existed in 1745 and was so named by 1759, when Pratt left six houses there.[96] On the south side of the high street the Gill mead estate of the Milborne family included the house leased as a workhouse until its sale in 1769.[97]

Hackney Wick in 1745 was reached through fields by Wick Lane. Apart from a few cottages where the lane turned east south of the brook, on the site of Silk Mill Row, the hamlet consisted of little more than the spacious Wick House, soon probably rebuilt, and its attendant buildings.[98]

In 1768 King's Head academy bought copyholds east of the Plough. Development by the academy, from 1823 Homerton College,[99] and the extension of Brooksby's Walk constituted the main changes in the high street and to the north in the late 18th and early 19th century.[1] Southwest of the high street more striking changes began with the leasing in 1780 of premises in

74 *Archaeologia*, xii. 186.
75 H.A.D., LBH/C/A2/1; below, manors (Ryder).
76 H.A.D., LBH/C/A2/1–13; M.L.R. 1717/2/170; Clarke, *Hackney*, 139; *Hackney Photos.* i. 54.
77 H.A.D., P/J/P/76, 91, 121, 150.
78 G.L.R.O., MR/LV3/116; MR/LV4/15; MR/LV6/79; ibid. P79/JN1/214, p. 81; ibid. M79/LH/13, pp. 1, 6, 16, 47.
79 Vestry mins. 23 Aug. 1729; Easter 1740.
80 Below, list of churches.
81 G.L.R.O., M79/LH/49, 18 Apr. 1718.
82 Ibid. M79/LH/48, 10 Apr. 1702; 21 Apr. 1704; M79/LH/49, 14 June 1722.
83 Ibid. M79/LH/14, pp. 4–6; H.A.D., D/F/TYS/38.
84 Below, list of churches; educ. (pub. schs.); Clarke, *Hackney*, 140–1.
85 G.L.R.O., M79/LH/13, pp. 46, 58–63; ibid. MR/TH/4, m. 1d.; MR/TH/34.

86 Ibid. M79/LH/18, pp. 1–7; M79/LH/19, pp. 211–12.
87 Ibid. M79/LH/20, pp. 26–9.
88 Ibid. M79/LH/50, 12 Apr. 1743.
89 Ibid. M79/LH/51, 3 Apr. 1744; 19 Apr. 1748; 24 Apr. 1750; M79/LH/13, pp. 162–73.
90 Ibid. M79/LH/14, pp. 137–44; M79/LH/15, pp. 186–90; 18, pp. 163–75.
91 Para. based on Rocque, *Map of Lond.* (1741–5), sheet 6.   92 Below, prot. nonconf. (Congs.).
93 G.L.R.O., H1/ST/E67/28/18; H1/ST/E67/32/7; H1/ST/E114/4/14; *Terrier*, Winter 1993/4.
94 G.L.R.O M79/LH/51, 19 Apr. 1748.
95 Ibid. Acc. 1449/1–2.   96 Ibid. M79/LH/15, p. 189.
97 Below, manors (Alvares); local govt. (par. govt.).
98 Rocque, *Map of Lond.* (1745–6), sheet 3; below, manors (Wick).   99 Below, prot. nonconf.
1 *Starling's Map* (1831).

Shepherd's Lane for Berger's paint factory, which led to the building of cottages around Thomas (later Ribstone) Street on St. Thomas's hospital's land along Water Lane.[2] To the west was the Woolpack inn, licensed probably by 1760, which gave its name to a brewery later owned by Ford Addison.[3] Much of the hospital's land was taken for residential housing which merged with that spreading from the south end of Hackney village. In Paradise Place (later the south end of Chatham Place), the New Gravel Pit chapel of 1809 was flanked by Hackney Free and Parochial school from 1811.[4] Behind, in Retreat Place, Robinson's Retreat was finished in 1813 and two pairs of houses, also designed by Samuel Robinson, were built to the east.[5] Chatham Place was built up from 1815 and new villas built by John Musgrove formed the east end of Retreat Place in 1824.[6]

Meanwhile the Charterhouse had built on 1¼ a. containing the remains of an old house, the Tanhouse or its successor, which had served as a school. A terrace of 12 houses was planned in 1796 as the south side of Sutton Place, with mews behind, but finally 16 were built under a lease of 1809 to William Collins, probably one of the family which also took land for the Paragon.[7] Houses and shops nearby in the high street, Bridge Street, and Morning Lane were leased by Susannah Musgrove in 1822.[8] In Brooksby's Walk, where her husband John had acquired William Frames's property, the younger John Musgrove made a building lease in 1821.[9]

The most respectable parts in 1821 were Upper Homerton,[10] around the later Urswick Road, with 19 merchants or gentry, and Sutton Place, with 15. A few lived nearby in Homerton Row, although most of the 80 householders in its extension Alderman's Walk, which had new cottages,[11] were tradespeople or labourers; so too were c. 130 in Brooksby's Walk and most of the 79 in 'Homerton', presumably the high street. To the south Homerton Terrace was largely middle-class but Morning Lane with 32 names and Water Lane with 99 were humbler, as were New Cut (later Ball's Buildings and from 1894 Link Street) with 41, Bridge (from 1938 Ponsford) Street with 29, and Shepherd's Lane with 60.

At Hackney Wick, where the White Lion was licensed by 1785,[12] a snuff mill was acquired c. 1787 for Leny Smith's silk factory.[13] W. H. Ashpitel held land between Wick Lane and Hackney brook from 1808 and had leased three small sites for building by 1813; c. 25 more cottages, presumably put up by Ashpitel, passed

to his sons in 1852.[14] Leny Smith in 1820 built or refronted 13 cottages, conveyed by his family to trustees in 1827 and to John Musgrove in 1828;[15] as Silk Mill Row, they stood south of the lane's junction with Cassland Road, which led from Well Street and near whose east end was a row of shanties built from 1806 called Hackney Bay, later nicknamed Botany Bay. Smith also built Sidney House, midway between Hackney Wick and Homerton, in 1808-9. A few buildings stood farther east near the old Wick House in 1831, where Wick Lane turned north towards a rope works and Froggatt's mill.[16] Smith and Froggatt were among 36 residents, most of them tradespeople or labourers, recorded at Hackney Wick in 1821; a further 76, including many gardeners, were at the Bay and 19 in Baker's Row, also at Hackney Wick. Listed under Homerton, although separated from it by the marsh, were 6 residents at Temple Mills.

Social decline may have started with the expansion of the workhouse, of Berger's factory, and of industry at Hackney Wick. It increased with speculative building and with the construction of the railway from 1847. Victoria Park station served Hackney Wick from 1856, although Homerton had its own station only from 1868.[17]

South of Retreat Place, small houses by 1843 formed Arthur, Margaret, and Brunswick streets (later Brooksbank and Collent streets and Cresset Road). They had been built by William Bradshaw (d. 1855), an auctioneer also active in Grove Street,[18] who was responsible for much of Homerton's expansion northward. In 1836 he bought the White House on the east side of Brooksby's Walk and in 1839 Home field on the west, with high street premises and c. 5 a. stretching back to the Grove (from 1907 Homerton Grove).[19] Part was sold for St. Barnabas's church and its attendant buildings in 1845 and 1847,[20] when the rest was being covered with cramped terraces: Albert (from 1887 Belshaw and from 1914 Wardle) Street, crossed by Victoria and Brook streets (from 1875 Holmbrook Street), which in 1860 were slums.[21] To the north-west land behind Homerton College was bought in 1852 by the East London union for a new workhouse and infirmary, under construction in 1854 and enlarged for imbeciles in 1858.[22]

Expansion southward produced both culs-de-sac and roads which passed under the railway, from Isabella Road in the west to Sidney Road, a renaming of most of Wick Lane (later Kenworthy Road), at the top of Marsh Hill.[23] The first presumably commemorated Isabella Ball, whose

---

[2] Below, econ. hist. (ind.); *Starling's Map* (1831).

[3] Clarke, *Hackney*, 188, 298 n.; G.L.R.O., MR/LV7/49; MR/LV9/136; *Hackney Dir.* (1849).

[4] Below, prot. nonconf. (Unitarians); educ. (pub. schs.).

[5] *Terrier*, Autumn 1991; below, misc. institutions.

[6] M.L.R. 1824/11/515.

[7] G.L.R.O., Acc. 1876/MP1/221 A – D; *Hackney Photos.* i. 52; above, Hackney village.

[8] M.L.R. 1820/5/614.

[9] G.L.R.O., M79/LH/20, pp. 26-9; M.L.R 1821/6/748.

[10] Two paras. based on H.A.D., P/J/CW/124, pp. 26-56.

[11] H.A.D., M 1282.

[12] G.L.R.O., MR/LV9/136.

[13] Below, econ. hist. (ind.); Clarke, *Hackney*, 160, 295 n.

[14] G.L.R.O., M79/LH/27, pp. 414-17.

[15] Ibid. M79/LH/22, pp. 179-80, 365.

[16] Ibid. M79/LH/25, pp. 430-2; M79/LH/26, pp. 75-6; Watson, *Gentlemen*, 35, 51; H.A.D., V 15; ibid. P/J/CW/115-17; *Starling's Map* (1831).   [17] Above, communications.

[18] Watson, *Gentlemen*, 53; below, Grove Street and Well Street.   [19] G.L.R.O., M79/LH/24, pp. 30-33, 363-8.

[20] Ibid. M79/LH/25, pp. 357-8, 362-3; below, list of churches.

[21] G.L.R.O., M79/LH/25, p. 24; M79/LH/28, pp. 75-83; *Ann. Rep. Bd. of Wks.* (1860).

[22] G.L.R.O., M79/LH/27, pp. 191-4; *Return of Inspections of Met. Workhos.* H.C. 50, p. 219 (1867), lxi; ibid. H.C. 50-1, pp. 466-7 (1867), lxi; Old O.S. Map Lond. 41 (1870).

[23] Two paras. based on Stanford, *Map of Lond.* (1862-5 edn.), sheet 8; Old O.S. Map Lond. 41 (1870).

father Robert Hopkins had left 17 copyholds from Sutton House to Bridge Street; she sold some land for the railway and in 1852 her son John Ball broke the entail of the rest.[24] Church (later Barnabas) Road had been planned as far as Hackney brook in 1849, when building land on either side was held by the auctioneer Marmaduke Matthews and his partner George Horatio Wilkinson, a timber merchant.[25]

South of the railway, housing by 1865 surrounded the grounds of Sidney House and stretched across the new Wick Road, an eastward route from Water Lane near the line of the culverted brook. Much of the road was built up after 1860 by Matthews and Wilkinson, who had bought some of the bankrupt Leny Smith's property.[26] Homerton thus reached the suburbs of south Hackney bordering Well Street common and Victoria Park. Housing also spread northward to merge with Lower Clapton. In 1867 the London & Suburban Land & Building Co. was diverting footpaths from the end of Brooksby's Walk, which it was to extend across its Clapton Park estate as Chatsworth Road.[27] The building of a fever (later the Eastern) hospital along the Grove filled the only large site west of Brooksby's Walk and was said in 1874 to have driven the wealthier inhabitants away.[28]

Shops lined much of the high street, with seven public houses, and a few had existed in Brooksby's Walk in 1849. By 1872 there were many more, along both sides of Wick Road.[29] The last private gardens between the high street and the railway, from King's (later Digby) Road to Crozier Terrace, made way for the culs-de-sac of Sedgwick and Nisbet streets (named from 1870).[30] Infilling south of the high street virtually ended with the expansion of the workhouse and infirmary and of Berger's factory and the building of Ballance Road (named in 1869) and Hassett Road over the grounds of Thomas Ballance's Sidney House.[31] Vacant plots in Retreat Place were leased in 1874, although the almshouses kept their garden on the north side.[32] Fields remained only between Homerton and the marsh. The lines of the G.N.R. and G.E.R. divided Hackney Wick, whose focus had shifted eastward to house industrial workers: spaces were being filled between an eastern section of Wick Lane called Gainsborough Road, the railways, and factories served by the Hackney cut.[33]

Housing spread east of Brooksby's Walk from the 1880s,[34] along parallel roads leading north: Pratt's Lane, renamed Glyn Road in 1881 and straightened at the high street end, was the longest and had been built up to Lower Clapton's Millfields Road by 1891. Roads to the east had been begun as far as Pincey (from 1905 Daubeney) Road, next to the moated site which still marked the eastern limit of building. South

of Marsh Hill there were houses along Sidney Road around a board school of 1882 east to Swinnerton Street, named in 1881 after the Milbornes' heirs, and beside the railway around Bartrip Street, named from 1876. Swinnerton Road replaced the north-west end of Red Path, leading from Marsh Hill to Hackney Wick; the south-east end of the path skirted G.N.R. sidings, next to where the rope works in 1880 was bought to house the Eton mission.[35] Meanwhile the acquisition of Sidney House as a convent in 1872 had been followed by the establishment of a Roman Catholic school and church where Sidney Road joined Wick Road.[36] Building joined Homerton to Hackney Wick, where by 1891 the triangle between the G.E.R. line, the cut, and Gainsborough Road had been almost wholly built over.

The high street had no tramways and sometimes appeared too quiet to deserve its name.[37] Congestion nonetheless led to changes, ranging from a widening of the entrance to Brooksby's Walk in 1876 to rebuilding of the range containing the Plough, where the street was narrowest, c. 1887. The north side of the Grove was to be widened around the junction with Brooksby's Walk in 1884.[38]

Signs of social decline in the high street included the use of no. 17, where the local benefactor Henry Sedgwick's daughter Marian had lived until 1860, by a pawnbroker's by 1872, the conversion of Upton House into a truant school in 1878, its rebuilding c. 1885, and the acquisition of the early 18th-century Eagle House at the corner of Homerton Row by a dyer; demolitions in Homerton Row c. 1887 were followed by denser building in Halidon Street.[39] Homerton as a whole was characterized c. 1890 by poverty. The well-to-do were confined to Urswick Road and its western offshoots St. John's Church Road and Sutton Place. Residents nearby were 'comfortable' around and opposite Ram's chapel, in Homerton Row and other streets in the angle with Urswick Road, in Isabella and Mehetabel roads south of Sutton House, and beyond the railway in Chatham Place and Retreat Place; others lived in avenues east of Brooksby's Walk, in Marsh Hill, Sidney Road, and around Hassett Road. The comfortable and the poor were mingled in the central stretch of the high street, the Grove, Brooksby's Walk, south of the railway in Morning Lane (which from 1887 included Water Lane), Digby, Wick, and Ballance roads, and at Hackney Wick in Gainsborough and Windsor (later Berkshire) roads. The poor lived mainly in side streets like College Street (later Row), Durham Grove, and Bradshaw's Margaret Street, the very poor behind the high street around Holmbrook Street to the north and Nisbet and Crozier streets to

24 G.L.R.O., M79/LH/27, pp. 26–32, 86–7.
25 Ibid. M79/LH/26, pp. 137–9, 177–9, 233, 351.
26 Ibid. M79/LH/25, pp. 186–191; 388–401; Watson, *Gentlemen*, 54; H.A.D., M 4232/13/8.
27 H.A.D., J/V/2, pp. 496, 504; above, Clapton.
28 Below, pub. svces.; Nat. Soc. files (letter from vicar of St. Barnabas's).   29 *Hackney Dir.* (1849, 1872).
30 Old O.S. Map Lond. 41 (1870).
31 Below, pub. svces.; econ. hist. (ind.).
32 *Terrier*, Autumn 1991.

33 Old O.S. Map Lond. 41 (1870); below, econ. hist. (ind.).
34 Para. based on Stanford, *Map of Lond.* (1891 edn.), sheet 8.
35 Old O.S. Map Lond. 41 (1870); Clarke, *Hackney*, 295 n.
36 Below, Rom. Cathm.
37 W. Besant, *E. Lond.* (1901), 267.
38 G.L.R.O., MBW 2471; *Hackney Photos.* i. 56, 58.
39 G.L.R.O., MBW 2471; Clarke, *Hackney*, 140, 143, 294 n.; *Hackney Photos.* i. 52, 54.

the south, and off Victoria Road which bisected Hackney Wick. All three of the poorest areas were the only ones in Hackney to contain the lowest, 'semi-criminal' class.[40]

Hackney Wick, notorious for its jerry building,[41] was described in 1879 as a district of 6,000 people who had sunk to the lowest depths.[42] They included many drifters and, being down-trodden, were found by the Salvation Army in 1897–8 to be less violent than those of Bethnal Green; Eton college's mission, despite lavish expenditure, had little moral influence. Houses had been built on layers of refuse, where brickearth had been excavated, and a recent insistence on concrete floors had led to higher rents. Several back-to-back cottages had already been demolished. Infant mortality, although not the general death rate, was the highest in Hackney.[43]

From the 1890s building continued on the few sites left near the marsh. On the south side of Marsh Hill the former tollhouse, having been a farmstead, made way in 1901 for the completion of Mabley Street,[44] thereafter the limit of permanent building east of Sidney Road. The moated site north of Marsh Hill was threatened in 1910 by Trehurst Street, started c. 1900 from the Clapton Park end and completed by 1913 along with most of Adley Street to the east.[45] On the marsh beyond, the first timber works at Homerton bridge existed from c. 1910.[46] Meanwhile the social standing of Homerton's west end declined further with the rehousing of Hackney parochial infants' school in Isabella Road in 1896, the building of Barlow's tin box factory immediately north of Sutton Place c. 1903, and the conversion of Sutton House into an institute, reopened in 1904,[47] Upton House's southern neighbour, built by the Ryders and owned from 1847 by the Rivaz family, had been demolished by 1905 for enlargement of the truant school.[48] Industry spread around Chatham Place: Grove House (no. 36 Chatham Place) became a clothing factory and had lost half of its garden by 1898; the nearby garden of Robinson's Retreat made way for Paragon shoe works in 1912.[49] William Bradshaw's heirs sold the site of Vine Cottage in the high street for a fire station in 1906; the family sold a block between Holmbrook and Belsham streets and Homerton Grove in 1910 but retained 189 houses in Homerton, including Eagle House, for sale in 1927.[50]

In the period between the World Wars, Homerton was equally residential and industrial. In 1928 it differed from much of Hackney in that industry occupied purpose-built premises

rather than converted dwellings. Tranby Place in the high street east of Brooksby's walk had been cleared and six factories had replaced houses north of Sutton Place. Hackney Wick also had purpose-built factories, mainly along the canal and older than the cheap terraces housing their workers.[51] Nisbet Street and parts of Hackney Wick were still the poorest areas in 1930.[52]

The built-up area spread only to the north-east, where in 1937 the L.C.C. took part of Hackney marsh for the Kingsmead estate. With 17 five-storeyed blocks, a school, and shops, it extended building from Adley Street to the factories at Homerton bridge.[53] Off the high street Hackney M.B. replaced slums behind the old Plough range, in Homerton Row and College Street, with 160 flats in Banister House, opened in 1935.[54] Clearances were also ordered for Nisbet Street in 1934, the south end of Bridge Street and part of Morning Lane in 1936, and Rosina Street in 1937.[55] Six-storeyed blocks forming Nisbet House, with 311 flats, were opened by Hackney in 1938.[56] Cramped rows off Morning Lane had made way by 1940 for Woolpack House and Ribstone House, the first blocks to form the north part of the L.C.C.'s Morningside estate. Beyond Retreat Place, streets were re-named between 1936 and 1938 and partly rebuilt; Lennox House had been built in Cresset Road by 1938.[57] Among buildings demolished were the 18th-century Grove House, empty since 1912, in 1921 and Ram's chapel, to widen the high street.[58] Longer streets to be renamed were Church Road, called Barnabas Road from 1936, and Sidney Road, called Kenworthy Road from 1938.

War damage led to an increase in public housing.[59] Demolitions included Homerton College for an extension of Banister House, with a further 235 flats by 1960,[60] and Robinson's Retreat for part of the Morningside estate, including Cresset House and Brooksbank House which by 1952 stretched south to Cresset Road. Building on the north part of the estate, where more blocks had been named early in the war, continued before and after 1950.

In 1960 Berger's factory closed,[61] whereupon almost the entire area south of the railway between Morning Lane and Barnabas Road was cleared for the L.C.C.'s Wyke estate. Early flats included Baycliffe House and Risley House in Digby Road from 1959 and Musgrove House in Barnabas Road from 1960. Nearby the L.C.C.'s Gascoyne estate, extending into south Hackney, included the ten-storeyed Kingscroft Point,

40 Clarke, *Hackney*, 129; *Booth's Map* (1889), NE.
41 *The Times*, 19 Sept. 1877, 11a; H.A.D., H/LD 7/4.
42 Nat. Soc. files.
43 Booth, *Life and Labour*, iii (1), 78, 96–8, 106; H.A.D., J/V/18/2, pp. 49–55.
44 *Hackney Photos.* i. 63.
45 Bacon, *Atlas of Lond.* (1910), sheet 40; Old O.S. Map Lond. 41 (1913).
46 *P.O. Dir. Lond. County Suburbs* (1909, 1911).
47 Below, educ. (pub. schs.); econ. hist. (ind.); *The Old Ho. at the Corner. St. John at Hackney Ch. Institute* (1906), 5; above, this section.   48 *Hackney Photos.* i. 53.
49 Ibid. ii. 36; G.L.R.O., H1/ST/E65/C/5/5/1; *Terrier*, Autumn 1991.

50 G.L.R.O., M79/LH/39, pp. 22–33, 158–64; M79/LH/40, p. 157; M79/LH/42.
51 Hackney M.B. *Rep. on San. Condition* (1928), 118–19.
52 *New Lond. Life and Labour*, iii (1), 361.
53 Hackney, *Official Guide* [1938]; below, pub. svces.
54 Hackney, *Official Guide* [1938]; *Hackney Photos.* ii. 88–9.
55 *Hackney Photos.* ii. 98; H.A.D., H/PD/3/4.
56 *Hackney Photos.* ii. 98; Hackney, *Official Guide* [1961].
57 *P.O. Dir. Lond.* (1934 and later edns.).
58 Below, list of churches; *Hackney Photos.* i. 59; ii. 36.
59 Four paras. based on *P.O. Dir. Lond.* (1939 and later edns.).   60 Hackney, *Official Guide* [1960].
61 *Hackney Photos.* i. 63; below, econ. hist. (ind.).

finished in 1967, and Heathcote, Vanner, and Ravenscroft points of 1968, all system-built and soon reinforced. In Berger Road, Latimer House and Gilby House were built as part of the Wyke estate c. 1982.[62]

Changes in Homerton High Street included the demolition of Eagle House in the early 1950s and of buildings to the east.[63] Hackney M.B.'s six-storeyed block of 75 flats called Marian Court[64] stood west of Ponsford Street by 1960 and the similar Bridge House to the east, opposite Banister House, by 1967. Priory Court had been built in Brooksby's Walk by 1970. The high street, as a shopping centre never a rival to Hackney village or Dalston, was characterized by such public buildings as the fire station and library, both Edwardian but rebuilt in 1974, and the gaunt piles of the extended workhouse which served as Hackney hospital.[65] Many terraces remained in Glyn Road and its neighbours east of Brooksby's Walk, but flats bordered Marsh Hill at Humberton Close and Newbury Court by 1980 and at Studley Close by 1985. Although Metal Box and other firms left, industry survived near the railway and in 1985 Homerton station was reopened.[66]

At Hackney Wick, which had public baths from 1935 and a library from 1947,[67] changes were more sweeping. South-west of the baths, the L.C.C.'s Eastway Park had been opened by 1960 as an old people's home. Opposite, between Eastway and the factories along the railway and the cut, the G.L.C.'s Trowbridge estate left only the north–south line of Osborne and Prince Edward roads from the centre of the old street pattern. First opened in 1965 and completed in 1969, the estate included 117 bungalow homes but was most striking for its seven 21-storeyed towers,[68] with mosaic facings and glass balconies.

The railway's division of Hackney Wick was reinforced from the 1970s by the partly sunken Cowdry Road and the elevated East Cross motorway. Construction of the East Cross route involved the demolition of Hackney Wick station, which had been closed since 1943, although a new station in Chapman Road was opened in 1980.[69] Plans to redevelop the Trowbridge estate were modified in 1987, after only three of the tower blocks had been demolished.[70]

In 1992 the railway sidings had made way for low-rise housing at Edmeston Close, still to be reached from Eastway along Red Path, which crossed Cowdry Road. Between Berkshire Road and the cut three-storeyed ranges formed Leabank Square, which was partly occupied. The only long terrace from late 19th-century Hackney Wick survived, partly neglected, north-east of the former baths as nos. 61–79 (consecutive) Eastway.

From the cut, Homerton Road and Eastway led straight between recreation grounds towards Temple Mills bridge. A few large factories stood near the end of Eastway and others bordered Waterden Road, which ran north to a busy intersection west of the bridge.[71] Where Temple Mills Road crossed the Lea, past the site of the mill and its cottages, a rebuilt successor to the White Hart stood empty. Nearby was the entrance to Lee Valley park authority's Eastway sports centre, beyond the boundary.[72]

Homerton has few pre-Victorian relics, apart from Sutton House, and Hackney Wick has none. The district is one of housing estates, factories, and small businesses. Apart from cleared sites west of Brooksby's Walk, there are spaces for recreation only where building gives way to Hackney marsh.

Homerton High Street is ill served by shops, although a few lie east of Brooksby's Walk. The dominance of municipal flats is relieved chiefly by St. Barnabas's church,[73] its churchyard, and attendant ragstone buildings. A few town houses remain on the south side of the street. No. 168, of three storeys over a basement and with a Tuscan doorcase, is the better preserved of a mid to late 18th-century pair, no. 170 having a warehouse covering its ground floor.[74] Nos. 140 and 142, east of Digby Road, have Tuscan doorcases and are probably early 19th- century.[75]

The gentility of Upper Homerton is recalled by Sutton Place, since 1969 part of the conservation area around Hackney church.[76] The south side, nos. 1–16, is a stock-brick terrace of three storeys over basements, nos. 1 and 2 having added mansards with dormers; details include pilastered doorcases, fanlights, and first-floor iron balconies.[77] The range was built under a lease of 1809, possibly to the design of the Charterhouse surveyor William Pilkington, who had been concerned with earlier plans, and forms a group with nos. 1–22 on the north side.[78]

Sutton House, to the south-east, is Hackney's oldest domestic building and one of the few urban properties of the National Trust.[79] Three-storeyed and built of brick on an **H** plan for Sir Ralph Sadler in the 1530s, Sutton House retains some of its original exterior diaper brickwork and of its early decoration and fittings. Fragments of painted decoration survive in the north-west room, the parlour, and there is 16th-century panelling in that room and in the large central room on the first floor. Only one original window, of six lights with a single transom, survives. The staircase in the west wing is 17th-century.

62 *Hackney & Stoke Newington Observer*, 14 Mar. 1969, 1; below, plate 34.
63 Hist. Mon. Com. *E. Lond.* 47; Pevsner, *Lond.* ii. 172; *Hackney Photos.* i. 55.
64 Hackney, *Official Guide* [1960].
65 Below, pub. svces.
66 Below, econ. hist. (ind.); above, communications.
67 Below, pub. svces.
68 *From Tower to Tower Block*, no. 51; *Hackney Echo*, 7 Oct. 1987, 1; G.L.C. Housing Dept. *Ann. Rep.* (1968–9), 25.
69 Above, communications; *Hackney Photos.* i. 74.
70 *Hackney Echo*, 7 Oct. 1987, 1.

71 Below, econ. hist. (ind.).
72 Ibid. econ. hist. (mills); social; *Hackney Photos.* i. 128.
73 Below, list of churches.
74 *List of Bldgs.* (1975).
75 Pevsner, *Lond.* ii. 172.
76 H.A.D., Conservation Areas file.
77 *List of Bldgs.* (1975).
78 G.L.R.O., Acc. 1876/MP1/221–2; Colvin, *Brit. Architects*, 637.
79 Para. based on Hist. Mon. Com. *E. Lond.* 45–6; *List of Bldgs.* (1990); *Sutton Ho., Hist. and Guide* (1988).

The eastern range housed the kitchen and service rooms. Its cellar was probably approached by an internal stair, whereas that under the west wing had an external stair. The house was divided into two dwellings c. 1752, when the central range was refaced and given sash windows and a second doorway, and sash windows were put into the fronts of the wings. The subdivision of the hall, and panelling and the staircase in the east wing, probably date from that time. The east wing was rendered in the later 19th century when there was some interior remodelling. Additions to the south culminated in a large meeting room, the Wenlock Barn, of 1904. Restoration, begun in 1990, has aimed to display the Tudor house in its undivided state while adapting the additions of c. 1904 for use by the community. The building was reopened to the public in 1992.[80]

Towards Hackney Wick, the former Sidney House survives as the north wing of the Sacred Heart convent. It is almost hidden by later buildings and is a brick villa of c. 1800, of five bays and three storeys beneath a stuccoed cornice and a mansard roof with dormers.[81] Housing of 1959–60 on the Wyke estate has been praised, both for the framework of low terraces around the towers and for landscaping.[82]

GROVE STREET AND WELL STREET.
Until joined by 19th-century building, two small settlements lay at road junctions. The first was where Grove Street, on the way from Old Ford Lane in Bethnal Green, met a footpath running from the south-west and continuing north-east as Grove Street Lane to Hackney Wick; the second was where Grove Street, slightly east of the modern Lauriston Road, met the way, called Well Street, running from Mare Street to Homerton.[83] From the 16th until the 19th century the hamlets were normally assessed and administered together.[84] This account covers south-eastern Hackney, east of Mare Street and south of Wick Road.

The names of Grove Street and of the Shoreditch family's Grove House, so called in 1327, may have had a common origin in a grove stretching westward from the hamlet to Shore Road.[85] Richard atte Grove left a house with a curtilage in Grove Street in 1392.[86] Until the way from Old Ford Lane was improved to form Grove Road c. 1800, the settlement there consisted of Londoners' scattered seats and a few

cottages.[87] Well Street, a busier route, presumably had a settlement by 1442, when common to the east was called Well Street field.[88] The moated site of the 'Pilgrim's house' to the west, on the north side of the street, may have had a house before the brick one was built.[89] Another moated house, on the south side, passed in 1658 from John Offley to his sons John and Thomas. It was occupied in 1664 by Sir John Gore and formed part of an estate of 14 houses and cottages in Well Street which was divided in 1686; the dwellings were decayed in 1695.[90] Well Street common in 1442 contained parcels which later passed to Henry Monger (d. by 1669), as did cottages in Grove Street recorded from 1516–17.[91] Later development around both hamlets was largely shaped by St. Thomas's hospital and the trustees of the Sir John Cass Foundation, and around Grove Street also by the Norris family. In the late 17th century the Norrises acquired a seat probably of the mid 16th.[92]

Mare Street, Grove Street, and Well Street were together represented by two chief pledges at the manor court in 1582.[93] From the 1650s Mare Street had its own chief pledge and Grove Street and Well Street were represented jointly under one or both of their names.[94] The two hamlets had 24 inhabitants who paid for church repairs in 1605,[95] and 26 assessed for hearth tax in 1664, when the largest house, Henry Monger's, had 18 hearths and 6 more houses stood empty.[96] Another resident was Nathaniel Barnardiston (d. 1680), of a prominent family with Dissenting sympathies.[97] In 1672 Grove Street had 16 assessed houses and Well Street 13.[98] Twelve residents of Grove Street paid poor rates in 1720 and 11 in 1735, 1761, and 1779, while those at Well Street increased from 15 to 24, 37, and 56.[99] Two of Hackney's select vestrymen lived in Grove Street in 1729 and 1740; one lived in Well Street in 1729 and 3 in 1740.[1]

Monger's almshouses, to which two cottages were annexed c. 1679,[2] slightly extended building from Well Street towards Grove Street. Towards Mare Street a house of six bays was built west of the Pilgrim's House; it was later held by the related De Kewer and Frampton families.[3] By 1745 a track led from the almshouses along the north side of the common towards Hackney Wick.[4] In Well Street the Green Dragon inn was recorded from 1724, the Cock, perhaps short-lived, in 1725, and the Two Black Boys from 1732.[5] In Grove Street the Three Colts stood across the street at the foot of

80 Terrier, Autumn 1992.
81 List of Bldgs. (1975).
82 Around Baycliffe Ho., Digby Rd., loosely described as Bentham Rd.: I. Nairn, Modern Bldgs. in Lond. (1964), 31.
83 Rocque, Map of Lond. (1741–5), sheet 6; Watson, Gentlemen, 16; above, communications.
84 Below, this section.
85 Watson, Gentlemen, 18; below, manors (Shoreditch Pl.).
86 Guildhall MS. 9171/1, f. 250v.
87 Watson, Gentlemen, 16, 18.
88 P.R.O., SC 2/191/62, m. 4d.; P.N. Mdx. (E.P.N.S.), 108.
89 Below, manors (Kingshold).
90 G.L.R.O., M79/KH/1, pp. 108, 113; 2, pp. 29–34, 102; 4, pp. 64–5.

91 S.J.C.F., 1A/1/D 61–70; ibid. unlisted deeds.
92 Below, manors (Shoreditch Pl.; Cass; Norris).
93 B.L. Eg. Ch. 2081.
94 G.L.R.O., M/93/1, f. 61; M/93/4, f. 106v.; M79/LH/45 sqq.   95 H.A.D., D/F/TYS/1, p. 65.
96 G.L.R.O., MR/TH/4, m. 2d.
97 Ibid.; P.R.O., PROB 11/363, f. 91; G.E.C. Baronetage, iii. 274–5; D.N.B.
98 G.L.R.O., MR/TH/34.
99 H.A.D., P/J/P/76, 91, 121, 150.
1 Vestry mins. 23 Aug. 1729, Easter 1740.
2 Below, charities.
3 Clarke, Hackney, 181, 297 n.; Hackney Photos. i. 67.
4 Rocque, Map of Lond. (1741–5), sheet 6; Watson, Gentlemen, 19.
5 G.L.R.O., MR/LV4/3; MR/LV4/15; P 79/JN1/214, pp. 45, 104.

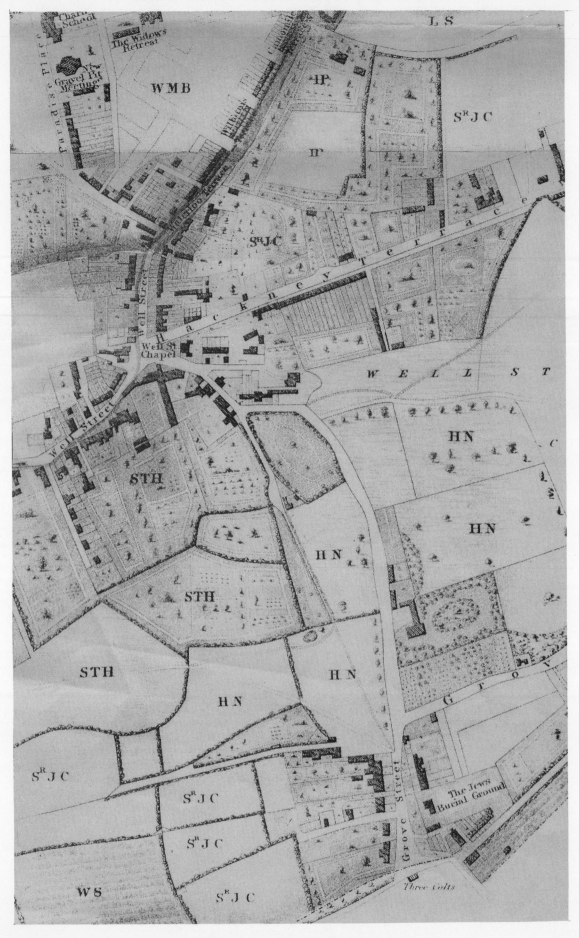

GROVE STREET AND WELL STREET c. 1830

the hamlet, a few yards south of the boundary.[6] Shore House (probably the former Grove House) was dilapidated in 1720, and by 1745 buildings called Water Gruel Row, on the east side of its approach road, housed labourers and market gardeners. There was little other building in the early 18th century.[7]

In 1768, on the demolition of Shore House, St. Thomas's hospital leased land east of the modern Shore Road, then called Shore Place, to Thomas Flight, a speculator. Flight put up three large houses fronting Well Street, a terrace of four or five along Shore Road, and a seat to the south-east later called Shore House; a few small houses were built south of his terrace in 1789. On the north side of Well Street a terrace of four was built in 1785 next to a semidetached pair. A nonconformist chapel of 1810–11 to the south and St. John's Anglican chapel of 1809–10 near a terrace in St. Thomas's Place were perhaps the only other nearby buildings until the 1840s, in contrast to development for the hospital farther north and beside Mare Street.[8]

In 1786[9] the Cass estate leased c. 70 a. north of the common to William Gigney, a baker, who put up a short terrace at the corner of Well Street and a new way which he laid out to the Wick (later Cassland Road). A row called Nursery Place to the east and Grove Cottage (later the Limes) and another row to the north were built by sublessees. Gigney himself was commemorated by Baker's Row in Grove Street Lane,[10] later taken for workers at the silk mills. On land subleased to Thomas Sell on the south side of Cassland Road were built two large houses, replaced in the 1840s for the estate manager's Cassland House. An adjoining plot was taken in the 1790s for the house later called Terrace Lodge; to the south, Common House was built to face the common in 1787.

On Gigney's bankruptcy in 1790 part of his land was taken by James Jackson, a City linen draper and Sell's assignee.[11] Jackson's undertenants William Fellowes, John Shillitoe, and Thomas Pickering in 1792 sought monthly payments which after four years would entitle a subscriber to one of 18 houses, allotted by ballot. Both Fellowes and Shillitoe were already involved in a similar but much larger scheme in Pollard's Row, Bethnal Green. Their Hackney Terrace gave directly on Cassland Road, while back gardens led to a communal pleasure ground with a gate to the common.[12] A stable block was built to the east. With 10 houses finished by 1796 and all 18 occupied in 1801, the terrace antedated the first known development by a conventional building society, near Preston (Lancs.).

From 1800 Well Street had an Independent chapel at the corner of Cassland Road.[13] Farther west semidetached villas called Greenwood's

Row had been built by 1811[14] in a southern offshoot of Well Street later called Percy Street (from 1938 Kingshold Road). They were followed by terraces along the north-west side of Well Street, from Waterloo Terrace at the corner of West (from 1877 Elsdale) Street to where the road ran into Water Lane.[15] Well Street's c. 200 households in 1821 probably included some in West Street; a further 37, all working-class, were in Orchard Street, an offshoot of West Street, and 49, many of them genteel, in Hackney Terrace, which had given its name to the western half of Cassland Road.[16] By 1831 building stretched the length of Well Street, although single houses and garden ground survived on the east side at the Homerton end. Space on the west side between Well Street and Retreat Place was filled from the late 1830s by William Bradshaw's building of Margaret Street and its neighbours.[17]

Elsewhere growth was piecemeal.[18] In 1831 the houses of Hackney Terrace appeared incongruously urban, with open views to the north. Scattered houses lay along the road of that name farther east; beyond were others, in a stretch called Wick Street, which led to Hackney Bay and Silk Mill Row. Grove Street was still separated from Well Street, there being no roadside housing between Monger's almshouses and the Norrises' seat. By 1811 the hamlet had been extended by cottages called Providence Row on the east side of the street, between the parish boundary and a burial ground which had been laid out from 1788 by the Hambro synagogue.[19] They contributed to a total of 38 households in 1821.[20] Grove Street Lane contained, apart from Baker's Row, only a few buildings on the verge beside the common.

Building joined the two hamlets[21] not along the road called Grove Street but along a more direct footpath to the west. Land west of the path was leased in 1833 by Jane, widow of John Wowen, for a brewery, while land to the east was given in 1834 by H. H. Norris for a school. When Wowen's former estate south-west of the junction with Well Street was sold in 1843, the part between the footpath and Grove Street was taken as an island site for St. John of Jerusalem's church,[22] with houses to the north, and for building at the corner with Cassland Road. The brewery was bought outright and the Albion built next to it, soon followed by Hampden chapel. Hackney Theological Seminary was established on Wowen's land to the west.[23] Most of the neighbouring land was taken by John Parr (d. 1853), who in 1844 built his first houses where the path formed a western branch of Grove Street (later the north end of Lauriston Road). From 1850 Parr and his son Samuel filled the angle between Grove Street (Lauriston Road) and Well Street with Manor (from 1878

6 Watson, *Gentlemen*, 19; *Starling's Map* (1831).
7 Below, manors (Shoreditch Pl.); Watson, *Gentlemen*, 26; Rocque, *Map of Lond.* (1741–5), sheet 6.
8 Watson, *Gentlemen*, 26–7, 52; above, Hackney village; Mare Street.
9 Para. based on Watson, *Gentlemen*, 28–9.
10 Above, Hackney Wick.
11 Para. based on Watson, *Gentlemen*, 28–34.
12 *Terrier*, Feb. 1986.
13 Below, prot. nonconf. (Congs).

14 H.A.D., P/J/Misc./II/1.
15 Watson, *Gentlemen*, 53.
16 H.A.D., P/J/CW/124, pp. 75–85.
17 *Starling's Map* (1831); above, Homerton.
18 Para. based on *Starling's Map* (1831).
19 Watson, *Gentlemen*, 54; below, Judaism.
20 H.A.D., P/J/CW/124, pp. 86–7.
21 Para. based on Watson, *Gentlemen*, 55–7.
22 Below, list of churches.
23 Below, prot. nonconf.

Holcroft) Road and its neighbours. A field south-west of Grove Street hamlet, acquired in 1841 by William Bradshaw, remained to be built over from 1845 as the north side of Morpeth Road and its offshoots,[24] where the Bradshaws retained 56 houses in 1927.[25]

The Crown's acquisition of land for Victoria Park,[26] opened in 1845 and absorbing the site of the old Three Colts,[27] stimulated building over the rest of south-eastern Hackney, although it prevented the southward extension of building from Grove Street, which it separated from Bethnal Green. The park was laid out mostly on fields of William Thompson but it also included land bought from the Cass trustees, St. Thomas's hospital, and the Sotheby family, whose estate straddled the boundary. The creation of the park soon led to the construction of Victoria Park Road from the south end of Mare Street into Grove Street Lane or Road (from 1878 the eastern section of Victoria Park Road). Belts of land immediately north of the park, both east and west of Grove Street, were reserved by the Crown. To the north comprehensive schemes were drawn up, further stimulated by the expiry of the leases to Gigney in 1847 and to Flight in 1848. Delay in building on the Crown estate and in providing approaches across the park, however, made it necessary to ensure access from other directions.[28]

Development for the Cass trustees,[29] who set up a Hackney estates committee in 1845, was largely decided by their surveyor George Wales, coiner of the name 'Cassland'. For St. Thomas's hospital, Henry Currey worked as surveyor from 1848. Agreements with landholders in Mare Street improved access, while exchanges which also involved the Norris family permitted the alignment of roads through all three estates. King Edward's Road, commemorating the hospital's benefactor, had been projected from the west in 1842; its eastern stretch was agreed in 1848. Shore Road and the Well Street end of St. Thomas's (from 1936 Ainsworth) Road were planned by 1850.[30] Comparatively large tracts, for nine or more double-fronted villas, were subleased by St. Thomas's, the first being to Charles Butters in 1848 south of Tudor Road.[31] Butters and from 1851 William Norris (unrelated to the landowning family) were the chief building contractors for the area around King Edward's Road in the 1850s and 1860s. Norris undertook to widen Well Street west of Shore Road in 1854.[32] In Victoria Park Road the Cass estate usually leased smaller plots between 1850 and 1862. South of King Edward's Road, behind Cambridge Lodge in Mare Street, cramped plots were allotted from 1855 by the St. Pancras, Marylebone and Paddington Freehold Land Society and slowly built up as Park (from 1877

Fremont) Street and the modern Warneford Street.[33]

Farther east change was slower, although in Grove Street an exchange with Monger's charity allowed the building of nos. 1–7 Blenheim Cottages, followed by the reconstruction of the almshouses. North and east of the common, building on the Cass estate spread along Well Street to Kenton Road, where land was leased in 1848 to George Oldfield for a ropery, and also along Cassland Road, involving the demolition of cottages at Hackney Bay and Nursery Place. Houses towards Hackney Wick, such as those begun by Oldfield along Bentham Road in 1851, were inferior to those nearer the common, where the surveyor George Wales's father took the first large villa in Gascoyne Road in 1848. Building around the west end of Cassland Road included Cassland Crescent opposite Hackney Terrace; it was to be begun by John Clark of Grove Cottage, registrar to the Cass trustees, in 1854 and was sufficiently complete for railings to be ordered in 1858.

Building east of the Cass estate, in the triangle between Victoria Park and Cassland roads, provided a link with Hackney Wick. It began on 3 a. sold by the Mann family in 1854, where from 1856 houses were built by the Suburban Villa and Village Association, a short-lived society which may have chosen too crowded a locality for a suburban village. Immediately to the east small terraced houses were built in a road named after John James Homer, to whom J. R. Mills leased the land c. 1858. Houses on the Victoria Road frontage were built by a contractor for the sublessee Thomas Peet Glaskin, who was active in much of Hackney. They looked across the northern apex of Victoria Park[34] and were soon complemented on the east side by Cadogan Terrace, under construction on the Crown estate in 1870.[35]

Between the west end of Well Street and where Hackney village had reached Paragon Road,[36] much of the land south of the later Loddiges Road had been held by John De Kewer (d. 1818) and then by Dr. Algernon Frampton (d. 1842);[37] beyond, it was partly the freehold of Conrad Loddiges[38] but mostly the leasehold of his family from St. Thomas's hospital until 1856. Darnley, Devonshire (from 1938 Brenthouse), and Loddiges roads had been planned to run east from Mare Street in 1853, their lines being modified towards West (later Elsdale) Street in 1854. They were linked by Stanley Road (later part of Frampton Park Road) continuing south[39] to permit the development of the Framptons' estate, on which Charles Butters and T. P. Glaskin began building in partnership in 1856; the larger houses were in Frampton Park and Glaskin roads. Abel Pilgrim was among builders on the

[24] Watson, *Gentlemen*, 53; G.L.R.O., M79/LH/28, pp. 86–9.   [25] G.L.R.O., M79/LH/42.
[26] Below, pub. svces.
[27] Watson, *Gentlemen*, 36.
[28] Ibid. 36–8, 59, 66, 70.
[29] Two paras. based on Watson, *Gentlemen*, 59–74.
[30] G.L.R.O., H1/ST/E114/5/1.
[31] Ibid. H1/ST/E40.
[32] Ibid. H1/ST/E65/C/28/1.

[33] Watson, *Gentlemen*, 77–80.   [34] Ibid. 76–7, 83.
[35] Ibid. 101; Old O.S. Map Lond. 41 (1870).
[36] Above, Hackney village. Rest of para. based on Watson, *Gentlemen*, 74, 82.
[37] *Gent. Mag.* lxxxviii. 377; cxii. 552; *Alum. Cantab. 1752–1900*, ii. 560.
[38] Clarke, *Hackney*, 180–1; below, econ. hist. (mkt. gdns.).
[39] G.L.R.O., H1/ST/E65/C/4/1/1–2; below, plate 23.

Loddigeses' land in 1857–8 and Butters in 1859.[40] No. 11 Loddiges Road was the birthplace of the engineer Herbert William Garratt (1864–1913).[41]

Grove Street saw little building in the 1850s.[42] Westward development, however, had been foreseen in 1850,[43] and in 1862 Henry Norris achieved the realignment of Grove Street (from 1877 Lauriston Road) west of the church, leaving the stretch on the east side to be renamed Church Crescent in 1878. He also laid out the western half of his estate with Speldhurst and other roads between the east end of King Edward's Road and Victoria Park Road; they had been built up, with most of Grove Street, by 1865, chiefly by Hugh Eastman and, in partnership, Henry Bagge and Robert Morley. The eastern half, south-west of Well Street common, was taken for the French hospital opened in 1865[44] and for Penshurst and neighbouring roads; the main builder was James Harman, who had completed the estate by 1867. On Cass land, south of the space at the intersection of Grove Street with Victoria Park Road, Rutland Road and its offshoots were built to the west from 1862 to 1865, followed by roads near the Jews' burial ground to the east; the neighbouring Lauriston Road frontage was finished in 1872.[45]

Towards Hackney Wick the space between Victoria Park and Cassland roads was filled after George Wales's departure in 1863.[46] Harrowgate Road was to be built up in 1863, by Bagge, and roads to the east in 1864, by John Wright, as far as the Suburban Villa and Village Association's Brookfield Road. From 1867 remaining sites were taken along the middle section of Cassland Road and in Bentham Road and others to the north, where most of the land had been market gardens.[47] The rest of Cassland Crescent was finished in 1865, when the parish vestry, as trustees of Poole's charity, made a building lease for the land between Well Street and Terrace Road on the west and Queen Anne Road.

Around the common, Gascoyne Road on the east was finished in 1870, Meynell Road on the north was occupied from 1877, a strip by Victoria Park Road on the south was taken for villas from 1891, and the lawn behind Hackney Terrace on the north-west was taken for Meynell Crescent from 1893.[48]

The last major phase of building was on the Crown's land bordering Victoria Park. Impressive villas had been planned in 1854 by James Pennethorne but, apart from keepers' lodges of 1857, construction on the Hackney side began only in 1860. Work had proceeded eastward along the south side of Victoria Park Road to the modern Skipworth Road by 1863 and was planned on the south side of Grove Street Lane in 1867, when St. Augustine's church was built

farther east. Public agitation ensured that stretches on either side of the church were saved from building by their sale to the M.B.W. in 1872. A slightly longer stretch nearer Grove Street was taken for Cawley and Rockmead roads of 1873–4, where single rows faced the park, as they did from 1872 along the curves of Gore Road, where Christ Church had been built as a western counterpart to St. Augustine's.[49]

Victoria Park was said to have initiated a new town in southern Hackney in 1862,[50] when building was at its busiest and when the M.B.W.'s completion of Burdett Road improved access by way of Grove Road through Bethnal Green.[51] Mainly residential, the area in 1869 was served by shops along Well Street, many of them around the junction with Cassland Road. A smaller group existed in the Broadway, where Grove Street widened south of the intersection with Victoria Park Road and where from 1879 trams passed on their way to Cassland Road.[52] Subdivision of premises or conversions for industry were controlled more carefully by the Cass trustees than by St. Thomas's, which allowed a wholesale bootmaker's to open at no. 74 Well Street in 1884. Ten years later the Well Street neighbourhood had 17 leatherworking or allied factories.[53]

About 1890 the well-to-do occupied most of the roads facing the park and Well Street common, or lived nearby east of St. John's church around Penshurst Road, to the west in Victoria Park and King Edward's roads, to the north along all but the easternmost stretch of Cassland Road, and in Darnley Road. Mixed with the 'fairly comfortable' they also lived along Well Street, around Frampton Park, Shore, and St. Thomas's roads, and west of Lauriston Road. Gore Road, although facing the park, and the nearby Rutland Road were only 'fairly comfortable'. Wick Road and some older enclaves were less prosperous. The poor were restricted to Wetherell Road and Bradshaw's Morpeth Road near the park end of Grove Street, to Percy Road off Well Street, and Hedgers Grove and Homer Road near Hackney Wick; Victoria Grove off Morpeth Road and Palace Road, opposite Percy Road, were very poor.[54]

By the 1890s there was room for building only in the grounds of Well Street's older residences,[55] notably Common (later Grove) House behind Monger's almshouses, Terrace Lodge immediately to the west, Cassland House at the end of Hackney Terrace, and Grove Cottage (later the Limes) nearby at the corner of Terrace Road. Cassland House was leased for technical education from 1897[56] and later replaced; Grove Cottage was taken for terraces in 1900. The other two were to survive until c. 1930. South Hackney county school was built in Cassland Road c. 1900

40 G.L.R.O., H1/ST/E40; HI/ST/E65/C/14/2/1–2; M.L.R. 1863/22/955–9.
41 D.N.B. Missing Persons.
42 Para. based on Watson, Gentlemen, 85–90.
43 H.A.D., V 33.
44 Below, misc. institutions.
45 Watson, Gentlemen, 93–5.
46 Para. based on ibid. 91–9.
47 Stanford, Map of Lond. (1862–5 edn.), sheet 8.
48 Watson, Gentlemen, 96–9.

49 Ibid. 100–102; below, list of churches.
50 G. R. Emerson, London: How the Great City Grew (1862), 281.
51 Watson, Gentlemen, 38.
52 Ibid. 109; Hackney Photos. i. 68, 72; above, communications.
53 Watson, Gentlemen, 106–7, 109.
54 Ibid. 105–6; Booth's Map (1889), NE.
55 Para. based on Watson, Gentlemen, 99.
56 Below, educ. (tech. educ.).

on the site of terraces of the 1860s between Bramshaw (formerly Brampton) and Bradstock (formerly Union) roads.[57]

Between the World Wars the district as a whole remained residential, except along Well Street and in offshoots near Mare Street such as Tudor Road. Elsewhere workshops were opened over a wide area, including Cassland, Wick, and Gascoyne roads by 1930, but were not concentrated.[58] Grove House and Terrace Lodge made way for Meynell Gardens after their purchase by Classic Estates, which also built Classic Mansions in Shore Road.[59] The Cass trustees objected to the L.C.C.'s proposed reduction of occupational density as more suitable for an outer suburb. They were reassured in 1937 that their estate as a whole would be zoned 'residential' rather than 'special residential' and that in principle they might build flats; the spread of shops and industry was restricted.[60]

Widening of Well Street west of Percy Road was planned in 1921.[61] The L.C.C. bought 3 a. between Well Street and King Edward's Road in 1926 for its Shore estate, finished in 1930, and 2½ a. to the south for the Kingshold estate, opened in 1932.[62] Smaller than some estates in northern Hackney, they had 184 and 140 dwellings respectively in 1938.[63] Templecombe Road, named in 1931, was built on a former nursery at the Kingshold estate's south-west corner and the private Sharon Gardens, named in 1934, on back gardens to the east.[64] Slum clearances were ordered in Lyme Grove, north of Loddiges Road, and in Wetherell Road in 1936–7.[65] The L.C.C.'s Banbury estate was built in 1936–7 with 203 dwellings on little more than 1 a. between Penshurst and Groombridge roads.[66]

Following widespread bomb damage in 1940,[67] redevelopment was most sweeping near Mare Street. After demolitions in King Edward's Road the Kingshold estate was extended by the opening of Weston House, Hackney's first post-war flats, in 1948.[68] North of Well Street, Glaskin and Palace roads were among those cleared on either side of Frampton Park Road, which survived with Loddiges Road as a way through the L.C.C.'s Frampton Park estate, begun in 1956, where blocks were up to 12 storeys.[69] The Gascoyne estate, started by 1949, extended south across the middle of Cassland Road to reach Well Street common.[70] The Parkside estate, with 152 dwellings, was built by Hackney M.B. in Rutland Road in the mid 1950s, as was Lauriston House in Lauriston Road.[71] There followed flats by the L.C.C. in Bentham Road and by the G.L.C. in Kenton Road.[72]

On the east side of Church Crescent, South

Hackney Rectory and a Toc H hostel had been rebuilt by 1965 as Prideaux House, with Sundridge House to the south and the 12-storeyed Chelsfield Point on the Banbury estate by 1967. The Kingshold estate had also been extended by 1970: Wakelyn House and other flats were built across Shore Road, curtailed and renamed Clermont Road south of Tudor Road, and Thornhill Point and other flats were built across King Edward's Road, curtailed and renamed Moulins Road to the east.[73] Yorke, Rosenberg & Mardall were architects for the extensions to Kingshold and Shepheard & Epstein for later work on the Banbury estate.[74]

Later redevelopment, mainly private, took place near Victoria Park. The 9-a. strip between Wetherell and Victoria Park roads on the north and Rockmead and Cawley roads on the south, with much damaged property, was to be cleared in 1976 by the Guinness trust, which provided 197 dwellings in 22 low-rise blocks; Guinness and Iveagh closes were so named in 1983.[75] On the Crown estate a bombed section of Gore Road was filled in 1966-7. Christ Church and the west end of the road made way for Christchurch Square and St. Agnes and Pennethorne closes; all three had been named by 1979, although Wates was building in Pennethorne Close in 1985.[76] Houses were also put up behind Hampden chapel, where a site to the south between the chapel and Balcorne Street awaited redevelopment in 1992. Thornhill Point and its companion Halston Point, with 21 storeys the tallest buildings in the area, then stood empty and partly boarded up.

A conservation area was proposed in 1976 for the north side of Victoria Park. It embraced the rows facing the park, houses stretching north along Lauriston Road to the church, and others facing Well Street common and at the west end of Cassland Road.[77] Thereafter the common, always less ornamental than the park and neglected for c. 20 years, was improved by tree planting.[78]

Well Street remains busy but lacks impressive public buildings. Most of the shops are near Mare Street and between Valentine Road and Morning Lane; the middle stretch retains a few mid 19th-century houses facing the Frampton Park estate. Near the west end nos. 23–5, Shuttleworth's hotel, is a four-storeyed pair built by 1785.[79]

The townscape to the south, despite much rebuilding, includes the spire of the Lauriston Road church. Beyond, Victorian terraces with some infilling define the edges of mature parkland in Victoria Park and, less clearly, of Well Street common.[80]

57 Below, educ. (pub. schs.); Watson, *Gentlemen*, 95.
58 Hackney M.B. *Rep. on San. Condition* (1928), p. 118.
59 Watson, *Gentlemen*, 99.   60 G.L.R.O., AR/TP/2/386.
61 Ibid. H1/ST/E65/2/28/3/1–12.
62 Hackney, *Official Guide* [1938].
63 L.C.C. *Lond. Statistics*, xli. 152–3.
64 Watson, *Gentlemen*, 99.   65 H.A.D., H/PD/3/4.
66 L.C.C. *Lond. Statistics*, xli. 150–1.
67 *Hackney Photos.* ii. 149–51; below, church extension.
68 L.C.C. *Ceremonial Pamphlets*, 18 Nov. 1948.
69 *Archit. Rev.* cxxi. 42–3.
70 Ibid. cv. 229; above, Homerton.
71 *P.O. Dir. Lond.* (1956, 1957); Hackney, *Official Guide*

[1961].
72 Nairn, *Modern Bldgs. in Lond.* 31; *P.O. Dir. Lond.* (1965, 1970).   73 *P.O. Dir. Lond.* (1965 and later edns.).
74 G.L.C. Housing Dept. *Ann. Rep.* (1969–70), 17; (1970–1), 11–12.
75 H.A.D., Statutory Lists file; ibid. Conservation Areas file; *P.O. Dir. Lond.* (1981, 1983).
76 *From Tower to Tower Block*, no. 52; *P.O. Dir. Lond.* (1978, 1979); *The Times*, 9 June 1985, 26.
77 H.A.D., Conservation Areas file.
78 'Parks and Open Spaces' (Hackney Soc.), 46.
79 Watson, *Gentlemen*, 52; above, this section.
80 H.A.D., Conservation Areas file.

The former Hackney Terrace, begun in 1792, is numbered 20–54 (even), Cassland Road. 'The earliest of Hackney's few palace-front terraces and the most ambitious of its Georgian survivals', it is of stock brick, each house being of three bays and three storeys over a basement; a central pediment bears the arms of the architect William Fellowes with those of the other two promoters. Balconies were the only permitted additions to the austere street front, although the interiors are asymmetrical and the rear elevations, which still overlook long gardens, contain many bay windows.[81] Opposite the terrace a small garden shields the mid 19th-century pairs of Cassland Crescent.[82]

In Church Crescent nos. 1–7 of 1847–8 were probably designed by George Wales, who rebuilt Monger's almshouses immediately to the east. Nos. 1–3 form a composition in Tudor style, of stock brick with red-brick dressings, and nos. 4–7 are two pairs, in pinkish brick, with quasiclassical features; all are two-storeyed and were known as Blenheim Cottages.[83]

Meynell Gardens, laid out as a close in 1932 by A. Savill on the site of Common House, is an 'oasis of Hampstead Garden Suburb cottages'. Gascoyne House, three five-storeyed blocks built by 1952, has been seen as more imaginative than most of the L.C.C.'s designs.[84] The White Lodge, at the northern tip of Victoria Park, predates the park; it was probably built for a market gardener under an agreement of 1837.[85]

SOCIAL AND CULTURAL ACTIVITIES

A tradition that the oldest inn was the Three Cranes in Church Street (later no. 359 Mare Street) apparently arose from association with the arms of the Heron family.[86] Seven alehouse keepers were licensed in 1552.[87] John Taylor, the 'water poet', in 1636 noted the King's or Prince's Arms at Kingsland and the Mermaid and the Rose, both in Hackney village.[88] A victualler's licence was suppressed in 1639 because of his wife's bad character.[89] Tokens record the Chequers at Kingsland (1663), the Flower de Luce at Clapton, and at least seven taverns in Hackney village: the Cock (1651), the Magpie (1656), the Green Man (1667), the Ferry and the White Hart (1668), the Mermaid, and the Lamb.[90] In 1660 another White Hart was at Kingsland and the Seven Stars, presumably an inn, was in Mare Street.[91] A victualler at Temple Mills in 1686 had lost his licence after a quarrel with Henry Rowe.[92] The Red Lion at Kingsland existed by 1682 and the Sun in Church Street by 1698.[93] A coffee house, in 1700 called Field's, was used for meetings to audit the parish accounts,[94] as in 1708 was the Flying Horse and in 1710 the Mermaid.[95] Church Street in 1719 had two coffee houses; one may have been a forerunner of Sir John Silvester's Hackney coffee house, which survived, with another at Shacklewell in 1785, until c. 1800.[96]

The number of licensed victuallers varied little in the 18th and early 19th centuries. Fifty-five licences were granted in 1723, 52 in 1750, 53 in 1785, and 58 in 1825.[97] Some 85 inns and taverns were listed in 1849 and more than 250, including 6 called hotels, in 1872.[98] There were 155 public houses and 68 beerhouses in 1906 and 148 public houses and 48 beerhouses, besides one licensed hotel, for a slightly smaller population in 1935.[99] Hackney village had the densest concentration in 1750, with 10 licensed victuallers in Church Street. A further 8 were strung along Mare Street, with 2 in Well Street, 1 at London Fields, and 1 at Cambridge Heath. At least 11 inns or taverns were on the high road through Kingsland, Newington, and Stamford Hill. Clapton had 7, Homerton 5 with 2 more at Marsh gate, and Dalston 2; the remaining 3 were at Shacklewell, a ferry, and Temple Mills.[1] The distribution showed wide social disparity in 1906, when Homerton and Kingsland wards had c. 700 persons for every licensed house and Clapton Park had 3,630.[2]

Pleasure grounds were attached to the better known taverns: the Sun on the west side of Church Street had a bowling green by 1698,[3] and the Plough at Homerton had a skittle ground in 1785.[4] Tea gardens, as at the Red Cow in Dalston Lane,[5] were popular in the early 19th century. While many gardens were taken for building, some survived in the more spacious districts: the Crooked Billet in Upper Clapton Road was rebuilt with a tea garden and covered bowling alley after 1840 and the Three Compasses in Dalston Lane was licensed with its gardens from 1858 to 1863.[6] The gardens of riverside inns, including the Horse and Groom

---

81 Watson, *Gentlemen*, 30–3; *Hackney Photos.* i. 69–71; *List of Bldgs.* (1975); below, plate 25.

82 Watson, *Gentlemen*, 49, 96.

83 Ibid. 62–3; *List of Bldgs.* (1975); below, charities.

84 Pevsner, *Lond.* ii. 173; *P.O. Dir. Lond.* (1951, 1952).

85 Watson, *Gentlemen*, 36.

86 Walford, *Old and New Lond.* v. 516; *Hackney Photos.* i. 10.

87 *Mdx. County Rec.* i. 11. Named in G.L.R.O., MR/LV1.

88 *Mdx. & Herts. N. & Q.* iv. 78–9. The Sun, also noted, was probably in Stoke Newington par.: *V.C.H. Mdx.* viii. 221.

89 Cal. Mdx. Sess. Bks. iA. 21.

90 *Trade Tokens in 17th Cent.* ed. G. C. Williamson, ii (1891), 815, 817, 822; Hackney mus.

91 P.R.O., C 54/4038/13; C 54/4038/19.

92 Cal. Mdx. Sess. Bks. vii. 163.

93 G.L.R.O., M79/LH/41; H.A.D., M 730.

94 Vestry mins. 22 Jan. 1694; 30 Nov. 1695; 16 Oct. 1698; 14 Jan. 1700.

95 Ibid. 28 July, 17 Aug. 1708; 14 June 1710.

96 Ibid. 5 Mar. 1719; G.L.R.O., MR/LV9/136; H.A.D., AP 258; below, manors (Spurstowe's ho.).

97 G.L.R.O., MR/LV3/107; MR/LV6/79; MR/LV9/136; MR/LV25/1.

98 *Hackney Dir.* (1849, 1872).

99 L.C.C. *Lond. Statistics*, xvi. 208; xxxix. 198, 206.

1 G.L.R.O., MR/LV6/79.

2 L.C.C. *Lond. Statistics*, xvi. 208.

3 H.A.D., M 730.

4 Ibid. LBH/C/A2/17; *Hackney Photos.* i. 57.

5 W. Wroth, *Cremorne and the later Lond. Gdns.* (1907), 96; H.A.D., M 549.

6 D. Howard, *Lond. Theatres and Music Halls, 1850–1950* (1970), no. 801; G.L.R.O., M79/LH/28, pp. 231–2.

at Lea bridge in 1821[7] and the Mount Pleasant at High Hill ferry in 1838,[8] remained an attraction, along with fishing and boating.[9]

The best known gardens, behind the Mermaid on the west side of Church Street,[10] included upper and lower bowling greens, presumably where Dudley Ryder in 1716 was amused by the earnestness of the players,[11] and a trap ball ground in 1810. They extended in 1766 beyond Hackney brook to a lime walk and in 1831 to a larger kitchen garden;[12] one green was used for archery in 1842. They witnessed successful balloon trips, notably by James Sadler in 1811, when the number of sightseers 'exceeded calculation',[13] and by Mrs. Graham and two other women in 1836. An ascent was advertised in conjunction with a fireworks display in 1822.[14] The Mermaid made way c. 1840 for J. R. Daniel-Tyssen's Manor House, which by the 1890s had been divided into shops, nos. 378 and 378A Mare Street. The gardens, 'much curtailed', survived in 1870 but had been bisected by Brett Road by 1877.[15] Another Mermaid, almost opposite and in the 19th century called the Old Mermaid,[16] was probably the 17th-century Mermaid and the tavern by the church where Pepys was refreshed in 1666; Pepys had eaten cherries and played shuffleboard at Hackney in 1664.[17] The Old Mermaid's entrance way was called Mermaid Yard in 1870;[18] a public house was kept until c. 1966 at no. 364 Mare Street, which building survived in 1993.

An assembly room adjoining the western Mermaid was said to have been kept by a Mr. Holmes (d. 1744).[19] Presumably it had been opened after 1716, when there had been 'no sociableness or familiarity kept up between families'.[20] Anthony Brunn, lessee of the Mermaid from 1766, advertised seasonal balls at his new assembly house in 1778 and 1780;[21] Thomas Rowlandson depicted the company in 1812.[22] The Mermaid's licences for music and dancing were granted from 1849 to J. R. Daniel-Tyssen for the assembly rooms,[23] which survived north of the gardens and behind Tyssen's Manor House and which came to be called the Manor rooms. Approached by a covered way from Mare Street, they continued to be licensed after Tyssen's departure in 1858 and were used by Hackney Literary and Scientific institution c. 1870.[24] As the Old Manor assembly

rooms, they were for sale in 1877, when they included a large concert hall and overlooked a skating rink on most of the remaining land to the south.[25] They had been demolished by 1894 and were partly replaced by the Manor theatre (later the Manor feature film theatre).[26]

Another assembly room was said to have been built at the 'Templars' house' when it was the Blue Posts inn, kept in 1760 and 1785 by Thomas Wright.[27] Music and dancing licences were also granted in 1849 for the Tyssen Arms in Dalston Lane, the Dolphin in Mare Street, and the Cat and Shoulder of Mutton at London Fields.[28] More than 40 inns were similarly licensed over the next 40 years, most of them briefly.[29] In 1905 music was licensed at only two inns but also at Hackney public baths, Morley hall, and the halls of the Eton mission, St. James's, and St. Mark's.[30]

Theatres mentioned in the 18th century were apparently all connected with private schools.[31] Three waits were licensed by Francis Tyssen in 1704 to play within the manor of Hackney, in an attempt to control revelry which had become a cloak for crime.[32] The parish, governed largely by Low Churchmen or those who had links with Dissent, opposed public performances: in 1768 strolling players at the Old Mermaid were banned, as were all puppet showmen and the like;[33] in 1778 a formal request for actors from Covent Garden to perform for two nights at the Blue Posts in Church Street was curtly dismissed; in 1824 the magistrates were asked not to license any theatre.[34]

Music at inns and the use of public halls by local societies prepared the way for purpose-built theatres. The Three Colts in Grove Street was licensed from 1863 until its failure to keep legal hours in 1875 and was known in 1867, after the licensee J. W. Scott, as Scott's music hall.[35] Amateur dramatic clubs included the Blackstone, at Luxembourg hall in 1869, and the Dalston, at Albion hall in 1860 and 1870.[36] Orion dramatic club, in 1869 the only group registered in the *Theatrical Journal*, won professional praise for its entertainments on behalf of local charities at the Manor rooms.[37]

Clapton Park theatre, designed by J. T. Robinson for nearly 600, was built for Thomas Turner behind nos. 79 and 81 Glenarm Road.

7 H.A.D., M 581.
8 Ibid. H/LD 7/2. Most of the dates in the source are MS. additions to cuttings.   9 Below, this section.
10 Para. based on Robinson, *Hackney*, i. 149–50; Clarke, *Hackney*, 109–11, 115–17, 292 n.; Wroth, *Cremorne and Later Lond. Gdns.* 46–7.
11 *Diary of Dudley Ryder*, ed. Matthews, 16, 200.
12 H.A.D., M 523; M 529; M550 (plans); *Starling's Map* (1831).
13 *Gent. Mag.* lxxxi(2), 184, 281; *D.N.B.*; below, plate 22.   14 *Hackney and Stoke N. Past*, illus. 42.
15 *Hackney Gaz.* 10 July 1869, 3d; Old O.S. Map 41 (1870); H.A.D., H/LD 7/4.
16 G.L.R.O., MR/LV9/136; MR/LV25/1; *Hackney Dir.* (1849). The inn W. of the street is confusingly called the Old Mermaid in Robinson, *Hackney*, i. 149–50.
17 *Diary of Sam. Pepys*, ed. Latham, v. 175, 182.
18 Old O.S. Map 41 (1870).
19 Robinson, *Hackney*, i. 149.
20 *Diary of Dudley Ryder*, ed. Matthews, 203.
21 H.A.D., M 523; M 529; ibid. H/LD 7/2, pp. 65, 71.
22 Below, plate 20.

23 G.L.R.O., MR/LMD card index.
24 Ibid.; Clarke, *Hackney*, 117–18; *Hackney Dir.* (1872).
25 H.A.D., H/LD 7/4.
26 Clarke, *Hackney*, 292 n.; Old O.S. Map Lond. 41 (1913); Howard, *Lond. Theatres*, no. 483; *Biograph Ann. and Trades Dir.* (1912, 1914).
27 Clarke, *Hackney*, 111; *Lost Hackney*, 36; G.L.R.O., MR/LV7/49; MR/LV9/136; below, manors (Kingshold).
28 G.L.R.O., LMD/149, 150.
29 Howard, *Lond. Theatres*, *passim*; G.L.R.O., MR/LMD card index.
30 L.C.C. *Lond. Statistics*, xvi. 194–5, 198, 201–3.
31 e.g. H.A.D., H/LD 7/3, p. 33; below, educ. (private schs.).   32 G.L.R.O., M79/LH/121/1.
33 Par. mins. 12 Dec. 1767.
34 Vestry mins. 21 Apr. 1778; 7 Dec. 1824.
35 Howard, *Lond. Theatres*, no. 798; *Hackney Gaz.* 2 Jan. 1875, 1.
36 *Theatrical Jnl.* xxx. 138; xxxi. 206; *Kingsland Times*, 8 Dec. 1860, 1.
37 *Hackney Gaz.* 11 Sept. 1869, 3d; 27 Nov. 1869, 3d; *Theatrical Jnl.* xxx. 4 and *passim*; xxxi. 81.

It had begun a precarious existence by 1875, was renamed the Hackney theatre in 1876, later known as the Theatre Royal, and licensed until 1884. After the theatre had served briefly as a forerunner of Clapton Park tabernacle, nos. 79 and 81 were partly rebuilt in 1894.[38] Dalston theatre in Roseberry Place, holding 1,030, was opened in 1886 and used for a circus until 1890 as the North London Colosseum or with similar names. A new building, designed by Wylson & Long for 3,516 and originally to be called Dalston Palace of Varieties, was opened in 1898[39] and had become Dalston Picture theatre by 1912.[40] Manor theatre, replacing the assembly rooms, was licensed from 1891 until 1903.[41]

The Hackney Empire theatre, nos. 381–91 Mare Street, was opened in 1901. Designed by Frank Matcham to seat 3,000, its ornate front had twin terracotta domes and a central pediment bearing a statue of Euterpe. The theatre, which belonged to Sir Oswald Stoll's Hackney & Shepherd's Bush Empire (later Empire Palaces) until his death in 1942, was used by many famous performers.[42] It served additionally as a cinema by 1910[43] and closed in 1956, reopening as a television studio before its purchase by Mecca Ltd. as a bingo hall. Removal of the domes and pediment in 1979 caused controversy which led to the building's external restoration, completed in 1988 at Mecca's expense. The theatre was reopened in 1986 by Hackney Empire preservation trust and was managed in 1989 by Hackney New Variety Management Co.[44]

Early cinemas included Henry Mason's cinematograph exhibition at no. 329 Mare Street in 1909,[45] the Premier Rink (later Clapton Rink), licensed for dancing in 1909 and as a cinema in 1910 at nos. 137–47 Lower Clapton Road, and Kingsland Palace of Animated Pictures, opened in Mrs. Clara Ludski's auction rooms at no. 105 Kingsland High Street in 1909.[46] Seven cinemas were listed for 1910–11: Gale's Electric Picture Palace at no. 329 Mare Street, Edgar Mason's Picture theatre (later Hackney Electric or Picture Palace) at no. 331,[47] the Manor theatre in Kenmure Road, Moss Empire's Stoke Newington Palace with a capacity of 3,000, F. W. Purcell's Amhurst hall for 1,000 at no. 42A Kingsland High Street, the Electric theatre or Kingsland Palace at no. 105, and the small Star Picture Palace at no. 110 Kingsland Road. Two

more were about to be built and films were also shown at the Hackney Empire and at Morley hall.[48] By 1912 seventeen premises were listed: all the cinemas and halls of 1910–11 except the Kingsland Palace, besides Clapton cinematograph theatre (later Kenning Hall) at no. 229 Lower Clapton Road, Dalston Picture theatre at nos. 17–19 Dalston Lane, the Electric Palace (later Majestic) at nos. 30–36 Stoke Newington High Street, the Electric theatre at no. 134 Homerton High Street, Hackney Electric theatre in Clarence Road, and Kingsland Imperial picture theatre at no. 538 Kingsland Road.[49] The former St. Thomas's Square Congregational church was licensed as the Empress electric theatre in 1912[50] and extended under a lease of 1920.[51] South Hackney Picture Palace was opened in Well Street in 1913, followed by the Castle electric theatre in Chatsworth Road, and the 'New', perhaps the Majestic, in Stoke Newington High Street.[52] Among London's grandest early cinemas was the Hackney Pavilion, no. 290 Mare Street, designed by George Billings and opened in 1914, seating 1,162 in an ornate auditorium 'the equal of any Edwardian theatre'.[53] The Renaissance style Kingsland Empire, designed by George Coles to seat over 1,000, replaced the Kingsland Palace at nos. 103–7 Kingsland High Street in 1915. Dalston Picture House, replacing the old theatre, was opened as 'Europe's first super cinema' in 1920.[54]

Sixteen cinemas, including the Hackney Empire, existed in 1934.[55] The earliest ones, at nos. 329 and 331 Mare Street, had closed, as had Morley hall and the Manor theatre.[56] The Stamford Hill Super, nos. 152–8 Clapton Common, designed by Coles, had opened in 1925 and the Regent, at the corner of Stamford Hill and Amhurst Park, designed for 2,182 by W.E. and W.S. Trent, in 1929. The Kingsland Imperial was renamed the Plaza in 1933, the Regal, at the corner of Mare and Well streets, was opened in 1936, and the Kingsland Empire was rebuilt as the smaller Classic in 1937.[57] The Odeon, designed by Andrew Mather at no. 505A Kingsland Road, and the Ritz, by W.R. Glen next to the Kenning Hall, were opened in 1939.[58] Thirteen cinemas, apart from the Hackney Empire, survived in 1947, when the Majestic had been renamed the Vogue. Amhurst hall, empty in 1942, was a theatrical store in 1951.[59]

38 Howard, *Lond. Theatres*, no. 360; *P.O. Dir. Lond. County Suburbs, North* (1880, 1888); *Hackney and Stoke N. Past*, 124–5, illus. 155; *Terrier*, Summer 1991; below, prot. nonconf. (Meths.); inf. from Isobel Watson.
39 Howard, *Lond. Theatres*, no. 208.
40 *Biograph Annual* (1912).
41 Howard, *Lond. Theatres*, no. 483.
42 Ibid. no. 359; *Tower to Tower Block*, no. 44; *Hackney Photos.* i. 22; posters in Hackney mus.
43 *Bioscope Ann. and Trades Dir.* (1910–11); *Kinematograph Year Bk.* (1916).
44 *Hackney Gaz.* (1864–1989 anniversary suppl.), 9; *Independent*, 2 Aug. 1988, 6.   45 *P.O. Dir. Lond.* (1909).
46 H.A.D., H/LD 7/24, p. 59; L.C.C. *Lond. Statistics*, xx. 209, 212; xxii. 241; E. Owen, 'Rio Centre' (TS. thesis, 1985, in H.A.D.), 7–8.
47 Adjacent cinemas illus. in D. Atwell, *Cathedrals of the Movies* (1980), 4, and *Hackney Camera*.
48 *Bioscope Ann. and Trades Dir.* (1910–11); *P.O. Dir. Lond.* (1911); L.C.C. *Lond. Statistics*, xxi. 238–9.

49 *Bioscope Ann. and Trades Dir.* (1912) (figure excludes premises in Bethnal Green and Stoke Newington listed under Hackney); L.C.C. *Lond. Statistics*, xxii. 241–2.
50 G.L.R.O., H1/ST/E21/2, p. 13; L.C.C. *Lond. Statistics*, xxiii. 267; *Hackney Photos.* i. 28.
51 G.L.R.O., H1/ST/E65/C/15/3/1–4.
52 *Kinematograph Year Bk.* (1914), 51, 53.
53 Atwell, *Cathedrals of the Movies*, 18–19 (illus.); *Lost Hackney*, 77; M. Webb, *Amber Valley Gaz. of Gtr. Lond.'s Suburban Cinemas* (1968), 37; *Hackney Photos.* ii. 129.
54 *Kinematograph Year Bk.* (1916), 85; Owen, 'Rio Centre', 16–19.
55 *P.O. Dir. Lond.* (1934). An additional King's cinema, nos. 432–4 Kingsland High Rd., is in Hackney, *Official Guide* [1933, 1935].   56 H.A.D., M 3573–4.
57 Webb, *Gaz. of Cinemas*, 21, 25, 38, 76; Hackney, *Official Guide* [1938], 59; Owen, 'Rio Centre', 22–3.
58 Pevsner, *Lond.* ii. 169; Webb, *Gaz. of Cinemas*, 21, 24.
59 *P.O. Dir. Lond.* (1947); insurance plan E 7 (1942, 1951).

Twelve cinemas remained in 1958,[60] when Dalston Picture House and the Empress had become Dalston Gaumont and the Essoldo, but only seven in 1964, after the successive closures of the Castle, Plaza, Stamford Hill Super, Dalston Gaumont, and Kingsland Odeon; the Regent had become the Stamford Hill Gaumont and then the Odeon. The Regal and the Ritz had both been renamed the ABC by 1970, when the Classic became the Tatler film club. There remained only the Kenning Hall, the Mare Street ABC, and the revived Classic in 1975;[61] the first closed in 1979 and the second, renamed the Mayfair, in 1981. The Classic was renamed the Rio in 1976 and ceased to be commercial in 1979, when a residents' group managed it as the Rio Centre. From 1982 it was a 'community cinema', offering films for minorities and live entertainments, financed by the G.L.C., which bought the lease in 1983, and Hackney L.B.[62]

Sports included horse racing, on Hackney Downs in 1733 and on the marsh, with an ox-roasting, in 1735. Less usual events included a swimming race between two horses in 1737[63] and women running for a linen shift from Tyler's ferry to Temple Mills in 1749.[64] Bird-shooting on the marsh was mentioned in 1754, a nearly lethal private boxing match in 1790, and bull-baiting, interspersed with prize fighting, before 3,000 people in 1791;[65] Sunday shooting was banned in 1809.[66] Pigeon-shooting was offered at High Hill ferry in 1838.[67] John Baum, landlord of the White Lion at Hackney Wick by 1825, provided a ring for more orderly boxing in the 1860s[68] but as late as 1875 a prize fighter was killed on Hackney marsh.[69] Part on the Leyton side of the mill stream at Temple Mills was used for recreation by Hackney Wick's Eton mission, founded in 1880, and later became Eton Manor sports ground.[70] The L.C.C.'s purchase of the marsh was prompted mainly by the need for games pitches; there were c. 100 by 1920[71] and in 1980.[72]

The river Lea's attractions were advertised by innkeepers: angling, rowing, and pleasure boating. A fishery was attached to the White House at Tyler's ferry in 1810 as a subscription water.[73] Annual charges were made by the Beresford family in 1848 both there and at the Horse and Groom on the Essex bank at Lea bridge, whereas above Lea bridge access was largely free.[74] Angling, also offered by the Mount Pleasant

in 1838,[75] may have been restricted to reaches farther north by 1869[76] and was destroyed by the pollution which made necessary the Lee Purification Act, 1886.[77] Rowing was at its most popular in the 1860s, when Spring Hill was 'the Henley of the Lea';[78] at the August regatta in 1869 tradesmen raced from Willow point for money prizes and amateurs, including Hackney rowing club, for trophies.[79] Processions of boats marked the opening and close of the season.[80] Many clubs were short-lived: at least 22 with boathouses in Hackney were defunct in 1899, although a few had changed names and were among the 39 active clubs, 20 of them amateur and 19 of them tradesmen's. Most were affiliated to the Amateur Rowing Association of 1879 or the Tradesmen's Rowing Club Association of 1882, or to branches which had been formed for the Lea. Nine clubs used V. Radley's boatyard in Waterworks Road at Lea bridge, 22, including Clapton ladies' boating club, were nearby at Middlesex wharf, 13 of them using C. Meggs's yard, and 8 used Verdon's at Spring Hill. Amateur races were held from May to July and tradesmen's, over a slightly shorter course, on three days in July or August.[81] Ladies and gentlemen raced in double skiffs in 1914.[82] High Hill ferry depended heavily on the seasonal income from river users:[83] pleasure boats and punts could be hired there and at the Jolly Anglers, Middlesex wharf, an area cleared in the 1930s.[84] The North London Amateur Rowing Association used Tyrrell's boathouse at Spring Hill, as did at least 7 of the 16 other clubs listed, in 1953.[85] Lee Valley regional park authority, established in 1967, redeveloped Radley's yard as Springfield marina in 1969.[86]

A Hackney cricket club dined at the Mermaid in 1778[87] and challenged a private school in 1789.[88] Matches for 500 guineas were played by Clapton gentlemen on London Fields and at Homerton by a local team against one from Hackney, Clapton, and Stoke Newington in 1802.[89] A women's match at Ball's Pond, perhaps Kingsland green, was caricatured by Rowlandson in 1811.[90] West Hackney cricket club, founded in 1840, played on a ground owned by J. Daly, landlord of the Green Man in Shacklewell Lane, and survived in 1855. Victoria Park club, of 1840, was not listed in 1855; neither was Stamford Hill club, of 1853 and also based on the Green Man, in 1856.[91] The Aurora club played at Pond

60 Para. based on *P.O. Dir. Lond.* (1958 and later edns.); Webb, *Gaz. of Cinemas, passim.*
61 The former Essoldo was sold in 1975: G.L.R.O., H1/ST/E65/C/16/10.
62 Owen, 'Rio Centre', 29, 32, 61, 82, 93.
63 H.A.D., 900.2, p. 14 (Hackney cuttings bk.); ibid. H/LD 7/2, p. 9.   64 Ibid. 900.2, p. 15.
65 Ibid. H/LD 7/2, pp. 17, 111, 269.
66 Vestry mins. 4 Apr. 1809.
67 H.A.D., H/LD 7/2, p. 259.
68 G.L.R.O., MR/LV 25/1; *Hackney and Stoke N. Past,* 48; below, plate 21.
69 *Hackney Gaz.* 6 Feb. 1875.
70 Hackney, *Official Guide* [1970], 27.
71 Ibid. [1920].
72 'Parks and Open Spaces in Hackney' (Hackney Soc. rep. 1980 in H.A.D.), 27.
73 *Hackney and Stoke N. Past,* illus. 59; below, plate 6.
74 Clarke, *Hackney,* 198; *Hackney Photos.* i. 128; *V.C.H. Mdx.* ii. 270.

75 H.A.D., H/LD 7/2, p. 259.
76 *Hackney Gaz.* 11 Sept. 1869, 4.
77 Grocott, *Hackney,* 63, 67; 49 & 50 Vic. c. 109 (Local Act).   78 Grocott, *Hackney,* 64.
79 *Hackney Gaz.* 28 Aug. 1869, 3f; 11 Dec. 1869, 3e.
80 *Hackney Gaz.* 20 Mar., 24 Apr., 24 July 1872.
81 G. T. Rees, *Rowing Club Dir. of Gt. Britain* (1898, 1899); *Hackney Photos.* i. 131; ii. 136.
82 *Hackney Gaz.* 6 July 1914.
83 Booth, *Life and Labour,* iii (1), 152–3.
84 H.A.D., H/LD 7/2, p. 259; *Hackney Photos.* i. 125, 127, 129.   85 Hackney, *Official Guide* (1953–4).
86 *V.C.H. Mdx.* v. 181; inf. from publicity manager, Lee Valley Regional Pk. Authy.
87 H.A.D., H/LD 7/2, p. 65.
88 *The Times,* 12 Aug. 1988, 12f.
89 *Hackney and Stoke N. Past,* 48; H.A.D., H/LD 7/2, p. 147.
90 *Hackney and Stoke N. Past,* illus. 56.
91 *Lillywhite's Guide to Cricketers* (1853, 1855, 1856).

Lane, adjoining South Mill field, before the formation in 1855 of its successor Homerton and Clapton club, which played on Norris's park opposite South Hackney church until 1857, when it was renamed Hackney. It then moved to a field near the end of Hackney Terrace which had been used until 1853 by an earlier Hackney club, perhaps a descendant of the 18th-century one.[92] Hackney cricket club played mainly at Clapton in 1875,[93] presumably on the ground by South Mill field which after 1894 was covered by the east end of Mildenhall Road.[94] Other clubs included in 1867 Norris Park, for employees of the builder William Turner,[95] and Colvestone,[96] in 1868 Albert, playing at Victoria Park,[97] and in 1869 Amhurst, which survived with Colvestone in 1890.[98] Clapton and the larger 'old established' Hope (Clapton) club were among the chief metropolitan clubs in 1872.[99] Most matches in 1869 took place in Victoria Park or on Hackney Downs, where Cricketfield Road was so called from 1864, or at Pond Lane (Millfields Road).[1] By 1890 c. 60 clubs, not all from Hackney, played in Victoria Park and at least 10 at Clapton, on North Mill and South Mill fields. Several represented churches or groups of workers. Wandering clubs included Colvestone, Dalston Albert, and Hackney Tradesmen; Clapton Wanderers used a private ground near Spring Hill.[2] Cricket continued on the large municipal open spaces of Hackney Downs and marsh, London Fields, the Mill fields, and Springfield park. A new cricket centre was opened on Arena fields, west of Hackney Wick stadium, in 1989.[3]

Football was played on Hackney Downs between the Sky Rockets and Oakfield clubs in 1872[4] and at Victoria Park, Hackney Downs, and Clapton in 1875–6. Association football clubs included Gresham, the Pilgrims, and the Ramblers in 1875 and Clapton and the Pilgrims in 1886.[5] Clapton, founded in 1877 as the Downs and renamed in 1878, moved in 1880 from Hackney Downs to North Mill field and in 1888 to a permanent home in West Ham (Essex). It became a leading amateur club, producing international players, and in 1954 was officially recognized as the first English club to have played on the continent, at Antwerp in 1890.[6] The best known association football club was an offshoot of Glyn cricket club, which had been started in 1881 at Homerton College, and first played as Glyn football club on waste ground near Glyn Road

in 1884. Renamed Eagle in 1886 and Orient in 1888, it headed the Clapton and District league in 1894, entered the London league, moved to its own Whittle's athletic ground, and in 1899 became Clapton Orient, playing at Millfields Road. The club turned professional in 1903, joined the 2nd division of the Southern league in 1905, and was reconstituted in 1906. After its ground had been taken for Clapton stadium, it played at Lea Bridge Road and then at Wembley before moving to Leyton in 1937 and acquiring the name Leyton Orient.[7]

Rugby union clubs included Clapton, Excelsior, Phoenix, and St. Vincent in 1875 and Upper Clapton in 1886.[8] The Saracens, established in 1876, played at South Mill field before moving to Walthamstow in 1885.[9] Upper Clapton had been founded as Orion in 1879 and had changed its name in 1882; it played at Spring Hill and after the First World War at Walthamstow and Enfield before moving in 1933 to Epping, where it retained three pitches in 1954.[10]

Athletics, long practised on the marsh, were organized by John Baum on a track at Hackney Wick immediately north-west of the White Lion. Races included several advertised as world championships and one by the American Indian Deerfoot, after whom Baum named a row of cottages.[11] The site was for sale in 1869, when W. Purnell was proprietor, although races continued until 1871; it was covered by Bartrip Street.[12]

Orion gymnastic club, founded in 1868 in Mile End and named after a rowing club, moved to St. Thomas's hall and in 1883 to a new building in Casterton Street. Debts led to the gymnasium's acquisition as a drill hall in 1912 but the club opened its Orion hall in East Bank in 1914; it claimed in 1948 to be the oldest of its kind under amateur control and it survived, after extension, in 1992.[13] A gymnasium was attached to the Havelock inn, Albion Road, in 1888 and a short-lived athletic club existed in Twemlow Terrace, London Fields, in 1890.[14] The Rhodes family supported a boys' institute in Woodland Road, including a gymnasium and rifle range, in 1914.[15] After extensive refurbishment, the Casterton Street hall was opened by Hackney L.B. in 1979 as George Sylvester sports centre, which included courts for ball games and a rifle range.[16] It closed in 1991, when a disused pool at the baths in Lower Clapton Road was converted into King's Hall leisure centre.[17] Lee Valley park

92 *Hackney Mag. in connection with Literary and Scientific Institution*, June 1858.
93 *Hackney Gaz.* 27 Mar. 1875, 3.
94 Old O.S. Maps Lond. 21 (1894, 1913).
95 *John Lillywhite's Cricketers' Companion* (1867).
96 *Hackney Gaz.* 24 Jan. 1872 (6th ann. mtg.).
97 *John Lillywhite's Cricketers' Companion* (1868).
98 *Hackney Gaz.* 17 July 1869, 3*d*; 31 July 1869, 4*b*; *Cricket and Lawn Tennis Clubs Dir.* (1890–1).
99 *Jas. Lillywhite's Cricketers' Annual* (1872); *Hackney Gaz.* 24 Jan. 1872.
1 *Hackney Gaz.* July, Aug. 1869, *passim*; L.C.C. *Names of Streets* (1901), 137.
2 *Cricket and Lawn Tennis Clubs Dir.* (1890–1); Booth, *Life and Labour*, iii (1), 102.
3 *Hackney Guide to Sports Facilities* [1990], 15.
4 *Hackney Gaz.* 16 Mar. 1872, 3.
5 *Football Calendar* (1875–6); *Football Assoc. Calendar*

(1886–7).
6 R. A. J. Ward, *Clapton F.C. 1878–1953*, 7–9; *V.C.H. Essex*, vi. 66–7.
7 *Hackney Gaz.* (1864–1989 anniversary suppl.), 53.
8 *Football Calendar* (1875–6); *Football Assoc. Calendar* (1886–7).
9 Inf. from press offr., Saracens football club.
10 H.A.D. H/LD 7/24, p. 177.
11 *Hackney and Stoke N. Past*, 48.
12 H.A.D., M 3552; ibid. 796.
13 Hackney, *Official Guide* [1930, 1938]; H.A.D., H/LD 7/16 [cutting, 1901].
14 G.L.R.O., LMD card index; *Kelly's Dir. Hackney* (1890).
15 *Hackney Gaz.* 19 June 1914, 1.
16 *Hackney Guide to Sports Facilities* [1990], 8–9; Hackney, *Official Guide* [1980].
17 Inf. from Hackney L.B., leisure svces. directorate.

authority's Eastway sports centre was opened in 1980, on the site of Eton Manor sports ground.[18]

Bicycling was pioneered in 1869 by the St. Katherine's velocipede club, which organized races and country rides. It often met at Dalston,[19] as did the Excelsior cycling club in 1890.[20] Stoke Newington cycling club met at the Swan, Clapton common, in the 1880s.[21] Ten clubs made regular rides in 1914.[22] Lee Valley regional park authority opened Eastway cycle circuit in Temple Mill Lane in 1975.[23]

Lawn tennis was offered by Clapton and Upper Clapton cricket clubs by 1890, when Atalanta and Springfield tennis clubs also served the northern end of the parish.[24] In Lea Bridge Road, Lee Valley park authority opened a riding school in 1973 and an ice centre in 1984.[25]

Greyhound racing, with a new type of electric hare, began at Clapton Orient's stadium in 1928. The stadium was converted to the design of Sir Owen Williams; improvements included a restaurant in 1930 and covered stands and a second restaurant in 1939. It was sold by the Greyhound Racing Association in 1969 and made way for Millfields estate.[26] Hackney Wick stadium, Waterden Road, was opened for both greyhound and motorcycle racing in 1932. The stands could hold 10,000 and terraces a further 15,000 in 1953. Greyhound racing was reintroduced after closure during the war, but motorcycling (speedway) not until 1963. The Kestrels, a speedway team among the founder members of the British league in 1965, raced weekly at Hackney Wick in 1989.[27]

The existence of a local volunteer corps,[28] formed in 1777 for the duration of the American war, was said to have deterred the Gordon rioters from entering Hackney in 1780. The first corps's red, white, and blue uniform was similar to that of the Loyal Hackney Volunteers, formed by the Hackney Association in 1794 with Mark Beaufoy as commander and containing two companies, one of them equipped by public subscription. They occasionally served in London and were recognized as the senior volunteer corps; in 1797 members who had paraded at Homerton were sued by a Channel Islander whom they had mistaken for a Frenchman.[29] Hackney in 1801 refused to join Whitechapel in opposing a continuance of the county's Tower Hamlets militia.[30] The volunteers were disbanded in 1802 and revived from 1803 until 1809 or later;[31] c. 40 members who had served before

1802, on being denied precedence, briefly formed a separate rifle corps.

The 9th (later 4th) Essex Rifle Volunteers[32] had their headquarters in 1872 and 1890 at no. 51 Mare Street and in 1892 at no. 208, where the 7th Battalion of the Essex Regiment remained until c. 1913. The 10th (Hackney) Battalion of the County of London Regiment had its headquarters in Hackney Grove (later Hillman Street) c. 1913 and soon had its orderly room at no. 208 Mare Street and a drill hall in Casterton Street. On the building of the third town hall a new headquarters was provided in Hillman Street, used by the 5th (Hackney) Battalion of the Royal Berkshire Regiment in 1937 and its successors as a Territorial Army centre in 1953.[33] The Tower Hamlets Artillery Volunteers were in Lansdowne Place and the Tower Hamlets Volunteer Rifles in Pembury Road in 1872.

Friendly societies registered in 1794 were a tradesmen's society at the Nag's Head, Mare Street, a women's society at the Ship, Church Street,[34] and societies at the White Hart, Clapton, and the Adam and Eve, Homerton.[35] Others at the Black Bull, Kingsland, and the Coach and Horses, Stoke Newington High Street, were registered in 1795 and at the Fountain, Clapton, and the Two Black Boys, Well Street, in 1796.[36] Five more societies met at inns by 1810.[37]

Hackney and Newington Auxiliary Bible society was established in 1812 to promote the aims of the British and Foreign Bible society.[38] Hackney savings bank, with the vicar as president, was opened at the vestry's committee room in 1818; it closed in 1894.[39] Hackney friendly institution, founded in 1829 with the vicar as patron, received contributions towards sickness and other benefits and also used the committee room.[40] Upper Clapton provident society loan fund was enrolled in 1836 as one of the first under the Act for the Establishment of Loan Societies.[41] Hackney Benevolent Pension society, founded in 1838, had Lord Amherst as president in 1898, when it supported 57 pensioners, and survived in 1962; a subsidiary body in 1843 collected funds for new almshouses.[42] Twenty or more friendly, loan, or building societies, some with members in neighbouring parishes, met at inns or schoolrooms by 1850.[43] The Hackney Association for Improving the Conditions of the Poor had existed for some years by 1869, when its office in the town hall first issued tickets for goods in an effort to suppress begging.[44] Many mid 19th-century

18 Inf. from publicity manager; *Hackney Gaz.* 23 Jan. 1981.
19 *Hackney Gaz.* 17 July 1869, 3; 21 Aug. 1869, 3.
20 Ibid. 24 Feb. 1890, 3.
21 *Hackney Photos.* i. 137.
22 e.g. *Hackney Gaz.* 26 June 1914, 7; 3, 10 July 1914, 6.   23 Inf. from publicity manager.
24 *Cricket and Lawn Tennis Clubs Dir.* (1890–1).
25 Inf. from publicity manager.
26 Hackney, *Official Guide* [1938, 1960]; *Stoke Newington & Hackney Observer*, 27 June 1969, 6.
27 *Hackney Gaz.* (1864–1989 anniversary suppl.), 48; Hackney, *Official Guide* (1953–4).
28 Para. based on *Terrier*, v (Dec. 1986); Robinson, *Hackney*, i. 244–5.   29 H.A.D., H/LD 7/2, p. 131.
30 Vestry mins. 23 Nov. 1801.
31 Disbanded 1811 in Robinson, *Hackney*, i. 246, although last mins. are 1809: H.A.D., D/F/DOB/37.

32 Para. based on *Hackney Dir.* (1872); *Kelly's Dir. Hackney* (1887 and later edns.); *P.O. Dir. Lond.* (1934 and later edns.).
33 *Terrier*, Mar. 1987; Hackney, *Official Guide* (1953–4).
34 P.R.O., FS 2/7/521, 652.   35 Ibid. FS 2/7/545, 708.
36 Ibid. FS 2/7/810, 821, 840, 1002.
37 Ibid. FS 2/7/924, 1052, 1057, 1242, 1436.
38 H.A.D., H/LD 7/2, p. 166; *Procs. of Public Mtg. for establishing Auxiliary Bible Soc. for Hackney* (1813).
39 Robinson, *Hackney*, ii. 335–6; vestry mins. 24 Mar. 1818; H.A.D., D/F/TYS/16, pp. 198, 208; ibid. 333.2.
40 H.A.D., D/F/TYS/16, pp. 223–5; ibid. 333.3; G.L.R.O., MC/R 1, f. 1; 2, f. 3; P.R.O., FS 2/7/1784; 10 Geo. IV, c. 56.   41 G.L.R.O., MC/R 1, f. 66.
42 Robinson, *Hackney*, ii. 310–13; H.A.D., H/LD 7/1; ibid. D/S/6/1–5, 19/1–19/4 (ann. reps.).
43 G.L.R.O., MC/R 1–3.
44 *Hackney Gaz.* 16 Oct. 1869, 3; 11 Dec. 1869, 1.

benevolent societies were branches of such national organizations as the Ancient Order of Foresters[45] and, from 1861, the Freemasons.[46] Others served localities, among them De Beauvoir Town Philanthropic society by 1869 and Southgate Road Philanthropic society, which gave bread and coal in 1875.[47] Those attached to churches included Hackney juvenile (later Bruce Hall) mission and the Old Gravel Pit sick and provident society.[48] The Borough of Hackney Co-operative society was formed in 1886, replacing an organization for south Hackney, and in London was second only to the Tower Hamlets society by 1888.[49]

A Kingsland branch of the Y.M.C.A. began its 8th session in 1869 and used a schoolroom behind Kingsland Congregational church.[50] Hackney Y.M.C.A. was founded by a meeting at Bethnal Green in 1883; it leased premises next to the town hall until 1886 and thereafter no. 275 Mare Street, part of which had recently been let in 1911 to the Y.W.C.A., until the Second World War. A branch at nos. 65 and 67 Stamford Hill, for which funds were sought in 1911 and 1914, was replaced by the Regent garage c. 1929.[51]

Cultural organizations included Hackney Literary and Philosophical society, first meeting in 1811 and perhaps short lived,[52] Hackney institute and subscription library from 1815 until 1817,[53] and Hackney Reading society from 1815 until 1911.[54] A horticultural society for Stamford Hill, formed in 1833 and often exhibiting at Craven Lodge in 1849, was 'strictly confined to the gentry'.[55] Hackney Debating society and Hackney and Clapton Amateur Musical society existed in 1842.[56] Hackney Choral society, formed in 1837 with weekly meetings and intended mainly as a school of music, proved too ambitious and faced dissolution in 1842,[57] although a Borough of Hackney Choral association existed in 1875 and a Hackney Choral society c. 1890.[58] Kingsland, Dalston, and Clapton all had choral societies in the 1860s,[59] besides popular groups which performed in taverns.[60] De Beauvoir Town, which had attracted many good teachers, was described as a particularly musical district in 1869.[61]

Hackney Literary and Scientific institution was founded in 1848 under the Tyssen-Amhursts'

patronage with gentleman and lady subscribers. In union with the Society of Arts, it used the Manor rooms, presumably until their demolition in or before 1894, and offered lectures and entertainments, a library, and classes in chess, French, book keeping, and a range of arts and sciences.[62] It produced its own magazine in 1858.[63] Albion hall, in Albion Square, was licensed from 1850 for Kingsland, Dalston and De Beauvoir Town Literary and Scientific institution. After several changes of tenant,[64] it was succeeded in 1869 by James Cox's Albion club, which resembled Hackney Literary and Scientific institution. Cox managed an adjacent swimming bath and conducted a school and evening classes which he called Dalston college. The hall was under separate management from both the baths and the college in 1888 and passed, with the baths, to the London school board in 1899; the L.C.C. bought the main lease in 1906.[65]

Public halls, in addition to the Manor rooms, Albion hall, and many church premises, included the town hall opened in 1866,[66] Luxembourg hall in Ashwin Street, and Morley hall at the Triangle from 1879.[67] The owner of Luxembourg hall was charged with staging an unlicensed play in 1869 and advertised dancing lessons to private schools in 1875;[68] the hall had gone by 1880 and was followed by Reeves's colour works.[69] Morley hall, begun as a 'masonic' hall and perhaps intended as a theatre, was completed by Cambridge Heath Congregational church, with help from Samuel Morley, and bought from the Tyssen estate in 1885. Designed to hold 1,500 and with rooms on three storeys in front, it was used for recreation in 1920 and by the clothiers Gerrish, Ames & Simpkins by 1924 until, after bomb damage, it made way for Hackney technical college's Triangle House.[70] Assembly rooms in Lyme Grove owned by William Youens in 1887 and the Misses Youens in 1890 and 1914 were probably a dancing school, called Hackney academy in 1936 and derelict by 1951.[71] Church halls were often used for public meetings, as was the People's hall of the Salvation Army, opened in Havelock Road by 1887.[72] All the denominations in Hackney provided for leisure activities.[73] One of many organizations to combine religious instruction with pleasure was the Grove Young

45 P.R.O., FS 2/7/4001, 4071, 4308, 4437, passim.
46 G.L.R.O., MC/R 5, pp. 311, 313 et seq.
47 Hackney Gaz. 7 Aug. 1869, 3; 10 Apr. 1875, 3; 21 Apr. 1875, 3.
48 Burdett's Hosp. Annual (1910); H.A.D., D/S/22/69; below, prot. nonconf. (undenom.).
49 Booth, Life and Labour, i (1), 112.
50 Hackney Gaz. 18 Sept. 1869, 1; 21 Apr. 1875, 3.
51 H.A.D., H/LD 7/1; Hackney Gaz. 19 June 1914, 5; G.L.R.O., H1/ST/E21/2, p. 21; P.O. Dir. Lond. County Suburbs (1928, 1930).
52 Hackney Literary Soc. Regulations (1811).
53 H.A.D., D/S/36/1.   54 Ibid. D/S/2/1–4.
55 Hackney Dir. (1849).
56 Reported in Hackney Jnl.: H.A.D., H/LD 7/4.
57 Robinson, Hackney, ii. 341–2.
58 Hackney Gaz. 10 Apr. 1875, 3; Kelly's Dir. Hackney (1887, 1890, 1893–4).
59 Hackney Gaz. 28 Aug. 1869, 3; 11 Sept. 1869, 1; 6 Nov. 1869, 3.
60 e.g. Dalston amateur musical soc.: ibid. 13 Nov. 1869, 3.
61 Ibid. 4 Dec. 1869, 3.

62 Hackney Dir. (1872); Hackney Gaz. 31 July 1869, 1; 25 Sept. 1869, 1; above, this section.
63 Hackney Mag. in connexion with Literary and Scientific Institution, June, July 1858.
64 Howard, Lond. Theatres, no. 11; H.A.D., LBH/C/A1/1–35; inf. from Isobel Watson.
65 Hackney Gaz. 17 July 1869, 1; 6 Nov. 1869, 3; 2 Jan. 1875, 1; below, educ. (private schs.); P.O. Dir. Lond. County Suburbs North (1888); P.O. Dir. Lond. (1902 and later edns.); H.A.D., LBH/C/A1/1–35.
66 Below, local govt. (local govt. after 1837).
67 Old O.S. Maps 40, 41 (1870); Hackney Photos. ii. 22.
68 Theatrical Jnl. xxx. 21; Hackney Gaz. 18 Sept. 1869, 3; 25 Sept. 1869, 1; 2 Jan. 1875, 1.
69 P.O. Dir. Lond. County Suburbs North (1880); Old O.S. Map 40 (1913).
70 H.A.D., D/E/233 CAM 1/22; D/F/AMH/555; Hackney, Official Guide [1920]; insurance plan E 20 (1924, 1958); Clarke, Hackney, 289 n.; Hackney Photos. ii. 22.
71 Kelly's Dir. Hackney (1887, 1890, 1914–15); insurance plan E 23 (1936, 1951).   72 Kelly's Dir. Hackney (1887).
73 Booth, Life and Labour, iii (1), 102.

Men's institute of 1876, in a schoolroom of the Old Gravel Pit chapel and later, until c. 1890, in Brooksby's Walk; it had a library and gave access to classes, debates, a band, and sports clubs.[74] The men's first-class swimming bath in Lower Clapton Road, opened in 1897, was boarded over in winter to form the King's hall and used for entertainments, many of them organized by the council.[75]

Specialist clubs abounded in the late 19th century. Some served only one district, such as Lea Bridge amateur horticultural society in 1869, others claimed a wider membership, including Hackney Scientific association in 1869,[76] Hackney Microscopical and Natural History society from 1878 to 1892 or later,[77] and Hackney Photographic society from 1889.[78] Clapton Naturalists' Field club, so called from 1886 to 1892, was a forerunner of the London Natural History society.[79]

Political meetings,[80] addressed by John Wilkes and other leading radicals and caricatured in 1796 by Gillray, took place at the Mermaid's assembly rooms; often they were concerned with parliamentary elections, which themselves took place at Brentford.[81] Hackney had a reputation for radicalism, partly because of the dissenters at New College, and in 1791 saw the earliest open-air demonstration by the London Corresponding society, probably on Hackney Downs. The Socratic union, which debated at the Mermaid, published its own periodical in 1808.[82] Local activity included the formation in 1792 of the Hackney Association, whose propaganda may have been subsidized by the government and which in 1793 met at the Mermaid. Revived agitation gave rise in 1835 to Hackney Conservative association and to Hackney Reform and Registration society, both of them apparently short lived.[83]

Radical institutions outside Hackney[84] included the Borough of Hackney club, a pioneer working men's club opened in 1863 in Shoreditch, the later Kingsland Progressive club, and Hackney 1 and Hackney 2 branches of the Reform League in Hackney Road, although the league's Homerton branch was at the Duke of Cornwall in the high street. A description of Hackney as the most heretical quarter of London was occasioned by the holding of three secularist meetings on a single Sunday in 1873;[85] two, including that of Hackney Secular association, were in Goldsmith's Row, Shoreditch. At Homerton a Social Democratic club, finally renamed Homerton Socialist club, met at the Lamb and Flag from 1881 until closed under threat in 1882. Hackney Radical club was at no. 5 the Grove by 1887, at no. 1A Brett Road in 1908, and later at no. 16 Kenmure Road, which served as Hackney Trades Council's headquarters during the general strike of 1926. Homerton Reform club was at no. 52 Well Street by 1888 and until 1931.[86] Homerton Progressive club may by 1892 have used no. 26 Brooksby's Walk, also used in the 1890s by Chatsworth social and athletic club, where it survived in 1935. A branch of the Fabian Society existed by 1893. Marxist meetings at Brotherhood church, Southgate Road, included the 5th London congress of the Russian Social Democrats in 1907.[87]

Hackney Conservative Union had offices at no. 33 Mortimer Road in 1872.[88] Hackney Advanced Liberal association, formed in 1874, had rooms at the Triangle in 1875, when a Liberal club was being prepared for use,[89] presumably in the Revd. H. F. Burden's former house at no. 206 Mare Street, which it occupied by 1880.[90] Local Liberals were among the first, in 1878, to remodel their party on the lines adopted in Birmingham.[91] Hackney Parliament or House of Commons was a new debating society in 1882 and was reported in the *Hackney Hansard*, the first publication of Horatio Bottomley.[92] Hackney Conservative club, formed c. 1882,[93] had moved to no. 206 Mare Street by 1886 and stayed until 1903 or later. Conservative associations had been formed for north, central, and south Hackney by 1886.[94] More localized were a Conservative group for Dalston and a Radical group for Hackney Wick in 1887[95] and Conservative groups for De Beauvoir Town[96] and for Victoria Park and Liberal and Radical groups for London Fields in 1890.[97] De Beauvoir Town and Dalston ratepayers' association was active in the 1880s.[98] Both the Conservative and Labour parties had separate organizations for central and for south Hackney in the 1930s.[99]

Hackney Community Action[1] and Hackney Ethnic Minorities Alliance acted on behalf of community and ethnic groups in 1991. Hackney Cypriot association, in Ball's Pond Road, was founded in 1978 and had 200 paid-up members in 1991.[2] Other ethnic organizations included a Turkish community centre at nos. 92–100 Stoke Newington Road, a Muslim welfare association in Mildenhall Road, an African

74 *Terrier*, Summer 1990, 7; H.A.D., D/S/41/1.
75 Hackney, *Official Guide* (1920 and later edns.).
76 *Hackney Gaz.* 11 Sept. 1869, 3; 23 Oct. 1869, 3.
77 Ann. reps. 1878–88 in B.L.; *Kelly's Dir. Hackney* (1892–3).
78 H.A.D., D/S/13/1–27 (min. bks. 1894–1983) and TS. note.
79 *Corresponding Socs. of Brit. Soc. 1883–1929* (1975), 83.
80 Para. based on H.A.D., H/LD 7/2, pp. 75, 79, and *passim*; *Terrier*, Sept. 1986.
81 *V.C.H. Mdx.* vii. 120.
82 *D.N.B.* s.v. Wooler, Thos. Jonathan.
83 *Hackney Mag.* July 1835, 107–8.
84 Para. based on B. Burke and K. Worpole, *Hackney Propaganda: Working Class Club Life in Hackney 1870–1900* (1980), *passim*; *Kelly's Dir. Hackney* (1887 and later edns.).
85 C. M. Davies, *Heterodox Lond.* (1874), 351.
86 *P.O. Dir. Lond. County Suburbs North* (1888); G.L.R.O., H1/ST/E21/3, p. 6.

87 J. Stalin, *Notes of a Delegate* (1941), 6–8 (copy with notes in Islington libr.); below, prot. nonconf. (other denom.).
88 *Hackney Dir.* (1872).
89 *Hackney Gaz.* 13 Feb. 1875, 3; 5 June 1875, 3.
90 Clarke, *Hackney*, 34; *P.O. Dir. Lond. County Suburbs North* (1880).
91 J. Davis, *Reforming Lond.* (1988), 69–70.
92 H.A.D., H/LD 7/4 (cutting from *Boro. of Hackney Express*); *Kelly's Dir. Hackney* (1887); below, local govt. after 1837.
93 *Hackney Gaz.* 14 Mar. 1890, 3 (9th ann. rep.).
94 *P.O. Dir. Lond.* (1886 and later edns.).
95 *Kelly's Dir. Hackney* (1887, 1890, 1892–3).
96 *Hackney Gaz.* 7 Mar. 1890, 3.
97 *Kelly's Dir. Hackney* (1890).
98 Davis, *Reforming Lond.* 27.
99 *P.O. Dir. Lond.* (1934 and later edns.).
1 Para. based on inf. from Hackney L.B. information bureau.
2 Inf. from Mr. A. Kyriacou.

women's association, a Hackney Hindu council, Agudas Israel Community Services, and Hackney Chinese Community Services.

Modern amenity societies have included the Hackney society, formed in 1969, affiliated to the Civic Trust and responsible for several publications on local buildings. The Friends of Hackney Archives, formed in 1985, published their newsletter the *Terrier* from that year.[3] Residents' associations existed for Cassland Green, Leswin Area, Rectory [Road] Area, and Graham Road in 1991,[4] although no longer for De Beauvoir Town.

The *Hackney Magazine and Parish Reformer* appeared monthly from 1833 to 1837 and as the *Hackney Magazine* in 1838. It was published by Charles Green, a printer of Church Street, and strongly advocated a more open local government.[5]

Early newspapers[6] circulating in Hackney included the *Shoreditch Observer* of 1857, continued as the *Shoreditch Observer and Borough of Hackney Express* from 1867 to 1868 and thereafter, under slightly different titles, until 1915. The reformist *Kingsland Times and General Advertiser* of 1860[7] was renamed the *Hackney and Kingsland Times* in 1862 and incorporated with the *Eastern Times* in 1863. Four short lived newspapers with more narrowly local circulation were the *Hackney Journal*, apparently published only in 1842, the *Hackney Ratepayer*, the *Kingsland Chronicle*, and the *Family Companion*.[8]

The most successful newspaper was launched in 1864 as the *Hackney and Kingsland Gazette*,[9] a vigilant local guardian which claimed to be the great Liberal organ of Hackney and the largest weekly newspaper in London.[10] Compiled at first by volunteers, it soon passed to the printer Charles Potter, whose sons formed Potter Bros. as a limited company in 1920 and changed the title to *Hackney Gazette and North London Advertiser* in 1926. The family acquired publications in St. Pancras and Tottenham before merging its business in 1987 with North West London Press Group to form Capital Newspapers, which published the *Hackney Gazette* weekly in 1990. The offices, originally no. 440 Kingsland Road,[11] moved to Lenthall works on the west side of the road, in 1924 in part to no. 505A Kingsland Road, and in 1958 to no. 250.

Other newspapers included the *Hackney Guardian* from 1874 to 1876, the *Hackney Mercury* from 1885 under slightly varied titles until 1910, the *North London Guardian* from the 1880s, renamed the *North London Guardian, Stoke Newington Chronicle, and Hackney Independent* 1910–16, and the *North London Chronicle* of 1939, continued as the *Stoke Newington and Hackney Chronicle* from 1940 until 1971. The *Hackney Echo* was distributed free from 1984[12] by Capital Newspapers, replacing a Tuesday edition of the *Hackney Gazette*.[13]

MISCELLANEOUS INSTITUTIONS

Robinson's Retreat was endowed by Samuel Robinson (d. 1833), surveyor to St. Thomas's hospital,[14] for 8 widows of Independent ministers and 4 widows of Baptists. He designed a two-storeyed Gothic range with a central chapel fronting his own tomb on the south side of Retreat Place and occupying part of 1 a. leased by the hospital in 1812; other parts were reserved for a garden and for houses. The founder was reburied in Abney Park cemetery and the almshouses were mostly let as flats in 1901, after the inmates had left and been given pensions; the range was acquired by the L.C.C. in 1935 and demolished after the war. Robinson's trustees bought the freehold in 1911 and sold nearly all the land in 1940 but retained funds for both the Retreat and a relief charity, founded under his will, in 1991.[15]

The London Orphan Asylum[16] was founded in 1813 by Andrew Reed (d. 1862),[17] who had been trained at Hackney College. The 8-a. site of Hackney school[18] off Lower Clapton Road, later

reached by Linscott Road, was bought in 1820 and the children were transferred to new buildings there in 1825. The asylum included boys' and girls' schools and was administered by the headmaster, who was also chaplain; numbers rose from 206 in 1826 to 453 in the 1860s. The building by W. S. Inman, 'very ambitious although rather cheaply executed',[19] had a frontage of 19 bays, the central 3 projecting beneath a pedimented Tuscan portico and the outer ones also projecting; it was extended behind in 1846 and included a chapel seating 400 in 1851.[20] After the orphans had moved to Watford (Herts.) in 1871, the building was occupied by the Metropolitan Asylums Board *c.* 1873–6 and the Salvation Army from 1882.[21]

Dalston infant orphan asylum, under royal patronage like the London Orphan Asylum, was founded by Reed in 1827. It moved from Bethnal Green to Dalston Lane in 1832, expanded to occupy three houses, with 170 children in 1842, and made way for the German

3 *Terrier*, 1985, *passim*.
4 Hackney L.B. inf. bureau; inf. from H.A.D.
5 *Hackney Mag.* 1833–8 (copies in H.A.D.).
6 Para. based on B.L. Newspaper Cat.
7 *Kingsland Times*, 7 July 1860, 2.
8 *Hackney Gaz.* (1864 to 1989 anniv. suppl.), 16.
9 Para. based on ibid. 16–17.
10 *Hackney Gaz.* 18 Sept. 1869, 1. The earliest surviving copies are 1869.
11 *Hackney Photos.* i. 82.
12 B.L. Newspaper Cat.; *Willing's Press Guide* (1988).
13 Inf. from H.A.D.
14 Colvin, *Brit. Architects*, 702.

15 Clarke, *Hackney*, 186, 298; *Terrier*, Autumn 1991; C. W. Ikin, *Sam. Robinson's Chars.* (1991) (notes in H.A.D.); H.A.D., 361.1 ROB, WP 12572; *Lost Hackney*, 49; below, plate 63.
16 Para. based on Robinson, *Hackney*, i. 132–9; *Terrier*, Winter 1991, 2–4; N. Alvey, *Educ. by Election, Reed's Sch.* (St. Albans and Herts. Archit. and Archaeol. Soc. 1990), 16–17 (plan); inf. from H.B.M.C. Lond; *Hackney and Stoke Newington Past*, 59.
17 *D.N.B.*   18 Below, educ. (private schs.).
19 Pevsner, *Lond.* ii. 171.
20 Below, plate 35; P.R.O., HO 129/11/4/1/5.
21 Below, prot. nonconf.

hospital after moving in 1843 to Essex, where it became the Royal Wanstead school.[22] The Bakers' Co. of London built almshouses in St. Thomas's Passage (later Lyme Grove) c. 1828; inmates moved to Epping (Essex) in 1973.[23] The Children's Friend Society supported its first home from 1830 to c. 1841 at Hackney Wick, to train boys for apprenticing in the colonies. It was called Brenton's asylum after the philanthropist Capt. Edward Brenton (d. 1839), who had no known connexion with the area,[24] and occupied Leny Smith's silk mill.[25] The girls' branch of a refuge for young ex-prisoners, opened in Lambeth in 1805, moved from Bethnal Green in 1849 to Manor House in Dalston Lane, where, as Dalston Refuge for Destitute Females, it continued as a reformatory under royal patronage, with 86 girls in 1857 supported largely by laundry-work. From 1925 it formed part of the Samuel Lewis trust dwellings.[26] The Elizabeth Fry refuge for women ex-prisoners opened in 1849 on the site of the later St. Joseph's hospice and moved in the 1860s to no. 195 Mare Street, which it left for Highbury in 1913; the institution amalgamated with Dalston Refuge in 1924.[27] The Goldsmiths' and Jewellers' annuity institution of Clerkenwell in 1853 built an asylum in Manor (later Holcroft) Road. A two-storeyed range of 16 almshouses, designed by W. P. Griffith in the Tudor style, it was replaced by Orchard primary school.[28] Almshouses for Sephardic Jews, with an average of seven inmates, were built at the south-east corner of London Fields with funds given in 1851 by Emanuel Pacifico. They were to be sold under a Scheme of 1897, having been supported since 1880 by the Spanish and Portuguese Jews' congregation of London, and had been demolished by 1900; the congregation, which had been reimbursed, then offered accommodation at new almshouses which it had built for Barrow's charity in Mile End.[29] Tre-Wint industrial home was at no. 201 Mare Street by 1859, when it received a parliamentary grant, until 1880 or later; by 1902 it was in Haverstock Hill, Hampstead.[30] The Hand in Hand asylum for aged Jews was at no. 23 Well Street by 1880; it was united with two other

institutions in 1894 and remained until c. 1907.[31]

The hospital for French protestants, founded in 1708, moved in 1865 from Bath Street, in St. Luke's, to a 3-a. site in Victoria Park Road. In effect an almshouse and larger than any other in Hackney, it opened with 60 inmates. The château-style buildings, designed free of charge by R. L. Roumieu, included an apsidal chapel and were of diapered brick with much ornate Franco-Flemish detail, 'very beefy'. They were taken over by St. Victoire's convent school in 1949 after the hospital had moved to Horsham (Suss.); Cardinal Pole school occupied them in 1990.[32]

A supporter of the German hospital,[33] Baron von Schröder (created Sir John Schröder, Bt., in 1892), in 1879 founded a German orphanage at no. 214 Dalston Lane. As the German orphan asylum it moved in 1884 to no. 106 Norfolk (from 1938 Cecilia) Road, where it survived until 1939. Sir John's nephew Freiherr Bruno von Schröder in 1910 established a German old people's home at no. 47 Nightingale Place, whence it moved to Stoke Newington in 1921 or later.[34] A girls' home, Lutherhaus, was established opposite the German church in 1932 and apparently closed in 1939.[35]

An orphanage was established in 1881 and managed by the Anglican community of the Holy Childhood, at no. 19 Clapton Common from c. 1897 until the Second World War.[36] The Woodlands, Clapton Common, was temporarily acquired c. 1882 as a boys' home by the Waifs and Strays Society, whose chairman Bishop Walsham How lived next door at Stainforth House.[37] The London City Mission moved the Ayahs' Home, an apparently unique institution for Indian women whose employers were staying in England, from Jewry Street (Lond.) in 1900 to no. 26 King Edward's Road and c. 1921 to no. 4 where, as the Ayahs' and Amahs' Home, it continued until c. 1942.[38] The London Female Penitentiary (later London Female Guardian society) was on the west side of Stoke Newington High Street from 1884 until 1939.[39] The Mission of Help for the Suffering Poor, founded in 1894, was a tenant at Sutton House from 1931 until 1947.[40]

[22] Robinson, *Hackney*, i. 141–2; H.A.D., D/F/TYS/16, pp. 258, 262; D. Grist, *A Victorian Char.* (1974), 1–7.

[23] H.A.D., bldgs. file.

[24] Robinson, *Hackney*, ii. 313, 315; G. Wagner, *Children of the Empire* (1982), 13; H.A.D., bldgs. file.

[25] Research by H.A.D. (1993).

[26] H.A.D., D/F/TYS/16, pp. 281–96; ibid. bldgs. file; ibid. D/S/4 (rec. inc. min. bks. to 1902); *Mins. of Educ. Cttee. of Council, 1857–8*, H.C. 2386, p. 56 (1857–8), xlv; below, manors (Graham); *P.O. Dir. Lond.* (1925); above, Dalston.

[27] H.A.D., bldgs. file.

[28] Ibid.; Watson, *Gentlemen*, 57; *Hackney and Stoke Newington Past*, 56 and illus. 68; W.J. Pinks, *Hist. of Clerkenwell* (1865), 319; Clarke, *Hackney*, 298 n.; below, educ. (pub. schs.).

[29] H.A.D., H/LD 7/4; N. Laski, *Laws and Chars. of Spanish and Portuguese Cong.* (1952), 149–50, 152; Stanford, *Map of Lond.* (1862–5 edn.), sheet 7; *Hackney and Stoke Newington Past*, 56; *Jewish Year Bk.* (1930).

[30] *Mins. of Educ. Cttee. of Council, 1859–60*, H.C. 2681, p. 687 (1860), liv; *P.O. Dir. Lond. Suburbs* (1880, 1884); *P.O. Dir. Lond.* (1902).

[31] *P.O. Dir. Lond. Suburbs* (1880); *Jewish Year Bk.* (1896–7 and later edns.).

[32] *Procs. of Huguenot Soc. of Lond.* xxi. 354; xxii. 244–5; *Hackney and Stoke N. Past*, 56; below, plate 37; Pevsner, *Lond.* ii. 167; H.A.D., bldgs. file; below, educ. (pub. schs.).

[33] Below, pub. svces.

[34] M. Neumann, 'Account of German Hosp. in Lond. 1845–1948' (Thos. Huxley coll. thesis, 1971, in H.A.D.), 73; H.A.D. D/F/AMH/555, p. 12; *Kelly's Dir. Stoke Newington* (1908–9 and later edns.); *P.O. Dir Lond.* (1934 and later edns.).

[35] *Hamburger Lutherische Kirche, London (1669–1969)*, 92.

[36] H.A.D., bldgs. file; *Kelly's Dir. Stoke Newington* (1897–8); *P.O. Dir. Lond. County Suburbs* (1928 and later edns.).

[37] H.A.D., D/F/BAG/1, p. 66. Not in *P.O. Dir. Lond. County Suburbs North* (1880, 1888).

[38] H.A.D., bldgs. file; *Lond. City Mission Mag.* lxv. 172–4; *Hackney and Stoke Newington Past*, 59 and illus. 72; *P.O. Dir. Lond.* (1920 and later edns.).

[39] H.A.D., bldgs. file.

[40] Inf. from H.A.D. The mission existed in 1994 as St. Martin's rest home, Westcliff-on-Sea (Essex).

MANORS

The manor of *HACKNEY* was not described by name in Domesday Book and was said in 1294 to have been held by the bishops of London from time immemorial as a member of their manor of Stepney.[41] Although accounted for separately from the 14th century and with its own courts by the 1580s,[42] Hackney remained with the bishops of London until it was granted in 1550 to the Wentworth family. It was mortgaged by way of a lease for 99 years by Thomas Wentworth, earl of Cleveland, in 1632.[43]

Both manors figured in the complicated transactions arising from Cleveland's debts, his forfeiture in 1650, and attempts to regain his lands after the Restoration.[44] Hackney, distinguished from Stepney, was usually described as a manor with lands and rights in Hackney, Kingsland, Shacklewell, Newington Street, Clapton, Church Street, Well Street, Grove Street, and Mare Street,[45] an area presumably covering most of the ancient parish. From the time of its purchase by Richard Blackwell, treasurer of prize goods, in 1653,[46] the main manor of Hackney was held by a succession of Londoners. The Wentworths' interest was finally surrendered in 1669 by Philadelphia, widow of the earl of Cleveland's son Thomas, Lord Wentworth (d. 1665), and her daughter Henrietta Maria, Baroness Wentworth.[47]

Richard Blackwell was recorded as lord of Hackney, as was William Hobson, the purchaser in 1660.[48] Hobson (d. 1661 or 1662), a haberdasher who settled in Hackney, was followed by his sons-in-law William Bolton, Patience Ward, both of them later lord mayor, and William White.[49] Their title was confirmed in 1663 by agreement with the Wentworths and in 1669 they sold the manor, again with the Wentworths' consent, to John Forth, an alderman.[50] Forth completed its sale to Nicholas Cary and Thomas Cooke, goldsmiths, in 1675. Cooke's assignees and Cary's widow Susan sold it to Francis Tyssen the elder, of Shacklewell, in 1697.[51] Tyssen acquired two other manors in Hackney,[52] for which separate courts had long been held. From the early 18th century the main manor, previously called simply Hackney, was styled lord's hold or *LORDSHOLD*.

The Tyssen family and its heirs thereafter held all three manors. Francis Tyssen the elder (d. 1699), a naturalized merchant from Flushing

(Netherlands), had married in London in 1649 and been granted arms in 1687.[53] He or his son Francis had been chosen a vestryman in 1689 and allotted the Rowe family's pew in 1690.[54] The younger Francis (d. 1710) left all his lands in Hackney, with 32 a. in Low Leyton marsh (Essex), to his son and namesake.[55] The third Francis married a daughter of Richard de Beauvoir of Balmes and was succeeded in 1717 by his posthumous son Francis John.[56]

Francis John Tyssen (d. 1781) left only illegitimate children. He settled the three Hackney manors and nearly all his lands[57] in trust for his sons Francis (d. 1813) and Francis John Tyssen (d. 1814), both of whom were childless, with remainder to his daughter Mary (d. 1800) wife of John Amhurst of Kent. Mary's daughter Amelia in 1814 married William George Daniel of Dorset, who took the surname Daniel-Tyssen.[58]

W. G. Daniel-Tyssen (d. 1838), the parish's largest landowner in 1831,[59] was succeeded by his eldest son William George Tyssen Daniel-Tyssen (d. 1885) of Foulden Hall (Norf.), who in 1852 took the surname Tyssen-Amhurst. His son William Amhurst Tyssen-Amhurst (d. 1909) of Didlington Hall, the bibliophile, changed the spelling of his surname to Tyssen-Amherst in 1877 and was created Baron Amherst of Hackney, with special remainder to his eldest daughter Mary Rothes Margaret, wife of Lord William Cecil, in 1892.[60] Lord Amherst, who was defrauded of much of his fortune by Charles Cheston, steward of the Hackney manors,[61] conveyed those manors in 1906 to his daughter, who settled them in tail male.[62] The manors passed with the barony from Lady Amherst of Hackney (d. 1919) to her great-grandson William Hugh Amherst Cecil, lord of the manors in 1990.[63]

The Tyssen estate was estimated to be c. 599 a. in 1809–10, when the densest building was at Kingsland and farther north along the high road, in Church Street, and at Shacklewell.[64] In 1903, when the freeholds were mortgaged and after housing had spread over most of the farmland, the estate consisted of blocks of freehold property at Stamford Hill, where a few leasehold sites were interspersed, at Upper Clapton, near Lea dock north of Lea bridge, and at Shacklewell.[65] Almost all of the family's property had been sold by 1990, some sales at Stamford Hill having occurred as recently as 1988.[66]

41 *Plac. de Quo Warr.* (Rec. Com.), 475.
42 Below, local govt. (manorial).
43 G.L.R.O., M79/LH/95.
44 *Complete Peerage*, xii (2), 502-4; *D.N.B.*; G.L.R.O., TS. index to M79. To be treated under Stepney.
45 e.g. G.L.R.O., M79/LH/95 (1632).
46 Ibid. M79/LH/99.
47 Ibid. M79/LH/106.
48 Ibid. M93/1, f.27; M93/4, f.7v.
49 Ibid. M93/4, f.115v.; P.R.O., PROB 11/307, no. 300; Beaven, *Aldermen*, ii. 86, 89, 106.
50 G.L.R.O., M79/LH/106; Beaven, *Aldermen*, ii. 102.
51 G.L.R.O., M79/LH/106 (endorsements); M79/LH/113; cf. below, this section (Shacklewell).
52 Below, this section (Kingshold; Grumbolds); M.L.R. 1712/1/134.
53 *Misc. Geneal. et Heraldica*, N.S. iii. 379–80.
54 Vestry mins. 14 Sept. 1689; 9 Apr. 1690.
55 P.R.O., PROB 11/518, f. 365; M.L.R. 1712/1/116.
56 Clarke, *Hackney*, 73; Robinson, *Hackney*, i, table facing p. 322; H.A.D., D/F/TYS/12/2, p. 192.
57 P.R.O., PROB 11/1082, f. 454; Robinson, *Hackney*, i, table facing p. 322; G.L.R.O., M79/LH/16, p. 214.
58 Robinson, *Hackney*, i, table facing p. 322.
59 *Starling's Map* (1831).
60 Ibid.; *Complete Peerage*, i. 124–5; *D.N.B.*
61 *D.N.B.*; H.A.D., H/LD 7/11; *The Times*, 18 Jan. 1909,13d.   62 G.L.R.O., M79/TA/21.
63 Burke, *Peerage* (1931); *Who's Who, 1987*; inf. from Ld. Amherst of Hackney.   64 G.L.R.O., M79/TA/28.
65 Ibid. M79/TA/20; M79/TA/21, map A.
66 Inf. from Ld. Amherst of Hackney.

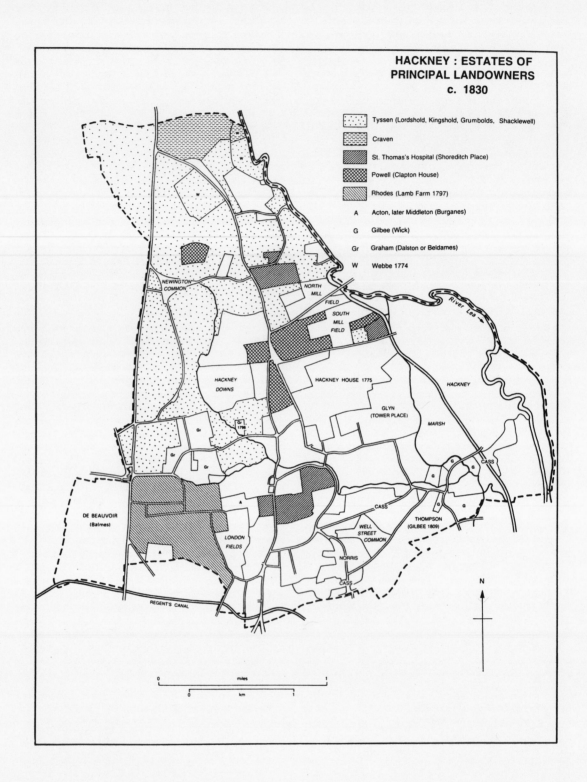

HACKNEY : ESTATES OF
PRINCIPAL LANDOWNERS
c. 1830

Tyssen (Lordshold, Kingshold, Grumbolds, Shacklewell)

Craven

St. Thomas's Hospital (Shoreditch Place)

Powell (Clapton House)

Rhodes (Lamb Farm 1797)

A   Acton, later Middleton (Burganes)

G   Gilbee (Wick)

Gr   Graham (Dalston or Beldames)

W   Webbe 1774

Three brothers of Francis Tyssen (d. 1717), John of Shacklewell, William, and Samuel (d. 1747 or 1748),[67] were buried in Hackney, as was John's son John Tyssen of Well Street.[68] Another Samuel (d. 1800), illegitimate son of Francis John, acquired land at Homerton by marriage to the first Samuel's granddaughter Sarah Boddicott. He lived in Norfolk, as did his son Samuel (d. 1845)[69] whose estate bordered Clapton common in 1807 and had grown by 1816;[70] part was sold in 1846 to Arthur Craven.[71] W. G. T. Daniel-Tyssen's brother John Robert acted as his steward and was prominent in local affairs.[72]

No manor house for Lordshold is known.[73] The manor house of Shacklewell was inhabited in the early 18th century by Tyssens and so sometimes called the Manor House.[74] So too was the early 19th-century house in front of the assembly rooms in Church Street where J. R. Daniel-Tyssen lived from 1845 until 1858, which was sold in 1877;[75] a three-storeyed yellow-brick composition of 2, 3, and 2 bays, with projecting modern shops on the ground floor, it formed nos. 387, 387A, and 387B Mare Street in 1991.[76]

The Knights Templars were given lands, probably early in the reign of Henry II, by the king's steward William of Hastings, presumably a kinsman of Richard of Hastings, master of the Temple in England. The lands, called Hastingmede in the 15th century, lay in the marsh and included 2 a. in Leyton (Essex).[77] The Templars also received land from Ailbrith, which they granted to Robert of Wick, in whose holding originated the reputed manor of Wick.[78] They acquired 6 a. quitclaimed by Alice de la Grave in 1231 and ½ hide quitclaimed by Ralph de Burgham, clerk, in 1232,[79] after a dispute between Ralph and a younger Robert of Wick.[80] Their estate comprised c. 35½ a. in Hackney, 9 a. in Leyton, and two mills in 1307–8, when they had pleas and perquisites of court.[81] It passed on their suppression in 1312 to the Knights Hospitallers, who acknowledged that 40 a. and the mills were held of the bishop's manor in Stepney in 1337.[82] At the Dissolution the lands passed to the Crown and were known as the manor of Hackney or *KINGSHOLD* in 1539–40.[83]

The king in 1614 granted the Hospitallers' manor to Thomas Land and Thomas Banks,

Londoners.[84] The two mills were reserved.[85] Land and Banks immediately conveyed their interest to Hugh Sexey (d. 1619), who established a rent charge to support his hospital at Bruton (Som.).[86] In 1633 the manor was sold by Sexey's feoffees to Humphrey Hurleston and then by Hurleston to William Benning, who in 1647 sold it to William Hobson.[87] Hobson's will, proved 1662, mentioned his manor of St. John of Jerusalem.[88] Courts were held for his sons-in-law and executors William Bolton, Patience Ward, and William White, who in 1668 jointly sold the manor to Sir George Vyner, Bt. (d. 1673).[89] It passed to Sir George's son Sir Thomas (d. 1683), a minor, whose coheirs were his father's cousins Edith Lambert, Elizabeth Tombs, and Elizabeth Marchant.[90] They and their heirs jointly sold their shares in 1693 to John Sikes, a London merchant, who in 1697 conveyed the manor to Francis Tyssen.[91] Their shares in other lands of the Vyners, held of Lordshold and Grumbolds manors, were later sold to the Ryders.[92]

There may have been no manor house for Kingshold.[93] The Hospitallers had a house (*domicilium*) in Hackney in 1416, inhabited by Richard Pande, servant and 'charioteer' of the bishop of London.[94] In 1693 a 'capital messuage or manor house' had an orchard and garden, adjoined by ground where the manor pound had stood and with 6 a. nearby, the existing pound being at the west end of Well Street.[95] It was presumably the 'Pilgrim's house', reputedly the oldest house in Hackney, built around a courtyard and described as formerly moated in 1741, when its two-storeyed front, of chequered brick and adorned with a cross, was of three bays, each under a stepped gable.[96] As a 'brick house at the bottom of Well Street, commonly called King John's Palace', it had been subdivided among poor tenants by 1795.[97] Said in 1797 to have been the prior of St. John's residence,[98] by 1842 it had made way for small houses forming St. John's Place, east of the junction of Well Street with Palace Road (later part of the Frampton Park estate).[99]

Another building, in Church Street nearly opposite Dalston Lane, was illustrated in 1805 as the 'Templars' house'. Apparently early 17th-century, it had four storeys and three projecting

67 P.R.O., PROB 11/518, f. 365.
68 Robinson, *Hackney*, i, table facing p. 322.
69 Ibid.; Burke, *Land. Gent.* (1952), 2576; G.L.R.O., M79/LH/19.   70 H.A.D., V 5; *Starling's Map* (1831).
71 G.L.R.O., M79/LH/25, M 127–30, 322–4.
72 Clarke, *Hackney*, 118.
73 Lysons, *Environs*, ii. 453. There is no evidence to support Clarke's belief that the bishops had a residence in Homerton: Clarke, *Hackney*, 146 and n. 87.
74 Robinson, *Hackney*, i. 116; below, this section (Shacklewell).
75 Clarke, *Hackney*, 118; H.A.D., D/F/AMH/555, p. 1.
76 *Hackney and Stoke N. Past*, illus. 39; *List of Bldgs.* (1975).
77 *Rec. of Templars in Eng. in 12th Cent.* ed. B. A. Lees (Brit. Acad. 1935), pp. 1, xc–xci; *V.C.H. Essex*, vi. 201.
78 *Rec. of Templars*, pp. xc, 17; below, this section (Wick).
79 B.L. Cott. MS. Nero E. VI, f. 65; P.R.O., CP 25(1)/146/8, no. 81; CP 25(1)/146/9, no. 104.
80 *Bracton's Note Bk.* ed. Maitland, ii, pp. 508–10.
81 *Rec. of Templars*, ed. Lees, 173; McDonnell, *Med. Lond. Suburbs*, 156.
82 B.L. Cott. MS. Nero E. VI, ff. 65–6.

83 P.R.O., SC 6/Hen. VIII/2402, m. 13 (copies in G.L.R.O., M79/KH/42/1/1, 3).
84 Para. based on G.L.R.O., M79/KH/44/28 (abs. of title 1614–97).   85 Ibid. M79/KH/42/2.
86 G.L.R.O., M79/KH/44/1/1; *V.C.H. Som.* iii. 22–3.
87 G.L.R.O., M79/KH/44/4; M79/KH/44/8/1; M79/KH/44/9.   88 P.R.O., PROB 11/307, no. 300.
89 G.L.R.O., M79/KH/1, p. 1; M79/KH/44/28/13.
90 G.E.C. *Baronetage*, iii. 31; G.L.R.O., M79/KH/1, p. 19; M79/LH/41; M79/G/3, p. 23.
91 G.L.R.O., M79/KH/44/22/1.
92 Below, this section.
93 The king's place, later Brooke Ho. (below, this section) has been mistaken for the manor ho. of Kingshold: Lysons, *Environs*, ii. 455; Robinson, *Hackney*, i. 110.
94 Guildhall MS. 9171/2, f. 342v. (not ref. given in McDonnell, *Med. Lond. Suburbs*, 24). The charioteer's function is not known.
95 G.L.R.O., M79/KH/44/22/1.
96 *Lost Hackney*, 26–7.   97 Lysons, *Environs*, ii. 456.
98 H.A.D., 900.2, pp. 36, 39.
99 Robinson, *Hackney*, i. 83 and illus.; Clarke, *Hackney*, 11, 113; *Lost Hackney*, 26–7.

bays, adorned with Ionic pilasters. It had served as the Blue Posts tavern in the mid 18th century, when an assembly room was added, and was later subdivided. In 1824 most of the building was said to have been demolished some ten years earlier; the assembly room survived as an auctioneer's hall in 1842. Part of the site came to be occupied by the Crown inn.[1]

A freehold estate was attached to a seat at Clapton called in the 16th century the *KING'S PLACE* and from the 18th *BROOKE HOUSE*.[2] After its addition to the Tyssens' holdings it was often assumed to have always formed part of Kingshold, although a separate history was sometimes recalled by its description as the reputed manor of Brooke.[3] Perhaps it originated in the 4 hides in Stepney held by Robert Fafiton in 1086. Fafiton's claim to be a tenant in chief was disputed by the bishop, although his lands had fallen in value since the Conquest and may therefore have lain partly along Ermine Street in the path of William I's army.[4] Probably it was the estate which Sir William Estfield (d. 1446), a London alderman, conveyed in 1439 to William Booth, rector of Hackney and later archbishop of York, one of whose feoffees in 1476 released his interest to William Worsley (d. 1499), dean of St. Paul's, whose brother had married into Booth's family.[5] Worsley sold it in 1496 to Sir Reginald Bray, K.G. (d. 1503), whose nephew John Bray had sold freeholds in Hackney, presumably once Worsley's, by 1513 to another courtier Sir Robert Southwell (d. 1514). The land apparently passed through Sir Robert's son Sir Richard (d. 1564) to a younger son Sir Robert (d. 1559), Master of the Rolls, who in 1536 married Margaret, daughter of the Speaker Sir Thomas Neville (d. 1542).[6] Neville was said to be the holder in 1531, presumably on his daughter's betrothal, and conveyed the estate to Henry Percy, earl of Northumberland (d. 1537), in exchange for lands in Sussex.[7] The impoverished earl surrendered it to the Crown in 1535 but died in Hackney.[8]

The king's 'manor of Hackney' and mansion were granted in 1547 to Sir William Herbert, later earl of Pembroke (d. 1570), who soon conveyed them to the diplomatist Sir Ralph Sadler (d. 1587).[9] Sadler sold them in 1548 to Sir Wymond Carew of Antony (Cornw.),[10]

whose grandson the antiquary Richard Carew (d. 1620) conveyed them in 1578 to Henry Cary, Lord Hunsdon (d. 1596).[11] They were bought in 1583 by Sir Rowland Hayward, twice lord mayor of London (d. 1593),[12] and in 1596 by Elizabeth, countess of Oxford (d. 1612 or 1613), from Hayward's executors. Elizabeth's husband Edward de Vere, earl of Oxford (d. 1604), was resident from 1596. The countess sold her interest to the poet Fulke Greville (d. 1628), later Baron Brooke, in 1609.[13]

It has sometimes been assumed that Greville received the Hospitallers' lands, which reverted to the Crown and came to form part of Kingshold.[14] The Grevilles, however, retained their Clapton estate, which was disputed between Sir Fulke Greville and Robert Greville, Baron Brooke (d. 1643),[15] and apparently were resident in the 1650s and 1660s.[16] Outlying lands in Hackney marsh and Hackney Downs of Francis Greville, Baron Brooke (later created Earl Brooke and earl of Warwick), were described in 1742.[17] Most of his 'reputed manor of Hackney', of which over 100 a. had been leased for 99 years in 1762, was conveyed in 1819 by his grandson Henry Richard Greville, earl of Warwick (d. 1853), to W. G. Daniel-Tyssen.[18] The earl also sold property at Clapton to James Powell and to Thomas Bros, land called Paradise to William Hurst Ashpitel, and parcels of Hackney Downs to John Alliston.[19] The Tyssens in 1834 claimed to hold the reputed manor of Brooke,[20] which descended thereafter with Lordshold.

Brooke House latterly was an imposing brick building at the north corner of Upper Clapton and Kenninghall roads.[21] It may have been the dean's hall on Worsley's estate, inspected in 1496 and 1498 by the Pewterers' Company of London as a model for its new hall. It was said, evidently in error, to have included a stone chapel of the Elringtons, which was mistakenly thought to have been depicted in 1642 by Wenceslaus Hollar. When the Crown acquired Northumberland's estate in 1535 Thomas Cromwell rapidly put a quadrangular house of the 15th century into a state for Henry VIII to use it in 1535, 1536 for a reconciliation with Princess Mary, and 1538.[22] Further repairs were effected before the grant of 1547 to Herbert included a 'fair house of brick', with a hall and parlour, large gallery, chapel, and library, en-

[1] H.A.D., 900.2, pp. 31, 39; Robinson, *Hackney*, i. 77–8; Clarke, *Hackney*, 111; *Lost Hackney*, 36; below, plate 14.

[2] Three paras. based on *Survey of Lond.* xxviii (1960), which revises E. A. Mann, *Brooke Ho.* (L.C.C. *Survey*, monograph v, 1904). [3] e.g. M.L.R. 1834/4/374.

[4] McDonnell, *Med. Lond. Suburbs*, 13–14; *V.C.H. Mdx.* i. 128.

[5] *Cal. Close*, 1476–85, 13; *Hist. Parl., Commons*, 1439–1509, 304; *D.N.B.*

[6] *Hist. Parl., Commons*, 1439–1509, 104; *D.N.B.*

[7] *Complete Peerage*, ix. 722; J. M. W. Bean, *Estates of Percy Fam. 1416–1537* (1958), 149, 152; *L. & P. Hen. VIII*, viii, p. 378.

[8] *L. & P. Hen. VIII*, x, p. 56; xii (1), pp. 557, 592; *Cat. Anct. D.* iii, A 4104; P.R.O., CP 25(2)/52/371, no. 12. Lysons and others state that Northumberland was granted the Hospitallers' estate, but the earl died before the order's suppression.

[9] *Cal. Pat.* 1547–8, 194, 209; *D.N.B.*

[10] *Cal. Pat.* 1548–9, 87–8; A. J. Slavin, *Politics and Profit, Sir Ralph Sadler* (1966), 202.

[11] *Cal. Pat.* 1575–8, 469; *D.N.B.*

[12] *T.L.M.A.S.* xii. 518.

[13] Lysons, *Environs*, ii. 455; P.R.O., PROB 11/83 (P.C.C. 24 Dixy); C. Ogbourne, *Mystery of Wm. Shakespeare* (1988), 672, 692–3.

[14] e.g. by Robinson, *Hackney*, i. 110.

[15] *Cal. S.P. Dom.* Addenda 1625–9, 739–40.

[16] Below, this section.

[17] G.L.R.O., M79/LH/50, 23 Apr. 1742.

[18] *Complete Peerage*, ii. 335–7; H.A.D., M 4038; M.L.R. 1763/3/351; M.L.R. 1819/4/277.

[19] M.L.R. 1819/6/16, 18, 20, 33; M.L.R. 1821/5/125–6; H.A.D., D/F/BAG/13A.

[20] M.L.R. 1834/4/374.

[21] Following archit. description based on Mann, *Brooke Ho., passim*; *Survey of Lond.* xxviii, *passim*.

[22] *Hist. of King's Works*, ed. H. M. Colvin, iv (1982), 125; *L. & P. Hen. VIII*, viii, p. 198; ix, pp. 13, 19, 30, 50, 87, 114, 136; xii (1), p. 597; xiii (1), p. 332; *Wriothesley's Chron.* i (Camden Soc. 2nd ser. xi), 51; *Lisle Letters*, ed. M. St. C. Byrne, v (1981), p. 114.

closed behind with a broad ditch.²³ Lord
Hunsdon rebuilt or remodelled the house *c.*
1580: his and his wife's arms adorned the ceiling
of a first-floor gallery which probably ran the
length of the **E**-shaped mansion, which faced the
high road from the west. Piecemeal additions
later closed the **E**, creating two courtyards: in
1750 there were gables, turrets, castellated sections of wall, a small wing projecting from the
south-east end, and two octagonal towers. The
whole was masked in the late 18th century by a
uniform brick front of nine bays, with a pediment over the central five.²⁴

Margaret Douglas, countess of Lennox (d.
1578), retired to the house, presumably as a
lessee, and Elizabeth I paid visits in 1583 and
1587.²⁵ As Lord Brooke's, it was assessed as the
largest in the parish in 1664 at 37 hearths²⁶ and
in 1672 at 36.²⁷ Evelyn in 1654 and 1656 found
Lady Brooke's garden 'one of the neatest and
most celebrated in England' and much superior
to the house,²⁸ as did Pepys in 1666.²⁹ There were
several tenants by 1719. A lease was renewed in
1750 to Thomas Pangbourne (d. 1758), whose
daughter sold it to William Clarke (d. 1777), who
secured a 99-year lease, converted the house
'called the King's Place' into an asylum, and
assigned it in 1781 to John Monro.³⁰ Called
Brooke House in 1786,³¹ it underwent alterations
which included the 19th-century division of the
long gallery and the later demolition of the small
south-west wing. The older parts, behind the
road front, were damaged in 1940 and the house
was sold with 5½ a. to the L.C.C. in 1944. The
house was demolished in 1954,³² 'Hackney's
greatest loss this century'.³³ Restored late 16th-
century panelling, said to be from Brooke
House, adorned the Alex Fitch room on its
opening in 1926 in the War Memorial building
at Harrow school.³⁴

The right of presentation to Hackney *REC-
TORY* and the rectory estate known by the mid
17th century as the manor of *GRUMBOLDS*³⁵
lay with the lord of Hackney manor and passed
in 1550 from the bishop of London to the
Wentworths.³⁶ Lands in Hackney for which
payments were made at Stepney courts included
an estate of Daniel in 1349, called 'Daniels now
Grumbolds' by 1384.³⁷ It may have been part
of a manor called Rumbolds otherwise Cobhams, with land in Hackney, Stepney, and
London, which was vested in trustees in 1462

and 1471³⁸ and was disputed 1518 × 1529.³⁹ The
name Cobhams probably derived from Reynold
Cobham, who surrendered his grandfather's
land in Hackney in 1404,⁴⁰ or Richard Cobham,
who surrendered in 1410,⁴¹ rather than from
Thomas de Cobham (d. 1327), bishop of
Worcester and rector of Hackney.⁴² A Grumbold
family was recorded in the early 13th century⁴³
and John Grumbold of Hackney made a will in
1452.⁴⁴ Perhaps, since many rectors were non-
resident, their lands came to be named after a
lessee.

Sir Thomas Heneage (d. 1553) was farmer for
the rector from 1540 and his nephew and namesake (d. 1595) was the first of several farmers
under Elizabeth I.⁴⁵ A lease, including both the
profits and the next presentation, was bought by
John Daniell and in 1601 offered as security for
payment of a heavy fine to the Crown.⁴⁶ Patronage of the rectory and the manor of Grumbolds
'to the said rectory belonging' were included in
the mortgage by the earl of Cleveland. They
were separated from Hackney manor in 1647 on
their sale to Henry White acting for William
Stephens, who formally acquired them in 1651.⁴⁷
It was later claimed that Stephens (d. 1658) also
extorted a 31-year lease from the rector.⁴⁸
Stephens soon sold the rectory manor to Raphael
Throckmorton, probably acting for Richard
Blackwell, who with Throckmorton sold it in
1654 to Thomas Fowkes, a London grocer.⁴⁹
The tithes had been sold to William Hobson by
1664, when Cleveland and his son confirmed
Fowkes's right to the rectory and its lands and
other profits.⁵⁰ Fowkes and the Wentworths sold
their interests in 1673 to John Forth, alderman,⁵¹
from whom the estate passed in 1675 to Daniel
Farrington and in 1680 to Thomas Cooke and
Nicholas Cary.⁵² Cooke and Cary's acquisition
of Lordshold⁵³ reunited the patronage of the
rectory and the manor of Grumbolds with the
lordship of Hackney. In 1697 Cooke and Cary
conveyed their interest to Francis Tyssen,⁵⁴
whose heirs presented to the rectory of the
ancient parish until the ecclesiastical division of
Hackney after the death of the last sinecure
rector in 1821.⁵⁵ In 1824 the church building
commissioners confirmed the manorial rights of
the Tyssens,⁵⁶ who thereafter held Grumbolds
with Lordshold and Kingshold.⁵⁷ The tithes, on
1,560 a., were redeemed in 1842.⁵⁸

By the 17th century it was the custom for a

²³ *King's Works*, ed. Colvin, iv. 124–5; P.R.O., SC
6/Hen. VIII/2103, m. 3d.
²⁴ *King's Works*, ed. Colvin, iv. 124–5; below, plate 16.
²⁵ *Hist. Parl., Commons*, 1558–1603, ii. 284.
²⁶ G.L.R.O., MR/TH/4, m. 3.
²⁷ Ibid. MR/TH/34.
²⁸ *Diary of John Evelyn*, ed. E. S. de Beer, iii. 96, 169.
²⁹ *Diary of Sam. Pepys*, ed. Latham, vii. 182.
³⁰ *Survey of Lond.* xxviii. 64–5; M.L.R. 1767/1/339;
below, pub. svces.   ³¹ M.L.R. 1789/5/461.
³² *Survey of Lond.* xxviii, pp. v, 66; Hist. Mon. Com. *E.
Lond.* 46; Pevsner, *Lond.* ii. 171; Clarke, *Hackney*, 300;
H.A.D., P 810–22.
³³ *Lost Hackney*, 28–9.
³⁴ Inf. from archivist, Harrow sch.
³⁵ G.L.R.O., M79/G/8/3.
³⁶ *Cal. Pat.* 1549–51, 404.
³⁷ P.R.O., SC 2/191/60; Guildhall MS. 10312/136.
³⁸ *Cat. Anct. D.* ii, C 2842; vi, C 4610, C 4664. Cobhams

to be treated under Stepney.   ³⁹ P.R.O., C 1/459/6.
⁴⁰ *Cat. Anct. D.* vi, C 4735.
⁴¹ McDonnell, *Med. Lond. Suburbs*, 155.
⁴² Hennessy, *Nov. Rep.* p. xxxii; *D.N.B.*
⁴³ McDonnell, *Med. Lond. Suburbs*, 24; cf. Guildhall
MS. 25516, f. 38v.   ⁴⁴ G.L.R.O., M79/G/3, p. 45.
⁴⁵ H.A.D., D/F/TYS/40, pp. 351, 355, 359, 367; *D.N.B.*
⁴⁶ *Cal. S. P. Dom.* 1601–3, 57–9, 94, 107, 129–30, 149,
245–6; ibid. Addenda 1580–1625, 410, 509; P.R.O., STAC
7/11/28.   ⁴⁷ G.L.R.O., M79/G/8/1.
⁴⁸ P.R.O., C 5/513/80.
⁴⁹ G.L.R.O., M79/G/8/3.   ⁵⁰ Ibid. M79/G/8/7.
⁵¹ Ibid. M79/G/8/10.   ⁵² Ibid. M79/G/8/14, 16.
⁵³ Above, this section (Lordshold).
⁵⁴ G.L.R.O., M79/G/8/19, 22, 24.
⁵⁵ Hennessy, *Nov. Rep.* 177; below, parish church.
⁵⁶ H.A.D., D/F/TYS/40, pp. 287–93.
⁵⁷ G.L.R.O., M79/G/2 (ct. min. bk.).
⁵⁸ H.A.D., rectory tithe award.

rector to lease his estate to the patron.[59] In 1650 the parsonage house and glebe land, but not the tithes, had been assigned to William Stephens.[60] In 1697 the Revd. Richard Roach leased the rectory, with its house, the tithes, and the manor of Grumbolds, to the new patron Francis Tyssen the elder for £20 a year.[61] Courts were held for Roach's predecessor Nehemiah Moorhouse, Thomas Cooke, as farmer,[62] and for Roach himself by Cooke and later by Tyssen.[63]

The rectory lands, probably all along the main street of Hackney, included Church field.[64] The parsonage house has not been identified but in 1487 was in the highway opposite the church, probably on the site of the Mermaid.[65] An orchard and fishpond were claimed by the rector c. 1580[66] and the house had barns and c. 5 a. attached to it on the west side in 1622.[67] It was occupied by John Eaton, a servant of Stephens, in 1650, when the rector lived in another, presumably smaller, house; a third house had been leased out. It was calculated that the parsonage house, land, and tithes might be let at an improved rent of £140 a year, almost three times the worth of the vicarage.[68] The court of Grumbolds in 1653 met at the parsonage house[69] but by 1688 had come to be held at an inn.[70] The house was last recorded, with 5 a., in 1762.[71] References to the 19th-century Rectory were to the former vicarage house, rebuilt c. 1826.[72]

The origins of the reputed manor of WICK lay in land which had been brought to the Templars by Ailbrith when he entered their order and, apart from two small holdings, had been granted by the master Richard of Hastings to Robert of Wick by 1185.[73] The land was held of the Templars and, after their suppression, of the Hospitallers.[74] It was held by Robert of Wick's son Edmund de la Grave and later with other parcels by Robert Belebarbe, who leased all his lands in Wick in 1301 and conveyed them to Simon of Abingdon, alderman, in 1316. Simon made further additions, as did his widow Eve and her second husband John of Causton, alderman, who sold Wyke and all their other lands in Hackney and Stepney to Adam Francis (d. 1375), mayor of London, in 1349; the manor then consisted of at least two houses and 114 a. After more purchases, some made through agents including Nicholas atte Wyke, a clerk, the estate passed to Adam's widow Agnes and then to his daughter Maud, who married John

Aubrey, Sir Alan Buxhall (d. 1381), and John de Montagu, earl of Salisbury.[75] The earl was executed in 1400, when his forfeited estates included the manor of Hackney Wick, with a tenement called the Wick, held half of the bishop of London and half of the Hospitallers.[76]

Wick was released in 1400 to Maud (d. 1424) and in 1425 to her son Sir Alan Buxhall.[77] Sir Alan Buxhall in 1436 conveyed Wick in remainder to Thomas de Montagu, restored as earl of Salisbury, and his wife, to whom Thomas Buxhall quitclaimed Wick in 1445.[78] Thereafter the estate presumably followed the vicissitudes of the earldom of Salisbury, which passed in 1460 to Richard Neville, earl of Warwick (d. 1471), and, after forfeitures, was held by George, duke of Clarence, from 1472 to 1478 and by Edward, son of Richard, duke of Gloucester (afterwards Richard III), from 1478 to 1484.[79] Wick was granted, perhaps only briefly, by Edward IV to Sir John Risley (d. 1512),[80] to whom it was regranted by Henry VII. Risley left no sons and in 1513 the Crown granted it to William Compton of Chigwell (Essex),[81] although presumably it soon passed to Clarence's reinstated daughter Margaret, countess of Salisbury (d. 1541). Margaret sold the manor of Wick to William Bowyer, later knighted as lord mayor of London, in 1538, when she and her son Henry Pole, Lord Montague, quitclaimed 470 a., including marshland, in Hackney and Stepney.[82]

Sir William Bowyer, by will proved 1544, left Wick to his younger sons William and Henry, with remainders to his eldest son John and daughters Elizabeth and Agnes, all of whom were infants and illegitimate. His death was followed by almost 20 years of litigation involving Richard Shepherd, to whom he had leased the manor. William and Henry Bowyer both died without issue. Francis Chaloner, husband of Agnes Bowyer, obtained a judgement against the executors in 1563[83] but died before a further judgement was given in favour of Francis Bowyer (d. 1598), infant son of Sir William's eldest son John Bowyer of Histon (Cambs.) in 1566.[84] Lands in Hackney marsh were held in 1578 by Mr. Bowyer of the Wick.[85] Apparently the manor was not held by an older Francis Bowyer, an alderman (d. 1581), who bought other property in Hackney[86] which in 1603 was occupied by his son John.[87]

Benedict Haynes (d. 1611), who also held land

59 Newcourt, Rep. i. 618; Lysons, Environs, ii. 474.
60 Home Counties Mag. iii. 224.
61 G.L.R.O., M79/G/8/23/1.   62 Ibid. M79/G/4/1/1.
63 Ibid. M79/G/4/1/2, 10. For the rectors, below, parish church.
64 McDonnell, Medieval Lond. Suburbs, 24; H.A.D., D/F/TYS/40. Tenants of Grumbolds manor are indexed alphabetically in G.L.R.O., M79/G/1 (index to ct. bks. 1716–1841).
65 H.A.D., D/F/TYS/40; rate bks. at H.A.D. Robinson suggests that Urswick, as 'vicar', lived in the ch. ho., later the free sch.: Robinson, Hackney, i. 91.
66 P.R.O., STAC 2/26/465.
67 Robinson, Hackney, ii. 148; vestry mins. 12 Aug. 1622.
68 Home Counties Mag. iii. 224; below, parish church.
69 G.L.R.O., M79/G/4/2/1/1; below, local govt. (manorial).
70 At the Sun, by 1762 at the Mermaid: G.L.R.O., M79/G/4/1/1–2, 10.   71 H.A.D., D/F/TYS/22.
72 e.g. Robinson, Hackney, ii. 147; below, parish church.
73 The grant was probably made after 1161: Rec. of

Templars, ed. Lees, pp. xc–xci, 165–6; Cal. of Cartularies of John Pyel and Adam Francis, ed. S.J. O'Connor (Camd. 5th ser. ii), 203–4.   74 Rec. of Templars, 166.
75 Cart. of Adam Francis, 49, 203–18; Beaven, Aldermen, i. 381, 383; McDonnell, Med. Lond. Suburbs, 159; Complete Peerage, xi. 392–3.   76 Cal. Inq. p.m. vii, pp. 11–12.
77 Cal. Close, 1399–1402, 153; 1422–9, 166.
78 Complete Peerage, xi. 395; Cat. Anct. D. vi, C 4104; Cal. Close, 1441–7, 348.
79 Complete Peerage, xi. 397–9.
80 Hist. Parl., Commons, 1439–1509, Biographies, 718.
81 L. & P. Hen. VIII, i (1), p. 759.
82 P.R.O., CP 25(2)/27/183, no. 19.
83 Ibid. PROB 11/30 (P.C.C. 11 Pynnyng); McDonnell, Med. Lond. Suburbs, 159; Hist. Parl., Commons, 1509–58, i. 477.   84 P.R.O., C 78/35/26; V.C.H. Cambs. ix. 95.
85 S.J.C.F., 'Note of Meadows in Hackney, 1578'.
86 P.R.O., PROB 11/63 (P.C.C. 27 Darcy).
87 Ibid. PROB 11/110 (P.C.C. 64 Huddlestone, will of Eliz. Bowyer).

in Surrey, had probably acquired Wick by 1602, when he was assessed in Hackney.[88] As a manor with 90 a. in Hackney and Stepney, formerly held of the Hospitallers and of the Crown, it was to be sold by the executors of his eldest son Henry Haynes (d. 1627).[89] In 1633 Thomas Haynes surrendered it to John Bayliffe,[90] a lawyer who lived in Hackney and who in 1642 vested it in his son-in-law Oliver Clobery (d. 1649)[91] and other creditors. Despite claims by representatives of the Haynes family and by Bayliffe's son William, Clobery's son Henry obtained possession in 1662 and left Wick by will proved 1665 to Abraham Johnson, his father's executor.[92] Abraham by will dated 1674 left it to his son Edward Johnson, who resisted renewed claims and in 1690 sold it to Edward Ambrose.

The Wick estate was conveyed in 1753 by Edward Woodcock to Joseph Barbaroux[93] and consisted of c. 112 a. in 1763, when Barbaroux sold it.[94] Most of it was bought back by Woodcock, a lawyer, who in 1776 acquired a copyhold parcel from John Mann.[95] The estate passed to Woodcock's son Edward (d. 1792), vicar of Watford (Herts.),[96] on the death of whose widow Hannah in 1796 it was sold to William Gilbee,[97] who held what was still described as the manor in 1809.[98] The estate belonged to a Capt. Gilbee in 1831 and was thought to remain in his family in 1842.[99] It may have been divided like the copyhold, which passed to William Gilbee's sons William and James in 1831, when the younger William sold his interest to the speculator William Bradshaw.[1] James was admitted to his share of the copyhold in 1838.[2] Catherine Habershon and Isabella Seymour were James's heirs in 1864 and surrendered to Mary Anne Bradshaw in 1866.[3]

A chief house existed in 1566[4] and 1627[5] and probably in 1399 when Richard Grey, a scion of the Barons Grey of Rotherfield (Oxon.), made his will at the Wick in Hackney.[6] A later house was said to have been built by John Bayliffe[7] and presumably was Henry Clobery's, which had 20 hearths in 1664, when it stood empty.[8] The Wick (Wyke) or Hackney Wick House was shown

mistakenly on the west side of Wick Lane in 1745[9] and on the east side, with pleasure grounds called the Islands covering c. 12 a., in 1763.[10] Joseph Barbaroux apparently lived there,[11] but the mansion and its grounds, with a mill house and field to the north, were not included in the sale of 1763 to Woodcock.[12] Wick House in 1809 was on lease with c. 32 a. from Gilbee to the astronomer and physicist Mark Beaufoy, who made a balloon ascent from Hackney Wick and left in 1815.[13] Apparently rebuilt after 1760, it was later rendered and given a new porch before serving as Wick Hall collegiate school from 1841. Wick Hall made way for Gainsborough Square c. 1862, when two other buildings on the estate, one a cottage possibly incorporating Bayliffe's house and the other called Manor Farm, were also demolished.[14]

The reputed manor of *SHOREDITCH PLACE*, later held by *ST. THOMAS'S HOSPITAL*, probably originated in lands accumulated by Sir John of Shoreditch (d. 1345), baron of the Exchequer, and his wife Ellen[15] and by his brother Nicholas of Shoreditch, a London citizen.[16] In 1324 Richard of Norton, a citizen, and his wife Maud conveyed to Sir John and Ellen first a house, 55 a., and rents in Hackney[17] and secondly a capital messuage called De La Grave, which Maud and her previous husband John Borewell had bought in 1319 from John of Bodley.[18] Sir John thereafter acquired several smaller properties in Hackney, as did Nicholas of Shoreditch[19] (d. by 1358).[20] The Hospitallers in 1349 granted Nicholas a building and adjacent places called Beaulieu in Hackney, which had been held by John of Banbury,[21] recorded from 1321.[22] John, son of Nicholas of Shoreditch, was active in Hackney until the 1380s.[23] Payments at the Stepney courts were made for Hackney lands of William de Ver in 1384 and of John Shoreditch, formerly of William de Ver, in 1405, suggesting that de Ver's Domesday holding may have lain in Hackney.[24] Elizabeth Shoreditch held lands late of John Shoreditch in 1412,[25] and John's grandson John received lands in Hackney and Ickenham in 1422.[26]

88 C.G. Paget, *Croydon Homes of the Past* (1937), 63–4; *V.C.H. Surr.* iii. 264; H.A.D., D/F/TYS/1.
89 P.R.O., PROB 11/155, f. 145; ibid. WARD 5/26, no. 5.
90 Robinson, *Hackney*, i. 320. Rest of para. based on Paget, *Croydon Homes*, 64–5.
91 Vestry mins. 8 Apr. 1634 et seq.; P.R.O., PROB 11/210 (P.C.C. 171 Fairfax).
92 P.R.O., PROB 11/316 (1665, f. 42).
93 M.L.R. 1763/1/230.   94 Ibid.; H.A.D. 3594.
95 G.L.R.O., M79/KH/6, p. 86. The copyhold is traceable to 1679: ibid. KH/1, pp. 114, 121.
96 H.A.D., V 140; *Cal. Inner Temple Rec.* v. 183; *Alum. Cantab. 1752–1900*, 565.
97 *Gent. Mag.* lxvi (2), 611; Robinson, *Hackney*, i. 321; G.L.R.O., M79/KH/6, pp. 313, 333.
98 H.A.D., V 28.
99 *Starling's Map* (1831); Robinson, *Hackney*, i. 321.
1 G.L.R.O., M79/KH/8, pp. 381–2; ibid. KH/9, p. 65; Watson, *Gentlemen*, 53.
2 G.L.R.O., M79/KH/10, p. 55.
3 Ibid. KH/14, pp. 389, 434, 443.
4 P.R.O., C 78/35/26.
5 Ibid. PROB 11/155, f. 145.
6 Guildhall MS. 9171/1, f. 434r.; *Complete Peerage*, vi. 149.   7 H.A.D., D/F/TYS/12/2, p. 49.
8 G.L.R.O., MR/TH/4, m. 1d.
9 Rocque, *Map of Lond.* (1741–5), sheet 3.

10 H.A.D., M 3594.
11 Ibid. H/LD 7/2, pp. 24, 39; H/LD 7/3, p. 39.
12 Ibid. M 3594.
13 Ibid. V 28; *D.N.B.*; Clarke, *Hackney*, 163, 292 n.
14 Clarke, *Hackney*, 162–3; H.A.D., P 12047–8; inf. from H.A.D.; below, educ. (private schs). Sidney Ho., on the W. side of what became Sidney (later Kenworthy) Road, was also called Wick Ho. in the early 19th cent.: Clarke, *Hackney*, 160; H.A.D., card index to illus.
15 *D.N.B.*
16 F. G. Parsons, *Hist. of St. Thos.'s Hosp.* i. (1932), 217; *T.L.M.A.S.* xxxvii. 149–51.
17 P.R.O., CP 25(1)/149/51, no. 311.
18 G.L.R.O., H1/ST/E65/C/1/1/8; H1/ST/E65/C/1/1/13.
19 Ibid. H1/ST/E65/C/1/1/1–26; H1/ST/E67/1; P.R.O., CP 25(1)/149/52, nos. 325, 342, 347; *Ft. of F. Lond. & Mdx.* i. 112–13, 115–16.
20 *Ft. of F. Lond. & Mdx.* i. 136; *V.C.H. Mdx.* iv. 102.
21 B.L. Cott. MS. Nero E. VI, f. 66.
22 *Ft. of F. Lond. & Mdx.* i. 100, 113.
23 *Cal. Close, 1364–8*, 192; *1377–81*, 335; *1381–5*, 247; G.L.R.O., H1/ST/E67/1.
24 Guildhall MSS. 10312/136, 25370.
25 *Feud. Aids*, vi. 488.
26 *T.L.M.A.S.* xxxvii. 152. Geneal. of Shoreditch fam. in ibid. 150 corrects that in H. Ellis, *Hist. Par. Shoreditch* (1798), 93.

Robert Shoreditch in 1452–3 successfully claimed lands in Chelsea and Hackney which had been held by his father John[27] and in 1473 leased 21 a. in Hackney to Simon Elrington.[28] In 1478, on his son George's betrothal to Elizabeth Tey or Taye, Robert promised to make a settlement out of his other Hackney lands,[29] including the Grove house which was presumably the capital messuage called De La Grave. Between 1487 and 1491 George Shoreditch conveyed most of the lands to Henry and John Tey, who allowed him to hold the Grove house for life, and to John's son William.[30] In 1488 George also quit-claimed 43 a. to John Elrington.[31] William Tey had recently held 100 a. in Hackney and Shoreditch in 1504–5, when quit rents were paid to the Hospitallers and the bishop of London.[32]

William Tey of Colchester in 1513 surrendered a house and c. 147 a. in Hackney and Tottenham, formerly the Shoreditches', to the executors of Henry VII[33] and in 1517 the bishop of London licensed their transfer from the executors to the hospital of the Savoy,[34] founded in 1505 and endowed under Henry's will.[35] The Savoy's estates included the manor of Shoreditch Place otherwise Ingilroweshold in 1535[36] and 61 a. in London Field with a toft called Barber's Barn, held of the Hospitallers, in 1539.[37] On the Savoy's dissolution in 1553 the manor was among the lands granted to the corporation of London for the royal hospitals of Christ, Bridewell, and St. Thomas, Southwark.[38]

Shoreditch Place, surveyed in 1560, may by then have been assigned to St. Thomas's hospital. It was estimated to contain 148 a. in 1560,[39] c. 107 a. in 1608,[40] 121 a. in 1628, when the lands lay mainly in blocks south of Well Street, south of Morning Lane, and at Upper Clapton,[41] as in 1697,[42] and 129½ a. in 1741.[43] Leases were made of the whole estate in the 17th century, often for 21 years.[44] Sir Thomas Player secured an extension in 1671 in return for having rebuilt the bowling green house. In 1720, after the expiry of a lease granted in 1697,[45] separate leases were negotiated directly with the undertenants.[46] The hospital leased most of its lands to builders from

the mid 19th century[47] and received more than 700 ground rents in south Hackney, besides many in Clapton, in 1931.[48] Only a small area, between the west side of Mare Street and the railway, was retained in 1990, when the hospital's trustees drew rents and held the reversion of ground rents on premises in Mare Street and Richmond Road.[49]

The capital messuage called De La Grave[50] was presumably the Grove house recorded in the later 14th and 15th centuries[51] and the 'manor place' which had two barns, two stables, and a dovehouse in 1504–5.[52] In 1612 the hospital's tenant William Cross was to rebuild the manor house in brick.[53] In 1628 it was formally depicted as a castellated building of five bays, with a yard on the west, an orchard, and gardens on the east of over 4 a.; it was approached by a drive (the modern Shore Road) running south from Well Street[54] and in the mid 17th century by Tryon's Place (later Tudor Road) from Mare Street. Nothing substantiates the tradition, recorded in 1720, that Edward IV's mistress Jane Shore lived there.[55]

The tenant in 1647 claimed that his improvements included brick garden walls;[56] the battlements on the house succumbed to storm damage c. 1661.[57] By 1720, when it was let annually with only 1 a. besides the garden, the house was in bad repair.[58] It was called Shoreditch House in 1697[59] and Shore Place (a name also applied to the immediate neighbourhood), or more commonly Shore House, in the 18th century.[60] Three storeys and five projecting bays were depicted c. 1730[61] and a brick wing had been added to the north by 1740.[62] Recorded but not named c. 1745,[63] the house disappeared soon after the grant of a building lease to a London speculator, Thomas Flight, in 1768. Flight's buildings in 1770 included a house subleased to Gedaliah Gatfield and later known as Shore House, on part of the garden south and east of the site.[64] Remains of c. 1320 and later were excavated in the garden of no. 18 Shore Road in 1978.[65]

The reputed manor of *HOXTON* or *BALMES*[66]

27 P.R.O., C 1/22/105.
28 G.L.R.O., H1/ST/E67/1/80.
29 Ibid. H1/ST/E65/C/1/1/27.
30 Ibid. H1/ST/E67/1/124; H1/ST/E 67/1/133.
31 B.L. Add. Ch. 15632.
32 G.L.R.O., H1/ST/E39/1.
33 P.R.O., CP 25(2)/27/178, no. 23; G.L.R.O., H1/ST/E67/1/51, 81.
34 Newcourt, *Rep.* i. 697.
35 *V.C.H. Lond.* i. 546.
36 *Valor Eccl.* (Rec. Com.), i. 358. 'Ingilroweshold' may have been a corruption of 'in Groves hold'; cf. *T.L.M.A.S.* xxxvii. 152.
37 P.R.O., SC 6/Hen. VIII/2402, m. 13.
38 *Cal. Pat.* 1553, 283–4; E. M. McInnes, *St. Thos.'s Hosp.* (1963), 24.
39 G.L.R.O., H1/ST/E103/1.
40 Ibid. H1/ST/E103/2.
41 Ibid. H1/ST/E103/3 [survey]; E114/2 [map].
42 Ibid. H1/ST/E39/2.
43 Ibid. H1/ST/E103/10.
44 e.g. ibid. H1/ST/E103/2; H1/ST/E67/3/30; H1/ST/E57. Tenants of the hosp. are listed in *T.L.M.A.S.* xxxvii. 157.
45 G.L.R.O., H1/ST/E57; H1/ST/E67/1/170; H1/ST/E67/15/8.   46 Ibid. H1/ST/E39/3.
47 Ibid. H1/ST/E114/9 [maps 1848]; Watson, *Gentlemen*,

70–4, 107.
48 Parsons, *St. Thos's. Hosp.* 217.
49 Inf. from est. manager, Special Trustees for St. Thomas's Hosp.
50 G.L.R.O., H2/ST/E65/C/1/1/8.
51 *T.L.M.A.S.* xxxvii. 151–2.
52 G.L.R.O., H1/ST/E39/1. The manor ho. has sometimes been identified with Beaulieu, e.g. Lysons, *Environs*, ii. 458.
53 G.L.R.O., H1/ST/E67/3/30.
54 Ibid. H1/ST/E103/3; H1/ST/E114/2; Watson, *Gentlemen*, 18.
55 Stow, *Survey*, ed. Strype, ii. 123; *T.L.M.A.S.* xxxvii. 152.
56 G.L.R.O., H1/ST/E57.
57 *T.L.M.A.S.* xxxvii. 153–4.
58 G.L.R.O., H1/ST/E103/9.
59 Ibid. H1/ST/E39/2.
60 Watson, *Gentlemen*, 25; G.L.R.O., H1/ST/E39/3; ibid. E103/10.
61 Below, plate 10; Shore Pl. is also a road on the Shore est.   62 *T.L.M.A.S.* xxxvii. 156.
63 Rocque, *Map of Lond.* (1742–5), sheet 6.
64 Watson, *Gentlemen*, 26; *T.L.M.A.S.* xxxvii. 157.
65 *T.L.M.A.S.* xxxvii. 158–85.
66 Para. based on L.C.C. *Survey of Lond.* viii (St. Leonard, Shoreditch), 4, 79–80.

lay north of the modern district called Hoxton
and from 1697 wholly within the south-western
corner of Hackney, where previously the parish
boundary with Shoreditch had been uncertain.
In 1351 Sir John of Aspley (d. 1355) leased out
all his manor of Hoxton in Hackney,[67] which
apparently Robert of Aspley had bought from
John and Maud Birtecurte in 1305–6, when it
consisted of a house, mill, 167 ½ a., and rents in
Hackney and elsewhere. Sir John's widow Elizabeth
sold the manor, leased for 10 years to St. Mary's
hospital, to John of Stodeye and others in 1372.[68]
John of Stodeye (d. 1376), mayor of London,
held land which came to his son-in-law Sir John
Philpot (d. 1384),[69] mayor of London, who in
1365 had received land in Stepney and Hackney
which had fallen to the Crown as creditor of
John Marreys and in 1375 more property from
Sir John at Hale and his wife Ellen.[70] By will
proved 1389 Philpot left all his lands to his
widow Margaret for life; the lands formerly of
John of Stodeye and the manor of Hulls in Mile
End were then to pass to his daughter and her
intended husband John at Hale and a place called
Hoxton was left to his sons Thomas and Edward.[71]

The Hoxton estate probably gained the name
Balmes from Adam Bamme (d. 1397), mayor of
London, who married Sir John Philpot's
widow.[72] Margaret had rents in Hackney of £6
13s. 4d. in 1412.[73] Sir John's descendant John
Philpot of Compton (Hants) (d. 1484)[74] left the
'manors' of Hoxton and Mile End, held of the
bishop of London for 12s. and 17s. respectively,
to his son John (d. 1502),[75] whose son Peter in
1510 claimed livery of lands which included the
manor of Hoxton 'otherwise called Bams', valued
at £16.[76] As the manor of Balmes, the estate
passed from Sir Peter Philpot (d. 1540) to his
sons Henry (d.s.p. 1567) and Thomas (d. 1586),
Thomas's son Sir George (d. 1624), and Sir
George's son Sir John, who in 1634 sold it to
Sir William Whitmore of Apley (Salop). Balmes
then consisted of a house, a cottage, two gardens,
an orchard, and 153 a. in Hackney, Shoreditch,
and Tottenham.[77]

Sir William Whitmore's father William, a
haberdasher, had held a lease of Balmes at his
death in 1593.[78] Sir William's purchase in 1634

was on behalf of his younger brother Sir George
(d. 1654), the royalist lord mayor, who received
Charles I at Balmes in 1641.[79] The estate was
sequestrated and in 1644 leased for three years
to Thomas Richardson,[80] but restored on Sir
George's discharge in 1651.[81] It passed to Sir
George's son William (d. 1678) and to William's
son William (d. 1684), on whose death under age
it was sold in 1687 to Richard de Beauvoir,
formerly of Guernsey.[82]

Richard de Beauvoir (d. 1708) was presumably
resident, since his memorial tablet was placed in
the church.[83] His son Osmond Beauvoir or de
Beauvoir (d. 1757) bought an estate at Downham
(Essex),[84] where he lived and was followed by
his youngest son the Revd. Peter (d.s.p. 1821),
the last sinecure rector of Hackney.[85] The Balmes
estate passed to Richard Benyon of Englefield
House (Berks.), grandson of Francis John
Tyssen's sister Mary Benyon and great-grandson
of Richard de Beauvoir's daughter Rachel, wife
of Francis Tyssen (d. 1717). For Benyon, who
assumed the surname Benyon de Beauvoir in
1822,[86] the Balmes estate comprising c. 150 a.
west of Kingsland Road was, after 10 years of
litigation with the developer William Rhodes (d.
1843), built up as De Beauvoir Town.[87] Richard
Benyon de Beauvoir was succeeded in 1854 by
his nephew Richard Fellowes (d. 1897), who
took the name Benyon and was succeeded by his
own nephew James Herbert Benyon (d. 1935) of
Englefield House.[88] In 1950, when owned by
Herbert Benyon, the estate had contracted since
1935;[89] it still embraced 20 wharves, a public
house, and property in 17 roads in 1992.[90]

Balmes House, built according to tradition by
two Spanish merchants and named after them
in the 1540s,[91] bore a name used in 1510[92] and
occupied a moated site. It stood on the present
De Beauvoir Road, midway between the canal
and Downham Road,[93] and was said to have had
a single entrance, by a drawbridge from the
south, until the late 18th century,[94] although in
1707 water was shown only as bounding its
pleasure grounds to the north and west. The
building depicted in 1707[95] has been attributed
to work done for Sir George Whitmore c. 1635[96]
and was assessed at 28 hearths in 1664 and

[67] Cal. Close, 1349–54, 477, 481.
[68] Ibid. 1369–74, 450–1.
[69] Beaven, Aldermen, i. 205; D.N.B. (s.v. Philipot).
[70] Cal. Pat. 1364–7, 365; P.R.O., CP 25(1)/151/74, no. 526.
[71] Cal. of Wills in Ct. of Husting, ii (1), 276; cf. Year Bk. 13 Ric. II, pp. xxxiii–xxxiv, 122; C.L.R.O., HR 118(30). Hulls may have been the property received from Sir John at Hale.
[72] S. L. Thrupp, Merchant Class of Medieval Lond. (1968), 322.   [73] Feud. Aids, vi. 489.
[74] Archaeologia Cantiana, lx. 24. Sir John's grandson John in 1433 acquired W. Twyford by exchange with Adam Bamme's son Ric.: Hist. Parl., Commons, 1439–1509, Biographies, 682; V.C.H. Mdx. vii. 174.
[75] H.A.D., D/F/TYS 70/5 ('Balmes Papers').
[76] Survey of Lond. viii. 80; P.R.O., E40/12856.
[77] H.A.D., D/F/TYS 70/5; P.R.O., C 142/64, no. 152; C 142/191, no. 85. Cf. descent in V.C.H. Hants, iii. 407.
[78] P.R.O., PROB 11/82 (P.C.C. 60 Neville). The est. was therefore probably not held by the Welds, as in Robinson, Hackney, i. 158; cf. Burke, Commoners, ii (1830), 409–10.
[79] Survey of Lond. viii. 80; D.N.B.
[80] Cal. Cttee. for Advance of Money, i. 120.

[81] Cal. Cttee. for Compounding, iv. 2890.
[82] Robinson, Hackney, i. 163; Survey of Lond. viii. 4; P.R.O., PROB 11/377, f.106; G.L.R.O., E/BVR/7.
[83] Vestry mins. 23 Apr. 1687; 19 Feb. 1694; 1 Oct. 1711; Stow, Survey (1720), ii, app. p.128.
[84] P. Morant, Hist. Essex, i (1768), 205.
[85] Robinson, Hackney, i. 177 and table facing p. 322; Hennessy, Nov. Rep. 177. De Beauvoirs often acted as trustees for Tyssens, e.g. P.R.O., PROB 11/1082, f.454; H.A.D., D/F/RHO/2/1–2.
[86] Robinson, Hackney, table facing p. 322; V.C.H. Essex. v. 208; Gent. Mag. xcii (2), 378.
[87] Robinson, Hackney, i. 163; The Times, 1 Nov. 1834, 6e; 3, 4, 12, 13 Nov.; 17 Nov., 3f–4b (judgement). Also in H.A.D., H/LD 7/3; ibid., D/F/TYS/59/1–3 (reps. of De Beauvoir v. Rhodes).   [88] Burke, Land. Gent. (1952), 162.
[89] G.L.R.O., E/BVR/174; cf. ibid. E/BVR/273.
[90] Inf. from Mr. W. R. Benyon, M.P.
[91] Robinson, Hackney, i. 154.
[92] Survey of Lond. viii. 80.   [93] Clarke, Hackney, 301.
[94] Robinson, Hackney, i. 156.
[95] Below, plate 2. Only the W. side of the moat is marked on Rocque, Map of Lond. (1741–5), sheet 6.
[96] Archit. Rev. cxxi. 445–6.

1672.[97] It was of brick and two-storeyed, with a steep roof containing two sets of dormers; the main front had five bays, separated by giant pilasters which were uncommon at that date and perhaps unique in England in that they were paired. A shallow two-storeyed projection to the east may have survived from an older house, as apparently did some early Jacobean woodwork in the 19th century. The house stood in formal gardens, with a gatehouse immediately to the south and farm buildings in the south-east corner; lines of trees stretched beyond and formed an avenue,[98] later called Balmes Walk, from the gatehouse to Hoxton. The avenue was re-planted and the entrance gate replaced c. 1794,[99] when Balmes served as a lunatic asylum.[1] Streets had been planned on all sides by 1831,[2] housing reached the gates by 1842,[3] and the mansion was demolished soon after 1852,[4] when it was recorded as 'one of our earliest specimens of brick-work and of the Italian school of architecture'.[5]

Sir John Heron of Shacklewell, formerly treasurer of the king's chamber,[6] by will dated 1522 left to his eldest son Giles, a minor, land including copyholds in Shacklewell, Kingsland, and Newington, which presumably formed the bulk of the reputed manor of *SHACKLEWELL*; a second son Edmund was to have a house at Hackney, with a close and all the Church field.[7] Sir John's widow was the most highly assessed parishioner for the subsidy in 1524.[8] Giles Heron entered parliament in 1529, when he married Cecily, daughter of Sir Thomas More. He disputed lands in Hackney with his brother Christopher in 1534 and was executed for treason in 1540.[9] His forfeited Shacklewell estate, including a 'manor or mansion' held of the bishop of London, was then in the hands of Sir Ralph Sadler,[10] to whom it was granted for 21 years in 1543.[11]

Sir Ralph, whose father Henry Sadler had recently bought a house in Hackney in 1521, was later said to be the richest commoner in England and also held Kingshold. He may have acquired Shacklewell to protect the Herons' interests: Giles's infant sons appealed to Sadler in 1540, when two of Giles's brothers were described as Sadler's servants.[12] In 1551 the bishop of London was licensed to convey his rights in the house and other lands lately occupied by Giles Heron to Lord Wentworth.[13] Thomas, Giles's elder

son, was restored in 1554 but sold Shacklewell to Alderman Thomas Rowe in 1566.[14]

Rowe, a merchant tailor, was knighted as lord mayor in 1569.[15] He had bought land in Hackney in 1550, 70 a. from Thomas Colshill and another 70 a. from Edward Pate,[16] and in 1557 30 a., called Mayfield and Broadleas, from Thomas Elrington.[17] He apparently lived at Shacklewell and in 1570[18] was succeeded by his son Sir Henry (d. 1612), who also became lord mayor.[19] Sir Henry left to his son Henry, later knighted and an alderman, the house at Shacklewell with 18 a. adjoining and other freehold and copyhold parcels in Hackney; land in Tottenham and Edmonton went to a second son Thomas.[20] The younger Sir Henry (d. 1661) built the Rowe chapel[21] and possibly was related to the regicide Col. Owen Rowe (d. 1661), who sometimes attended the vestry with him and was buried at Hackney.[22] Sir Henry was succeeded at Shacklewell by his grandson Henry Rowe (d. 1670),[23] whose son Henry sold most of the family's freehold estate in 1685 to Francis Tyssen (d. 1699),[24] who complained about its encumbrances[25] and who by 1697 was described as of Shacklewell.[26] The Rowes, who had given up their pew in Hackney church by 1690, left their chapel to be disputed between the vestry and a more prosperous branch of the family at Muswell Hill.[27] Henry Rowe returned to Hackney in 1706 to seek parish relief, which he received, exempted from wearing a pauper's badge in 1710, until 1711.[28]

Sir John Heron had a house at Shacklewell,[29] presumably the 'ancient manor house' recorded in 1720. It was then a three-storeyed brick building, with tall sash windows and a pair of Dutch gables and glass displaying the arms of the Rowes.[30] The house was assessed at 25 hearths in 1664[31] and 1672.[32] It was occupied by Francis Tyssen (d. 1710) and his son Francis (d. 1717)[33] and came to be called the manor house.[34] In 1743 Richard Tillesley, a Shoreditch carpenter, assigned his lease of the house and grounds to Charles Everard, a Clerkenwell brewer. By 1762 the house had gone and 12 new houses occupied the grounds of 3 a.[35] west of Shacklewell green. Ancient gate piers survived in 1824, when a second manor house stood closer to the road; it made way for Seal Street c. 1880.[36]

97 G.L.R.O., MR/TH/4, m. 4; MR/TH/34.
98 *Archit. Rev.* cxxi. 445–6; *Lost Hackney*, 34–5; below, plates 2 and 19.
99 Lysons, *Environs*, ii. 488 and illus.; Robinson, *Hackney*, i. 154–6 and illus.   1 Below, pub. svces.
2 *Starling's Map* (1831).
3 Robinson, *Hackney*, i. 155.
4 Clarke, *Hackney*, 301; H.A.D., H/LD 7/11 (undated cutting).
5 *Illus. Lond. News*, 5 June 1852; watercolours in Brit. Mus. and H.A.D.   6 *L. & P. Hen. VIII*, i (1), p. 276.
7 P.R.O., PROB 11/21 (P.C.C. 33 Bodfelde).
8 Ibid. E 179/141/116, m. 1.
9 *Hist. Parl., Commons*, 1509–58, ii. 350.
10 B.L. Add. MS. 35824, f. 28b.
11 *L. & P. Hen. VIII*, xviii (1), p. 284.
12 *Hist. Parl., Commons*, 1509–58, ii. 350; iii. 249; Slavin, *Sir Ralph Sadler*, 4, 8–12, 138–9, 201.
13 *Cal. Pat.* 1550–3, 50.
14 Ibid. 1553–4, 472; 1563–6, 417.
15 *Visit. Mdx.* (Harl. Soc. lxv), 8; Beaven, *Aldermen,* ii. 35.   16 P.R.O., CP 25(2)/61/474, nos. 36, 57.

17 Ibid. CP 25(2)/74/630, no. 54.
18 Ibid. PROB 11/52 (P.C.C. 29 Lyon).
19 Beaven, *Aldermen,* ii. 41, 46; cf. *V.C.H. Mdx.* vi. 144.
20 P.R.O., PROB 11/120 (P.C.C. 96 Fenner).
21 Below, parish church.
22 Vestry mins. 12 May 1650; 24 Aug. 1657; *D.N.B.*
23 P.R.O., PROB 11/308, f. 101.
24 G.L.R.O., M79/LH/47, 3 Apr. 1684, 25 Aug. 1687.
25 P.R.O., C 8/525/106.
26 Robinson, *Hackney*, i. 116; G.L.R.O., M79/LH/113.
27 Vestry mins. 9 Apr. 1690, 17 May 1692; below, parish church.
28 Vestry mins. 10 Oct. 1706; 14 June 1710; 3 Apr. 1711.
29 P.R.O., PROB 11/21 (P.C.C. 33 Bodfelde).
30 Stow, *Survey of Lond.* ii, app. 1, p. 123; below, plate 11.   31 G.L.R.O., MR/TH/4, m. 3d.
32 Ibid. MR/TH/34.
33 Stow, *Survey of Lond.* ii, app. 1, p. 123.
34 Robinson, *Hackney*, i. 116.
35 H.A.D., M 517; Lysons, *Environs*, ii. 459.
36 H.A.D., M 752; M 3230, pp. 22, 96; Old O.S. Map Lond. 30 (1868); *Lost Hackney*, 33.

The hospital of St. Mary without Bishopsgate[37] in 1535 received c. £80 a year from its Middlesex estate, derived almost equally from a manor called *HICKMANS* and from *BURGANES* lands in Hackney, Stepney, and Shoreditch.[38] It had a rent in Hackney in 1232.[39] John of Banbury gave 33 a. in Hackney and Enfield for a chantry in 1338 and a further 28 a. in Hackney in 1349. The prior acquired other lands in Hackney, Stepney, and Shoreditch in 1349, including 24 a. from Nicholas of Shoreditch,[40] and in 1362;[41] he was allowed to retain 60 a. in Hackney, which had been held without licence, in 1363.[42] More land in the three parishes was acquired in 1376.[43] By 1412 the prior had lands worth £10 in Hackney.[44] In 1507 cottages in Church Street, held of Hackney rectory, were seized for non-payment of rent over 20 years.[45]

The estate in 1540 included London Field of c. 100 a. and parcels in the other common fields and marsh, many of which had been leased out shortly before the hospital's suppression in 1538.[46] Royal grantees of the divided estate included Francis Jobson in 1544 (followed by William Beryff in 1545),[47] Sir Ralph Warren, alderman, who secured Burganes lands in 1544–5,[48] and Sir Thomas Darcy, who received London Field in 1546.[49] Robert Heneage, an officer in the court of Augmentations and brother of Sir Thomas (d. 1553), bought some of the lands and had sold c. 27 a. to Alexander Avenon by 1551[50] and a further 25 a. in 1553.[51] Avenon, knighted as lord mayor of London, settled his Hackney lands in trust in 1570.[52] His son or grandson Alexander held c. 40 a. in Hackney as a minor in 1594[53] and conveyed c. 25 a. to Sir Robert Lee (d. 1605), a former lord mayor, in 1604.[54] Seven a. which Lee leased in 1605 to Ralph Treswell included a new house where Treswell lived.[55]

Sir Robert Lee[56] bought land in Suffolk and was succeeded by his son Sir Henry Lee (d. 1620)[57] who left the reversion of Burganes land to his son Sir John, a minor.[58] Middlesex property was disputed between Sir John's three daughters and his infant grandson Thomas Lee in 1674.[59] Presumably it passed to Baptist Lee of Ipswich, who by will proved 1768[60] left his property in and around London to his late niece's husband Nathaniel Acton (d. 1795) for life, with remainder to Nathaniel's son, who was to take the name Nathaniel Lee Acton.[61]

In 1836 Nathaniel Lee Acton was succeeded by his sisters Caroline Acton and Harriot (d. 1852), widow of Sir William Middleton, Bt. (d. 1829), of Shrubland Park (E. Suff.).[62] Harriot's son and heir Sir William Fowle Fowle Middleton, Bt. (d. 1860), was succeeded by his sister Sarah, wife of Adm. Sir George Nathaniel Broke, Bt. (d. 1887) (later Broke-Middleton), who was also childless. The Middlesex estates were entailed in favour of Sir William's great-niece Jane Broke, from 1882 wife of James Saumarez, Baron de Saumarez (d. 1937). Lady de Saumarez (d. 1933)[63] sold her Hackney property by auction in 1921.

The estate, c. 95 a. in 1777[64], lay mainly in Shoreditch. A field near Kingsland Road stretched into Hackney, south and west of the later Middleton and Queensbridge roads, and a separate piece of land stretched from Mare Street to the south end of the later Eleanor Road, bordering London Fields;[65] another detached portion lay in Bethnal Green. In 1838 Sir W. F. F. Middleton bought part of the former Spurstowe estate with a view to extending development northward along the entire length of Eleanor Road.[66] An Act of 1808 had removed a restriction of leases to 21 years, under Baptist Lee's and other wills, permitting building leases of up to 99 years.[67] In Hackney planned development began along Middleton Road in 1840 and was facilitated by agreements and some exchanges of land, mainly with the Rhodes family, from 1843.

The estate centred on *CLAPTON HOUSE* originated in acquisitions by the Woods, a Lancashire family of courtiers. Thomas Wood (d. 1649), Serjeant of the Pantry, lived in Hackney in 1597 and in 1627,[68] when he became a vestryman.[69] He left the 'manor house' where he dwelt to his eldest son Sir Henry (d. 1671), treasurer to Queen Henrietta Maria and a baronet, whose heir was apparently his brother Thomas (d. 1692), bishop of Lichfield and Coventry.[70] The bishop, who had been admitted to copyholds of c. 15 a. at Clapton in 1651,[71] normally lived in Hackney. Subject to provision for his almshouses, he left all his lands to his nephew Henry

37 *V.C.H. Lond.* i. 531.
38 *Valor Eccl.* (Rec. Com.), i. 400.
39 P.R.O., CP 25(1)/146/8, no. 87.
40 *Cal. Pat.* 1338–40, 14; 1349–50, 363.
41 P.R.O., CP 25(1)/151/69, no. 401.
42 *Cal. Close,* 1360–4, 470.
43 *Cal. Pat.* 1374–7, 388.
44 *Feud. Aids,* vi. 487; *V.C.H. Mdx.* v. 331.
45 H.A.D., D/F/TYS/40.
46 P.R.O., SC 6/Hen. VIII/2396, mm. 79d.–8or., 93.
47 *L. & P. Hen. VIII,* xix (1), p. 625; xx (1), p. 661.
48 Ibid. xix (2), p. 75; xx (2), p. 329; xxi (1), p. 351.
49 Ibid. xxi (1), p. 764.
50 W.C. Richardson, *Hist. Ct. of Augmentations* (1961), 352 n.; P.R.O., SC 6/Hen. VIII/2396, m. 93d.; G.L.R.O., M79/LH/83.   51 *Cal. Pat.* 1553–4, 361.
52 G.L.R.O., M79/LH/86.
53 Ibid. LH/88.
54 Ibid. LH/90; Beaven, *Aldermen,* ii. 45.
55 H.A.D., M 505 (i). Part of Avenon's land was held in 1707 by John Woodfield: ibid. M 935.
56 Three paras. based on inf. and TS. notes from Isobel Watson.

57 Beaven, *Aldermen,* ii. 53, 177; W. A. Copinger, *Manors of Suff.* i (1905), 129; P.R.O., PROB 11/108, no. 137; PROB 11/135, no. 87. The wills do not mention Hackney lands.
58 P.R.O., WARD 5/25, no. 5; WARD 5/27, no. 6.
59 Ibid. C 7/544/69.
60 P.R.O., PROB 11/938, no. 168.
61 Ibid. PROB 11/1260, no. 107; 19 Geo. III, c. 21 (Priv. Act).
62 P.R.O., PROB 11/1858, no. 262; *Hist. Parl., Commons,* 1754–90, iii. 137; *Gent. Mag.* cxxxi. 436.
63 Burke, *Peerage* (1949).
64 H.A.D., M 530.
65 *Starling's Map* (1831).
66 Below (Spurstowe's ho.); G.L.R.O., M79/KH/12, pp. 296, 325.
67 48 Geo. III, c. 123 (Local and Personal).
68 Robinson, *Hackney,* i. 429.
69 Vestry mins. 14 Oct. 1627.
70 *Hist. Parl., Commons,* 1660–90, iii. 755; P.R.O., PROB 11/212, f. 85; G.E.C. *Baronetage,* iii. 18; J. R. Woodhead, *Rulers of Lond. 1660–89* (1965), 173.
71 P.R.O., PROB 11/212, f. 85; G.L.R.O., M79/LH/49, 15 June 1720.

Webb (d. 1713).[72] In 1720 the estate was divided between Charles, son of the bishop's sister Mary Cranmer, Henry's daughters Elizabeth and Anne Webb, and the four daughters of Henry's elder brother Thomas Webb, including Elizabeth, wife of Sir William Chapman, Bt.[73] Chapman soon acquired the shares of the others in Hackney but as a result of the failure of the South Sea Co. they were sold in 1723 to a Huguenot silk merchant René de Boyville (d. by 1743).[74] René's widow Louise sold the mansion house in 1749 to a gem merchant Jacob de Moses Franco, who had paid rates in Hackney since 1736.[75] Jacob, whose younger brother Joseph also held copyholds in Clapton,[76] bought more copyholds[77] and by will proved 1777 left his Clapton estate to his grandson Jacob Franco.[78] The grandson by will dated 1780 left it to his brother David, afterwards Francis, Franco of Great Amwell (Herts.),[79] who acquired the copyholds which had been left by Joseph to a nephew Raphael Franco and who sold his enlarged estate of c. 22 a. in 1799 to James Powell.[80]

James Powell (d. 1824), a wine merchant,[81] was the youngest son of David Powell (d. 1784), scion of a Suffolk family who had prospered in London in partnership with James Baden and who had bought and perhaps remodelled the later Byland House.[82] He may have been related to James Powell, a vintner who had held land in Hackney since 1718 and whose sons James and Joshua succeeded in 1765.[83] James Powell (d. 1824) built up a substantial estate between 1785 and 1821 by purchases from, among others, F. J. Tyssen's trustees, the Revd. Benjamin Newcome's heirs, and the earl of Warwick.[84] He also inherited the Suffolk lands of his brother Baden (d. 1802) and bought Newick Park (E. Suss.) in 1809. Most of the lands went to James's son Thos. Baden Powell (d. 1868), rector of Newick, whose heirs disposed of them piecemeal.[85]

Some of James's purchases in Clapton went to his elder daughter Hester,[86] wife of her cousin Baden Powell (d. 1844) of Langton Green (Kent), who in 1798 enlarged his estate at Stamford Hill;[87] he was father of the Revd. Baden Powell (d. 1860), Savilian professor of geometry,[88] and

grandfather of Robert, Baron Baden-Powell (d. 1941), founder of the Boy Scouts. A younger brother of Baden was James Powell (d. 1840), who bought the Whitefriars glass works and in 1839, when described as of Shore Place,[89] took a lease of Clapton House from the Revd. T. B. Powell, his cousin and brother-in-law. James was followed at Clapton House by his sons James Cotton Powell, the first incumbent of St. James's, and Arthur, who continued the glass firm, until c. 1851.[90] Other purchases of James Powell (d. 1824) went to his daughter Anne, wife of the Revd. Robert Marriott.[91] They passed to Anne's heir the Revd. James Powell Goulton Constable, whose estate included Noble's nursery, Cromwell Lodge, and five other large houses when it was auctioned in 1882.[92]

The Woods' house, which Thomas probably inherited rather than built,[93] stood on the east side of Lower Clapton Road. It was assessed at 14 hearths in 1672, as when Bishop Wood lived there.[94] It was called the bishop's mansion for over a century, Lizhards or Leezhards (a name that is unexplained) in 1749, and Clapton House in 1799.[95] Improvements 'nearly equal to rebuilding' were made for the lessee Israel Levin Salomons (d. 1788). Features included a marble paved hall, a library,[96] and, in the 5 a. of pleasure grounds, a structure resembling an orangery or banqueting room, which was built as a private synagogue.[97]

Tenants occupied the house in 1749 and 1799.[98] They always did so under James Powell (d. 1824), who lived in a house bought from the Tyssens on the west side of the road,[99] and his son, who leased Clapton House both as a residence and a school.[1] It stood empty in 1884, an imposing building of three storeys and attics; the road front, behind ornate iron gates, was of seven bays, separated by pilasters and with rustication at the corners, beneath a bold cornice. It was demolished c. 1885 to make way for Thistlewaite Road.[2] The neighbouring residence later called Byland House (no. 185 Lower Clapton Road), which bore David Powell's initials on a cistern of 1761, served as a vicarage for the second and third incumbents of St. James's, both of them related to the Revd. T. B. Powell. It passed to

[72] Clarke, *Hackney*, 93; P.R.O., PROB 11/410, f. 142; W. A. Copinger, *Manors of Suff.* ii (1908), 20; v (1909), 135; vii (1911), 256, 276; below, charities.
[73] G.L.R.O., M79/LH/49, 26 Apr. 1717; 15 June 1720; G.E.C. *Baronetage*, v. 53.
[74] G.L.R.O., M79/LH/49, 15 June 1720; 14 Apr. 1721; 7 Oct. 1723; M79/LH/51, 17 May 1743; *Jewish Hist. Soc. Trans.* xxx. 74.
[75] M.L.R. 1749/2/95–6; *Jewish Hist. Soc. Trans.* xxx. 74.
[76] P.R.O., PROB 11/1008, f. 229.
[77] G.L.R.O., M79/LH/13, pp. 87–94; M79/LH/14, p. 316.   [78] P.R.O., PROB 11/1033, f. 308.
[79] G.L.R.O., M79/LH/17, pp. 53–4, 113–14.
[80] Ibid. M79/LH/18, pp. 25–6, 104–5; H.A.D., D/F/BAG/5, pp. 31–4 (sales parts.); M.L.R. 1799/3/871.
[81] P.R.O., PROB 11/1325, f. 421 (will of Jas. Powell's father-in-law, Revd. Thos. Cornthwaite).
[82] *Home Counties Mag.* iii. 144; E. Powell, *Pedigree of the Fam. of Powell* (1891), chart; P.R.O., PROB 11/1113, no. 96; Copinger, *Manors of Suff.* i. 387, 391; H.A.D., D/F/BAG/8, pp. 7, 12; below, this section.
[83] G.L.R.O., M79/LH/49, 18 Apr. 1718; M79/LH/14, p. 336; H.A.D., P/J/P/76, p. 2.
[84] G.L.R.O., M79/LH/17, p. 47; M79/LH/18, p. 142; M79/LH/19, pp. 299–301; M.L.R. 1789/3/362, 1819/6/33–4, 1821/5/125–6. Jas. Powell described all his acquisitions in a

memo., copy among notes on Powell fam. in H.A.D., D/F/BAG/13A.
[85] *Home Counties Mag.* iii. 144; P.R.O., PROB 11/1683, no. 173; below, this section.
[86] P.R.O., PROB 11/1683, no. 173. Geneal. details in following para. from tables in H.A.D., D/F/BAG/13A.
[87] Powell, *Powell Fam.* 28–9; G.L.R.O., M79/LH/18, p. 153.
[88] *D.N.B.*
[89] H.A.D., D/F/BAG/13A.
[90] Ibid.; below, list of churches.
[91] P.R.O., PROB 11/1683, no. 173.
[92] H.A.D., M 3548.   [93] Ibid. D/F/BAG/5, p. 24.
[94] G.L.R.O., MR/TH/34.
[95] M.L.R. 1749/2/95; 1799/3/871.
[96] H.A.D., D/F/BAG/5, p. 32 (sales parts.); *Jewish Hist. Soc. Trans.* xxxi. 193–4.
[97] H.A.D., D/F/BAG/13A (memo. by Jas. Powell); *Jewish Hist. Soc. Trans.* xxx. 75; xxxi. 194–5; *Lost Hackney*, 39; below, Judaism.
[98] M.L.R. 1749/2/95; 1799/3/871.
[99] H.A.D., D/F/BAG/13A (memo. by Jas. Powell).
[1] Ibid. D/F/BAG/5, pp. 26–7, 38, 52 (prospectus); D/F/BAG/13A; *Lost Hackney*, 38 (litho. from earlier prospectus); below, educ. (private schs).
[2] *Lost Hackney*, 39; *Hackney Photos.* i. 44.

his younger son James David (d. 1919), whose trustees sold it to Hackney council in 1932.[3]

The compact estate of the *NORRIS* family began with purchases by Hugh Norris (d. 1661), the scion of a Somerset family who became an alderman and treasurer of the Levant Co. In 1653 he bought a large house and 31 a. in Hackney[4] from Edward Misselden (d. 1654), another London merchant.[5] The land, enfranchised by Richard Blackwell in 1654 but later treated as copyhold of Lordshold manor,[6] lay partly in Broomfield and the marsh but mainly on the east side of Grove Street in the middle field of Well Street common.[7] It passed to Hugh's eldest son Hugh (d. 1693)[8] and then to the younger Hugh's children Hugh, Henry, and Hester, whose shares by agreements of 1709 and 1715 were reunited under Henry (d. 1762).[9] Thereafter it descended in a direct line to Henry Norris (d. 1790),[10] to Henry Handley Norris (d. 1804), a Russia merchant,[11] and to Henry Handley Norris (d. 1850), rector of South Hackney. The rector's son Henry Norris (d. 1889) of Swalcliffe Park (Oxon.)[12] managed the estate from 1843, when it contained *c.* 34 a.[13] The land was enfranchised in 1853[14] and built over in the 1860s.[15] Most of the freeholds were sold by Henry Everard Du Cane Norris in the 1920s and 1930s.[16]

Hugh Norris (d. 1661) and his son lived in Hackney.[17] Henry Norris (d. 1762) leased his Hackney residence in 1725 but resumed possession after four years.[18] Henry Norris (d. 1790) moved to Essex, leasing the Hackney house rebuilt by his father,[19] but both Henry Handley Norris (d. 1804) and his son the rector lived in Hackney.[20] The last resident Norris was the rector's widow Henrietta Catherine (d. 1854).[21]

The Norrises' house, on the east side of Grove Street, was a large rambling structure in 1725,[22] when it was drawn by William Stukeley as 'a model of our ancient way of building'. Ornate plasterwork adorned a long range of two storeys, with an attic and north and south wings towards the road; two stair turrets, their jettied upper floors forming polygonal pavilions, were in the style used at Nonsuch Palace, begun in 1538.[23] Henry Norris replaced it with a more compact house, commissioned in 1729 and finished in 1730, designed probably by James

Shephard, a London builder, with three storeys over a basement; the main front was of five bays, with a central Doric porch.[24] The house, with well stocked gardens, was leased to Paul Amsinck, a London merchant, in 1761[25] and, after serving as Henry Handley Norris's rectory, made way in the 1860s for the west end of Penshurst Road.[26]

The copyhold land of the *CASS* estate, enfranchised in 1770[27] for the trustees of the Sir John Cass Foundation, formed the largest estate in southern Hackney in 1843.[28] Most of it came from Henry Monger, who acquired part through marriage to Bridget, daughter of William Swayne (d. 1649).[29] Parcels of Swayne's land had been in varied ownership in the late 15th and 16th centuries: they included land in Well Street common field recorded from 1442[30] and land in Grove Street sold by William Leigh to John Bowes in 1535, by John's son Jeremy to Arthur Dericote, a draper, in 1557, and by Arthur's son Thomas to William Swayne's uncle and namesake in 1599.[31]

Monger, by will proved 1669, founded almshouses in Well Street and divided the residue of his estate between his son-in-law Thomas Chamberlain, Joan, widow of William Martin, and his maidservants Hester and Alice Eames.[32] By surrenders from 1673 and by Joan Martin's will, proved 1681, *c.* 75 a. passed to Hester (d. 1681) and her husband Thomas Cass, carpenter to the Royal Ordnance. They descended in 1699 to Thomas's son[33] John (d. 1718), later knighted as a Tory M.P. and alderman.[34]

Sir John died in Hackney, 'neither loving nor beloved in the parish'. His intention to establish schools in St. Botolph's, Aldgate, and in Hackney went unfulfilled with regard to Hackney, but after a Chancery decree the trustees of the Sir John Cass Foundation held his lands in Hackney and elsewhere, paying a rent charge towards Monger's almshouses. The Hackney estate, to which Sir John's widow Elizabeth (d. 1732)[35] was admitted in 1719,[36] was estimated in 1817 at *c.* 87 a. around Grove Street, east of Well Street, and in the north and south fields of Well Street common; another *c.* 13 a. lay in Bethnal Green, and *c.* 50 a. in the marsh.[37] The trustees, like the governors of St. Thomas's hospital, were

3   H.A.D., D/F/BAG/8, pp. 7, 12.
4   Ibid. D/F/NOR/1/1/1–3; Burke, *Land. Gent.* (1952), 1898; Woodhead, *Rulers of Lond.* 122.
5   *D.N.B.*
6   H.A.D., D/F/NOR/1/2/1.
7   Ibid. D/F/NOR/1/1/2; Watson, *Gentlemen*, 10 (map), 17, 19.
8   H.A.D., D/F/NOR/1/1/8–9; J. Nicholl, *Hist. Ironmongers' Co.* (1851), 369.
9   H.A.D., D/F/NOR/1/1/18, 1/2/6; *Gent. Mag.* xxxii. 294; G.L.R.O., M79/LH/14, pp. 274–7.
10   G.L.R.O., M79/LH/17, pp. 228–31; *Gent. Mag.* lx (2), 674.
11   G.L.R.O., M79/LH/19, pp. 204–6; *Gent. Mag.* lxxiv (1), 482; *Alum. Cantab. 1752–1900*, 563.
12   Burke, *Land. Gent.* (1952), 1898; *V.C.H. Oxon.* x. 231.
13   Watson, *Gentlemen*, 20, 41, 85; G.L.R.O., H1/ST/E114/5/1.
14   G.L.R.O., M79/LH/26, pp. 400–405.
15   Watson, *Gentlemen*, 86, 90.
16   H.A.D., D/F/NOR/6/2–7.
17   P.R.O., PROB 11/306, f. 188; PROB 11/414, f. 56.
18   H.A.D., D/F/NOR/4/4; below, this section.
19   Ibid. D/F/NOR/4/10; *Gent. Mag.* lx (2), 674.
20   *Gent. Mag.* lxxiv (1), 482; *D.N.B.*
21   Watson, *Gentlemen*, 85.
22   H.A.D., D/F/NOR/4/4; below, educ. (private schs.).
23   *T.L.M.A.S.* xxii (1), 28–9; above, plate 12.
24   H.A.D., D/F/NOR/3/1 (inc. elevation and plan). 'A very early example of a highly developed form of bldg. contract': Watson, *Gentlemen*, 116.
25   H.A.D., D/F/NOR/4/10.
26   Watson, *Gentlemen*, 18–19, 90. The ho. was still marked in Stanford, *Map of Lond.* (1862–5 edn.), sheet 8.
27   G.L.R.O., M79/LH/15, pp. 387–90.
28   Watson, *Gentlemen*, 10, 17–20.
29   *Visit. Lond.* (Harl. Soc. xvii), 106.
30   S.J.C.F., 1A/1/D61–70.
31   Ibid. unlisted deeds; vestry mins. 11 Apr. 1619; 3 June 1627.   32   P.R.O., PROB 11/330, f. 96.
33   *T.L.M.A.S.* viii. 246–7; P.R.O., PROB 11/368, f. 143. Thos. Cass's accumulations of copyholds in G.L.R.O., M79/LH/47.   34   *D.N.B.*
35   *T.L.M.A.S.* viii. 248–52; below, charities.
36   G.L.R.O., M79/LH/49, 3 Apr. 1719.
37   S.J.C.F., survey (1817).

for long concerned chiefly with letting the lands in the largest possible segments. Joseph Sureties, a local farmer, took nearly 70 a. from Well Street towards Hackney Wick in 1765 and was followed by William Gigney from 1786; the land thus came to be known as Sureties's or Gigney's farm. Development was attempted by Gigney and from 1790 by underlessees of James Jackson, but systematic building was possible only from 1847 on the expiry of Gigney's lease.[38] The Cass Foundation held c. 73 a. in Hackney, excluding lands in the marsh, in 1843, when the land in Bethnal Green was about to be sold to the Crown for Victoria Park. Building in the 1850s and 1860s[39] produced an income which permitted the establishment of the Sir John Cass technical institute.[40]

The extent of the estate changed little until after the Second World War. It contained 1,178 separate leases in 1957.[41] By 1964 large tracts on either side of Bentham Road had been taken for the municipal Wyke estate and some sites had been sold near Victoria Park in Redruth and Rutland roads.[42] Later sales included bombed sites in Danesdale Road near Hackney Wick and Hackney Terrace.[43] In 1976 the bulk, in Cassland, Victoria Park, and adjoining roads, was leased to the World of Property Housing Trust (later the Sanctuary Housing Association).[44] By 1990 the Cass Foundation retained a few other isolated parcels in Hackney, including a supermarket leased to Tesco Stores in Well Street.[45]

Buildings acquired by Cass included a cottage in Grove Street of 1516–17 and another of 1519–20, besides a house with a curtilage which Leigh had sold to John Bowes by 1539–40.[46] The first cottage was probably among lands granted to Thomas Wood in 1618[47] and one of two houses held in 1658 by Henry Monger, whose other house may have been that of Bowes, later of the Dericotes.[48] One of Monger's houses was the largest near Grove Street, assessed at 18 hearths, in 1664.[49] He leased a house called the George, on the west side of Grove Street (later the southern end of Lauriston Road), in 1664[50] and left another house, occupied by Edward English, to Hester Eames in 1669.[51] Thomas Cass leased English's house in 1694[52] and lived in one on the site of the George, as did his son

Sir John. Both houses were capital messuages in 1699, as was a third which had passed from Monger to Cass; English's house was described as on the east side of Grove Street and the third house as on the west in 1699 but vice versa in 1719.[53] Sir John's widow leased his former residence, with its furnishings, to Henry Norris in 1722.[54] It stood empty in 1770, when English's house was occupied by the Huguenot merchant Peter Thelluson (d.1797).[55] The trustees' property on the west side of Grove Street was leased to their surveyor Jesse Gibson in 1779.[56] By 1807 Gibson had replaced Cass's dilapidated seat with two houses, one of them later Grove House school, whose name was to be appropriated for a school at Common House.[57]

Members of the Rhodes family were active as brickmakers and land speculators in the late 18th and early 19th centuries. William Rhodes (d. 1769), from Cheshire, bought land in St. Pancras and was succeeded by his son Thomas (d. 1787),[58] who occupied most of Balmes farm by 1773.[59] Thomas's son Samuel Rhodes (d. 1794) in 1775 held 97 a. of the Hackney House estate[60] and had formerly held c. 22 a. near the Rosemary Branch.[61] As Samuel Rhodes of Balmes, yeoman, he was granted leases by the Revd. Peter de Beauvoir of c. 10 a. of Balmes farm with power to dig brickearth in 1785[62] and of the farmhouse which he already occupied near Balmes House, with over 40 a. near the Rosemary Branch, in 1789.[63] As Samuel Rhodes of Hoxton, farmer, he bought the lands of F. J. Tyssen's trustees east of Kingsland Road, including the Lamb inn[64] and all or part of London Fields farm,[65] in 1788–9. Those lands were later said to form the *LAMB FARM* estate of c. 140 a., stretching from behind the buildings along Kingsland Road eastward to London Fields, northward to Dalston Lane and Pigwell brook, and southward to the parish boundary.[66]

Samuel's property, in Hackney and elsewhere, was divided in 1795 between his sons Samuel Rhodes of Islington (d. 1822), Thomas (d. 1856), and William (d. 1843).[67] William, who failed to fulfil his plants for the Balmes House estate, had wharves in Haggerston[68] and acquired his brother Samuel's third part of the Hackney lands, which he shared with his brother Thomas.[69] The bulk of their estate, after a minor

38 Ibid.; Watson, *Gentlemen*, 23–4, 27–30, 35.
39 Watson, *Gentlemen*, 20–1, 35–6, 81–2, 93.
40 *Endowed Chars. Lond. V*, H.C. 181, p. 626 (1903), xlix.
41 G.L.R.O., AR/TP/2/386.
42 S.J.C.F., map (1850); ibid. photocopies of O.S. maps (from 1946).
43 Inf. from archivist, S.J.C.F.
44 S.J.C.F., deed.
45 Inf. from archivist.
46 S.J.C.F., unlisted deeds.
47 Ibid. 1A/1/D31.
48 Ibid. 1A/1/D91.
49 G.L.R.O., MR/TH/4, m. 2d.
50 S.J.C.F., 1A/1/D260.
51 P.R.O., PROB 11/330, f. 96.
52 S.J.C.F., 1A/1/D16.
53 G.L.R.O., M79/LH/47, 20 Oct. 1699; LH/48, 3 Apr. 1719.
54 S.J.C.F., 1A/1/D29 (inc. schedule of furnishings). A much larger seat, probably unconnected with Hackney, is illus. ibid. on cover of parts. of Cass trustees' holdings in Hackney marsh (1787).

55 G.L.R.O., M79/LH/15, p. 388.
56 S.J.C.F., survey (1817).
57 Ibid.; *Endowed Chars. Lond. I*, H.C. 394, pp. 362, 364 (1897), lxvi (2); below, educ. (private schs.). The first sch. was also the home of Geo. Offer, probably demolished in the 1860s: Clarke, *Hackney*, 172, 296 n. Another Grove Ho. was Braidwood's academy: below, pub. svces.
58 *D.N.B.*, s.v. Rhodes, Cecil; *Survey of Lond.* xxiv. 71. Dates for members of the fam., commemorated in Old St. Pancras ch., are from F. T. Cansick, *Epitaphs of Mdx.* i (1869), 49–51.
59 G.L.R.O., E/BVR/430.
60 H.A.D., V 31.
61 M.L.R. 1776/2/373.
62 Ibid. 1787/3/456.
63 Ibid. 1789/7/369. Lease renewed 1802: ibid. 1803/1/556.
64 Ibid. 1789/3/361.
65 Ibid. 1790/1/57 (also in H.A.D., D/F/RHO/2/1–2).
66 Ibid.; H.A.D., D/F/RHO/8, 3rd schedule; H.A.D., V 70; *Starling's Map* (1831).
67 H.A.D., D/F/RHO/1.
68 Above; *Holden's Triennial Dir.* (1802–4); *Robinson's Lond. Dir.* (1820); *Robson's Lond. Dir.* (1830, 1840).
69 H.A.D., D/F/RHO/2/3–4.

exchange with Sir William Middleton in 1843, passed to Thomas's grandson Thomas William Rhodes (d. 1885) of Flore (Northants.) and to William's sons William Arthur (d. 1856), whose chief legatee was Thomas William, and the Revd. Francis William (d. 1878). The Lamb Farm estate consisted of terraced housing stretching from Dalston Lane south to Albion Road (later Drive) and bounded east by Greenwood and Lansdowne roads in 1874–5, when it was divided between Thomas William, who received the north-eastern and south-western quarters, and Francis William, who received the other two quarters.[70] Fragmentation followed except in the north-west, where a block between Dalston Lane and Queen's (later Queensbridge) and Lenthall roads passed to Francis William, whose fifth son was the imperialist Cecil Rhodes (d. 1902).[71] Family trustees retained the property, mostly let on weekly tenancies, in 1939.[72]

A new farmhouse, which gave its name to the estate, stood in 1789 on the site of the Lamb inn.[73] Presumably it was reached from the high road both by a cartway which became Lamb Lane (later the west end of Forest Road) and by Swan Lane; it may have been the 'Old Lamb' marked east of Mayfield Road c. 1823.[74] A more central house, probably built by 1807 for James Grange, was reached from Swan Lane (later Grange, then Lenthall, Road) and, as a 'retired mansion' in walled grounds opposite St. Philip's church, was called Richmond Lodge in 1870.[75] None of the Rhodes family is known to have lived there: Thomas Rhodes (d. 1856) retired to Tottenham and his brother William (d. 1843) to Leyton (Essex).[76]

Sir Francis Bickley, Bt. (d. 1670), master of the Drapers' Company, was a Hackney vestryman from 1630.[77] He retired to Norfolk and in 1667 sold his copyhold estate of DALSTON, centred on BELDAMES (later called GRAHAM HOUSE) to Sir Stephen White (d. 1678), who left it to his cousin Stephen White (d. 1681). It passed to Stephen's son Thomas, of the Middle Temple, whose son Thomas was admitted in 1743 and conveyed it to James Graham in 1753.[78] James's son Sir Robert (d. 1836) was admitted to c. 35 a. in 1795.[79] Sir Robert, later a baron of the Exchequer, who first mortgaged the estate in 1797,[80] held in 1796 most of the houses which formed the hamlet of Dalston and c. 47 a. lying

mainly between Pigwell brook and Shacklewell Lane.[81] The estate passed to his sister Catherine Graham (d. 1840) and then to their niece Catherine Massie and her brother Henry George Massie, R.N. (d. by 1864). The Massies sold land for the railway and in the 1850s and 1860s on building leases for Graham Road and streets to the north.[82] The copyhold was enfranchised in 1864.[83]

A house assessed at 15 hearths was occupied in 1664 by Bickley[84] and later by Sir Stephen and Stephen White.[85] It was called Beldames in 1682 but not in 1743, when James Graham was already resident.[86] Probably it was the house in Dalston Road or Lane which was on lease with c. 2 a. to Mr. Pitt in 1796, opposite the later entrance to the German hospital.[87] By 1849 called Graham House and rebuilt,[88] it was inhabited in 1864 and 1880 by William Hodson, the speculative builder, and afterwards by convalescents from the hospital.[89] The three-storeyed stock-brick house of c. 1800, with a later stuccoed porch and single-storeyed addition, was an office of Circle Thirty Three housing trust at no. 113 Dalston Lane in 1992.[90] In the 1890s it was thought to have lost the eastern part of its grounds to a building called Manor House,[91] perhaps the residence of 13 hearths[92] to which Alderman Thomas Blackall (d. 1688) and his wife Mary, née Offspring, the parents of Offspring Blackall, bishop of Exeter (d. 1716), had been admitted in 1660; as a copyhold of Lordshold it passed to their son John Blackall in 1705 and may have been acquired by Thomas White.[93] Manor House, an old brick house let as lodgings by 1795 but not among the Grahams' copyholds in 1796, later served as Dalston Refuge for Destitute Females.[94]

Moses Keeling, a lawyer, and his wife Joanna were admitted in 1653 to copyholds of Lordshold manor, including TOWER PLACE with 11 a. and a further 30 a. or more. Joanna was the wife of John Pinchbeck in 1676; in addition she held freeholds to the west, abutting Cobb's (later Pratt's) Lane (later straightened as Glyn Road) and recorded in 1565. Her children John and Mary Keeling[95] sold the copyholds to Thomas Hussey in 1684. Hussey conveyed them in 1720 to Sir William Lewen (d. 1722), a former lord mayor, who was succeeded by his nephews George, Charles, and Robert Lewen.[96] All the shares passed after a dispute to George,[97] whose daughter Susanna married her kinsman Richard

70 Ibid. D/F/RHO/8, 27/2.   71 D.N.B.
72 H.A.D., D/F/RHO/27/3, 4.
73 Ibid. D/F/RHO/8, 3rd schedule. The inn apparently survived in 1788: M.L.R. 1789/3/361.
74 Ibid. D/F/TYS/59 (map, exhibit H in De Beauvoir v. Rhodes).
75 M.L.R. 1807/5/119; Starling's Map (1831); Clarke, Hackney, 240 and n.; H.A.D., V 70; Old O.S. Map Lond. 40 (1870).
76 H.A.D., D/F/RHO/4/1; W. Robinson, Hist. Tottenham, i (1840), 55; V.C.H. Essex, vi. 187.
77 G.E.C. Baronetage, iii. 230; vestry mins. 6 Jan. 1630 et seq.
78 P.R.O., PROB 11/358, no. 329; G.L.R.O., M79/LH/13, pp. 47–57; M79/LH/50, 12 April 1743; M93/90, pp. 102, 121, 124.
79 G.L.R.O., M79/LH/18, pp. 70–3; D.N.B.
80 G.L.R.O., M79/LH/18, pp. 73–4, 148–9, 374; M79/LH/19, pp. 1–3, 123–5, 128.
81 H.A.D., V 14.
82 G.L.R.O., M79/LH/26, pp. 273–4, 277, 282–3;

M79/LH/27, pp. 218–30; M79/LH/28, pp. 72–4; M79/LH/29, passim; Stanford, Map of Lond. (1862–5 edn.), sheet 7.   83 G.L.R.O., M79/LH/42.
84 Ibid. MR/TH/4, m. 4.
85 Ibid. MR/TH/34; P.R.O., PROB 11/367, f. 102.
86 G.L.R.O., M79/LH/50, 12 Apr. 1743.
87 H.A.D., V 14.
88 Hackney Dir. (1849); Old O.S. Map Lond. 40 (1870).
89 M.L.R. 1864/9/1012; P.O. Dir. Lond. Suburbs, North (1880); below, pub. svces.
90 Clarke, Hackney, 302; List of Bldgs. (1975).
91 Clarke, Hackney, 242–3.
92 G.L.R.O., MR/TH/4, m. 4.
93 Clarke, Hackney, 243; D.N.B. A crossed out entry referring to the Blackalls' property precedes a record of the admission of Thos. White: G.L.R.O., M79/LH/50, 12 Apr. 1743.
94 Lysons, Environs, ii. 463; H.A.D., V 14; above, social.
95 H.A.D., M 1553; M 1564; P.R.O., PROB 11/306 (P.C.C. 158 May).   96 G.L.R.O., M79/LH/49, 12 June 1723.
97 H.A.D., M 1560; M 1564.

Glyn (d. 1773), later lord mayor of London, a baronet, and co-founder of the bank of Glyn, Mills & Co.[98] In 1769 Sir Richard bought more land at Homerton from the heirs of the Marlowe family.[99] His son Sir George (d. 1814)[1] was admitted to Tower Place in 1763.[2] Col. Thomas Glyn (d. 1813), half-brother of Sir George, who conveyed the whole estate to him in 1803, granted leases from 1797. The colonel's son the Revd. Thomas Clayton Glyn (d. 1860) was succeeded by his eldest son Clayton William Feake Glyn (d. 1887).[3] T. C. Glyn in 1849 held 41 a. of copyhold land on the north side of Marsh Hill and Homerton Road, from the later Glyn Road to the Hackney cut, besides a field west of Brooksby's Walk and c. 23 a. of freehold. C. W. F. Glyn made leases from 1862, enfranchising the land in 1868 and 1880.[4]

An unnamed capital messuage on the north side of Homerton Street was recorded in 1565 and stood in 1649 and 1683 on the west corner of Cobb's Lane. It was claimed to have been freehold and may have been acquired separately from Tower Place. Tower Place was described in 1653 as near Hackney marsh and in 1797 was presumably represented by a rectangular moated enclosure of 2 a. 3 r. on the north side of the road at Marsh gate.[5] From its size it may have been one of the unidentified houses in Homerton occupied by a nobleman in 1605.[6] It was a ruin by 1684, when its site included a dovecot and a cottage.[7] The Moat House, shown as apparently inside the enclosure in 1849 but gone by 1870, was remembered in the 1890s as having been an 'old fashioned square built' residence.[8] The moat, visible in 1891, was about to be covered by Trehurst Road in 1910.[9]

Separate estates were held by two families named *ALVARES*, whose relationship has not been established. A copyhold house in Homerton Street was surrendered in 1624 with 10 a. by Rachel Denham and acquired in 1643 by Robert Johnson, whose daughters, including Elizabeth Carteret, were admitted in 1662.[10] Sir Edward Carteret sold it in 1674 to Isaac Alvares (d. 1684), a London jeweller, whose daughter Deborah and her husband David Alvares sold it to George Bonnett, cutler of London, in 1698.[11] Sarah, wife of Charles Milborne, was admitted under Bonnett's will in 1707. George Milborne (d. 1758) held Bonnett's house, two others on the south side of the high street with closes of 4 a., and

10 a. called Gill mead east of Wick Lane and south of Marsh Hill.[12] Bonnett's may have been the gabled house leased as a workhouse.[13] George Milborne's son Charles, like George, lived in Monmouthshire.[14] Under his will dated 1774 Charles's Marsh Hill estate, copyhold of Lordshold, was conveyed to his granddaughters Martha, Mary, and Elizabeth Swinnerton in 1812.[15]

Jacob Alvares the elder, otherwise Alvaro da Fonseca (d. 1742), in 1716 had gone from a burnt down house in Clapton and in 1717 was in Mare Street, where in 1730 he bought a capital messuage and 6 other copyhold houses for his great-grandson Isaac Jessurun Alvares. The residence, once Thomas Byfield's, had been left by a London mercer Thomas Blackmore to his grandson Raymond Blackmore by will dated 1708.[16] Isaac acquired neighbouring sites,[17] began building a house next to his own, and left copyholds by will proved 1809[18] to his illegitimate sons George Jenkins of Woodford (Essex) and Richard Jenkins and their mother Catherine (d. 1811). George replaced the main residence with small houses and by will proved 1846 left the 'Lamb Lane estate' to his widow Matilda and children, subject to provision for Richard's widow.[19] In 1852 Matilda Jenkins held property on either side of Pembroke House and stretching back to London Fields, containing 41 houses in Helmsley Street, Place, and Terrace; it included Melbourne Lodge asylum and West House, both leased to Dr. Williams.[20] Immediately to the south a house facing London Fields passed to Richard and in 1852 to Catherine Jenkins, who sold it to John Graves.[21]

Another Jewish family, that of the tobacco merchant Joshua Israel Brandon who came to Clapton in 1742,[22] likewise held property at Homerton and London Fields. Trustees under the will of his widow Esther (d. 1789) assigned quit rents for the Homerton residence to her son Jacob da Fonseca Brandon in 1832[23] and a nursery ground south of Exmouth Place was sold for his daughters Esther, Caroline, and Jesse Brandon in 1846.[24]

The estate of the *RYDER* family[25] originated in copyholds of Lordshold, Kingshold, and Grumbolds bought by Richard Ryder (d. 1733), a draper and member of the Skinners' Company. His father Dudley had perhaps been drawn to Hackney as the brother-in-law of the Congregationalist Robert Billio, William Bates's

98 *Hist. Parl., Commons*, 1754–90, ii. 505–6.
99 M.L.R. 1770/3/173.
1 Burke, *Peerage* (1890), 586.
2 G.L.R.O., M79/LH/14, pp. 267–73.
3 Ibid. M79/LH/19, pp. 100, 137; M79/LH/26, pp. 159–66 sqq.; Burke, *Peerage* (1890), 586.
4 G.L.R.O., M79/LH/26, pp. 127–33 (inc. plan); M79/LH/41.
5 H.A.D., M 1564; G.L.R.O., M79/LH/26, p. 166 (plan).
6 H.A.D., D/F/TYS/1, p. 66; above, Homerton.
7 G.L.R.O., M79/LH/49, 12 June 1723.
8 Ibid. M79/LH/26, p. 131; Old O.S. Map Lond. 41 (1870); Clarke, *Hackney*, 153.
9 Stanford, *Map of Lond.* (1891 edn.), sheet 8; Bacon, *Atlas of Lond.* (1910), sheet 40.
10 H.A.D., M 1463–5.
11 Ibid. M 944, 1196, 1198–9, 1205; P.R.O., PROB 11/375, f. 11; *Jewish Hist. Soc. Trans.* xxx. 71–3.
12 G.L.R.O., M79/LH/41; M79/LH/50, 3 Apr. 1730; *Gent.*

Mag. xxviii. 46.
13 Below, local govt. (par. govt.).
14 G.L.R.O., M79/LH/16, pp. 12–13; *Gent. Mag.* xlvi. 47.
15 H.A.D., V 3; G.L.R.O., M79/LH/20, pp. 32, 138; G.E.C. *Baronetage*, ii. 411.
16 *Jewish Hist. Soc. Trans.* xxx. 73–4, 76; P.R.O., PROB 11/722, f. 345; G.L.R.O., M79/LH/48, 29 Apr. 1709; M79/LH/50, 12 Aug. 1730.
17 G.L.R.O., M79/LH/17, p. 182.
18 P.R.O., PROB 11/1496, f. 326.
19 G.L.R.O., M79/LH/20, pp. 63–71, 176–9; M79/LH/27, pp. 96–7; P.R.O., PROB 11/2031, f. 117.
20 G.L.R.O., M79/LH/27, pp. 99, 100–1 (plan).
21 Ibid. pp. 37–8, 83–4.
22 *Jewish Hist. Soc. Trans.* xxx. 83.
23 G.L.R.O., M79/LH/23, pp. 61–6, 82.
24 Ibid. M79/LH/25, pp. 158 (plan), 253.
25 Fam. descent based on *Complete Peerage*, vi. 331–2; Burke, *Peerage* (1931), 1187–8.

1. Brickfields in Kingsland Road *c.* 1830

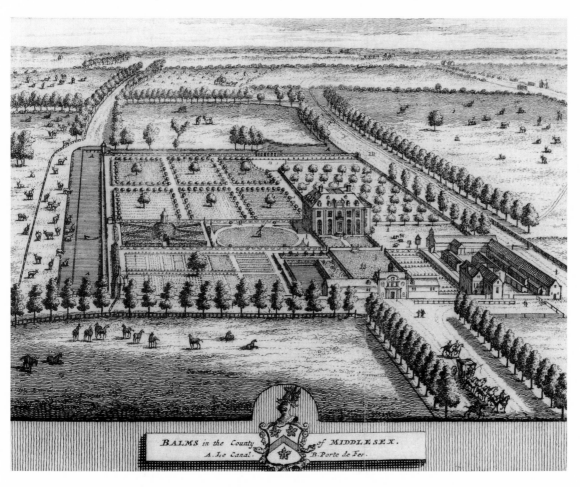

BALMS in the County of MIDDLESEX.
A. Le Canal. B. Porte de Fer.

2. Balmes House from the south in 1707

4. High Street, Homerton, the Plough range c. 1830

3. Spring Lane, looking east, c. 1840

6. The White House, Hackney Marsh, in 1885

5. Hackney Wick, looking south towards the ropeworks, c. 1825

7. The new Lea Bridge in 1821

8. Kingsland Road, looking south to Kingsland Crescent, in 1852

9. Church Street *c.* 1750, showing the ford across Hackney brook

10. Shore Place *c.* 1730

11. Shacklewell Manor House *c.* 1720

12. Norris's house, Grove Street, in 1725

13. Barber's Barn, Mare Street, *c.* 1800

14. The Templars' house, Church Street, *c.* 1800

15. Brooke House from the south-east in 1750

16. Brooke House from the east in 1844

17. Ward's house, Church Street, showing the junction with Dalston Lane *c.* 1830

18. Hackney House *c.* 1730

19. Balmes House *c.* 1825

22. Balloon ascent from the Mermaid's gardens in 1811

20. Assembly at the Mermaid in 1812

21. Boxing match between Mace and King at Hackney Wick in 1862

24. Chapman Road, nos. 86-100. Demolished early 1960s

26. Pond Lane *c.* 1891

23. Frampton Park Road, northward from no. 49. Demolished *c.* 1970

25. Cassland Road, nos. 20-54 (Hackney Terrace)

27. Beechwood Road, northward from no 17. Demolished 1960s

28. Lower Clapton Road, no. 162 (Pond House)

30. De Beauvoir Square, nos. 13 and 14

29. Laura Place, looking east from no. 13

31. Paragon Road and Trelawney estate tower

33. Amhurst Road, Evelyn Court flats

34. Morning Lane, from east. The former Berger's laboratory on the left

32. Gibson Gardens, Stoke Newington High Street, flats

35. The London Orphan Asylum in 1826

36. Hackney Town Hall, built in 1865, after extension

37. The French Hospital, built in 1865

38. Brick kilns at Upper Clapton *c.* 1830. Buccleuch Terrace in the background

39. Lea Bridge Mills *c.* 1845

40. Spill's Ivoride Works, High Street, Homerton, *c.* 1880

41. Matthew Rose's new store, Amhurst Road, in 1868

42. Berger's factory *c.* 1865. Ornamental water has been diverted from Hackney brook

43. Hackney Metropolitan Borough's electricity generating station, Millfields Road, in 1937.
The Hackney Cut is in the foreground.

44. The New Parish Church and Hackney Proprietary Grammar School *c.* 1840

45. The Old Parish Church, partly demolished, in 1798

46. West Hackney Church c. 1850

47. St James's Church, Lower Clapton Road, in 1841

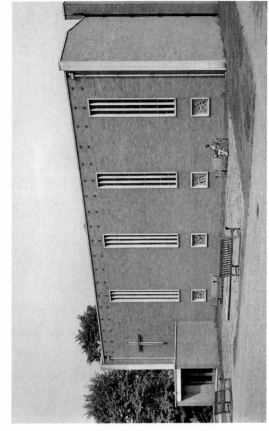

48. St. Matthew's Church Mount Pleasant Lane. Demolished 1974

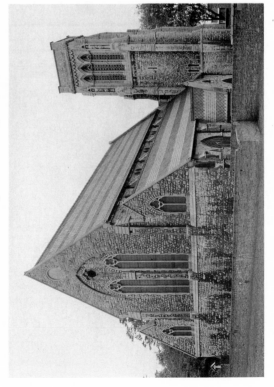

49. St. Paul's (West Hackney) Church, Stoke Newington Road

51. St. John of Jerusalem's Church in 1941

50. St. Mark's Church, Sandringham Road

53. Church of the Ark of the Covenant (Agapemonite), Rookwood Road

55. St Barnabas's Church, Shacklewell Row

52. St. Matthew's Church, Mount Pleasant Lane

54. Clapton Park Congregational Church (the 'Round Chapel')

57. The New Synagogue, Egerton Road

58. Mare Street Baptist Church. Demolished after 1945

56. Church of the Ark of the Covenant (Agapemonite), Rookwood Road

59. Clapton House School c. 1830. The former synagogue is on the right

60. Newcome's Academy (Hackney School) c. 1815

61. Hackney Free and Parochial Schools in 1886

62. Design for the Grocer's Company's School, 1857

64. Hackney Workhouse from the south c. 1830

66. The German Hospital, Ritson Road: extension at rear

63. Robinson's Retreat c. 1830, with the tomb of the founder

65. Monger's Almshouses in 1815, before rebuilding

successor.[26] Richard in 1704 bought some of Sir Thomas Cooke's property on behalf of his son Richard (d. by 1739), also a skinner. It included the later Upton House, the family home until 1721 of Sir Dudley Ryder (d. 1756), the judge and diarist.[27] The Ryders had built more houses at Homerton by 1717 and moved to Church Street, where property of Sir George Vyner's heirs, including the Black and White House, was added from 1706.[28]

Under the elder Richard Ryder's will his son Sir Dudley (d. 1756) received property at Homerton.[29] Sir Dudley's son Nathaniel, Baron Harrowby (d. 1803), made leases in 1757 and 1759 and sold 12 houses and the Plough in 1785.[30] The buyers included David Powell (d. 1810), elder brother of James (d. 1824), whose house was sold to Charles Rivaz in 1847.[31]

Meanwhile the younger Richard left all his Hackney lands to his widow Ann (née Lomax), who was admitted in 1740, with remainder to his son Lomax, who was admitted in 1759[32] and acquired more Vyner property in 1765.[33] Lomax Ryder (d. 1779) was succeeded by his brother Thomas (d. 1812), who was licensed to make leases for up to 61 years.[34] Thomas's heirs were the sons of Nathaniel Ryder, Baron Harrowby: Dudley, earl of Harrowby (d. 1847), Richard (d. 1832), and Henry, bishop of Lichfield and Coventry (d. 1836).[35] After the bishop's nine sons had been admitted in 1840 the eldest, Canon Henry Dudley Ryder (d. 1877), acquired the others' interests and also those of the earl's younger son Granville Dudley Ryder. Many leases were granted by the canon's sons Henry Dudley (d. 1904) and Lieut. Harry Lefevre (d. 1880), the first of whom acquired the interest of H. L. Ryder's widow Frances Elizabeth and left copyholds to his sister and four half-sisters.[36] In the 1840s the four houses of Ryder Place, together with Bohemia Place and Bell's Yard, formed the built-up corner along Church Street of land stretching from the churchyard across Hackney brook to Morning Lane.[37] Part, including Ryder Place, was sold to the E. & W. India Docks & Birmingham Junction Railway in 1847.[38] The canon's last surviving daughter Mary Emma Ryder paid compensation for enfranchisement of property in Chalgrove Road in 1931.[39]

Upton House, the home of Richard Ryder (d. 1733) but not apparently of his heirs,[40] was a three-storeyed brick building of the late 17th century, probably rebuilt in 1776–7. As no. 10

Upper Homerton and finally as no. 2 Urswick Road it became a truant school and was demolished c. 1885.[41]

William Spurstowe,[42] former vicar of Hackney, left to his brother Henry (d. 1677) part of his copyhold estate, comprising six houses and 7 a. and including SPURSTOWE'S HOUSE.[43] The estate passed to Henry's granddaughter Anne Spurstowe, whose husband William Skrine sold it in 1719 to Francis Douce (d. 1760), a physician,[44] who acquired more land to the west. Douce's nephew and namesake in 1761 sold a house and some land to the vestry clerk Richard Dann[45] and much of the estate including Spurstowe's house to Sir John Silvester, an army physician, who built five houses in the later Sylvester Road which he retained for his son John on selling the rest of the property to Dann in 1777.[46] Dann and his son Richard, who succeeded in 1800, took leases of adjoining lands. Executors in 1838 sold parts of Dann's estate to Sir William Middleton and parts to Samuel Nelme, a retired silversmith and already a tenant at no. 2 Grove Place, where he may have resided rather than in Spurstowe's house when murdered in 1847.[47] Other parts had been sold to Thomas Wilkinson, who also bought much of Nelme's property, although Spurstowe's house was sold with c. 6 a., as Nelme had agreed, to the E. & W. India Docks & Birmingham Junction Railway Co.[48]

Spurstowe's house was assessed at 16 hearths, the third highest in Church Street, in 1664.[49] It stood immediately south of the confluence of Pigwell and Hackney brooks, which fed ornamental canals in the 1720s, when the water's diversion led to litigation. The brooks formed the garden's northern boundary in 1761, by which date the canals had largely made way for less formal features.[50] Landscaping was continued by Silvester, who employed the young Conrad Loddiges and whose garden and parkland in 1777 included a Chinese bridge, soon to be broken down, a grotto, a Gothic hermitage, and five waterfalls. Silvester often resided at Bath[51] and may not have much altered the house, which presumably was built in the 17th century and was enlarged c. 1800 for the Danns. It was tenanted in 1838, called Park House in the 1840s, used as a home for Islington's pauper children from c. 1849 to 1855, and demolished by 1862, to be replaced by a terrace on the south side of Amhurst Road.

[26] Diary of Dudley Ryder, ed. Matthews, 3–4; below, prot. nonconf.
[27] H.A.D., LBH/C/A2/1 & 2; Terrier, Autumn 1993; below; D.N.B.
[28] M.L.R.   1717/2/170;   G.L.R.O.,   M79/LH/41; M79/KH/22; H.A.D., M 95–6; M 98–9.
[29] H.A.D., LBH/C/A2/8, 10–11.
[30] Ibid. 12–13, 17–18; M.L.R. 1785/2/609; Harrowby MSS. Trust, Sandon Hall, vol. 438, p. 63.
[31] H.A.D., LBH/C/A2/19–20, 29–30; Hackney Photos. i. 53.
[32] P.R.O., PROB 11/694, no. 153; G.L.R.O., M79/LH/50, 15 May 1740; M79/LH/14, p. 80.   [33] H.A.D., M 158(b).
[34] V.C.H. Herts. ii. 223; G.L.R.O., M79/LH/16, pp. 166–8.   [35] G.L.R.O., M79/LH/24, pp. 358, 375.
[36] Ibid. M79/LH/42; M79/KH/42.
[37] Starling's Map (1831); G.L.R.O., M79/KH/10, p. 337; H.A.D., V 9.   [38] G.L.R.O., M79/KH/12, pp. 289–309.

[39] Ibid. M79/KH/20, pp. 292–4.
[40] Ibid. M79/LH/14, p. 79; ibid. LBH/C/A2/1 & 2; Diary of Dudley Ryder, ed. Matthews, 30; P.R.O., PROB 11/694, no. 153; Hist. Parl., Commons, 1754–90, iii. 388–9.
[41] Hackney Photos. i. 52; below, educ. (special schs.).
[42] Two paras. based on Terrier, Winter 1991/2.
[43] Other parts were devoted to Spurstowe's charity or sold to the Tyssens. Below, charities.
[44] G.L.R.O., M79/KH/3, pp. 108, 124, 127. Douce was great-uncle of the antiquary Fras. Douce: D.N.B.
[45] G.L.R.O., M79/KH/5, p. 225.
[46] Ibid. M79/KH/9, p. 380.
[47] Ibid. M79/KH/10, p. 229; Clarke, Hackney, 52; The Times, 13 Nov. 1847, 8e; 19 Nov. 1847, 5d; 26 Nov. 1847, 5a.   [48] G.L.R.O., M79/KH/12, pp. 243–6 (inc. plan).
[49] Ibid. MR/TH/4, m. 2.   [50] H.A.D., M 3513.
[51] P.R.O., PROB 11/1185, f. 561.

ECONOMIC HISTORY

AGRICULTURE. Hackney was not mentioned in Domesday Book, which included most of it in the bishop of London's Stepney manor. Four hides in Stepney held by Robert Fafiton may have been the later manor of Kingshold and had land for 3 ploughs, of which Roger the sheriff had 1 hide, 2 villeins had 26 a., and an unspecified number of bordars had 3 virgates; there was woodland for 60 pigs.[52] Hackney (later Lordshold) manor was still administered with Stepney in 1318 and probably until after the Black Death. By 1386–7 separate account rolls signified the lord's policy of retaining a few meadows while leasing out the other lands piecemeal.[53] The total receipts of c. £142 for Hackney included £18 in fixed rents and £16 for parcels of the demesne let to 10 tenants, in some instances for five years.[54] Rents from the demesne, both arable and pasture, were higher in the 1390s than in the 1380s but much lower in the early 15th century; they were stable, totalling £12 16s. 8d., for much of the early 16th century.[55]

On the Templars' estate in 1185 the land given by William of Hastings had 13 tenants of whom eight held 5 a. apiece and paid 1s. 6d. rent and provided one man's labour for the hay harvest; tenants of 10 a. or ½ virgate paid and owed twice as much, and the single holder of a virgate twice as much again, from which figures a virgate has been estimated at 20 a. and a hide at 80 a. Similar services and slightly higher rents were owed on land given by Ailbrith. The customary works were all done on meadow land.[56] Mowing works survived in 1307–8 and, for the Hospitallers, in 1331.[57] On the bishop's manor commuted works were worth £23 17s. 6d. in 1386–7, when mowing and carting hay were among the expenses, and in 1464–5.[58] The Hospitallers complained in 1384 that their rights of free warren in Hackney had been infringed.[59]

Hay from the demesne was carted to Stepney for the bishop's use in 1386–7 and in 1464–5, when some was taken to London. Hay was also sold, while in the 1380s corn was bought.[60] Arable was rarely recorded: Wick manor supported 26 cattle and 4 horses in 1400[61] and pasture predominated on the Hospitallers' estate at the Dissolution.[62] By the early 17th century little arable apparently survived, other than in Hackney Downs, in the open fields which became known as the Lammas lands.[63]

Copyhold tenure was confirmed as gavelkind by an Act of 1623,[64] itself confirming a Chancery decree on the customs of Hackney and Stepney manors. The form of descent was division among a tenant's sons or, in default, his daughters, the youngest coheir to have first choice. It applied to named copyholders who had compounded with Thomas, Lord Wentworth (d. 1640), or his father, as did other benefits including the right to fell trees, dig the waste before their houses, let their buildings decay, or make leases for up to 31 years 4 months without licence.[65] Such subdivision and short leasing were to militate against substantial planned development on the north-east side of London.[66]

The demesne of Hackney manor in 1652 consisted of Scotland farm, c. 138 a., with another 30 a. south of Homerton, 6 a. abutting Millfield Lane, and 64 a. dispersed in the marsh. Nearly half of its value of £101 7s. came from fines, almost as much from quitrents, and £7 from fishing, which had been leased in the 1460s, and two ferries.[67]

Grass, whether for pasture or mowing, covered some three-quarters of the land subject to tithe in 1711, when 1,004 a. were 'upland' and 382 a. marsh. Apart from hay, the largest crops were oats on 146 a., peas on 106 a., barley on 86 a., wheat on 60 a., and rye on 26 a.; beans and potatoes took up 80 a.[68] Four ploughed fields stretched from the west end of Dalston Lane southward to the parish boundary and eastward from Kingsland Road to London Fields in 1745, when their depiction as the only arable was probably a simplification.[69] Arable was recorded in 1794 between Stoke Newington and Clapton and in 1800 in small patches in most parts of the parish and in Hackney Downs.[70]

In the 1790s the farms were occupied mainly by cowkeepers, who bred few animals but fed c. 600 on rich grass.[71] Hackney had 1,570 a. of grass, including the marsh, and 580 a. of arable in 1811.[72] The titheable land included 1,062 a. of grass and 154 a. of arable in 1842,[73] when there had been some recent reversion to arable on Hackney Downs and pasturage rights had been infringed by delays in moving crops.[74] Agriculture was said to employ only 49 of the 3,125

52 *V.C.H. Mdx.* i. 128.
53 McDonnell, *Medieval Lond. Suburbs*, 35–6. Acct. rolls, with gaps, are for 1386–7 to 1422, 1438–9, 1465–6, and 1468–9: P.R.O., SC 6/915/29–32; SC 6/1093/17; SC 6/1139/1–12; SC 6/1140/24.   54 P.R.O., SC 6/1139/1.
55 P. J. Taylor, 'Estates of Bishopric of Lond. from 7th to early 16th cent.' (Lond. Univ. Ph.D. thesis, 1976), 321, 341–2.
56 *Rec. of Templars*, ed. Lees, pp. xciv–xcv, 16–17; *T.L.M.A.S.* xiii. 229–33; above, manors (Kingshold).
57 *T.L.M.A.S.* xiii. 232; B.L. Cott. MS. Nero E. VI, f. 66v.
58 P.R.O., SC 6/1139/1; SC 6/1140/24, m. 2.
59 *Cal. Pat.* 1381–5, 496, 601.
60 P.R.O., SC 6/1139/1–2; SC 6/1140/24, m. 2 and d.
61 *Cal. Inq. Misc.* vii, p. 45.
62 P.R.O., SC 6/Hen. VIII/2402; (Eng. translation in

G.L.R.O., M 79/KH/42/1/3).
63 Vestry mins. 7 July 1605; *Terrier*, Spring 1988; H.A.D., H/LD 7/2, pp. 144–5, 241–3.
64 21 Jas. I, c. 6 (Priv. Act); cf. *Statutes of the Realm*, iv, p. lxxiv..   65 Robinson, *Hackney*, i. 354–408.
66 N. G. Brett-James, *Growth of Stuart Lond.* (1935), 110.
67 Robinson, *Hackney*, i. 409–40; P.R.O., SC 6/1140/24, m. 2d.; cf. H.A.D., M 1279.
68 G.L.R.O., M79/LH/44.
69 Rocque, *Map of Lond.* (1741–5), sheets 3–6.
70 Middleton, *View*, frontispiece map; T. Milne, *Land Use Map of Lond.* (1800) (Lond. Topog. Soc. 1975–6).
71 Foot, *Agric. of Mdx.* 80; Middleton, *View*, 330–1.
72 Lysons, *Environs*, Suppl. 163.
73 H.A.D., tithe award.
74 Robinson, *Hackney*, i. 76.

families in 1811, compared with 838 in trade or industry, but 582 families out of 6,307 in 1831.[75]

The extensive commonable lands of the parish, on which landholders enjoyed rights of pasturage from 1 August (Lammas rights), comprised Hackney Downs, London Fields, Well Street common, North and South Mill Fields, and most notably Hackney marsh. The regulation of Lammas rights chiefly concerned the marsh, where in 1185 the *humbra* or marshy meadow was distinguished from the *quabba* or bog.[76] Hackneymead was an alternative name for Hackney marsh in 1535.[77] Annual appointments of manorial drivers and the lord's charge for impounding were confirmed in the Act of 1623,[78] after intrusions by newcomers. In 1804 no records could be found of the extent of the lands or of the vestry's right to permit encroachment.[79] The lord's ancient scale of rights, allowing from three head of cattle for parishioners' holdings rented at £10–£15 a year to an unlimited number for those worth more than £100, was amended in 1836 to favour the poor.[80] Cattle and horses were to be branded HM in 1736, and often were rescued illegally from the pound. Asses and mules were to be impounded as not commonable in 1802 and goats, sheep, and pigs in 1814. An account of all impounding was to be kept by the marsh keeper, the drivers' deputy, from 1802.[81] The profits from marking and impounding were to be spent on improving the marsh in 1817; gates were to be set up and tolls paid by strangers riding across the land during the closed season.[82] The traditional grazing period ran from Lammas day (12 August from 1752) to Lady Day; premature entry was condemned in 1605 and the start of the season was sometimes postponed, for 10 days in 1692 and until 14 August in 1696 and 1703.[83] A shorter season, from 26 August until 25 March, was ordained in 1817.[84]

A later start for grazing enabled crops, whether hay or corn, to be harvested after bad weather. The marsh in 1745 comprised 283 strips of very variable size with 35 owners, the chief being Stamp Brooksbank with 74 a. in 17 strips and F. J. Tyssen with 72 a. in 61 strips. Only six other holdings exceeded 10 a. and most were less than 5 a.; Brooksbank's was exceptional in including a large block, c. 46 a. astride the later cut between Homerton bridge and Cow bridge.[85] The lands of the poor of Hackney, 29 a. in 27 strips, were staked out in 1786.[86] Larger divisions existed in Well Street common, by 1700 in two fields held by the Cass family and one each by the Norris family and the parochial charities,[87] and in London Fields, in 6 strips with 4 owners in the early 19th century and with five owners

in 1860.[88] The Mill fields and Hackney Downs, like the marsh, lay in narrow strips in the mid 18th century, when F. J. Tyssen, Lord Brooke, William Parker, and St. Thomas's hospital held parcels in all three. Stoke Newington common was apparently owned by the lord but subject to rights of common pasture throughout the year.[89]

In 1605 the early lifting of hay from London Fields was held to be no justification for the owner having put his cattle to grass before the accepted date.[90] In 1837 Adamson, the tenant farmer of 20 a. of Hackney Downs, failed to gather his harvest by Lammas, whereupon one parishioner turned cows on to the land and another seized part of the wheat. Their acquittal by the magistrates prompted rumours that the crop was public property and led to its despoilment by a crowd estimated at 3,000–4,000.[91] If such activity curbed any tendency to revert to arable, the increasing isolation of the detached commons combined with encroachments to lessen their value as pasture. Brickmaking and building were planned on part of London Fields called Nursery field, once used for sick cattle, in 1812.[92] Hopeful vendors in 1862 stressed London Fields' appeal to builders and dismissed the Lammas rights as rarely used and of little value.[93] It was gravel digging which brought riots and litigation after most of the commons had passed into public ownership in 1872, although continued grazing postponed Hackney marsh's final conversion to recreation until 1893.[94]

Sheep and pigs made up most of the sales from Marsh farm c. 1815 to 1840.[95] Livestock in the parish in 1867 included 534 cattle, 600 sheep or lambs, and 95 pigs. Sheep and pigs had fallen in number by 1880, risen again to 450 and 65 respectively by 1890, and disappeared by 1914. Cattle, mainly dairy cows, numbered 571 in 1870, 1,116 in 1880, 719 in 1890, and 140 in 1914. Thirty-nine people in 1880 and 25 in 1890 farmed land, while another 44 in 1880 and 30 in 1890 merely kept livestock, as 11 still did in 1914. The decline of both groups was attributable to the spread of building and also to the extinction of Lammas rights: no corn and very few green crops were grown from the late 1860s, and perhaps earlier, whereas in 1890, before Hackney marsh was taken over for recreation, there were c. 600 a. of permanent grass, of which c. 320 a. were not to be cut that year for hay.[96]

Cowkeepers who had no land suffered from increasingly stringent safeguards for public health. Eighty-three cowsheds and 65 slaughterhouses were inspected in 1876 and 81 cowsheds and 47 slaughterhouses were licensed in 1889;

75 *Census*, 1811–31.
76 *T.L.M.A.S.* xiii. 231.
77 P.R.O., SC 6/Hen. VIII/2101, m. 3d.
78 Robinson, *Hackney*, i. 404–5.
79 Vestry mins. 31 July 1614; 15 Oct. 1804.
80 Robinson, *Hackney*, i. 74–5.
81 G.L.R.O., M79/LH/41–2, *passim*.
82 Ibid. M79/LH/21, p. 197.
83 Vestry mins. 7 July 1605; 26 July 1692; 19 July 1696; 26 July 1703.
84 G.L.R.O., M79/LH/21, p. 197.
85 Robinson, *Hackney*, i, map facing p. 1. Brooksbank's successor's total was c. 68 a. in 1775: H.A.D., V 31.

86 Robinson, *Hackney* i, map facing p. 1; G.L.R.O., M78/LH/17, p. 123.
87 Watson, *Gentlemen*, 17; H.A.D., M 3589.
88 H.A.D., M 3590; ibid. J/V/1, pp. 354–5.
89 Ibid. M 3587; M 3591; V 32.
90 Vestry mins. 7 July 1605.
91 *Terrier*, Spring 1988; H.A.D., H/LD 7/2, pp. 144–5, 241–3.   92 Par. mins. 16 Dec. 1812.
93 H.A.D., H/LD/ 7/4.
94 Below, pub. svces.
95 H.A.D., D/F/ADM.
96 P.R.O., MAF 68/136; MAF 68/250; MAF 68/706; MAF 68/1276; MAF 68/2644.

licences had dwindled to 39 and 33 in 1900, to 18 and 21 in 1912, and to 3 and 13 by 1930. A Stapleton at Brookfield farm, Northwold Road, had 5 sheds in 1889 and 1900 and 3 in 1912. The Welford family, prominent dairymen on the north-west side of London, had 3 sheds in 1901 and one in 1912. Welford's made way c. 1928 for United Dairies and Stapleton's later for Home Counties Dairies. The largest cowkeeper in 1930 was Edward Mason, with 29 in Downham Road, although the longest survivor was S. P. Snewin, relicensed in Oldhill Street in 1946 and still there with a dairy in the 1960s.[97]

MILLS. On a site where there was apparently no mill in 1185 the Templars had in 1278 a watermill in Leyton and in 1307–8 adjoining mills under the same roof, one in Leyton and one in Hackney. Both watermills passed with the Templars' estate to the Hospitallers and in 1540 to the Crown, which in 1593 leased them for 40 years with adjoining lands, as Ruckholt and Temple mills, to Clement Goldsmith.[98] They were subleased in 1600 by Goldsmith to Edward Ryder, who sold his interest to George Bromley in 1601 but reserved all fishing and the right to operate his recently built flood gates. A former leather mill on the premises was the forerunner of many industrial buildings, but the main mills were still to be used for grinding corn.[99] They were sold by the Crown, probably in 1633, to Richard Trafford, whose son John leased them to Abraham Baker in 1637. Baker as tenant had already improved the old mills and built new ones, all of which were sold in 1668 by John Trafford's son Sigismund to John Samyne, grocer of London, whose family sold them soon after 1680.[1] Several short lived industries were later started by owners or lessees of the mills.[2] Adjoining land which had been sold with the mills in 1668 and probably in 1601 was mortgaged in 1769 on behalf of George Petty, together with a rent charge on the mills;[3] it was conveyed without the rent charge in 1772 to Edward Leeds,[4] whose son Richard conveyed it in 1812 to William Turner, a farmer on the Ruckholt estate in Leyton.[5]

The mills in 1812 adjoined the south side of a bridge across the Lea, through whose centre ran the parish boundary. Buildings immediately to the west included the White Hart, south of

which a narrow peninsula stretched between the river and a wide ditch or sewer. On the Essex bank were c. 6½ a. in Leyton and West Ham.[6] The mills had been demolished by 1854,[7] probably by a new owner whose heir offered the entire estate, which was underlet, for sale in 1899.[8]

A mill from which North Mill field in 1381 and South Mill field in 1443 were named[9] was presumably the forerunner of corn mills at Lea bridge which were for sale in 1791.[10] The flour mills in 1829 lay south-east of Lea bridge across an arm of the river to an island at the north end of the Hackney cut.[11] The buildings apparently survived but their island had been joined to the East London Waterworks Co.'s land to the south by 1865.[12]

MARKET GARDENS AND NURSERIES. A field called Gardenplot belonged to the king's manor in 1535[13] and artichokes were grown on an orchard of Grumbolds c. 1580.[14] The herbalist John Gerard (d. 1612) praised small turnips grown in Hackney for sale in London.[15] He also obtained foreign seeds from Lord Zouche, whose collection at Homerton was supervised by Matthias de Lobel (d. 1616), after whom the lobelia was named.[16] Both Evelyn in 1654 and Pepys in 1666 admired Lord Brooke's garden, where oranges grew.[17]

The garden of James Thynne at London Fields in 1666 was presumably the nursery advertised in 1694 and occupied by John Thynne in 1695.[18] By 1745 nurseries and market gardens lined both sides of Mare Street and stretched south of Wick Lane.[19] Middlesex's main market gardens lay farther west[20] and Hackney was less noted for horticulture than was Hoxton[21] until building drove nurserymen farther from London.

Johann (John) Busch, from Hanover, had small nursery sites on the west side of Mare Street from 1756 and may have sold them to another Hanoverian, Conrad Loddiges, in 1771. He then worked in Russia, as did his son Joseph Charles Bush, who was born in Hackney.[22] Conrad Loddiges (d. 1826), who produced a trilingual catalogue from 1777, began business from a shop at the corner of London Lane and Mare Street. He held scattered fields before moving c. 1786 to grounds east of Mare Street, where he later acquired Barber's Barn.[23] The

97 Hackney bd. of wks. *Ann. Rep. of M.O.H.* (1877), 44; (1889–90), 47–50; Hackney M.B. *Ann. Rep. of M.O.H.* (1900), 86–7; (1912), 61, 165–6; (1930), 81; H.A.D., H/PD/2/7/3–4; *V.C.H. Mdx.* vii. 224; ix. 234; *P.O. Dir. Lond.* (1934 and later edns.).
98 *V.C.H. Essex*, vi. 201; H.A.D., M 793.
99 H.A.D., M 793; below, ind.
1 *V.C.H. Essex*, vi. 201; H.A.D., M 795.
2 Below, ind.
3 H.A.D., M 793; M 795; M 1420–1.
4 Ibid. M 1422–4.
5 Ibid. M 1425–6; *V.C.H. Essex*, vi. 195.
6 Ibid. M 1426, M 3562 (plans).
7 *V.C.H. Mdx.* vi. 201; Clarke, *Hackney*, 166.
8 H.A.D., M 3562.
9 *Cal. Close*, 1381–5, 247; *P.N. Mdx.* (E.P.N.S.), 107.
10 H.A.D., H/LD 7/2. p. 107; ibid. D/F/BAG/13A.
11 H.A.D., M 3604; above, plate 39. Two additional mill islands lay in Leyton.
12 Stanford, *Map of Lond.* (1862–5 ed.), sheet 4.

13 P.R.O., SC 6/Hen. VIII/2101, m. 3d.
14 Ibid. STAC 2/26/465.
15 J. Gerard, *Herball* (facsimile edn. 1974), i. 178; ii. 786; *D.N.B.*
16 R. Desmond, *Dict. of Eng. and Irish Botanists and Horticulturists* (1977), 391, 683.
17 *Diary of John Evelyn*, iii. 96, 169; *Diary of Sam. Pepys*, vii. 182.
18 G.L.R.O., M79/KH/1, p. 2b; M79/KH/9, pp. 321–3; J. Houghton, *Colln. for Improvement of Husbandry and Trade* [weekly newsheet], v, nos. 102, 106.
19 Watson, *Gentlemen*, 17; Rocque, *Map of Lond.* (1741–5), sheet 6. 20 Foot, *Agric. of Mdx.* 16.
21 Desmond, *Dict. Botanists*, 727–8; *Terrier*, Autumn 1991.
22 Desmond, *Dict. Botanists*, 110; *Terrier*, Winter 1991/2; for Loddiges cf. H.A.D., D/F/LOD.
23 Desmond, *Dict. Botanists*, 392; J. Harvey, *Early Nurserymen* (1974), 89; *T.L.M.A.S.* xxiv. 184; ibid. xxvi. 298; Robinson, *Hackney*, i. 90; *Terrier*, Winter 1991/2.

firm, soon noted for exotics,[24] flourished under his younger son George (d. 1846), publisher of the *Botanical Cabinet*. With glasshouses up to 40 ft. high and an arboretum begun in 1816, Loudon considered Loddiges's a commercial botanic garden of model design. The arboretum was imitated at Chatsworth for the duke of Devonshire (d. 1858), a frequent visitor, whose protégé Sir Joseph Paxton probably secured the finest specimens for the Crystal Palace in 1854,[25] when the main lease was shortly to expire. After St. Thomas's had sold most of the land, George's son Conrad (d. 1898) kept some small glasshouses and remained at no. 222 Mare Street.[26]

John Abercrombie (d. 1806) was at Hackney by 1767, when he published *Every Man His Own Gardener*, but by 1779 was in Tottenham.[27] In 1786 he listed the Smiths' nursery at Dalston, Shoobert's in Homerton, Richards's in Kingsland, and Ross's in Stoke Newington Road.[28] The first, founded by Warren Luker (d. 1784) between Dalston Lane and the later Graham Road, was known as Luker, Smith & Lewis from 1780 and as Smiths' from 1785 until 1849.[29] Under Edward and Samuel Smith it offered foreign flowers in 1794 and covered 30 a. by 1800.[30] John Smith traded in 1842 and part of the grounds survived until shortly after 1865.[31] John Shoobert or Shuport had previously held 3 a. in south Hackney.[32] Thomas Richards was assessed 1784–1802 and Mary Richards in 1805 held a nursery which was probably the large ground between Lamb Farm and London Fields occupied 1811–24 by James Grange.[33] The Ross family was represented from 1811 to 1837 by John Ross, in 1825 a landscape gardener at the Caledonian nursery; his ground lined the south side of Wellington Road in 1837, when it was partly built upon and when he secured a long building lease.[34] Unlisted nurserymen included John Meek, successor to Thomas Meek, in Lamb Lane by 1782,[35] William Archer, lessee from Meek in 1803, and James Kelvington, Archer's underlessee in 1807.[36] Meek's lands, originating in a lease of 1746 to his grandfather, were the subject of lawsuits which led to his widow's imprisonment.[37] A nursery of c. 4 a. west of London Fields in 1790 survived until building spread south of Wilman Grove.[38] Early 19th-century nurserymen[39] included the

Scots Thomas Shepherd, who with his son Thomas William emigrated in the 1820s, John MacKay in Upper Clapton Road, and Hugh Low (d. 1863), who joined MacKay in 1823. Hugh Low's son Stuart Henry (d. 1890) and grandsons continued at Clapton until their move to Enfield in 1882; another son Sir Hugh (d. 1905) was an authority on tropical plants.[40] Nurserymen in the 1830s included Thomas Gellan at Shacklewell, Richard Mitchell in Lower Clapton, Thomas Waredraper in Well Street,[41] and William Dulley at Lamb Farm, perhaps as James Grange's successor. William Holmes, gardener to Dr. Frampton in 1848, acquired Frampton Park nursery, where his son William succeeded him; Eliza Jane Holmes's nursery was listed at no. 1 Frampton Park Road in 1902.[42] William Chitty (d. 1894), with a nursery at Stamford Hill, was connected with the horticultural writer Shirley Hibberd.

Commercial gardening was still concentrated in southern Hackney c. 1800.[43] Market gardeners were estimated to occupy 110 a. and nurserymen 40 a. in 1806;[44] together they held 139 a. out of the 1,560 a. subject to tithe in 1842.[45] Business was driven northward by builders, although in 1865 gardens remained at London Fields and at the eastern end of Cassland Road; a patch was kept by the builder Charles Butters's son Walter behind King Edward's Road in 1891.[46] The main areas by 1865 were behind Stoke Newington High Street and Road as far as Rectory Road, south of Hackney Downs between Amhurst and Pembury roads, around the sites of Navarino Grove (formerly Smiths') and Colvestone Crescent, and east of Brooksby's Walk.[47] All were soon built up, although in 1868 a large, presumably temporary, nursery bordered the projected Fountayne Road.[48] Watercress beds lay between the railway and Morning Lane, on the site of Chalgrove Road, until the 1870s.[49]

Later nurseries included Brick's in Shacklewell Row, Baddeley's on the site of Alvington Crescent, Hollington's in Downs Road, Allen's in Downs Park Road, and Prince's.[50] J. Noble's Pond Lane (later Millfield Road) nursery, established in the 1840s, supplied trees for municipal open spaces in the 1880s; potential building land in 1882, it made way for Elmcroft and Hilsea streets in 1896.[51]

[24] 'American and Botany Bay plants' by 1794: Foot, *Agric of Mdx.* 16.
[25] *D.N.B. Missing Persons*; *London's Pride*, ed. M. Galinou (Mus. of Lond. exhib. cat. 1990), 169; Robinson, *Hackney*, i. 90–1; Harvey, *Early Nurserymen*, 89; Clarke, *Hackney*, 39–40; *Terrier*, Spring, Summer 1992, Winter 1992/3. Original plan in J. C. Loudon, *Encyc. of Gardening* (1835), 1217.
[26] H.A.D., TS. notes on gdns. exhib. 1986; ibid. BW/E/13/2, 3; *Terrier*, Summer 1992.   [27] *D.N.B.*
[28] *T.L.M.A.S.* xxvi. 299.
[29] Harvey, *Early Nurserymen*, 88; *T.L.M.A.S.* xxiv. 184.
[30] Desmond, *Dict. Botanists*, 566, 570; Foot, *Agric. of Mdx.* 16; *T.L.M.A.S.* xxiv. 184; cf. H.A.D., M 545.
[31] Robinson, *Hackney*, i. 7; Desmond, *Dict. Botanists*, 569; Stanford, *Map of Lond.* (1862–5 edn.), sheet 7; Old O.S. Map Lond. 40 (1870).   [32] Watson, *Gentlemen*, 17.
[33] Desmond, *Dict. Botanists*, 263, 518; *T.L.M.A.S.* xxvi. 299; H.A.D., D/F/RHO/2/3; H.A.D., V 10; V 15.
[34] Desmond, *Dict. Botanists*, 531; *T.L.M.A.S.* xxvi. 299; H.A.D., M 718.   [35] H.A.D., M 3064.

[36] Ibid. M 3070–1.
[37] *Case of Mrs. Piggott* (1836), 15, *passim*.
[38] H.A.D., V 2/6; Stanford, *Map of Lond.* (1862–5 edn.), sheet 7; above, Mare Street and London Fields.
[39] Para. based on Desmond, *Dict. Botanists*, *passim*.
[40] D. Pam, *Hist. Enfield 1837–1914* (1992), 148; *Who Was Who* (1897–1916), 439.   [41] H.A.D., BW/E/13/16.
[42] *P.O. Dir. Lond.* (1902).
[43] Foot, *Agric. of Mdx.* frontispiece map (also in Middleton, *View*); Milne, *Land Use Map of Lond.* (1800).
[44] Lysons, *Environs*, Suppl. 163.
[45] H.A.D., Rectory tithe award (1842).
[46] Stanford, *Map of Lond.* (1862–5 edn.), sheets 7 and 8; H.A.D., TS. notes on gdns. exhib. 1986.
[47] Stanford, *Map of Lond.* (1862–5 edn.), sheets 3–4, 7–8.
[48] Ibid. (1891 edn.); Old O.S. Map Lond. 30 (1868) (called Foulden Rd.).
[49] Old O.S. Map Lond. 41 (1871); Walford, *Lond. Old and New*, v. 515.
[50] H.A.D., M 3230, pp. 51, 54, 75, 77, 88.
[51] Ibid. TS. notes on gdn. exhib. 1986; ibid. M 3548.

TRADE AND INDUSTRY. Hucksters from Hackney, selling cheese in London, were accused of regrating in 1377.[52] Occupations included those of sawyer in 1566,[53] embroiderer and joiner in 1598,[54] locksmith in 1613, poulterer and hackneyman in 1614, carpenter and cordwainer in 1615, blacksmith, tailor, and baker in 1616, cutler in 1617, and butcher and shoemaker in 1618.[55] More numerous were 'moniers' (presumably money-changers or bankers),[56] victuallers or vintners,[57] brickmakers,[58] and silkweavers,[59] the two last representing activities for which parts of Hackney were later noted. Tradesmen's tokens, mostly of innkeepers, included one issued by a chandler in 1656.[60]

Brickhill and the Gravel Pit were crofts at Clapton in 1535.[61] Brickmaking on 1½ a. near Balmes was banned on the complaint of Sir George Whitmore in 1631.[62] The Whitmores in 1660 leased land immediately south of the grounds of Balmes House to John Waxham, a Hoxton brickmaker,[63] and from 1670 to Ralph Harwood, a brickmaker later described as a gentleman.[64] The Rowes in 1687 had forfeited land for having dug brickearth near Kingsland Road.[65] Some gravel pits south of Morning Lane, soon to be commemorated in the name of a meeting house, were old in 1697.[66] A lease by Thomas Lee of land east of Mare Street in 1704 allowed digging to make bricks.[67] Thomas Scott, brickmaster of Shoreditch, reserved the brickearth when settling land in Hackney, Stepney, and Shoreditch in 1706 on the marriage of his son Thomas, who soon moved to Hackney.[68] Brickmaking was allowed north of Dalston Lane in 1709,[69] on unidentified sites in 1717–18,[70] by Thomas Waxham at Stamford Hill in 1721,[71] on part of the poor's land in 1729,[72] and east of Stamford Hill in 1760.[73] The earl of Warwick owned three brickfields at Upper Clapton, totalling c. 17 a., in 1762.[74] Balmes farm had fields called Further, Hither, and Middle Bricklands, totalling c. 27 a., in 1756;[75] Samuel Rhodes (d. 1794), as lessee of the farm, could dig brickearth in 1785.[76]

'Vast quantities' of bricks and tiles had been made around Kingsland by 1795.[77] By 1798 manufacturers' rent for brickfields had trebled within 20 years to £300 an acre.[78] The Tyssen

estate required £500 an acre in 1803 from Richard Dann for land behind Church Street[79] and supplements of £400 in 1805 from Edward and Samuel Smith for their nursery ground, where they might also extract potter's clay.[80] Brickfields occupied 170 a., more than market gardens and nurseries, in 1806.[81] Spurstowe's charity leased 14 a. for digging brickearth to Dann in 1818.[82] Several leases, as of land at Shacklewell in 1806 and High Hill ferry in 1822, exacted a premium rather than additional rent.[83] Alternatively a charge was levied, 1s. 9d. for every 1,000 bricks at Shacklewell in 1845, when it was hoped to make 3 million within four years, and 3s. 3d. at Upper Clapton in 1865.[84] Many leases were made by the Tyssens to Thomas (d. 1856) and William Rhodes (d. 1843).[85] William was still extending their holding in 1843, when the Middletons leased him 24 a. south of Shrubland Road, in Haggerston.[86] Among his successors were Robert and William Webb of Newington green, whose land in 1845 included pug or chalk mills at the south-west corner of the projected intersection of Downs Park and Amhurst roads.[87]

Although exhausted brickfields were always to be manured for return to cultivation, lessors increasingly reserved the right to reclaim and build. On land between Stoke Newington Road and Shacklewell Lane leased in 1806 and 1815 the high road frontage accordingly was to be dug first;[88] parts of 61 a. leased in 1814, near the high road or Downs and Dalston lanes, could be resumed.[89] Whereas De Beauvoir Town was built up largely with materials shipped from outside to Kingsland basin,[90] in 1845 brickearth from Shacklewell was not to be sold for manufacture elsewhere.[91] When other areas were built over, Clapton became the centre of brickmaking: the victims of a boating accident in 1840 were nearly all the sons of brickmakers from Caroline and Brook streets.[92] A brickfield leased with a wharf at Lea dock, north-west of Lea bridge, to James and Alfred Stroud in 1865[93] was the only one marked in 1883; probably it had gone by 1901.[94]

Silkweavers were recorded from 1609,[95] apprentices were bound to a local weaver and a silk stocking and frame maker in 1647,[96] and the

52 *Memorials of Lond.* ed. H. T. Riley (1868), 406.
53 *Mdx. County Rec.* i. 59.
54 H.A.D., D/F/TYS/1, ff. 33, 35.
55 *Mdx. Sess. Rec.* i. 181; ii. 74, 99; iii. 8, 120, 150, 153, 293; iv. 86, 339, 355.
56 H.A.D., D/F/TYS/1, pp. 45–7.
57 *Mdx. Sess. Rec.* i. 316; ii. 63; iii. 138, 143; iv. 241.
58 Ibid. i. 396; ii. 123; 215.
59 Ibid. i. 315; ii. 221, 265; iii. 153, 295; iv. 347; Guildhall MS. 9171/21, ff. 168v.–70.
60 *Trade Tokens*, ed. Williamson, ii. 817; above, social.
61 P.R.O., SC 6/Hen. VIII/2101, m. 3d.
62 Ibid. PC 2/41, p. 212; N. G. Brett-James, *Growth of Stuart Lond.* (1935), 111.
63 G.L.R.O., E/BVR/23.
64 Ibid. 24–7; H.A.D., M 506–7.
65 H.A.D., D/F/TVS/40, pp. 173, 215.
66 *Terrier*, Winter 1993/4.
67 H.A.D., M 734–5.
68 Ibid. M 3519–20.
69 Ibid. M 510.
70 M.L.R. 1717/2/24, 3/161; 1721/5/267.
71 Ibid. 1721/5/243.
72 Vestry mins. 20 June, 23 Aug., 6 Dec. 1729.
73 H.A.D., M 515.
74 M.L.R. 1763/3/351; above, plate 38.
75 G.L.R.O., E/BVR/430.
76 M.L.R. 1787/3/456; cf. ibid. 1789/7/369.
77 Lysons, *Environs*, ii. 451; above, plate 1.
78 Middleton, *View*, 24–6.
79 H.A.D., M 543.   80 Ibid. M 545.
81 Lysons, *Environs*, Suppl. 163.
82 Below, charities.
83 H.A.D., D/F/RHO/3/2; M 570.
84 Ibid. M 725; M 760.
85 e.g. ibid. D/F/RHO/3/1–3; above, manors (Lamb Farm).   86 H.A.D., M 724.
87 *V.C.H. Mdx.* viii. 191–2; H.A.D., M 725.
88 H.A.D., D/F/RHO/3/2–3.
89 Ibid. M 557; cf. ibid. M 536.
90 G.L.R.O., E/BVR/458.   91 H.A.D. M 725.
92 Ibid. H/LD 7/3, p. 173.   93 Ibid. M 760.
94 Ibid. BW/E/13/20; H/LD 7/16; still shown in Bacon, *Atlas of Lond.* (1910), sheet 33.
95 Guildhall MS. 9171/21, f. 168v.
96 Cal. Mdx. Sess. Bks. ib, 102.

parish supplied an old silkweaver with a loom in 1659.[97] Local expertise perhaps contributed to the choice of Hackney Wick for a factory by Leny Smith, who from 1787 was leased 31 a. with a tobacco or snuff mill, previously a fulling mill, and who had a London office by 1791. Described as a silk throwster and later as a crêpe manufacturer,[98] he or his son Leny Deighton Smith[99] was the country's largest producer in 1811, with a mainly female workforce of 600–700 at Hackney Wick and another at Taunton (Som.).[1] The elder Smith mortgaged property to the Hope Insurance Co. in 1831,[2] shortly before the mill was taken for Brenton's asylum.[3] Smith's family had long been out of business by 1842, when a smaller workforce at the mills produced flock and horsehair for George Kent.[4] Part of the old snuff mill estate was offered in 38 plots by Marmaduke Matthews in 1849 and later built up as Wick Road. Sir John Musgrove was also among the estate's developers.[5]

Water power at Temple Mills served many industries.[6] Before 1593 a little leather mill had stood there,[7] where there was later a powder mill, itself probably replaced c. 1627 by a mill for grinding smalt. A watermill built on Hackney marsh for Prince Rupert (d. 1682), where the secret of 'prince's metal' for guns was reputedly lost on his death, may have been at Temple Mills.[8] A company formed in 1695 to make brass, tin, and latten utensils was disputed between its past and present managers in 1721.[9] Manufacture of sheet lead had begun by 1757 and continued until 1814 or later. In 1792 the points of needles were ground by Messrs. Sharpe, under a lease of 1783, and tree trunks were bored to make water pipes.[10] Flockmaking was probably the last activity there c. 1829–32.[11] Turner & Sons, papermakers and embossers, sold up a recently built mill in 1765; called Hackney Wick House, its site had abundant water and was probably by Hackney brook.[12]

A calico ground at Temple Mills lay on the Leyton side in 1772.[13] Two calico printers and a calenderer recorded in 1795[14] were probably at Spring Hill, where there was a large calico factory in 1774,[15] or at High Hill ferry, where George Baker and William Burch occupied intermingled buildings, backed by drying grounds, in 1826. Burch was normally styled a calico printer and Baker a dyer.[16] They were there c. 1845[17] and may have been represented in 1855 by Baker & Hudden, calenderers, and James Burch, who had a carmine works.[18] Baker's Hill by 1880 contained the Lea Valley bleaching and dyeing works of William Connell & Co., whose Lea Valley laundry was taken over in the 1960s by Initial Services.[19] Also at High Hill ferry were Robert Lyon, a bleacher in 1826 and 1838,[20] and George Wickenden, a glazier or presser in 1845 and 1855.[21] Another calico printer was John Hammond, who was building immediately south of Lea dock in 1832 and acquired more land in 1838.[22]

Trade, manufacture, and handicrafts were said to employ 838 families by 1811 and 2,505 by 1831, but the figures appear unreliable.[23] Industries of note included an unlocated 18th-century porcelain factory, a rope works in the 1820s on the site taken for the church of St. Mary of Eton, a perforating works in John Street, London Fields, employing c. 50 in 1842,[24] and an optical glass works, mentioned in 1849, which was presumably that of Samuel Froggatt, by 1821 an optician at Hackney Wick, where Frogatt's mill stood east of the rope works.[25]

Riverside or canalside wharves served builders, industry, and later public utilities. By 1830 the De Beauvoir Town estate had made leases of 4 wharves on the Regent's canal west of Whitmore bridge and of 16 in Shoreditch (later Kingsland) basin.[26] In 1870 most received manure or building materials, those on the east side of the basin having frontages to Kingsland Road.[27] Wharves accounted for 7 per cent of the probate value of the De Beauvoir Town estate in 1935[28] and for c. 15 per cent of its rental in 1950.[29]

Early wharves on the Lea were at Hackney Wick, the neighbourhood of Lea bridge, High Hill ferry, and Spring Hill. Three were at Spring Hill in 1774.[30] Near Lea bridge, where Paradise (later Lea bridge) dock and Lea dock existed by 1831,[31] the boundary crossed the river to include Essex wharf, opposite Middlesex wharf, where a lease was renewed to Thomas Saunders, a coal merchant, in 1815.[32] North of Hackney Wick the cut was almost deserted in 1865 but industry had spread to Marsh gate or Homerton bridge by 1891 and had filled any gaps there by 1910. Hackney district board had a wharf or stone

97 Vestry mins. 15 June 1659.
98 M.L.R. 1788/2/159; G.L.R.O., M79/LH/18, pp. 30–1; Lond. Dir. (1791); P.O. Ann. Dir. (1800 and later edns.).
99 G.L.R.O., M79/LH/22, pp. 179–80.
1 Lysons, Environs, Suppl. 163.
2 G.L.R.O., M79/LH/23, pp. 41–2; H.A.D., M 3607; Watson, Gentlemen, 54.
3 Above, misc. institutions; research by H.A.D.
4 Robinson, Hackney, i. 209, 242.
5 H.A.D., M 3616; Watson, Gentlemen, 54; above, Hackney Wick.
6 Para. based on V.C.H. Essex, vi. 201.
7 H.A.D., M 793.
8 D.N.B.; Robinson, Hackney, i. 68–9.
9 H.A.D., H/LD 7/2, p. 2b.
10 Ambulator (1792), 103; H.A.D., D/F/BAG/13A.
11 V.C.H. Essex, vi. 201; above, econ. hist. (mills).
12 H.A.D., H/LD 7/2, p. 24.
13 Ibid. p. 49.
14 Lysons, Environs, ii. 451.   15 H.A.D., V 6.
16 Ibid. M 596; M.L.R. 1834/4/374, nos. 269–72; Pigot, Com. Dir. (1826–7 and later edns.); Pigot's Lond. Dir. (1838).

17 H.A.D., M 3629–30.
18 Hackney Dir. (1855).
19 P.O. Dir. Lond. County Suburbs, North (1880); Old O.S. Map Lond. 22 (1894); P.O. Dir. Lond. (1960 and later edns.).
20 Pigot, Com. Dir. (1826–7); Pigot's Lond. Dir. (1838); Robinson, Hackney, i. 207.
21 P.O. Dir. Six Home Counties (1845); Hackney Dir. (1855).   22 H.A.D., M 710.
23 Census, 1811–31.
24 Robinson, Hackney, i. 206–8; H.A.D., J/BW/E/13/15; above, plate 5.
25 Lewis, Topog. Dict. Eng. (1849), iv. 364; H.A.D., P/J/CW/124, p. 53; Pigot, Com. Dir. (1826–7); Starling's Map (1831); S. Tymms, Family Topographer, vii (1843), 17.
26 G.L.R.O., E/BVR/29, pp. 1–2.
27 Old O.S. Map Lond. 40 (1870).
28 G.L.R.O., E/BVR/273, p. 81.
29 Ibid. 174.
30 Starling's Map (1831); H.A.D., V 6; above, Clapton.
31 M.L.R. 1834/4/474, no. 280.
32 H.A.D., M 559; P.O. Dir. Six Home Counties.

depot at the Homerton end of the later Lee Conservancy Road (so named from 1907) and another at Kingsland basin, no. 297A Kingsland Road;[33] in 1913 the council also used a wharf leased from the Lee Conservancy board for bringing coal to the electricity works and refuse destructer. Homerton wharf was retained for refuse disposal until the 1970s.[34] James Latham, 18th-century timber merchants from Liverpool who in 1815 had moved to Shoreditch, from 1912 were also in Hackney, where in 1991 they employed 100–250 at a site which included Middlesex wharf.[35] Building contractors included Frederick Wise, by 1899 at no. 146 Dalston Lane; the site was sold in 1985 to Travis Perkins, which in 1991 also occupied Metropolis wharf at no. 305A Kingsland Road.[36]

The manufacture of colour, later of paint,[37] was brought to Hackney from Shadwell in 1780 by Lewis Berger (formerly Steigenberger, d. 1814). At Homerton he rented a farmhouse in Shepherd's Lane with a field stretching west to Hackney brook. The farmhouse was rebuilt as a residence, a factory was set up at the southern end of the field, near a well, and the brook was diverted through the grounds to prevent floods in Water Lane.[38] The business was expanded by Lewis's sons Samuel (d. 1855) and John (d. 1860) and from 1860 by John's sons Capel Berrow and Lewis Curwood Berger, who began making paint and varnish. A limited company called Lewis Berger & Sons, formed in 1879, was bought in 1905 by the American paint makers Sherwin-Williams. Overseas expansion was accompanied in 1926 by the establishment of a public company and in 1960 by a merger with Jensen & Nicholson, itself taken over in 1970 by Hoechst AG, which sold Berger, Jensen & Nicholson in 1988 to Williams Holdings, who sold to Crown Paints.

Berger's occupied almost all the land between Shepherd's and Water lanes, c. 5 a.[39] bounded on the north from 1848 by the N.L.R. line. Samuel and John replaced the original works with a Lower factory and added an Upper factory near the house. In 1860 the site contained only the two factories, Berger House, an adjoining clock tower of 1805, and ornamental water representing the diverted brook, but by 1890 it had been almost entirely built over. Employees numbered 60–70 at Homerton and at a City office in 1860 and 400 at Homerton alone by 1910; they were noted for long service, although industrial sickness led strikers in 1911 to de-

nounce the company's 'sheds of death'.[40] Berger's ended its connexion with Homerton in 1960. The buildings were replaced, except for a laboratory of 1934 at no. 205 Morning Lane,[41] used in 1991 by Hackney L.B.'s social services.

The first plastics in Britain[42] were patented, as parkesine, by Alexander Parkes in 1862 and produced from 1866 at a works next to the waterproofers George Spill & Co. in Wallis Road, Hackney Wick. The company went bankrupt in 1868 but Spill's brother Daniel continued at the same works with improved material from 1869 until 1874, when his Xylonite Co. also failed. In 1875 he moved to no. 124 High Street, Homerton, and L. P. Merriam, who had tried to promote celluloid, the American equivalent of xylonite,[43] moved into no. 122. In 1877 they respectively formed the British Xylonite Co. and the Homerton Manufacturing Co., which merged in 1879. Merriam (d. 1889), whose factory in the garden made combs from the sheet xylonite made next door, assumed sole control in 1884 and finally prospered after acquiring the Impermeable Collar and Cuff Co. of Bower Road, Hackney Wick. His son C. F. Merriam moved sheet production to Suffolk in 1887. The Homerton site was sold after the production of finished articles was moved in 1897 to Hale End (Essex).

Water provided access and a means of waste disposal for noxious industries at Hackney Wick. George Spill had a works there by 1862 and James G. Ingram & Son, vulcanized rubber manufacturers founded in Hoxton, from 1866.[44] The Victorian iron works west of Wallis Road, a ropery in Gainsborough Road, an aniline dye works north of the parkesine works, and a varnish works all lay within Hackney by 1870, when the Hackney cut led to an isolated rubber works and a tar and chemical works beyond Wick Lane bridge.[45] The group of works at Hackney Wick included several using noxious substances on the Bow side of Wallis Road and in White Post Lane.[46] In 1875 the aniline dye works was the Atlas works of Brooke, Simpson & Spiller, and Ingrams had extended their factory in Chapman Road.[47] By 1880 the Hackney side of Wallis Road had a printer and makers of printing ink, bedsteads, paving, and book cloth.[48]

Clarke, Nickolls & Coombs,[49] confectionery and jam makers established in 1872, were at Hackney Wick by 1879 and on both sides of Wallis Road by 1910, when they had also spread

33 Stanford, *Map of Lond.* (1862–5 edn.), sheet 8; (1891 edn.); Bacon, *Atlas of Lond.* (1910), sheet 40; insurance plan 390 (1891, 1924).

34 Hackney M.B. *Ann Rep.* (1913), 79–80; H.A.D., H/LD 7/16; *P.O. Dir. Lond.* (1975, 1980).

35 *P.O. Dir. Lond.* (1879 and later edns.); inf. from marketing svces. manager, Jas. Latham (Southern).

36 *P.O. Dir. Lond.* (1899 and later edns.); inf. from Travis Perkins plc.

37 Two paras. based on *Terrier*, Autumn 1988; T. B. Berger, *Cent. and Half of Ho. of Berger* (1910); H.A.D., D/B/BER (TS. notes and index); ibid. D/B/BER 2/7/51 (TS. hist. by F. Armitage); insurance plan E 28 (1924, 1951).

38 H.A.D., D/B/BER 1/61.

39 Valuations of 1897, 1907, and 1935: ibid. D/B/BER 2/9/13.

40 Above, plate 42; H.A.D., D/B/BER 2/7/59.

41 *Hackney Photos.* i. 63.

42 Para. based on *E. Lond. Record*, vi. 6–12; Brit. Xylonite Co. Ltd., *Fifty Years 1877–1927*; *Xylonite Group,1877–1952* (booklets in H.A.D.); *Beetle Bulletin* 36 (1975)(ho. jnl. of Brit. Industrial Plastics), 5–7.

43 *Terrier*, June 1986.

44 Hackney bd. of wks. *Ann. Rep.* (1866), 6; *P.O. Dir. Lond.* (1862); *Cent. of Progress, J. G. Ingram & Son, 1847–1947* (booklet in H.A.D.), 11.

45 Old O.S. Map Lond. 41 (1870).

46 Ibid.; e.g. Giles & Barringer, starch makers, and Carless, Blagden & Co., manufacturing chemists: *P.O. Dir Lond.* (1867).

47 *P.O. Dir. Lond.* (1875); *Ingram & Son, 1847–1947*, 11.

48 *P.O. Dir. Lond. County Suburbs, North* (1880).

49 Para. based on Hackney, *Local Govt. and Ind.* (1948), 135–7; *P.O. Dir. Lond.* (1875 and later edns.).

south of the G.E.R. line and to the previously underdeveloped east bank of the Hackney cut in both Hackney and Bow.[50] The company, probably the district's leading employer, was one of the first to introduce profit sharing in 1890,[51] acquired a convalescent home at Clacton (Essex), and formed many social clubs.[52] It was registered as Clarnico in 1946 and described as having been the country's largest confectioners in 1948, when war damage had led to plans for a factory in Waterden Road. Clarnico moved to Waterden Road c. 1955 and, as Trebor Sharps, left Hackney c. 1975.

The industries which employed the greatest numbers were widespread away from the river and were often organized in small firms. Furniture trades were noted in the 1890s, although fewer than in Shoreditch or Bethnal Green.[53] Small carpentry or cabinet factories abounded in side streets, as around the G.E.R. line between Mare Street and London Fields or by the G.N.R. line south of Homerton's high street.[54] In 1901 over 5,000 people worked in wood, including 1,852 cabinet makers and 504 french polishers.[55] Piano making was well represented: of 34 north London manufacturers listed in 1880, 14 were in Hackney, besides a piano warehouse. There were fewer by 1900 but in 1924 they included the Helmsley works of Broadwood, White & Co., which in 1951 was an office equipment factory.[56] Charles Crop & Sons in Brooksby's Walk made tobacco pipes by 1872; by 1898 the London exporters Adolph Frankau & Co. had a steamworks at no. 112 (later no. 154) High Street, Homerton, where briar pipes were later made by Marechal Ruchon and in the 1970s by Fairfax Traders.[57] Large furniture firms included from 1895 the Acme Wood Flooring Co. from Vauxhall, perhaps supplied by the neighbouring timber merchants G. Ellis & Co., in Gainsborough (later Lee Conservancy) Road until the 1920s,[58] and Greaves & Thomas, inventors of the Put-U-Up settee-bed, in Northwold Road, where their premises included the Amherst works, from 1911 until c. 1965.[59]

The making of clothes and footwear employed over 15,000 in 1901. One third, including 2,686 bootmakers, were men; women included over 2,000 dressmakers, over 2,000 shirtmakers or seamstresses, 1,000 tailors, over 900 milliners, and over 900 artificial flower makers.[60] Although never so concentrated as they were farther south, clothing workers multiplied until by 1964 there were almost as many in Hackney as in London's old East End. Both areas were centres of Jewish enterprise: Hackney in 1964 was noted for its large factories for men's tailoring, its dispersed production of shirts and underwear, and for clothing accessories. The industry ranged from factories with their own retail outlets to home-workers paid by contractors.[61]

Simeon Simpson in 1894 established a firm in Stoke Newington[62] which opened a model factory in 1929 at nos. 92–100 Stoke Newington Road, where 2,000 were employed. The company patented Daks clothing in 1934 and, despite war damage and the opening of factories elsewhere,[63] remained until c. 1982; Halkevi Turkish community centre used the premises in 1991. Gerrish, Ames & Simpkins, of Basingstoke (Hants), bought Morley hall during the First World War, built the adjoining Carlington works[64] in 1932, and remained until c. 1962. Horne Bros. had a model factory at Durigo House, King Edward's Road, from 1922 until c. 1987, and Swears & Wells were at no. 1 Downs Park Road by 1938 until c. 1976.[65] Barrymore's made clothing in Retreat Place in 1934 and later at Pembury works in Glaskin Mews off Pembury Road.[66] Their successors Willerby & Co. employed 410 there in 1955[67] and remained until after 1964. The outfitters Moss Bros. had a workshop between Ball's Pond and Bentley roads by 1961.[68]

The East End clothing firm of Alfred Polikoff (d. 1943) had a plant in London Lane by 1915, when a factory was built at nos. 148–50 Mare Street which was burned down in 1932. New premises were opened in 1933 in Chatham Place, where part, used by a subsidiary called Sportown, was rebuilt after bomb damage. Polikoff's, which opened Welsh and Irish factories, was acquired by Great Universal Stores in 1948 but kept its own name in the 1970s. Amenities for its staff included a sports ground at Springfield park from c. 1955. By 1952 Polikoff's shared premises with Burberry's, which had had a London shop from 1901; Burberry's was also taken over by G.U.S. and employed c. 315 at nos. 29–53 Chatham Place in 1991.[69]

Bootmaking was at first concentrated south and south-east of London Fields: in 1880, of 43 wholesale boot manufacturers listed in north London, 38 were in Hackney, including all but one of the 8 businesses in Ash Grove and 6 of the 10 in Mentmore Terrace.[70] Poverty in the 1890s was attributed to the hangers-on of boot finishers, whose northward drift from Bethnal

50   Bacon, *Atlas of Lond.* (1910), sheet 40.
51   Clarke, Nickolls & Coombs, *Proof of the Pudding. Notes on Co-partnership* (1919).
52   *Clarnico News* (nos. from 1963 in B.L.).
53   Booth, *Life and Labour*, iii (1), 110; L.C.C. *Rep. on Tech. Educ.* (1892), map 3.
54   Insurance plan 384 (1891); ibid. E 29 (1899).
55   *Census*, 1901, table 35.
56   Booth, *Life and Labour*, iii (1), 110; *P.O. Dir. Lond. County Suburbs, North* (1880, 1900); insurance plan E 20 (1924, 1951).
57   *P.O. Lond. Suburban Dir.* (1872 and later edns.).
58   *P.O. Dir. Lond.* (1894 and later edns.).
59   Hackney, *Local Govt. and Ind.* (1948), 133.
60   *Census*, 1901, table 35.
61   L.C.C. *Rep. on Tech. Educ.* (1892), maps 6, 7; Institute of Brit. Geographers, *Trans. and Papers*, xxviii. 157–60; J.

T. Coppock and H. C. Prince, *Gtr. Lond.* (1964), 248–52; F. Payne, 'Clothing Ind. with regard to Hackney Based Firms' (TS. rep. 1980 in H.A.D.), 3–6.
62   Para. based on Hackney, *Local Govt. and Ind.* (1948); *Kelly's Dir. Hackney* (1915–16); *P.O. Dir. Lond* (1934 and later edns.).
63   *Dict. Business Biog.* ed. D. J. Jeremy and C. Shaw, v (1986), 184.
64   Insurance plan E 20 (1958).
65   Ibid. E 6 (1961).   66   Ibid. E 26 (1945).
67   *N. Lond. Observer, clothing trade suppl.* (1955), vi.
68   Insurance plan E 6 (1961).
69   Inf. from Miss E. Wright and asst. co. sec., Burberry's Ltd.; *P.O. Dir. Lond.* (1952).
70   *P.O. Dir. Lond. County Suburbs, North* (1880). Individual craftsmen, listed as bootmakers, were more widespread.

Green had made a second centre for their trade.[71] In 1938 London's footwear industry was centred on Hackney,[72] where long established firms, all with Jewish names, were to survive until the 1960s. Jacob Kempner, at no. 236 Mare Street and Paragon Road in 1898, was at nos. 31 and 33 Well Street by 1911, called Kempner & Brandon by 1920, at Victory works in Shore Road in 1934 and 1948, and later in Dalston Lane.[73] Reuben Lazarus, in Hackney Grove by 1911, had one of three boot factories between Richmond and Ellingfort roads in 1934 and was in Kenworthy Road in 1948.[74] Eleazer Phillips, who replaced a Barnardo's home and the Y.M.C.A. at nos. 273–5 Mare Street, claimed to be Hackney's oldest shoemakers in 1948.[75]

The varied industries included several other firms which became household names. A large works of the King's printers Eyre & Spottiswoode (before 1831 Eyre & Strahan), originally for producing bibles, was in Shacklewell by 1829[76] and until c. 1936; later occupants included Swears & Wells. Reeves & Sons moved their artists' colour factory in 1866 from the City to Beech (later Ashwin) Street, replacing Luxembourg hall, surviving war damage c. 1940, and moving away c. 1955. Tyer & Co., inventors of a railway signalling system, were also in Ashwin Street until the 1960s.[77] W. J. Bush & Co., England's first makers of flavouring essences, had moved from the City by 1880 to Ash Grove, where their Grove chemical works had expanded by 1930 and was occupied by the firm, from the 1960s called Bush Boake Allen, until c. 1973. Achille Serre, the dyers and cleaners, were in White Post Lane from c. 1896 to c. 1928.[78] Nalder Bros. & Thompson moved in 1899 to Dalston Lane, where they made electrical measuring instruments and employed c. 400 in 1948 and remained until c. 1969. Siemens Bros., based at Woolwich, made electric tantalum lamps at Dalston from 1908 until 1923.[79] E. C. Barlow & Sons had moved from Shoreditch to Urswick Road by 1903, where from 1929 they formed a branch of Metal Box, enlarged the factory in 1940, and employed 320 in 1948; the company left Urswick Road c. 1983 and a second local works in Theydon Road c. 1987. Venus Pencil Co. was at nos. 169 and 171 Lower Clapton Road from 1903[80] until c. 1970. The War Department's National Projectile factory was opened in 1915 on part of the marsh near the G.N.R.'s sidings and the Hackney cut.[81] Mentmore Manufacturing Co., at no. 16 Mentmore Terrace in 1921, moved c.

1923 to Tudor Grove, where in 1948 it claimed to be Europe's biggest fountain pen maker at Platignum House; it moved to Hertfordshire c. 1963.

In 1904 Hackney had 374 factories and 855 workshops, employing 17,714 people. Nearly a third worked in the clothing industry, while almost a tenth, mainly men, made articles of wood and almost as many, mainly women, worked in laundries; over 1,000 were employed in the respective manufactures of fine instruments, of paper (or in printing), and of chemicals or drugs.[82] That industrial workforce was less than a fifth of all those occupied, in 1901 estimated at 101,606, of whom 65,379 were male.[83] The larger figure included those in offices, in domestic service, or with no fixed workplace, and perhaps many who worked on their own.[84] In Hackney, as in London as a whole, domestic service was the largest single employer,[85] with over 8,000, mostly unmarried women. Men in commercial occupations formed a still larger category, but one with wide subdivisions: 2,335 were merchants, agents, or accountants, 6,146 were clerks, and 1,199 dealt in money or insurance, most of them presumably in the City. Building, including such allied trades as plumbing or glazing, occupied 6,382 and transport nearly 5,000. The availability of sites presumably explained why in 1892 proportionately more people were employed by builders in Hackney and Stoke Newington than elsewhere on the north and east sides of London.[86]

By 1938 the pattern of industrial employment had not greatly changed, despite much small-scale conversion of private premises.[87] Hackney had 2,071 factories and workshops, of which 922 made clothing or footwear, 401 made furniture, and 310 were concerned with engineering. Only 5 of London's 28 boroughs had more factories and only 3 exceeded Hackney's industrial workforce of 46,333. Clothing employed nearly 23,000, furniture making 7,580, and engineering 5,850. More than 2,000 worked in the production of food, drink, and tobacco, and in papermaking and printing. A few firms, chiefly furniture makers, had moved farther north or east; both Hackney and St. Pancras had experienced an overall loss of 21 factories, more than in any other metropolitan borough, since 1932.[88]

The departure of large firms was part of the decentralization of London's industry which gathered pace after the Second World War.[89] At Hackney Wick the rubber makers Ingrams and

71 Booth, *Life and Labour*, iii (1), 77.
72 J. H. Forshaw and P. Abercrombie, *County of Lond. Plan* (1943), 85. Rest of para. based on *P.O. Dir. Lond. County Suburbs, North* (1880 and later edns.); *P.O. Dir. Lond.* (1902 and later edns.).
73 Hackney, *Local Govt. and Ind.* (1948), 162.
74 Insurance plan E 23 (1936); Hackney, *Local Govt. and Ind.* (1948), 162.
75 Insurance plan E 24 (1924, 1951); Hackney, *Local Govt. and Ind.* (1948), 154.
76 *Cruchley's New Plan* (1829); E. Howe, *Lond. Compositor* (1947), 49–50, 357. Rest of para. based on *P.O. Dir. Lond.* (1902 and later edns.); *P.O. Dir. Lond. County Suburbs, North* (1880 and later edns.); Hackney, *Local Govt. and Ind.* (1948).   77 Clarke, *Hackney*, 45, 290.
78 *Hackney Photos.* ii. 62.
79 J. D. Scott, *Siemens Bros. 1858–1958* (1958), 153,

201–4.
80 H.A.D., D/F/BAG/8, p. 70.
81 H.A.D., H/E 66/1.
82 L.C.C. *Lond. Statistics*, xix. 42–3. Slightly different figures, making instrument makers outnumber laundry workers, are in ibid. xvii. 54–6, 58; different totals of workshops are in Hackney M.B. *Ann. Reps. of M.O.H. passim.*
83 Rest of para. based on *Census*, 1901, table 35.
84 Outworkers' premises were inspected from 1904: Hackney M.B. *Ann. Rep. of M.O.H.* (1904), 68.
85 L.C.C. *Rep. on Tech. Educ.* (1892), 12.
86 Ibid. map 1.
87 Hackney M.B. *Ann. Reps. of M.O.H.* (1928), 116–20; (1930 and later); *New Lond. Life and Labour*, iii (1), 362.
88 Forshaw and Abercrombie, *County of Lond. Plan*, 88–9, 90, 94.
89 Para. based on *P.O. Dir. Lond.* (1862 and later edns.).

the manufacturing chemists E. Beanes, of the Falcon works, survived for almost a century into the 1960s, as did the only slightly younger timber merchants G. Ellis, the drysalters Jessop & Co., and several firms on the Bow side of the boundary. In Bentham Road the Cassland ropeworks established in 1848 by George Oldfield similarly survived.[90] The most spectacular modern advance was made by Lesney Products, pressure die casters at no. 1A Shacklewell Lane by 1950, in Eastway by 1959, and Lee Conservancy Road by 1975. Lesney began to make Matchbox model vehicles in 1953.[91] With a workforce of 1,500, it was thought to be Hackney L.B.'s largest employer in 1982, when it went into receivership and was bought by the Hong Kong based Universal (International) Holdings.[92]

Industrial decline became more marked from the 1970s, although statistics such as the 38 per cent fall in the manufacturing workforce between 1971 and 1980 applied to the wider area of the L.B.[93] The clothing industry was critically threatened in 1980, both by recession and by ephemeral back-street shops,[94] often using immigrant labour.[95] Burberry's was one of the few well known names to survive in 1991.[96] A large factory might be taken over by several businesses: Reeves's former works at no. 18 Ashwin Street was occupied by 5 firms, all concerned with clothing or accessories, in 1964 and by 8 in 1975.[97]

In 1826 a wide variety of shops in Church Street served Hackney village and one in the high road served Kingsland, Dalston, and Stoke Newington. They included booksellers, watchmakers, wine merchants, and, in Hackney, 2 perfumers and 4 confectioners. Both Clapton and Homerton had shops for everyday needs.[98] Local retailers included Thomas Gibbons, who started as a china and glass dealer in Morning Lane in 1831. His daughter Elizabeth Gibbons moved from Brett Road to Amhurst Road, where, after making room for Matthew Rose & Sons c. 1890, her cash furnishers' business acquired a row of nine shops and remained a family firm at nos. 1–17 in 1991.[99] Matthew Rose, Hackney's leading department store c. 1900,

began as a draper's at no. 335 Mare Street and from 1868 expanded to include nos. 347–57 Mare Street and nos. 2–18 Amhurst Road, closing in 1936.[1] T. B. Stephens, a modest draper's in 1904, built a three-storeyed department store at nos. 230–240 Stoke Newington High Street, where it survived until c. 1973.[2] Cooke's eel and pie business, from Shoreditch, in 1910 opened a branch at no. 41 Kingsland High Street; as F. Cooke's, the shop retained its ornate interior in 1991.[3] Hackney and District chamber of commerce was founded in 1897 and renamed Hackney and Tower Hamlets chamber of commerce in 1982.[4]

Street markets were held in 1893 in Kingsland Road, Mare Street, Well Street, and the Broadway, London Fields. The Kingsland Road market moved to Kingsland High Street, and in 1930 was in Ridley Road, where it remained among the best known in London; Clapton had a similarly large market, with 200 or more licensed pitches, in Chatsworth Road, but Mare Street's had disappeared.[5] Market streets contained c. 350 food stalls in 1927, besides itinerant food sellers, and over 400 in 1930.[6]

National retail chains included Home & Colonial Stores, the grocers, with branches by 1895 at nos. 52 Kingsland High Street and 400 Kingsland Road, by 1898 at nos. 303 Mare Street, 218 Well Street, 120 Stoke Newington High Street, and 50 Chatsworth Road, and by 1920 at no. 166 Stamford Hill. Boots cash chemists were at no. 382 Mare Street by 1911 and moved to nos. 398 and 400 c. 1920. W. H. Smith & Sons, the booksellers, were at no. 80 Stoke Newington High Street by 1912. Marks & Spencer was at no. 297 Mare Street by 1914, as the London Penny Bazaar, and also at no. 156 Stoke Newington High Street by 1915; in Mare Street it moved in the 1930s to part of Matthew Rose's former premises. F. W. Woolworth & Co. was at nos. 144–6 Stoke Newington High Street by 1917 and at no. 333 Mare Street by 1922.[7] In 1991 Hackney was served by national chains, by individual shops, many of them catering for ethnic minorities, by markets including a daily one in Ridley Road, and by Dalston Cross shopping centre, opened in 1989.[8]

LOCAL GOVERNMENT

MANORIAL GOVERNMENT. In 1294 the bishop of London claimed view of frankpledge, infangthief, outfangthief, the assize of bread and of ale, fugitives' goods, tumbril, pillory, gallows, and fines in Hackney, as part of his manor of Stepney.[9] Separate bailiffs accounted for Hack-

ney and Stepney by the 1380s[10] but courts for the whole manor, sometimes with pleas for Hackney entered separately, were still held at Stepney in the 16th century.[11] The bishop was paid 16s. as the common fine from Hackney in 1349.[12]

90 Watson, *Gentlemen*, 65.
91 Colln. in Hackney mus.
92 *Hackney Gaz.* 28 Sept. 1982, 1, 6.
93 Survey based on inf. from 33 cos., 18 of them in Shoreditch: *Lond. Jnl.* xiii (1), 29–30, 37.
94 Payne, 'Clothing Ind.' 8, 10–11.
95 e.g. Gadek Ltd. in Tyssen Street: *Daily Telegraph*, 28 Feb. 1989, 2.   96 *P.O. Lond. Business Dir.* (1991).
97 *P.O. Dir. Lond.* (1964, 1975).
98 Pigot, *Com. Dir.* (1826–7).
99 *Hackney Gaz.* (1864 to 1989 anniv. suppl.), 34; inf. from Mr. F. J. Gibbons Smith.

1 *Hackney Photos.* i. 12, 18; above, plate 41.
2 Hackney, *Local Govt. and Ind.* (1948); *P.O. Dir. Lond.* (1973).   3 *Hackney Photos.* ii. 56; *List of Bldgs.* (1991).
4 *Handbk. and Dir.* (1949–50 and later edns.) in H.A.D.
5 *New. Lond. Life and Labour*, iii (1), 294, 321, map facing p. 328; *Hackney Photos.* i. 81; ii. 19, 54.
6 Hackney M.B. *Ann. Rep. of M.O.H.* (1927), 102; (1930), 84.   7 *P.O. Dir. Lond.* (1895 and later edns.).
8 *Hackney Echo*, 11 Oct. 1989, 5.
9 *Plac. de Quo Warr.* (Rec. Com.), 475.
10 McDonnell, *Medieval Lond. Suburbs*, 35.
11 P.R.O., SC 2/191/60–4.   12 Ibid. 60, m. 16.

Proceedings for Hackney are recorded on Stepney court rolls for 1349, 1442, 1509, and 1581–2 and in books for Stepney for 1654–64.[13] Two officers, perhaps constables, were elected for Hackney in 1509, when two chief pledges were elected for Shacklewell and one each for Clapton and Homerton.[14] A general court baron for Hackney, held immediately after a Stepney court in December 1581, was concerned largely with copyholds which had changed hands during the previous year; it also proposed two names for the choice of bailiff or collector.[15] The next court for Hackney, after a view of frankpledge at Stepney in April 1582, chose 2 constables, 2 aletasters, and 6 chief pledges or headboroughs: one and a deputy for Clapton, 2 for Mare Street, Well Street, and Grove Street, and 2 for Kingsland, Newington, Shacklewell, and Dalston. Three common drivers were chosen two days later.[16] In 1641 the steward of Hackney, who was also steward of Stepney, summoned the copyholders to meet in Hackney[17] and in 1642 courts at Stepney were held for Hackney alone in April and October. The first dealt with ditches, the assize of bread, and the elections of a constable and 2 aletasters for the parish and of a headborough for each of 7 wards: Kingsland and Dalston, Newington and Shacklewell, Church Street and part of Clapton, Clapton, the upper end of Homerton, Mare Street, and the lower end of Homerton.[18] By 1654, although the manors still had the same lord, Hackney courts were held at Homerton; much less frequent than those for Stepney, they consisted of a general court baron in April and December and a view in April, with one special court in 1655 and three in 1656.[19]

Separate courts were held for the Hackney manors of Lordshold, Kingshold, and Grumbolds, despite the acquisition of all three by the Tyssen family. Court books or draft court books exist for Lordshold for 1658–1940[20] and for Kingshold for 1666–1936,[21] with minutes and extracts.[22] It had been claimed in 1331 that the Templars had possessed pleas and perquisites of court for what became Kingshold manor; the Hospitallers, fined in 1511 for default at the bishop's law day, had held a court at Hackney in the early 16th century, when rolls had allegedly been lost.[23] For Grumbolds there are extracts for 1486–1741; later records include a minute book to 1925.[24] In 1711 the lord received 83 quitrents for Lordshold, 21 for Kingshold,

and 5 for Grumbolds.[25] Uncertainty was such that a Kingshold transaction of 1798 was wrongly entered under Lordshold.[26]

The busiest court, that of Lordshold, consisted of a view of frankpledge, followed by a court baron, in April and sometimes special courts.[27] The view was held at first usually at Homerton, where the Coach and Horses was the meeting place in 1752, and later at Kingsland, at the King's Arms by 1753[28] and at the Tyssen Arms from 1815.[29] After 1845, no longer called a view, the court met at the Manor rooms until 1885 or later;[30] enfranchisements[31] and property transactions were done in lawyers' chambers until 1924. For Kingshold a view was likewise followed by a court baron, in Church Street and perhaps from 1666 at the Green Man, named as the usual meeting place in 1723; it was held at the Cock in the late 18th century, later at the Mermaid, the Tyssen Arms, the Manor rooms, and finally in London.[32] Grumbolds courts, annual c. 1500 but later less regular, also met latterly at the Manor rooms.[33] Probably all three manors had a single steward, normally a lawyer. Stewards exploited the family's absence before and after the term of J. R. Daniel-Tyssen from 1829 until 1852: Thomas Tebbutt and his son were involved in William Rhodes's building schemes[34] and Charles Cheston, son and successor of Chester Cheston, ruined Lord Amherst of Hackney by embezzlement.[35]

Until 1840 or later[36] the Lordshold court appointed 2 constables, 2 aletasters, and normally 8 headboroughs; it also suggested 2 names for the choice of a reeve and appointed 6 or 7 common drivers. A magistrate was excused serving as headborough in 1718, partly because the headborough's was an inferior office.[37] Aletasters were active in the late 17th century and continued to present the use of false weights and measures in 1740.[38] Reeves and drivers were substantial landowners and were still being appointed in 1885.[39] Kingshold courts appointed a constable, an aletaster, and 2 headboroughs until 1841 or later but no officers by 1845.[40]

Manorial and parochial authority overlapped. The common drivers reported in 1605 to a large meeting of inhabitants, which then passed a resolution on the commons, as did the vestry in 1614 and later. Parishioners claimed to be upholding ancient customs, which were set out by agreement between the lord and the copyholders in 1617.[41] The vestry instructed the constables

13 P.R.O., SC 2/191/60, 62–3; B.L. Eg. Ch. 2080–1; G.L.R.O., M93/1–4. Also abstracts from 1651: G.L.R.O., M93/89– 92.   14 P.R.O., SC 2/191/63, m. 3d.
15 B.L. Eg. Ch. 2080.
16 Ibid. 2081.   17 B.L. Eg. MS. 3006, f. 87.
18 Ibid. ff. 66, 149–50.
19 G.L.R.O., M93/1, ff. 15, 56, 61, 64, 108, 142, 145, 154, 156, 160, 213.
20 G.L.R.O., M79/LH/1–40 (ct. bks., some unfit for consultation); M79/LH/45–56 (draft ct. bks.); M79/LH/41–2 (indexes).
21 Ibid. M79/KH/1–20 (ct. bks., some unfit for consultation); M79/KH/23–5 (draft ct. bks.); M79/KH/21–2 (indexes).
22 Ibid. M79/LH/57–82; M79/KH/26–41.
23 B.L. Cott. MS. Nero E. VI, ff. 66–7; P.R.O., C 1/314/8; C 1/465/31.
24 H.A.D., D/F/TYS/40; G.L.R.O., M79/G/1 (index); M 79/G/2–7.   25 Ibid. M79/LH/44.

26 Ibid. M79/LH/18, p. 150.
27 Two paras. based on ct. bks. and draft ct. bks.
28 G.L.R.O., M79/LH/13, pp. 1, 24.
29 Ibid. 20, p. 435.
30 Ibid. 36, p. 372. Ct. book for 1886–96 unfit for consultation.
31 Listed from 1836 to 1923 at back of G.L.R.O., M79/LH/42.
32 Listed from 1666 to 1852 at back of ibid., M79/KH/22.
33 H.A.D., D/F/TYS/40; G.L.R.O., M79/G/2.
34 Above, manors (Balmes).
35 Above, manors (Lordshold).
36 Ct. bk. for 1841–4 wanting.
37 Cal. Mdx. Sess. Bks. xi. 155–6.
38 G.L.R.O., M79/LH/4.
39 Ibid. M79/LH/36, p. 372.
40 Ibid. M79/KH/10, p. 393; ibid. 12, passim.
41 Vestry mins. 7 July 1605; 31 July 1614; 19 July 1696; 26 July 1703; Robinson, Hackney, i. 353–408.

and headboroughs about the poor in 1618, before it had its own beadle,[42] and again in 1701 and, after offering payment, in 1712; it barred manorial officers from serving as beadle in 1781.[43] In addition to safeguarding the commons, the Lordshold court in its turn gave orders about the stocks and whipping post, which the parish had failed to repair, in 1744.[44] The steward denied intentional infringement of parochial privileges in 1804, after the vestry's protest at not having been informed of inclosures, and the vestry promised in 1806 to keep better records, after the court's complaint that their inadequacy made it difficult to appoint officers. The vestry disclaimed any connexion with manorial officers when asked to meet parliamentary election expenses in 1833.[45]

PARISH GOVERNMENT TO 1837. Hackney, where parish meetings were recorded from 1581,[46] had an unusual dual form of government from 1613, when a select vestry was instituted by a faculty from the bishop of London. In most parishes a select vestry tolerated open meetings only to add occasional weight to its own decisions. In Hackney, perhaps because it attracted so many rich merchants, the parish officers 'and other inhabitants' continued to meet every few months and shared power with the 'gentlemen of the vestry', for whom the faculty was reissued in 1679. Both bodies were merged in an open vestry in 1833,[47] by which time they had surrendered responsibility for the poor and for lighting and watching to trustees under Acts of 1763 and 1810; separate vestries for South and West Hackney had also been created by the subdivision of the rectory in 1831. Hackney vestry's continued influence through the election of parish officers and others as trustees was diminished by the establishment of the poor-law union in 1837.[48]

In 1547 Church House of c. 1520 was said to have been built for meetings on the king's, the church's, or parochial business. Presumably it was so used until taken for the free school c. 1616.[49] Officers recorded from 1554 were 2 churchwardens and 4 *laici* or sidesmen,[50] and 2 surveyors of the highways, 4 surveyors of the poor, and 2 collectors for the poor from 1581. One churchwarden was elected in 1583, the second one presumably being named by the vicar.[51] A steady source of income which came

to form the 'unappropriated funds' was foreshadowed in 1590, when the vicar and 15 others excused Thomas Audley from parish offices in return for money towards repair of the church.[52] Inhabitants were first listed by district for the collection of church rates in 1605.[53]

The faculty of 1613 was requested by the vicar and others after trouble from 'the meanest sort being greater in number'. It appointed the rector, vicar, assistant curate, churchwardens, and 32 named parishioners, or any 10 of them, to meet as vestrymen at the church.[54] Vacancies thereafter were filled by co-option. In the 1620s the vestry usually appointed annually 2 churchwardens, 4 sidesmen, 2 surveyors, and 2 collectors; later in the century overseers, rather than collectors, and 2 sidesmen were chosen. At least 4 of the original vestrymen and in 1628 both churchwardens signed with a cross.[55] There was a parish clerk before 1625, when the vicar's installation of his own nominee led to an action in King's Bench which upheld the traditional right of election claimed for the parish and exercised by the vestry.[56] In 1711 the parish clerk was also given the office of vestry clerk, apparently a new post whose duties were again defined in 1756.[57] A sexton was paid an increased salary in 1632 and one was succeeded by his wife as sextoness in 1690;[58] the office was lucrative enough to be shared in 1744 and entailed the employment of pew openers in 1759.[59] A beadle was to be appointed in 1657 'for the preventing of multiplying of the poor' and again in 1671; his duties were reviewed in 1694, when all new lodgers were to be reported.[60] Two beadles were paid in 1732–3 and again, as home and out beadles, with partly differing functions until 1771, in 1753;[61] there were three beadles by 1810.[62] Searchers, to examine corpses, were originally appointed by magistrates but from c. 1727 by the vestry until they were discontinued in 1836.[63] A verger was first appointed in 1799.[64] Most salaried offices, like those of the early schoolmasters and of lecturers and others connected with the church,[65] were renewed annually; in 1730 they were those of vestry clerk, beadle, organist, sextoness, clock minder, organ minder, organ bellows blower, churchyard keeper, and midwife. Holders of all the offices save that of organ minder were reappointed in 1760, by which date 6 bearers were also chosen.[66] Records include a summary minute book for 1581–1613, vestry

42 Vestry mins. s.v. 1618; below (parish govt. to 1837).
43 Vestry mins. 26 May 1701; 26 June 1712; 17 Apr. 1781.
44 G.L.R.O., M79/LH/52, ct. 3 Apr. 1744.
45 Vestry mins. 3 Apr., 14 Oct. 1804; 22 Dec. 1806; 24 Jan. 1833.
46 H.A.D., D/F/TYS/1.
47 S. and B. Webb, *Eng. Local Govt., Par. and County* (1924), 193, 228–9 n., 246 n., 264. Both types of mtg. were sometimes recorded in same bk., e.g. vestry mins. 10 Aug., 26 Dec. 1724.
48 4 Geo. III, c. 43; 50 Geo. III, c. 190 (Local and Personal); vestry mins. 30 June 1831; G.L.R.O., P79/JN1/157.
49 *Lond. Rec. Soc.* xvi. 68; below, educ. (preamble).
50 Guildhall MSS. 9537/1, f. 78; 9537/2, f. 106r. Four *oeconomi* or churchwardens in 1577: ibid. 9537/4.
51 H.A.D., D/F/TYS/1, pp. 1–3. Officers 1581–1607 listed in ibid. D/F/TYS/12/2, pp. iii–iv.

52 H.A.D., D/F/TYS/1, p. 5; Webb, *Eng. Local Govt.* 229 n.
53 H.A.D., D/F/TYS/1, pp. 66–7.
54 Ibid. D/F/TYS/2, pp. 2–3; Robinson, *Hackney*, ii. 85–7.   55 H.A.D., D/F/TYS/2, *passim*.
56 Vestry mins. 20 July 1628; G.L.R.O., P 79/JN1/239/1–3.
57 Vestry mins. 13 Dec. 1711; 12 June 1756.
58 Ibid. 1 May 1632; 22 Apr. 1690.
59 Ibid. 23 Jan. 1744; 16 Apr. 1745; 16 June 1759.
60 Ibid. 1 May 1657; 24 May 1658; 25 Apr. 1671; 17 Sept. 1694.
61 Ibid. 18 Dec. 1731; 11 Apr. 1732; 27 Mar. 1733; 24 Apr. 1753; 16 Dec. 1771.
62 Ibid. 24 Apr. 1810.
63 Ibid. 29 July 1727; 5 July 1736; 30 Mar., 30 May, 24 Sept. 1748; 7 Aug. 1836.   64 Ibid. 15 Apr. 1799.
65 Below, ch.; educ. (preamble).
66 Vestry mins. 31 Mar. 1730; 8 Apr. 1760.

minutes from 1613,[67] parishioners' meetings minutes for 1762–1824,[68] churchwardens' accounts, some with overseers' accounts, from 1732,[69] poor rate books from 1716,[70] churchwardens' rate books from 1743 and statute labour books from 1720, with gaps,[71] and lamp and watch rate books from 1764.[72]

The vestry met at Easter, for appointments and audits,[73] and also irregularly: 4 times in all in 1620, 9 in 1660, 16 in 1700, 4 in 1740 and 1770, 8 in 1810, and 3 in 1820. Attendances ranged from 7 to 22 in 1660, with an average of nearly 16 which varied little thereafter. In 1712 absentees were to be asked to attend and in 1719 it was agreed that if numbers should fall below 13 a churchwarden and 4 others might prepare proposals for the next vestry;[74] nine meetings were dissolved between 1729 and 1753 for lack of a quorum. It was planned in 1732 and 1759 to summon one at least every two months and in 1790, without success, to observe fixed dates in June and August.[75] The chair was normally taken by the vicar or his curate. A suggestion that the vestry should meet at the 'parish house' (Church House) rather than its room at the church was rejected in 1781.[76] Church House, in use in 1795, was replaced in 1802 by the building later called the old town hall.[77]

Wider parish meetings obtruded, as in 1723 when the vestry insisted on its right to choose a lecturer, although the general public might afterwards voice its opinion. On legal advice, the right was conceded to all who paid poor rates.[78] Such parishioners were sometimes present in the vestry, as in 1700 when 'others' were noted after the named attenders.[79] In 1725 a separate book was reserved for general meetings and in 1739 the select vestry forced several outsiders to withdraw.[80] The vicar and parish officers attended the parish meetings, of which there were 11 in 1763 and 7 in 1770. The parish meetings submitted names to the magistrates for appointment as highway surveyors and were concerned particularly with the poor, although all matters of parish interest were discussed.[81] Petitioners for an inquiry into the leasing of Lammas lands were accused of treating a session of the select vestry as a public meeting in 1804. A new local Act, to create more vestrymen, was sought in 1813. The vestry claimed that parochial rates and expenditure had always been effectually controlled by parish meetings, when it finally admitted an additional 49 inhabitants in 1833.[82] The merger resulted from legal opinions that the bishop's faculty, a copy of which

had been withheld by the clerk, was an unsafe foundation for a select vestry.[83]

In 1581 the collectors for the poor raised money to bring up a fatherless child and in 1598 they made 37 payments, including one to the 'poor house'.[84] Pensioners were to attend church twice a week in 1620 and were to number not more than 15 in 1628, when a separate book for poor rates was to be bought.[85] Some pensions were paid for looking after the young or the sick.[86] The poor's stock was separated in 1628 from the church stock and consisted of the income from parish lands which had been acquired through charitable gifts and which were leased out by the vestry; money in the church box was added.[87] When the magistrates decided that Hackney could afford to contribute to relief in Stepney in 1676, the vestry claimed that it was already burdened with extraordinary poor. In 1708 bread was distributed to up to 74 people, 'as was usual in this parish', whether or not the amount was covered by gifts.[88] In 1710 badging was to be strictly enforced on all paupers except Henry Rowe.[89]

Responsibility by 1741 had devolved upon a workhouse committee, which fixed the poor rate and was answerable to the parish meetings rather than the vestry.[90] An Act of 1763 committed the poor to a board of trustees, being the vicar, parish officers, and anyone eligible for office, including those who had compounded; any five of them could fix the poor rate.[91] The early meetings of the trustees, rarely numbering more than 12, were held weekly in the vestry room. Separate rates were introduced, for the poor and for lighting and watching, and five collectors were appointed in 1764; an initial sum was raised by the promise of annuities secured on the rates.[92] An Act of 1810 allowed all householders rated for the poor at £40 a year to act as co-vestrymen, sharing the vestry's responsibility for relief although not in other fields. It also increased the number of trustees, who might be vestrymen or co-vestrymen, from 53 to 72, and provided for them to form 12 committees of six, which would meet weekly in rotation, and to delimit six districts: Clapton, Homerton, Church Street, Mare Street, Kingsland, and Newington.[93] The enlarged board of trustees in 1811 met 17 times at the parish house, with an average attendance of 28.[94] It was elected annually after the opening of the vestry in 1833.[95]

Revenue for the poor in 1628 was £14 10s. from charities' lands and £2 10s. from £50 stock.[96] The poor rate, increasingly important as

67 In H.A.D. and G.L.R.O.
68 G.L.R.O., P79/JN1/157.
69 H.A.D., P/J/CW/1–36, 119–23; G.L.R.O., P79/JN1/218–28.
70 H.A.D., P/J/P/71–195.
71 Ibid. P/J/CW/37–118; P/J/H/7–10, 12–62.
72 Ibid. P/J/L/1–82.
73 Para. based on vestry mins. passim.
74 Vestry mins. 16 July 1712; 12 Dec. 1719.
75 Ibid. 8 Jan. 1732; 16 Apr. 1759; 6 Apr. 1790.
76 Ibid. 26 May; 4 Aug. 1781.
77 Lysons, Environs, ii. 512; Robinson, Hackney, i. 91; below, local govt. after 1837.
78 Vestry mins. 18 Nov. 1723; 1 Apr., 27 May 1724.
79 Ibid. 27 May, 17 June 1700.
80 Ibid. 11 Jan. 1725; 1 May 1739.

81 G.L.R.O., P79/JN1/157, passim.
82 Vestry mins. 15 Oct. 1804; 16 Dec. 1813; 9 Apr. 1833.
83 Hackney Mag. Nov. 1833, 17–20.
84 H.A.D., D/F/TYS/1, ff. 1, 37.
85 Vestry mins. 19 Nov. 1620; 1 Dec. 1628.
86 Ibid. 1 Dec. 1628; 22 Apr. 1650.
87 Ibid. 1 Dec. 1628; below, charities.
88 Vestry mins. 16 Sept. 1676; 20 June 1708.
89 Ibid. 14 June 1710; above, manors (Shacklewell).
90 Par. mins. 4 July 1763.
91 50 Geo. III, c. 190 (Local and Personal).
92 G.L.R.O., P/JN1/158, pp. 16–17 and passim.
93 50 Geo. III, c. 190 (Local and Personal).
94 H.A.D., P/J/P/2.
95 Robinson, Hackney, ii. 322.
96 Vestry mins. 1 Dec. 1628.

the payers multiplied, raised £120 in 1669 and £326 in 1710.[97] In 1720 nearly two thirds of expenditure was on monthly payments to 52 pensioners, some with children, a tenth was on nursing, and the rest on children's clothing.[98] The cost of maintaining the poor was £1,725 17s. 5d. in 1775–6,[99] when the rate was 2s. in the £,[1] and an average of £2,376 8s. 5d. for the three years to Easter 1785.[2] It was £5,158 in 1803, over £13,000 in 1813 and 1821, and slightly less in 1831; the rise, more uneven than that of the population, produced an expenditure per head of 15s. 8d. in 1813 and less than half of that amount in 1831.[3] Nearly £14,349 was levied but only £8,849 spent on the poor in 1834–5.[4]

A workhouse where a child was to be sent in 1709 was presumably outside the parish.[5] In 1732 rented premises were repaired as a workhouse.[6] A house on the south side of Homerton's high street was leased from the Milborne family in 1741 and in 1761; the parish officers assigned the lease in 1764 to the new trustees for the poor[7] and in 1769 lent them money to buy the site.[8] The workhouse management committee met weekly in the 1740s and 1750s,[9] when the number of inmates ranged from 41 to 74.[10] At first the committee arranged quarterly contracts for supplies but the poor were farmed by 1755 and in 1764;[11] direct management was resumed in 1765.[12] One of the six overseers was to attend on every weekday at the workhouse under the Act of 1810.[13] Accommodation was for 220 in 1775–6[14] and expensive enlargement was carried out in 1810–11 and again in 1813.[15] Stricter discipline and more profitable work were sought in 1811 but many rules were not kept by 1822.[16] The parish claimed to manage a model workhouse in 1831, when it held 102 men and 153 women, housed separately, 80 boys, and 60 girls; work was provided there and a few inmates were farmed out. In addition outdoor relief was paid to 398 pensioners and for 35 children to be nursed.[17] The buildings apparently had no special accommodation for the religious services which were held and the schooling which was recommended in 1815.[18]

LOCAL GOVERNMENT AFTER 1837.

Although the body of trustees continued until 1899,[19] the Poor Law Amendment Act, 1834, vested practical responsibility for the poor from 1837 in Hackney union until the London Government Act, 1929, substituted the L.C.C. in 1930. The union combined the old parishes of Hackney and Stoke Newington;[20] initially, Hackney contributed seven eighths of the annual cost[21] and elected 13 guardians (20 by 1872) to Stoke Newington's 5.[22] Weekly meetings were held at the parish house and later at the town hall and at the workhouse.[23] The old workhouse was replaced by a building begun in 1838 and finished by 1842,[24] which the trustees sold to the guardians in 1845,[25] when further building had to be done.[26] The premises in 1849 included a range along the high street, in front of women's wards and a small infirmary to the west and men's wards, with a stone yard, to the east; farther south stood a chapel of 1848 seating 500 and schools, behind which the grounds stretched to beyond the new railway line.[27] The schools were criticized in 1854, when attended by 45 boys and 79 girls, but had improved by 1857, when the numbers had risen by 50.[28] The union maintained 459 indoor and 2,034 outdoor poor, 42.6 for every 1,000 inhabitants, in 1850; the proportion fell to 28.9 for every 1,000 inhabitants in 1860 but was 55 in 1870.[29] Although some buildings were adapted and others added for the infirmary, later Hackney hospital, the workhouse continued to receive both the able bodied and the infirm and was certified for 1,090 inmates in 1885.[30] As Homerton central institution it was certified for 1,404 in 1930, when the guardians derived most of their income from Hackney M.B. as overseers and when they also had nearby branch homes, besides one for children at Ongar (Essex).[31]

From 1833 the trustees and the enlarged vestry[32] were still seen as unrepresentative by the *Hackney Magazine*, which publicized their proceedings.[33] The vestry in 1836 set up a 20-member highways board, soon renewed under a new Act,[34] and in 1837 accepted the continuance of the trustees'

97 Robinson, *Hackney*, i. 253.
98 H.A.D., D/J/P/76.
99 *Rep. Cttee. on Returns by Overseers, 1776*, p. 100.
1 G.L.R.O., P/JN1/158, p. 295.
2 *Abstract of Returns by Overseers, 1787*, H.C. 1st ser. ix, p. 143.
3 *Rep. Com. Poor Laws*, H.C. 44, p. 99f (1834), xxxv, app. B2, pt.1. Half yearly rates detailed in trustees' min. bks.: H.A.D., P/J/P/2–23.
4 *Poor Law Com. 2nd Rep.* H.C. 595–II, p. 214 (1836), xxix.　　5 Vestry mins. 15 Dec. 1709.
6 Ibid. 4 Jan. 1737; *Hackney and Stoke Newington Past*, 79; *Hackney Par. Workho. Rules* (facsimile pub. by H.A.D. 1986).　　7 H.A.D., P/J/P/68/1–2, 5.
8 G.L.R.O., M79/LH/15, p. 120; H.A.D., P/J/P/2, p. 60.　　9 H.A.D., P/J/P/35; G.L.R.O., P79/JN1/160–1.
10 H.A.D., P/J/P/35, 18 Sept. 1742; 25 Oct. 1746.
11 Ibid. *passim*; ibid. P/J/P/68/3–4. Mins. and outdoor relief payments are ibid. P/J/P/37–40.
12 G.L.R.O., P/JN1/158, pp. 85, 100; cf. H.A.D., P/J/P/2, pp. 289, 308, *passim*.
13 50 Geo. III, c. 190.
14 *Rep. Cttee. on Returns by Overseers, 1776*, p. 100.
15 Robinson, *Hackney*, i. 253; par. mins. 31 Aug. 1812; *Hackney Par. Workho. Rules*; H.A.D., P/J/P/2, pp. 4, 148, and *passim*.
16 *Hackney Par. Workho. Rules*; H.A.D., P/J/P/2, pp.

43–7.　　　　　　　　　　　　　　17 *Rep. Com. Poor Laws*, 98g.
18 *Hackney and Stoke Newington Past*, 80, illus. 99- 100; above, plate 64; H.A.D., P/J/P/2, pp. 238, 243.
19 H.A.D., P/J/P/11–23; *Hackney Dir.* (1872 and later edns.); A. Bassett Hopkins, *Boros. of the Metropolis* (1900), 21, 29, 57.
20 4 & 5 Wm. IV, c. 76; 19 Geo. V, c. 17; *V.C.H. Mdx.* viii. 197.
21 *Poor Law Com. 4th Rep.* H.C. 147, app. D, p. 81 (1840), xviii.　　　　22 *Hackney Dir.* (1849 and later edns.).
23 G.L.R.O., Ha BG 1–137 (min. bks. 1837–1940).
24 Robinson, *Hackney*, ii. 343–4.
25 G.L.R.O., M79/LH/26, p. 115.
26 *Statement relating to Metropolitan Workhos.* H.C. 474, p. 3 (1866), lxi.
27 G.L.R.O., M79/LH/26, pp. 118–19 (plan); P.R.O., HO 129/11/4/1/2.
28 *Mins. of Educ. Cttee. of Council, 1854–5*, H.C. 1954, p. 35 (1854–5), xlii; *1857–8*, H.C. 2386, p. 49 (1857–8), xlv.
29 *Return of Paupers in each Union*, H.C. 214, p. 2 (1876), lxiii.
30 *Return relating to Accn. in Workhos. and Infirmaries in Metropolis*, H.C. 93, p. 4 (1888), lxxxvii.
31 G.L.R.O., Ha BG 137, pp. 4, 590–1.
32 Para. based on G.L.R.O., P79/JN1/147, *passim*.
33 *Hackney Mag.* Nov. 1833 sqq.
34 Ibid. pp. 55–8, 105–7.

lamp board.[35] It also protested at the high property qualification for election as guardian and in 1841 opposed the rates sought by the Tower Hamlets commissioners of sewers.[36] Meetings were normally chaired by the rector or a church-warden and spent much time over repeated and rising demands to abandon church rates.

A new administrative vestry, for the whole parish but with more limited responsibilities, was installed under the Metropolis Local Management Act, 1855. The Act replaced the metropolitan commissioners of sewers, successors to the Tower Hamlets commissioners, with the Hackney district of the Metropolitan Board of Works (M.B.W.); the district, which included Stoke Newington, returned one member to the M.B.W.[37] The new vestry superseded the three church vestries for all but church purposes. It met, erratically, less than once a month. In addition to the rector and churchwardens, it consisted of 119 vestrymen, of whom one third was elected annually, representing the seven wards of Stamford Hill, Homerton, Dalston, De Beauvoir Town, Hackney, South Hackney, and West Hackney.[38] It chose the district board and, after some doubts about their continued existence, the trustees of the poor.[39] Resenting the link with Stoke Newington and the division and vagueness of its own powers, the vestry criticized the bookkeeping of the former highway and lighting boards and unsuccessfully sought to control those parochial charities which had been apportioned to South and West Hackney.[40] It appointed a fire engine committee, as did the trustees, and a finance committee.[41] Through a joint committee also representing the trustees and the district board, it was responsible for building a new town hall.[42]

Hackney district board, meeting weekly from 1855 at the town hall, consisted of 51 members for the eight Hackney wards and 5 for Stoke Newington. At first it was often chaired by J. R. Daniel-Tyssen and represented on the M.B.W. by George Offor, an earlier opponent of church rates. The board appointed general purposes and finance committees and superseded the highway and lighting boards. Officers included a clerk, a medical officer of health, a surveyor, and an inspector of nuisances.[43] From 1856 the trustees of the poor met twice a year to make a parish or poor trust rate, chiefly for the guardians, the Metropolitan Police, and the fire engines, and separate general, lighting, and sewers' rates for the district board of works. Many other meetings dealt with appeals against assessments. The trustees' delays in meeting financial calls forced the guardians to postpone the settling of bills in 1856.[44]

The district board of works was dissolved in 1894.[45] No longer linked with Stoke Newington except in the poor-law union, Hackney was administered again by the vestry, which maintained the district board's officers and worked, as the board had done, through committees;[46] it called itself a corporate body and was quick to seek a transfer of powers from the trustees of the poor, since many vestrymen were also trustees.[47] Both vestry and trustees were superseded by Hackney metropolitan borough council under the London Government Act, 1899, which also introduced a single rate.[48]

BOROUGH OF HACKNEY. *Per fess in chief the dexter side gules with a representation of Hackney tower proper and the sinister side per fess sable and argent with a maltese cross per fess argent and gules, and in the base six pieces barry wavy argent and azure*

[Granted 1924]

Hackney metropolitan borough council was first elected in 1900 and consisted of a mayor, 10 aldermen, and 60 councillors representing 8 wards which remained unchanged until 1936: Stamford Hill, Clapton Park, Homerton, the Downs, Kingsland, Hackney, South Hackney, and West Hackney.[49] In 1903 the town hall was the meeting place of the council twice monthly; in addition to the town clerk, treasurer, and solicitor, there were departments for the accountant, the engineer and surveyor, public health, electricity, and libraries.[50] The borough received a grant of arms in 1924.[51] From 1936 there were 8 aldermen and 48 councillors for 16 wards. Most of the wards were altered and renamed in 1955 but there were still 16 in 1965 when, under the London Government Act, 1963, the metropolitan borough was joined with those of Stoke Newington and Shoreditch to form the London Borough of Hackney.[52] The new borough had 20 wards in 1971 and 23, of which 15 lay in Hackney, by 1978.[53]

The first town hall, which in 1802 had replaced Church House,[54] remained in use until 1866. Rooms were then leased to the M.B.W., the guardians, who disputed ownership with the vestry, and several provident societies, and public meetings might still be held there.[55] A plain

35 Ibid. pp. 78, 84.
36 Ibid. pp. 90–1, 289–90.
37 18 & 19 Vic. c. 120; Grocott, *Hackney*, 18, 21–4.
38 *Hackney Dir.* (1872); *Kelly's Dir. Hackney* (1890).
39 H.A.D., J/V/1, pp. 3–7, 54, 165–7, and *passim*.
40 H.A.D., J/V/1, pp. 64–5, 99, 165–7, 216 sqq.
41 Ibid. J/V/1, p. 89 and *passim*; J/V/2, *passim*; ibid. P/J/P/15, p. 71.   42 Ibid. J/V/1, p. 219; 2, pp. 52–3.
43 H.A.D., BW/1; G.L.R.O., P79/JN1/166, *passim*.
44 H.A.D., P/J/P/15, pp. 16, 62–6 and *passim*.
45 Metropolis Management (Plumstead and Hackney) Act, 56 & 57 Vic. c. 55.
46 H.A.D., J/V/18/1–5 (ann. reps. 1895–1900); mins. and letter bks. in H.A.D.

47 Ibid. J/V/18/1, pp. 3, 19–21.
48 62 & 63 Vic. c. 14; Hopkins, *Boros. of Metropolis*, 21, 29, 57.
49 *The Times*, 3 Nov. 1900, 14a; 3 Nov. 1934, 7b; L.C.C. *Lond. Statistics*, xli. 24.
50 *Kelly's Dir. Hackney* (1902–3).
51 C. W. Scott-Giles, *Civic Heraldry* (1953), 251.
52 L.C.C. *Lond. Statistics*, xli. 24; ibid. N.S. iii. 20; *Census*, 1951–61; Lond. Govt. Act, 1963, c. 33.
53 *Census*, 1971; H.A.D., Hackney L.B. *Ward Map* (1978); *Hackney Herald*, June 1986 (suppl.).
54 Lysons, *Environs*, Suppl. 173.
55 H.A.D., J/V/2, pp. 588, 622; J/V/3, p. 80; *Terrier*, Mar. 1987.

two-storeyed block of four bays, the central two slightly projecting, it was given a stone cladding in 1900, with a pediment, balustrades, and more elaborate doorway. Part was occupied from 1899 by the London City & Midland Bank, which remained there as the Midland Bank in 1991.[56] The second town hall, begun in 1864, was opened in 1866 in the centre of the rectangular space called Hackney Grove.[57] Designed in the

LONDON BOROUGH OF HACK-NEY. *Per fess in chief per fess sable and argent a maltese cross per fess argent and gules between two oak tress eradicated or fructed gules and in the base gules three bells or, the whole within a bordure barry wavy argent and azure*

[Granted 1969]

'French-Italian' style by Hammack & Lambert and faced with Portland stone, it was of two storeys over a basement and consisted of a five-bayed central block, balustraded and with a Doric porch, projecting beyond single-bay wings.[58] The estimated building costs were greatly exceeded.[59] Extensive alterations by Gordon, Lowther, & Gunton, opened in 1898, included wider two-storeyed wings producing an ornate frontage of 11 bays.[60] A third town hall was begun in 1934, finished in 1936, and opened in 1937, replacing houses behind the second one, of which the site thereafter formed a garden. 'Conventional but not showy', the building was designed by Lanchester & Lodge and faced in Portland stone; it was flat-roofed and four-storeyed, with a front of nine bays, the central five slightly projecting. From 1965 it was the municipal centre of Hackney L.B.[61] The building in 1991 retained its unaltered interiors in the Art Deco style.[62]

Conservatives outnumbered Liberals on the first borough council, elected in 1900. As Municipal Reformers they averted Progressive control in 1906, by allying with Independents (Ratepayers' Association), and took overall control in 1912.[63] Labour, which in 1900 had unsuccessfully run 9 candidates in Homerton, the most radical ward, narrowly took control in 1919 but lost every seat to an alliance of Municipal

Reformers and Progressives in 1922 and 1925.[64] It regained a majority only in 1934 but kept it thereafter, both on the metropolitan borough council and, except in 1968, on its successor. One Communist was elected in 1945 and two were elected in 1949.[65] Apart from Springfield, all the wards in the former borough elected Labour members to Hackney L.B. in 1990.[66] The turnout in municipal elections was close to London's average until the Second World War but lower thereafter.[67]

Two parliamentary seats were allotted to Hackney by the Representation of the People Act, 1867.[68] Liberals were always returned until the constituencies of North, Central, and South Hackney were created in 1885.[69] Hackney North returned a Conservative or Unionist until 1945, except in 1906. Hackney Central voted Conservative until 1900, then Liberal until 1923, Conservative again in 1924 and 1931, and Labour in 1929 and 1935. Hackney South generally returned a Liberal, with Conservatives only in 1895, 1900, at a by-election in 1922, and 1931; it was the first to vote Labour, in 1923, as it did again in 1929 and 1935. All M.P.s were elected as Labour from 1945, the boundaries being redrawn to form the two seats of Hackney Central and of Hackney North and Stoke Newington in 1955. Hackney South and Shoreditch formed a third constituency in the 1970s but Hackney Central was divided between the other two Hackney seats in the 1980s. The M.P. for Hackney South, who had joined the Social Democrat party, was defeated in 1983.[70] Members included Sir Charles Reed (d. 1881), chairman of the London school board, and his successor Henry Fawcett (d. 1884), the 'member for India', and for South Hackney Sir Charles Russell from 1885 until 1894, when he became Lord Russell of Killowen and lord chief justice.[71] The financier Horatio Bottomley (d. 1933) represented South Hackney from 1906, despite local opposition from his own party, and as an independent from 1918 until his imprisonment in 1922.[72] Herbert Stanley Morrison (d. 1965), later Lord Morrison of Lambeth, was co-opted as mayor of Hackney in 1919 and began his parliamentary career as M.P. for Hackney South in 1923.[73]

From 1889 Hackney's three parliamentary seats each returned two members to the L.C.C.[74]

56   Robinson, *Hackney*, i. 91; Pevsner, *Lond.* ii. 168; *Lost Hackney*, 31; *Hackney Photos.* i. 6; *Terrier*, Mar. 1987; *List of Bldgs.* (1975).
57   The rector hoped that it would be on the cramped site of its predecessor: H.A.D., J/V/2, pp. 52–3, 65–6.
58   *Illus. Lond. News*, 13 Oct. 1866, 371–2; *Hackney Photos.* ii. 70; *Terrier*, Mar. 1987.
59   H.A.D., J/V/2, pp. 286, 288–9; ibid. H/LD 7/5.
60   Ibid. J/V/18/2, 30; Hackney *Official Guide* [1925], 58–9; *Terrier*, Mar. 1987; above, plate 36.
61   *Terrier*, Mar. 1987; Pevsner, *Lond.* ii. 167; Hackney, *Official Guide* [1938]; *Daily Telegraph*, 11 Dec. 1989, 4c.
62   H.B.M.C. Lond., HAC 65; *List of Bldgs.* (1991).
63   Election results in *The Times*, 3 Nov. 1900, 14a; 3 Nov. 1906, 5a, b; 2 Nov. 1912, 11b.
64   Ibid. 4 Nov. 1919, 12f, 14a; 3 Nov. 1922, 14d, 16c.
65   Ibid. 3 Nov. 1934, 7b; 3 Nov. 1937, 19a; 3 Nov. 1945, 2c; 14 May 1949, 2b; G.L.C. *Ann. Abstract of Gtr. Lond.*

Statistics, ii. 8; vii. 11; x. 6; xii; *Hackney Herald*, June 1986.
66   *Hackney Gaz.* 9 May 1990, 16.
67   L.C.C. *Lond. Statistics*, xvii sqq.
68   30 & 31 Vic. c. 102, pt. II.
69   F. W. S. Craig, *Brit. Parl. Election Results 1832–85* (1989), 11; Redistribution of Seats Act, 48 & 49 Vic. c. 23. Boundaries in H.A.D., BW/E/13/19.
70   F. W. S. Craig, *Brit. Parl. Election Results 1885–1918* (1989), 19–20; ibid. *1918–49* (1969), 20–2; *1950–73* (1983), 17–18, 42; *1974–83* (1984), 20–1; H. Pelling, *Social Geog. of Brit. Elections 1885–1910*, 30, 33, 37–9; L.C.C. *Lond. Statistics*, N.S. iii. 12; *Whitaker's Almanack* (1983 and later edns.).   71   *D.N.B.*
72   Ibid.; Craig, *Election Results 1885–1918*, 20.
73   *D.N.B.*; Herb. Morrison, *An Autobiography* (1960), 82–3 and *passim*.
74   *Whitaker's Almanack* (1890); G. Alderman, *Lond. Jewry and Lond. Politics 1889–1986* (1989), 28.

PUBLIC SERVICES

WATER SUPPLY. Six excellent wells were noted *c.* 1720, including those commemorated in the names Pigwell brook and, by the 15th century, Shacklewell and Well Street. One, a disused chalybeate spring between Church Street and Dalston,[75] may have been the source near Dalston from which pipes were laid to Aldgate after Londoners had voted funds in 1535.[76] Hackney was among the places from which London was authorized to draw water by an Act of 1543, which eventually led to the creation of the Hampstead Water Co., and the Lea at Hackney marsh figured as a possible source in unrealized proposals of 1610.[77] Church Well Path records a well, on the site of Hackney bus depot, which had been abandoned by 1850.[78] Conduit field lay in the north angle of Kates Lane and Upper Clapton Road in 1790; an ancient conduit there in 1831 was to be commemorated in Conduit Place off Wood (later Rossington) Street.[79]

Clapton and some other parts were supplied in 1720 from the Lea through pipes which had recently been laid by the Tyssen family.[80] In 1753, however, Hackney and Homerton were losing summer visitors because of the lack of 'soft' water.[81] From 1760 Abraham Ogier and other lessees of the Tyssens' corn mill at Lea bridge increased the waterwheel's power by making a weir, which in 1766 pumped water for Hackney. Assisted in 1784 by a reservoir at Clapton and with profits from the waterworks rising in 1791, they continued as suppliers until a new lease was granted in 1820 to a Mr. Killick. The lease and freehold were bought by the East London Waterworks Co. in 1830.[82]

The East London Waterworks Co., incorporated to supply Hackney and other parishes from the Lea in 1807, secured further powers in 1829[83] and had made a waterworks channel from Lea bridge to Old Ford alongside the Lee trustees' Hackney or New cut by 1834. The supply was increased by reconstruction at Lea bridge in 1837. Lea bridge reservoir was built between the river, the cut, and the new channel and in 1838 the reservoir at Clapton was replaced by one at Stamford Hill, where by 1891 it had

made way for houses on the west corner of Portland Avenue and Darenth Road.[84] Under an Act of 1853 filter beds were built at Lea bridge, one on the Essex side of the Lea and the other replacing Lea bridge reservoir. A new engine was installed in 1854 and two more filter beds, on the Essex bank, were built under an Act of 1867.[85]

In 1850 the vestry unanimously resolved to seek the establishment of a public body to improve the metropolitan water supply.[86] In 1874 the East London Waterworks Co. supplied most of Hackney; the New River Co. served the north-west corner of the parish, Shacklewell, Dalston, and De Beauvoir Town.[87] The New River Co.'s supply was not yet constant in 1888 and the East London's was disrupted in 1894.[88] Under the Metropolis Water Act, 1902, both companies were superseded in 1904 by the Metropolitan Water Board,[89] itself superseded under the Water Act, 1973, by the Thames Water Authority in 1974.[90]

SEWERAGE posed a problem by 1845 and preoccupied the new district board's medical officer of health in 1856, when the spread of housing had turned Hackney brook into an open sewer.[91] In 1859–60 the M.B.W. completed its northern high-level sewer along the line of Hackney brook to Church Street and thence south-eastward across Victoria Park to Old Ford,[92] where it joined the Marsh sewer skirting the Lea from Tottenham and, in the 1860s, the Wick Lane branch sewer. The high-level and Ratcliff storm relief sewer, running due south along Mare Street to join the middle-level sewer in Shoreditch, was built between 1881 and 1884. The L.C.C. built a more northerly middle-level sewer, passing through De Beauvoir Town and south Hackney to Old Ford, between 1906 and 1911. It also built storm relief sewers and curbed flooding on the marsh with a main sewer from Abbey Mills in Stratford, passing mainly between the Lea and the Marsh sewer, which was finished in 1908.[93]

Local sanitation[94] from 1856 was the respon-

75 Stow, *Survey* (1720), ii. 123; above, intro.
76 Stow, *Survey*, ed. Kingsford, i. 128; H. W. Dickinson, *Water Supply of Gtr. Lond.* (1954), 12.
77 Dickinson, *Water Supply*, 12–13, 43; *V.C.H. Mdx.* ix. 76, 138; Lond. Water Supply Act, 35 Hen. VIII, c. 10; Lond. Water (Hackney) Act, 7 Jas. I, c. 9.
78 *Starling's Map* (1831); D. Mander, *St. John-at-Hackney* (1993), 29.   79 Ibid.; H.A.D., V 2/4.
80 Stow, *Survey* (1720), ii. 123.
81 H.A.D., H/LD 7/2, pp. 18, 107; ibid. D/F/BAG/13A.
82 Ibid. 3, p. 39; Dickinson, *Water Supply*, 89–90; River Lee Navigation Act, 7 Geo. III, c. 51; Robinson, *Hackney*, i. 11, 49.
83 East Lond. Waterworks Co. Act, 47 Geo. III, Sess. 2, c. 72 (Local and Personal); ibid. 10 Geo. IV, c. 117 (Local and Personal).
84 Dickinson, *Water Supply*, 89–90; Robinson, *Hackney*, i. 50–1, 58; J. Wyld, *Map of Lond. and its Environs* [*c.* 1845]; Old O.S. Map Lond. 21 (1868); Stanford, *Map of Lond.* (1891), sheet 3.
85 Dickinson, *Water Supply*, 91–4; East Lond. Water-

works Co. Act, 16 & 17 Vic. c. 166 (Local and Personal); ibid. 30 & 31 Vic. c. 149 (Local and Personal); Stanford, *Map of Lond.* (1862–5 edn.), sheet 4; Old O.S. Map Lond. 31 (1894).
86 G.L.R.O., P79/JN1/148.
87 J. F. B. Firth, *Municipal Lond.* (1876), map facing p. 381.
88 P. Scratchley, *Lond. Water Supply* (1888), map facing p. 45; H.A.D., J/V/18/1, pp. 11–12.
89 2 Edw. VII, c. 41; Dickinson, *Water Supply*, 124, figs. 21, 38.
90 *Annual Abstract of Gtr. Lond. Statistics*, ix. 68.
91 H. Jephson, *Sanitary Evolution of Lond.* (1907), 17, 100.
92 *Rep. of M.B.W. 1861*, H.C. 11, p. 391 (1862), xlvii.
93 G. W. Humphreys, *Main Drainage of Lond.* (L.C.C. rep. 1930), plan 2 and p. 30; L.C.C. *Main Drainage of Lond.* (1909), 8, 10–12.
94 Para. based on Jephson, *San. Evolution*, 103, 123, 136, 197–8, 266–7, 309, 373; *Returns of San. and Street Improvements since 1855*, H.C. 298, pp. 42–3 (1872), xlix.

sibility of Hackney district board of works, which spent most of its money on paving and sewerage and much of its time on prosecutions for nuisances. Although until 1866 the staff was too small to carry out inspections except after complaint, the medical officer reported that 1,518 houses had been connected to sewers and 1,839 nuisances abated in 1858 alone. Perhaps made unusually vigilant by the rapid pace of building, Hackney was one of the first parishes to take advantage of the Sanitary Act, 1866,[95] by regularly inspecting all houses with a rental of under £20. By 1870 it claimed to have paved and drained most yards and alleys, improved ventilation, and enforced the emptying of 5,715 cesspools for houses served by main drains. It again took the lead when further powers were conferred by the Sanitary Laws Amendment Act, 1874,[96] but was still short of staff, to inspect c. 2,000 work places, in 1891.

MEDICAL SERVICES. The vestry granted a weekly sum to keep a patient at Kingsland hospital in 1613,[97] and made payments to the father of a consumptive child in 1657 and to a surgeon in 1659 and 1704.[98] Precautions against the plague in 1665 were to include procuring four bearers, a sedan chair for the sick, and four nurses who would be pensioned for life.[99] In 1716 most of the poor rate was spent on pensions, often for the sick, but £94 18s. out of £352 7s. provided monthly payments to 14 women for nursing.[1] A midwife was paid weekly in 1665 and probably thereafter[2] for over a century, her office being among those renewable at Easter.[3] An apothecary received gratuities for treating the workhouse and out poor from 1741 until 1744, when he was granted a salary,[4] and a successor was retained in 1764 by the trustees, who in 1767 appointed a new surgeon and apothecary to attend both the workhouse and the poor at home.[5]

Hackney workhouse infirmary, the forerunner of Hackney hospital, at first consisted merely of beds for the sick or idiots. In 1764 the trustees felt that they had taken over an infirmary rather than a workhouse.[6] In 1836 the diet was wrong for inmates who were mostly old or infirm.[7] In 1837 the guardians reappointed one apothecary for the workhouse and three others for the districts as medical officers of health.[8] The infirmary in 1849 consisted of a single range on the west side of the grounds, immediately south

of the women's wards;[9] a smallpox ward was put up with the help of the inmates in 1860[10] and an iron building for sick children by 1866.[11] The parish had subscribed to a smallpox hospital at King's Cross since 1815[12] and to the county lunatic asylum since 1836 or earlier,[13] but the workhouse admitted a few smallpox cases and held some harmless imbeciles in 1866, when 119 of the 613 inmates were visited daily by the medical officer's assistant. The sick were not classified, were tended by only two paid nurses, and had no day rooms.[14]

Extensions and adaptations from 1869[15] led to a distinction between the workhouse, later called Hackney and Homerton central institution and entered from Sidney Road, and the infirmary, called Hackney hospital.[16] The workhouse in 1890 had 90 beds, chiefly for the aged bedridden and attended by three paid nurses, while the infirmary had 437 beds, with 35 nurses.[17] The infirmary expanded to fill the angle between Homerton's high street and Sidney Road and was largely rebuilt in the early 20th century to include four pavilions, two on each side of an administration block, with 800 beds by 1929. The institution underwent less change,[18] although its area included a pavilion opened in 1926 and on the west side a new nurses' home and mental block, all of which served the hospital.[19] Both sites passed in 1930 to the L.C.C., which in 1933 completed improvements to the hospital which had been planned by the guardians and in 1937 opened a six-storeyed nurses' home, partly replacing terraced houses acquired by the institution in Sidney Road.[20]

Hackney hospital passed in 1948 to the northeast metropolitan region's Hackney group management committee, under which it had 1,310 beds in 1949 and 920, mostly acute, in 1968.[21] The site was cramped and most of the buildings were outdated in 1976, when prefabricated operating theatres were being installed and one ward block offered 'arguably the worst general hospital psychiatric facility in the country'.[22] In 1985, when administered by the City and Hackney health authority as part of its Hackney/Homerton unit, it served as an acute hospital during the rebuilding of the Eastern hospital. From 1986 Hackney hospital retained 244 beds for old and psychiatric patients, whom it was planned to move to an extension at Homerton.[23] Demolition on the west side of the site was in progress in 1993.

95 29 & 30 Vic. c. 90.
96 37 & 38 Vic. c. 89.
97 Vestry mins. Dec. 1613.
98 Ibid. 6 Apr. 1657; 15 June 1659; 26 Sept. 1704.
99 Ibid. 16 July 1665; Lysons, Environs, ii. 482.
1 H.A.D., D/J/P/71.
2 Vestry mins. 28 Mar. 1665; 7 Apr. 1713.
3 e.g. ibid. 31 Mar. 1730; 17 Apr. 1750; 17 Apr. 1770.
4 H.A.D., P/J/P/35, 2 May 1741, 12 May 1744.
5 G.L.R.O., P79/JN1/158, pp. 1, 159.
6 Ibid. p. 31.   7 H.A.D., P/J/P11, p. 134.
8 G.L.R.O., Ha BG 1, pp. 16–17, 22–3.
9 Ibid. M79/LH/126, pp. 118–19.
10 Return of Metropolitan Workhos. H.C. 50, p. 136 (1867), lxi.
11 Rep. on Metropolitan Workho. Infirmaries, H.C. 372, p. 153 (1866), lxi.
12 H.A.D., P/J/P/2, p. 283; V.C.H. Mdx. v. 297.
13 H.A.D., P/J/P11, p. 1.
14 Rep. on Metropolitan Workho. Infirmaries, 153–6.
15 Ret. on Bldgs. for Paupers in Metropolis, H.C. 86, p. 2 (1876), lxiii.
16 Return relating to Accn. in Workhos. and Infirmaries in Metropolis, H.C. 93, p. 4 (1888), lxxxvii.
17 Return of Beds for Sick in Workhos. H.C. 365, p. 1 (1890–1), lxviii.
18 G.L.R.O., AR/CB/3/1, vol. I (inc. plan).
19 Ibid.; Ha BG 1, p. 591.
20 L.C.C. Ceremonial Pamphlets, 15 Oct. 1937.
21 Hosps. Year Bk. (1949, 1970).
22 'Hackney's Hosps. Investigation by Hackney Trades Council, 1976' [TS. in H.A.D.], 7, 9.
23 Hosps. and Health Svces. Year Bk. (1985); Hackney Echo, 17 Apr. 1986, 11.

The Eastern, later Homerton, hospital was opened in 1871 as one of the first three foundations of the Metropolitan Asylums Board. The buildings, on 6 a. north of Homerton Grove, at first were used solely to meet a smallpox epidemic but were designed as a pair of hospitals, the northern for 112 smallpox cases and the southern for 200 fever cases.[24] The M.A.B., which was in dispute with Hackney district board of works over health precautions, in 1882 stressed the pair's wide catchment area by calling it the North-eastern fever hospital.[25] An ambulance station had been attached by 1889, when there were 400 beds,[26] classes on infectious diseases were introduced in 1891,[27] and a small isolation block was added in 1900. Accommodation was increased to 561 beds by the M.A.B.'s purchase in 1921 of the City of London's institution, originally the East London workhouse, immediately to the west.[28] The Eastern hospital was administered from 1930 by the L.C.C. and from 1948 by the regional board's Hackney group management committee, under which it had 621 beds in 1949 and 495 in 1968.[29] A new isolation block was opened in 1935[30] and major rebuilding was planned in 1939, but demolition started only in 1981.[31] The hospital was reopened in 1986 as Homerton hospital, the City and Hackney health authority's general hospital for the district, with four two-storeyed brick wards containing 444 beds.[32]

The German hospital[33] was opened in 1845 in Dalston Place on the south side of Dalston Lane, in three houses bought from the infants' asylum.[34] Financed by subscriptions and patronized by royalty, the hospital offered free treatment to Germans or German speakers and had dispensing branches in both east and west London;[35] a few 'sanatorium' beds attracted fees but most of the out-patients were poor English. Two linked blocks of red brick with patterning, designed by T. L. Donaldson[36] and E. A. Gruning in Tudor style, were opened in the garden in 1864, whereupon most of the Dalston Lane frontage was let for building. The new hospital, with 100 beds, was approached by Alma (from 1877 Ritson) Road and from 1867 by a road from Dalston Lane across the railway. Later additions included the Sister's House designed by C. G. F. Rees in 1911 and a five-storeyed buff-brick wing by Burnet, Tait & Lorne, opened in 1936 and facing Fassett Square.[37] A small convalescent

home was opened at Graham House, no. 113 Dalston Lane, in 1883 and replaced in 1908 by one at Hitchin (Herts.). The hospital had 142 beds in 1890, when the London dispensaries survived,[38] 161 including 12 private beds in 1931, and 192 in 1935. It passed in 1948 to the Hackney group management committee as a general hospital, with 217 beds in 1949 and 1968.[39] It was reserved for psychiatric and psychogeriatric patients from 1974, was partly empty by 1976, and closed in 1987.[40] The original block, a very early pavilion-plan hospital, with its contemporary lodge and the noteworthy eastern extension,[41] survived in 1991.

The Salvation Army's Mothers' hospital originated in a maternity home for unmarried women opened in 1894 by Mrs. Bramwell Booth at Ivy House, on the corner of Mare Street and Richmond Road. It closed in 1912, when the semidetached nos. 153–63 Lower Clapton Road were bought and when wards were built in their gardens to form a general maternity hospital, opened in 1913. The hospital also trained Salvationist and other midwives;[42] it had 90 beds in 1935. It passed to Hackney group management committee in 1948, with 107 beds in 1949 and 114 in 1968,[43] and despite opposition[44] was closed on the opening of Homerton hospital in 1986.[45] Most of the site was sold to Newlon housing trust for Mothers' Square. The scheme was partly finished in 1988, when a small psychogeriatric hospital was to be included.[46]

The Salvation Army kept a maternity home, at first called a rescue home, at nos. 27 and 29 Devonshire Road from c. 1898 until 1927 or later. By 1922 there were homes later called Cotland at no. 9 Amhurst Park and Hope Lodge at no. 4 Clapton Common (formerly the Salvationists' training college). Sapsworth House was at nos. 122 and 124 (later also at nos. 126 and 128) Clapton Common, when by 1934 all three maternity homes had 20–30 beds. All had closed by 1970. Crossways, opened by 1898 as a rescue home at no. 13 Laura Place, had 20 maternity beds in 1970 and remained a hostel for girls in the 1980s.[47]

The Metropolitan Free hospital, founded in 1836, moved from Stepney to the south corner of Kingsland Road and St. Peter's Road (from 1936 St. Peter's Way), where out-patients were received by 1886.[48] It was intended for a poor area, treating subscribers, and in 1888 only 50

24 G. M. Ayers, *Eng.'s First State Hosps. 1867–1930* (1971), 32, 49–51, 54; G. Rivett, *Development of Lond. Hosp. System, 1823–1982* (1986), 88–9.
25 Ayers, *Eng.'s Hosps.* 76 n., 83.
26 *Burdett's Hosp. Annual* (1890).
27 Ayers, *Eng.'s Hosps.* 195.
28 L.C.C. *Ceremonial Pamphlets*, 26 July 1935; G.L.R.O., MAB 2355.
29 Ayers, *Eng.'s Hosps.* 274; *Hosps. Year Bk.* (1949, 1970).
30 L.C.C. *Ceremonial Pamphlets*, 26 July 1935.
31 'Hackney's Hosps.' 13; *Hackney Gaz.* 13 Jan. 1981, 1.
32 *Hackney Echo*, 17 Apr. 1986, 11–14.
33 Para. based on M. Neumann, 'Account of German Hosp. in Lond. 1845–1948' (Thos. Huxley Coll. thesis, 1971, in H.A.D.), *passim*.
34 Above, misc. institutions.
35 *The Times*, 17 Oct. 1845, 7f; *Lond. & Provincial Medical Dir.* (1847, 1854).
36 *D.N.B.*

37 *List of Bldgs.* (1988); R.C.H.M. *Newsletter*, spring 1991; Pevsner, *Lond.* ii. 167; above, plate 66.
38 *Burdett's Hosp. Annual* (1890).
39 *Hosps. Year Bk.* (1931, 1935, 1950–1, 1970).
40 'Hackney's Hosps.' 20; *Hackney Gaz.* 17 Apr. 1987, 17.
41 *List of Bldgs.* (1988).
42 *Terrier*, Winter 1990; H.A.D., D/F/BAG 8, pp. 66, 69, 71.
43 *Hosps. Year Bk.* (1935, 1950–1, 1970).
44 'Hackney's Hosps.' 18–19.
45 *Hackney Echo*, 17 Apr. 1986, 11, 14; *Hackney Herald*, June 1986, 6.
46 *Hackney Echo*, 16 Nov. 1988, 1; *Daily Telegraph*, 30 Nov. 1988, 37.
47 *P.O. Dir. Lond. County Suburbs, North* (1898); *P.O. Dir. Lond.* (1902 and later edns.); *Hosps. Year Bk.* (1950–1, 1970).
48 *Lond. & Provincial Medical Dir.* (1854); *P.O. Dir. Lond.* (1879); *The Times*, 15 May 1886, 14c.

of its 160 beds were in use, from lack of funds;[49] 12 of the beds were for Jews. In 1890 it was governed by a committee, with the lord mayor as president, and by 1902 the king was patron.[50] All 150 beds remained free in 1935. It passed to the region's Central group management committee in 1948 and to the new East London committee in 1966, when it was linked with St. Leonard's hospital, Shoreditch.[51] The Metropolitan remained open, with a chest clinic, in 1975 but was closed to in-patients in 1977.[52] The yellow- and red-brick building, mainly of four storeys, later housed workshops and survived in 1991.

A dispensary for Stamford Hill, Stoke Newington, Clapton, West Hackney, Kingsland, and Dalston was opened in 1825 on the Hackney side of Stoke Newington High Street but moved to the opposite side in 1864.[53] The union guardians in 1870 acquired a site in Roseberry Place for a dispensary[54] which was open by 1872, when there was also a homoeopathic dispensary at no. 100 Stoke Newington High Street;[55] the Roseberry Place dispensary survived until c. 1961.[56] Hackney Provident dispensary, established in 1877 as a branch of the Metropolitan Provident Medical Association, had 370 subscribers at no. 8 Brett Road in 1910.[57] A disinfecting station and shelter designed by Gordon & Gunton, to isolate people whose homes were being disinfected, was built by the council in Millfields Road in 1900 and retained in the 1980s.[58] There were health centres in 1985 at no. 205 Morning Lane, no. 36 Lower Clapton Road, no. 200 Wick Road, no. 3 Mandeville Street, no. 210 Kingsland Road, and in Fountayne Road and Somerford Grove.[59] A mortuary, initially for cholera victims, was housed in the old church tower by 1875; part of the Rectory's garden was taken in 1890 for a new mortuary, which was opened with rooms for a coroner's court in 1893.[60]

Hackney was associated with lunatic asylums,[61] although less notoriously than Hoxton by the 1670s or Bethnal Green later. The longest lived was Brooke House, taken in 1759 by John Monro (d. 1791), who was physician to Bethlehem hospital like his father and many of his descendants.[62] The house was licensed for 50 patients c. 1840, when it was dilapidated and rarely visited by Henry Monro, whose family

owned it until the late 19th century and retained an interest until it was bombed in 1940.[63] Whitmore (formerly Balmes) House had by 1756 been taken for an asylum by the physician Meyer Schomberg (d. 1761)[64] and in 1773 was occupied by Roger Devey and another doctor, John Silvester.[65] It passed by marriage to Thomas Warburton, an unqualified man with influential contacts, who supplied keepers for George III in 1788 and reserved Whitmore House for rich patients; they included Henry Addington (d. 1823), son of the former prime minister and lodged separately in the grounds, and John Murray, marquess of Tullibardine and later duke of Atholl (d. 1846).[66] Conditions were praised by Edward Wakefield (d. 1846) in 1815 but fiercely attacked in the 1820s.[67] The asylum passed to Thomas's son Dr. John Warburton (d. 1845) and was closed in the mid 19th century, although more crowded madhouses in Bethnal Green remained in the family. A house which Thomas held from 1801 in Mare Street was to be demolished in 1847 and was commemorated in Warburton Road.[68]

In the same part of Mare Street the old 'Black and White House' was a madhouse in 1724.[69] The nearby Pembroke House was taken by Dr. George Rees in 1818 for insane employees of the East India Co. It was under Dr. Walter Davis Williams by 1844 and had 135 inmates by 1870; the site was then bought by the G.E.R. and the house soon replaced by Bayford Street.[70] London House, also nearby, was an asylum c. 1826 under Samuel Fox[71] and in 1830 and 1844 under William Oxley, who joined its grounds to those of a house in Mare Street, possibly the later Tre-Wint industrial home; presumably they constituted the male and female asylums with 15 and 22 inmates in 1861.[72] Wick (later Sidney) House was marked in 1831 as Dr. Tuke's lunatic asylum.[73] Dr. Thomas Ruston, a propagandist for inoculation,[74] offered treatment in Mare Street in 1768 but was apparently forced to leave by threats of prosecution.[75]

Charitable institutions with medical functions included a school for the deaf and dumb, which Thomas Braidwood (d. 1806) moved in 1783 from Edinburgh to Bowling Green (renamed Grove) House and in 1799 to Pembroke House, where it was continued by his family until c. 1810.[76] The British Asylum for Deaf and Dumb

49 *The Times*, 3 Dec. 1888, 6d.
50 *Burdett's Hosp. Annual* (1890); *P.O. Dir. Lond.* (1902). 51 *Hosps. Year Bk.* (1935, 1949–50, 1970).
52 *P.O. Dir. Lond.* (1975); 'Hackney's Hosps.' 21.
53 *V.C.H. Mdx.* viii. 203; H.A.D., D/S/28.
54 G.L.R.O., Ha BG 182. 55 *Hackney Dir.* (1872).
56 *P.O. Dir. Lond.* (1961, 1962).
57 *Burdett's Hosp. Annual* (1910).
58 Hackney M.B. *Ann. Rep. of M.O.H.* (1900), 32 and illus.; (1912–13), 79; Hackney, *Official Guide* [1920 and later edns.]; *P.O. Dir. Lond.* (1987).
59 *Hosps. and Health Svces. Year Bk.* (1985).
60 Clarke, *Hackney*, 102; H.A.D., H/LD 7/24; Hackney bd. of wks. *Ann. Rep.* (1890–1), 6; (1892–3), 4; datestone 1891.
61 Para. based on W. L. Parry Jones, *Trade in Lunacy* (1972), *passim*.
62 *D.N.B.*; G.L.R.O., Acc. 1063/1, 49–57.
63 e.g. *Hosps. Year Bk.* (1931).
64 G.L.R.O., E/BVR/430; *Hackney and Stoke Newington Past*, 58; *D.N.B.* 65 G.L.R.O., E/BVR/430.

66 A. D. Morris, *Hoxton Madhos.* (1958) (TS. copy in H.A.D.); *Complete Peerage*, i. 321; xi. 735.
67 Morris, *Hoxton Madhos.*; *D.N.B.*
68 Morris, *Hoxton Madhos.*; G.L.R.O., M79/KH/10, pp. 57–8 (plan); ibid. 12, pp. 50–3, 83, 86–7, 119–22; above, Mare Street and London Fields.
69 G.L.R.O. M79/LH/49, 10 Apr. 1724.
70 *Hackney and Stoke Newington Past*, 58; G.L.R.O., M79/LH/26, p. 33; ibid. 27, pp. 100–1 (plan); *Lond. and Provincial Med. Dir.* (1847).
71 *Pigot's Com. Dir.* (1826–7); H.A.D., M 4404/7.
72 H.A.D., M 4404/5/1–2; Clarke, *Hackney*, 30; *Imperial Gaz. of Eng. and Wales*, ed. J. M. Wilson [1866–9], iii. 831.
73 *Starling's Map* (1831).
74 T. Ruston, *Essay on Inoculation for the Smallpox* (1767).
75 H.A.D., H/LD 7/3, p. 43; par. mins. 7, 14 Mar., 21 Apr. 1768; 9 Jan. 1769.
76 *D.N.B.*; H.A.D., bldgs. file; *Gent. Mag.* lxxvii (1), 38, 130, 305; G.L.R.O., H1/ST/A6/7, p. 44; *Terrier*, Winter 1993/4.

Females was founded by two ladies at Stamford Hill in 1851, moved to Eagle House, Homerton, in 1857 and to no. 179 Lower Clapton Road in 1864.[77] After demolition of the house in 1933,[78] the Deaf and Dumb Home continued at no. 26 Clapton Common, a four-storeyed building designed by A. Rubens Cole, until c. 1986.[79] The East London Home and School for Blind Children, founded c. 1894 by Miss S. Rye at no. 120 Lower Clapton Road, moved in 1901 to nos. 2 and 4 Warwick Road (from 1938 Warwick Grove), where it was licensed for 15 by the Education Department and replaced c. 1948 by a municipal welfare centre, itself replaced by Warwick Court.[80] The Anglican sisters of St. Francis maintained a home for bedridden women at no. 157 Richmond Road from 1920 until 1962.[81] St. Mary's home for mothers and babies moved in 1918 from Paddington to no. 153 Stamford Hill, where it remained in 1975.[82]

PUBLIC ORDER. A cage, a cucking stool, and a whipping post were to be set up in 1630. The cage was at the south-west corner of the churchyard in 1657 and, with the stocks, was repaired in 1659; a new cucking stool was ordered in 1690.[83] A manorial court demanded that the public stocks and whipping post be mended in 1744[84] and a pillory near the pond in Mare Street was used in 1748.[85]

A nightly watch was the responsibility of a headborough in 1617.[86] Quarter sessions in 1681 ordered those magistrates who lived in Hackney to form 16 night watchmen into companies; in 1686 the constables were to be prosecuted for not keeping a proper watch.[87] A watchhouse was to be built in 1696 and one at Cambridge Heath was paid for by voluntary contributions in 1714; there were watchhouses at Cambridge Heath and nearby at the Shoulder of Mutton in 1728.[88] Watchmen, to be fined in 1725 for unpunctuality, were in 1740 to patrol both the road and footway to London in pairs, those on the road to be mounted. The expense was to be met from the 'unappropriated funds',[89] as were rewards and prosecution costs[90] until subscriptions had raised enough for rewards by 1778.[91] Hackney turnpike trust employed its own eight watchmen under an Act of 1756, when guns and bayonets

were bought, beats defined, the two watchhouses to be continued, and four more to be provided.[92] There was no lock-up, however, in 1763, when the landlord of the Mermaid and Bird in Hand refused to guard prisoners taken by the turnpike trust's watchmen.[93]

Watching, with lighting, devolved in 1763 upon the parish trustees,[94] although the vestry continued to issue orders and offer rewards.[95] It replaced a road patrol with four local watchmen in 1764 and because the lighting and watching rate sufficed only for the winter it agreed in 1785 to pay for a nine-man summer patrol out of the 'unappropriated funds'.[96] The parish meeting also offered rewards and in 1782 sought subscriptions for armed patrols whose cost was too heavy for the rates.[97] To avoid taking all prisoners to Hackney, a cage at Kingsland was promised in 1819 and again in 1822.[98] In May 1828 the lighting and watching trustees took pride in having recently freed the parish from all night-time robberies: four inspectors had charge of an evening patrol of 26 and a night patrol of 30, the numbers being much greater in winter, when boxes were used; horse patrols had been replaced by foot and in addition eight parish constables saw to inns, shops, and the serving of warrants. Claiming to have driven criminals away to Tottenham, Hackney advised other parishes to copy its vigilance[99] and was one of only two petitioners against the Metropolitan Police Act, 1829.[1] It was nonetheless included in the metropolitan police area, with stations next to the old church tower and in Kingsland High Street south of Shacklewell Lane by 1842.[2] The Hackney station had moved to the north-west corner of the churchyard (later no. 422 Mare Street) by 1865;[3] the site was that of a police barracks in 1910, the station having moved to a building of 1904 at the north-east corner,[4] where it remained in 1991. The Kingsland station had moved by 1872 to Dalston Lane, where its building at no. 39, dated 1914, had recently closed in 1991. A station in Wick Road, west of Hedgers Grove, was in use by 1892 and until the Second World War.

STREET LIGHTING. Oil lamps were set up in 1756 by Hackney turnpike trustees,[5] who

77 *Hackney and Stoke Newington Past*, 58; *Hackney Photos.* ii. 40–1; H.A.D., bldgs. file; ibid. D/S/14.
78 *Lost Hackney*, 41–3.
79 H.A.D., D/F/BAG/1, p. 104; *Hackney Photos.* ii. 40.
80 H.A.D., H/LD 7/16; *Kelly's Dir. Stoke Newington* (1892–3 and later edns.); *P.O. Dir. Lond.* (1947 and later edns.).
81 H.A.D., bldgs. file.
82 *St. Mary's 37th Ann. Rep.* (booklet in H.A.D.); *P.O. Dir. Lond.* (1975).
83 Vestry mins. 17 May 1630; 27 Nov. 1657; 10 May 1658; 12 Apr. 1659; 7 Aug. 1690; Clarke, *Hackney*, 70, 107–8.
84 G.L.R.O., M79/LH/51, 3 Apr. 1744.
85 Cal. Mdx. Sess. Bks. xxii. 9.
86 *Mdx. Sess. Rec.* iv. 221, 241.
87 Cal. Mdx. Sess. Bks. vi. 76; viii. 15.
88 Vestry mins. 26 July 1696; 10 Oct. 1705; 30 June 1716; 13 July 1728.
89 Above, local govt. (par. govt.); ibid. 11 Jan. 1725, 1 Sept. 1740.
90 e.g. vestry mins. 6 Dec. 1742, 29 Apr. 1745.
91 Ibid. 21 Apr. 1778.

92 Shoreditch to Stamford Hill Road Act, 29 Geo. II, c. 41; H.A.D., P/J/T/5, ff. 2, 4, 15–16.
93 Par. mins. 13 Aug. 1763.
94 Hackney (Poor Relief) Act, 4 Geo. III, c. 43.
95 e.g. G.L.R.O., P79/JN1/157 (notice on back cover); H.A.D., H/LD 7/2, pp. 61, 76.
96 Vestry mins. 6 Nov. 1764; 26 May 1785.
97 Par. mins. 28 Oct. 1776; 2 Sept. 1782.
98 Par. mins. betw. 10 June and 22 July 1819; 1 Feb. 1822.
99 *Rep. Cttee. on Police of Metropolis*, H.C. 533, pp. 209–11 (1828), vi.
1 F. H. W. Sheppard, *London 1808–70: the Infernal Wen* (1971), 35; 10 Geo. IV, c. 44.
2 Robinson, *Hackney*, i. 247; *Hackney Dir.* (1849).
3 Rest of para. based on Stanford, *Map of Lond.* (1862–5 edn.), sheet 7; (1891 edn.); *Bacon's Atlas of Lond.* (1910), sheet 39; *P.O. Lond. Suburban Dir., North* (1872 and later edns.); *P.O. Dir. Lond.* (1902 and later edns.).
4 Designed by John Dixon-Butler: *List of Bldgs.* (1990).
5 Shoreditch to Stamford Hill Road Act, 29 Geo. II, c. 41; Robinson, *Hackney*, i. 244.

ordered five for 130 yd. of Church Street and offered a contract to light all the lamps from Shoreditch. In 1757 their surveyor stored 154 lamps during the summer.[6] The parish trustees, responsible for lighting under the Act of 1763, established a lamp board,[7] whose legality was questioned in the 1830s[8] but which was superseded only in 1856 by Hackney district board of works, which fixed the lighting rate.[9] For 1841–2 the lamp board paid £2,290 to the Imperial Gas Co. and £611 to a contractor for the oil lamps.[10] With 30 miles of road and 1,047 lamps, the parish was comparatively well lighted in 1854.[11] The oil lamps were converted to gas in 1856–7 under the district board,[12] whose area was part of that supplied by the Imperial Gas Co.[13]

Electric street lighting, under an order of 1893, was provided only in 1901, after Progressive electoral gains had ensured that Hackney would have its own power station.[14] The station, at the east end of Millfields Road, was built in brick with stone dressings to the design of Gordon & Gunton.[15] An adjacent refuse destructor supplied heat, and a wharf was built on land leased by the Lee Conservancy for bringing coal and removing waste.[16] Allegations that profits from the electricity supply had been misused proved harmful locally to the Labour party in 1922.[17] The power station passed to London Electricity Board in 1947 and still operated, as a substation, in 1994.[18]

FIRE ENGINES were required by law in 1708, when Francis Tyssen offered to supply one cheaply and all landholders were to pay in proportion to their poor rates.[19] An engine house was to be sited on the south side of the churchyard, where churchwardens were to inspect the equipment twice a year in 1712, and was built or rebuilt in 1725. A second engine, under a further law, was needed in 1774.[20] A new large engine was to be bought in 1823 and the existing one assigned to Kingsland.[21] In 1849 engines were kept in Church Street, in the workhouse, and at Kingsland (probably the later De Beauvoir Town station in St. Peter's Road),[22] and in 1858 one was bought for west Hackney and

Stoke Newington and installed on the east side of the high street.[23] By 1861 the parish had five engines tended by eight men.[24] Under the Metropolitan Fire Brigade Act, 1865, the vestry leased its engine houses and sold most of the equipment to the M.B.W., whose duties later passed to the L.C.C.'s London Fire Brigade.[25] The M.B.W. in 1868 rented and in 1874 bought a site for Hackney fire station at the corner of Amhurst and Bodney roads.[26] In 1870 there were fire stations in Amhurst Road, St. Peter's Road, and, for south Hackney, Perry (later Kingshold) Road.[27] Stoke Newington's station was moved in 1886 to the corner of Brooke and Leswin roads and a station at the corner of Kingsland and Downham roads, presumably replacing the one in St. Peter's Road, was built in 1895.[28] Hackney Wick, which factories made particularly vulnerable, was served only by a substation moved from Poplar to the north end of Wallis Road in 1897,[29] until a full station was opened in 1902 on the site of nos. 97 and 99 Homerton High Street.[30] Hackney fire station survived until c. 1921 and Leswin Road until 1977, after it had temporarily housed firemen from Homerton and Kingsland, whose rebuilt stations were reopened in 1974 and 1977.[31]

PUBLIC LIBRARIES[32] were the subject of a rowdy meeting in 1878 and were successfully opposed by a small popular vote.[33] Private institutions[34] or circulating libraries[35] were supplemented in 1885 by a gift of records and books to the vestry from the executors of J. R. Daniel-Tyssen. Kept at the Manor House and then at the town hall, with its own librarian, the Tyssen library came to form the basis of Hackney's local history collection.[36] After adopting the Public Libraries Acts in 1903, the council bought land in Mare Street from the L.C.C. for a central library, designed by Henry Crouch,[37] built with funds from Andrew Carnegie, and opened in 1908. Branch libraries, also paid for by Carnegie, were opened for Dalston in 1912 in Forest Road on land given by the Rhodes family, for Homerton, to the design of Edwin Cooper, in Brooksby's Walk, and for Clapton in

[6] H.A.D., P/J/T/5, ff. 11, 14–15, 79, 137, 139.
[7] Hackney (Poor Relief) Act, 4 Geo. III, c. 43; Robinson, *Hackney*, ii. 323.
[8] *Hackney Mag.* Oct. 1834, June 1835; vestry mins. 1 Dec. 1836; 23 Feb. 1837.
[9] H.A.D., BW/1, pp. 10, 34, 163.
[10] Robinson, *Hackney*, ii. 324; *Hackney Dir.* (1849).
[11] *Return on Paving, Cleansing, and Lighting Metropolitan Dists.* H.C. 127, p. 7 (1854–5), liii.
[12] Hackney bd. of wks. *Ann. Rep.* (1856–7), 7; *V.C.H. Mdx.* viii. 202.
[13] J. F. B. Firth, *Municipal Lond.* (1876), map facing p. 340.
[14] H.A.D., H/LD 7/5, 16.
[15] Ibid. H/LD 7/16; *Hackney Photos.* ii. 77.
[16] Hackney M.B. *Ann. Rep.* (1912–13), 78–9.
[17] *Politics and People of Lond. 1889–1965*, ed. A. Saint (1989), 113.
[18] Electricity Act, 10 & 11 Geo. VI, c. 54; inf. from London Electricity; above, plate 43.
[19] Vestry mins. 3 June, 25 Nov. 1708.
[20] Ibid. 7 Apr. 1709; 13 Jan. 1712; 30 Mar. 1725; 5 Apr. 1774.
[21] Par. mins. 14 Aug. 1823.
[22] *Hackney Dir.* (1849); *Green's Hackney Dir.* (1869–70).
[23] *V.C.H. Mdx.* viii. 202; H.A.D., J/V/1, pp. 82–3, 121, 150.

[24] *Amounts paid by Metropolitan Pars. for Fire Engines, 1861–3*, H.C. 322, p. 9 (1864), l.
[25] 28 & 29 Vic. c. 90; H.A.D., J/V/2, pp. 301–2, 324, 346; M.B.W. *Mins. of Procs.* 22 June 1866.
[26] M.B.W. *Rep.* (1868–9), 52; *Mins. of Procs.* 6 Mar. 1868; 2 Oct. 1874.
[27] *Green's Hackney Dir.* (1869–70).
[28] *V.C.H. Mdx.* viii, 202; *P.O. Dir. Lond.* (1898); inf. from Lond. Fire Brigade Mus.
[29] L.C.C. *Mins. of Procs.* 26 June, 23 Oct., 18 Dec. 1900; 4 Feb. 1902.
[30] Ibid. 18 Dec. 1900; 2 Apr., 16 July 1901; 4 Feb., 21 Oct. 1902.
[31] *P.O. Dir. Lond. County Suburbs* (1921 and later edns.); *P.O. Dir. Lond.* (1947 and later edns.); inf. from Lond. Fire Brigade Mus.
[32] Para. based on *Golden Jubilee of Hackney Pub. Librs.* (1958), *passim*.
[33] *The Times*, 23 May 1878, 5f; 18 June 1878, 7f; H.A.D., H/LD 7/4.
[34] Above, social.
[35] e.g. Barker's and Morris's circulating librs.: *Hackney and Kingsland Gaz.* 17 July 1869, 1.
[36] Hackney, *Official Guide* [1960]; D. Mander, *Guide to Lond. Local Hist. Sources*, Hackney L.B. (1990), 93.
[37] H.A.D., cutting from *Hackney Gaz.* 29 May 1908.

1914 in Northwold Road.[38] A fourth branch, in a converted motor showroom at no. 158 Stamford Hill, was open part time from 1936 and full time from 1939. Dalston library was bombed but reopened in temporary premises, extended in 1946, at nos. 80–82 Dalston Lane and on a permanent site at nos. 24–30 in 1959.[39]

Part-time libraries[40] had been opened by 1942 at no. 160 Victoria Park Road, no. 71A Englefield Road, and Kingsmead Way. A further branch was opened in 1947 in a prefabricated building in Eastway, where it was enlarged in 1948, and in 1951 at no. 24 Somerford Grove. The Englefield Road branch was reopened at no. 105 Mortimer Road in 1962 and the Victoria Park branch, called Parkside, at nos. 92–6 Victoria Park Road in 1964.[41] New two-storeyed libraries were opened for Stamford Hill on the site of the Congregational church in 1968 and for Homerton in the high street in 1974; Eastway library was rebuilt as part of a shopping precinct in 1979.[42] Rose Lipman library, beneath a community hall in De Beauvoir Road, replaced Mortimer Road in 1975; thereafter it held Hackney archives department, established in 1965 and first housed in Shoreditch.[43] Hackney museum was opened in the Central hall, Mare Street, in 1987[44] but three branch libraries were closed in 1988.[45]

BATHS. Public baths designed by Harnor & Pinches were opened in 1897 in Lower Clapton Road; proposed alterations caused controversy in 1990.[46] Slipper baths were opened in Wardle Street in 1922, Gayhurst Road in 1928, Shacklewell Lane in 1931, Englefield Road in 1932, and Gainsborough Road (later Eastway), together with a laundry, in 1935. All remained open c. 1980, as did the first municipal launderette opened in Oldhill Street in 1958 and a more recent one in Morning Lane.[47] The more westerly of Victoria Park's bathing lakes lay within Hackney, although not the Lido which superseded them in 1936.[48] The L.C.C.'s improvements to Hackney marsh included the formation of a bathing pool, unused in 1898 as the Lea had still to be purified.[49] An open air pool was opened at West Side, London Fields, c. 1931.[50] It survived, with Eastway baths, c. 1987, but swimming pools were open only in Lower Clapton Road in 1989.[51]

PARKS AND OPEN SPACES. The first large open space maintained from public funds was Victoria Park,[52] created under Acts of 1841 and 1842[53] on lands compulsorily purchased with money from the Crown's sale of York (later Lancaster) House. The park, intended for east Londoners as a whole, extended from Bethnal Green into south Hackney mainly over parts of the Cass and St. Thomas's hospital estates. It was unofficially open from 1845, when still being laid out by the commissioners of Woods and Forests, whose architect Sir James Pennethorne planned gardens at the west end and open grass for recreation at the east. A quarter, later reduced to a sixth, of the purchased land could be leased for building until the M.B.W. bought c. 24 a. from the Woods and Forests to add to the park's 193 a. in 1872;[54] a small plot was added by Wilberforce Bryant in 1876. Maintenance of the park had passed in 1851 from the Woods and Forests to the office of Works and Public Buildings, which received annual parliamentary grants until an Act of 1887[55] transferred the charges to Londoners. Thereafter management was by the M.B.W., the L.C.C., the G.L.C., and from 1986 a board representing Hackney L.B., which contained 27.92 of the park's 88.02 ha., and Tower Hamlets.[56]

Victoria Park, whose first lake was authorized in 1846, was noted for its landscaping[57] and for amenities ranging from floral displays to concerts and sports contests. Ornamental furnishings included a Tudor lodge of 1845 and imposing gates at Approach Road, Bethnal Green, a pagoda ordered in 1847, a Moorish arcade designed by Pennethorne, a polygonal Gothic fountain designed by H. A. Darbishire and given by Baroness Burdett-Coutts in 1861, a palm house of 1892, a refreshment pavilion of 1940, and two alcoves from the 18th-century London Bridge. Many did not survive the Second World War or subsequent neglect, but in 1988 it was planned to restore the fountain, which stood within Hackney, and to re-erect other monuments.[58]

Enough commons and Lammas lands were preserved from 19th-century building to make Hackney relatively rich in open spaces,[59] although most were useful rather than ornamental. Under the Metropolitan Commons Act, 1866, the district board organized a petition for the inclosure of nearly 180 a. collectively described as Hackney commons, whose transfer to the M.B.W. was confirmed in an Act of 1872. The lands were Clapton common (9¼ a.), Stoke Newington common (5½ a.), North and South Mill fields (57½ a.), Hackney

38 Municipal Year Bk. (1909); Hackney M.B. Ann. Rep. (1912–13), 78, 109–10; List of Bldgs. (1981).
39 Hackney, Official Guide (1920 and later edns.); P.O. Dir. Lond. (1934 and later edns.).
40 Para. based on Golden Jubilee of Hackney Pub. Librs.; P.O. Dir. Lond. (1946 and later edns.).
41 H.A.D., H/LD 3/13, 15.
42 Opening programmes in H.A.D.
43 Inf. from H.A.D.
44 Hackney Herald, Jan. 1987, 8; Aug. 1987, 8.
45 Hackney Gaz. (1864–1989 anniversary suppl.), 4.
46 Municipal Year Bk. (1909); Hackney M.B. Ann. Rep. (1912–13), 78; H.B.M.C. Lond., HAC 52.
47 L.C.C. Lond. Statistics, xli. 176; Hackney, Official Guide (1920 and later edns.).
48 Old O.S. Map Lond. 41 (1870); C. Poulsen, Victoria

Pk. (1976), 50.
49 J. J. Sexby, Municipal Pks. of Lond. (1898), 363; below.
50 L.C.C. Lond. Statistics, xxxvi. 148.
51 British Telecom, The Phone Bk. (1987); Hackney L.B. Guide to Sports Facilities (1989).
52 Two paras. based on Poulsen, Victoria Pk. passim; Sexby, Municipal Pks. 553–71.
53 York House Act, 4 & 5 Vic. c. 27; Victoria Park Act, 5 & 6 Vic. c. 20.
54 Victoria Park Act, 35 & 36 Vic. c. 53.
55 London Parks and Works Act, 50 & 51 Vic. c. 34.
56 Hackney Echo, 26 Oct. 1988, 4; Ann. Abstract of Gtr. Lond. Statistics, vii. 396.   57 Pevsner, Lond. ii. 173.
58 Hackney Echo, 26 Oct. 1988, 4; London's Pride, ed. M. Galinou (Mus. of Lond. exhib. cat. 1990), 151.
59 Para. based on Sexby, Municipal Pks. 334–61.

Downs (50 a.), Hackney or Well Street common (30 a.), London Fields (27 a.), and strips of waste in Dalston Lane and Grove Street (later Lauriston Road).[60] The lord, while repudiating his agent's digging for gravel on Stoke Newington common, in 1875 provoked protests by inclosing part of Hackney Downs and the Mill fields. His fences were torn down, as were notices put up by the Grocers' Co. in 1877, but Chancery upheld him against the M.B.W. in 1879.[61] His rights were purchased by the M.B.W. under an Act of 1881 and those of other freeholders under a further Act of 1884.[62]

Hackney marsh (337 a.)[63] where Lammas rights were still exercised, was excluded from the M.B.W.'s scheme in 1872. The possibility that the owners might unite to convert it into building land led the district board to seek its purchase by the L.C.C. in 1889, when further agitation was caused by the manorial drivers' ban on football by boys from the Eton mission. After the Board of Agriculture had drafted a Scheme in 1890 the owners negotiated to sell their rights to the L.C.C. for £75,000, the district board contributing £15,000 and private subscribers £10,000. The marsh was open to the public from 1893, when transferred under the London Open Spaces Act, and formally dedicated in 1894. Flood prevention works by the L.C.C. included four cuts across bends in the Lea, the old channels being retained to form islands; a bathing pool was created by the northernmost cut. West of Lee Conservancy Road 37½ a. taken in 1915 for the National Projectile factory were to be retained by the government in 1922 but later were cleared for Mabley Green recreation ground.[64] Kingsmead estate was built on 20½ a. exchanged with the L.C.C. in 1937.[65] Thereafter it separated Hackney Marsh recrea-

tion ground (later Daubeney Fields) from Mabley Green ground to the south.[66]

Springfield park (32½ a.) was opened in 1905 after its purchase from T. K. Bros under the L.C.C. (General Powers) Act, 1904. As the SpringWeld estate, it had contained Thomas Garland's Spring Hill House, the Chestnuts, and SpringWeld House, the last of which was retained for refreshments and staff accommodation; it also included Spring Lane, which was diverted closer to the Lea, and the island at Horse Shoe Point.[67]

Smaller plots were bought or held for nominal rents by Hackney district board and its successors, the vestry and the metropolitan borough, which respectively cared for 11 a. in 1895, and 13½ a. in 1912.[68] They included the freeholds of Shacklewell green, the Triangle in Mare Street, Stonebridge common, and strips along Stamford Hill, all acquired by the board in 1883, and strips in Dalston Lane and Lauriston Road handed over by the M.B.W. in 1884. With grants from the Metropolitan Gardens Association, the M.B.W., and the L.C.C., gardens were created in Well Street burial ground, bordering St. Thomas's Place, and West Hackney, St. John's, and South Hackney churchyards under faculties granted in 1884, 1885, 1893, and 1900, and also in De Beauvoir Square and St. Thomas's Square, leased from 1891 and 1892. West Bank at Stamford Hill was bought in 1891, East Bank in 1894, and Clapton pond and gardens and Albion Square in 1898.[69] Clapton Square, neglected as a residents' garden, was acquired by the L.C.C. and passed to Hackney M.B. in 1924, by which date 621 a., almost one fifth, of the borough was open space.[70] Encroachment on parks by sports pitches and playgrounds, notably on London Fields and Hackney Downs, brought complaints in 1980.[71]

THE PARISH CHURCH

THE parish church of Hackney was a sinecure rectory,[72] presumably by 1275 when it had a vicar[73] and until 1821 when the incumbent vicar became rector and the rectory and vicarage were merged.[74] The rectory was in the gift of the bishop of London and from 1550 of his lay successors as lords of Hackney or Lordshold manor. Licences to appropriate the rectory to the precentorship of St. Paul's in 1352[75] and to the bishop's table temporarily c. 1385 and permanently in 1391[76] had no lasting effect. From

the former dedication of the church to St. Augustine,[77] a connexion has been assumed with the Knights Hospitallers or Knights Templars, whose rules derived from those of St. Augustine of Hippo.[78] The church was said to be exempt from the archdeacon's jurisdiction and subject wholly to the bishop in 1708.[79]

Although there were proprietary chapels in the 18th century at Kingsland, Homerton, and Stamford Hill and a chapel of ease from 1810 for southern Hackney,[80] the parish remained

60 M.B.W. *Mins. of Procs.* 26 Feb. 1869; *Hackney Gaz.* 29 May 1875. Slightly smaller acreages in Sexby, *Municipal Pks.* 334; Hackney M.B. *Ann. Rep.* (1912–13), 43.
61 *The Times*, 13 Dec. 1875, 9f; 17 Jan. 1876, 11f; 8 June 1877, 8b; 2 Apr. 1879, 4a.
62 M.B.W. (Hackney Commons) Act, 44 & 45 Vic. c. 148 (Local); M.B.W. (Various Powers) Act, 47 & 48 Vic. c. 223 (Local).
63 Para. based on Sexby, *Municipal Pks.* 361–3; L.C.C. *Ceremonial Pamphlets*, 21 July 1894.
64 H.A.D., H/E 66/1.
65 Hackney, *Official Guide* [1970]; H. P. Clunn, *Face of Lond.* (1951), 459.
66 'Pks. and Open Spaces' (Hackney Soc.), 23–4, 30.
67 L.C.C. *Ceremonial Pamphlets*, 5 Aug. 1905; *Hackney Photos.* ii. 17.
68 H.A.D., J/V/18/2, p. 26; Hackney M.B. *Ann. Rep.*

(1912–13), p. 50.
69 G.L.R.O., MBW 2471, plans 22–22B; Hackney bd. of wks. *Ann. Rep.* (1890–1), 14; ibid. (1892–3), 9–10; Hackney M.B. *Ann. Rep.* (1912–13).　　70 H.A.D., H/LD 7/25, p. 67.
71 'Pks. and Open Spaces' (Hackney Soc.), 10.
72 For the rectory estate, above, manors (Grumbolds).
73 *Cal. Close*, 1272–9, 165.
74 Vestry mins. 9 Apr. 1822; Hennessy, *Novum Rep.* 177–8.　　　　　　　　75 *Cal. Pat.* 1350–4, 239.
76 *Cal. Papal Reg.* iv. 410.
77 Below, this section (building).
78 R. Simpson, *Memorials of St. John at Hackney*, i (1882), 42. Apart from the dedication, there is no evidence that the ch. belonged to the Knights of St. John (Hospitallers), as in Guildhall MS. 9557A, f. 31.
79 Newcourt, *Rep.* i. 617.
80 Below, this section (church extension).

undivided until in 1825 the church building commissioners established the three rectories and parishes of Hackney, South Hackney, and West Hackney.[81] Several new churches, to which parishes were assigned, were founded within the reduced parish of Hackney;[82] in 1971 a Scheme united the benefice and parish of the mother church with those of St. James with Christ Church, Clapton.[83]

The vicarage had evidently been endowed by 1291.[84] Its patronage belonged to the rector, but by 1650 it was customary for the rectors to lease the rectory to the lords of Hackney manor, who thereby presented both rectors and vicars.[85] The vicar Calybute Downing unsuccessfully petitioned parliament in 1640 for institution to the rectory also,[86] the Crown's presentation in 1664 of the vicar to the rectory was revoked,[87] and only Nehemiah Moorhouse and Robert Wright were both rector and vicar[88] before the benefices were merged in 1821. Thereafter the lord of the manor retained the advowson of the mother church, Lord Amherst of Hackney being patron in 1987.[89]

The value of the sinecure rectory was comparatively high, at £33 6s. 8d. in 1291,[90] £26 in 1535,[91] and £140 in 1650. In 1622 its house stood in 5 a., and in 1650 there were three glebe houses.[92] The vicarage, valued at £8 in 1291,[93] may thereafter have been augmented at the expense of the rectory, being valued in 1535 at £20,[94] which sum the vicar received in 1548.[95] By 1657 the vicar had a share of the tithes, which he was then leasing to the vestry,[96] and of which the records could not be found in 1690.[97] The vicarage was valued in the mid and late 18th century at £400.[98] It included two payments of 20s. for sermons from Thomas Jeamson's charity from 1679,[99] a share of the fees,[1] £10 a year from the vestry to replace burial fees lost when new vaults were banned in 1759,[2] and the option of £10 a year from the vestry for doing the duty of the assistant curate or reader appointed from 1704.[3] The vestry combined and increased its payments in the 1780s to £21, in 1800 to £30, and in 1802 to £40,[4] which the incumbent J. J. Watson gave up in 1822 to help pay for services at the workhouse.[5]

In 1825, following the merging of the rectory and vicarage, the newly established rectories of South and West Hackney were endowed with their respective portions of the rectorial and vicarial tithes.[6] The average net income of Hackney rectory 1828–31 was £1,082 a year.[7] There were nearly 3 a. of glebe in 1887,[8] when a rent charge of £981 10s. was received for commuted tithes.[9]

Land for a dwelling house was licensed in 1345 to be settled by William Langford on the vicar and his successors.[10] It may have been next to the churchyard, where the vicar had a house and 1 a., besides 2 a. in parcels in Hackney marsh, in 1622.[11] In 1650 he was leasing his house from year to year for £12, though it was thought to be worth £50.[12] The Vicarage stood north of the churchyard and immediately south of the Old Mermaid's garden in 1698.[13] It was 40 ft. long, with three rooms on the ground floor and three above, in 1705, when no vicar had lived there for more than 60 years; adjoining the north-east corner stood a brewhouse and cellar, with one room over, behind which a boarded barn served as stabling. The new vicar was licensed to replace all three buildings with a brick residence of two storeys, garrets, and cellars, set back farther from the road in the garden.[14] Subscriptions were raised from 94 benefactors, the old house was taken in part payment by the chief builder John Hill, and the new one was inhabited from 1706.[15] As the Rectory, it was refronted and extended to the design of James Spiller in 1828–9 with three storeys and six bays, the four central ones being slightly recessed.[16] It formed a 'very respectable residence' in 1842 and survived, as no. 356 Mare Street, in 1952.[17] It was demolished and a smaller house was built on the site in 1956.[18]

Benefactions suggest that the church was served by a priest and two chaplains in the late 14th and early 15th century but that later there were only two priests, since bequests were made for more services in 1349 and 1453. Various wards maintained lights[19] and there were fraternities for Church Street ward by 1428 and, of the Blessed Virgin, for Homerton ward by 1451.[20] A guild of the Holy Trinity and the Virgin Mary recorded in 1453 was to be re-established by the rector and Simon and John Elrington in 1478, with two wardens for

81 *Lond. Gaz.* 19 Mar. 1825, p. 460.
82 Below, this section (church extension).
83 G.L.R.O., P79/JSG/38; below, list of churches.
84 *Tax. Eccl.* (Rec. Com.), 17b.
85 *Home Counties Mag.* iii. 224; Newcourt, *Rep.* i. 617; Robinson, *Hackney*, ii. 79.
86 Hist. MSS. Com. 3, *4th Rep., H.L.* p. 33.
87 *Cal. S.P. Dom.* 1663–4, 671, 642.
88 Below, this section (vicars).
89 *Crockford* (1980–2); inf. from rector.
90 *Tax. Eccl.* (Rec. Com.), 17b.
91 *Valor Eccl.* (Rec. Com.), i.433–4.
92 H.A.D., D/F/TYS/2, pp. 53–4 (copy of cert. of ch. lands in vestry mins., mentioned in Newcourt, *Rep.* i. 618); *Home Counties Mag.* iii. 224.
93 *Tax. Eccl.* (Rec. Com.), 17b.
94 *Valor Eccl.* (Rec. Com.), i. 433–4.
95 *Lond. and Mdx. Chantry Cert.* (Lond. Rec. Soc. xvi), 68.   96 Vestry mins. 6, 27 Nov. 1657; 10 May 1658.
97 Ibid. 29 Nov. 1690.
98 Guildhall MSS. 9556, f. 51; 9557, f. 31.
99 Vestry mins. 13 June 1679; below, charities.
1 Vestry mins. 1 Jan., 9 Apr. 1690; 16 Mar., 7 Apr., 1

Dec. 1801.   2 Ibid. 4 Aug. 1759; 19 Apr. 1760.
3 Ibid. 22 June 1704; 15 Aug. 1705; 19 Apr. 1760.
4 Par. mins. 5 Mar. 1781; vestry mins. 26 Mar. 1799; 15 Apr. 1800; 7 Apr. 1801.
5 Vestry mins. 9 Apr. 1822; 1 Apr. 1823.
6 *Lond. Gaz.* 19 Mar. 1825, p. 460.
7 *Rep. Com. Eccl. Revenues*, 649.
8 *Return of Glebe Lands*, H.C. 307, p. 85 (1887), lxiv.
9 *Return of Tithes Commuted*, H.C. 214, p. 122 (1887), lxiv.   10 *Cal. Pat.* 1343–5, 471.
11 H.A.D., D/F/TYS/2, p. 53.
12 *Home Counties Mag.* iii. 224.
13 G.L.R.O., M79/G/11/1–2.
14 H.A.D., D/F/AMH/527.
15 G.L.R.O., P79/JN1/24 (list of donations at back of reg.).
16 H.A.D., print F 97 (anon. pencil sketch); D. Mander, *St. John-at-Hackney* (bicentenary booklet, 1993), 27–8.
17 Robinson, *Hackney*, ii. 79, 117 (plan); Lysons, *Environs*, ii. 474; Pevsner, *Lond.* ii. 168.
18 Inf. from rector.
19 McDonnell, *Med. Lond. Suburbs*, 146.
20 Guildhall MSS. 9171/3, f. 211v.; 9171/5, 42v.

its brothers and sisters. Sir James Bartholomew, a former mayor, in 1480 left property in London to the guild, [21] which at its dissolution in 1548 was served by a brotherhood priest and an additional priest. Other chantry lands in 1548 supported 6 obits, 2 lights, church repairs and ornaments, and a church house built by the parishioners for meetings.[22]

The sinecure rectors were mostly absentee pluralists.[23] They included Thomas de Cobham, bishop of Worcester, the French cardinal Gaucelin Jean Deuza (d. 1348),[24] William Booth (d. 1464), archbishop of York, the diplomatists Christopher Urswick (d. 1522), dean of Windsor, and Richard Sampson (d. 1554), bishop of Chichester and later of Lichfield and Coventry, the Jesuit Thomas Darbyshire (d. 1604), and the scholar Christopher Carlile (d. ? 1588).[25] Darbyshire was a Marian intruder whose predecessor John Spendlove was reinstated under Elizabeth I.[26] The royalist George Moore, rector 1622–64, having leased his rights, was apparently not formally deprived: in 1653 courts were held in the name of the parliamentarian Richard Blackwell.[27]

Most medieval vicars were probably resident.[28] Exceptionally Robert Bromyard, chaplain to Archbishop Booth, was licensed to hold the vicarage with one other benefice in 1455.[29] Many later vicars were pluralists. John Willoughby, vicar 1546–8, Robert Stokes, 1549–70, Henry Wright, 1570–1,[30] Thomas Knell, 1571–3, the verse writer,[31] and Hugh Johnson, 1573–1619,[32] held benefices in London or nearby in Essex. David Dolben (d. 1633), vicar from 1619, acquired a Welsh living and prebend and in 1631 became bishop of Bangor, but he died in London and was buried in Hackney. Gilbert Sheldon (d. 1677), later archbishop of Canterbury, was vicar 1633–6 and at the same time a canon of Gloucester.[33]

Calybute Downing (d. 1644), vicar 1636–43, grandson of a Hackney resident, was alleged to have sought royal favour through the earl of Strafford before 1640, when his charges against the rector marked the start of an association with the parliamentary cause.[34] William Spurstowe (d. 1666), vicar 1643–62, a moderate puritan, was deprived of the mastership of Catharine Hall, Cambridge, in 1650 after opposing the king's trial; he supported the Restoration but welcomed the presbyterian Richard Baxter at his vicarage house and resigned over the Act of Uniformity in 1662, thereafter living in retirement at Hackney.[35] The 'able and godly minister' serving the parish in 1650[36] was presumably Spurstowe. Downing and Spurstowe may have established a tradition that was reinforced when George Clarke's charity of 1668 provided for a protestant sermon on the anniversary of Elizabeth I's coronation.[37]

Thomas Jeamson or Jameson, vicar 1662–87, was pulled from the pulpit by his congregation for preaching that London ought not to be rebuilt after the Great Fire.[38] Neither he nor his successors Nehemiah Moorhouse, 1687–89, Robert Bruce, 1690–1703, and Peter Newcome, 1704–38, held other preferments with Hackney.[39] Newcome (d. 1738), who published some sermons, was grandfather of the antiquary of the same name.[40] Despite competition from nearby nonconformist meeting houses,[41] the church drew both rich residents and visitors such as Pepys, who found it full in 1667.[42] The vestry spent much time in allocating pews, which in 1700 it vainly decided not to grant to individuals,[43] and in 1753 the beadles were instructed to control the crowd of coaches trying to draw up at the church steps.[44]

Robert Wright, vicar 1738–53 and rector from 1730, was also a chaplain to the prince of Wales, a canon of Lichfield, and from 1746 rector of Downham (Essex), but apparently spent much time at Hackney until 1749.[45] Thomas Cornthwaite, vicar 1753–99 and perpetual curate of Mortlake (Surr.), normally lived in Hackney until 1786[46] but later was non-resident, probably through ill health.[47] Services were held twice on Sunday in the mid and late 18th century;[48] c. 1790 communion was administered monthly to c. 100 people and the children were catechized in Lent.[49]

The vicar's assistants had varying titles and functions. William Barnard was chosen jointly by the vicar and vestry in 1628 to give Sunday afternoon lectures for one year.[50] His reappointment was not recorded but Samuel Tomlins was chosen lecturer in 1634, to be assisted in reading prayers and administering communion by the schoolmaster Mordecai Keydon.[51] Tomlins was described as curate at vestry meetings, which the vicar Gilbert Sheldon rarely attended.[52] There

---

21 Ibid. 9171/5, ff. 110–111; *Cal. Pat. 1476–85*, 126; *Cal. of Wills in Ct. of Husting*, ii (2), 588.
22 *Lond. and Mdx. Chantry Cert.* 67–8.
23 Rectors from 1306 are listed in Hennessy, *Novum Rep.* 177–8.
24 Le Neve, *Fasti, 1300–1544, Coventry and Lichfield*, 11.
25 *D.N.B.*
26 Hennessy, *Novum Rep.* p. xxxv; Darbyshire was a nephew of Bishop Bonner: ibid. p. xlvi.
27 G.L.R.O., M79/G/4/2/1/1; P.R.O., C 5/513/80.
28 Vicars from 1328 are listed in Hennessy, *Novum Rep.* 178. Earlier vicars were Thomas in 1275 and John of Foxcote in 1292: *Cal. Close, 1272–9*, 165; P.R.O., JUST 3/87, m. 29. Thos. of Wickham was vicar by 1326: *Cal. Pat. 1324–7*, 287.
29 *Cal. Papal Reg.* xi. 95; *D.N.B.*
30 Hennessy, *Novum Rep.* 178; Newcourt, *Rep.* i. 483, 540; ii. 680.
31 Newcourt, *Rep.* i. 505; *D.N.B.*
32 Le Neve, *Fasti, 1547–1857, St. Paul's, Lond.* 60.
33 *D.N.B.*
34 Ibid.

35 *D.N.B.*; *Cal. S.P. Dom.* 1659–60, 420.
36 *Home Counties Mag.* iii. 224.
37 *12th Rep. Com. Char.* H.C. 348, p. 137 (1825), x.
38 *Cal. S.P. Dom.* 1665–7, 283.
39 Vestry mins. *passim*. Not John Bruce, as in Hennessy, *Novum Rep.* 178.
40 *D.N.B.* s.v. Newcome, Hen.
41 Below, prot. nonconformity.
42 *Diary of Sam. Pepys*, viii. 174.
43 Vestry mins. 8 July 1700; *passim*.
44 Ibid. 24 Apr. 1753.
45 *Alum. Cantab. to 1751*, iv. 477; Guildhall MS. 9556, f. 74; vestry mins. *passim*.
46 Vestry mins. *passim*; *Rec. of Old Westminster*, i (1928), 215.
47 Guildhall MS. 9557, f. 31; *Gent. Mag.* lxix. 530.
48 Guildhall MSS. 9550; 9558, f. 441.
49 Ibid. MS. 9557, f. 31.
50 Vestry mins. 31 Aug. 1628.
51 Ibid. 8 Apr. 1634.
52 Ibid. 1634–6, *passim*.

may have been no need for an assistant until 1657, when Spurstowe was to have one, supported by subscriptions. The first two appointed failed to arrive;[53] at the Restoration Spurstowe was assisted by Ezekiel Hopkins (d. 1690), later bishop of Derry.[54]

In 1631 and 1671 the schoolmasters were not ordinarily to perform pastoral functions,[55] but several acted occasionally as assistant curate and attended the vestry in the vicar's absence. Robert Skingle did so between 1661 and 1670;[56] his teaching was unsatisfactory in 1666, when he was not to be paid from parish funds if the vicar insisted on employing him as reader.[57] The lectureship, apparently in abeyance, was revived in 1669 for John Worthington (d. 1671), formerly master of Jesus College, Cambridge, who was to receive £80 a year from subscriptions.[58] In 1670 the vestry agreed that there should also be a reader, under the vicar and Dr. Worthington.[59] Jonathan Bowles, Skingle's successor as schoolmaster in 1671, was made lecturer in 1683, and a curate was employed from 1684. On Bowles's death in 1686 Nehemiah Moorhouse was made lecturer, and when Moorhouse became vicar Timothy Hall (d. 1690),[60] already curate, and appointed by James II as bishop of Oxford in 1688, became lecturer.[61] John Lupton, who succeeded Bowles as schoolmaster and so remained until his death in 1741,[62] acted as assistant curate between 1690 and 1700; he was not to be paid from the poor's money in 1692 but was voted an annual gratuity from 1694.[63] It is not clear whether an assistant curate was employed between 1704, when the vicar was voted £10 a year for that purpose, and 1724. John Lewis, licensed in 1726,[64] took over the parish school on Lupton's death and continued as curate.[65]

The lectureship again became a separate office in 1689 with the appointment of the historian John Strype (d. 1737), who remained vicar of Leyton (Essex) but spent his later years at the Hackney home of a surgeon, Thomas Harris. He held the lectureship, renewed annually, until 1724,[66] when all ratepayers were allowed a voice in the appointment and four lecturers were chosen in rotation and, to calm public dissension, two more were added in survivorship.[67]

The lectureship was held by the curate John Lewis (d. 1770), whose son Robert succeeded him as a joint lecturer.[68] Robert, who had been licensed curate in 1765, continued as joint lec-

turer for 57 years, for most of which time he was rector of Chingford (Essex). His fellow lecturers were Robert Bromley, who from 1775 held a London rectory and in 1791 was accused of neglecting Hackney,[69] and from 1806 George Paroissien, who served for many years as assistant curate before becoming the first rector of West Hackney. In 1828 J. J. Watson relieved the parish by himself paying for the afternoon sermon.[70]

Watson, vicar from 1799 and incumbent rector 1821–39, was also rector of Digswell (Herts.) from 1811 and later archdeacon of St. Albans and a canon of St. Paul's.[71] He was normally resident at first[72] but c. 1828 lived partly at Digswell.[73] The 'Hackney Phalanx', formed around Watson, his younger brother Joshua (d. 1855), treasurer of the National Society, and their brother-in-law Henry Handley Norris (d. 1850), the 'bishop-maker', largely inspired a national High Church revival. In 1811 Joshua took a house in the parish, where Norris, a native and, like the Watsons, the son of a rich merchant, was already unpaid minister of a chapel which he had helped to establish in South Hackney. Too informal to be termed a pressure group, the Phalanx was a body of friends whose religious and political beliefs made them prominent both in the National Society, founded in 1811, and in its offshoot, the commission formed under the Church Building Act, 1818. J. J. Watson, although hampered by ill health, encouraged both church and school building, providing his own parish as a field where the group's ideals could be put into practice.[74]

J. J. Watson made possible the division of his parish by enlisting public support for new churches and by surrendering part of his own income. In particular he stressed the need for large endowments, so that most pews should be free.[75] Although his later years saw repeated assaults on the church rates, as in South and West Hackney, vestrymen of all denominations praised his generosity and moderation.[76] Watson bought many ornaments for the church[77] and opposed the formation of an Auxiliary Bible Society, fearing unnecessary trouble with dissenters and preferring the older S.P.C.K.[78] His churchmanship was not so high as that of T. O. Goodchild, his successor 1839–77, who followed Bishop Blomfield's charge of 1842 by wearing a surplice in the pulpit. Faced with a dwindling congregation and a 'tempest of popular indignation',

53 Ibid. 19 Apr., 7 June, 23 Aug. 1657.   54 D.N.B.
55 Vestry mins. 5 July 1631; 5 Nov. 1671.
56 Ibid. 25 Oct. 1661; 5 Apr. 1670; passim.
57 Ibid. 9 Jan., 5, 6 Feb. 1666.
58 Ibid. 30 Nov. 1669; D.N.B.
59 Vestry mins. 5 June 1670.
60 Ibid. 10 Apr. 1683; 6 Apr. 1686; 17 Apr. 1688; D.N.B.
61 Vestry mins. 1684–6, passim; D.N.B.
62 Vestry mins. 22 Mar. 1686; Alum. Oxon. 1500–1714, 950.
63 Vestry mins. 22 Apr. 1690; 17 May 1692; 29 May 1694; 17 June 1700.
64 Ibid. 22 June 1704; 8 June 1724; Guildhall MS. 9550.
65 Vestry mins. 23 Nov. 1741.
66 Ibid. 2 Apr. 1689; passim; V.C.H. Essex, vi. 216–17; D.N.B.
67 Vestry mins. 18 Nov. 1723; 27 May, 8 June 1724.
68 Par. mins. 10 Apr. 1769; 11 Aug., 10 Nov. 1770.

69 Guildhall MS. 9557A, f. 31.
70 Par. mins. 27 Oct. 1806; 13 Dec. 1823; vestry mins. 3 Jan. 1828; Robinson, Hackney, ii. 220–1.
71 J. Foster, Index Eccl. 1800–40 (1890), 185; D.N.B. s.v. Watson, Joshua.   72 Guildhall MS. 9558, f. 441.
73 Ibid. 9560; V.C.H. Herts. iii. 85.
74 D.N.B. s.vv. Watson, Joshua; Norris, H. H.; M. H. Port, Six Hundred New Chs. (1961), 2, 4, 15; A. B. Webster, Joshua Watson (1954), 18–32; O. Chadwick, Victorian Ch. (1970), 78, 152, 340.
75 Guildhall MS. 9557 (loose insertion); vestry mins. 31 Mar. 1807.
76 Vestry mins. 7 Aug. 1835; Hackney Mag. Mar., Aug., Oct. 1834. For S. and W. Hackney, G.L.R.O., P79/JN1/166, 168.
77 e.g. vestry mins. 9 Apr. 1822; 5 Aug. 1824; 10 Nov. 1828.
78 Vestry mins. 2 Nov. 1812.

the rector withdrew several innovations, while asserting his right to preach in a surplice on days when the sacrament was administered.[79]

Several assistant curates were appointed in the late 18th century, normally with stipends of £100, including Jelinger Symons, who published some sermons and in 1802 became minister of Stamford Hill chapel.[80] Distinguished assistants to J. J. Watson were Frederick Nolan (d. 1864), George Townsend (d. 1857), and Renn Dickson Hampden (d. 1868), later bishop of Hereford.[81] In 1810 two assistant curates were resident, a third being available on Sundays.[82] There were three for the reduced parish in 1835, with stipends totalling £340,[83] and in 1889 and 1907.[84]

Morning and evening services at St. John's had attendances of 700 and 500 in 1851,[85] of 1,093 and 960 in 1886,[86] and of 714 and 756 in 1903.[87] Numbers were higher than at any other Hackney church in 1886, although they were nearly equalled by those at West Hackney, which had taken the lead by 1903.[88] In 1882 a mission house was opened at nos. 21-3 the Grove (later Hackney Grove), where in 1903 there were 150 morning and 135 evening worshippers. It was rebuilt in 1938 with proceeds from the sale of St. John's Institute (Sutton House) and survived in 1988. An additional hall was opened in 1929. Two halls were let in 1988 to the I.L.E.A. and one to Dr. Barnardo's.[89]

Rectors in the 19th and 20th centuries included Arthur Brook, 1877–88, a prebendary of Lincoln, A. G. Lawley, later Baron Wenlock (d. 1931), 1897–1911, and H. A. S. Pink, 1951–65, who were prebendaries of St. Paul's, and Henry Mosley, 1911–19, later bishop of Stepney and then of Southwell.[90] After 1907 there were often two curates until 1971, from which time Hackney had a rector and two team vicars, aided in the 1980s by a non-stipendiary curate. One team vicar was responsible for the church of St. John, the other for that of St. James, Clapton.[91]

There was a strong musical tradition. An organ bought by 1500[92] presumably did not survive the Reformation, as one by Ralph Dallam (d. 1672) was to be set up in 1666 and a salary was ordered for the organist in 1667.[93] It was the new organ, together with the young ladies at school, which

drew Pepys to Hackney church.[94] Organists' appointments were renewed every Easter with those of other parish officers. In 1720 the vestry warned against long voluntaries and 'light, airy, and jiggy tunes'.[95] Edward Henry Purcell, grandson of the composer Henry, was appointed in 1753 and was rebuked for lightness and for irregular attendance,[96] as was his successor.[97] Singing was a qualification sought in the parish clerk, in 1778 without success.[98] Francis Edward Bache (d. 1858) served briefly as organist in 1855.[99]

The church of *ST. JOHN*, which stood east of Church Street,[1] was called St. Augustine's from the 14th to the 17th century.[2] From *c.* 1660 it was known as St. John of Jerusalem,[3] St. John the Baptist,[4] or simply as St. John at Hackney.[5] Only the 16th-century tower survives from what may have been a complete rebuilding, formerly commemorated by the arms of Sir John Heron (d. 1521) carved between each arch of the nave and also placed, with those of the rector Christopher Urswick (d. 1522), in the chancel. Thereafter the church consisted of a chancel, aisled and clerestoreyed nave, and south-west tower.[6] The so-called Rowe chapel, properly a mausoleum, was built on the south side of the chancel in 1614[7] and a vestry was added on the north side. In 1741 the church measured 105 ft. along its north wall and 64 ft. across; the tower bore a vane surmounted by a crown which reached to 118 ft. The walls, with fenestration of *c.* 1500, showed a variety of materials,[8] as they did at the time of the church's demolition, when the exterior presented 'an incomprehensible jumble of dissonant repairs, without a trace of the original building, except the windows of part of it'.[9]

Repairs were paid for by bequests, recorded from 1378,[10] and by periodic assessments from 1586 or earlier;[11] some parish funds were set aside in 1628 as church stock, distinct from the poor's stock. Major repairs were needed in 1659[12] and 1720.[13] Plans for rebuilding proved too expensive in 1756, when it was decided to repair the existing fabric, and 1779.[14] The Rowe chapel, built by Sir Henry Rowe with a monument to his father the lord mayor (d. 1612),

79 *The Times*, 18 Feb. 1845, 7d; 4 Mar. 1845, 5f.
80 Guildhall MS. 9557A, f. 31; Robinson, *Hackney*, ii. 219. Symons was grandfather of the writer Jelinger Cookson Symons (d. 1860): *Alum. Cantab. 1752–1900*, 102; *D.N.B.*
81 *D.N.B.*
82 Guildhall MS. 9558, f. 441.
83 *Rep. Com. Eccl. Revenues*, 649.
84 *Mackeson's Guide* (1889), 70; *Crockford* (1907).
85 P.R.O., HO 129/11/4/1/1.
86 *Brit. Weekly*, 19 Nov. 1886, 4a.
87 Mudie-Smith, *Rel. Life*, 63.
88 Below, list of churches.
89 *P.O. Dir. Lond. County Suburbs, North* (1894 and later edns.); Mudie-Smith, *Rel. Life*, 63; Mander, *St. John-at-Hackney*, 33,35-6; inf. from Mr. S. E. Piesse, chwdn.
90 *Clergy List* (1881, 1915); *Crockford* (1926 and later edns.).
91 *Crockford* (1935 and later edns.); G.L.R.O., P79/JSG/38; inf. from rector.
92 Guildhall MS. 9171/8, f. 234v.
93 *D.N.B.*; vestry mins. 9 Jan. 1666; 9 Apr. 1667.
94 *Diary of Sam. Pepys*, viii. 174.
95 Vestry mins. 6 Apr. 1686 sqq.; 21 Jan. 1714; 19 Apr. 1720.

96 Ibid. 22 Sept. 1753; 25 Sept. 1756; 17 Oct. 1763; *D.N.B.* s.v. Purcell, Hen.
97 Vestry mins. 27 Dec. 1780.
98 Par. mins. 19 Oct., 7 Dec. 1778; 30 Oct. 1786.
99 *D.N.B.*
1 Rocque, *Map of Lond.* (1741–5), sheet 6; Root's map (1741); L.C.C. *List of Streets* (1901), 330.
2 Guildhall MS. 9171/1, ff.64v. (1378), 77 (1380); *Lond. and Mdx. Chantry Cert.* 68; Stow, *Survey* (1720), ii, app. p. 122.
3 Newcourt, *Rep.* i. 617.
4 Guildhall MSS. 9556, f. 50; 9558, f. 441.
5 Vestry mins. *passim.*
6 Stow, *Survey* (1720), ii, app. p. 122; Lysons, *Environs*, ii. 460-1; Simpson, *Memorials of St. John*, i (1882), 43–5.
7 Lysons, *Environs*, ii. 464-5; vestry mins. 16 May 1614.
8 Root's map (1741).
9 *Gent. Mag.* lxvi (1), 273; above, plate 45.
10 Guildhall MS. 9171/1, ff. 64v., 77 sqq.
11 Vestry mins. 23 May 1585; 12 Sept. 1596; 17 May 1604 sqq.   12 Ibid. 1 Dec. 1628; 17 Oct. 1659.
13 Ibid. 17 Oct. 1719; 19 Apr. 1720.
14 Ibid. 25 Sept., 6, 20, 27 Nov. 1756; par. mins. 28 July 1779.

proved difficult to maintain: the parish was obliged to repair it in 1691.[15] Further negotiations took place with the Rowes' heirs in 1719 and again in 1768, when the earl of Hillsborough agreed to repair the chapel but warned that he would insist on a new one if the parish should rebuild the church.[16] Other embellishments included a clock, which was to be bought in 1628,[17] and bells, of which there were at least four in 1596 and six from 1678; a peal of eight bells and a new clock were ordered in 1743.[18]

To increase space subscriptions were collected for a gallery in 1659.[19] Another gallery was needed in 1671 and piecemeal additions had raised the seating to 1,000 by 1789.[20] The need for seats, rather than disrepair, led the vestry to secure an Act to rebuild in 1790, amended by a further Act in 1795.[21] The body of the church was pulled down in 1798, regretted by some as an antiquity that was sound, spacious, and unusually rich in monuments.[22]

The tower was spared lest its eight bells should be too heavy for the new church, although in 1854 they were moved there after it had been underpinned.[23] Fragments of monuments were kept beneath the tower in 1811, including that of Lucy, Lady Latimer,[24] which was also moved. In 1992 the tower, maintained from 1912 by Hackney M.B.,[25] survived as an early 16th-century Kentish ragstone structure, of four stages beneath a restored parapet and with diagonal buttressing;[26] a paved area to the east marked the site of the old church. The Rowe chapel, dominating the surrounding tombs and repaired c. 1835 and after 1877, was demolished in 1896.[27]

The new church of St. John was begun in 1791, in a field north-east of the old church, and consecrated, after a costly delay caused by contractors' bankruptcies, in 1797.[28] Designed by James Spiller,[29] it is on the plan of a large Greek cross, with massive yellow-brick walls that were to have been mostly stuccoed, and white stone dressings. The windows are round-headed in two storeys and the walls have broad Tuscan pilasters beneath boldly projecting eaves. The semicircular porch on the north side and smaller porches for the east and west lobbies are additions of 1812–13. So too are a white stone tower

and clock steeple, 'of the most unconventional shape', also on the north side. After a fire in 1955, restoration by N. F. Cachemaille-Day and W. C. Lock involved the removal of the north and south pediments. The building was rededicated in 1958.[30]

Spiller's church came to be much criticized both for its plan and for its appearance,[31] although recently an appreciation of its originality has evoked comparisons with the work of Hawksmoor and Soane.[32] Attitudes to its seemingly disembodied tower illustrate the changes in taste: in 1909 it was 'only prevented by a perpetual miracle from crashing through the structure';[33] later it was held to add a touch of fantasy, floating 'in sublime independence of the sturdy brown temple which really supports it'.[34]

The interior is reached through vestibules, which in the 1880s were derided as resembling those of a theatre or town hall.[35] It is almost square, measuring 104 ft. into the shallow arms of the Greek cross,[36] of which the eastern one forms the chancel. Galleries fill the other arms and curve round the north-west and south-west corners. A shallow stuccoed vault, reinforced in 1929, covers the wide central area; like the walls, it is plain and has been rendered white as a result of the fire of 1955. There was seating for 2,700 in 1811.[37] A chapel beneath the gallery on the south side of the altar was moved to the north side after the fire, the area to the south being partitioned off as a parish room. At the same time the entrances through the porches on the east side of the church were closed and the north-eastern vestibule was converted into the Urswick chapel.[38] Many fittings were burned in 1955, including the 18th-century organ in the west gallery, which was replaced by an organ from All Saints', Ennismore Gardens (Kensington). A new east window, by Christopher Webb, was installed in 1958.[39]

Monuments which have survived from the old church include, in the Urswick chapel, the combined altar-tomb and Easter sepulchre of Christopher Urswick (d. 1522), beneath a recessed canopy and with inscriptions behind.[40] Nearby are brasses to John Lymsey (d. 1545) and to Arthur Dericote (d. 1562) and his four

[15] Vestry mins. 16 May 1614; 25 Feb., 1 June 1691; 17 May 1692.
[16] Ibid. 11, 18 July 1719; par. mins. 21 Apr. 1768.
[17] Vestry mins. 1 Dec. 1628.
[18] Ibid. 12 Sept. 1596; 25 Sept., 9, 13 Dec. 1677; Robinson, *Hackney*, ii. 103.
[19] Vestry mins. 16 May, 1 June 1659.
[20] Ibid. 26 Nov. 1671 sqq.; par. mins. 23 Mar. 1789.
[21] Par. mins. 23 Mar. 1789; 30 Geo. III, c. 71; 35 Geo. III, c. 70.
[22] Lysons, *Environs*, Suppl. 164; *Gent. Mag.* lxvi (1), 273. The monuments dated from 1399: Stow, *Survey of Lond.* ed. J. Strype, ii (1720), 124–9; J. Weaver, *Ancient Funeral Monuments* (1768), 305.
[23] Walford, *Old and New Lond.* v. 518; Clarke, *Hackney*, 84; vestry mins. 28 Aug. 1851.
[24] Lysons, *Environs*, Suppl. 164; below.
[25] Hackney M.B. *Ann. Rep. of Boro. Engineer* (1912–13), 75.
[26] Pevsner, *Lond.* ii. 163; Hist. Mon. Com. *E. Lond.* 43–4.
[27] Vestry mins. 22 Sept. 1835; Clarke, *Hackney*, 64, 291 n. 40; Robinson, *Hackney*, illus. facing p. 3; Mander, *St. John-at-Hackney*, 25.
[28] Inscription over N. door. Following three paras. based

on Pevsner, *Lond.* ii. 163–4; Clarke, *Lond. Chs.* 64. Fullest details of rebldg. are by A. Saint in *Terrier*, Autumn 1992; Mander, *St. John-at-Hackney*, 16–22.
[29] Colvin, *Brit. Architects*, 773.
[30] Wooden tablet inside N. porch; Mander, *St. John-at-Hackney*, 39–40; above, plate 44.
[31] e.g. J. H. Sperling, *Ch. Walks in Mdx.* (1849), 128; Walford, *Old and New Lond.* v. 518; T. F. Bumpus, *Lond. Chs. Ancient and Modern*, ii (1908), 88–9; J. Tavenor-Perry, *Memorials of Old Mdx.* (1909), 36–7.
[32] e.g. Pevsner, *Lond.* ii. 163–4; Clarke, *Lond. Chs.* 64.
[33] W. W. Hutchings, *Lond. Town: Past and Present*, ii (1909), 949.
[34] J. Summerson, *Georgian Lond.* (1978), 214.
[35] Walford, *Old and New Lond.* v. 518.
[36] Lysons, *Environs*, Suppl. 165.
[37] Ibid.
[38] Inf. from Mr. S. E. Piesse.
[39] *Brief Guide to Par. Ch. of St. John* (leaflet in ch. 1991); Mander, *St. John-at-Hackney*, 40.
[40] Its re-erection, with 4 other monuments, in the new ch. was paid for out of the unappropriated fund: vestry mins. 30 Apr. 1798. The vicar could sell unclaimed monuments: ibid. 15 Apr. 1800.

wives, besides a wall monument to David Dolben (d. 1633). In the north porch the reconstructed tomb-chest of Lucy (d. 1583), widow of John Nevill, Lord Latimer, has an alabaster effigy 'of a quality good enough for Westminster Abbey', and the marble wall monument to Thomas Wood (d. 1649) and his wife is noteworthy for its advanced style. There are also figures from the monuments to Sir Thomas Rowe (d. 1570) and to Henry Banister (d. 1628) and his wife. The crest to the epitaph to James Sotheby (d. 1750) is by Roubiliac.[41] Memorials designed for the new church include those to Capt. Henry Newcome (d. 1797) and to Lieut. Harry Sedgwick (d. 1811) by Charles Regnart, to Mary Field (d. 1825) by J. E. Carew, to Philip Lucas (d. 1830) by Samuel Nixon, and to Eliza Livermore (d. 1831) by John Soward.[42]

The churchyard was enlarged in 1671 by the gift of part of Church field from Sir George Vyner.[43] In 1707 it was to have a brick wall[44] and in 1741 it had gates to Church Street on each side of the school house.[45] A cleaner for the churchyard was regularly appointed from 1723, paving was to be laid from the church to the road in 1724, and lamps were ordered in 1756, by which time more land was needed.[46] In 1759 no more vaults were to be made without the vestry's leave either in the churchyard or in part of Church field which had been bought as an extension. The new ground was consecrated in 1763, when burials in the old ground, except in family vaults, were forbidden.[47] Some 4½ a. of Church field, bought under the Act of 1790, were consecrated for the new building and its churchyard in 1797.[48] The ground was well planted with chestnuts and other trees but, lacking a yew and being intersected by busy walks, was later held to be unsuitable for sober reflection.[49] Burials were restricted in 1854[50] and were to cease, except in family graves, from 1859.[51] Nineteenth-century monuments, many in railed enclosures, existed around the church in 1992; they included that of the hydrographer Sir Francis Beaufort (d. 1857).[52]

The plate includes two flagons of 1638 × 1657 given by Sir George Vyner, two cups and covers of 1637, patens of 1663 and 1781, that of 1781 presented in 1822 by J. J. Watson, a dish of 1671, and a fine seal-topped spoon perhaps of 1641, all silver gilt, and pewter almsdishes of 1758 and later. Four electroplate dishes were also acquired

in 1822.[53] The registers of baptisms date from 1555, of marriages from 1590, and of burials from 1593.[54]

CHURCH EXTENSION. Additional places of worship in the 18th century were provided only by the proprietary chapels of Kingsland, Homerton (Rams's chapel), and Stamford Hill.[55] Stephen Ram bought land in Hackney in 1723, when he vainly sought a pew in the parish church.[56] The vestry declined to take responsibility for Ram's chapel in 1764,[57] although the parish plate could be used there,[58] and from 1771 until 1776 it compensated the vicar, whose outgoings as lessee of the chapel, including £50 for a curate, exceeded the chapel's pew rents.[59] In 1776 and 1779 the vestry declined to support Stamford Hill chapel, also leased to the vicar.[60]

The division of the mother parish[61] into three rectories was presaged by the opening of St. John's chapel of ease, which the vestry agreed to keep in repair[62] and which became the church of South Hackney. It was served by H. H. Norris, who acted as J. J. Watson's unpaid curate.[63] Both its establishment and its later rebuilding resulted from the personal benevolence and the promotional activities of the Hackney Phalanx, as did the early building of many daughter churches.[64]

In 1839 a local committee under J. J. Watson found that there was accommodation for less than one fifth of the increased population of the central parish. With promises of grants from the church building commissioners and the bishop of London, the committee raised much of the money to build and endow St. Philip's, Dalston, and St. James's, Clapton,[65] both of which were consecrated in 1841. St. Peter's, De Beauvoir Town, was also consecrated in 1841 and St. Barnabas's, Homerton, in 1847. Including Ram's chapel and Stamford Hill chapel, there were nine Anglican churches within the ancient parish by 1851, when services were also held at the workhouse and the London Orphan Asylum.[66] After a pause, eight more churches were opened between 1866 and 1872: St. Michael and All Angels', St. Augustine's, and Christ Church, all in South Hackney, St. Matthew's, All Saints', and Christ Church, in Clapton, St. Mark's, Dalston, and St. Luke's, Homerton. There followed Holy Trinity, Dalston, All Souls', Clapton Park, and St. Michael and All Angels',

41 Hist. Mon. Com. *E. Lond.* 43–4, plates 93–5; Pevsner, *Lond.* ii. 164–5; *Complete Peerage*, s.v. Latimer; *D.N.B.* s.v. Cornwallis, Wm. A brass to Hugh Johnson (d. 1619) was extant in 1958 but not in 1993: Mander, *St. John-at-Hackney*, 52.

42 Gunnis, *Sculptors*, 80, 88, 273, 317–18, 361; full inscriptions in Robinson, *Hackney*, 126–9. Newcome's memorial was not extant in 1993.

43 Vestry mins. 26 Nov. 1671.

44 Ibid. 15 Apr. 1707.

45 Root's map (1741).

46 Vestry mins. 27 July 1723; 6 Nov. 1727; 14 Feb., 25 Sept. 1756.

47 Ibid. 4 Aug. 1759; 17 Oct. 1763.

48 Lysons, *Environs*, Suppl. 165.

49 Robinson, *Hackney*, ii. 37.

50 *Lond. Gaz.* 31 Jan. 1854, p. 273.

51 Ibid. 6 Nov. 1857, p. 3701; 10 June 1862, p. 2290.

52 *D.N.B.*; inf. from Miss E. Wright.

53 Freshfield, *Communion Plate*, 22–3; Hist. Mon. Com. *E. Lond.* 45; inf. from Mr. Piesse; cf. Guildhall MS. 9537/20; vestry mins. 2 Oct. 1738; 9 Apr. 1822.

54 In G.L.R.O.   55 Below, list of churches.

56 Vestry mins. 4 Feb., 22 Oct. 1723.

57 Par. mins. 10, 17 Mar., 22 Dec. 1764.

58 Ibid. 3 June 1765.

59 Ibid. 31 Dec. 1771; 17 Aug. 1772; 12 Oct. 1776.

60 Ibid. 28 Oct. 1776; 19 Apr., 31 May, 7 June 1779.

61 What follows summarizes the detail given below for the several churches.

62 Vestry mins. 23 Nov. 1809.

63 Webster, *Joshua Watson*, 25.

64 Plaques to commemorate J. J. Watson, Joshua Watson, and H. H. Norris were placed in the S. Hackney chs. of St. Augustine and St. Mic.: H.A.D., D/F/NOR/8/2.

65 Robinson, *Hackney*, ii. 205; H.A.D., P/J/CW/128, *passim*.

66 P.R.O., HO 129/11/2–5.

Stoke Newington Common, and, in the 1890s, St. Paul's, Homerton, St. Mary of Eton, Hackney Wick, and St. Bartholomew's, Dalston. Thus Hackney contained 23 Anglican churches by 1902, many of them with missions.[67] The last daughter church, St. Barnabas's, Shacklewell, was begun in 1909.

Anglican church attendance in 1886 was roughly equal to that of all protestant nonconformists: excluding missions it was 25,162.[68] Anglicans were still the largest single denomination in 1902, by which time numbers had fallen to 15,414 at the churches and c. 2,000 at missions, while the nonconformists had gained.[69] Hackney, still with many prosperous inhabitants, had the best worship attendance in east London; numbers were particularly high in Dalston, although they were very low in the working-class Hackney Wick.[70]

Closures began with that of Ram's chapel in the 1930s and continued after damage during the Second World War. A Church Commissioners' Scheme of 1953 converted ten benefices into five united benefices, permitting the demolition of the bombed churches of Christ Church, Clapton, St. Philip, Christ Church, South Hackney, and St. Augustine, and the use of St. Bartholomew's as a hall. A sixth bombed church, St. Michael's, South Hackney, was to be replaced on a new site. Thirteen damaged churches were to be restored, including that of West Hackney, which in the event was rebuilt with a new dedication,[71] to St. Paul, its benefice being united with that of St. Barnabas, Shacklewell.[72] In the 1970s St. Matthew's and All Souls' were rebuilt and All Saints' was demolished. St. Paul's, Homerton, was later taken over by spiritualists. By 1982 there were fifteen Anglican churches within the ancient parish, of which two served central Hackney, three South Hackney, two West Hackney, four Clapton, two Dalston, one Homerton, and one the borders of Stoke Newington.[73] The introduction of team ministries, beginning with one for Hackney (St. John the Baptist and St. James, Clapton) in 1971,[74] continued with the establishment of the benefice of Hackney Marsh (St. Barnabas, Homerton, and All Souls, Clapton Park) in 1985.[75]

Two Sisters[76] of St. Margaret, an order based at East Grinstead (Suss.), moved from Soho to Ash Grove, off Cambridge Heath Road, in 1865 and opened an orphanage and guild for working girls as a centre for work in South Hackney, Haggerston, and Shoreditch. In 1866 the Revd. R. Tuke, from St. Anne's, Soho,[77] turned two houses in Ash Grove into a small orphanage, initially for boys orphaned by cholera. He also held classes there and acted as spiritual director of the nearby sisters. Tuke's so-called order of St. Joseph, which adopted the Franciscan habit, was disbanded on his conversion to Roman Catholicism in 1867, when several sisters followed him. Sister Kate Warburton, who remained, moved briefly to no. 334 Kingsland Road, in 1869 called St. Saviour's priory, and then to Great Cambridge Street in Shoreditch.

Sisters of the Holy Childhood established a children's home[78] at their mother house, no. 19 Clapton Common, in 1881, where they also did parish work and remained until c. 1940.

The community of St. Augustine of Hippo, for men skilled in a trade or profession who did not yet feel able to live in a strict community, briefly existed at no. 58 Pedro Street, Clapton, c. 1920, before moving to Clapham.

Sisters of St. Francis, on their return to London from Hull (Yorks.), in 1908 moved into a small house in Malvern Road, Dalston, and soon afterwards into no. 155 Richmond Road, acquiring no. 157 in 1920.[79] A convent chapel was consecrated in 1924. The sisters, who did missionary work, remained until the site was taken by the L.C.C. in 1962, when they moved to Compton Durville (Som.).

LIST OF CHURCHES

Inf. about patrons is taken from *Clergy List, Crockford,* and *Lond. Dioc. Year Bk.* (various edns.); seating and attendance figs. 1851 are from P.R.O., HO 129/11/2–5 attendance Wgs. 1886 from *Brit. Weekly,* 19 Nov. 1886, 1903 from Mudie-Smith, *Rel. Life,* 63. Liturgical directions are used in all architectural descriptions. The following additional abbreviations are used: aft., afternoon; asst., assistant; Dec., Decorated; demol., demolished, demolition; evg., evening; mem., memorial; mtg., meeting; min., minister; Perp., Perpendicular; R., rector; temp., temporary; V., vicar. Most ch. regs. are at G.L.R.O.

ALL SAINTS, Blurton Rd., Clapton Pk.[80] Site for ch., Vicarage, and sch. on N. side at corner of Elderfield Rd. bought by Chas. Jacomb 1868. Iron ch. seating 500 bought from St. Mat. 1869. Half bldg. costs of permanent ch. borne by Jacomb. Dist. formed from St. John 1873.[81] Patron rector of St. John, Hackney. High Ch.

---

[67] Mudie-Smith, *Rel. Life,* 63. The total excludes St. John's, Vartry Rd., partly in Tottenham: *V.C.H. Mdx.* v. 352. A few streets in S. Hackney were served from All Saints' or St. Paul's, Haggerston: Booth, *Life and Labour,* iii (1), map between pp. 113 and 115.

[68] *British Weekly,* 19 Nov. 1886, 2a, allowing for the deduction in respect of Stoke Newington chs. and St. John's, Vartry Rd.

[69] Totals for Hackney in Mudie-Smith, *Rel. Life,* 63, 67, 287–8, deducting for St. John's, Vartry Rd. Some mission attendances were probably from Islington.

[70] Mudie-Smith, *Rel. Life,* 26–7.

[71] G.L.R.O., P79/JSG/37/2; below.

[72] J. Carrow, *By Faith–With Thanksgiving* (booklet 1960).   [73] *Crockford* (1980–2).

[74] Above, this section.

[75] *Crockford* (1987–8); inf. from the Revd. S. J. W. Cox.

[76] Four paras. based on *P.O. Dir. Lond.* (1869 and later edns.) and P. F. Anson, *Call of the Cloister* (1964), *passim; Official Year Bk. of Ch. of Eng.* (1921).

[77] Not St. Mary's, as in Anson: *Clergy List* (1866).

[78] Above, misc. institutions.   [79] Above, pub. svces.

[80] Para. based on N. G. J. Stiff, *Our Neighbourhood, Our Par., and Our Ch.* (1907); *Mackeson's Guide* (1870 and later edns.); Clarke, *Lond. Chs.* 68, fig. 46.

[81] *Lond. Gaz.* 18 July 1873, p. 3400.

svces. as at All Saints, Margaret Street (Westm.).
Attendance 1886: 663 a.m., 634 p.m.; 1903: 387
a.m., 378 p.m. Bldg. of Kentish rag with Bath
stone dressings in Early Eng. style, seating 800,
by F. T. Dollman 1870–1: chancel, nave with
low aisles and tall clerestory, bellcot; SW. tower
and steeple not built. Interior of red and black
brick, with reredos by Earp.[82] Par. united with
St. John, St. Jas., and All Souls 1972.[83] Ch.
demol. 1973[84] and replaced by All Saints Ct.
flats. Mission in iron chapel in Rushmore Rd.
by 1881; later called Good Shepherd mission.
Attendance 1903: 46 a.m., 71 p.m. Closed c.
1919.[85]

ALL SOULS, Pedro Street (rebuilt in Overbury
Street), Clapton Pk.[86] Svces. for populous E.
part of All Saints par. held at no. 1 Bellevue
Terr., Pedro Street, before gift of land between
Overbury Street and Pedro Street by Chas.
Jacomb, where iron ch. seating c. 400 opened
1880. Dist. formed from All Saints and St.
Barnabas, Homerton, 1884.[87] Patron five trustees, inc. R. of Hackney, V. of All Saints, and
Jacomb.[88] High Ch. 1884. Attendance 1886: 373
a.m., 350 p.m.; 1903: 254 a.m., 300 p.m. Bldg.
of brick with stone dressings in Early Eng. style,
seating 760, by F. T. Dollman 1882–3: chancel,
NE. and SE. chapels, chancel continued over
aisled and clerestoreyed nave, NW. and SW.
porches, bellcot.[89] Declared redundant 1976 and
demol., with Vicarage to N. and sch. to W. New
ch. of the Risen Christ and All Souls, facing
Overbury Street, consecrated 1977: flat roofed
red-brick bldg. of secular appearance, seating
150, by Fred. To, with free-standing concrete
cross. Served by team V. as part of new par. of
Hackney Marsh from 1985.[90]

CHRIST CHURCH, Gore Rd., South Hackney.[91]
Site at W. end of rd., opposite North (later
Northiam) Street. Dist. formed from South
Hackney, St. Mic. and All Angels, St. Jas.,
Bethnal Green, St. John, Bethnal Green, and St.
Steph., Haggerston, 1871.[92] Patron J. C. Egan,
first V.,[93] thereafter R. of South Hackney. Attendance 1886: 333 a.m., 209 p.m.; 1903: 241
a.m., 151 p.m. Bldg. of brick with stone dressings in Dec. style, seating 850, by W. Wigginton
1871: apsidal chancel, aisled and clerestoreyed
nave. Demol., after war damage, between 1944
and 1952.[94] Par. united with St. John of Jerusalem, South Hackney, 1953.[95] Mission svces. in
room in East Street 1889 and hall in North
Street 1889 to 1914 or later.[96]

CHRIST CHURCH, Rendlesham Rd., Clapton.[97]
Iron ch. seating 350, served by asst. curate from
St. Jas., opened 1868 in Walsingham Rd.[98] Site
at S. corner of Kenninghall Rd. bought from
Brit. Land Co. by Chas. Jacomb 1866 and
conveyed to Eccl. Com. 1870. Dist. assigned
from West Hackney and St. Jas. 1871.[99] Patron
R. of West Hackney and V. of St. Jas. alter-
nately. Increasingly High Ch., until 'full
Catholic ceremonial' achieved 1911. Attendance
1886: 388 a.m., 120 p.m.; 1903: 153 a.m., 161
p.m. Bldg. of brick with brick and stone dressings in Dec. style, seating c. 700, by W.
Wigginton 1870–1: chancel, N. and S. chapels,
aisled and clerestoreyed nave, bellcot; interior of
variegated brickwork.[1] Demol., after war damage, between 1944 and 1952.[2] Svces. in par. hall
1940–4 and in St. Jas. 1945–53. Par. united with
St. Jas. 1953.[3]

GOOD SHEPHERD, High Hill Ferry, see ST.
MATTHEW.

GOOD SHEPHERD, Rushmore Rd., see ALL
SAINTS.

HOLY TRINITY, Woodland Street, Dalston.[4]
Finance for ch. on W. side of street from proceeds of demol. of Merchant Taylors' Co.'s ch.
of St. Martin Outwich (Lond.). Dist. formed
from St. Phil. and St. Mark 1879.[5] Patron
Merchant Taylors' Co. to 1937,[6] thereafter bp.
Attendance 1886: 461 a.m., 465 p.m.; 1903: 95
a.m., 197 p.m. Bldg. of red brick in Early Eng.
style, seating 600, by Ewan Christian 1878–9:
very short chancel flanked by vestries, N. and S.
transepts, crossing tower with NE. stair turret,
aisled and clerestoreyed nave. Reopened after
war damage, with S. transept reduced in height,
1952. Svces. in neighbouring red-brick hall of
1908 in Beechwood Rd. in 1987, during renovation of ch., which served par. of Holy Trinity
with St. Phil. from 1953. Patron bp.[7]

HOLY TRINITY, Lea Bridge, see ST. MATTHEW.

KINGSLAND CHAPEL, Kingsland Rd.[8] Chapel of
Kingsland leper hosp., founded c. 1280 and
annexed to St. Bart.'s 1549, on S. side of Ball's
Pond Rd.[9] Continued as proprietary chapel on
closure of Kingsland hosp. 1760. Min., nominated by governors of St. Bart.'s, to maintain
fabric and be supported by congregation. Attendance 1842: c. 20. Small stone medieval bldg. on
par. boundary, which ran through N. and S.
doorways, had bell-turret, chancel with squints.
Floor lay c. 3 ft. below level of highway when
chapel demol. 1845.[10]

[82] T. F. Bumpus, Lond. Chs. Ancient and Modern, ii
(1908), 301–2; H.A.D., Y54, Vol. III, p. 46; G.L.R.O.,
photo. (1972).   [83] G.L.R.O., index to P79/ALL/17.
[84] N.M.R., photos.   [85] P.O. Dir. Lond. (1919, 1920).
[86] Para. based on Stiff, Our Neighbourhood, 47–8, 51–2,
65; Mackeson's Guide (1881 and later edns.); Clarke, Lond.
Chs. 69.   [87] Lond. Gaz. 2 Jan. 1885, p. 19.
[88] Hennessy, Novum Rep. 179.
[89] G.L.R.O., photos. (1975, 1977).
[90] Inf. from Revd. S. J. W. Cox and Mrs. C. O. David,
chwdn.
[91] Para. based on Mackeson's Guide (1871 and later
edns.); G.L.R.O., index to P79/CTC/1.
[92] Lond. Gaz. 22 Dec. 1871, p. 5717.
[93] Hennessy, Novum Rep. 182.
[94] N.M.R., photos.; P.O. Dir. Lond. (1952).
[95] G.L.R.O., P79/JSG/37/2.
[96] H. W. Harris and M. Bryant, Chs. and Lond. (1914),
393.

[97] Para. based on G.L.R.O., P79/CTC2/16 (R. H.
Parker, Christ Ch. Clapton, 1871–1931); Mackeson's Guide
(1870 and later edns.); G.L.R.O., index to P79/CTC/2.
[98] Stiff, Our Neighbourhood, 26.
[99] Lond. Gaz. 7 Nov. 1871, p. 4505.
[1] H.A.D., Y54, Vol. IV, p. 19; N.M.R., photos. (1905);
G.L.R.O., photos. (1944).
[2] G.L.R.O., photos.(1944); P.O. Dir. Lond. (1952).
[3] G.L.R.O., P79/JSG/37/2.
[4] Para. based on Mackeson's Guide (1881 and later
edns.); Clarke, Lond. Chs. 69; G.L.R.O., index to P79/TRI.
[5] G.L.R.O., P79/TRI/44.
[6] Lond. Gaz. 31 Oct. 1879, p. 6174.
[7] G.L.R.O., P79/JSG/37/2.
[8] Para. based on V.C.H. Mdx. i. 210; Robinson, Hackney, i. 127–30; Clarke, Hackney, 238–9.
[9] Starling's Map (1831).
[10] Bldg. materials to be sold 1846: Islington libr., sale
cat.

RAM'S CHAPEL, High Street, Homerton.[11] Site on N. side of street in gdn. of ho. of Steph. Ram (d. 1746). Proprietary chapel, left to Ram's son-in-law Revd. Reeve Ballard, who employed preacher before leasing it to V. of Hackney 1765[12] and whose son sold it 1775; vested in 12 trustees 1791. Small dist. allocated by V. of St. Barnabas, Homerton, from 1891, chapel min. being licensed as curate and otherwise independent. Evangelical svces. to be held by ordained clergymen; adaptations, inc. admission of lay preachers, led to description of chapel as Meth. 1795[13] but established Low Ch. practices soon restored. John Eyre (d. 1803) was min. c. 1785.[14] Tradition, with emphasis on preaching, maintained by trustees 1924, 1930. Compensation paid to V. from ch. rates 1765–76,[15] as pew rents inadequate, but 19th-cent. chapel maintained by pew rents, collns., and, from 1883, endowment. Attendance 1851: 400 a.m., 600 p.m.; 1886: 295 a.m., 249 p.m.; 1903: 257 a.m., 179 p.m. Bldg. of 1729,[16] with 21 rented pews and gallery 1771,[17] seating 600 in 1851 and 500 in 1881. Long, nondescript exterior, of brick with stone dressings, 2 rows of round-headed windows along street, W. cupola.[18] Closed when in disrepair 1933, svces. being held at Sun. sch. in Urswick Rd. until 1934. Trust dissolved 1936, when endowment and money for site, taken for rd. widening, transferred with plate to St. Mary, Becontree Heath (Essex). Among other fittings, pulpit and 2 stained-glass windows went to St. And., Whitehall Pk., Islington.[19]

ST. ANDREW, Well Street, see ST. JOHN'S CHAPEL.

ST. AUGUSTINE OF CANTERBURY, Victoria Pk. Rd., South Hackney.[20] Svces. by clergy of South Hackney in sch. room when Crown granted site for ch. on NW. side of pk. c. 1865. Bldg. costs from Bp. of Lond.'s Fund, Lond. Diocesan Ch. Bldg. Soc., and subscriptions. Dist. assigned from South Hackney 1867.[21] Patron rector of South Hackney. Attendance 1886: 333 a.m., 436 p.m.; 1903: 225 a.m., 261 p.m. Bldg. in Early Eng. style, seating 1,086, by J. H. Hakewill 1867: chancel, aisled nave, pinnacled W. tower.[22] Closed after war damage 1944, demol. 1952 or later.[23] Par. united with St. Mary of Eton 1953.[24]

ST. BARNABAS, High Street, Homerton.[25] Purchase of lands W. of Brooksby's Walk from 1845 largely financed by ch. bldg. com. and Joshua Watson. Dist. assigned 1846.[26] Patron bp. At-

tendance 1851: 500 a.m., 400 p.m.; 1886: 287 a.m., 301 p.m.; 1903: 153 a.m., 241 p.m. Bldg. of Kentish rag with Bath stone dressings in Dec. style, seating 600, by A. Ashpitel 1845–7: chancel with N. vestry, nave with S. aisle, S. porch, W. tower; N. aisle, planned if nos. should rise, added 1851–2.[27] 'A good country ch.'[28] but criticized by Ecclesiologist; some proposed decoration excluded as too High Ch. Damaged 1944 but restored by W. C. Lock, with remains of chancel converted into vestries, and rededicated 1958. Ch. formed part of group with Ashpitel's Tudor Vicarage and sch. to W.

ST. BARNABAS, Shacklewell Row.[29] Hindle Street mission, for part of West Hackney par.,[30] succeeded by svces. on upper floor of Merchant Taylors' sch. mission ho. opened E. side of Shacklewell Row 1890.[31] Attendance 1903: 69 a.m., 145 p.m. Finance for ch. inc. grants from sch., Bp. of Lond.'s Fund, and Eccl. Com. Patron Merchant Taylors' sch. by 1935. Bldg. of stock brick and concrete, not oriented, with round-headed windows and externally plain because hidden behind mission ho. but internally Byzantine in plan and style, seating 400, by C. H. Reilly 1909–10, consecrated 1929: apse, chancel with aisles carried round as ambulatory, SE. chapel, tunnel-vaulted nave with aisles carried round W. end as baptistery; vestry 1937. Shallow dome over chancel. Altar fittings by Reilly; pulpit from Christ Ch., Clapton. Widely praised: 'the best ch. of its date in Lond.'.[32] Served par. of West Hackney, with smaller ch. of St. Paul, from 1955. Patron bp.[33]

ST. BARTHOLOMEW, Dalston Lane.[34] Svces. of 'Free Ch. of Eng.', seceders from St. Phil. under dismissed asst. curate R. S. Daniell, in iron ch. NW. side of rd., opposite Graham Rd., 1874. Iron ch. sold to evangelical mission 1882 but site acquired for chapel of ease to St. Mark. Financed by St. Mark's congregation. Dist. assigned from St. Mark and St. Phil. 1897.[35] Patron trustees, later Church Patronage Soc. Attendance 1886: 407 a.m., 472 p.m.; 1903: 216 a.m., 286 p.m. Bldg. of brick with stone dressings in Early Eng. style, seating 800, by J. Johnson 1884–5: chancel under same roof as aisled and clerestoreyed nave. Closed during Second World War. Members remained together without incumbent until par. merged with St. Mark 1953.[36] Bldg., assigned as hall for united par., survived as storeho. for ch. fittings

[11] Para. based on H.A.D., D/E/211/RAM/1 (trustees' mins. 1847–1936); ibid. M 3955 (TS. 'Recollections' by E. K. Packard); Robinson, Hackney, ii. 267–8; Mackeson's Guide (1867 and later edns.).
[12] Par. mins. 3 June 1765.
[13] Lysons, Environs, ii. 473.
[14] D.N.B.
[15] Par. mins. 31 Dec. 1771, 17 Aug. 1772, 12 Oct. 1776.
[16] Memorial to Ram's wife Anne in the chapel gave its foundation as 1729.   [17] Par. mins. 17 Aug. 1772.
[18] H.A.D., Y54, Vol. III, p. 45; G.L.R.O., photo. (1935).
[19] V.C.H. Mdx. viii. 94.
[20] Para. based on H.A.D., D/F/NOR/8/2 (prospectus and subscription list); Mackeson's Guide (1868 and later edns.).
[21] Lond. Gaz. 24 Dec. 1867, p. 7000.
[22] H.A.D., Y54, Vol. IV, p. 14; N.M.R., photos. (c. 1890, c. 1905). A different bldg. was projected in H.A.D., D/F/NOR/8/2.
[23] N.M.R., photos.; Pevsner, Lond. ii. 165.

[24] G.L.R.O., P79/JSG/37/2.
[25] Para. based on Mackeson's Guide (1867 and later edns.); Clarke, Lond. Chs. 66–7.
[26] G.L.R.O., M79/LH/25, pp. 355–65; Lond. Gaz. 16 Jan. 1846, p. 159.
[27] Memoir of Josh. Watson, ed. E. Churton, ii (1861), 296.
[28] Gent. Mag. cxvii. 173.
[29] Para. based on H.A.D., M 3230 (scrapbk. on hist. of Shacklewell); Clarke, Lond. Chs. 70.
[30] Carrow, By Faith–With Thanksgiving; below, W. Hackney ch.
[31] Official Year Bk. of Ch. of Eng. (1910), 61; datestone.
[32] I. Nairn, Nairn's Lond. (1966), 169. 'The bldg. I should like to be remembered by': C. H. Reilly, Scaffolding in the Sky (1938), 113; above, plate 55.
[33] Inf. from Preb. F. Preston, R. of West Hackney.
[34] Para. based on St. Mark's, Dalston, 1860–1960 (booklet 1962), 15, 48, 58; Mackeson's Guide (1889).
[35] 50th Rep. Eccl. Com. [C. 8766], p. 55 (1898), xxi.
[36] G.L.R.O., P79/JSG/37/2.

1962 but demol. by 1980.[37] Adjoining Gothic Vicarage derelict 1991.

ST. BARTHOLOMEW'S CHAPEL, *see* KINGSLAND CHAPEL.

ST. JAMES, Lower Clapton Rd.[38] Site on W. side of rd. opposite Clapton Ho. given by Revd. Thos. Baden Powell, owner of Clapton Ho., 1840. Financed by Hackney ch. bldg. cttee. as chapel of ease. Jas. Cotton Powell first min., followed by cousin Geo. Powell and Geo.'s nephew Geo. Powell Irby.[39] Asst. curates inc. Nathaniel Woodard (d. 1891), founder of Woodard schs.[40] Dist. assigned from St. John 1863.[41] Patron rector of Hackney. Low Ch., pioneer of evg. svces., *c.* 1892.[42] Attendance 1851: 400 a.m., 300 p.m.; 1886: 554 a.m., 282 p.m.; 1903: 481 a.m., 416 p.m. Bldg. of brick with stone dressings in Early Eng. style, seating 1,050 in 1851 and 900 in 1881, by E. C. Hakewill 1840–1: unusual variant of cruciform plan, with chancel with N. vestries and S. octagonal bell turret, N. and S. transepts with entrance porches, wide nave, W. baptistery. Chancel rebuilt with S. chapel by W. D. Caroë, rest of ch. reseated, 1902. E. window by Burlison & Grylls. Floors, served by NW. stair and lift turret of steel and glass, have been inserted into nave. Ch. served par. of St. Jas. with Christ Ch. from 1953. Patron R. of Hackney.[43] Par. united with St. John at Hackney 1971.[44] Mission svces. at rooms in Lea Bridge Rd. by 1888.[45] Attendance 1903: 34 p.m. Closed *c.* 1922.[46]

ST. JAMES, Stoke Newington Rd., *see* WEST HACKNEY.

ST. JOHN AT HACKNEY, *see above* (the old parish church).

ST. JOHN'S CHAPEL, Well Street.[47] Site at corner of St. Thos.'s Pl. given by John De Kewer for chapel of ease to serve South Hackney. Finance for bldg. and endowment from J. J. and Joshua Watson, H. H. Norris, and others, inc. grant from vestry, which agreed to maintain structure 1809.[48] Fund vested in 5 trustees, inc. V. of Hackney, 1810.[49] Served without payment by H. H. Norris 1825.[50] Many seats free. Became ch. of new rectory of South Hackney, with dist. assigned 1831. Patron W. G. Daniel-Tyssen.[51] Plain bldg., seating 750, by Jas. Savage[52] 1809–10; not oriented. Later enlarged,[53] having round-headed windows and pedimented W. front with Ionic pillars beneath pillared cupola 1843. Superseded by ch. of St. John of Jerusalem

(q.v.) 1848. Mission ch. of St. And., served from St. John of Jerusalem, built on part of site 1880.[54] Attendance 1886: 290 a.m., 228 p.m.; 1903: 78 a.m., 135 p.m. Survived, as St. And.'s hall, until *c.* 1942.[55]

ST. JOHN OF JERUSALEM, Lauriston Rd., South Hackney.[56] Island site for new ch. to serve South Hackney rectory, between Lauriston Rd. and Church Crescent, bought with donation from H. Wroxton Norris. Subscriptions raised largely by H. H. Norris.[57] Dist. and patron those of St. John's chapel. Attendance 1851: *c.* 700 a.m.; 1886: 592 a.m., 758 p.m.; 1903: 284 a.m., 401 p.m. Bldg. of Kentish rag with Speldhurst stone dressings in Early Eng. style, seating 1,100, by E. C. Hakewill 1845–8: apsidal chancel with N. vestry, N. and S. transepts, aisled and clerestoreyed nave supported by flying buttresses, W. tower with broach spire. 'One of largest par. chs. built in or near Lond. since Reformation';[58] design and decoration both welcomed for Catholic spirit and criticized for ostentation.[59] Much ornamental stonework removed as dangerous in 1880s.[60] Glass by Wailes destroyed in Second World War, after which stone spire was replaced by slender copper spire by Cachemaille-Day. Ch. served par. of St. John of Jerusalem with Christ Ch. from 1953. Patron Ld. Amherst of Hackney.[61]

ST. LUKE, Homerton Terr.[62] Svces. in Ram's chapel boys' sch., Durham Grove, then in mission room at no. 176 Well Street 1871. Secluded site for ch. between terr. and Chatham Pl. given by St. Thos.'s hosp. Dist. assigned from St. John, St. Barnabas, St. John of Jerusalem, and St. Augustine 1873.[63] Patron first V., W. H. Langhorne,[64] then bp. to 1898, then trustees of St. Olave, Hart Street (Lond.),[65] who contributed to stipend. Attendance 1886: 813 a.m., 800 p.m.; 1903: 238 a.m., 362 p.m. Bldg. of ragstone with stone dressings in early Dec. style, seating 900, by Newman & Billing 1871–2: chancel, short N. transept, SE. chapel, aisled and clerestoreyed nave; SW. tower and spire completed 1882. Mission svces. at hall in Kenton Rd. by 1881. Attendance 1903: 48 a.m., 96 p.m. Superseded, with other premises used by ch., by new St. Luke's hall, Rivaz Pl., *c.* 1935.

ST. MARK, Sandringham Rd., Dalston.[66] Iron ch. in Ridley Rd. opened 1860, destroyed by storm 1865. Site for permanent ch. at E. corner of St. Mark's Rd. given by W. A. Tyssen-Amhurst. 'Notorious for its Evangelism' under first

37 G.L.R.O., photo. (1980); *List of Bldgs.* (1975).
38 Para. based on Robinson, *Hackney*, ii. 211–19 (inc. illus. and plan); *Mackeson's Guide* (1867 and later edns.); Clarke, *Lond. Chs.* 65.   39 H.A.D., D/F/BAG/8, p. 10.
40 *D.N.B.*
41 *Lond. Gaz.* 15 Sept. 1863, p. 4488.
42 Clarke, *Hackney*, 41.
43 G.L.R.O., P79/JSG/37/2; above, plate 47.
44 Ibid. P79/JSG/38.
45 *P.O. Dir. Lond. County Suburbs, North* (1888).
46 *P.O. Dir. Lond. County Suburbs* (1922, 1923).
47 Para. based on Robinson, *Hackney*, ii. 171–4 and illus.
48 Vestry mins. 23 Nov. 1809.
49 H.A.D., D/E/211/JOH/J/1.
50 *Lond. Gaz.* 19 Mar. 1825, p. 460.
51 Hennessy, *Novum Rep.* 182.
52 T. F. Bumpus, *Lond. Chs.* ii (1908), 155.
53 Accn. said to be *c.* 900 in 1825 but 800 in 1831: *Lond. Gaz.* 19 Mar. 1825, p. 460; *Rep. Com. Eccl. Rev.* 649.

54 G.L.R.O, P79/JNJ/219, 223; *Mackeson's Guide* (1884).   55 *P.O. Dir. Lond.* (1942, 1947).
56 Para. based on *Mackeson's Guide* (1867 and later edns.); Clarke, *Lond. Chs.* 66 and illus.
57 H.A.D., D/F/NOR 8/1.
58 Bumpus, *Lond. Chs.* ii. 157; above, plate 51; cf. below, St. Mark.
59 *Gent. Mag.* cxvii. 173.
60 Bumpus, *Lond. Chs.* ii. 157; H.A.D., D/F/NOR 8/2.
61 G.L.R.O., P79/JSG/37/2.
62 Para. based on *Mackeson's Guide* (1881 and later edns.); Clarke, *Lond. Chs.* 68; C. May, *Centenary 1872–1972, St. Luke's Ch., Hackney.*
63 *Lond. Gaz.* 21 Nov. 1873, p. 5131.
64 Hennessy, *Novum Rep.* 180.
65 *51st Rep. Eccl. Com.* [C. 9195], p. 52 (1899), xix.
66 Para. based on *St. Mark's, Dalston, 1860–1960, passim*; *Mackeson's Guide* (1867 and later edns.); Clarke, *Lond. Chs.* 67 and illus.; above, plate 50.

min. W. Y. Rooker (d. 1869).[67] Dist. assigned from West Hackney and St. Matthias, Stoke Newington, after disputes over boundaries, 1871.[68] Patron bp. Attendance 1886: 796 a.m., 726 p.m.; 1903: 357 a.m., 445 p.m. Bldg. of brick with stone dressings in Early Eng. style, seating 1,800, by Chester Cheston 1864–5, consecrated 1870: apsidal chancel, short N. and S. transepts, aisled and clerestoreyed nave, base of SW. tower. Tower in early Continental Gothic style completed, with spirelet and corner turrets instead of intended spire, by E. W. Blackburne 1877–80. Chancel roof raised and apse rewindowed, to take mosaic reredos, c. 1880. Criticized for size by W. A. Tyssen-Amhurst, who, however, gave adjoining site for Vicarage, by Cheston 1873; 'largest area of any Lond. ch.' 1880s. Ornate interior, with polychrome brickwork, iron columns, and stained glass by Lavers & Barraud in all windows. Unusual glazed openings in roof spandrels over crossing. The only working external turret barometer in Europe c. 1979, when bldg. termed 'the cathedral of the East End'.[69] Served par. of St. Mark with St. Bart. from 1953. Patron Church Patronage Soc. Mission by Highgate sch. transferred at instance of V., E. A. B. Sanders, old pupil and later prebendary of St. Paul's, from Whitechapel to no. 18 John Campbell Rd. 1897 and to new Cholmeley hall, Boleyn Rd., opened 1899.[70] Attendance 1903: 47 p.m. Taken over by Church Army after Second World War, closed 1955, reopened as club 1958.

ST. MARTIN, Ada Street, see ST. MICHAEL AND ALL ANGELS, London Fields.

ST. MARY OF ETON, Gainsborough Rd., Hackney Wick.[71] Mission established in upper room of undertaker's shop in Mallard Street 1880. Iron ch. behind shop, seating 250, opened 1881. Site of ropeworks on W. side of Gainsborough Rd. acquired through Ric. Foster and other subscribers 1880: mission hall and, to its S., iron ch. seating 350 opened 1884. First missioner was W. M. Carter, later abp. of Capetown.[72] All clergy Old Etonians until 1918. Dist. assigned from St. Augustine and St. Barnabas, Homerton, 1893. Patron Eton Coll.[73] Attendance 1886: 181 a.m., 331 p.m.; 1903: 223 a.m., 436 p.m. Missioner (V. of St. Mary's), 4 assistant curates, and lay helpers 1910. Bldg. of red brick with Bath stone dressings in Dec. style, seating 800, by Bodley & Garner 1890–2: continuous chancel with N. vestry, tall, narrow-aisled nave, SE. chapel; two W. bays and porches, baptistery, and large NE. gate-tower to mission bldgs., by Cecil Hare 1910–12. Interior has tall piers without

capitals and painted wagon roof; altar and reredos by W. Ellery Anderson 1930. E. window by Fras. Spear, replacing one by Comper, 1953; Eton Ho., in Tudor style, built behind ch. and hall for clerical and lay staff and visiting Etonians 1898. Group of bldgs. inc. 2 hos. and 5 halls 1938.[74] Par. united with St. Augustine 1953. Patron Eton mission trustees.[75] College last raised funds for mission 1958 and surrendered freehold 1973. Mission svces. at room in Chapman Rd. by 1894.[76]

ST. MATTHEW, Mount Pleasant Lane, Upper Clapton.[77] Svces. in sch. built at High Hill Ferry 1862. Leasehold of site on W. side of lane given by Chas. Jacomb and freehold by W. A. Tyssen-Amhurst, where iron ch. opened 1866. Served by L. E. Shelford, asst. curate of St. John's and later prebendary of St. Paul's. Dist. assigned from St. Thos. and St. Jas., Clapton, 1866.[78] Patron bp., from c. 1876 dean and chapter of Canterbury on augmentation of living from par. of St. Dionis Backchurch (Lond.). Attendance 1886: 866 a.m., 806 p.m., highest in Hackney after St. John's; 1903: 631 a.m., 550 p.m. Bldg. of Kentish rag with stone dressings in Early Eng. style, seating 750, by F. T. Dollman 1867–9: apsidal chancel, N. chapel, aisled and clerestoreyed nave, SE. tower with spire. Praised as landmark on commanding site. Interior inc. mosaics, delicate carving, metalwork by Skidmore, and stained glass by Powell.[79] Restored 1953, after war damage, but spire demol. 1962. After fire 1976 demol. 1977 and replaced by ch. to S.: low building of brown brick in contemporary style; not oriented.[80] Mission ch. of Holy Trinity, Southwold Rd., for Lea Bridge, built by W. Richards of Springfield 1877, opened 1878 and extended at his expense 1885. Attendance 1903: 99 a.m., 54 p.m. Bldg. of brick, enlarged by Wm. Bradbury to have 2 aisles with round-headed windows, bellcot.[81] Svces. in boys' sch. at High Hill Ferry from 1874, where mission ch. of Good Shepherd, Harrington Hill, built as extension to sch., seating 200, by J. E. K. Cutts 1879. Attendance 1903: 131 a.m., 73 p.m. Survived as mission hall 1934[82] and again used for svces. after war damage to St. Mat.'s; leased 1947, sold to L.C.C. 1957, and replaced by Valley Ho. flats.[83]

ST. MICHAEL AND ALL ANGELS, London Fields.[84] Svces. held in bldg. belonging to Dr. Williams of Pembroke Ho., who gave site for ch. at W. end of Lamb Lane, E. side of Lond. Fields. Dist. assigned from St. John of Jerusalem and St. Jude, Bethnal Green, 1865.[85] Patron R. of South Hackney. Attendance 1886: 360

67 Hackney Gaz. 25 Sept. 1869, 3.
68 Lond. Gaz. 4 July 1871, p. 3064.
69 St. Mark's, Dalston (appeal leaflet c. 1979).
70 Official Year Bk. of Ch. of Eng. (1910), 60.
71 Para. based on Mackeson's Guide (1884 and later edns.); Pevsner, Lond. ii. 166; Clarke, Lond. Chs. 69; M. Chapman, St. Mary of Eton with St. Augustine, 1880–1980, passim.   72 Crockford (1926).
73 Lond. Gaz. 29 Aug. 1893, p. 4903.
74 Hackney, Official Guide [1938].
75 G.L.R.O., P79/JSG/37/2.
76 P.O. Dir. Lond. County Suburbs, North (1894).
77 Para. based on L. E. Shelford, Twenty Years at St. Mat.'s, 1866–86 [booklet 1886]; Stiff, Our Neighbourhood,

25; Mackeson's Guide (1867 and later edns.); Clarke, Lond. Chs. 68 and illus.
78 Lond. Gaz. 25 May 1866, p. 3125.
79 Bumpus, Lond. Chs. ii. 299; above, plates 48 and 52.
80 G.L.R.O., photos. (1977); Hackney Gaz. 15 Mar. 1977, 20.
81 N.M.R., photos. (1905); G.L.R.O., P79/MTW/17/1.
82 P.O. Dir. Lond. (1934).
83 D. V. Cosser, 'One Hundred Years of St. Mat.'s' (TS. in G.L.R.O., P79/MTW/75).
84 Para. based on Illus. Lond. News, 13 Jan. 1866; Mackeson's Guide (1867 and later edns.); Clarke, Lond. Chs. 71.
85 Lond. Gaz. 4 Apr. 1865, p. 1876.

a.m., 283 p.m.; 1903: 289 a.m., 252 p.m. Bldg. of rag with stone dressings in Early Eng. style, seating 1,050, by E. C. Hakewill 1864:[86] chancel, aisled nave, later SW. tower. After bomb damage 1945,[87] svces. held in Vicarage, Lamb Lane, and then in mission hall, Wilman Grove.[88] Ch. rebuilt in Lansdowne Drive on W. side of Lond. Fields. Bldg. of yellow brick and concrete in contemporary style, seating 150 excluding gallery,[89] by N. F. Cachemaille-Day 1959–61: square plan beneath shallow central dome, W. gallery over vestibule, adjoining hall which can be opened into ch. Glass by Cachemaille-Day. Par. united with St. Paul, Haggerston, 1971.[90] Mission svces. at hall in Ada Street by 1894. Attendance 1903: 18 a.m., 65 p.m. Svces. presumably replaced by those in premises opened as ch. of St. Martin, Ada Street, 1906, closed 1939.[91]

ST. MICHAEL AND ALL ANGELS, Stoke Newington Common.[92] Site at E. corner of Northwold and Fountayne rds. given by W. A. Tyssen-Amherst for ch. planned in 1883. Svces. in iron ch., seating 400, 1884. Dist. assigned from St. Thos. and West Hackney pars. 1886.[93] Patron bp. Attendance 1903: 508 a.m., 451 p.m. Bldg. of red brick with stone dressings in Early Eng. style, seating 750, by J. E. K. Cutts, 1884–5: chancel with N. vestry, short N. transept, S. chapel, aisled and clerestoreyed nave, W. porch substituted for projected tower. Glass by Heaton, Butler, & Bayne. W. end of nave converted into hall 1972.[94]

ST. PAUL, Glyn Rd., Homerton.[95] Svces. in King's Coll. Sch. mission chapel, seating 250, from 1885. Site at angle with Chelmer Rd., where ch. built and endowed by Grocers' Co. of Lond. under Lady Slaney's (Trust) Estate Act, 1869. Dist. assigned from St. Barnabas, Homerton, 1889.[96] Patron Grocers' Co. Attendance 1903: 157 a.m., 171 p.m. Bldg. of red brick in Early Eng. style, seating 1,000, by Grocers' architect H. C. Boyes 1890–1: chancel with aisle carried round E. end as vestry, central tile-hung tower with spire reached from turreted circular stair at NE. corner, N. and S. transepts, aisled and clerestoreyed nave, SW. porch. Served jointly with St. Barnabas from 1981.[97] Closed 1982 and leased by diocese to Celestial Ch. of Christ 1983.[98]

ST. PAUL, Stoke Newington Rd., see WEST HACKNEY.

ST. PETER, Northchurch Terr., De Beauvoir

Town.[99] Site at SW. corner of De Beauvoir Sq. given by Ric. Benyon de Beauvoir, who built and endowed ch. in memory of Peter de Beauvoir, last sinecure R. of Hackney. Dist., intended to be coextensive with De Beauvoir Town est., from West Hackney by 1851.[1] Patron R. B. de Beauvoir. Attendance 1851: 950 and 77 Sun. sch. a.m., 900 p.m.; 1886: 328 a.m., 507 p.m.; 1903: 91 a.m., 136 p.m. Bldg. of stock brick with stone dressings in Middle Gothic style, seating c. 1,000, by W. C. Lockner 1840–1: pre-ecclesiological plan, nave with galleried aisles and pinnacled W. tower flanked by vestibules with stairs to galleries; octagonal corner turrets; sch. rooms below. Chancel, with N. aisle and S. organ chamber, in Romanesque style added by H. R. Gough 1884.

ST. PHILIP, Richmond Rd., Dalston.[2] Site in NE. angle with Park (later Parkholme) Rd. given by Wm. Rhodes for ch. financed by Hackney ch. bldg. cttee. Dist. assigned from St. John 1848.[3] Patron R. of Hackney. Attendance 1886: 380 a.m., 395 p.m.; 328 a.m., 425 p.m. Bldg. of brick with stone dressings in Early Eng. style, seating c. 1,000, by Hen. Duesbury 1841: chancel, aisled nave, W. tower with spire; 3 W. doorways in Tudor style; octagonal corner turrets. 'A specimen of modern economical ch. bldg.' Bombed 1940, whereupon svces. held at Holy Trinity, and demol. between 1947 and 1952.[4] Par. united with Holy Trinity 1953.[5] Mission ch. 1867 was probably iron ch. of St. Saviour, Dalston Lane, with registers for 1874–82 and 1885.[6]

ST. SAVIOUR, Dalston Lane, see ST. PHILIP.

ST. THOMAS, Stamford Hill.[7] Site on S. side of Clapton Common at end of Hill (later Oldhill) Street. Proprietary chapel built by John Devall for tenants and other residents at Stamford Hill c. 1774. Leased for first 5 years to V. of Hackney, but pew rents insufficient and vestry declined to compensate him for losses 1779.[8] Served 'for many years' by Jelinger Symons (d. 1810), asst. curate of Hackney.[9] Various owners until sold by Geo. Richards, V. of St. Martin-in-the-Fields, to Joshua Watson and 3 other trustees 1827; trustees were to enlarge chapel and R. of Hackney was to contribute towards min. until dist. assigned. Repair costs disallowed by Hackney chwdns. 1835.[10] Dist. assigned from St. John 1828.[11] Patron R. of Hackney. C. J. Heathcote, incumbent 1827–61, High Ch.; successor F. W. Kingsford sued 3 times in Ct. of Arches for structural changes and ritualism

[86] E. C. Hakewill in *Illus. Lond. News*, J. H. Hakewill in Clarke, op. cit.
[87] H.A.D., Y54, Vol. I, p. 27; *Hackney Photos.* i. 79; G.L.R.O., photo. (1944).   [88] Inf. from vicar.
[89] Ibid.   [90] G.L.R.O., index to P79/MAA.
[91] *P.O. Dir. Lond. County Suburbs, North* (1894); G.L.R.O., index to P79/MAA.
[92] Para. based on *Mackeson's Guide* (1884 and later edns.); Clarke, *Lond. Chs.* 171.
[93] *Lond. Gaz.* 9 Feb. 1886, p. 615.   [94] Plaque in hall.
[95] Para. based on *Mackeson's Guide* (1889 and later edns.); Clarke, *Lond. Chs.* 69.
[96] *Lond. Gaz.* 4 June 1889, pp. 3041–2.
[97] Inf. from Preb. J. F. D. Pearce.
[98] Ibid.; inf. from ch. asst.; below, prot. nonconf. (Spiritualists).
[99] Para. based on Robinson, *Hackney*, 180–91 and illus.; *Mackeson's Guide* (1867 and later edns.); Clarke, *Lond. Chs.*

66 and illus.
[1] P.R.O., HO 129/11/3/1/1.
[2] Para. based on Robinson, *Hackney*, ii. 205–8 and illus.; *Mackeson's Guide* (1867 and later edns.).
[3] *Lond. Gaz.* 25 Apr. 1848, p. 1607.
[4] G.L.R.O., index to P79/PH1/1–2; *P.O. Dir. Lond.* (1947, 1952). Remembrance svces. on site until 1960 or later: H.A.D., H/E 88/5.   [5] G.L.R.O., P79/JSG/37/2.
[6] Ibid. index to P79/SAV/1.
[7] Para. based on Robinson, *Hackney*, ii. 197–204 and illus.; *Mackeson's Guide* (1867 and later edns.); Clarke, *Lond. Chs.* 65; H. S. Kingsford, *Short Account of St. Thos.'s Ch.* (1913); H.A.D., D/F/BAG/2.
[8] Par. mins. 28 Oct. 1776; 19 Apr., 31 May, 7 June 1779.
[9] The chapel was probably leased to Symons: Lysons, *Environs*, ii. 473.
[10] Vestry mins. 7 Aug., 3 Dec. 1835; 22 Apr. 1836.
[11] *Lond. Gaz.* 4 July 1828, p. 1298; 8 July 1845, p. 2027.

1866–7.[12] Attendance 1851: 400 a.m., 600 evg.; 1886: 425 a.m., 239 p.m.; 1903: 371 a.m., 288 p.m. Rectangular bldg. of brick with stone dressings, seating c. 400,[13] enlarged to seat 800 and given E. clock-tower surmounted by open lantern and with stuccoed and rusticated wings by Jos. Gwilt 1828–9; recessed altar beneath tower, galleried nave with 2 rows of square-headed windows. Piecemeal changes made from 1864, followed by remodelling, copying ch. of San Clemente in Rome, by Wm. Burges 1873: half-domed recess for altar, galleries removed, single row of windows, new coffered ceiling, W. narthex.[14] Body of ch. destroyed by bombing in Second World War and rebuilt in yellow brick by N. F. Cachemaille-Day: aisled and clerestoreyed nave with square-headed windows. Svces. at mission of Holy Cross, Ravensdale Rd., built 1884. Attendance 1903: 25 p.m. Bldg. sold when part of par. transferred to St. Bart., Stamford Hill (Tottenham).[15]

SOUTH HACKNEY, see ST. JOHN'S CHAPEL; ST. JOHN OF JERUSALEM.

STAMFORD HILL, see ST. THOMAS.

WEST HACKNEY church, Stoke Newington Rd.[16] Site for ch. to serve new West Hackney rectory at SE. corner of Church (later part of Evering) Rd. given by Wm. Geo. Daniel-Tyssen. Paid for by com., reputedly as first of 9 chs. built with money from Portuguese govt., none of which was given dedication;[17] often called St. Jas. from 1881. Patron W. G. Daniel-Tyssen and successors. First R. was Geo. Paroissien 1825, formerly asst. curate of St. John's. Thos. Hugo, R. 1868–76, a noted antiquarian, and attacked for ritualism.[18] H. C. Montgomery Campbell, R. 1919–26, later bp. of Lond.; J. R. G. Easthaugh, R. 1952–6, later bp. of Hereford.[19] Largest attendances in Hackney 1851: 1,980 a.m. (inc. Sun. sch.), 480 aft., 1,400 evg.; 1886: 1,004 a.m., 988 p.m.; 1903: 640 a.m., 878 p.m. Bldg. of white Suffolk brick [20] with stone dressings in Greek Doric style, seating c. 1,900, by Rob. Smirke 1821–4: recessed altar of scagliola, rectangular galleried nave with round-headed windows, 4-column W. portico with pediment surmounted by circular tower and cupola. Later embellishments inc. glass by Holder in E. window 1842, pulpit by Jas. Brooks, altarpiece by Earp, and alterations by G. F. Bodley 1879. Bombed 1940, whereupon svces. held in hall in former Nat. sch. Par. united with St. Barnabas, Shacklewell, 1955.[21] New pale brown-brick ch. of St. Paul, seating c. 120, by N. F. Cachemaille-Day 1958–60: flat-roofed bldg. with tall rectangular windows, not oriented, opening at right angles to similar ch. hall; free standing altar, wall paintings by Chris. Webb. Churchyard to E., closed to burials 1879,[22] survived as public gdn., with gravestones against wall. Mission room in Hindle Street built by 1884. Chapel in Clevedon Street, later called St. Paul's, served partly from ch. by 1889. Attendance 1903: 25 a.m., 59 p.m. Closed c. 1924.[23]

ROMAN CATHOLICISM

William, Lord Vaux of Harrowden, who had been arrested for harbouring Edmund Campion, was allowed to live from 1583 at Hackney and remained there, apart from a further period of imprisonment at the time of the Armada, until 1590. He rented a house from Lord Mordaunt, where several priests stayed and c. 18 people attended a mass in 1584; the conspirator Anthony Babington, one of whose servants was exorcised there, was a visitor in 1585.[24] Those indicted for recusancy between 1583 and 1587 included Lord Vaux, his sons Henry and George, Andrew Mallory, gentleman, and their retainers. They probably formed more than one household, since some were also described as of Tottenham.[25]

Recusants in 1609 were Sir Rhys Griffin of Hackney[26] and in 1610 Isabel Oliver, in 1615 William Deane, and in 1617 and 1619 Richard Abington, gentleman, and his wife, all late of Hackney.[27] Samuel Hodgson, who had been ordained in Lisbon, joined the Jesuit mission to England in 1761 and died at Homerton in 1766.[28] Fourteen papist families were reported c. 1790; they had no place of worship, whereas protestant dissenters had four meeting houses.[29]

Roman Catholics could attend the chapel of St. Mary, Moorfields, from 1820.[30] In Hackney their first services were probably held in 1843, a mission was established in 1847, and the church of St. John the Baptist opened near the southern end of Mare Street in 1848. In Kingsland a mission was started in 1854 and the church of Our Lady and St. Joseph, built over a school at the corner of Culford and Tottenham roads, opened in 1856. In Clapton a mission was started in 1862 and the church of St. Scholastica opened as part of a school in Kenninghall Road.

12 *1st Rep. Royal Com. on Ritual* [3951], p. 110, H.C. (1867), xx; F. W. Kingsford, *Case of St. Thos.*, Stamford Hill (1867), *passim*.
13 Lysons, *Environs*, ii. 473.
14 Bumpus, *Lond. Chs.* 98–9.
15 *V.C.H. Mdx.* v. 354.
16 Para. based on Robinson, *Hackney*, ii. 178–80 and illus.; Hennessy, *Novum Rep.* 183; *Mackeson's Guide* (1866 and later edns.); Bumpus, *Lond. Chs.* ii. 108–10; Clarke, *Lond. Chs.* 70.
17 Hackney, *Official Guide* [1938], 90.
18 *D.N.B.*; *Hackney Gaz.* 4 Sept. 1869, 3; 23 Oct. 1869, 3.
19 Carrow, *By Faith–With Thanksgiving*.
20 Hackney, *Official Guide* [1938]. 90.
21 Carrow, *By Faith–With Thanksgiving*; *Hackney Pho-*

tos. i. 80; *Lost Hackney*, 58–60; above, plate 46; inf. from Preb. F. Preston.
22 Above, plate 49; *Lond. Gaz.* 29 Aug. 1879, p. 5273.
23 *P.O. Dir. Lond. County Suburbs* (1924, 1925).
24 *Complete Peerage*, xii (2), 221; G. Anstruther, *Vaux of Harrowden* (1953), 149, 153–4, 159, 162–3, 217; G. Anstruther, *Seminary Priests*, i (1969), 127, 227, 303.
25 *Mdx. County Rec.* i. 144, 158, 163, 167, 173; *V.C.H. Mdx.* v. 355.
26 *Cal. S.P. Dom.* Addenda 1603–10, 493.
27 *Mdx. County Rec.* ii. 69, 114, 131, 146, 215.
28 Anstruther, *Seminary Priests*, iv (1977), 140.
29 Guildhall MS. 9557, f. 31.
30 Para. based on *Cath. Dir.* (1838 and later edns.); A. Rottman, *Lond. Cath. Chs.* (1926); accounts of individual chs. below.

In Homerton a mission was started in 1873 and used a school chapel until the church of the Immaculate Heart and St. Dominic, Ballance Road, opened in 1875. The church served Hackney Wick, a poor district where its success was ascribed in 1903 to the presence of Irish or Italian immigrants.[31] The four Roman Catholic churches had a Sunday attendance of 1,801 in 1886 and 3,312 in 1903, both of which figures were much smaller than those for Congregationalists, Methodists, or Baptists.[32] Kingsland's church was replaced by one nearby in Ball's Pond Road, Islington, in 1964, and another church in Clapton, St. Jude's, opened in 1965.[33] The churches, followed by convents and many charitable institutions, are described below.

The following abbreviations are used: consecr., consecrated; demol., demolished; evg., evening; reg., registered; temp., temporary. Attendance figs. 1886 are from *Brit. Weekly*, 19 Nov. 1886, 4*b*; figs. 1903 are from Mudie-Smith, *Rel. Life*, 66.

ST. JOHN THE BAPTIST, King Edward's Rd.[34] Svces. said to have begun as evg. mtgs. in a room and later held by Revd. John Rolfe in old brewery behind Black Boys in Elsdale Street. Spaniard John Lecuona was missionary priest when ch. built on N. side of King Edward's Rd. near the Triangle at rd.'s junction with Mare Street.[35] Attendance 1851: 300 a.m., 150 evg.;[36] 1886: 191 a.m., 175 evg.; 1903: 648 a.m., 128 evg. Bldg. of Kentish rag with Caen stone dressings in Early Eng. style, seating *c*. 300, by W. W. Wardell 1847–8: chancel, nave, N. aisle and chapel, tower with spire; S. aisle and chapel added later. Consecr. 1899. Served Hackney union and workho. at Bethnal Green 1863. After war damage, svces. on ground floor of no. 14 Gore Street, reg. 1945, and chapel of St. Joseph's hospice, Mare Street, reg. 1947.[37] New ch. in King Edward's Rd. reg. 1956: brown-brick bldg. with pantiled roof, seating *c*. 300, by Peter Lamprell-Jarrett.[38]

OUR LADY AND ST. JOSEPH, Kingsland.[39] Mission begun by Wm. Lockhart, Father of Charity, 1854. Temp. chapel opened at no. 83 Culford Rd. North 1855. Ch. on S. side of Tottenham Grove (later Rd.) near E. corner with Culford Rd. reg. 1856.[40] Attendance 1886: 428 a.m., 220 evg.; 1903: 912 a.m., 438 evg. Bldg. by A. W. N. Pugin: aisleless ch., reached by external staircase, over sch. and hall.[41] Served Hoxton

1858, Shoreditch workho. 1863. Moved to no. 100A Ball's Pond Rd., Islington, 1964.[42]

ST. SCHOLASTICA, Kenninghall Rd., Clapton.[43] Svces. begun by Fathers of Charity (Rosminians) from Kingsland in libr. hall of St. Scholastica's Retreat (q.v.), on part of site given by Miss Eliz. Harrison, 1862. Reg. 1870.[44] Ch. intended to form N. side of rectangular gdn., with Retreat to E. and W. and Kenninghall Rd. to S. Land and pastoral charge transferred to diocese 1868. Sch. chapel to be built instead of ch., with presbytery for first full-time par. priest, 1879. Reg. as temp. ch., at NE. corner of gdn., 1887:[45] plain bldg. with rectangular windows. Attendance 1886: 128 a.m., 140 evg.; 1903: 272 a.m., 127 evg. Reg. again 1963.[46] Permanent ch. built next to new sch. after demol. of Retreat. Bldg. of pale grey brick and concrete in contemporary style, seating 400, by J. E. Sterrett, consecr. 1987. Sch. chapel and old sch. bldgs. used as par. centre 1988.

THE IMMACULATE HEART of Mary and St. Dominic, Homerton.[47] Mission begun by Geo. Akers, asst. priest at St. John the Baptist, at no. 21 Sidney Terr., Sidney Rd., 1873. Temp. sch. chapel opened 1873, reg. 1874.[48] Ch. on S. side of Ballance Rd., at corner of Sidney (later Kenworthy) Rd., reg. 1877.[49] Attendance 1886: 211 a.m., 308 evg.; 1903: 646 a.m., 141 evg. Bldg. of yellow brick with red-brick dressings in Romanesque style by A. E. Buckler 1875–7: basilican plan, with apse, aisled and clerestoried nave, round-headed windows, campanile, not oriented. Consecr. 1884. Damaged in Second World War; svces. in hall of convent of Sacred Heart (q.v.) 1951; ch. restored after 1952.[50]

ST. JUDE, Clapton Pk. Yellow-brick former tabernacle, S. side of Blurton Rd., reg. 1965.[51]

St. Scholastica's Retreat (later home)[52] was founded by Wm. Harrison and sis. Eliz., out of est. of their bro. Rob. (d. 1852) and his wid. Charlotte Scholastica, for 40 poor Caths. aged 60 or more from gentry, professions, or commerce. Each man or woman had self-contained residence in hos. forming E. and W. sides of gdn. on N. side of London (later Kenninghall) Rd. Bldgs. in Gothic style by E. W. Pugin begun 1861, partly occupied by 1863, when under spiritual care of Fathers of Charity.[53] Demol. 1972, but Retreat survived as home for aged gentlefolk in Princes Risborough (Bucks.) 1988.[54]

31 Mudie-Smith, *Rel. Life*, 27.
32 *Brit. Weekly*, 19 Nov. 1886, 4*b*; Mudie-Smith, *Rel. Life*, 66.
33 *V.C.H. Mdx.* viii. 101; below.
34 Para. based on *Cath. Dir.* (1846 and later edns.); Rottman, *Lond. Cath. Chs.* 204–5.
35 G.L.R.O., M79/LH/25, pp. 118–22, 422–3, 433–5.
36 P.R.O., HO 129/11/5/1/5.
37 Pevsner, *Lond.* ii. 166; H.A.D., H/LD 7/24, p. 185; G.R.O. Worship Reg. nos. 61059, 61705.
38 H.A.D., H/LD 7/24, pp. 185, 195; G.R.O. Worship Reg. no. 65650; inf. from par. priest.
39 Para. based on *Cath. Dir.* (1856 and later edns.); Rottman, *Lond. Cath. Chs.* 210.
40 G.R.O. Worship Reg. nos. 7481, 7522.
41 Pevsner, *Lond.* ii. 166, says that ch. was converted from a manufacturing bldg. by Wardell.
42 *V.C.H. Mdx.* viii. 101.
43 Para. based on *Cath. Dir.* (1863 and later edns.);

Rottman, *Lond. Cath. Chs.* 203–4 and illus.; *Hist. of St. Scholastica's* (consecr. pamphlet 1987); inf. from par. priest.
44 Old O.S. Map Lond. 30 (1868); G.R.O. Worship reg. no. 19486.
45 G.R.O. Worship Reg. no. 30296.
46 Ibid. no. 69248.
47 Para. based on *Cath. Dir.* (1900 and later edns.); Rottman, *Lond. Cath. Chs.* 200–2.
48 G.R.O. Worship reg. no. 21938.
49 Ibid. no. 23767.
50 *Hackney Photos.* i. 60; Pevsner, *Lond.* ii. 165.
51 G.R.O. Worship Reg. no. 70032; below, prot. nonconf. (Meths.).
52 Para. based on *Hist. of St. Scholastica's* and inf. from par. priest.
53 *Cath. Dir.* (1863 and later edns.); Old O.S. Map Lond. 30 (1868); *Babe of the Retreat* (TS. by caretaker's son in H.A.D.).
54 *Westm. Year Bk.* (1969); *Cath. Dir.* (1979).

Little Sisters of the Poor were in Queen's (later Queensbridge) Rd., Dalston, before moving to Manor Rd., Stoke Newington, where they built St. Ann's Ho. 1878.[55]

Sisters of the Sacred Hearts of Jesus and Mary[56] moved from Stratford to Sidney Ho., Homerton, 1872. Chapel and orphanage opened 1883, when ho. was at SE. end of new Hassett Rd.[57] Orphanage closed during Second World War. Hostel for 60 women opened 1948 and closed 1978, whereupon hostel and chapel were replaced by Chigwell Ct. old people's flats. Old ho. altered to inc. convent chapel, in use 1988, when St. Anne's wing was on lease to priests of order of St. Camillus, who cared for sick.

Ursulines of Jesus were at no. 164 Culford Rd., De Beauvoir Town, by 1897 until c. 1959.[58]

The Institute of Our Lady of the Retreat in the Cenacle occupied convent at no. 63 Stamford Hill by 1900.[59] Chapel reg. from 1905 to 1941.[60] One of order's four Eng. convents, where retreats held and religious instruction given. Replaced by ho. in West Heath Rd., Hampstead, by 1946.[61]

Irish Sisters of Charity came to Mare Street, where anonymous donor gave them Cambridge Lodge Villas, 1900. Originally intending to supply home nursing for the dying, they opened St. Joseph's hospice in 1905; hospice was one of first of its kind, although preceded by Anglican hostel in Clapham and by St. Luke's hosp., which settled finally in Bayswater. Sisters occupied only no. 6 in 1905 but whole row by 1911. Private nursing home advertised from 1930s until c. 1951 was later absorbed into hospice. Old bldgs. replaced by Our Lady wing 1957, St. Patrick's wing 1965, new convent 1969, Heenan House 1977, and Norfolk wing, containing study and day centres, 1984. Hospice, which retained home care svce., had 108 beds 1988.[62]

Servite Sisters, who managed Our Lady's Convent high sch. at nos. 14 and 16 (later 6 to 16) Amhurst Pk. from c. 1931, came from St. Mary's priory, St. Ann's Rd., Tottenham.[63]

Little Sisters of the Assumption, nursing sisters of the poor, occupied no. 11 Amhurst Pk. from c. 1946 to c. 1960. Ursulines of Jesus had taken their place by 1965.[64]

PROTESTANT NONCONFORMITY

A circulating preacher called Davenport, possibly the puritan John Davenport (d. 1670), was reported in 1637 at Hackney,[65] where in 1641 a crowd gathered for rebaptism in the Lea.[66] Daughters of the independent divine Philip Nye (d. 1672) were baptized at Hackney in 1634 and 1636, as was a son of the preacher Adoniram Byfield (d. 1660) in 1636. The republican John Goodwin (d. 1665), later ejected from his London vicarage, made his will as of Hackney in 1659.[67] One of the earliest and largest of the parish's noted girls' schools was founded before 1650 by a Presbyterian, Mrs. Salmon. Hannah Woolley, a puritan critic of the more wordly schools, opened her own establishment in 1655.[68]

After the Restoration many ejected ministers came to Hackney, where the vicar William Spurstowe was sympathetic and where London merchant families could patronize dissenters' schools. Spurstowe, the employer of Ezekiel Hopkins and host to Richard Baxter, remained in the parish after his resignation in 1662. His widow in 1669 was to marry Anthony Tuckney, formerly master of St. John's College, Cambridge, and father of the Hackney Presbyterian Jonathan Tuckney, who also had been ejected from St. John's.[69] Friends' meetings took place in 1662[70] and secret meetings were reported in

1664, when the passage of the first Conventicle Act was expected.[71] Some 25 people in 1665 attended a conventicle at the house of Margaret Hammond of Hackney, widow, whereupon eight were fined, including Thomas Barnardiston, gentleman, and members of his family.[72] The biblical commentator Matthew Poole (d. 1679) wrote to Baxter from Hackney in 1667–8.[73]

An early instance of dissenters' co-operation was provided at Hackney in a 'lecture by combination', reported in 1669. The lecturers, all well known preachers, were Philip Nye, John Owen (d. 1683), formerly vice-chancellor of Oxford University, Thomas Goodwin (d. 1680), formerly president of Magdalen College, John Griffith, formerly minister at the London Charterhouse, Thomas Brooks, Thomas Watson, and William Bates (d. 1699), all ejected from London livings, and Peter Sterry, who had been chaplain to Oliver Cromwell. Watson, Bates, and possibly Sterry were Presbyterians, the others Congregationalist. Relief under the Declaration of Indulgence allowed a more enduring weekly lecture, financed by City merchants, to be established in London at Pinners' Hall in 1672.[74]

Nine houses in Hackney and one in Kingsland were licensed as Presbyterian meeting places in 1672. They included the houses of two London

55 P.O. Dir. Lond. County Suburbs, North (1884); V.C.H. Mdx. viii. 211.
56 Para. based on inf. from superior, Sacred Heart convent; Cath. Dir. (1900 and later edns).
57 P.O. Dir. Lond. Suburban, North (1880);Bacon, Atlas of Lond. (1910), sheet 40.
58 P.O. Dir. Lond. (1897 and later edns.);Cath. Dir. (1900 and later edns.).
59 Cath. Dir. (1900).
60 G.R.O. Worship reg. no. 41201.
61 Cath. Dir. (1938, 1946).
62 P.O. Dir. Lond. (1905 and later edns.);Cath. Dir. (1931 and later edns.); M. Manning, Hospice Alternative (1984), 42, 44, 106, 126; inf. from hospice sec.
63 Cath. Dir. (1931 and later edns.); V.C.H.Mdx. v. 356;

below, educ. (private schs.).
64 Cath. Dir. (1946 and later edns.).
65 Cal. S.P. Dom. 1636–7, 545; D.N.B.
66 Robinson, Hackney, ii. 302; Bk. of Common Prayer in H.A.D.
67 Calamy Revised, 227, 370; D.N.B.; Lysons, Environs, ii. 479.   68 V.C.H. Mdx. i. 251–2.
69 Calamy Revised, 457, 496; D.N.B.
70 W. Beck and T. F. Ball, Lond. Friends' Mtgs. (1869), 37.   71 Cal. S.P. Dom. 1663–4, 587.
72 Mdx. County Rec. iii. 345, 347.
73 D.N.B.
74 Orig. Rec. of Early Nonconf. ed. G. L. Turner, i. 92; ii. 957–8; iii. 91; M. R. Watts, The Dissenters (1978), 289; D.N.B. s.vv. Nye; Owen; Goodwin; Bates.

aldermen, John Forth, the son-in-law of Sir Henry Vane, and Henry Ashurst (d. 1680), a friend of Baxter and treasurer of the Society for the Propagation of the Gospel.[75] Philip Sterry, as a resident of Hackney, procured a licence for a friend's house. Four of the houses belonged to men who had suffered ejection: Thomas Senior and Jonathan Tuckney from Cambridge, Arthur Barham from London, and Martin Morland from Weld (Hants).[76]

Local Dissent drew much of its strength from rich residents with London connexions, who themselves conformed but whose sympathies were shown in their wills. William Spurstowe and Ezekiel Hopkins were remembered by Sir Thomas Vyner (d. 1665)[77] and William Bates was remembered by Sir Stephen White, by Nathaniel Barnardiston, together with Arthur Barham, and by Thomas Cooke (d. 1695).[78] Dame Jane Barnardiston, her son Nathaniel, and White all referred to their kindness to suffering ministers.[79]

Private schools continued to be run largely by dissenters. George Fox (d. 1691), founder of the Society of Friends, visited a school at Shacklewell in 1671 and again in 1684, when its principal was Jane Bullock,[80] who had been among Hackney residents cited for not attending church in 1669–70.[81] Thomas Cruttenden, ejected from Magdalen College, Oxford, assisted at the school of his mother-in-law, Mrs. Salmon, and Martin Morland, brother of the diplomatist Sir Samuel, probably also taught in Hackney, where his son Benjamin in 1685 founded a long lived academy.[82] Sir Thomas Marsh was reported c. 1682 to have turned his house into an academy for training nonconformist ministers, who were up at all hours of the night.[83]

Twenty fines, amounting to £600, were levied in 1682 on Arthur Barham, for preaching at conventicles in his own house.[84] The churchwardens complained that fines for attending conventicles had been unlawfully disposed of in 1683 and at least two other conventicles were reported in 1686.[85] After persecution had declined, three Presbyterian ministers were active c. 1690; two of them had a 'competent supply', one of them being the former combination lecturer William Bates.[86]

Many national figures served as ministers in the 18th and early 19th centuries, although secessions and changes of name obscured the continuity of their churches. The oldest ministry was later seen as originally Presbyterian, passing from Nye through Bates to Matthew Henry (d. 1714) and then to John Barker (d. 1762),[87] whose disputed election in 1714 led to the establishment of the Old Gravel Pit meeting. In 1731 Barker's followers were 'declaimed Calvinists' and the Old Gravel Pit worshippers were 'accounted Arminians'; later the Gravel Pit meeting was normally described as Congregationalist or Independent, as in due course was the older meeting.[88] Barker, a friend of Philip Doddridge, was suspicious of the Methodist upsurge inspired by George Whitefield,[89] who in 1739 preached three times in a field at Hackney or on the marsh to crowds of 2,000 and 10,000.[90] John Wesley preached in 1741.[91]

Hackney village had two meeting houses in 1761, when unidentified Presbyterians were said also to worship at Clapton.[92] It still had its Presbyterian and Independent meeting houses in 1778, when Methodists were using Ram's chapel,[93] but by 1790 there were four meeting houses, the Methodists having recently acquired two of their own.[94] At least eight places of worship were registered by dissenters in the 1790s, including a schoolroom in the house of John Eyre, minister of Ram's chapel, and possibly a forerunner of Hackney's first Baptist church.[95] Attendance at the parish church had not lessened in 1810, despite the existence of seven meeting houses, apart from Ram's chapel.[96]

The most famous pastor at either of Hackney's established 18th-century meetings was the theologian and scientist Joseph Priestley (d. 1804), who in 1791 briefly succeeded his friend Richard Price (d. 1791) at the Old Gravel Pit chapel.[97] Their Unitarian views gained ground under Priestley's successors and led to the opening of the New Gravel Pit chapel, the old one later passing to Independents.[98] Priestley, although not chosen unanimously, found advantages for his studies which led him to recall his time at Hackney as the happiest that he had so far known.[99] He and many other dissenters were active not only in pastoral work; they made Hackney noteworthy for academies which, while offering a general education, pioneered the work of the later theological colleges.[1]

Homerton College,[2] the most long lived of the institutions, was known as King's Head academy

75 *Early Nonconf.* ed. Turner, ii. 956–7; *D.N.B.* s.vv. Ashurst; Vane.
76 *Early Nonconf.* ed. Turner, ii. 956–7; *Calamy Revised*, 28, 355, 433, 496.   77 P.R.O., PROB 11/316, f. 55.
78 Ibid. PROB 11/358, no. 329; PROB 11/363, f. 101; PROB 11/425, f. 46.
79 Ibid. PROB 11/330, f. 101; PROB 11/363, f. 91; PROB 11/358, no. 329.
80 *Jnl. of Geo. Fox*, ed. N. Penney, ii. 169, 424; *Short Jnl. and Itinerary Jnls. of Geo. Fox*, ed. N. Penney, 89, 305.
81 Guildhall MS. 9537/19, ff. 75, 78v., 81 sqq.
82 *Calamy Revised*, 153, 355; *V.C.H. Mdx.* i. 243; *D.N.B.* s.v. Morland, Sam.   83 *Cal. S.P. Dom.* 1682, 610.
84 *Calamy Revised*, 28.
85 Cal. Mdx. Sess. Bks. vii. 30, 149–50.
86 *Freedom after Ejection*, ed. A. Gordon, 72.
87 Robinson, *Hackney*, ii. 243–4; *D.N.B.*
88 Robinson, *Hackney*, ii. 245; A. R. Ruston, *Unitarianism and Early Presbyterianism in Hackney* (1980), 10; below,

Congs.
89 R. T. Jones, *Congregationalism in Eng. 1662–1962* (1962), 148.
90 *Geo. Whitefield's Jnls.* (1960), 276–7, 315.
91 *Works of John Wesley* (1872), i. 319. His retirement near Hackney in 1754 was to Bishop's Hall in Bethnal Green: ibid. ii. 317.
92 *Lond. and its Environs Described*, iii (1761), 121.
93 Guildhall MS. 9558; above, list of churches.
94 Guildhall MS. 9557, f. 31.
95 Ibid. 9580/1, pp. 13, 15, 56, 68, 76, 146; 9580/2, p. 41; below, Congs., Bapts.   96 Guildhall MS. 9558.
97 Robinson, *Hackney*, ii. 249; *D.N.B.*
98 Robinson, *Hackney*, ii. 250; below, Congs.; Unitarians.   99 *Memoirs of Jos. Priestley* (1809), 130.
1 *V.C.H. Mdx.* i. 250.
2 Para. based on T. H. Simms, *Homerton Coll. 1695–1978* (1979); Robinson, *Hackney*, ii. 272–3, 278–84; *V.C.H. Mdx.* i. 250.

when it moved in 1768 from Plasterers' Hall, London, to a large copyhold house on the north side of Homerton's high street. Its trustees, who were appointed by the King's Head Society, remained strict Calvinists and so avoided what in the 1790s might have proved to be the fatal taint of Unitarianism and Jacobinism. John Pye Smith (d. 1851),[3] founder of Mill Hill school, was residential tutor and in effect principal at Homerton from 1800. The King's Head Society was replaced in 1817 by the Homerton Academy Society, concerned solely with maintaining the academy. In 1819 the house held masters, students, and a large library, and three other houses were let; 12 of the 18 students were supported by the society and 6 by the Congregational Fund Board.[4] The name was changed to Homerton College in 1823, graduates qualified for degrees from London University from 1840, and an amalgamation with Highbury and Coward colleges formed the purely theological New College, Hampstead, in 1852. Largely owing to the Liberal philanthropist Samuel Morley (d. 1886),[5] who then lived in Lower Clapton, the Homerton premises were transferred to the Congregational Board of Education for trainee teachers and a model school. In 1892 they moved to the former Cavendish College, Cambridge, where the name Homerton was retained.

The main house in Homerton's high street was enlarged in 1811 and replaced by a two-storeyed brick building, originally of seven bays and with the central three stuccoed and pedimented, to the design of Samuel Robinson in 1823. Dormitories and a school, designed by Alfred Smith, were built in the garden behind c. 1852. Bought by the London school board and used as a school for the deaf, the buildings made way for flats after 1945.[6]

Hackney College or Hackney New College[7] was founded in 1786 by Dr. Price of the Old Gravel Pit chapel and other eminent liberal dissenters, in consequence of the closure of Hoxton Square academy in Shoreditch. Hackney House at Lower Clapton was bought and enlarged to take 75 students, although a smaller number resided and not all were intended for the ministry. Tutors included the controversialist Gilbert Wakefield (d. 1801),[8] who objected to public worship, and Priestley, whose appointment led to the college being denounced as the 'slaughterhouse of Christianity'. Unorthodoxy and political radicalism infected the students, whose indiscipline undermined public support, hastening a financial crisis which led to closure in 1796. Thomas Belsham (d. 1829),[9] Priestley's successor at the Old Gravel Pit and, like him, a

tutor at the college, took pupils at his own house in Grove Place after 1796.

Hackney Theological Seminary,[10] at first popularly called Hackney academy and later, officially from 1871, Hackney College, was founded in 1803, largely with a gift from Charles Townsend of Homerton. It was intended to fulfil the plans of the late John Eyre, minister of Ram's chapel,[11] to educate preachers for his Village Itinerancy or Evangelical Association for the Propagation of the Gospel. The academy was managed by a committee, with George Collison of Walthamstow (Essex) as tutor,[12] and used Eyre's house in Well Street, where the students lived in converted stabling until new quarters were built after purchase of the freehold in 1843.[13] Training of Congregational ministers came to predominate over missionary work, although in 1898 the college's trustees had built or enlarged over 50 chapels, many of which they still maintained. The college moved to Finchley Road, Hampstead, in 1887.[14]

Many new places of worship were registered in the early 19th century by Independents or by unspecified Protestants.[15] Several meetings founded Congregationalist chapels, although from 1813 the Unitarians who had moved to the New Gravel Pit chapel legally formed a new denomination.[16] By 1851, out of 24 Middlesex districts, Hackney was among the 10 with the highest number of protestant nonconformist worshippers. In that respect it was like its neighbours Islington and Bethnal Green, which it surpassed in being one of six districts where nonconformists formed more than half of all the worshippers.[17] Nonconformists still predominated in 1886, when they accounted for 23,458 attendances at churches and chapels within the ancient parish, while Anglicans accounted for 20,238; mission services were not included.[18] The contrast was greater by 1903, when, without including Salvation Army meetings, nonconformist attendances had risen slightly while Anglican attendances, including those at missions, had fallen to 17,705.[19]

Congregationalists, easily the largest nonconformist body in the metropolitan area c. 1850, were well supported in Hackney, where many leading families had long been linked with the City, Dissent, and Radical politics. Hackney Congregational association had been formed in 1846, two years before the London Congregational Chapel Building Society. Chapels were often attached to schools and formed part of an impressive range of buildings, as at Clapton Park, the successor to the Old Gravel Pit chapel, in 1871. Such expense testified to the munificence

3 D.N.B.   4 2nd Rep. Com. Educ. of Poor, 94–5.
5 D.N.B.
6 Simms, Homerton Coll. 12, 89–90, and illus.; Lost Hackney, 70–1.
7 Para. based on Robinson, Hackney, i. 117–19; ii. 291–3; V.C.H. Mdx. i. 250–1.
8 D.N.B.
9 Ibid.
10 Para. based on A. Cave, Story of Founding of Hackney Coll. (1898); Robinson, Hackney, ii. 295–7, 301–2.
11 Above, list of churches; D.N.B.
12 V.C.H. Essex, vi. 226.

13 Cong. Year Bk. (1846).
14 V.C.H. Mdx. ix. 154.
15 Guildhall MSS. 9580/2–8, passim.
16 G. Hague and others, Unitarian Heritage, Architectural Surv. (1986), 9; Doctrine of the Trinity Act, 53 Geo. III, c. 160.
17 V.C.H. Mdx. i. 147.
18 Figs. for Hackney census dist. in Brit. Weekly, 19 Nov. 1886, 4, excluding City workho., chs. in Stoke Newington, and St. John's, Vartry Rd., Tottenham.
19 Figs. for Hackney census dist. in Mudie-Smith, Rel. Life, 67, 287, excluding St. John's Vartry Rd.

of individuals, notably of Samuel Morley, to the middle-class character of much of the parish,[20] and perhaps particularly to the strength of nonconformity in Clapton.[21] Congregationalists, although challenged in the poorer parts of London, were still dominant in Hackney in 1886, with 11,636 attendances. The various Methodists had 6,284 attendances, mostly Wesleyan, and the Baptists 4,226.[22] Wesleyans, the most numerous Methodists, by 1872 were organized into a Hackney circuit, which included some churches in metropolitan Essex, and a Dalston circuit.[23]

New arrivals c. 1850[24] included the Brethren, who were encouraged by William T. Berger of the paint firm, his brother-in-law James van Sommer, a solicitor who published a magazine called *The Missionary Reporter*, and Samuel Morley's brother John, senior partner of the family's textile firm.[25] Latter-Day Saints and the Free English Church appeared in the 1850s, Presbyterians in the 1860s, and the Catholic Apostolic Church and German Lutherans in the 1870s. The Agapemonites' only London church, at Clapton Common, was opened in 1896 but was little used.

The Salvation Army, recorded from 1880, had early links with Hackney: its founder Gen. William Booth (d. 1912) and his wife Catherine (d. 1890) lived at no. 1 Cambridge Lodge Villas from 1865 and at no. 3 Gore Road (later demolished) from 1868. Their move to Clapton Common in 1880 enabled them to equip the Gore Road house as the Army's first training home, for 30 women cadets. A similar home for men was opened at Devonshire House, no. 259 Mare Street, in 1881. The Army soon attracted much publicity to Clapton by adapting the London Orphan Asylum as its chief hall and training centre, called Congress Hall, which often drew enormous crowds.[26] The Army's National Headquarters of Women's Social Work, replacing offices at no. 259 Mare Street and a temporary branch in Lower Clapton Road, opened at no. 280 Mare Street in 1911.[27]

The older sects' relative strength had changed very little by 1903, when the Congregationalists had 11,640 attendances, the Methodists 6,332, and the Baptists 4,791. The Salvation Army had 4,083, followed by the Brethren with 1,498.[28] Hackney was still credited with the best attendance in east London, but by that date social changes were beginning to have an effect. Dalston, still largely middle-class, had a high proportion of worshippers, whereas Hackney Wick's was very low.[29] In 1904 a correspondent of the secretary of the London Congregational Union lamented the decay of Cambridge Heath church, whose supporters had moved away,

leaving their houses to Jews or working people who let rooms. He knew of 28 places of worship within a half-mile radius, of which 18 were run on free church lines and all in difficulties. Although he did not admit that church activities had become less important in social life, he noted that there were many more places where people could meet and he feared that indebtedness could be avoided only by amalgamations.[30]

The forces affecting the churches' attendance and solvency continued in the period 1918-39,[31] when most new places of worship were registered by Jews. Presbyterians had no place after 1936, but few other major churches were forced to close. The greatest change was carried out by Wesleyans, who in 1914 merged their Hackney circuit with Victoria Park circuit to form Hackney (South) circuit, itself merged in 1931 with Hackney Central mission, which had been created on the opening of the long-projected Hackney Central Hall in 1925.[32]

The Second World War brought many closures. Some churches were demolished then or soon afterwards, others reopened for a while, often in halls or schoolrooms. From the 1950s amalgamations became common, although a few churches were rebuilt on a more modest scale. The Salvation Army gave up its Congress Hall for smaller premises in 1970. Surviving buildings were sometimes sold to other denominations, to Roman Catholics, to Jews, and especially to Pentecostalists serving the growing Afro-Caribbean population. In 1988 Hackney had five United Reformed (formerly Congregational) churches, of which the 'Round Chapel' at Clapton Park remained the finest example of Victorian affluence. There were three Baptist churches, two of which had been built since the war. The Methodists, whose circuits had undergone many changes, had five churches, of which only the one in Stoke Newington High Street was 19th-century.

The following abbreviations are used: Bapt., Baptist; Cong., Congregationalist; Dec., Decorated; demol., demolished; evg., evening; Ind., Independent; Meth., Methodist; mtg., meeting; min., minister; perm., permanent; reg., registered; temp., temporary; Utd. Ref., United Reformed; Wes., Wesleyan. Attendance figs. 1886 are from *Brit. Weekly*, 19 Nov. 1886, 4; figs. 1903 are from Mudie-Smith, *Rel. Life*, 64-6. Locations of the bldgs. are from Stanford, *Maps of Lond.* and Old O.S. Maps Lond. Liturgical directions are used in architectural descriptions.

CONGREGATIONALISTS. MARE STREET mtg.,[33] seen as oldest in Hackney, claimed de-

20 *Cong. Year Bk.* (1847); *Trans. Cong. Hist. Soc.* xx (1), 22-4, 26, 34; *D.N.B.*
21 *Hackney Gaz.* 31 July 1869, 4.
22 Figs. for Hackney census dist. in *Brit. Weekly*, 19 Nov. 1886, 4, excluding Stoke Newington.
23 *Hackney Dir.* (1872); H.A.D., TS. catalogue, D/E/234/A.
24 Para. based on lists of individual chs. below.
25 F. R. Coad, *Hist. of Brethren Movement* (1968), 166, 174, 222.

26 R. Collier, *General Next to God* (1965), 49, 56, 88; below.
27 *P.O. Dir. Lond.* (1902); *Deliverer*, June 1911, 91-2; inf. from Salv. Army International Heritage Centre.
28 Mudie-Smith, *Rel. Life*, 64-7.   29 Ibid. 26-7.
30 *Trans. Cong. Hist. Soc.* xx (12), 372.
31 Two paras. based on lists of churches below.
32 H.A.D., TS. catalogue, D/E/234/A.
33 Para. based on Robinson, *Hackney*, ii. 243-5; Ruston, *Unitarianism and Early Presbyterianism*, 2-5, 10.

scent from ministries of Phil. Nye and Wm. Bates. Bates preached in Hackney 1669 and was min. of first perm. mtg. ho., reg. 1694. Bldg. on W. side of street, with 3 galleries, formed out of dwelling hos. Fewer than 100 communicants 1712. Normally called Presb. or Calvinist. Distinguished pastors were Bates, John Barker, whose election led seceders to found Old Gravel Pit chapel (below), and nonconf. biographer Sam. Palmer (d. 1813),[34] who presided over move to St. Thos.'s Sq. (below) 1773, whereupon old mtg. ho. was demol.

OLD GRAVEL PIT mtg.[35] formed by seceders from Mare Street, inc. Ryder fam., on election of John Barker 1714. Site at gravel pit near bowling green in Mare Street, opposite St. Thos.'s Sq., leased by St. Thos.'s hosp. to Allard Denn, Clapton brewer. Bldg. of brick S. of Morning Lane and E. of Chatham Pl. 1715–16; enlarged by one third 1787, after which it had three parallel hipped roofs.[36] Dan. Mayo (d. 1733) co-pastor until 1723, while retaining ministry at Kingston-on-Thames (Surr.).[37] Colleague and successor Geo. Smyth was Arminian, perhaps preparing way for move towards Unitarianism under Ric. Price, who often entertained John Adams, American envoy to London 1785–8 and later president. Unitarianism strengthened under Jos. Priestley, who reg. chapel for Presbs. 1792,[38] and Thos. Belsham, but formally acknowledged only after move to New Gravel Pit chapel in 1809 (below, Unitarians). Old Gravel Pit chapel considered unsafe and leased 1810 to Congs. who had formed ch. under John Pye Smith at Homerton Coll. 1804. Two schoolrooms added 1841, when windows may have been rearranged and stone dressings and cornice added.[39] Attendance 1851: 468 a.m. and 149 Sun. sch. with 85 children at separate svce. in schoolroom, 397 evg.[40] Bldg. enlarged 1853, when it may have received its late 19th-cent. pedimented front.[41] Last Cong. svce. 1871 but still used as Sun. sch. 1872 after cong. moved to Clapton Pk. (below). Reopened 1874 as undenom. Old Gravel Pit mission (below, undenom.), sometimes listed as Cong.[42]

ST. THOMAS'S SQUARE ch.[43] Mare Street mtg. under Sam. Palmer moved from W. to E. side of street 1773.[44] New bldg. on SW. side of St. Thos.'s Sq., enlarged 1824, altered and sch. rooms added 1841, seating 900 in 1851.[45] Pal-

mer's successor 1814 was Hen. Forster Burder (d. 1864). Thos. Braidwood (d. 1806),[46] teacher of deaf and dumb, was buried in adjoining churchyard. Attendance 1851: 414 and 120 Sun. sch. a.m., 125 aft., 400 evg.;[47] 1886: 109 a.m., 141 evg. Bldg. of brick, two-storeyed and with stuccoed and pedimented street front 1891.[48] Listed as Cong. until 1879, although min. J. A. Picton allegedly introduced modified Anglican svces. without members' full support 1869.[49] Conveyed to Presbs. (below), who reg. ch. 1896–1912,[50] and later became cinema, then bingo hall.[51]

KINGSLAND ch.[52] Prayer mtgs. for brickmakers held in foreman's ho. by Thos. Cranfield 1789. Larger room found 1790, with Sun. sch. (previously in Cranfield's ho.) overhead 1791. Summer evg. svces. also on Kingsland green. Site for chapel in middle of Robinson's Row, W. side of Kingsland High Street, leased by Wm. Robinson 1792. Chapel next to no. 16 opened and reg. by Ind. 1794,[53] whereupon Calvinistic worshippers temporarily withdrew to ho. of John Truman[54] in Providence Pl. Svces. also in new Sun. sch. and day sch., reg. 1808.[55] Ministers inc. philanthropist and traveller John Campbell (d. 1840) from 1802 and writer Thos. Aveling (d. 1884) from 1838.[56] Chapel, seating c. 400, enlarged 1840 and 1845, to seat 950 by 1851. Attendance 1851: 664 a.m. and 20 Sun. sch., 100 aft., 763 evg.[57] New chapel on E. side of street, at corner of later Sandringham Rd., reg. 1852.[58] Site, previously leased, bought from Tyssen est. 1858.[59] Bldg. of brick with stone and terracotta dressings, seating 1,350 with schoolroom below for 800, in Dec. style by Fras. Pouget 1852: chancel, nave, SW. tower with crocketted spire; buttresses, pinnacles, large W. window by Wailes.[60] Attendance 1886: 430 a.m., 456 evg.; 1903: 196 a.m., 305 evg. Bldg. survived 1947, closed by 1951.[61] Mission in Castle Lane, seating 150, by 1881 and to 1894 or later; mission in John (later Dunn) Street, Shacklewell Lane, seating 300 in 1894, from 1871; attendance 1903: 172 a.m., 26 evg.; closed between 1926 and 1932.[62]

CLAPTON PARK ch.[63] Seceders from Ram's episcopal chapel after d. of John Eyre met at Homerton Coll. and chose John Pye Smith as first pastor 1804. Took lease of Old Gravel Pit chapel (above), vacated by increasingly Unitarian cong., 1810. Site on E. side of Lower Clapton

34 D.N.B.
35 Para. based on Robinson, Hackney, ii. 248–50; Ruston, Unitarianism and Early Presbyterianism, 7–20; J. Davies, Acct. of Old Gravel Pit Mtg. Ho. (1853), passim.
36 H.A.D., WP 2497/1–2.
37 D.N.B.   38 Guildhall MS. 9580/1, p. 24.
39 H.A.D., WP 2497/3 (proposed elevations).
40 P.R.O., HO 129/11/4/1/9.
41 H.A.D., Y54, Vol. II, p. 15; E. Matthews, Clapton Pk. Utd. Ref. Ch. 1804–1984 (1984), 10; A. Peel, Clapton Pk. Cong. Ch. as seen in its Mins. 1804–1929 (reprint from Trans. Cong. Hist. Soc. 1929), 19.
42 e.g. Cong. Year Bk. (1875 and later edns.); Brit. Weekly, 19 Nov. 1886, p. 4a.
43 Para. based on Robinson, Hackney, ii. 245.
44 Ruston, Unitarianism and Early Presbyterianism, 2. Mtg. ho. under construction 1769: H.A.D., D/E/230/THO/13.
45 P.R.O., HO 129/11/5/1/2.
46 D.N.B.   47 P.R.O., HO 129/11/5/1/2.
48 Clarke, Hackney, plate facing p. 32.

49 Cong. Year Bk. (1878, 1879); Hackney Gaz. 11 Sept. 1869, 3.   50 G.R.O. Worship Reg. no. 35491.
51 Clarke, Hackney, 290 n.
52 Para. based on Robinson, Hackney, ii. 252–4; A. S. Aveling, Memories of Kingsland (1887), 7–12, 31–35.
53 Guildhall MS. 9580/1, p. 76.
54 Ibid. 8 Oct. 1794.
55 Ibid. 3, 25 Feb. 1808.   56 D.N.B.
57 P.R.O., HO 129/11/3/1/6.
58 G.R.O. Worship Reg. no. 55; further reg. 1861: ibid. no. 11656.
59 G.L.R.O., M79/TA/15, no. 2.
60 Cong. Year Bk. (1853).
61 P.O. Dir. Lond. (1947, 1952); G.R.O. Worship Reg. no. 52646.
62 A. Mearns, Guide to Cong. Chs. of Lond. (1884), 65; Cong. Year Bk. (1881 and later edns.). Dunn Street mission later said to have originated in 1848.
63 Para. based on S. C. Tongue, 'One Hundred and Seventy Years On' (TS. 1971 in H.A.D.); Peel, Clapton Pk. Cong. Ch.; Matthews, Clapton Pk. Utd. Ref. Ch. passim.

Rd., with adjacent ground to prevent bldg. of shops, acquired in 1868. Imposing 'Round Chapel' of Redhill stone with Portland stone dressings in Romanesque style, seating 1,150 in 1894, by Hen. Fuller 1869–71:[64] semicircular W. end flanked by octagonal towers; refaced with pale Ancaster stone 1906. Bldg. in similar style to N., entered from Powerscroft Rd., for Sun. sch.[65] Attendance 1886 largest of all Hackney Cong. chs.: 845 a.m., 659 evg.; 1903: 787 a.m., 708 evg. Utd. Ref. ch. from 1972. United with Middleton Rd., Dalston (below), 1975. Grove mission, Brooksby's Walk, from 1863, presumably first in 'Gravel Pit chapel mission rooms' in the Grove (later Homerton Grove), W. of Brooksby's Walk, later taken for hosp.[66] New mission room on E. side of Brooksby's Walk, seating 400 in 1894, reg. by unsectarian Christians 1881 and by Congs. 1899.[67] Attendance 1903: 179 a.m., 243 evg. Temp. closed in Second World War, taken over by Lond. City Mission (below, undenom.) 1952. Mission in Chapman Rd., Hackney Wick, from 1864, seating 200 in 1894. Attendance 1903: 34 a.m., 78 evg.; closed by 1910.[68] Mission at corner of Pratt's (later Glyn) Rd. and Presburg Street, where Sun. sch. previously held in Elizabeth Ho., from 1882. Hall and adjoining sch. of Kentish rag with Bath stone dressings in free Early Eng. style, extended 1890 and seating 500 in 1894, by E. M. Whitaker 1882: bellcot. Attendance 1903: 31 a.m., 148 evg.; closed 1939, when bldg. served as wareho. before being bombed.[69]

WELL STREET chapel. Mtg. said to have been founded by Geo. Collison, who from 1803 was tutor at new Hackney Theological Seminary in John Eyre's former ho. in Well Street.[70] New bldg. on E. side of street, in angle between Grove Street (later Lauriston Rd.) and Hackney Terr. (later Cassland Rd.) reg. 1805.[71] Bldg. probably rendered, of two storeys, with round-headed windows and one-storey wings.[72] Superseded by Hampden chapel (below) 1847[73] and demol. by 1870.[74]

UPPER CLAPTON ch.[75] Svces. by theology students at home of John Rumbal, Manor Ho. opposite Brooke Ho. in Upper Clapton Rd., 1812. Superseded by bldg. on W. side of rd., for which registration was sought by Wm. Slack and others 1813.[76] Bldg. was probably mtg. ho. opposite Mount Pleasant Lane, on part of Conduit field bought by Slack and others,

opened 1816, enlarged 1841, seating 530 when closed 1850. Estimated average attendance 1850: 530 and 150 Sun. sch. a.m., 530 and 50 Sun. sch. evg.[77] Bldg. on enlarged site faced with Caen stone in Transitional style, seating 900–1,000, by T. Emmet 1851–2: nave, aisles, corner pinnacles, E. front 'bold and abbey-like'.[78] Attendance 1886: 359 a.m., 254 evg.; 1903: 424 a.m., 480 evg. Large assembly hall at rear for Sun. sch. 1891. Chapel damaged 1944; svces. in renovated large assembly hall, seating 300, from 1950. New chapel and adjoining rooms, seating 240 in 1988, by W. B. Attenbrow opened and reg. 1956. Utd. Ref. ch. from 1972.[79] Mission in Conduit (later Rossendale) Street, where Congs. had sch., seating 300, from 1882. Attendance 1903: 48 a.m., 111 evg.; closed between 1926 and 1932.[80]

TRINITY chapel, Devonshire Road.[81] Mtg. formed by seceders from Well Street chapel (above). Bldg., seating c. 1,500 and inc. 2 schoolrooms, at end of East Pl., later NE. corner of Devonshire (later Brenthouse) and Stanley (later Frampton Pk.) rds. by Mat. Habershon 1832:[82] square-headed windows, stone-faced front with projecting pediment and Ionic pilasters.[83] Millenarian min. 1843. Attendance 1886: 510 a.m., 248 evg.; 1903: 248 a.m., 250 evg. Closed by 1907. Devonshire hall recorded on site from 1911.[84]

HAMPDEN chapel, Grove Street (later Lauriston Rd.).[85] Blt. on W. side of rd. to replace Well Street chapel. Stock-brick bldg. with round-headed windows and pedimented front, seating 340 and with schoolrooms beneath, 1847.[86] Attendance 1851: 65 and 6 Sun. sch. a.m., 29 Sun. sch. aft., 40 evg. First cong. moved to Stepney 1858. Probably Bapt. by 1863.[87]

MIDDLETON ROAD ch., Dalston.[88] Ch. formed in disused chapel in Phillip Street, Kingsland Rd., Shoreditch, 1838. Bldg. of yellow brick with rusticated stone on N. side of rd. in Dec. style, seating 1,000, 1847; reg. 1848. Attendance 1851: 774 and 181 Sun. sch. a.m., 330 and 286 Sun. sch. aft., 733 evg.;[89] 1886: 343 a.m., 403 evg.; 1903: 249 a.m., 233 evg. Reg. again 1860.[90] Closed and united with Pownall Rd. ch., Shoreditch, c. 1948. United with Clapton Pk. Utd. Ref. ch. (above) 1975. Bldg. rebuilt behind street front and used by Pentecostals (below). Mission in Canal Rd., Shoreditch, seating 100 by 1883, from 1860 to 1898 or later.

64 Cong. Year Bk. (1872); reg. by Congs. 'being Paedobaptists': G.R.O. Worship Reg. no. 20098.
65 List of Bldgs. (1975); above, plate 54.
66 G.R.O. Worship Reg. no. 15781; Old O.S. Map Lond. 14 (1870).
67 Cong. Year Bk. (1894); G.R.O. Worship Reg. nos. 25812, 37035.
68 Cong. Year Bk. (1894 and later edns.); G.R.O. Worship Reg. no. 16417.
69 Cong. Year Bk. (1883 and later edns.); H.A.D., Y54, vol. IV, p. 19. Reg. only in 1899: G.R.O. Worship Reg. no. 37036.
70 Robinson, Hackney, ii. 245.
71 Starling's Map (1831); Guildhall MS. 9580/2, p. 146.
72 H.A.D., P 12492.
73 P.R.O., HO 129/11/5/1/3.
74 Old O.S. Map Lond. 41 (1870).
75 Para. based on Robinson, Hackney, ii. 251; Upper Clapton Cong. Ch. 1812–1962 (booklet in H.A.D.), passim.

76 Guildhall MS. 9580/4, 23 Apr. 1813.
77 P.R.O., HO 129/11/2/1/2.
78 Cong. Year Bk. (1853); H.A.D., Album I, p. 86.
79 G.R.O. Worship Reg. no. 65653; inf. from ch. sec.
80 Cong. Year Bk. (1894 and later edns.).
81 Para. based on Robinson, Hackney, ii. 256–7.
82 Guildhall MS. 9580/7, p. 78.
83 H.A.D., P 987 (from lithograph c. 1840).
84 P.O. Dir. Lond. (1907 and later edns.); Old O.S. Maps Lond. 41 (1913).
85 Para. based on P.R.O., HO 129/11/5/1/3.
86 Guildhall MS. 9580/8, p. 286.
87 Cong. Year Bk. (1862, 1863); below, Bapts.; other denom.
88 Para. based on Cong. Year Bk. (1847 and later edns.); Mearns, Guide to Cong. Chs. 16.
89 Guildhall MS. 9580/8, p. 307; P.R.O., HO 129/11/4/1/10.
90 G.R.O. Worship Reg. no. 9404.

PEMBURY GROVE chapel, Lower Clapton.[91] Ch. formed by seceders from St. Thos.'s Sq. under Burder's co-pastor Geo. Thompson. Leased chapel on N. side of rd. (probably from Bapts.) 1850. Bldg. of brick with stone dressings, seating 330 in 1851: small central pediment above cornice with inscription and porch.[92] Attendance 1851: 275 and 85 Sun. sch. a.m., 285 evg.[93] Meth. by 1886, after Congs. had moved to Lower Clapton ch. (below).

LOWER CLAPTON ch., Amhurst Road.[94] Congs. from Pembury Grove (above) reg. new ch. at NW. corner of intersection with Dalston Lane and Pembury Rd. 1864.[95] Bldg. of Kentish rag with Box Hill stone dressings in Dec. style, seating 1,000 by 1894, by Hen. Fuller: clerestory formed by rose windows, elaborate buttresses, SE. tower with spire;[96] adjoining rooms and sch. to W. Attendance 1886: 310 a.m., 248 evg.; 1903: 421 a.m., 433 evg. Replaced by Downs Ct. flats[97] after cong. moved to former Clapton Presb. ch. (below), seating 400 in 1951, reg. 1936–63.[98] Mission in Morning Lane, seating 150 by 1881, from 1878 to c. 1926,[99] when acquired by Brethren (below). Attendance 1903: 143 a.m., 213 evg. Mission in Castle Street, Norfolk Rd., seating 150 by 1881; closed by 1883.

SOUTHGATE ROAD chapel. Ind. chapel adjoining sch. at N. corner of Balmes Rd. reg. 1860–9. Reg. as Brotherhood ch., on same site, 1897.[1] Attendance 1886: 204 a.m., 237 evg.; 1903: 57 a.m., 205 evg. Reg. as Cong. but only sometimes so described.[2] Closed between 1935 and 1938.[3]

VICTORIA PARK tabernacle, South Hackney. Seceders from Victoria Pk. Approach Rd., Bethnal Green, met from 1862 at Scott's music hall and then in Patriot Sq., Bethnal Green, before moving to new iron ch. on NW. side of Wetherell Rd., seating 1,500 before enlargement with gallery.[4] New bldg. 1869–70, reg. 1871.[5] Attendance 1886: 404 a.m., 442 evg. Closed 1901 on union with Trinity ch., Lauriston Rd. (below).[6]

CAMBRIDGE HEATH ch., Mare Street.[7] Iron chapel[8] on E. side of street, S. of Cambridge Lodge Villas, for ch. formed 1861. Replaced by ch. reg. 1866.[9] Bldg. of Kentish rag with Bath stone dressings, seating 1,200 in 1894, in Dec.

style by Jos. James 1865–6: pinnacled tower with spire.[10] Attendance 1886: 296 a.m., 244 evg.; 1903: 253 a.m., 269 evg. Repairs needed 1904, when membership in decline.[11] Closed between 1936 and 1938. Orchard mission in hall at no. 179 Well Street, seating 350 in 1894, from 1865; reg. 1907.[12] Attendance 1903: 43 a.m., 77 evg. Closed between 1951 and 1960. Mission in Dove Row, Shoreditch, seating 350 in 1894, from 1871 to c. 1898. Morley hall built for Sun. schs.[13]

SHRUBLAND ROAD ch., London Fields.[14] Ch. formed 1870. Took over Dalston (Eng.) Presb. ch. on S. side of rd. but did not reg. bldg. for Congs. until 1894.[15] Seating for 500 in 1894, 350 by 1910; Attendance 1886: 133 a.m., 226 evg.; 1903: 63 a.m., 74 evg. United with Trinity ch., Lauriston Rd., 1971. Bldg. acquired by Evangelical and Reformed ch.[16]

SOUTH HACKNEY or Bethany ch., Victoria Park Road.[17] Formed 1871 as South Hackney ch. In Cadogan Terr. 1880, 1883 when supplied by students from Hackney Coll.[18] Moved to former Bapt. Park chapel (below) at corner of Victoria Pk. and Homer rds. Bldg., seating 450 in 1894, reg. 1893.[19] Attendance 1886: 129 a.m., 129 evg.; 1903: 65 a.m., 94 evg. Ch. and Bethany hall recorded 1940, hall alone c. 1946–8.[20] Disused yellow-brick bldg. survived 1988.

RECTORY ROAD.[21] Trinity Introductory ch., often listed under Stoke Newington, formed from Harecourt chapel, Islington, as Paedobaptist ch. in Walford Rd., S. Hornsey, 1865.[22] Moved to temp. ch. on site later bought from Tyssen est. in SE. angle of Rectory and Evering rds., opened and reg. as Cong. ch. 1882. Bldg., seating 1,200 in 1894, by R. A. Lewcock, built and reg. 1887.[23] Attendance 1886: 374 a.m., 384 evg.; 1903: 346 a.m., 427 evg. Bombed 1940. New brown-brick bldg. with pantiled roof, seating c. 180, by Harrison & Stevens 1954–5. Utd. Ref. ch. from 1972.[24] Mission called Christian Institute in Hoxton Market, Shoreditch, seating 150 in 1894, from 1886; 'moribund' 1950, closed 1983.

STAMFORD HILL ch.[25] Site on E. side of Stamford Hill in S. angle with Portland Ave. bought by Thos. Kelsey, worshipper at Harecourt ch., Islington. Imposing building[26] of Kentish rag with stone dressings in Dec. style, seating 1,200,

91 Para. based on Mearns, *Guide to Cong. Chs.* 14; H.A.D., D/E/233/LOW/1.   92 H.A.D., P 1054.
93 P.R.O., HO 129/11/4/1/8.
94 Para. based on *Cong. Year Bk.* (1863 and later edns.).
95 G.R.O. Worship Reg. no. 16315.
96 H.A.D., Y54, vol. IV, p. 20.
97 Clarke, *Hackney*, 302 n.
98 G.R.O. Worship Reg. no. 56988; H.A.D., D/E/LOW/5.
99 G.R.O. Worship Reg. no. 24219.
1 Ibid. nos. 9483, 35958; below, other denom.
2 e.g. in Harris and Bryant, *Chs. and Lond.* 394; not listed in *Cong. Year Bk.*
3 *P.O. Dir. Lond.* (1935, 1938).
4 *Hackney Gaz.* 18 Dec. 1869, 3; H.A.D., D/E 233 CAM.
5 G.R.O. Worship Reg. no. 19990.
6 *P.O. Dir. Lond.* (1901, 1902); G.R.O. Worship Reg. no. 38769.
7 Para. based on *Cong. Year Bk.* (1864 and later edns.); H.A.D., D/E 233 CAM.
8 Mearns, *Guide to Cong. Chs.* 20.
9 G.R.O. Worship Reg. no. 17291.

10 H.A.D., P 12122.
11 *Trans. Cong. Hist. Soc.* xx. 372.
12 G.R.O. Worship Reg. no. 42202.
13 Above, social.
14 Para. based on *Cong. Year Bk.* (1871 and later edns.).
15 G.R.O. Worship Reg. no. 34619; below, Presbs.
16 *Terrier*, Summer 1992; H.A.D., D/E 233 CAM; below, other denom.
17 Para. based on *Cong. Year Bk.* (1894 and later edns.).
18 *P.O. Dir. Lond. County Suburbs, North* (1880); A. Mearns, *Lond. Cong. Dir.* (1883), 35.
19 G.R.O. Worship Reg. no. 33995.
20 *P.O. Dir. Lond.* (1940 and later edns.).
21 Para. based on *Cong. Year Bk.* (1865 and later edns.); H.A.D., TS. catalogue, D/E/233/REC; D/E/233/REC/2/1.
22 *V.C.H. Mdx.* viii. 213; Mearns, *Guide to Cong. Chs.* 38.   23 G.R.O. Worship Reg. nos. 26165, 30486.
24 Ibid. no. 65147; H.A.D., D/E/233/REC/9/9; inf. from min.
25 Para. based on J. Bristow, *Stamford Hill Cong. Ch. 1871–1971*; *Cong. Year Bk.* (1871 and later edns.).
26 H.A.D., Y54, vol. IV, p.21; a 'Cong. cathedral': Clarke, *Hackney*, 225.

adjoining lecture hall to E., by J. Tarring & Son 1869–71: semicircular apse, tall W. tower and spire. Opened 1871, reg. 1872.[27] Attendance 1886: 615 a.m., 446 evg.; 1903, when Sun. total larger than that at any other place of worship in Hackney except Salvation Army's Congress Hall: 1,119 a.m., 1,336 evg. Old ch. demol. 1966. Lecture hall adapted for svces. 1965; seated *c.* 200 in 1988.[28] Utd. Ref. ch. from 1972.[29] Mission in St. Ann's Rd., Tottenham, from 1878, seating 150 in 1894.[30]

HOMERTON EVANGELICAL hall, no. 116 High Street, Homerton, reg. by Congs. 1878–96.[31]

CHATSWORTH ROAD tabernacle. Bldg. on W. side at angle with Elderfield Rd. reg. by Congs. 1887.[32] Attendance 1886: 350 a.m., 447 evg. Bapt. by 1894 (below).

TRINITY ch., Lauriston Road.[33] Mtg. of 1823 moved from Hanbury Street, Mile End New Town, to bldg. of red brick with stone dressings in Tudor style, seating 800 in 1926, adjoining halls to W. in SW. angle with Rutland Rd. 1901: two copper spirelets above main doorways in Lauriston Rd. Dated and reg. 1901,[34] but inc. older foundation stone of 1861 (? from Victoria Pk. tabernacle). Attendance 1903: 231 a.m., 357 evg. From 1972 Utd. Ref. ch.[35] Closed 1988.[36]

MISSIONS. From late 18th cent. Inds. used various premises apparently briefly. Room in Eliz. Farrow's ho. 'at Stoke Newington', 1791.[37] Room in Wm. Hartwell's ho., Shacklewell, 1793.[38] Bldg. in Shore Pl., by Jas. Thurgood, min. (possibly later used by Bapts.), 1794.[39] Hall adjoining Chas. Buck's ho. 1797.[40] John Knight's ho. at Clapton, 1799.[41] Premises were later reg. specifically for Inds. Ho. in Brewhouse Lane, 1812.[42] John Gardner's ho., Stoke Newington High Street, 1820.[43] Mr. Hemsley's ho., no. 27 Charles Street, Dalston, 1825.[44] Thos. Geo. Williams's ho., no. 3 Orchard Street, 1828.[45] Jas. Alloway's ho., no. 8 Sheep Lane, Lond. Fields, 1834.[46] No. 4 Orchard Street, 1834.[47] No. 5 Morning Lane, 1834.[48] Rob. Butt's room, Church Street, 1837.[49] No. 4 High Hill Ferry, 1839.[50] 'New chapel', Upper Clapton (possibly repeat reg. of Upper Clapton Cong. ch., above), 1840.[51] No. 3 Perseverance Row,

Sanford Lane, W. Hackney, 1842.[52] No. 1 Stratford Pl., Richmond Rd., 1843.[53] Other premises were reg. for unspecified Protestant dissenters, perhaps Inds. Wm. Everett's ho. at Kingsland, 1811.[54] Ho. in Paradise Row, Church Street, 1816.[55] Ho. near Bath Pl., Dalston, 1820.[56] Dye factory at High Hill Ferry, 1821.[57] No. 2 Wick Street, 1825.[58] No. 2 Buck Bldgs., Morning Lane, 1827.[59] Thos. Geo. Williams's premises, Mare Street, 1827.[60] Hos. in Coldbath Lane (later Kenmure Rd.), Jerusalem Sq., Sheep Lane, and Bennett's Yard, Well Street, 1829.[61] Strawberry Cottage, Kates Lane (later Brooke Rd.), Clapton, 1830.[62] No. 5 Wick Street and no. 3 Hackney Wick, 1832.[63] No. 11 Beauvoir Terr., Kingsland Rd., 1846, and no. 28, 1847.[64] Sch. in Manor Rd., S. Hackney, 1851.[65]

BAPTISTS. MARE STREET.[66] Aft. mtgs. of worshippers from Little Prescot Street, Whitechapel,[67] under John Rance at small ho. in Shore Pl. 1796. Ch. formed with Rance, ordained at St. Thos.'s Sq. Ind. chapel, as first pastor 1798. New ch. on W. side of Mare Street N. of Flying Horse Yd. (later Exmouth Pl.) 1812.[68] Plain bldg., apparently rendered, with two rows of windows,[69] seating 1,150 by 1851 after addition of galleries. 'Well filled' 1830. Attendance 1851: 800 and 300 Sun. sch. a.m., 300 and 500 Sun. sch. aft., 850 and 300 Sun. sch. evg.[70] F. A. Cox (d. 1853), instrumental in founding *Bapt. Mag.* and Lond. Univ.,[71] was pastor from 1811. After fire of 1854, new stone-faced ch. in Classical style, seating 1,200, by W. G. and E. Habershon built 1856: round-headed windows for galleries over square-headed windows, projecting cornice, Tuscan pillared pediment over main entrance.[72] Reg. by Particular Bapts. 1858.[73] Attendance 1886: 462 a.m., 568 evg.; 1903: 311 a.m., 537 evg. Supported Bapt. Union and in Lond. Bapt. Soc. 1928.[74] Ch. bombed 1940, when svces. held in St. Andrew's hall, Well Street, and 1944; repaired but damaged again 1945, when svces. moved to Congs.' Orchard mission, Well Street; demol. after war. Replaced by Frampton Pk. Rd. ch. (below).

HOMERTON ROW chapel.[75] Mtgs. under Thos.

27 G.R.O. Worship Reg. no. 20460.
28 Inf. from ch. sec.
29 Ibid.
30 *V.C.H. Mdx.* v. 362.
31 G.R.O. Worship Reg. no. 23985; *P.O. Dir. Lond. County Suburbs, North* (1880 and later edns.).
32 G.R.O. Worship Reg. no. 30341.
33 Para. based on *Cong. Year Bk.* (1926 and later edns.).
34 G.R.O. Worship Reg. no. 38769.
35 *P.O. Dir. Lond.* (1973).
36 H.A.D., D/E 233 CAM.
37 Guildhall MS. 9580/1, p. 13.
38 Ibid. 9580/1, p. 56.
39 Ibid. 9580/1, p. 68.
40 Ibid. 9580/1, p. 146.
41 Ibid. 9580/2, p. 41.
42 Ibid. 9580/3, 4 Jan. 1812.
43 Ibid. 9580/5, 8 Nov. 1820.
44 Ibid. 9580/6, pp. 16–17.
45 Ibid. 9580/6, p. 214.
46 Ibid. 9580/7, p. 128.
47 Ibid. 9580/7, p. 138.
48 Ibid. 9580/7, p. 153.
49 Ibid. 9580/7, p. 252.
50 Ibid. 9580/8, p. 26.
51 Ibid. 9580/8, p. 59.

52 Ibid. 9580/8, p. 135.   53 Ibid. 9580/8, p. 155.
54 Ibid. 9580/3, 22 Oct. 1811.
55 Ibid. 9580/4, 18 Oct. 1816.
56 Ibid. 9580/5, 5 Aug. 1820.
57 Ibid. 9580/5, 30 June 1821.
58 Ibid. 9580/6, p. 67.
59 Ibid. 9580/6, p. 137.   60 Ibid. 9580/6, p. 158.
61 Ibid. 9580/6, pp. 247–8, 264–5.
62 Ibid. 9580/6, p. 282.
63 Ibid. 9580/7, pp. 57, 77.
64 Ibid. 9580/8, pp. 257, 284.
65 Ibid. 9580/9, p. 78.
66 Para. based on J. Ivimey, *Hist. Eng. Bapts.* iv (1830), 405–6; C. M. Moore-Crispin, *Ter-Jubilee Memories of Mare Street Bapt. Ch. 1798–1948.*
67 E. F. Kevan, *Lond.'s Oldest Bapt. Ch.* (1933), 103.
68 1803 according to min.'s return 1851: P.R.O., HO 129/11/5/1/4.
69 H.A.D., P 12077/1–2 (pencil sketch of 'Bapt. chapel, Shore Place' [*sic*]).
70 P.R.O., HO 129/11/5/1/4.   71 *D.N.B.*
72 H.A.D., P 12554–5; Y54, Vol. II, p. 15; above, plate 58.
73 G.R.O. Worship Reg. no. 8270.
74 W. T. Whitley, *Bapts. of Lond.* (1928), 141, 279.
75 Para. based on Ibid. 150, 279.

Eason 1817. Ch. formed 1820. Bldg. on S. side of Homerton Row opened and reg. 1822;[76] seating for 350 in 1851. Attendance 1851: 225 and 58 Sun. sch. a.m., 40 aft., 195 evg.;[77] 1886: 69 a.m., 51 evg.; 1903: 121 a.m., 117 evg. In Metropolitan Assoc. of Strict Bapt. Chs. 1928. Closed between 1959 and 1964.[78]

SHACKLEWELL chapel.[79] Bldg. of 1822 in Wellington Pl., Wellington (later Shacklewell) Rd., vested in trustees 1827. New bldg., seating 564, 1843–4, when min. was F. A. Cox of Mare Street ch.[80] Attendance 1851 (estimated average): 160 a.m., 90 aft., 180 evg.;[81] 1886: 57 a.m., 61 evg. Merged with Particular Bapt. former Devonshire Sq. ch. in Stoke Newington Rd., S. Hornsey, 1884.[82]

PEMBURY GROVE chapel, Lower Clapton, reg. by Hen. Robinson of Grove Cottage, Clarence Rd., 1848. Probably bldg. leased to Meths. 1850.[83]

WEST (later ELSDALE) STREET chapel. Seceders from Mare Street under W. Emmet had ch. in West Street 1851.[84]

HOCKLEY STREET chapel. Mtg. in former street N. of Durham Grove off Morning Lane recorded 1862–8.[85] Perhaps same as Salem chapel, Hockley Street, reg. by Particular Bapts. 1875[86] and dissolved 1880.[87]

HAMPDEN chapel, Grove Street (later Lauriston Rd.). Bapt. mtg. said to have been formed 1863 and to have gone by 1883[88] was probably group which took over Congs.' Hampden chapel, which name it later adopted.[89] Attendance 1886: 156 a.m., 147 evg.; 1903: 114 a.m., 116 evg. Closed 1927,[90] when sold to Assemblies of God.[91]

CHATSWORTH tabernacle, Chatsworth Rd., Lower Clapton.[92] Mtg. formed as Kingsland tabernacle 1864. New bldg. at corner of Enfield Rd. 1873. Moved to bldg. on W. side of Chatsworth Rd. at angle with Rushmore Rd. 1877, then to former Cong. ch. at angle with Elderfield Rd. reg. by Bapts. 1894.[93] Bldg. of brick with stone dressings, seating 800 in 1928: round-headed windows, octagonal corner tower with bellcot, halls beneath.[94] Attendance 1886: 103 a.m., 61 evg.; 1903: 296 a.m., 313 evg. Left Metropolitan Assoc. of Strict Bapt. Chs. by 1905; in no assoc. 1909; in Lond. Bapt. Soc. 1928. Closed c. 1948.[95]

PARK chapel, Victoria Park Rd. Mtg. formed at St. Thos.'s hall 1864 moved to iron chapel

probably replaced by bldg. at W. corner of Homer Rd. marked as Bapt. 1870.[96] Later South Hackney Cong. ch. (above).

FOREST ROAD chapel, Dalston. Svces. in schoolroom on Grange Rd. before ch. formed in Forest Rd. 1865. Bldg. on N. side of rd. between Woodland and Holly streets. Attendance 1886: 87 a.m., 92 p.m. Served as Holy Trinity par. room by 1898.[97]

BLOMFIELD STREET. Svces. in Albion hall, Dalston,[98] 1866. New bldg. in Downham Rd. 1871. Later moved to Blomfield Street. In Lond. Bapt. Assoc. Closed c. 1880.[99]

ASHWIN STREET ch., Dalston Junction.[1] Svces. in Luxembourg hall, N. end of street, 1868.[2] New bldg. on opposite side, seating 1,250 in 1928, 1871; reg. 1873.[3] Attendances largest of all Hackney Bapt. chs. 1886: 693 a.m., 770 evg.; 1903: 532 a.m., 715 evg. Supported Bapt. Union and in Lond. Bapt. Assoc. 1928. Became Shiloh Pentecostal ch. (below).

SPELDHURST ROAD chapel, South Hackney. Mtgs. in schoolroom on W. side of rd. winter 1867–8. New bldg., seating c. 300, 1869. In Metropolitan Assoc. of Strict Bapt. Chs. Bought by Chas. W. Banks 1873. Closed c. 1886.[4] Bldg. presumably acquired by Ch. of Martin Luther.[5]

DOWNS chapel, Lower Clapton.[6] Open membership ch.[7] formed by worshippers at Mare Street and reg. 1869. Site intended to be in Avenue Rd. (later Midhurst Way) but moved to corner of Downs and Queen's Down (later Queensdown) rds. in expectation that rly. station wd. be opened at NE. corner of Hackney Downs. Bldg. of red brick with black- and white-brick bands and Bath stone dressings and round-headed windows, seating 1,008 in 1928, by Morton M. Glover 1868–9: W. corner turrets and rose window over double porch; halls beneath and to E.[8] Attendance 1886: 480 a.m., 432 evg.; 1903: 540 a.m., 651 evg. Supported Bapt. Union and in Lond. Bapt. Assoc. 1928. Mission in Rendlesham Rooms, at corner of Heatherley and Landfield streets, from 1872. Attendance 1903: 74 a.m., 145 evg.; closed on expiry of lease by 1923.[9] Mission in Waterloo Rooms, Prout Rd., seating 80 in 1928, from 1877. Attendance 1903: 36 a.m., 68 evg.; closed after 1929.

ALBION hall, Dalston,[10] used by Bapts. who moved to Blomfield Street (above) and by Strict Bapts. who celebrated anniversary in hall 1875.[11]

76 Guildhall MS. 9580/3, 28 Aug. 1822.
77 P.R.O., HO 129/11/4/1/12.
78 P.O. Dir. Lond. (1959, 1964).
79 Para. based on Whitley, Bapts. of Lond. 106.
80 Robinson, Hackney, ii. 251.
81 P.R.O., HO 129/11/3/1/7.
82 V.C.H. Mdx. viii. 214. Wellington Rd. chapel briefly reg. again by Bapts. 1888–9: G.R.O. Worship Reg. no. 30885; later W. Hackney synagogue (below, Judaism).
83 Guildhall MS. 9580/8, p. 302; below, Meths. (Pembury Grove).   84 Whitley, Bapts. of Lond. 176.
85 Ibid. 191.   86 G.R.O. Worship Reg. no. 22510.
87 Whitley, Bapts. of Lond. 216.
88 Ibid. 193.
89 Above, Congs.; G.R.O. Worship Reg. no. 35365.
90 Whitley, Bapts. of Lond. 280.
91 Tower to Tower Block, no. 33; below, Pentecostals.
92 Para. based on Whitley, Bapts of Lond. 195, 279.
93 G.R.O. Worship Reg. no. 34579.
94 H.A.D., P 10368.
95 P.O. Dir. Lond. (1948, 1949).

96 Whitley, Bapts. of Lond. 195; Old O.S. Map Lond. 41 (1870).
97 Ibid. 197; P.O. Dir. Lond. County Suburbs, North (1894, 1898).
98 Earlier reg. by Free Eng. Ch.: below, this section.
99 Whitley, Bapts. of Lond. 200.
1 Para. based on ibid. 205, 279.
2 Hackney Gaz. 13 Nov. 1869, 3.
3 G.R.O. Worship Reg. no. 21096.
4 Hackney Gaz. 9 Oct. 1869, 3; Whitley, Bapts. of Lond. 205.
5 Below, other denom.; Old O.S. Map Lond. 41 (1870).
6 Para. based on Whitley, Bapts. of Lond. 207, 279; Downs Chapel, Diamond Jubilee Programme (1929).
7 A. C. Underwood, Hist. of Eng. Bapts. (1947), 207 n.
8 G.R.O. Worship Reg. no. 19259; Hackney Gaz. 18 Sept. 1869, 4; datestone.
9 Reg. 1886–1923: ibid. no. 29388. The same or a neighbouring mission was also reg. 1901–25: ibid. no. 38571.
10 Earlier reg. by Free Eng. Ch.; below, this section.
11 Hackney Gaz. 5 June 1875, 4.

RETREAT PLACE. Mtg. begun nearby in Mead Pl. 1879. Belonged to Old Bapt. Union 1928.[12] Perhaps used Ram's sch., Retreat Pl., reg. 1900, although registration was cancelled 1925.[13]

MALLARD STREET chapel, Hackney Wick. Bldg. at S. corner of Percy Terr. Attendance 1886: 17 evg.; 1903, when called Bethsaida, 23 evg. Closed c. 1911.[14]

NORFOLK (later CECILIA) ROAD. Bapt. mtg. (probably in Shacklewell Green mission hall recorded 1894)[15] formed by 1902. Attendance 1903: 40 a.m., 42 evg. Belonged to Old Bapt. Union. Closed between 1914 and 1928.[16]

LODDIGES ROAD chapel. Bapt. ch. (perhaps Christian ch. recorded 1894 and Loddiges Rd. chapel reg. by Independents 1900)[17] recorded by 1902.[18] Closed c. 1947.[19]

FRAMPTON PARK ROAD ch. Ch. on W. side of Frampton Pk. Rd., reg. as successor to Mare Street ch. 1955. Bldg. of brown brick, seating 320 and with adjoining halls, by Spalding, Myers & Attenbrow 1953–4; opened 1956.[20]

BARNABAS ROAD ch. Strict Bapts. reg. ch. at corner of Barnabas Rd. and Daley Street 1963.[21] Bldg. of pale grey brick in modern style, with small clock tower and inc. hall.

MISSIONS. From early 19th cent. Bapts. reg. several premises. Bldg. called Stoke Newington chapel, behind no. 16 High Street, 1812.[22] Thos. Frankland's ho. near Marsh Gate, Lower Homerton, and David Ramsay's ho., no. 6 Homerton Row, 1817.[23] John Lee's ho. at Hackney Wick and Rob. Fletcher's schoolroom in Bridge Street, Homerton, 1819.[24] Hen. Simonds's ho., no. 3 Down Cottage, Shacklewell, 1836.[25] Schoolrooms at no. 5 Wick Street, 1840, and in Charles Street, Dalston, 1844.[26] No. 1 Jerusalem Sq. 1845.[27] Room at no. 8 Homerton Terr. 1848.[28]

METHODISTS. PLEASANT PLACE. Newly formed Wes. mtg. at ho. in Grove Lane[29] moved to mtg. place in Shore Pl. vacated by Bapts. 1812.[30] Rent paid by members of City Rd. chapel. New smaller bldg. on N. side of Pleasant Pl. (later Paragon Rd.) c. 1816, enlarged 1825, seating c. 400 in 1843. Replaced by Richmond Rd. chapel (below) and later used by Brethren (below) as Providence chapel.

STOKE NEWINGTON HIGH STREET.[31] Wes. chapel on E. side of street N. of Tyssen Rd. built and reg. 1816.[32] Enlarged c. every 7 years, seating c. 500 by 1843 and 640 by 1851.[33] Attendance 1851: 334 and 94 Sun. sch. a.m., 342 evg. Rebuilt in brick with stone dressings in vaguely Romanesque style 1851: three gable ends and two turrets on street front, which was largely obscured until removal of cottages and enlargement of ch. to seat 1,000 by T. Scott 1875.[34] Attendance 1886: 376 a.m., 427 evg.; 1903: 351 a.m., 461 evg. Again rebuilt as plain red-brick bldg. with hall behind and reopened 1958. Seating for 200 in 1970.[35]

BAKER'S ROW, Hackney Wick. Calvinistic dissenters, probably Meths., reg. room in Wm. Edwards's ho. 1817.[36]

KATES LANE (later BROOK STREET, then NORTHWOLD RD.). Wes. chapel built 1833, seating 120 in 1851 when sold by Meths. to 'moderate Calvinists'.[37]

HOPE STREET, no. 2 reg. by 'Revivalist Methodists' 1834.[38]

ROSEBERRY PLACE, Dalston. Wes. chapel built and reg. 1844, seating 226 by 1851. Attendance 1851: 130 and 30 Sun. sch. a.m., 35 aft., 158 evg.[39] Reg. again 1854–61.[40] Demol. for rly. 1865 and replaced by Mayfield Terr. chapel (below).[41]

RICHMOND ROAD. Site leased from St. Thos.'s hosp. at E. end of later Richmond Rd., on S. side, 1846. Wes. chapel to replace one in Pleasant Pl., seating 1,110 in 1851, built and reg. 1846.[42] Bldg. of brick with stone dressings; rectangular plan, tall square-headed windows, pedimented street front with Ionic pillars flanking doorway.[43] Attendance 1851: 350 and 64 Sun. sch. a.m., 45 aft., 400 evg. Reg. again 1854.[44] Attendance 1886: 524 a.m., 475 evg.; 1903: 235 a.m., 294 evg. Closed 1925 and leased to Central Hackney synagogue on opening of Hackney Central hall, Mare Street (below).[45]

LONDON LANE. Lecture room reg. by Primitive Meths. 1859–66.[46]

NORTHWOLD ROAD, Stoke Newington Common. Primitive Meths. reg. chapel on S. side of rd. 1861 and again, perhaps after rebuilding, 1895–1954.[47] Street front of red brick with stone dressings in Gothic style, masking yellow-brick octagon beneath skylight.[48] Attendance 1886: 85 a.m., 73 evg.; 1903: 258 a.m., 339 evg. Reg. as Northwold Rd. synagogue 1955.[49]

12 Whitley, *Bapts. of Lond.* 224, 280.
13 G.R.O. Worship Reg. no. 38110.
14 Mudie-Smith, *Rel. Life*, 64; *P.O. Dir. Lond. County Suburbs* (1911, 1912).
15 *P.O. Dir. Lond. County Suburbs, North* (1894).
16 Whitley, *Bapts. of Lond.* 258, 280; Harris and Bryant, *Chs. and Lond.* 393
17 *P.O. Dir. Lond. County Suburbs, North* (1894); G.R.O. Worship Reg. no. 37938.
18 Whitley, *Bapts. of Lond.* 255, 280.
19 *P.O. Dir. Lond.* (1946, 1947).
20 *Bapt. Union Dir.* (1988-9); G.R.O. Worship Reg. no. 65049; datestone.
21 G.R.O. Worship Reg. no. 69122.
22 Guildhall MS. 9580/3, 15 Feb. 1812.
23 Ibid. 9580/4, 27 Feb., 5 Aug. 1817.
24 Ibid. 9580/5, 22 Feb., 12 Aug. 1819.
25 Ibid. 9580/7, p. 240.
26 Ibid. 9580/8, pp. 91, 215.
27 Ibid. 9580/8, p. 242.
28 Ibid. 9580/8, p. 293.
29 Para. based on Robinson, *Hackney*, ii. 255-6.

30 Above, Bapts. (Mare Street).
31 Para. based on Robinson, *Hackney*, ii. 254.
32 Guildhall MS. 9580/4, 2 Oct. 1816.
33 P.R.O., HO 129/11/3/1/5.
34 *Hackney Gaz.* 5 June 1875, 3; *Meth. Recorder*, 9 Oct. 1902, 15; Clarke, *Hackney*, 230.
35 G.R.O. Worship Reg. no. 66779; *Meth. Statistical Return*, i. 8.
36 Guildhall MS. 9580/4, 10 Nov. 1817.
37 P.R.O. HO 129/11/2/1/3.
38 Guildhall MS. 9580/7, p. 155.
39 Ibid. 9580/8, p. 224; P.R.O., HO 129/11/3/1/4.
40 G.R.O. Worship Reg. no. 1797.
41 H.A.D., TS. catalogue, D/E/234/A.
42 Guildhall MS. 9580/8, p. 271; P.R.O., HO 129/11/4/1/7. 43 H.A.D., Album I, p. 9.
44 G.R.O. Worship Reg. no. 3990.
45 H.A.D., TS. catalogue, D/E/234/A; below, Judaism.
46 G.R.O. Worship Reg. no. 8987.
47 Ibid. nos. 11780, 34665.
48 When used as synagogue, 1987.
49 G.R.O. Worship Reg. no. 64951; below, Judaism.

LONDON FIELDS. Primitive Meths. had chapel at SE. corner of Lond. Fields, W. of Exmouth Pl., from 1863,[50] reg. 1865.[51] Attendance 1886: 106 a.m., 74 evg.; 1903: 60 a.m., 68 evg. Also held open-air svces. 1872. Called Jubilee chapel 1873.[52] Closed between 1935 and 1938.[53]

CLAPTON METH. ch.[54] Wes. ch. founded from Richmond Rd. on W. side of Lower Clapton Rd. N. of corner of Downs Rd., reg. 1865.[55] Bldg. of ragstone with stone dressings in Dec. style, seating 1,000, 1863–5; not oriented; apse, pinnacled W. tower with tall spire over central porch facing Lower Clapton Rd.[56] Attendance 1886: 372 a.m., 325 evg.; 1903: 326 a.m., 328 evg. Closed 1934 and later demol. Replaced by lecture hall (later sch.) in Downs Rd., remodelled as ch. and reg. 1934.[57] Bldg. of stone faced in Dec. style, with bellcot, built by 1880. Damaged 1940 and reopened 1949. Seating for 160 in 1970.[58]

MAYFIELD TERRACE, Dalston.[59] Wes. reg. chapel on NW. corner of Mayfield and Richmond rds. to replace Roseberry Pl. chapel 1865.[60] Bldg. in Dec. style, seating 1,000, 1865.[61] Attendance 1886: 374 a.m., 404 evg.; 1903: 225 a.m., 593 evg. Bombed 1945. Replaced on same site by Dalston, Richmond Rd., ch. (reg. as Dalston Meth. mission at no. 15 in 1954)[62] 1961.[63] Seated 203 in 1970.[64] Demol. by 1979.[65]

PEMBURY GROVE, Lower Clapton. Utd. Meth. Free Ch. reg. bldg., acquired from Congs., 1866–1954.[66] Attendance 1886: 163 a.m., 134 evg.; 1903: 293 a.m., 268 evg. Bombed in Second World War and later closed.[67]

CHURCH ROAD, Homerton. Wes. ch. on W. side of Church (later Barnabas) Rd. founded by 1868. Attendance 1903: 118 a.m., 109 evg. Reg. as Homerton Meth. mission 1937. Damaged in Second World War and closed.[68]

CASSLAND ROAD. Wes. reg. chapel at W. corner of Queen Anne Rd. 1872.[69] Bldg., seating 1,000, in Dec. style; octagonal corner turret with spirelet.[70] Attendance 1886, largest of all Hackney Meth. chs.: 579 a.m., 518 evg.; 1903: 395 a.m., 373 p.m. Closed and probably demol. by 1946.[71]

DAINTRY STREET, Hackney Wick. Chapel on E. side existed by 1879, reg. by Wes. Meths. 1886. Closely associated with Cassland Rd. Per-

haps was ch. sometimes said to be in Chapman Road. Attendance 1903: 97 a.m., 150 evg. Closed 1951.[72]

CLAPTON PARK tabernacle, Blurton Rd.[73] Primitive Meths. started mission when Thos. Jackson took over Theatre Royal, Glenarm Rd., reg. 1884–96.[74] Tabernacle on S. side of Blurton Rd. E. of Chatsworth Rd. opened 1885 and reg. 1887–1958.[75] Bldg. of ragstone with stone dressings: round-headed windows, small porch with Ionic pillars.[76] Attendance 1886: 204 a.m., 243 evg.; 1903: 137 a.m., 170 evg. Remained headquarters of mission, which had holiday home at Southend (Essex) and later at Herne Bay (Kent), until damaged in Second World War. Replaced by Chatsworth Rd. ch. (below) 1958. Former tabernacle became St. Jude's Rom. Cath. ch.[77]

BROOKFIELD ROAD, South Hackney. Primitive Meths. in Brookfield Rd. by 1886[78] reg. Tyndale Memorial ch. on W. side of rd. 1888–1941.[79] Attendance 1886: 112 a.m., 124 evg.; 1903: 74 a.m., 153 evg. Closed c. 1951.[80] Replaced by Tyndale Ct. flats.

SOUTHWOLD ROAD, Upper Clapton. Primitive Meths. reg. chapel at W. corner of Theydon Rd. 1888–1951.[81] Attendance 1903: 59 a.m., 46 evg. Closed c. 1951.[82]

OLINDA ROAD, Stamford Hill. Primitive Meths. had mission hall on S. side of rd. by 1898, perhaps Beulah hall there by 1894.[83] Attendance 1903: 88 a.m., 49 p.m. Possibly replaced by Ravensdale Rd. ch. (below).

RAVENSDALE ROAD, Stamford Hill. Primitive Meths. reg. chapel on S. side of rd. 1905.[84] New bldg. on N. side of rd., red-brick with stone dressings, with Perp. style windows and short tower, 1925;[85] reg. 1927.[86] Seated 300 in 1970.[87]

HACKNEY CENTRAL HALL, Mare Street.[88] Site on E. side, between Salvation Army hall and central libr., secured 1909 to replace Richmond Rd. ch. Bldg. of three storeys and seven bays, faced in yellow stone, with cornice and Ionic pilasters, 1924–5: headquarters of Hackney mission, inc. hall seating 1,500, three halls for 700 Sun. sch. children, gymnasium, ground-floor shops; reg. 1925.[89] Memorial chapel for silver jubilee opened on ground floor 1950. Seating for 350 in 1970.[90] Sold to Hackney L.B. 1979 but 4

50 *Hackney Dir.* (1872).
51 G.R.O. Worship Reg. no. 16917.
52 *Hackney Dir.* (1872); O.S. Map 1/2,500, Lond. XVIII (1873 edn.).
53 *P.O. Dir. Lond.* (1935, 1938).
54 Para. based on *Clapton Pk. Meth. Ch. 1865–1965* (booklet in H.A.D.); H.A.D., TS. catalogue, D/E/234/A.
55 G.R.O. Worship Reg. no. 16648.
56 H.A.D., Album I, pp. 41–3, 49; *Meth. Recorder,* 9 Oct. 1902, 13.
57 G.R.O. Worship Reg. no. 55314.
58 *Meth. Statistical Return.* i. 7.
59 Para. based on H.A.D., TS. catalogue, D/E/234/A.
60 G.R.O. Worship Reg. no. 16723.
61 *Meth. Recorder,* 9 Oct. 1902, p. 13.
62 G.R.O. Worship Reg. no. 64476.
63 H.A.D., 234 DAL (2) P (cutting).
64 *Meth. Statistical Return.* i. 7.
65 O.S. Map 1/10,000, TQ 38 SW. (1979 edn.).
66 G.R.O. Worship Reg. no. 17636.
67 H.A.D., TS. catalogue, D/E/234/A.
68 Ibid.; G.R.O. Worship Reg. no. 57812.
69 G.R.O. Worship Reg. no. 20666.
70 *Meth. Recorder,* 9 Oct. 1902, 14.

71 *P.O. Dir. Lond.* (1940, 1946).
72 H.A.D., TS. catalogue, D/E/234/A; G.R.O. Worship Reg. no. 29087. Attendance figs. for 2 Wes. chapels at Hackney Wick are in *Brit. Weekly,* 19 Nov. 1886, p. 4.
73 Para. based on H.A.D., TS. catalogue, D/E/234/A.
74 G.R.O. Worship Reg. no. 28043.
75 Ibid. nos. 30322, 66665.
76 H.A.D., Y54, Vol. IV, p. 21.
77 Above, Rom. Cathm.
78 *Brit. Weekly,* 19 Nov. 1886, p. 4.
79 G.R.O. Worship Reg. no. 31061.
80 *P.O. Dir. Lond.* (1950, 1951).
81 G.R.O. Worship Reg. no. 31090.
82 *P.O. Dir. Lond.* (1951, 1952).
83 *P.O. Dir. Lond. County Suburbs, North* (1894, 1898).
84 G.R.O. Worship Reg. no. 41327.
85 Datestone.   86 G.R.O. Worship Reg. no. 50693.
87 *Meth. Statistical Return.* i. 8.
88 Para. based on *After Twenty-Five Years. Ann. Rep. of Hackney Meth. Mission 1925–50; New Central Hall, Programme of Stone-Laying 1924* (photocopy in H.A.D.); H.A.D., TS. catalogue, D/E/234/A.
89 G.R.O. Worship Reg. no. 49891.
90 *Meth. Statistical Return.* i. 7.

shops retained by mission and converted into place of worship 1982.[91]

CHATSWORTH Road, Clapton Pk. Ch. reg. as new headquarters of Clapton Meth. Union 1958.[92] Bldg. S. of Elderfield Rd., yellow-brick and concrete, seating 200 in 1970.[93]

UNITARIANS.[94] Growing Unitarianism of Old Gravel Pit mtg. formally acknowledged after move under Rob. Aspland (d. 1845) to New Gravel Pit chapel on E. side of Paradise Pl. (later S. part of Chatham Pl.). Octagonal bldg. in Gothic style, 'naked and angular', 1809; repaired 1824, when svces. held in Mermaid inn, and seated 500 in 1851. Attendance 1851: 400 and 28 Sun. sch. a.m., 150 and 28 Sun. sch. evg.[95] Rebuilt in Gothic style and reg. 1858.[96] Bldg. of ragstone with stone dressings in Dec. style: chancel, N. and S. transepts, SW. spirelet.[97] Attendance 1886: 93 a.m., 71 evg.; 1903: 54 a.m., 57 evg. Aspland hall, by R. P. Jones, opened 1913. Ch. damaged 1940, renovated hall used for worship 1946, ch. reopened under part-time min. 1953. Tercentenary of Wm. Bates's mtg. celebrated 1966 but ch. closed 1969 and all bldgs. demol. by G.L.C. 1970. Char. Com. Scheme established fund from sale proceeds and trust funds, used for maintenance of Unitarian chapel at Newington Green.[98] Worshippers inc. economist David Ricardo (d. 1823), theologian Chas. Hennell (d. 1850), and radical politician Daniel Whittle Harvey (d. 1863), first commissioner of Metropolitan Police, who was buried in churchyd.[99] John Boucher (d. 1878) min. 1848–53; Rob. Aspland's s. Rob. Brook Aspland (d. 1869),[1] min. from 1858, was 'practically the head of Eng. Unitarianism'.

BRETHREN. ST. THOMAS'S SQUARE. Group probably mtg. at Ellis's rooms, between nos. 183 and 185 Well Street, 1847 had moved to schoolroom in St. Thos.'s Sq. by 1854. Members inc. Jas. van Sommer, who started Brethren's journal *Missionary Reporter*, his brother-in-law Wm. Berger, and zoologist Phil. Hen. Gosse (d. 1888). 'Open' or independent, rather than 'exclusive,' Brethren after schism of 1848.[2] Moved to Providence chapel (below).

PARAGON ROAD. Providence chapel, originally Pleasant Pl. Meth. chapel and by 1851 Ind. Calvinist,[3] was acquired on lease by Berger 1850s[4] and reg. 1866.[5] Thereafter known as Paragon Rd. mtg. room. Attendance more than 200 in 1870s; 1903: 66 a.m., 93 evg. Compul-

sorily bought by Post Office to make way for telephone exchange 1926.[6] Paragon gospel hall, Morning Lane (former Cong. Old Gravel Pit chapel, used as undenominational mission from 1874), renamed by Brethren and reg. 1926.[7] Damaged in Second World War, whereupon mtgs. held in elder's ho. until new Paragon hall (later chapel) in Glyn Rd. was reg. 1952.[8]

CLAPTON hall, replacing iron hall of 1867, paid for by John Morley and opened on E. side of Alkham Rd. 1880. Among largest of all Brethren's halls, with more than 700 members 1888.[9] Reg. from 1891.[10] Attendance 1903: 286 a.m., 324 evg.

BLURTON hall,[11] N. side of Blurton Rd. near corner of Chatsworth Rd., used by 1884. Attendance 1903: 123 a.m., 95 evg. Normally listed as used by Brethren, before and after its reg. by undesignated Christians 1965.[12]

DOWNHAM ROAD hall, N. side at no. 68, used by 1894. Attendance 1903: 63 a.m., 77 evg. Served as Meth. mission room 1907 after Brethren moved to Bedford hall, no. 54 at corner of Mortimer Rd., which closed c. 1952.

TWEMLOW TERRACE, Lond. Fields. Mission room at no. 6 (later no. 49A Westgate Street) used by 1894. Attendance 1903: 26 a.m., 29 evg. Closed c. 1916.

LONDON FIELDS gospel hall, NW. corner of Lond. Fields, reg. by Bethesda mission 1889–97 and as undenominational 1897–1913.[13] Called West Side gospel hall 1903, when cong. described as Brethren. Attendance 1903: 28 a.m., 27 evg. Later served as League of Helpers' hall.[14]

TOWER (later MARTELLO) gospel hall, E. side of Lond. Fields, used c. 1911–1920. Cong. described as Brethren 1914.[15]

FERRY gospel hall, Little Hill, Upper Clapton. Attendance 1903: 96 evg. Listed as used by Brethren 1914[16] and as undenominational by 1934. Closed c. 1948.

BUCKINGHAM ROAD, Kingsland. Room at rear of no. 27 reg. 1909–12 and again, after replacement by room at rear of no. 6 Kingsland Green 1912–13, 1913–14.[17] Replaced by room at no. 36A Stamford Hill 1914–41.[18]

MABERLY hall, Ball's Pond Rd. Former Cong. chapel, in Islington until 1900,[19] reg. by Brethren 1922–52.[20] Replaced by Maberly (probably former Lond. City mission) hall, Crossway, reg. 1952–86.[21]

FREE ENGLISH CHURCH. ALBION hall, W. side of Albion Sq., Dalston, reg. by 'members

91 *Hackney Gaz.* 12 Apr. 1979, 1; 17 Sept. 1982, 4.
92 G.R.O. Worship Reg. no. 66665.
93 *Meth. Statistical Return.* i. 7.
94 Para. based on A. R. Ruston, *Unitarianism and Early Presbyterianism in Hackney*, 23–4, 30–8.
95 P.R.O., HO 129/11/4/1/13, which says chapel blt. 1812.   96 G.R.O. Worship Reg. no. 8264.
97 H.A.D., P 10510.
98 *V.C.H. Mdx.* viii. 213.   99 *D.N.B.*
1 Ibid.
2 *Jnl. of Christian Brethren Research Fellowship*, xxi. 34, 42 n.; F. R. Coad, *Hist. of Brethren Movement* (1968), 159, 166; *D.N.B.* s.v. Gosse.
3 P.R.O., HO 129/11/4/1/11.
4 D. J. Beattie, *Brethren, Story of a Great Recovery* (1940), 80.   5 G.R.O. Worship Reg. no. 17266.
6 Beattie, *Brethren*, 80, 82.

7 Ibid. 84; G.R.O. Worship Reg. no. 50452.
8 *Jnl. of Christian Brethren Research Fellowship*, xxi. 34; G.R.O. Worship Reg. no. 62766.
9 Beattie, *Brethren*, 82; Coad, *Hist. Brethren*, 174.
10 G.R.O. Worship Reg. no. 32721.
11 Following accounts of Brethren's halls based on *P.O. Dirs. Lond., Lond. Suburban, North*, and *Lond. County Suburbs* (1880 and later edns.).
12 G.R.O. Worship Reg. no. 69947.
13 Ibid. nos. 31334, 36282.   14 Below, undenom.
15 Harris and Bryant, *Chs. and Lond.* 393.
16 Ibid.
17 G.R.O. Worship Reg. nos. 43562, 45083, 45659.
18 Ibid. no. 46123.
19 *V.C.H. Mdx.* viii. 104; H.A.D., TS. catalogue, D/E/233/MAB/1.   20 G.R.O. Worship Reg. no. 48656.
21 Ibid. no. 63565.

of the Free Ch.' 1859 and by 'English Free Ch.' 1861.[22] Sect was presumably Free Ch. of Eng., which used slightly amended Bk. of Common Prayer and whose bp. had ch. at Teddington.[23] Albion hall was Bapt. by 1875.[24]

CHRIST CHURCH, near the Triangle, Cambridge Heath, reg. 1861, disused by 1866.[25]

HOLY TRINITY ch., the Triangle, Mare Street, reg. 1864, closed between 1880 and 1884.[26]

CLAPTON PARK. Bldg. occupied by Chas. Geary, no. 6 Clarke's Terr., Pratt's Lane (later Glyn Rd.), reg. 1878–96.[27]

ST. ANDREW'S ch., Chatsworth Rd., reg. by 'reformed Episcopal Ch.' 1892–4.[28]

CHRIST'S mission ch., Rushmore Rd., reg. by 'Reformed Ch. of Eng.' 1894–1913.[29]

DALSTON. No. 1 Colvestone Cres. reg. 1900–13.[30]

ST. ANDREW'S ch., Robinson's Retreat, Retreat Pl., reg. 1934–7.[31]

PRESBYTERIANS. DALSTON Presb. ch. Iron ch. built on Rhodes land on S. side of Shrubland Rd. 1858, reg. by Presb. Ch. of Eng. 1863.[32] Cong. by 1871. Bldg., with lancet windows and spirelet, acquired by Evangelical and Reformed Ch. c. 1970.[33]

DOWNS PARK ROAD ch., Lower Clapton. Presb. Ch. of Eng. reg. ch. at corner of Cricketfield Rd. 1872 and 1877–1936.[34] Bldg. of Kentish rag with stone dressings in Dec. style, seating 630 in 1872, begun 1863:[35] apsidal chancel, NE. and SE. chapels, N. transept over hall, aisled and clerestoreyed nave, S. porch, pinnacled SW. tower with spire.[36] Attendance 1886: 111 a.m., 60 evg.; 1903: 114 a.m., 143 evg. Closed and reopened for Lower Clapton Cong. ch. 1936. Later used by New Testament Ch. of God.[37]

ALBION Presb. ch. (formerly at Albion ch., Lond. Wall) advertised svces. at St. Thos.'s hall, E. side of St. Thos.'s Rd., 1875.[38] Presb. chapel and ch. ho., recorded 1894,[39] presumably replaced by St. Thos.'s Sq. ch. (below).

ST. THOMAS'S SQUARE. Presb. Ch. of Eng. reg. former Cong. ch. 1896–1912.[40] Attendance 1903: 67 a.m., 83 evg. Bldg. used as cinema 1913.[41]

LATTER-DAY SAINTS. CHURCH STREET lecture hall reg. 1854–66.[42]

JOHN STREET chapel, Shacklewell, reg. 1856–96.[43]

Two Mormon elders from U.S.A. held regular mtgs. at Chatsworth Rd. Meth. ch. 1977.[44]

SALVATION ARMY. CONGRESS HALL, Linscott Rd., Lower Clapton, opened and reg. 1882.[45] Bldg., formerly Lond. Orphan Asylum, adapted by demol. of chapel and excavation of quadrangle, roofed over to create hall seating 4,700. Wings formed training barracks for 150 men and 150 women cadets, with classrooms on ground floor, work rooms below, and bedrooms above.[46] Attendance largest at any place of worship in Hackney 1903: 914 a.m., 1,635 evg. Huge crowds at lying-in-state of 'Army Mother' Cath. Booth 1890 and of founder Gen. Wm. Booth 1912. Renovated 1931.[47] Most of bldg. demol. after army's move to Clapton Congress hall (below) 1970, but façade survived 1988.

CLAPTON CONGRESS HALL, no. 122 Lower Clapton Rd. Brown-brick hall and hostel by Alex. Dalziel, replacing Congress hall, Linscott Rd., opened 1970.[48]

MISSIONS. People's hall, Havelock Rd., Well Street, reg. by Christian Mission of army 1880–97.[49] Perhaps same as later premises in Havelock Rd. Attendance 1903: 66 a.m., 72 evg. Citadel in rd. reg. 1908–41.[50] Clapton Pk. theatre, Glenarm Rd., reg. 1881.[51] Probably taken over by Meths. as forerunner of Clapton Pk. tabernacle (above). Nisbet Street, Homerton, barracks reg. 1888–96.[52]

High Street, Homerton, barracks at no. 97 reg. 1889–96.[53] Perhaps same as later premises in High Street. Attendance 1903: 48 a.m., 149 evg. Hall behind no. 98 reg. 1910–80.[54] Durham Grove, barracks reg. 1892–1903.[55] Mallard Street, Hackney Wick, barracks at no. 34, reg. 1892–1911.[56] Attendance 1903: 35 a.m., 57 evg. Replaced by Hedgers Grove hall (below). Kingsland Rd., hall, at no. 383, reg. 1893–1931.[57] Havelock Rd., Well Street, hall recorded 1894.[58] The Temple, Almack Rd., Lower Clapton. Bldg. behind Congress hall reg. 1895–1971.[59] Attendance 1903: 105 a.m., 124 evg. Ball's Pond Rd., barracks at no. 83, reg. 1898–1911.[60] Attendance 1903: 55 a.m., 115 evg. Rossington Street, Upper Clapton, mission ho. reg. 1903–64.[61] Cambridge Heath citadel, Mare Street, reg. 1908–57. Presumably Mare Street premises with attendance 1903: 249 a.m., 459 evg. Bombed in Second World War. Yellow-brick and concrete

22 G.R.O. Worship Reg. nos. 8869, 11959.
23 V.C.H. Mdx. iii. 80.
24 Above, Bapts.
25 G.R.O. Worship Reg. no. 14238.
26 Ibid. no. 16320; P.O. Dir. Lond. County Suburbs, North (1880, 1884).
27 G.R.O. Worship Reg. no. 24249.
28 Ibid. no. 33080.
29 Ibid. no. 34575.
30 Ibid. no. 37880.
31 Ibid. no. 54980.
32 Terrier, Summer 1992; G.R.O. Worship Reg. no. 15488; above, Congs.
33 Below, other denom.
34 G.R.O. Worship Reg. nos. 21047, 23385.
35 Hackney Dir. (1872), which says built 1871; datestone has 1863.
36 H.A.D., Y54, Vol. II, pp. 21, 23.
37 G.R.O. Worship Reg. no. 56988; below, other denom.
38 Hackney Gaz. 2 Jan. 1875, 1.
39 P.O. Dir. Lond. County Suburbs, North (1894).
40 G.R.O. Worship Reg. no. 35491.
41 Clarke, Hackney, 290 n.
42 G.R.O. Worship Reg. no. 5288.
43 Ibid. no. 7556.
44 Hackney Gaz. 7 Apr. 1977, 4.
45 G.R.O. Worship Reg. no. 26277.
46 The Times, 15 May 1882, 8f.
47 D.N.B. s.vv. Booth, Cath.; Booth, Wm.; H. V. Rohu, 'Short Hist. of Congress Hall (TS. in H.A.D.).
48 G.R.O. Worship Reg. no. 72274; War Cry, 25 July 1970, 7
49 G.R.O. Worship Reg. no. 25304.
50 Ibid. no. 43303.
51 Ibid. no. 25559.
52 Ibid. no. 30845.
53 Ibid. no. 31755.
54 Ibid. no. 44403.
55 Ibid. no. 33405.
56 Ibid. no. 33422.
57 Ibid. no. 33739.
58 P.O. Dir. Lond. County Suburbs, North (1894).
59 G.R.O. Worship Reg. no. 34922.
60 Ibid. no. 36923.
61 Ibid. no. 39986.

hall by Wm. Charles opened 1957.[62] Clapton Common, no. 4 (formerly W. Springfield) acquired as training coll. *c.* 1909 and as Army's maternity home *c.* 1922–50.[63] Hedgers Grove, Cassland Rd., hall reg. 1911–20.[64] Middlesex Wharf, Lea Bridge, hall reg. 1925–41.[65] Lawrence Bldgs., Northwold Rd., hall reg. 1935.[66] Florence Booth hall, Valette St., reg. 1947.[67]

GERMAN LUTHERAN CHURCH.[68] Site on S. side of Alma (later Ritson) Rd., ch., and minister's ho. paid for by compensation from Metropolitan Dist. Rly. Co., which had bought old Hamburg Lutheran ch. in Gt. Trinity Lane (Lond.). Bldg. of yellow brick with stone dressings in Dec. or 'German Gothic' style, seating 280, by Habershon & Brock 1875–6:[69] chancel, N. and S. transepts, aisleless nave; (probably later) tower with broach spire next to S. transept; not oriented. Reredos, attributed to Grinling Gibbons, and organ from old ch. Partly served adjacent hosp.,[70] whose chapel was converted into a ward, and other German homes. Attendance 1886: 120 evg.; 1903: 86 a.m., 132 evg. Hall added to E. wing 1899, enlarged as Luther hall 1932. Pentecostal 1983.[71]

AGAPEMONITES.[72] Ch. of the Ark of the Covenant at corner of Rookwood and Castlewood rds., N. end of Clapton common, reg. by 'Ch. of the Son of Man' 1896,[73] followers of Hen. Jas. Prince (d. 1899), who had Agapemone or Abode of Love at Spaxton (Som.).[74] Bldg. of Bristol stone with Portland stone dressings and spire in eclectically ornamental Gothic style, seating *c.* 400, by J. Morris of Reading 1893–5: apse, aisleless nave, W. tower with symbols of 4 Evangelists in place of pinnacles at base of spire, other sculptures at corners of ch. Ornate interior, with hammerbeam roof, mosaic wall in sanctuary, and stained glass, illustrating woman's submission to man, by Wal. Crane. Scene of enthronement of Prince's successor John Hugh Smyth-Pigott as second Messiah, attended by hostile crowd, 1902. Ch., a tribute to sect's early wealth, probably not long used for regular svces.[75] and closed 1920s. Ownership doubtful 1955.[76] Acquired by Ancient Cath. Ch. (below).

JEHOVAH'S WITNESSES. KINGDOM hall, no. 383 Kingsland Rd., reg. 1944–54.[77]

KINGDOM hall, ground-floor room at no. 72A Woodland St., Dalston, reg. 1949 and 1972. Moved to Pitfield St., Shoreditch, 1974 and to rear of nos. 1–7 Fassett Rd., Dalston, 1974.[78]

PENTECOSTALS. ASSEMBLIES OF GOD reg. Hampden chapel, Lauriston Rd. (formerly Bapt.) 1928.[79]

ANGLO-WEST INDIAN ASSEMBLY (later EVANGELICAL REFORMED CHURCH) reg. by Pentecostals at nos. 2, 4, and 6 Sandringham Rd. 1961. Reg. again in Lauriston Rd. 1989.[80]

SHILOH PENTECOSTAL ch., previously worshipping in St. Luke's ch. hall, Morning Lane, took lease of Ashwin Street Bapt. ch. 1968 and bought bldg. 1976.[81]

UNITED PENTECOSTAL CHURCH OF GOD reg. at no. 16 Rossendale Street, Clapton, 1977.[82]

CLAPTON PENTECOSTAL ch. reg. at no. 171 Rushmore Rd. 1977.[83]

HACKNEY PENTECOSTAL APOSTOLIC ch. (formerly MIDDLETON RD. CONG. ch.) used by W. Indian Fellowship 1979[84] and reg. 'as heretofore for worship by Pentecostals' 1982.[85]

FAITH TABERNACLE CHURCH OF GOD acquired and began to worship in former German Lutheran ch., Ritson Rd., 1982,[86] where Ch. had international headquarters 1989.

REFUGE TEMPLE OF CHURCHES OF JESUS CHRIST (APOSTOLIC) reg. room at no. 109 Brooke Rd. 1987.[87]

OTHER DENOMINATIONS. FREE CHURCH reg. bldg. at corner of Albert (later part of Middleton) and Lansdowne rds., Lond. Fields, 1860-4.[88]

CHRISTIANS (unspecified) reg. no. 199 Richmond Rd., Dalston, 1863–96.[89]

INDEPENDENTS reg. St. Thos.'s hall, St. Thos.'s Rd., 1864. Used by former Anglican curate J. Allen, on doubtful authority, for svces. like those at Ram's chapel 1869.[90]

EVANGELICAL FREE CHURCH reg. Christ Ch., at corner of Amhurst and Rectory rds., 1876–86.[91]

CHURCH OF MARTIN LUTHER, Speldhurst Rd., reg. by Evangelical Christians 1887–1941.[92] Attendance 1886: 212 a.m., 351 evg.; 1903: 21 a.m., 37 evg.

GOSPEL hall, Wellington Rd., reg. by sect refusing to be designated 1888–1903.[93]

BROTHERHOOD church, Southgate Rd., reg. 1897 in Cong. ch. (above)[94] for mtg. formed 1891 by John Bruce Wallace, who preached mixture of Christianity and Marxism and opened food

[62] Ibid. nos. 43267, 66451. *War Cry*, 5 Oct. 1957, 3
[63] H.A.D., D/F/BAG/1, p. 103; *Kelly's Dir. Stoke Newington, Stamford Hill, and Clapton* (1909–10, 1921, 1922); P.O. Dir. Lond. (1950).
[64] G.L.R.O. Worship Reg. no. 44789.
[65] Ibid. no. 49826.   [66] Ibid. no. 56174.
[67] Ibid. no. 61699.
[68] Para. based on *Hackney Gaz.* 8 May 1875, 3.
[69] G.R.O. Worship Reg. no. 22959; *List of Bldgs.* (1988).
[70] Above, pub. svces.   [71] Below, Pentecostals.
[72] Para. based on *Cathedral Ch. of the Good Shepherd* (booklet *c.* 1953 in H.A.D.); D. McCormick, *Temple of Love* (1962), 69–70, 169; C. Mander, *Revd. Prince and his Abode of Love* (1976), 134, 137–8.
[73] G.R.O. Worship Reg. no. 35401.
[74] *V.C.H. Som.* vi. 124.
[75] Not recorded in Mudie-Smith, *Rel. Life.* The Agapemone in Som. became a girls' reformatory in 1920s:

Mander, *Revd. Prince*, 141. Above, plates 53 and 56.
[76] H.A.D., H/LD 7/24, pp.182, 193–4.
[77] G.R.O. Worship Reg. no. 60684.
[78] Ibid. nos. 62429, 73206, 73619, 73788.
[79] Ibid. no. 51153; *Tower to Tower Block*, no. 33.
[80] G.R.O. Worship Reg. nos. 68059, 68066–8, 77948.
[81] Ibid. no. 71889; inf. from Revd. W. P. Ryan.
[82] G.R.O. Worship Reg. no. 74716.
[83] Ibid. no. 74803.
[84] *Hackney Gaz.* 20 Apr. 1979, 10.
[85] G.R.O. Worship Reg. no. 76175.
[86] Inf. from Bp. R. Thomas; ch. reg. 1983: G.R.O., Worship Reg. no. 76317.   [87] G.R.O. Worship Reg. no. 77459
[88] Ibid. no. 9472   [89] Ibid. no 15707
[90] Ibid. no. 16412; *Hackney Gaz.* 11 Sept. 1869, 1; 25 Sept. 1869, 4   [91] G.R.O. Worship Reg. no. 23104.
[92] Ibid. no. 30310.   [93] Ibid. no. 31251.
[94] Ibid. no. 35958.

co-operative in Downham Rd.[95] Continued sometimes to be described as Cong. Closed between 1935 and 1938.[96]

THE SANCTUARY, nos. 2 and 4 Cassland Rd., reg. by 'King's Cross Higher Life Mission' 1892–4. Reg. again by Christians 1894, closed c. 1902.[97]

CHRISTIAN SCIENTISTS reg. rooms at no. 43A Stamford Hill 1910.[98] Comprised reading room and, in 1912, Fourth Ch. of Christ Scientist, both at Stamford hall. Closed c. 1914.[99]

CHRISTIAN TULIPEANS reg. Tulip hall, on ground floor of no. 55 King Edward's Rd., 1941–67. Replaced by Tulip hall on ground floor of no. 64 Holly Street, Dalston, reg. 1967–85.[1]

SPIRITUALISTS reg. Kenton hall, Kenton Rd., 1954–64.[2]

CHRISTIANS (undesignated) reg. rooms at no. 28 Alcester Cres. as 'Baltic Svce.' 1962.[3]

NEW TESTAMENT CHURCH OF GOD reg. former Presb. ch. in Downs Pk. Rd. 1964.[4]

EVANGELICAL AND REFORMED CHURCH occupied former Cong. ch. in Shrubland Rd. from c. 1970.[5]

FIRST DEEPER LIFE MINISTRY reg. basement at nos. 101–7 Chatsworth Rd. 1984–6 and, as Deeper Life Ministries International, no. 1 Sandringham Rd. 1986.[6]

CHURCH OF THE CALL OUT reg. room at no. 9 Urswick Rd. 1985.[7]

UNDENOMINATIONAL MISSIONS. Christian Mission hall reg. in Loddiges Rd. (presumably distinct from later Loddiges Rd. Bapt. chapel) 1874–1906.[8] Attendance 1886, when described as 'Christian Ch.': 37 a.m., 43 evg.

Christian Mission hall in Stoke Newington High Street reg. 1875–96.[9]

Old Gravel Pit chapel,[10] Chatham Pl., vacated by Congs. who moved to Clapton Pk. 1871. Taken for 'new Independent ch.'[11] under Revd. J. De Kewer Williams 1874,[12] reg. 1875, and again sometimes listed as Cong.[13] Attendance 1886: 309 a.m., 297 evg. Lease acquired for Old Gravel Pit undenom. mission, by young men who formed Sick and Provident soc. 1888 and reg. mission 1898,[14] survived until 1969.[15] Attendance 1903: 245 a.m., 364 evg. On expiry of lease name was transferred to new bldg. at corner of Valette Street and Morning Lane, called Old Gravel Pit hall, 1913. Valette Street hall was taken for rd. widening and Trelawney est. 1959. Old Gravel Pit office was opened in new bldg. in Morning Lane 1961 but mission was liquidated 1971. Chapel in Chatham Pl. survived as part of factory, with plaque to commemorate Jos. Priestley 1985.[16]

Bruce hall, Lyme Grove, reg. for mission 1885–97. Bruce hall, Havelock Rd., reg. by unsectarian Christians 1897–1906.[17] Attendance 1903: 241 evg. Bruce hall mission, founded as Hackney juvenile mission 1871,[18] was in Chatham Pl. c. 1908–20.

League of Helpers' hall (formerly Bethesda mission, then London Fields gospel, hall),[19] West Side, Lond. Fields, reg. by undesignated Christians 1913–46 and by London Fields fellowship 1946–64.[20]

London City Mission had Kingsland mission hall on S. side of Castle Street (later Crossway) by 1880; reg. 1930–52.[21] Attendance 1903: 71 evg. Also had hall at no. 1 Hassett Rd. by 1888; reg. 1900–13.[22] Attendance 1903: 129 evg.

Morley hall, the Triangle, Mare Street, was reg. for unsectarian worship 1901–25.[23] Attendance 1903: 175 evg. Welsh svces. also held there 1903, attendance 31 evg.

Kingsland Gospel mission was presumably at hall, no. 493 Kingsland Rd., reg. 1908–41.[24] Attendance 1903: 26 a.m., 39 evg.

Brunswick hall free gospel mission, S. side of Retreat Pl. Attendance 1903: 23 a.m., 47 evg. Closed c. 1950.[25]

OTHER CHRISTIAN CHURCHES

CATHOLIC APOSTOLIC CHURCH. Ch. on E. side of Mare Street at no. 184, next to Lady Holles sch. (later part of Cordwainers' coll.), reg. 1874.[26] Bldg. of yellow brick with white-brick and stone dressings in Dec. style: aisled nave, shallow transepts, flèche over crossing. Attendance 1886: 227 a.m., 168 evg.; 1903: 199 a.m., 213 evg. Still listed as Cath. Apostolic in 1964 but served as Greek Orthodox ch. of St. John the Theologian from 1966.[27]

ANCIENT CATHOLIC CHURCH. Former Agapemonite ch. (above) leased 1956 to Harold Percival Nicholson, who, as abp. of Karim, perhaps already used it as his cathedral ch. of the Good Shepherd. Ch., which had premises in Lower Sloane Street, Chelsea, claimed to be older than Rom. Cath. Ch. by virtue of descent from Syrian Orthodox Ch. at Antioch. Spiritual healing practised in Clapton bldg., where chapel for animals also opened.[28]

95 *Cong. Year Bk.* (1895); B. Burke and K Worpole, *Hackney Propaganda* (1980), 31.   96 Above, Congs.
97 G.R.O. Worship Reg. nos. 33550, 34580; *P.O. Dir. Lond.* (1901, 1903)   98 G.R.O. Worship Reg. no. 44580.
99 *P.O. Dir Lond. County Suburbs* (1911–15).
1 G.R.O. Worship Reg. nos. 59734, 70844.
2 Ibid. no. 64243.   3 Ibid. no. 68862.
4 Ibid. no. 69522.
5 H.A.D., P 4877–9; *P.O. Dir. Lond.* (1969, 1970).
6 G.R.O. Worship reg. nos. 76563, 77190.
7 Ibid. no. 76929.   8 Ibid. no. 21929.
9 Ibid. no. 22252.
10 Para. based on C. M. Gardner, 'Old Gravel Pit Sick and Provident Soc.' (TS. 1972 in H.A.D.).
11 *Hackney Gaz.* 24 Apr. 1875, 3.
12 G.R.O. Worship Reg. no. 22427.

13 e.g. *Cong. Year Bk.* (1875 and later edns.). Williams did not use the term 'Congregational'.
14 G.R.O. Worship Reg. no. 36547.
15 H.A.D., D/S/22/69.
16 Clarke, *Hackney*, 291 n.; *Hackney and Stoke Newington Past*, 74.   17 G.R.O. Worship Reg. nos. 28709, 36344.
18 *Burdett's Hosp. Annual* (1910)
19 Above, Brethren.
20 G.R.O. Worship Reg. nos. 45653, 61500.
21 Ibid. no. 52379.   22 Ibid. no. 37760.
23 Ibid. no. 38580.   24 Ibid. no. 43221.
25 *P.O. Dir. Lond.* (1949, 1950).
26 Clarke, *Hackney*, 28; G.R.O. Worship Reg. no. 21971.
27 *P.O. Dir. Lond.* (1964); below, Greek Orthodox Ch.
28 *Cathedral Ch. of Good Shepherd* (booklet c. 1953 in H.A.D.), 3–6; H.A.D., H/LD 7/4, p. 194.

GREEK ORTHODOX CHURCH. Former Cath. Apostolic ch. (above) at no. 184 Mare Street opened as Greek Orthodox ch. of St. John the Theologian 1966; reg. 1986. Bldg. seated c. 250 in 1988, when ch. also ran Greek language sch. and Sun. sch.[29]

JUDAISM

Jews were among the Londoners who bought property in Hackney,[30] the first recorded purchase by a Jew being that of a house in Homerton by Isaac Alvares, a jeweller, in 1674. Jacob Alvares alias Alvaro da Fonseca, not known to have been a relation, left Clapton in 1716 and soon acquired the estate between Mare Street and London Fields which his descendants held for nearly a century.[31] Moses Silva and Jacob Cohen were already in Mare Street, as was Benjamin Mendes da Costa from 1727 until he moved to Homerton near his brother Jacob and Gabriel Lopes Pinheiro. Fonseca, Pinheiro, and the da Costas convinced the magistrates in 1733 that they had been rated more highly than 'other gentlemen in as good or better circumstances'.[32] They and others were Sephardim mostly of Iberian origin, who were elected to parish and manorial offices from which they often paid to be excused. Benjamin Mendes da Costa and Jacob de Moses Franco were among the first members of the Jewish Board of Deputies in 1760,[33] when every member of the London *Mahammed* had a house in Hackney. The Francos' lessee Israel Levin Salomons between 1779 and 1781 spent lavishly on a building which in 1799 formed a 'chapel or private synagogue' at Clapton House.[34]

In 1786 land east of Grove Street (later Lauriston Road) was sold to Leon Gompertz and other Ashkenazim acting for the Germans' Hambro synagogue, one of whose overseers was Israel Salomons. The land, including buildings and once part of that occupied by Sarah Tyssen (d. 1779), widow of Samuel,[35] was used for burials by 1788[36] and until the closure of the Hambro synagogue in Great St. Helen's (Lond.) in 1892.[37] The disused ground survived in 1990.

Stamford Hill[38] claimed eminent Jewish residents from the time of the Italian-born Moses Vita Montefiore (d. 1789), who was there by 1763.[39] His son Joseph (d. 1804) married Rachel Mocatta and his grandson Abraham Montefiore (d. 1824) married Henrietta, whose father the financier Nathan Meyer Rothschild (d. 1836)[40] lived from 1818 to 1835 near the later Colberg Place. The Montefiores' property, a little farther south, was to be turned by Abraham's grandson Claude Montefiore into Montefiore House school.[41] With the spread of building, such distinguished families moved away: in 1842 there were few of the wealthy Jews who had once settled in Hackney.[42]

Increasing immigration from London had by c. 1880 brought perhaps 5,000 Jews to Hackney, Dalston, and neighbouring parts of Islington.[43] Thence the more prosperous tended to move farther north to Stamford Hill, Highbury, and Stoke Newington, while southern Hackney received an overspill from Stepney and Bethnal Green.[44] In 1895 Hackney synagogue served a district 'thickly populated by the better class of Jewish working man', and in 1902 settlement in Dalston or Canonbury was 'among the first steps upwards of the Whitechapel Jew'.[45] Attendances on the first day in Passover week, 1903, totalled 1,274.[46] Moving from London to Dalston and Stoke Newington was encouraged by the Four Per Cent Industrial Dwellings Co.[47]

Bolstered by arrivals from Russia and Poland, from central Europe, from parts of London cleared for rehousing or by bombing, and finally by survivors of the east European holocaust, North London's Jewry may have reached 40,000 by 1929, 50,000 by 1938, and 100,000 by 1950. A recognition that the area was seen as likely to become more important than London's East End was the transfer of the New Synagogue to Stamford Hill in 1915.[48] Both the rector of Hackney and the vicar of St. Thomas's, Stamford Hill, claimed in 1931 that any moneyed residents were likely to be Jews.[49]

A statement that Hackney in the early 1950s had the largest and densest Jewish population in the country assumed that Hackney included Stoke Newington's Woodberry Down estate.[50] Two estates in Amhurst Road alone, however, contained 1,500 to 2,000 working-class Jews, while half of the boys at Hackney Downs school were Jewish. Some families prospered and, as before, moved away, with the result that less than a third of the school's boys were Jewish by 1972, many newcomers being Afro-Caribbean immigrants.[51]

[29] Inf. from priest in charge; G.R.O. Worship Reg. no. 77032; below, educ. (special schs.).
[30] Para. based on *Jewish Hist. Soc. Trans.* xxx. 71–89.
[31] Above, manors (Alvares).
[32] G.L.R.O., P79/JN1/214, p. 80.
[33] A. M. Hyamson, *Sephardim of Eng.* (1951), 125–6, 135.
[34] *Jewish Hist. Soc. Trans.* xxxi. 193–6; above, manors (Clapton Ho.).
[35] G.L.R.O., M79/LH/17, p. 59; Robinson, *Hackney*, i. 210.
[36] Lysons, *Environs*, ii. 480.
[37] V. D. Lipman, *Social Hist. of Jews in Eng. 1850–1950* (1954), 130; B. Holmes, *Lond. Burial Grounds* (1896), 157.
[38] Para. based on M. Bernstein, *Stamford Hill and the Jews bef. 1815* (1976), 17–20; *Jewish Hist. Soc. Trans.* xxx. 81–3.
[39] G.L.R.O., M79/LH/41.

[40] *D.N.B.*
[41] Below, educ. (private schs.).
[42] Robinson, *Hackney*, i. 210.
[43] Lipman, *Social Hist. of Jews*, 77, 169.
[44] *Jewish Hist. Soc. Trans.* xxi. 86–8.
[45] Bernstein, *Stamford Hill and Jews*, 34; Booth, *Life and Labour*, iii (1), 152.
[46] Mudie-Smith, *Rel. Life*, 67.
[47] H. Pearman, *Excellent Accn.* (1985), 82; *V.C.H. Mdx.* viii. 170.
[48] B. A. Kosmin and N. Grizzard, *Jews in an Inner Lond. Suburb* (1975), 32; Lipman, *Social Hist. of Jews*, 158, 169–70.
[49] Nat. Soc. files.
[50] Kosmin and Grizzard, *Jews in Lond. Suburb*, 33; *V.C.H. Mdx.* viii. 150.
[51] Kosmin and Grizzard, *Jews in Lond. Suburb*, 33; G. Alderman, *Hist. Hackney Downs Sch.* (1972), 79.

Remarkable growth took place at Stamford Hill, partly in consequence of the establishment in 1926 of the Union of Orthodox Hebrew Congregations, most of whose constituents were affiliated to the Adath Yisroel Synagogue, in Stoke Newington.[52] Schools and other institutions followed[53] and, after the Second World War, ultra-orthodox Hassidic or Chassidic sects, which had little save some practical educational contact with the older, declining, synagogues. In 1977 c. 2,500 strictly observant families, of whom over half were Chassidim proper, attended c. 35 conventicles, either a *shtibl* (little room) or *beth hamedrash* (house of study), within Stamford Hill's 'square mile of piety'. Chassidic groups, deriving their names from places in eastern Europe, had multiplied through secession, the main ones being the Belzer, themselves divided, the Gerer, the Satmarer, the Bobover, the Vishnitzer, and the Lubavitcher. Rapid progress was claimed by the American-based Lubavitch movement,[54] also known as Chabad, which administered its own schools and many activities from its Foundation at no. 107 Stamford Hill.[55] In 1991 the area remained distinctively Jewish, with schools, study centres, specialized shops, and residents in traditional clothes, which had been tested for acceptability in the Shaatnez research laboratory.[56]

The earliest public services were those of Dalston synagogue (below), which later moved west, in 1874. A *minyan* or small group, sometimes claimed as a forerunner of Hackney synagogue, had worshipped in Hackney Road East, Bethnal Green, in 1862 but failed to find permanent accommodation.[57]

The following abbreviations are used: Fed., Federation; reg., registered; syn., synagogue; Utd., United.

DALSTON SYNAGOGUE, for those too far from North London syn. in Barnsbury, began 1874 at Colvestone Ho., Ridley Rd. Synagogue opened in Birkbeck Rd. in 1874 but moved 1876 to a new iron bldg. at no. 120 Mildmay Rd., Islington, while keeping old name.[58]

HACKNEY SYNAGOGUE began 1881 at no. 43 Darnley Rd., moved 1885 to Dalston's vacated premises in Mildmay Rd. and back to Hackney 1892 as South Hackney synagogue in Devonshire (from 1938 Brenthouse) Rd.[59] Constituent of Utd. Syn. from 1897, with 352 seat-holders

1910; renamed Hackney 1936.[60] Red-brick building, designed by Delissa Joseph, consecrated 1897 and again after enlargement 1936, seated c. 1,000 1991.[61]

STOKE NEWINGTON SYNAGOGUE began 1887 at no. 23 Alvington Crescent as New Dalston syn., which was opposed by Dalston. Moved 1888 to Birkbeck Rd. and belonged by 1896 to Fed. of Syn.[62] New bldg., renamed, opened 1903 on site of Limes in Shacklewell Lane as constituent of Utd. Syn., with 434 seat-holders 1910. Amalgamated with Dalston syn. 1967 and closed c. 1976.[63] Ornate bldg. of red brick with stone dressings, designed by Lewis Solomon.[64] Served as mosque 1990.[65]

MONTAGUE ROAD BETH HAMEDRASH began 1902. Belonged to Fed. of Syn., reg. 1919 at no. 62 and again 1934 and 1935. Syn. had 200 members 1918 and closed between 1980 and 1985.[66] Octagonal bldg., with red-brick façade, used by Dalston Community Centre Project 1992.

WEST HACKNEY SYNAGOGUE began 1903 as Wellington Rd. syn. at no. 23A, formerly Shacklewell Baptist chapel. Belonged 1939 to Fed. of Syn. (when rd. renamed Shacklewell Rd.), reg. again 1950 at no. 233A Amhurst Road and soon renamed;[67] 'typical Fed. syn.' 1975,[68] an affiliated member 1990.[69]

YAVNEH SYNAGOGUE began 1904, presumably as North-East Lond. Beth Hamedrash recorded first at no. 47 Victoria Pk. Rd. and reg. 1909 as unnamed *beth hamedrash* at no. 25 St. Thomas's (later Ainsworth) Rd. As South Hackney syn. 1930 and North-East Lond. Beth Hamedrash 1939 it belonged to Fed. of Syn. and as Yavneh, reg. 1966, it was a constituent member 1990,[70] when the stuccoed bldg., once St. Thos.'s hall, survived.

THE NEW SYNAGOGUE, one of Lond.'s three 18th-cent. Ashkenazi syn., was re-erected 1915 in Egerton Rd., Stamford Hill.[71] Ample premises served several organizations 1930 but advance of Chassidim left it 'only as a residuary legatee' of Utd. Syn. 1977, a constituent member in 1990.[72] Bldg. in Grt. St. Helen's since 1838 was reproduced in red brick with bold stone dressings by Ernest M. Joseph, with addition of tetrastyle Doric portico, and connected by loggia to contemporary sch.[73]

DALSTON TALMUD TORAH,[74] founded 1909, was at no. 62 Montague Rd. 1918–19, at no. 141 Amhurst Rd. 1920, and in addition at no. 187 by 1930. Dalston Fed. syn. and Talmud Torah

52 *Jewish Year Bk.* (1939); *V.C.H. Mdx.* viii. 216.
53 Yesodey Hatorah and Lubavitch Ho.: below, educ. (private schs.).
54 *Jewish Chron. Colour Mag.* 27 May 1977.
55 Ibid. 8 June 1979.
56 Ibid. 27 May 1977; *Jewish Year Bk.* (1990).
57 *Jewish Hist. Soc. Trans.* xxi. 86.
58 Ibid.; J. Rabbinowitz, *Hist. Sketch of Dalston Syn.* (1935), 9–10; *V.C.H. Mdx.* viii. 117.
59 Lipman, *Social Hist. of Jews*, 158.
60 A. Newman, *United Syn. 1870–1970* (1976), 216.
61 *Jewish Year Bk.* (1990); G.R.O. Worship Reg. nos. 33066, 56873; inf. from sec.
62 Bernstein, *Stamford Hill and Jews*, 34; *Jewish Year Bk.* (1896–7).
63 H.A.D., M 3230, p. 74; Lipman, *Social Hist. of Jews*, 158; Newman, *United Syn.* 168, 216.
64 Datestone; *Hackney Photos.* i. 79.

65 Below, Islam.
66 *Jewish Year Bk.* (1918 and later edns.); G.R.O. Worship Reg. nos. 47524, 55026, 56290.
67 H.A.D., M 3230, p. 56; *Jewish Year Bk.* (1939 and later edns.); G.R.O. Worship Reg. nos. 39524, 62752; datestone.
68 Kosmin and Grizzard, *Jews in Lond. Suburb*, 33.
69 *Jewish Year Bk.* (1990).
70 Ibid. (1905–6 and later edns.); G.R.O., Worship Reg. nos. 43606, 70513.
71 *V.C.H. Mdx.* i. 149; Lipman, *Social Hist. of Jews*, 158; G.R.O. Worship Reg. no. 46435; *Jewish Year Bk.* (1930).
72 *Jewish Year Bk.* (1939 and later edns.); *Jewish Chron. Colour Mag.* 27 May 1977.
73 Above, plate 57; *List of Bldgs.* (1991).
74 Rest of section based on *Jewish Year Bk.* (1904–5 and later edns.).

were reg. at no. 213 Amhurst Rd. 1935 and were at nos. 213 and 215 by 1939 and until *c.* 1975.[75]

STAMFORD HILL BETH HAMEDRASH may have been congregation at no. 35 Clapton Common 1914[76] and reg. at no. 26 Grove Lane (from 1938 Lampard Grove) 1918 and 1936.[77] Belonged to Fed. of Syn. 1930, when it included Stamford Hill Talmud Torah at no. 116 Stamford Hill; moved to no. 50 Clapton Common after 1960.

SANDRINGHAM ROAD SYNAGOGUE reg. 1917–41 at no. 1 as a *beth hamedrash.*[78] Belonged to Fed. of Syn. and also known as Schiff's Beth Hamedrash 1930, 1939.

CLAPTON FEDERATION SYNAGOGUE or Sha'are Shomayim began 1919 and was reg. 1932 at no. 47 Lea Bridge Rd.[79] Constituent member of Fed. of Syn. and its 'cathedral synagogue' 1975.[80] Brick bldg., with polychrome façade decorated in mosaic, in use 1991.

NORTH LONDON PROGRESSIVE SYNAGOGUE began 1921 for Liberal Jews in Stoke Newington. Moved 1928 to Belfast Rd. and later to Montefiore Ho., to no. 30 Amhurst Pk., and to no. 100 Amhurst Pk., where, after reconstruction 1961, it remained in 1991.[81]

SPRINGFIELD SYNAGOGUE begun 1929, was reg. 1937 at no. 202 Upper Clapton Road.[82] Belonged 1939 to Fed. of Syn., an affiliated member 1991.

KNIGHTLAND ROAD SYNAGOGUE was reg. in 1931.[83] As Succath Sholom, belonged 1939 to Union of Orthodox Hebrew Congregations. As Knightland Rd. syn. of the Law of Truth Talmudical college, it remained at no. 50 in 1991.

Persian and Bokharan Jews, akin to the Sephardim in ritual, were in Stamford Hill before the Second World War.[84] The first were at no. 5A East Bank by 1945, although registered only in 1955 and 1966, and remained there in 1991.[85] The second registered rooms at no. 7 Amhurst Park in 1957.[86]

Early synagogues of the Union of Orthodox Hebrew Congregations, besides Knightland Rd. (above), were: Central Hackney in former Richmond Rd. Wes. chapel 1925–58;[87] Kehillath Jacob, no. 81 Cazenove Rd., 1930; Beth Israel, no. 51 Upper Clapton Rd., reg. 1931; Chabad, no. 158 Amhurst Rd., reg. 1931,[88] Northfields, nos. 109–11, Stamford Hill, also used by Yeshivah or Yisroel, made way for Lubavitch (below); Amhurst Pk., no. 93 Amhurst Pk. 1931, reg. at no. 36 1953, at no. 86 1960;[89] Amhurst Pk. and North Fields served Jewish Secondary Schs. Movement; Biala, no. 10 St. Mark's Rise 1931,

1960; Beth Joseph, no. 22 Dunsmure Rd. 1940,[90] 1960.

A *beth hamedrash* was registered from 1919 until 1941 at no. 62 Colvestone Crescent and another at no. 144 Amhurst Road.[91] Other synagogues were: Chevra Ahavas Torah, reg. at no. 34 Sandringham Rd. 1930–64; Rossens, reg. at no. 8 Dunsmure Rd. 1932–41, Congregation of Jacob, reg. at no. 81 Cazenove Rd. 1939–54; Beth Israel (Trisker), reg. at no. 111 Cazenove Rd. 1942–72; Ohel Yisrael Beth Hamedrash (later Northwold Rd. syn.), reg. at no. 116 Brooke Rd. from 1943; Voydislav syn. at no. 8 Leweston Pl. from 1945 to 1954.[92] South Hackney Talmud Torah at no. 76 King Edward's Rd. from *c.* 1920 may have been succeeded by a study circle reg. at no. 6 1939–54 and then at no. 11.[93]

Most of the groups established since the Second World War belonged to the Union of Orthodox Hebrew Congregations, whose associated schools had their own synagogues: Yesodey Hatorah at nos. 2–4 Amhurst Park from 1950 and the Lubavitch foundation, from its establishment in 1959, in Cazenove Road. Lubavitch soon moved to Stamford Hill, where a synagogue registered at nos. 109–11 in 1959 was replaced by one at nos. 113–15 in 1968; another was registered at no. 126 in 1967.[94] The Agudah Youth movement had a *beth hamedrash* at no. 93 Stamford Hill in 1960, registered in 1965.[95]

Many of the Union's congregations were small and occupied converted rooms: Dameshek Eliezer, no. 121 Clapton Common 1952[96] until 1960 or later; Beth Levy syn., no. 48 Alkham Rd. 1954 until 1980 or later; Northwold Rd. syn., 1955 until 1985 or later;[97] Beth Hamedrash Torath Chaim, no. 36 Bergholt Crescent from 1955, although reg. there only 1981–6 until it reg. Torah Chaim Liege syn. at no. 145 Upper Clapton Rd;[98] Ahavet Israel syn., no. 97 Stamford Hill 1956–60, no. 2 Colberg Pl. 1975[99] and, as Ahavat Israel D'Chasidey Vishnitz, no. 89 Stamford Hill from 1976; Beth Hamedrash D'Chasidey Gur, no. 95 Stamford Hill by 1959 and reg. at no. 2 Lampard Grove 1965, 1980; Beth Hamedrash Yeshivas D'Chasidey Gur, nos. 4–6 Lampard Grove from 1984;[1] Beth Hamedrash D'Chasidey Belz, in Bethune Rd., Stoke Newington, by 1959, had recently formed two groups in 1977[2] and reg. one at no. 2 Leweston Pl. 1978–82, then probably moving to no. 96 Clapton Common;[3] Mesifta syn., at no. 84 Cazenove Rd. by 1960, reg. at nos. 82–4 from 1968; Kehillath Chassidim syn., at no. 82 in 1960, reg. at no. 85 from 1971;[4] Beth Israel (Trisker)

75 G.R.O. Worship Reg. nos. 56306, 65373.
76 H. W. Harris and M. Bryant, *Chs. and Lond.* (1914), 394.
77 G.R.O. Worship Reg. nos. 47412, 56958.
78 Ibid. no. 47073.
79 Ibid. no. 53531.
80 Kosmin and Grizzard, *Jews in Lond. Suburb,* 33.
81 G.R.O. Worship Reg. no. 51626; *V.C.H. Mdx.* viii. 216.
82 G.R.O. Worship Reg. no. 57156.
83 Ibid. no. 53317.
84 Hyamson, *Sephardim of Eng.* 413.
85 G.R.O. Worship Reg. nos. 65164, 70407.
86 Ibid. no. 66227.
87 G.L.R.O., H1/ST/E65/C/19/3/1–6.
88 G.R.O. Worship reg. nos. 53101, 53367.

89 Ibid. nos. 64001, 67855.
90 Ibid. nos. 52975, 59442, 66490.
91 Ibid. nos. 47424, 47559.
92 Ibid. nos. 52769, 53528, 58644, 60314, 60560, 61201.
93 Ibid. nos. 58916, 64389.
94 Ibid. nos. 67571, 70786, 71495; inf. from dir. of educ.
95 *V.C.H. Mdx.* viii. 217; G.R.O. Worship Reg. no. 70017.   96 G.R.O. Worship Reg. no. 63603.
97 Ibid. nos. 64270, 64951, 70842.
98 Ibid. nos. 75661, 77267.
99 Ibid. nos. 65896–7.
1 Ibid. nos. 70287, 75639, 76490.
2 *V.C.H. Mdx.* viii. 217; *Jewish Chron. Colour Mag.* 27 May 1977, 13.
3 G.R.O. Worship Reg. nos. 74988, 76204.
4 Ibid. nos. 71261, 72569.

syn., at no. 111 Cazenove Rd. by 1960, reg. at no. 146 Osbaldeston Rd. by 1980;[5] Beth Hamedrash Yetiv Lev, no. 86 Cazenove Rd. 1962;[6] Beth Hamedrash Ohel Naphtoli, at no. 5 Darenth Rd. by 1964, reg. nos. 3–5 1968–80, until reg. of Ohel Naphtoli and Ohel Moshe syn. of Bobor at no. 67 Egerton Rd.; Ohel Moshe Beth Hamedrash, reg. at no. 202 Upper Clapton Rd. in 1982.[7]

Among more recent conventicles of the Union of Orthodox Hebrew Congregations, each one a *beth hamedrash* in converted rooms, were: Ohel Shmuel Shalom, no. 37 Craven Walk by 1975, reg. 1983;[8] Tchechenover, established *c.* 1896, no. 38 Ickburgh Rd. until 1985 or later; Atereth Zvi, replacing Dameshek Eliezer, no. 121 Clapton Common until 1980 or later; Birketh Yehuda (Halaser), no. 47 Moundfield Rd. 1975;[9] Beis Nadvorna, no. 45 Darenth Rd. from 1984;[10]

D'Chasidey Sanz-Klausenberg, no. 42 Craven Walk by 1985; D'Chasidey Square, no. 22 Dunsmure Rd. (formerly Beth Joseph); Imrey Chaim D'Chasidey Vishnitz-Monsey, no. 121 Clapton Common 1990.

A Sephardi Eastern Jewry synagogue, established in 1955, was at no. 13 Amhurst Park in 1960 and registered as Ohel David at Gan Eden hall, no. 140 Stamford Hill, in 1972. It may have been the one registered at no. 7 Stamford Hill from 1956 to 1958[11] and was renamed Jacob Benjamin Elias synagogue at no. 140 *c.* 1980.

Diure Shir synagogue was registered in 1970 at no. 50 Clapton Common,[12] where the Federation's Stamford Hill Beth Hamedrash moved after 1985. Jews from Aden were at no. 117 Clapton Common *c.* 1979 to *c.* 1985[13] and at no. 127 in 1992.

ISLAM

No. 82 Forburg Rd. opened for worship 1974 by Naquibul Islam soc., trust formed 1973, closed 1978 on opening of North London mosque at no. 70 Cazenove Rd.[14]

Sufis worshipped at an unnamed terrace house in Hackney in 1981.[15]

Turkish mosque reg. in former Stoke Newington synagogue, Shacklewell Lane, 1981.[16] Central dome added by 1987.

Medina mosque reg. at no. 2A Lea Bridge Rd. 1984.[17] Red-brick bldg. with domes and minarets erected by 1991.

Aziziye mosque reg. at nos. 117–19 Stoke Newington Rd. 1986. Bldg., former Apollo cinema in Stoke Newington parish and serving much of Hackney, refurbished with marble-like facing and two gilded domes.[18]

EDUCATION

The vestry's appointment of a schoolmaster in 1613 has normally been seen as the origin of Hackney's first parochial school.[19] A schoolmaster (*ludimagister*) had been recorded in 1580 and 1586,[20] however, and William Snape, a parishioner, had left 40*s*. 'for the better maintaining of the grammar school' by will proved 1587.[21]

The vestry specified different rates for teaching some parishioners' children to read and others to write and cypher; fees for outsiders' children were left to the master.[22] Margaret Audley's charities, by will dated 1616, included £20 a year for a schoolmaster, to be appointed by the vicar, churchwardens, and 12 leading inhabitants.[23] Although the foundation was presumably intended as a second school, perhaps to prepare for the learned professions,[24] a separate master was not recorded. Its 12 boys were taught, as were the other children, in the Church House,[25] in 1620 called the 'common schoolhouse of the parish'.[26] Robert Skingle, parish schoolmaster from 1644, taught both sets of pupils: in 1665

he was said to neglect his schools and not to deserve his £20 salary.[27] The vestry's and Mrs. Audley's schools were later believed to have been the same.[28]

A parochial charity school was founded in 1714[29] and finally absorbed the old free school in 1772, when it took in Mrs. Audley's pupils. As a National school, whose funds also supported a Sunday school from 1804, it became known as Hackney Free and Parochial school. A school of industry, proposed in 1772, was founded in 1790; both boys and girls were taught in Dalston Lane from *c.* 1810, although only the girls remained in 1833. A Unitarian school also originated in 1790. Another industrial school, for girls, was founded in 1803 and survived in 1824 in Bohemia Place with the support of Independents. At Homerton, Ram's episcopal chapel established a girls' school in 1792 and a boys' in 1801. At Kingsland a school later connected with Kingsland Congregational church was opened in 1808 on the Stoke Newington

5 Ibid. no. 76959.
6 Ibid. no. 68682.
7 Ibid. nos. 71353, 75482, 75994.
8 Ibid. no. 76355.
9 Ibid. no. 74068.
10 Ibid. no. 76579.
11 Ibid. no. 73023; *V.C.H. Mdx.* viii. 217.
12 G.R.O. Worship Reg. no. 72314.
13 Ibid. no. 75253.
14 G.R.O. Worship Reg. no. 75345; Char. Com. files; inf. from sec.
15 *Hackney Gaz.* 2 Jan. 1981, 12.
16 Ibid. 26 Aug. 1981, 8.
17 G.R.O. Worship Reg. no. 76718.
18 Ibid. no. 77130; Char. Com. files; *V.C.H. Mdx.* viii.

177; *Hackney Gaz.* (1864–1989 anniv. suppl.), 21.
19 Vestry mins. Dec. 1613; J. Baldry, *Hackney Free and Parochial Schs.* (1970), 17.
20 Guildhall MS. 9537/4; ibid. 6, f. 5.
21 Ibid. 9171/17, f. 96.
22 Vestry mins. Dec. 1613.
23 *2nd Rep. Com. Educ. of Poor*, H.C. 547, p. 94 (1819), x.   24 Lysons, *Environs*, ii. 512.
25 Baldry, *Free Schs.* 18.
26 Vestry mins. 1 Aug. 1620.
27 Baldry, *Free Schs.* 19; vestry mins. 11 Dec. 1665, 9 Jan. 1666.   28 Lysons, *Environs*, ii. 512.
29 Para. based on Lysons, *Environs*, ii. 512–13; ibid. Suppl. 173–4; Robinson, *Hackney*, ii. 231–4, 246–7, 258–9, 270–1; accounts of individual schs., below.

side of the boundary.[30] South Hackney had a free school founded from Well Street chapel in 1807 and St. John's chapel school founded by the Revd. H. H. Norris in 1810. Infants attended a school near the brickfields at Upper Clapton, which had been built by the Revd. J. J. Watson, in 1811, when some girls from the Sunday school went on to a school supported by Mrs. Watson.

In 1819 the poor were said to have ample means of obtaining education.[31] The four endowed schools were Hackney Free and Parochial, in so far as it served Mrs. Audley's charity, and those of Norris, Ram's chapel, and Well Street chapel. In addition to the workhouse and the school of industry, there were 12 other schools supported entirely by voluntary contributions, six of them being Sunday schools. At least one Sunday school, held by Methodists, in 1821 taught writing on some weekdays.[32] The numbers included a second National school at Stamford Hill, which perhaps was a short lived forerunner of St. Thomas's, Upper Clapton, and a new Independents' school in St. Thomas's Square, but excluded a new Lancasterian or British school for boys in Homerton Row.

Provision had greatly increased by 1833,[33] when there were 4 infants' and 59 day schools. The day schools included 8 connected with the Church of England, among them the Cumberland benevolent institution and 2 started in 1828 at Upper Clapton, and 6 connected with dissenters, among them a girls' Lancasterian school, Brenton's asylum school at Hackney Wick which prepared boys for the colonies, and the London Orphan Asylum. The last two, like the Cumberland institution, were not restricted to local children. The other day schools were for fee payers, some of them boarders: 2,109 children were educated at their parents' expense.[34]

National schools, promoted by the Hackney Phalanx,[35] were opened in connexion with the new Anglican churches. By 1846–7, in addition to Hackney Parochial or St. John's, Ram's chapel, and St. Thomas's schools, there were National schools for South Hackney (formerly Norris's school) and West Hackney, and for St. James's, Clapton, St. Philip's (later Holy Trinity), Dalston, and St. Peter's, De Beauvoir Town. The National Society found least provision in the poorer parts of South Hackney.[36] Later National schools were those of St. Barnabas, Homerton, and St. Thomas (later St. Matthew) at Upper Clapton, St. Augustine, Victoria Park, and St. Michael and All Angels, London Fields. Dissenters were served by Congregational schools in Stoke Newington High Street and

Upper Clapton, in addition to those at South Hackney, Kingsland, Homerton, and St. Thomas's Square, by Wesleyan ones at Homerton and Dalston, and by the Unitarian school. Roman Catholics had a school at the Triangle, later St. John the Baptist's, by 1849 and at Kingsland, later Our Lady and St. Joseph's, from 1855. Ragged schools were opened at Kingsland in 1848 and in Sanford Lane, off Stoke Newington High Street, in 1849.[37]

Parliamentary grants were paid to the Parochial school and West Hackney school, which had also received a building grant, by 1851.[38] Eight schools or institutions received annual grants by 1868[39] and thirteen by 1870.[40] All were listed in 1871 among Hackney's 42 public elementary schools, a number exaggerated by the counting of some departments as separate schools and the inclusion of such institutions as the London Orphan Asylum, with 439 inmates, and the smaller Dalston refuge, Elizabeth Fry refuge, and Silesia orphanage. Dalston refuge, like the privately managed Tre-Wint industrial home, had received a parliamentary grant since 1868. Of 6,762 daytime attenders in 1871, 4,917 went to public schools or institutions, a further 288 to 13 privately managed schools, institutions, or missions, and 1,557 to 88 private adventure schools.[41]

Under the Education Act, 1870, the Hackney division of the school board for London included Shoreditch and Bethnal Green.[42] The board, whose divisional committee hired offices at no. 205 Mare Street from 1873,[43] was warned in 1872 that compulsory attendance could be achieved only after a building programme in the poorest districts, where absentees were 'of such a low order' as to be unfit to mix with children in regular attendance.[44] Despite the poor state of existing accommodation, lack of places forced the board to take over Kingsland and Shacklewell ragged school as soon as its managers threatened closure.[45] Most of the board's early building took place outside the parish: 7 of the division's 19 board schools in 1873 were in Hackney and only one, in John Street replacing Kingsland ragged school, was a new foundation.[46]

The most effective defence of denominational education against the dominance of the board was in South Hackney, where the vicar of St. Michael's pressed ahead with the building of a large National school near the board's school in Lamb Lane, although he gave up a proposed infants' school.[47] There was a mild demurral at the board's plans to build near St. Matthew's school at Upper Clapton in 1874[48] and proposals to build opposite the Free and Parochial school

30 Above, prot. nonconf.; V.C.H. Mdx. viii. 219.
31 Para. based on Educ. of Poor Digest, 546.
32 H.A.D., D/F/TYS/16, pp. 57–8.
33 Para. based on Educ. Enq. Abstract, 562–3.
34 Below, private schs.
35 Above, parish church (church extension).
36 Nat. Soc. Inquiry, 1846–7, Mdx. 6–7.
37 Based on accounts of individual schs. below.
38 Mins. of Educ. Cttee. of Council, 1851 [1357], p. clxx, H.C. (1851), xliv(1); 1852–3 [1623], pp. 124, 238, H.C. (1852–3), lxxix.
39 Rep. of Educ. Cttee of Council. 1868–9 [4139], pp.

569–71, H.C. (1868–9), xx.
40 Ibid. 1870–1 [C. 406], p. 495, H.C. (1871), xxii.
41 G.L.R.O., SBL 1518, pp. 90–99; Rep. of Educ. Cttee. of Council, 1868–9, pp. 569–70
42 33 & 34 Vic. c. 75; Stanford, Sch. Bd. Map of Lond. [undated].
43 Sch. Bd. for Lond. Mins. of Procs. 30 Apr. 1873
44 Ibid. 12 June 1872
45 Ibid. 10 July, 10 Oct. 1872
46 Ibid. (1872–3), midsummer returns.
47 Nat. Soc. files.
48 Sch. Bd. for Lond. Mins. of Procs. 18, 25 Mar. 1874.

were defeated in 1875.[49] Hackney vestry joined neighbouring authorities in 1876 in charging the board with extravagance.[50] Proposals for a board school in Cassland Road were opposed by residents and by the Cass Foundation in the 1890s.[51]

The board had opened 13 permanent schools, besides 3 temporary ones, by 1880 and 16 by 1890. A National school was opened for St. Michael and All Angels, Stoke Newington common, although it proved short lived; the schools connected with St. Augustine's, St. Barnabas's, and St. Peter's also closed. Two more Roman Catholic schools had opened by 1890. Of the four protestant nonconformist schools which then still received grants,[52] only Dalston Wesleyan survived in 1903.[53]

By 1903 the 28 board schools in Hackney M.B. had accommodation for 33,758 and a total average attendance of 27,435.[54] Nearly all had separate departments for boys, girls, and infants; Millfields Road school was higher elementary, Queen's Road and Wilton Road included higher grade classes, and Cassland Road was entirely higher grade. In addition the board's 7 special schools were attended by 258 handicapped children.[55] Eighteen other schools received grants and were attended by 4,869. Ten were connected with the Church of England.[56] Only Hackney Free and Parochial school, including a branch for infants on a separate site and with a total attendance of 779, was comparable in size to a normal board school.

The L.C.C.'s education committee succeeded the London school board in 1904.[57] By 1909 there were county secondary schools at Hackney Downs (taken over from the Grocers' Company), Colvestone Crescent, and Cassland Road.[58] A central school was opened at Lauriston Road in 1910, another at Millfields Road to replace the higher elementary department in 1911, and another at Wilton Road to replace the higher grade departments of Wilton and Queen's roads in 1913.[59] Of 43 maintained schools in 1927, 32 were county, 7 connected with the Church of England, St. Matthew's and West Hackney parochial schools having closed, and 4 Roman Catholic.[60] Three of the Anglican and all the Roman Catholic schools survived the Second World War, to become voluntary aided primary schools. In 1951 there were also 23 county primary schools, a county nursery school called Wentworth in Cassland Road, and 16 county secondary schools.[61] Many county schools were renamed in 1949.[62]

Under the London Government Act, 1963, Hackney L.B. formed a division of the new I.L.E.A.[63] By 1976 several of the county primary schools had been divided into adjoining junior mixed and infants' schools, while the number of county secondary schools had been reduced by reorganization on comprehensive lines, although some formed upper and lower schools on separate sites.[64] In 1989 there were 50 I.L.E.A. primary schools,[65] most of which had nursery classes, besides Wentworth nursery school; they included the 3 Anglican and 4 Roman Catholic schools and an eighth voluntary school, the Jewish Simon Marks.[66] Of the 8 I.L.E.A. secondary schools only Clapton, Homerton House, and Kingsland had originated as county schools; the others were Our Lady's Convent High and the Skinners' Company's,[67] Hackney Downs, Cardinal Pole's, originally in Shoreditch, and a secondary division of Hackney Free and Parochial.

Hackney L.B. became a local education authority on the abolition of the I.L.E.A. in 1990.[68] The education directorate, which occupied the former Edith Cavell school building from 1992, had carried out six amalgamations of junior and infants' schools by 1993.[69]

Public schools.[70] Except where otherwise stated, basic historical information and figures of accommodation and average attendance have been taken from: files on Church of England schools at the National Society; *Mins. of Educ. Cttee. of Council, 1848- 9* [1215], H.C. (1850), xliii; *1850- 1* [1357], H.C. (1850-1), xliv(1); *1859-60* [2681], H.C. (1860), liv; *Rep. of Educ. Cttee. of Council, 1867-8* [4051], H.C. (1867-8), xxv; *1868-9* [4139], H.C. (1868-9), xx; *1869-70* [C.165], H.C. (1870), xxii; *1870-1* [C.406], H.C. (1871), xxii; *1871-2* [C.601], H.C.(1872), xxii; *1880-1* [C.2948-I], H.C. (1881), xxxii; *1890-1* [C.6438-I], H.C. (1890-1), xxvii; *Return of Non-Provided Schs.* H.C. 178-XXXIII (1906), lxxxviii; *Bd. of Educ.*, *List 21, 1908-38* (H.M.S.O); L.C.C. *Educ. Service Particulars* (1937 and later edns.); L.C.C. (I.L.E.A from 1965), *Educ. Service Inf.* (1951 and later edns.). Inf. on Church of England schools 1846 is from National Society, *Inquiry, 1846-7*, Mdx. Roll and attendance figures for 1871 are from G.L.R.O., SBL 1518, pp. 91-2. Schools renamed in 1949 are listed in L.C.C. *Educ. Cttee. Mins.* (1949-50), 269. Primary school rolls for 1989 have been supplied by the education officer, I.L.E.A. division 4; rolls for 1993, including

49 Baldry, *Free Schs.* 54.
50 Sch. Bd. for Lond. *Mins. of Procs.* 29 Mar., 5 Apr. 1876.
51 P.R.O., ED 14/8.
52 *Rep. of Educ. Cttee. of Council, 1880–1* [C. 2948–I], p. 639, H.C. (1881), xxxii; *1890–1* [C. 6438–I], p. 637, H.C. (1890–1), xxvii.
53 G.L.R.O., SBL 1527 (return of elem. schs. 1903).
54 Para. based on ibid.
55 Below.
56 Inc. St Paul's, Brougham Rd., the infants' branch of a sch. in Shoreditch
57 Education (London) Act, 3 Edw. VII, c. 24.
58 L.C.C. *Educ. Svce. Partics.* (1909–10). Other sec. schs. were Lady Eleanor Holles's and the Skinners' Co.'s: below, private schs.

59 L.C.C. *Educ. Svce. Partics.* (1913–14).
60 *Bd. of Educ., List 21, 1927* (H.M.S.O.). The 45 maintained schs. listed inc. Bay Street temp. and Derby Rd. (qq.v.).
61 L.C.C. *Educ. Svce. Inf.* (1951).
62 L.C.C. *Educ. Cttee. Mins.* 7 Dec. 1949
63 *Ann. Abstract of Gtr. Lond. Statistics* (1967), 119.
64 I.L.E.A. *Educ. Svce. Inf.* (1976).
65 Rest of para. based on inf. from educ. officer, I.L.E.A. division 4.
66 Below, pub. schs.
67 Below, private schs.
68 *Whitaker's Almanack* (1991), 452
69 Inf. from inf. officer, research and statistics, Hackney educ. directorate.
70 Private schs. are treated separately below.

nursery classes, have been supplied by the research and statistics team, Hackney education directorate.

The following abbreviations are used in addition to those in the index: a.a., average attendance; accn., accommodation; amalg., amalgamated; B, boy, boys; bd., board; C, county; C.E., Church of England; Cong., Congregationalist; demol., demolished; dept., department; G, girl, girls; I, infant, infants; J, JB, JG, JM, junior, junior boys, girls, mixed; M, mixed; Meth., Methodist; Nat., National; parl., parliamentary; perm., permanent; R.C., Roman Catholic; reorg., reorganized; roll, numbers on roll; S,SB,SG,SM, senior, senior boys, girls, mixed; S.B.L., School Board for London; sec., secondary; Sun., Sunday; temp., temporary; vol., voluntary; Wes., Wesleyan. The word 'school' is to be understood after each named entry. Separate departments are indicated by commas: B,G, I; JM, I.

ADA STREET C.E.[71] Temp. I sch. opened 1840 or 1841 in premises of Sir John Cass's char. in Wick Street, followed by schs. for 120 I in Goring Street and 30 I in Well Street. Intended partly to serve South Hackney Parochial schs. but founded as separate venture by asst. curate C. J. Daniel. Larger site leased to cttee. by 1847, in Ada Street,[72] where I sch. used also as mixed sch. 1870. Roll 1871: 192; a.a. 106. Listed 1871 as St. Mic. and All Angels, Ada Street, and probably replaced by St. Mic.'s Nat. sch., Lamb Lane (q.v.).

AMHERST. Formerly Sigdon Rd. bd. (q.v.), renamed 1949. JM, I by 1951. Rolls 1989: 220 JM, 200 I. Amalg. as primary sch. 1992. Roll 1993: 472.

BADEN-POWELL, Ferron Rd. Opened 1970 for 280 JM & I.[73] Roll 1989: 190 JM & I; 1993:247.

BALLANCE RD., see St. Dominic.

BAY STREET TEMP. BD. Opened 1906 in former Dalston Cong. sch. (q.v.) for 260 M, 60 I. Closed 1923.

BENTHAL. Opened 1876 as Rendlesham Rd. bd.[74] for 532 SM, 300 I, and 1887 for 379 JM. Called Benthal Rd. by 1903, Benthal by 1951. Rebuilt after war damage 1949 for JM & I[75]; reorg. by 1955 for I only, by 1976 for JM, I. Rolls 1989: 194 JM, 187 I; 1993: 220 JM, 244 I.

BERGER, Anderson Rd. Opened 1877 in former St. Barnabas sch. (q.v.),[76] moved 1878 as Berger Rd. temp. bd. to iron bldg. in Wick Rd., and 1879 to perm. sch. for 720 M, 356 I. Iron bldg. reopened 1879–83, 1883–4;[77] inc. temp. accn. for 30 I in 1913. Reorg. 1920 for 328 B, 338 G, 356 I, again 1932/6 for 480 JB, 313 I, and again by 1951 for JM, I. Renamed Berger 1949. Rolls

1989: 192 JM, 188 I. Amalg. as primary sch. 1993. Roll 1993: 455.

BERKSHIRE RD. BD. Opened 1899 as Windsor Rd. bd. (Berkshire Rd. from 1906), on site of dyeworks, for 348 B, 348 G, 390 I. Inc. temp. accn. for 50 B in 1913. Reorg. 1927/32 for 340 SB, 340 SG, 397 I. Renamed Lea Marsh primary and sec. schs. 1949. Reorg. by 1951 as sec. for SM. Closed by 1966, when pupils sent to Clapton Pk. or Upton Ho. (qq.v.).[78]

BOHEMIA PLACE INDUSTRIAL. Opened 1803 for G, most of whom were placed in domestic svce. Not identifiable with any sch. listed 1819 or later but supported 1821–4, when 33 G educ. and clothed, by sermons at Old Gravel Pit and Well Street chapels.[79]

BROOKE HO. SEC., Kenninghall Rd. Opened 1960 for 960 SB from Joseph Priestley and Mount Pleasant (qq.v.) in bldgs. designed by Armstrong & MacManus on site of Brooke Ho.[80] Amalg. with Upton Ho. to form Homerton Ho. (qq.v.) 1982. Bldg. later adapted for Hackney Coll.[81]

CADOGAN TERR. TEMP. BD. Opened 1879 for B. Closed 1883 on opening of Sidney Rd. (q.v.).[82]

CARDINAL POLE R.C. SEC., Kenworthy Rd. Opened 1959 in Wenlock Rd., Shoreditch, as vol. aided sch. with older children from Kingsland R.C. (later Our Lady and St. Joseph, q.v.). Moved 1964 to new bldg. in Kenworthy Rd. Annexe in former French hosp., Victoria Pk. Rd., for lower sch. from 1974.[83] Roll 1993: 992.

CASSLAND RD. HIGHER GRADE, see South Hackney C.

CASSLAND RD. C. Opened 1913 as temp. county sch. for 160 JM, 192 I. SM dept. opened 1916, closed 1917 on opening of Derby Rd. (q.v.). Reorg. 1932/6 for 285 I only.

CASSLAND SEC., see South Hackney.

CHAPMAN RD. CONG. Opened by 1870 for BG. Described 1871 as at Chapman Rd. mission rooms, Hackney Wick.[84] Roll 1871: 161; a.a. 116. Nothing further known.

CHATSWORTH RD. TEMP. BD. Opened 1901 for 60 G in Sun. schoolroom below tabernacle and managed from Rushmore Rd. (q.v.).[85] Closed 1908.

CLAPTON C, Laura Pl. Opened 1916 for SG. Renamed John Howard sec. 1949. Amalg. with Clapton Pk. to form Clapton comprehensive in Howard bldg. and 4 new perm. bldgs. for 1,080 SG 1977. Roll 1993: 781 SG.[86]

CLAPTON JEWISH DAY, see Simon Marks.

CLAPTON PK., Oswald Street. Formerly Mandeville Street (q.v.), renamed for SB 1949. Closed 1953, when bldg. occup. by Pond Ho. Reopened by 1961 for SG, with lower sch.

71 Based on Nat. Soc. files, S. Hackney Parochial.
72 H.A.D. D/F/TYS/16, p. 31.
73 I.L.E.A. *Educ. Cttee. Mins.* 17 July 1968; 20 May 1970.
74 P.R.O., ED 7/75.
75 L.C.C. *Ceremonial Pamphlets,* 18 Nov. 1949.
76 G.L.R.O., SBL 1527 (return of temp. schs. 1903), p. 12.
77 Ibid.
78 L.C.C. *Educ. Cttee. Mins.* 3 Mar. 1965.
79 H.A.D., D/F/TYS/16, pp. 53–6.
80 L.C.C. *Educ. Cttee. Mins.* 27 Jan. 1960; *Archit. Rev.*

cxxi. 48; L.C.C. *Ceremonial Pamphlets,* 16 Feb. 1961.
81 Below, tech. educ.
82 G.L.R.O., SBL 1527 (return of temp. schs. 1903), p. 12; P.R.O., ED 14/8.
83 L.C.C. *Educ. Cttee. Mins.* 7 Oct. 1959; 20 July 1960; inf. from head teacher.
84 Old O.S. Map Lond. 41 (1870); G.L.R.O., SBL 1518, pp. 91–2.
85 G.L.R.O., SBL 1527 (return of temp. schs. 1903), p. 12; P.R.O., ED 14/8.
86 I.L.E.A. *Educ. Cttee. Mins.* 10 Feb., 13 Apr. 1976; inf. from head teacher.

between Oswald and Mandeville streets and annexe (later upper sch.) in Chelmer Rd. Amalg. with John Howard to form Clapton comprehensive.

CLAPTON R.C., see St. Scholastica.

CLAPTON, UPPER, AND STAMFORD HILL, see St. Thomas.

CLAPTON, UPPER, CONG., Conduit (later Rossendale) Street. Opened by 1871, when paid parl. grant, by Upper Clapton Cong. ch. Roll 1871: 251 M; a.a. 170. Transferred 1875 to S.B.L., closed 1876 on opening of Rendlesham Rd. (later Benthal, q.v.), briefly for I 1877.[87]

COLVESTONE. Opened as Colvestone Crescent by 1949, when renamed Colvestone. I only 1951, 1955, JM & I by 1970. Roll 1989: 163 JM & I; 1993: 205.

CRAVEN PK., Castlewood Rd. Opened 1896 by S.B.L. for 336 M, 215 I. Reorg. by 1919 for 404 SM, 228 JM & I, and again 1932/6 for 300 JM, 262 I. JM, I 1951, with annexe at synagogue in Egerton Rd., JM & I by 1976. Roll 1989: 164 JM & I; 1993: 221.

DALSTON CENTRAL, Wilton Rd. Opened 1913[88] for 388 Higher Grade M from Wilton Rd. (q.v.). Closed 1938/51.

DALSTON CONG., Bay Street. Opened 1855 as Dalston Training sch. by Dalston Cong. ch.[89] In 1873 had separate bldgs. for 229 B and 169 I in Bay Street and school room for 98 G above chapel vestry; styled 'Middle-class', although only 81 of 297 pupils paid more than 9d. a week. Managers unsuccessfully sought transfer to S.B.L. 1873[90] and maintained sch., with accn. for 580 by 1880, until 1890 or later.

DALSTON C, Shacklewell Lane. Opened 1876 as Hindle Street bd. for 469 B, 464 G, 546 I. Called the Shacklewell by 1903. Reorg. 1932/1936 for 353 SB, 342 SG, 414 I. New yellow-brick bldg. in Shacklewell Lane by E. P. Wheeler 1937.[91] Renamed Dalston county sec. bef. 1949, when renamed Dalston. For SG only 1951. Renamed Dalston Mount after enlargement on closure of Mount Pleasant (q.v.) by 1974. Amalg. with Edith Cavell, South Hackney (q.v.), and Shoreditch to form Kingsland (q.v.) 1982.

DALSTON MOUNT, see Dalston C.

DALSTON SCH. OF INDUSTRY.[92] Opened 1790 for 30 B at Shacklewell and 30 G in par. churchyard; by 1795 40 G, who had moved to Jerusalem Sq. by 1799. B educ. and 20 of them taught tailoring 1799, when G taught reading and needlework. B moved 1803 to Dalston Lane,[93] where G had moved by 1810. Financed by subscriptions and sermons 1811. 20 B and 35 G in 1819, as Hackney sch. of ind.; 40 G only by 1833. New bldg. by Jas. Edmeston for 80 G with ho. for mistress on site leased from Tyssen est. at corner of Dalston Rise (later Lane) and projected Am-

hurst Rd 1837.,[94] but a.a. only 40 G in 1843. Roll 1871: 49 G; a.a. 24. probably closed by 1880 and later acquired for North-East Lond. Institute.[95]

DALSTON TRAINING, see Dalston Cong.

DALSTON WES., Mayfield Terr. (later Rd.). Opened by 1871, when paid parl. grant. Roll 1871: 105 M; a.a. 97. Accn. for 526 by 1880. 'Middle-class', not transferred to S.B.L. Closed after 1906.[96]

DAUBENEY. Opened 1886 as Daubeney Rd. bd. for 540 B, 530 G, 436 I. Inc. temp. accn. for 50 B in 1913. Reorg. 1927/32 for 422 JB, 435 JG, 306 I, by 1976 for JM, I. Renamed Daubeney 1949. Rolls 1989: 233 JM, 216 I. Amalg. as primary sch. 1993. Roll 1993: 517.

DE BEAUVOIR, Tottenham Rd. Opened by 1951 for JM, I. Rolls 1989: 203 JM, 183 I. Amalg. as primary sch. 1993. Roll 1993: 397.

DERBY RD. Opened 1917 for 440 SM from Cassland Rd. county (q.v.). Reorg. 1926. Amalg. 1927 with Lauriston (q.v.).

DETMOLD RD. BD. Opened 1884 in iron bldgs.[97] and 1886 as perm. sch. for 407 B, 364 G, 445 I. Reorg. 1932/36 for 560 JM, 324 I. Renamed Southwold (q.v.) by 1951.

DOWNS SIDE, Rendlesham Rd. Opened 1969 for JM & I in new bldgs.[98] Roll 1993: 235 JM & I.

EDITH CAVELL, see Enfield Rd. and Kingsland.

ELIZABETH CARR, see Glyn Rd.

ELEANOR RD. BD. Opened 1898 for 295 B, 295 G, 310 I from Lamb Lane (q.v.).[99] Inc. temp. accn. for 20 B, 20 G in 1913. Reorg. 1927/32 for 300 JM, 262 I, and again 1936/38 for 510 SB. Closed by 1947.

ENFIELD RD. BD. Opened 1894 for 355 B, 355 G, 438 I. Reorg. 1932/36 for 273 SB, 275 SG, 312 I. Renamed Kingsland (q.v.) 1949, for SM only by 1951. Renamed Edith Cavell by 1963. Premises housed Hackney L.B. educ. directorate from 1992.[1]

ETON MISSION SCHS., Hackney Wick. Opened probably as char. schs. supported by mission. Govt. inspection sought for small sch., not in receipt of grant, by sister in charge 1889. Upper grade sch., under govt. inspection, closed 1891.[2]

FLEETWOOD. Formerly Stoke Newington bd.(q.v.), renamed 1949. JM, I in 1951, JM & I by 1970. Closed by 1978.

FOUNTAYNE, see Jubilee.

GAINSBOROUGH. Opened 1875 as Gainsborough Rd. bd. for 468 B, 468 G, 496 I. Reorg. 1927/32 for 353 JB, 355 JG, 307 I. Renamed Gainsborough by 1938, after rd. renamed Eastway. JM, I in 1951. In Berkshire Rd. as JM & I by 1970. Roll 1989: 124 JM & I; 1993: 216.

GAYHURST.[3] Opened 1894 as Gayhurst Rd. bd. for 358 B, 358 G, 363 I. Reorg. 1927/32 for 560

87 P.R.O., ED 14/8; G.L.R.O., SBL 1527 (return of temp. schs. 1903), p. 11.
88 P.R.O., ED 7/75.
89 Ibid.
90 S.B.L. Mins. of Procs. 30 July 1873.
91 Pevsner, Lond. ii. 167.
92 Based on Robinson, Hackney, ii. 258–9; Lysons, Environs, ii. 512–13; ibid. Suppl. 173; H.A.D., D/F/TYS/16, pp. 348, 353 et seq.
93 G.L.R.O., M79/LH/19, pp. 114–15.
94 Ibid. P79/JNI/282-3.   95 Below, technical educ.
96 G.L.R.O., SBL 1527 (return of elem. schs. 1903), p. 8; P.O. Dir. Lond. (1902).
97 G.L.R.O., SBL 1527 (return of temp. schs. 1903), p. 12.
98 Inf. from head teacher; Tower to Tower Block, no. 54.
99 P.R.O., ED 7/75.
1 Inf. from Hackney educ. directorate.
2 Ibid. ED 14/8.
3 Tower to Tower Block, no. 41.

SG, 328 I. Primary only by 1949, when renamed Gayhurst. JM, I in 1951. Rolls 1993: 269 JM, 269 I.

GLYN RD. BD., Chelmer Rd. Iron bldg. opened 1884, closed 1886 on opening of Daubeney (q.v.), reopened 1891–2 and 1893– 4.[4] Perm. sch. opened 1892 for 420 B, 418 G, 488 I. Inc. temp. accn. for 40 B in 1913. Reorg. 1927/32 for 360 SB, 360 SG, 325 I. Renamed Glyn 1949; I sch. renamed Elizabeth Carr 1951.[5] Glyn closed 1958[6] and Eliz. Carr by 1961, when Chelmer Rd. premises occup. by Clapton Pk. (q.v.).

HACKNEY BRITISH, see Homerton Cong.

HACKNEY DOWNS, Downs Park Rd.[7] Opened 1876 as grammar sch. for 500 B by Grocers' Co. of Lond. on site bought from Tyssen est. Fees of £3 to £6 p.a., raised to £8 to £10 in 1888. Offered to L.C.C. 1904, renamed Hackney Downs sch., formerly the Grocers' Co.'s sch., 1905, and managed by L.C.C. from 1907. Thereafter popular and usually overcrowded. Roll 1906: 426; 1931: 675; 1952: 539. Main bldg. in Gothic style by Theophilus Allen damaged by fire 1963, when sch. temporarily dispersed, and demol. 1970. New bldg., intended for grammar sch., opened 1967, but further bldg., for comprehensive intakes from 1969, carried out 1968–70. Roll 1993: 441 SB. Pupils inc. playwright Harold Pinter (b. 1930).[8]

HACKNEY FREE AND PAROCHIAL SCHS.[9] Originated in parochial sch. recorded in 1580s and supported by Marg. Audley's foundation by will of 1616 for 12 B (by 1732 called the free sch.) and by char. sch. established for 30 B and 20 G aged 7 to 12, also clothed, in 1714. Free sch. held in Church Ho. and char. sch. in rented ho. in churchyard. Char. sch., managed by subscribers of 40s. a year, financed largely by sermons. Temporarily closed 1734 but revived with Stephen Ram as treasurer 1738[10] and absorbed free sch. 1772. Premises in Plough Lane, Homerton, until 1811, then new two-storeyed bldg. with central pediment in Paradise Fields (later Chatham Pl.), with accn. for master and mistress, largely paid for by legacy from Jas. Gadsden. 50 B and 40 G educ. and clothed by 1811, besides 50 B and 30 G at Sun. sch. opened 1804. Nat. system by 1819, when 179 B educ., inc. 100 clothed, and 80 G educ. and clothed.[11] I sch. opened 1826 in rented premises in Bridge (later Ponsford) Street, moved temporarily 1856 to Chatham Pl., then to new bldg. in Paragon Rd. Name Hackney Free and Parochial Charity schs. adopted under Chancery decree of 1842, to remove doubts about legacy to Hackney's 'free' school. 180 B, 110 G, and 120 I by 1846. Schs. financed by subscribers and benefactors, inc. Gadsden's legacy for 15 medals presented

annually from 1820, parl. grant in 1850, and sch. pence (1d.–2d.) from 1856. Master and mistress not certificated 1858.[12] 100 B and all G clothed 1861.[13] Rolls 1871: 330 BG, 296 I; a.a. 252 BG, 158 I. Bldg. in grounds of Sutton Ho., Isabella Rd., opened 1896, replacing condemned Chatham Pl. BG and I schs., with accn. for 829, formed boro.'s largest non-bd. sch. 1903.[14] Associated with Ram's chapel I (q.v.) from 1936. Isabella Rd. bldg. condemned 1937, rebuilt, and alone used as vol. aided sch. 1946, after bomb damage to Paragon Rd. and requisitioning of Ram's sch. in Tresham Ave. Temp. transfer to Berger Rd. 1950. New sch. for c. 320 SM opened 1952 on Paragon Rd. site; designed by Howard V. Lobb as first post-war C.E. sec. sch. completed in Lond. Overcrowding relieved 1963 by acquisition of former Wilton Rd. sch. (q.v.). Roll 1993: 670 SM. Isabella Rd. bldg. remodelled after seniors' move and site later extended after compulsory purchase of Tresham Ave. Rolls 1989: 197 JM in Isabella Rd., 139 I in Mehetabel Rd. Amalg. as Ram's Episcopal primary sch. (q.v.). Sale of Wilton Rd. site and re-establishment of SM sch. in Paragon Rd. planned for 1994.[15]

HACKNEY SCH. OF INDUSTRY, see Dalston sch. of industry.

HACKNEY UNITARIAN, Paradise Fields (later Chatham Pl.).[16] Established 1790 by Ric. Price and other subscribers as Sun. and day sch. for BG; to be inspected by members of cong. and Hackney New Coll. Called New Gravel Pit mtg. sch. 1819, when 30 B and 30 G clothed and educ. By 1833 only 25 G attended daily, besides 14 B at Sun. sch. in Water Lane which closed 1840. Roll 1871, when called Hackney Unitarian: 56 G; a.a. 48. Improved after having been found inefficient 1872.[17] Day sch. closed 1884.

HACKNEY WORKING MEN'S INSTITUTE, West Street.[18] Two rooms on first floor of institute[19] were lent for sch., under uncertificated mistress, by 1871. Financed by pence (1d.–2d.). Roll 1871: 102; accn.: 50. Presumably closed soon afterwards, when premises found inadequate and transfer was rejected by S.B.L.

HARRINGTON HILL PRIMARY. Opened 1970/2 for JM & I. Roll 1989: 183 JM & I; 1993: 222.

HINDLE STREET, see Dalston C.

HOLCROFT RD., see Orchard primary.

HOLMLEIGH PRIMARY, Dunsmure Rd. Opened 1970 for JM & I in new bldgs.[20] Roll 1989: 147 JM & I; 1993: 206.

HOLY TRINITY C.E. PRIMARY, Beechwood Rd.[21] Opened by 1842 as St. Philip's Nat. for 60 G. 40 G, 35 I by 1846. Schoolroom for 100 BGI built 1851 on site in Woodland Street leased for 99 yrs. by Thos. and Wm. Art. Rhodes; enlarged

4 G.L.R.O., SBL 1527 (return of temp. schs. 1903), p. 12.
5 L.C.C. *Educ. Cttee. Mins.* 4 July 1951.
6 Ibid. 22 Jan. 1958.
7 Based on G. Alderman, *Hist. Hackney Downs Sch.* (1972).
8 *Who's Who, 1992,* 1476
9 Based J. Baldry, *Free Schs.* passim; Nat. Soc. files.
10 H.A.D., D/F/TYS/70/18 (char. schs. min. bk.).
11 Above, plate 61; *2nd Rep. Com. Educ. of Poor,* 94. Many annual attendance nos. 1802–47 are in H.A.D., D/F/TYS/16, pp. 349–95 (notices of sermons).

12 P.R.O., ED 7/75.
13 *Crockford's Scholastic Dir.* (1861).
14 G.L.R.O., SBL 1527 (return of schs. 1903), p. 8.
15 Mander, *St. John-at-Hackney,* 50.
16 Based on E. H. Green, *Hist. New Gravel Pit Ch. Sun. Sch.* (1913), 3–6.
17 P.R.O., ED 14/8.
18 Based on S.B.L. *Mins. of Procs.* 26 July, 11 Oct. 1871.
19 Below, tech. educ.
20 Inf. from head teacher.
21 Based on P.R.O., ED 7/75; *Endowed Chars. Lond. I,* 260–1.

1865. Roll 1871: 150 BGI; a.a. 138. Financed 1873 by vol. contributions and sch. pence (2d.); parl. grant by 1876. Iron room for I built nearby 1879 and replaced by perm. bldg. 1880, when management transferred to new dist. of Holy Trinity. Site for new GI sch. leased 1882 by Rhodes fam. in Mayfield (later Beechwood) Rd.[22] Accn. 1890: 568 BGI; a.a. 506. Reorg. 1927/32 for 120 G, 156 I, by 1951 vol. aided for JM & I. Roll 1993: 232 JM & I.

HOMERTON CONG., Homerton Row. Opened 1819 as Homerton (sometimes called Hackney) Brit. or Lancasterian sch. in new bldg. 215 B, most paying 1d., in 1822; overcrowded by 1824;[23] 273 B in 1833. GI sch. in separate bldg. 1820, at first under different managers.[24] Both schs. probably transferred to Cong. Bd. of Educ. (responsible for Homerton Coll.) 1852.[25] Parl. grant by 1869. a.a. 1869: 50 G, 70 I. B sch. continued under Homerton Practising sch. (below), but lease of GI sch., with accn. for c. 275, transferred to bd. 1871.[26]

HOMERTON HO., Homerton Row. Opened 1982 as SB comprehensive on amalgamation of Brooke Ho. with Upton Ho. (qq.v.), on site of former Upton Ho. annexe. Roll 1990: 700 SB; 1993: 591.

HOMERTON PRACTISING, High Street. Model sch. for BG built c. 1852, designed by Alf. Smith, behind Homerton Coll. and managed, like coll., by Cong. Bd. of Educ.[27] Parl. grant by 1869. Rolls 1871: 490 BG; a.a. 346; 89 B; a.a. 74. Children drawn from wider area than those at Homerton Cong. sch.[28] (above), which was taken over as Homerton Row training sch. Roll 1871: 130; a.a. 115. Transfer to S.B.L., reserving right for coll. students to practise teaching, rejected by bd. 1888.[29] Schs. closed 1893, when S.B.L. bought bldgs.[30]

HOMERTON RAGGED, John (later Dunn) Street. So named 1871, when night sch. with roll and a.a. 30.[31] Probably offshoot of Kingsland ragged sch. (q.v.). Acquired as John Street bd. sch. (q.v.) 1872.

HOMERTON R.C., see St. Dominic.

HOMERTON ROW BD. Opened 1883 for 1,180 BGI (I opened 1882). Reorg. 1927/32 for 355 JB, 360 JG, 411 I and again 1932/6 for 360 JG, 409 I. Closed after 1938.

HOMERTON WES., Church Rd. Opened probably in connexion with Wes. Meth. ch. of 1868.[32] Roll 1871: 77; a.a. 68. Parl. grant by 1876. 1890 accn. 627; a.a. 187. Closed by 1899.

HOWRAH HO., see St. Victoire's.

ISAAC WATTS, see Stoke Newington Road.

JOHN HOWARD, see Clapton C.

JOHN STREET TEMP. BD.[33] Opened 1872 for BG.

a.a. 1873: 70.[34] Schoolroom in Dunn's Pl., John (later Dunn) Street, stated 1872 to have been used by Kingsland, Dalston, and Shacklewell ragged sch. Closed 1875 and replaced by Hindle St. bd. sch. (see Dalston C).

JOSEPH PRIESTLEY SEC., Morning Lane. Opened by 1951 for SB. Annexe at Homerton Row by 1958. Amalg. with B from Mount Pleasant to form Brooke Ho. (q.v.) 1960. Annexe used by Upton Ho. 1961.

JUBILEE, Filey Ave. Opened 1970/2 for JM & I as Fountayne. Roll 1989: 316 JM & I; 1993: 365.

KINGSLAND, Shacklewell Lane. Enfield Rd. sch. (q. v.) renamed Kingsland 1949 for SM. Kingsland renamed Edith Cavell for SM by 1961, with upper sch. in Enfield Rd. and lower in former Queen's Rd. sch. (see Queensbridge) in Albion Drive. Edith Cavell amalg. 1982 with Dalston Mount (see Dalston county), South Hackney C (q.v.), and Shoreditch to form Kingsland comprehensive, by 1990 with whole sch. at Shacklewell Lane. [35] Roll 1993: 880 SM.

KINGSLAND R.C., see Our Lady and St. Joseph.

KINGSLAND RAGGED, Kingsland High Street.[36] Opened 1848 after mtg. at Maberly schoolroom, presumably part of Maberly Cong. chapel, Islington, in no. 14 Providence Row. Moved 1848 to rented room at Kingsland British sch., Stoke Newington,[37] but served wide area, with annual mtgs. at Kingsland Cong. ch., and therefore named Kingsland, Dalston, and Shacklewell ragged sch. from 1851. a.a. 1850: 70 B and 80 G, taught on separate evgs. by 14 vol. teachers; also industrial class of 10 G.[38] B and G taught together from 1855, when day sch. also started. a.a. 1861: 240 day, 166 evg.[39] Bldg. fund started with legacy 1866,[40] apparently followed by move to Abbott Street, where a.a. 1871 was 124, and John Street. Transferred with Homerton ragged to John Street bd. (qq.v.) 1872.[41]

KINGSMEAD, Kingsmead Way. Opened 1953 for I.[42] JM & I after 1976. Roll 1993: 221 JM & I.

LAMB LANE BD. Opened 1873 for 120 G, 120 I.[43] Children moved to Eleanor Rd. (q.v.), when Lamb Lane bldg. converted into centre for special instruction.[44]

LAURISTON, Rutland Rd. Opened 1892 as Lauriston Rd. bd. for 300 B, 300 G, 377 I. Reorg. 1926. Accn. 1927, after taking children from Derby Rd.: 440 B, 424 G, 384 I. Reorg. 1932/6 for 640 JM, 408 I, and again by 1938 for 438 SM, 400 JM, 336 I. Separate SM and primary schs. by 1949, when both renamed Lauriston. Sec. sch. amalg. with Cassland to

22 Bp. of Lond.'s Fund made grant not towards sch. but towards 'mission bldgs.' where day sch. might be held: Nat. Soc. files.
23 17th Rep. Brit. and Foreign Sch. Soc. (May 1822), 69, 134; 19th Rep. (May 1824), 54.
24 20th Rep. (May 1825), 49.
25 P.R.O., ED 7/75.
26 Ibid. ED 4/37.
27 T. H. Simms, Homerton Coll. 1695–1978 (1979), 21–2.
28 S.B.L. Mins. of Procs. 11 Oct. 1871.
29 P.R.O., ED 4/36.
30 Ibid. ED 14/8; Simms, Homerton Coll. 89.
31 G.L.R.O., SBL 1518, pp. 91–2.
32 Above, prot. nonconf. (Meths.).
33 Based on G.L.R.O., SBL 1527 (return of temp. schs. 1903), p. 11.
34 P.R.O., ED 7/75.
35 Inf. from head teacher.
36 Based on Ragged Sch. Union Mag. ix. 74–8.
37 V.C.H. Mdx. viii. 219.
38 Ragged Sch. Union Mag. ii. 233.
39 Ibid. xiii. 72.   40 Ibid. xviii. 96.
41 S.B.L. Mins. of Procs. 10 July, 10 Oct. 1872.
42 L.C.C. Educ. Cttee. Mins. 6 May 1953.
43 S.B.L. Mins. of Procs. (1872–3), 754.
44 G.L.R.O., SBL 1527 (list of schs. 1899), 48.

form South Hackney C (q.v.) 1958. primary sch. in Derby Rd. 1970, Rutland Rd. by 1976. Roll 1993: 254 JM & I.

LAURISTON RD. CENTRAL. Opened 1910 at Lauriston Rd. bd. for 340 M. Closed by 1919.

LEA MARSH, see Berkshire Rd.

LONDON FIELDS, Westgate Street. Opened 1874 for 453 B, 442 G, 577 I. Reorg. 1927/32 for 360 JB, 360 JG, 408 I, and again 1932/6 for 640 JM, 408 I. Rolls 1989: 137 JM, 153 I; 1993: 400 JM & I.

MANDEVILLE, Oswald Street. Opened 1902 as Mandeville Street bd. for 300 B, 300 G, 302 I. Reorg. 1927/32 for 280 JB, 240 JG, 276 I, and again 1936/8 for 352 JM, 276 I. Sec. sch. by 1949, when renamed Clapton Pk. (q.v.). Replaced 1977 by Mandeville primary, with J sch. in old Oswald Street bldg. and I in new adjoining bldg.[45] Roll 1993: 224 JM & I.

MAYFIELD TERRACE, see Dalston Wes.

MILLFIELDS, Elmcroft Street. Opened 1895 as Millfields Rd. bd. for 1,539 MI. Opening of higher grade dept., attended by many pupils from outside Hackney, led to curtailment of senior sch. and to local complaints 1901.[46] Accn. 1909: 300 SM (higher elem.), 650 M, 379 I; 1919, after opening of Millfields Rd. central (below): 590 M, 404 I. Reorg. 1927/32 for 490 JM, 398 I. Rolls 1989: 243 JM, 211 I. Amalg. as primary sch. 1993. Roll 1993: 517.

MILLFIELDS RD. CENTRAL. Opened 1911 at Millfields Rd. bd. for 354 M. Accn. 1922: 414 M. Renamed North Hackney central by 1927. Reorg. 1927/32 for 374 SG. Renamed Pond Ho. 1951.[47] Closed 1955/63.

MORNINGSIDE, Chatham Pl. Formerly Morning Lane bd. (q.v.), renamed as JM & I by 1951. Roll 1989: 275 JM & I; 1993: 359.

MORNING LANE BD. Opened 1884 for 465 B, 465 G, 578 I; inc. temp. accn. for 60 I in 1913. Reorg. 1927/32 for 371 SB, 379 SG, 443 I. Replaced by Joseph Priestley and Morningside (qq.v.) by 1951.

MOUNT PLEASANT COUNTY SEC., Mount Pleasant Lane. Opened by 1938 for 320 SB, 320 SG. SB amalg. with Joseph Priestley to form Brooke Ho. (q.v.) 1960. SG remained in Mt. Pleasant Lane until bldgs. taken over as lower sch. for Skinners' Co.'s sch. 1972.[48]

NORRIS'S CHARITY, see South Hackney Parochial.

NORTH HACKNEY CENTRAL, see Millfields Rd. central.

NORTHWOLD, Northwold Rd. Opened 1902 as Northwold Rd. bd. for 366 SM, 306 JM, 306 I. Reorg. 1923 for 440 B, 440 G, 480 I. Separate SM and primary schs. by 1949, when both renamed Northwold. Sec. sch. closed by 1955. Rolls 1993: 198 JM, 213 I.

OLDHILL STREET, see Tyssen.

OLINDA RD. TEMP. BD. Opened 1891 for B & G

in two iron bldgs. on land owned by S.B.L. Superseded 1896 by Craven Pk. (q.v.).

ORCHARD PRIMARY, Holcroft Rd. Opened 1926 as Holcroft Rd. county for 232 B, 232 G, 276 I. Renamed Orchard county by 1927. Reorg. 1932/6 for 240 JB, 240 JG, 251 I. Roll 1989: 294 JM & I; 1993: 374.

ORCHARD STREET BD. Opened 1874 in former Well Street chapel (q.v.) and Orchard Street schs.; closed 1875, reopened 1875, closed again 1876.[49] Perm. sch. opened 1875 for 246 B, 239 G, and 1876 for 303 I. Closed 1926.

ORCHARD STREET SCHS., see Well Street chapel.

OUR LADY AND ST. JOSEPH R.C. PRIMARY, Tottenham Rd. Opened 1855 as Kingsland R.C. on ground floor of ch. Financed by vol. contributions and sch. pence (1d.–6d.) 1870;[50] parl. grant by 1871, when also called St. Joseph's: 92 BGI; a.a. 71. Accn. 1880: 355 BGI. Remained all-age sch., later vol. aided, until transfer of older children to Cardinal Pole (q.v.) 1959.[51] Primary sch. continued in Tottenham Rd., renamed Our Lady and St. Joseph by 1976. Roll 1989: 205 JM & I; 1993 251.

OUR LADY'S CONVENT HIGH SCH., see below, private schs.

POND HOUSE, see Millfields Rd. central.

QUEEN'S RD. BD., see Queensbridge.

QUEENSBRIDGE, Queensbridge Rd. Opened 1898 as Queen's Rd. bd., apparently as successor to Dalston Cong. or Training sch., for 418 SM (higher grade), 420 JM, 405 I. Reorg. 1923 for 454 B, 448 G, 368 I, and again 1927/32 for 549 SB, 275 JM, 310 I. Renamed Queensbridge Rd. 1939. Sec. and primary schs. both renamed Queensbridge 1949. I sch. only by 1951. Roll 1993: 120.

RAM'S EPISCOPAL CHAPEL SCHS., Homerton. Char. sch. to educ. and clothe 25 G aged 8 to 14 opened 1792 in rented ho.; additional 4 G taught reading at Sun. sch. 1819 under legacy from Judith Lambe. Sch. to educ. and clothe 25 B opened 1801. Financed 8 by vol. contributions 1819,[52] when all classes perhaps held in later B sch. in Durham Grove. Separate bldg. for G, with teacher's ho., built 1836 in Retreat Pl.[53] 60 B, 70 G, and 137 I by 1846, when G sch. praised by inspector. G had certificated teacher, supported by endowment and subscriptions, 1856;[54] G still clothed 1861, when master took some paying pupils.[55] Parl. grant probably paid by 1869. Rolls 1871: 60 B in Durham Grove, 101 G in Retreat Pl., 140 I at corner of Urswick Rd. and College (later Tresham) Ave.; a.a. 54 B, 76 G, 90 I. B and G schs. probably closed by 1880. Accn. 1903: 175 I; a.a. 118.[56] Management transferred to Hackney Free and Parochial schs. (q.v.) 1936.[57] Remodelled Hackney Free and Parochial I sch. renamed Hackney Free and Parochial (Ram's Episcopal) 1951.[58]

45 Inf. from head teacher. 46 H.A.D., H/LD 7/16.
47 L.C.C. *Educ. Cttee. Mins.* 9 May 1951.
48 Inf. from Skinners' Co., schools clerk.
49 G.L.R.O., SBL 1527 (return of temp. schs. 1903), p. 11. 50 P.R.O., ED 7/75.
51 L.C.C. *Educ. Cttee. Mins.* 7 Oct. 1959.
52 *2nd Rep. Com. Educ. of Poor*, 96–7; H.A.D., D/F/TYS/16, pp. 116, 449. 53 P.R.O., ED 7/75.
54 Ibid. Many annual attendance nos. 1822–41 are in H.A.D., D/F/TYS/16, pp. 428–49 (notices of sermons).
55 *Crockford's Scholastic Dir.* (1861). Presumably the 'first-class day sch. for young gentlemen' advertised in *Hackney Gaz.* 2 Jan. 1875, 4.
56 G.L.R.O., SBL 1527 (return of schs. 1903), p. 8.
57 Baldry, *Hackney Free Schs.* 82.
58 L.C.C. *Educ. Cttee. Mins.* 9 May 1951.

RAM'S EPISCOPAL PRIMARY established 1993 on amalgamation of Hackney Free and Parochial JM, I schs. Roll 1993: 319 JM & I.

RENDLESHAM RD., see Benthal.

RUSHMORE. Opened 1877 as Rushmore Rd. bd. for 432 B, 432 G, 382 I, and 1908 for 330 JM, inc. pupils from Chatsworth Rd. temp. (q.v.). Reorg. 1924 for 432 B, 384 G, 330 J & I (B), 334 J & I (G), and again 1927/32 for 472 SB, 418 SG, 326 I. Primary sch. only by 1949, when renamed Rushmore. Rolls 1989: 211 JM, 213 I; 1993: 220 JM, 260 I.

ST. AUGUSTINE, Cassland Rd. Roll 1871: 96; a.a. 78. Presumably connected with ch. in Victoria Pk. Only Sun. sch. and recently started night sch. existed 1878.[59] Nothing further known.

ST. BARNABAS NAT., Queen's (later Berger) Rd.[60] Opened 1855 for BGI on site bought 1853 mainly with money from Revd. J. J. Watson. Parl. grant by 1868. Roll 1871: 342; a.a. 241. Debts incurred by opening of separate G sch. to satisfy Educ. Dept. 1875.[61] Closed 1877, when rented to S.B.L. for Berger Rd. sch. (q.v.).[62] Proceeds of sale spent c. 1880 on new Sun. sch. and other bldgs. next to St. Barnabas's ch.

ST. DOMINIC R.C. PRIMARY, Ballance Rd. Opened 1873 as Homerton or Ballance Rd. R.C. for BGI in new bldg. next to ch. on site given by Revd. Geo. Akers. Financed by vol. contributions and sch. pence (1d.–2d.) 1873;[63] parl. grant by 1876, when a.a. 136. Accn. 1890: 420; a.a. 182. G taught by Sisters of Sacred Hearts, who also kept nearby boarding sch.[64] Renamed St. Dominic, vol. aided, 1949. Roll 1989: 215 JM, 169 I; 1993: 236 JM, 238 I.

ST. JAMES NAT., Powell Rd.[65] Opened by 1846 for G, I. Perhaps not permanent until land settled in trust by Powell fam. 1853.[66] Financed by vol. contributions, sch. pence (1d.–2d. 1873), and parl. grant by 1870. Neighbouring B sch. probably opened before 1863, when new I sch. built adjoining G sch.[67] Roll 1871: 105 B, 62 G, 80 I; a.a. 81 B, 52 G, 46 I. Closed as day schs. 1876, after inspector's report,[68] but reopened by 1880. Accn. 1886: 286. Accn. 1906: 342; a.a. 267. Reorg. by 1909: accn. 122 B. Closed after 1938. I sch. under same management opened at Lea Bridge by 1846. Roll 1871: 120; a.a. 77. Closed after 1880.

ST. JOHN OF JERUSALEM C.E., Ainsworth Rd. Opened 1956 in new bldg. on site of bombed South Hackney Parochial schs. (q.v.). Enlarged 1968. Roll 1993: 238 JM & I.[69]

ST. JOHN THE BAPTIST R.C., King Edward's Rd. Opened by 1849 as Triangle or Hackney Triangle R.C. for BG in rented bldg. New bldg. for BGI, adjoining presbytery, built 1851. Fi-

nanced by vol. contributions and sch. pence (1d.–2d.) 1868;[70] parl. grant by 1869. Roll 1871: 152; a.a. 100. Accn. 1890: 528; a.a. 236. Accn. 1909: 100 B, 101 G, 114 I. Reorg. 1932/6 for 100 B, 196 GI. As St. John the Bapt., vol. aided, occupied part of London Fields sch. by 1951 to c. 1968, when it moved to Bonner Rd., Bethnal Green.[71]

ST. JOHN'S CHAPEL, see South Hackney Parochial.

ST. MATTHEW NAT., Harrington Hill.[72] Opened 1862 for I in new bldg. at High Hill Ferry granted to clergy of St. Thos., Stamford Hill, by W. A. Tyssen-Amhurst. Parl. grant by 1870. Management by new dist. of St. Mat. from 1871, when sch. enlarged for GI. Sch. for B opened 1874, designed, like master's ho., by F. T. Dollman.[73] Further additions to allow separation of G from I 1881. Accn. 1890: 364; a.a. 215. I sch. accn. improved after threat to grant 1893. BG sch. closed by 1906, I sch. in 1909. Derelict bldgs. remained Ch. property 1936.

ST. MICHAEL AND ALL ANGELS NAT., Lamb Lane. Probably replaced Ada Street (q.v.) as Ch. sch. Opened 1873 for 500 B and 250 G, to serve also as ch. hall, on part of site of Pembroke Ho., bought in 1871 from G.E.R. Co.[74] Financed by sch. pence (6d.–8d.) 1874;[75] parl. grant by 1876. Accn. 1890: 534; a.a. 237. Accn. 1909: 231 M, 110 I. Closed after 1939.

ST. MICHAEL AND ALL ANGELS NAT., Rossington Street. Probably opened 1884 in former premises of Upper Clapton and Stamford Hill Nat. sch. (see St. Thomas C.E.).[76] Accn. 1890: 151; a.a. 89. Nothing further known.

ST. PETER NAT., De Beauvoir Rd. Opened by 1846 for B, G. Financed by vol. contributions and sch. pence. Roll 1871: 260; a.a. 182. Parl. grant, as De Beauvoir Town Nat., by 1876. Accn. 1880: 365. Closed by 1890.

ST. PHILIP, see Holy Trinity.

ST. SCHOLASTICA R.C. PRIMARY, Kenninghall Rd. Opened 1868 as Clapton R.C. for BG in bldg. also used as temp. chapel. New bldg. for BGI 1879. Financed by vol. contributions and sch. pence (2d.–9d.) 1881,[77] parl. grant by 1890. Accn. 1909: 90 MI. Vol. aided JM & I in Kenninghall Rd. 1951, in Elmcroft Street 1970. Called St. Scholastica from c. 1972. In Kenninghall Rd. by 1976. Roll 1993: 251 JM & I.

ST. THOMAS C.E. PRIMARY, Lynmouth Rd. Opened 1828 for BG and 1831 for I as Upper Clapton and Stamford Hill Nat. in leased bldg. in Wood (later Rossington) Street.[78] 100 B, 53 G, 80 I by 1846. Enlarged 1855. Roll 1871: 202; a.a. 160; also sch. for 75 I in Chapel Rd., improved after being found inefficient 1872.[79] Financed by endowment, vol. contributions, and

59 G.L.R.O., SBL 1518, pp. 91–2; Nat. Soc. files.
60 Based on *Endowed Chars. Lond.* I, 258–60; Nat. Soc. files.
61 *Hackney Gaz.* 8 May 1875, 3.
62 S.B.L. *Mins. of Procs.* 18 Apr., 2 May 1877.
63 P.R.O., ED 7/75.
64 *Kelly's Dir. Hackney* (1890); below, private schs.
65 Rec. in G.L.R.O., P79/JSG/119–52.
66 Nat. Soc. files.
67 P.R.O., ED 7/75.
68 Ibid. ED 14/8.
69 H.A.D., H/LD 7/24 (cutting); Nat. Soc. files (inspec-

tor's rep. 1983).
70 P.R.O., ED 7/75.
71 I.L.E.A. *Educ. Cttee. Mins.* 15 Dec. 1965; 7 Feb. 1968.
72 Based on L. E. Shelford, *Twenty Years of St. Mat.'s* (1886), i, 4–5.
73 G.L.R.O., P79/MTW/17/1/
74 Nat. Soc. files.
75 P.R.O., ED 7/75.
76 H. L. Kingsford, *Short Acct. of St. Thos.'s Ch.* (1913), 78.
77 P.R.O., ED 7/75.
78 Ibid. Many annual attendance nos. 1833–43 are in H.A.D., D/F/TYS/16, pp. 124–33 (notices of accts.).
79 P.R.O., ED 14/8.

sch. pence (1*d*.–3*d*.) 1872;[80] parl. grant, after closure 1875 and reopening for GI,[81] by 1876. New bldg. for GI in Grove (later Lynmouth) Rd. on site given by W. A. Tyssen-Amherst 1884, when old bldgs. assigned to St. Mic. and All Angels, Rossington Street (q.v.).[82] Accn. 1909: 126 G, 84 I. Reorg. 1927/32 for 210 M & I, and again 1932/6 for 194 JM & I. Called St. Thomas by 1938. Vol. aided JM & I by 1951. Roll 1993: 91 JM & I.

ST. THOMAS'S SQ. MEETING. Opened by 1819, when 20 G educ. and clothed in addition to 120 BG at Sun. sch. of Ind. chapel.[83] 120 G, of whom 25 clothed and oldest trained as servants, 1833.[84] Financed mainly by vol. contributions. New schoolrooms 1841.[85] Apparently survived only as St. Thos.'s Sq. I sch., Loddiges Rd., 1871: accn. 33; a.a. 18. Probably closed after S.B.L. refused to accept transfer 1871.[86]

ST. VICTOIRE'S CONVENT R.C., Victoria Pk. Rd.[87] Opened as Howrah Ho. high sch. for G next to convent of Faithful Companions of Jesus in E. India Dock Rd. (Poplar).[88] After war damage and use of temp. premises, moved as vol. aided grammar sch. with 161 G to former French hosp. on edge of Victoria Pk. 1949. Name changed from Howrah Ho. convent sch. to St. Victoire's convent sch. 1952, although no convent attached. Closed between 1972 and 1974.

SANDFORD LANE RAGGED, Stoke Newington High Street. Opened C. 1846 as Stoke Newington ragged in ho. on n. side of Stoke Newington common. Accn. 1850: 60; a.a. 36 B and 12 G week days, 16 B evgs., and Sun. classes, taught by 33 vol. and 2 paid teachers.[89] Moved 1854 to single-storeyed bldg. at S. end of Lawrence's Bldgs. Accn. 1871: 208; a.a. 176. Closed on transfer to S.B.L. as temp. accn. 1872.[90]

SHACKLEWELL, THE, see Dalston C.

SHACKLEWELL PRIMARY, Shacklewell Row. Opened by 1951 for JM, I. New bldgs. 1971. Rolls 1993: 191 JM, 216 I.

SIDNEY RD. BD. Opened 1882 for 471 G, 634 I, and 1883 for 471 B. Reorg. 1927/32 for 387 JB, 392 JG, 468 I, and again 1932/6 for 468 I. Closed after 1938.

SIGDON RD. BD. Opened 1898 for 328 B, 328 G, 350 I. Inc. temp. accn. for 25 B, 25 G, 25 I in 1913. Reorg. 1932/6 for 392 JB, 391 JG, 470 I. Renamed Amherst (q.v.) 1949.

SIMON MARKS, Kyverdale Rd. Opened 1956 as Clapton Jewish day sch., vol. aided, in purpose built Zion Ho. Renamed Simon Marks primary 1973. Roll 1993: 214.[91]

SKINNERS' CO.'S SCH., see below, private schs.

SOUTH HACKNEY C, Cassland Rd. Opened by 1902 as Cassland Rd. higher grade with single dept. for 816.[92] Bldg. of red brick in elaborate Renaissance style.[93] Called South Hackney sec. for G in 1910. Transferred to Clapton C (q.v.) 1916.[94] South Hackney central sch. for 440 M was in former SM premises of Cassland Rd. (q.v.) in 1919. Accn. 1938: 500 SM. Renamed Cassland 1951[95] on amalg. with Lauriston (q.v.) but renamed South Hackney 1958,[96] with upper sch. in Cassland Rd. and lower in Lauriston Rd. Amalg. with Dalston C (q.v.), Edith Cavell, and Shoreditch to form Kingsland (q.v.) 1982.

SOUTH HACKNEY CENTRAL, see South Hackney C.

SOUTH HACKNEY I, see Ada Street.

SOUTH HACKNEY PAROCHIAL.[97] Opened 1810 as St. John's chapel (also known as Norris's char.) sch. in new bldg. with wings for 50 B and 50 G flanking rooms of master and mistress; land in Park Pl., Grove Street, given by Revd. H. H. Norris, whose endowment was assisted by J. De Kewer.[98] 57 B and 24 G in 1814, when G clothed; financed mainly by subscriptions. 82 B and 32 G in 1833. Settled in trust by Norris as South Hackney Parochial or charity schs. 1834. 140 B, 40 G by 1846.[99] Bldg. of St. John of Jerusalem ch. necessitated move 1848 to site given by St. Thos.'s hosp. in Greenwood's Row (later Percy and later Kingshold Rd.), where sch. for BG designed by Hen. Currey.[1] Master and mistress certificated 1855. 50–60 B partly and 30 G completely clothed 1861, when master took some paying pupils.[2] Parl. grant by 1860. Roll 1871: 126; a.a. 114. Transfer of G sch. rejected by S.B.L. 1871. I sch. built on adjoining site, given by St. Thos.'s hosp., 1875. BG sch. enlarged 1883. Total accn. 1890: 535; a.a. 422. Accn. 1909: 266 M, 110 I. Reorg. for JM & I 1939.[3] Bombed in war and replaced by St. John of Jerusalem (q.v.).[4]

SOUTHWOLD, Detmold Rd. Formerly Detmold Rd. (q.v.), renamed by 1951. JM, I, in 1951. Roll 1989: 261 JM & I; 1993: 316.

STOKE NEWINGTON, STAMFORD HILL, AND UPPER CLAPTON, Stamford Hill. Roll 1871: 88 I; a.a. 72. Possibly connected with Stoke Newington British (below) and transferred to S.B.L. 1872.[5]

STOKE NEWINGTON BRITISH, High Street. Opened 1838 for BG in new bldg. near S. corner of later Northwold Rd. Financed by vol. contributions and sch. pence (4*d*.–9*d*.) 1869, when principal teacher trained at Homerton Coll. but not certificated.[6] Roll 1871: 143; a.a. 132. Transferred to S.B.L. 1872 and replaced by bd. sch.[7]

80 Ibid. ED 7/75.   81 Ibid. ED 14/8.
82 Kingsford, *St. Thos.'s Ch.* 78.
83 *Educ. of Poor Digest*, 546.
84 *Educ. Enq. Abstract*, 562.
85 Robinson, *Hackney*, ii. 245.
86 S.B.L. *Mins. of Procs.* 9 Aug., 11 Oct. 1871.
87 Based on G.L.R.O., EO/PS/12/NP S304/1.
88 *P.O. Dir. Lond.* (1932).
89 H.A.D., D/5/34/1-5; *Ragged Sch. Union Mag.* i. 134; ii. 233.   90 S.B.L. *Mins. of Procs.* 2 Oct. 1872.
91 Inf. from headmistress.
92 *Tower to Tower Block*, no. 43; G.L.R.O., SBL 1527 (return of schs. 1903), p. 7.
93 *List of Bldgs.* (1975).
94 L.C.C. *Lond. Statistics*, xxvi. 259.

95 L.C.C. *Educ. Cttee. Mins.* 4 July 1951.
96 Ibid. 17 July 1957, 22 Jan. 1958.
97 Based on Nat. Soc. files, inc. hist. of sch. from *Lond. Dioc. Mag.* Apr. 1895; G.L.R.O., P79/JNJ/314-400.
98 Lysons, *Environs*, Suppl. 174; *2nd Rep. Nat. Soc.* (1814), 45.
99 Nat. Soc. nos. of 18 I and 88 I may refer to schs. in Goring and Well streets: above, s.v. Ada Street.
1 H.A.D., D/F/TYS/16, p. 30.
2 *Crockford's Scholastic Dir.* (1861).
3 G.L.R.O., note in index to rec. of ch.
4 H.A.D., H/LD 7/24.
5 S.B.L. *Mins. of Procs.* (1872-3), 754.
6 P.R.O., ED 7/75.
7 S.B.L. *Mins. of Procs.* 10 Apr., 1, 29 May 1872.

STOKE NEWINGTON BD., High Street. Opened 1876 for 236 B, 213 G, 234 I in new bldg. on site of British sch. (above). Primary sch. renamed Fleetwood (q.v.) 1949. Sec. sch. renamed Isaac Watts and closed by 1951.

STOKE NEWINGTON RAGGED, see Sandford Lane.

TOTTENHAM RD. BD. Opened 1874 for 230 B, 230 G, 443 I, and 1887 for 480 JM. Reorg. 1932/6 for 360 JB, 320 JG, 333 I. Closed after 1938 and replaced by De Beauvoir (q.v.).

TOTTENHAM SQ. TEMP. BD., Tottenham Rd. Opened 1877 in temperance hall, rented weekly. Closed 1882 on transfer to Tottenham Rd. bd.[8]

TRIANGLE R.C., see St. John the Baptist.

TYSSEN, Oldhill Street. Bldg. for Oldhill Street primary partly completed 1939 and used as temp. accn. by 1948.[9] Renamed Tyssen 1949. JM, I by 1951, in Firsby Rd, off Oldhill Street. Roll 1989: 261 JM & I; 1993: 431.

UPTON HO., Urswick Rd. Opened 1928 as Upton Ho. central sch. for 361 SB in former truant or industrial sch. Sec. sch. for SB 1951; annexe in Homerton Row by 1958 and another annexe there, formerly of Joseph Priestley sch., by 1961. Amalg. with Brooke Ho. to form Homerton Ho. (qq.v.) 1982.

WELL STREET CHAPEL FREE SCHS.[10] Established 1807 by Wm. Pearson and others to educ. up to 60 B according to principles of C. of E. 'in their Calvinistic sense'. Premises between Well Street and later Orchard Street settled in trust 1811[11] on Revd. Geo. Collison and 11 other members of Well Street Ind. chapel or cttee. of Village Itinerancy soc., with provision for reversion to Brit. and Foreign Schs. Soc.; inc. master's ho., and adjoining ground let on bldg. lease. I sch. built 1830 with gift from Pearson. 70 B, chosen by subscribers and attending chapel, educ. 1843 at free sch.,[12] whose management was vested in Village Itinerancy soc. 1850. Free sch. united with I sch. under soc. by Char. Com. Scheme 1868. Bldgs. enlarged for 160 B and 180 GI by 1869, when master and mistress not certificated. Financed by endowment and sch. pence (1d.–6d.) 1869;[13] parl. grant by 1871. Leased to S.B.L. from 1873 as temp. accn. for Orchard Street bd. (q.v.). Compulsorily purchased by S.B.L. 1877 but part of proceeds awarded to Brit. and Foreign Sch. Soc. 1878 and devoted to Orchard Street Schs. Endowment, providing scholarships at Hackney elem. schs., 1881, and to Hackney and Spitalfields Exhibition Foundation from 1894.

WEST HACKNEY PAROCHIAL SCHS.[14] Probably opened c. 1830 for 70 B, 50 G,[15] although West Hackney Nat. recorded 1833 as having 47 G and mistress's ho.,[16] while rector in 1837 claimed that

there was provision only for Sun. schs. and that sch. room for G was beyond par. boundary. Sch. for 200 B and 200 G, on site leased by W. G. Daniel-Tyssen in Church (later Evering) Rd., built 1837[17]. 98 B, 113 G by 1846. Parl. grant by 1849. Roll 1871: 157 BG, 58 I; a.a. 114 BG, 37 I. Rebuilt c. 1873, largely at expense of Ric. Foster. Fees (previously 1d.–2d.) raised 1877 and again 1882. Accn. 1880: 498; a.a. 395. Closed 1906. Bldg. survived 1992.

WICK RD. TEMP. BD., see Berger.

WILTON RD. BD. (later WILTON WAY C). Opened 1886 for 477 B (higher grade), 477 G (higher grade), 560 I. Reorg. 1927/32 for 457 JB, 417 JG, 420 I. Sec. sch. for SM by 1951. Closed by 1963.

WINDSOR RD. BD., see Berkshire Rd.

Special schools.[18] The opening in 1899 of three special day schools, in Berkshire Road, Enfield Road, and Lamb Lane, was followed in 1900 by that of a residential deaf school at Homerton.[19] By 1903 the board administered 7 special schools in Hackney, with a total of 324 places and an average attendance of 258. The school for the deaf and one in College Lane for the physically defective had their own buildings; the other five, for the mentally defective, shared the premises of ordinary schools. The L.C.C. likewise administered 7 schools in 1909, although some of the sites had changed.[20] The older and privately financed East London Home and School for Blind Children[21] was later listed with the council's schools, which are described below. Downsview, Ickburgh, and Stormont House were maintained by the I.L.E.A. in 1990.[22]

BERGER RD. Opened 1902 for 80 mentally defective. For 90 and 10 temp. by 1924, for 113 SG and JM by 1935. Classes for maladjusted continued at Berger primary sch. until 1967 or later, when perhaps moved to Morningside (q.v.).

BERKSHIRE RD. Opened 1899 as Windsor Rd. for 65 mentally defective. For 90 and 10 temp. by 1924. Reopened 1925 for 45 partially blind. Renamed Ryder sch., sec. and primary, for partially sighted by 1951. Moved to Tollet Street, Stepney, by 1958.

COLLEGE LANE. Opened 1903 for 60 physically defective in former Homerton Practising sch.[23] Accn. 1921: 125; roll 152. For 135 SG and JM by 1935. Closed c. 1940.

DOWNSVIEW, Downs Rd. Opened 1968 as purpose-built sch. for children aged 5 to 16 with moderate learning difficulties. Roll 1993: 130.[24]

ENFIELD RD. Opened 1899 for 65 physically defective, perhaps replacing manual training centre of 1897.[25] Reopened 1929 for 45 blind. Closed by 1935.

8 G.L.R.O., SBL 1527 (return of temp. schs. 1903).
9 L.C.C. *Educ. Cttee. Mins.* 10 Mar. 1948.
10 Based on *Endowed Chars. Lond.* I, 156–7, 183–8.
11 The statement that sch. was behind chapel perhaps refers to years before 1811: Clarke, *Hackney*, 185, 298.
12 Robinson, *Hackney*, ii. 248.
13 P.R.O., ED 7/75.
14 Para. based on Nat. Soc. files.
15 H.A.D., D/F/TYS/16, p. 319 (5th ann. rep., 1835).
16 *Educ. Enq. Abstract*, 562.
17 Datestone.
18 Para. based on L.C.C. *Educ. Svce. Partics.* (1909–10

and later edns.).
19 *Final Rep. of S.B.L. 1870–1904*, 182.
20 G.L.R.O., SBL 1527 (return of elem. schs. 1903), p. 8.
21 Above, pub. svces.
22 Inf. on the schs. listed below is from L.C.C. *Educ. Svce. Partics.* and L.C.C. (I.L.E.A. from 1965) *Educ. Svce. Inf.* Except where otherwise stated, schs. are for mixed day pupils.
23 G.L.R.O., EO/PS/12/SP/28/1. Wrongly listed as for the deaf in ibid. SBL 1527 (return of elem. schs. 1903), p. 8.
24 Officially opened 1969: inf. from head teacher.
25 G.L.R.O., SBL 1527 (return of schs. 1899), p. 48.

HOMERTON ROW. Opened 1920 for 45 partially blind. Closed *c.* 1940.

HOMERTON SCH. FOR DEAF CHILDREN, High Street. Opened 1900 for 45 boarders and 25 day pupils. Moved to Penn (Bucks.) 1921.[26]

ICKBURGH, Ickburgh Rd. Opened 1970 for children aged 2 to 19 with severe learning difficulties, in bldg. which had been acquired from Hackney L.B. health dept. and built by L.C.C. in early 1960s. Steel framed single-storeyed bldg. by Foster Associates 1972-3. Roll 1993: 86.[27]

LAMB LANE. Opened 1899 for 65 mentally defective, upgrading centre for special instruction which had replaced bd. sch. 1898.[28] Closed *c.* 1926. Unit for partially deaf open at London Fields primary sch. by 1951 to 1974 or later.

MARSH HO., Millfields Rd. Opened by 1972 for children with severe learning difficulties. Listed as annexe of Ickburgh (q.v.) 1976 and probably closed soon afterwards.

MORNING LANE. Opened by 1903 for 24 blind, probably as temp. sch.[29] Closed *c.* 1926.

MORNINGSIDE, Morning Lane. Classes for maladjusted held at Morningside primary sch. 1970, perhaps in place of those at Berger (q.v.). Discontinued by 1972.

NORTHWOLD RD. Opened 1903 for 65 mentally defective, perhaps replacing centre for physically and mentally handicapped of 1898.[30] For SG and JM by 1930. Closed *c.* 1932.

RENDLESHAM RD. Room for special instruction of defective children in temp. use 1898-9.[31]

RYDER, see Berkshire Rd.

STORMONT HO., Downs Pk. Rd. Opened 1919 as 'open air' sch. for 75 tuberculous children. Bombed in Second World War and reopened 1964 in new bldg. for delicate children aged 5 to 16. Roll 1993: 133.[32]

UPTON HO., Urswick Rd. Opened 1878 for 60 B nominally as industrial sch., to avoid disputes about legality of detentions, although only truants admitted. Rebuilt 1885 for 100 B and enlarged on provision of new infirmary 1887.[33] 1909 accn.: 150 B aged 5 to 14. Truant sch. closed by 1913. Opened 1928 as 'open air' sch. for 130 delicate children. Closed *c.* 1940.

WINDSOR RD., see Berkshire Rd.

Adult and technical education. Well Street chapel, in addition to providing day and Sunday schools, was the scene in 1822 of the seventh general meeting of the Hackney Society for Teaching Adult Persons to Read.[34] A successful course of lectures for parents was given in 1854 at Kingsland ragged school, where adults may

have attended the evening classes from 1855, by which time children could attend classes in the day.[35] Adults may have been in the mind of the vicar of St. Barnabas when he hoped to start an evening school in 1855.[36]

In 1871 there was a total roll of 531 and an attendance of 459 at night classes held in both public and private schools. Apart from Hackney Working Men's Institute (below), the largest numbers enrolled were 72 at an evening school at the printing house, Shacklewell, and 70 at Sandford Lane ragged school. Churches and missions, notably St. Matthew's, also offered many places.[37]

The school board provided several centres for cookery, of which the first, each with 14 places, were opened at Benthal Road in 1881, at Homerton Row in 1883, and Tottenham Road in 1887. Centres for laundrywork and handicrafts followed in the 1890s.[38] In addition to those centres and to the classes at Hackney technical institute (below), 17 ordinary evening schools or continuation classes were held by 1901, all of them in the board's buildings save one at Holy Trinity school.[39] The L.C.C. in 1910 administered one science and art and two commercial evening centres, besides 16 ordinary evening schools; it aided the technical institute and Clapton and Stamford Hill school of art, which had their own governing bodies.[40]

Hackney Working Men's Institute was at no. 6 West (later Westgate) Street, the Triangle, by 1860. It held a yearly tenancy in 1871, when listed as a private adventure school with 94 on the roll, and apparently had closed by 1880.[41]

The North-East London institute school of music, science, and art, at nos. 236 and 238 Dalston Lane, by 1894 occupied enlarged premises on the site of Dalston school of industry.[42] They were to be acquired in 1897 as a central site for Hackney institute[43] and by 1904 served as its northern branch, being transferred to the L.C.C. with the southern branch in 1909.[44]

South Hackney technical institute, so called in 1900 but later known as Sir John Cass's Hackney institute,[45] originated in the annual tenancy of Cassland House taken by the L.C.C.'s technical education board in 1897. With money assigned to technical instruction in Hackney under a Charity Commission Scheme, a building trade school was opened and placed under the same governing body as that of the institute in Dalston Lane.[46] After transfer to the L.C.C. in 1909,[47] the two branches constituted the L.C.C. Hackney institute, renamed in 1928 the L.C.C. Hackney technical institute[48] and in 1947 Hackney

[26] Ibid. EO/PS/12/SP/54/1; L.C.C. *Educ. Svce. Partics.* (1928-9).
[27] *Archit. of Lond.* 376; inf. from head teacher.
[28] G.L.R.O., SBL 1527 (return of schs. 1899), p. 48; above, pub. schs.
[29] Ibid. (return of elem. schs. 1903), p. 8.
[30] Ibid.   [31] Ibid.
[32] Inf. from head teacher.
[33] *Final Rep. of S.B.L. 1870-1904*, 252-4.
[34] H.A.D., D/F/TYS/16, p. 113.
[35] *Ragged Sch. Union Mag.* vi. 240; above.
[36] Nat. Soc. files.
[37] G.L.R.O., SBL 1518, pp. 90-2, 98-9.
[38] L.C.C. *Educ. Svce. Partics.* (1909-10), 195, 204, 209,

214.
[39] H.A.D., H/LD 7/16: nos. inc. Bailey's Lane, Tottenham, but not Maidstone Rd., Haggerston.
[40] L.C.C. *Educ. Svce. Partics.* (1909-10), 222, 228-9, 259.
[41] *P.O. Lond. Suburban Dir.* (1860 and later edns.); S.B.L. *Mins. of Procs.* 11 Oct. 1871.
[42] *Kelly's Dir. Hackney* (1894-5); above, pub. schs.
[43] H.A.D., H/LD 7/1; *P.O. Dir. Lond.* (1904).
[44] L.C.C. Educ. Cttee. *Mins. of Procs.* 13 Oct., 10 Nov. 1909.   [45] *P.O. Dir. Lond.* (1900-10).
[46] H.A.D., H/LD 7/1.
[47] L.C.C. Educ. Cttee. *Mins. of Procs.* 13 Oct., 10 Nov. 1909.   [48] Ibid. 25 July 1928.

technical college.[49] In 1974 it was amalgamated with Poplar technical college and Hackney and Stoke Newington college of further education to form Hackney College, whose Poplar sites were transferred in 1990 to the new Tower Hamlets college of further education.[50]

Hackney's technical college expanded from the mid 1960s, when its department of building took over Triangle House at nos. 15-35 Mare Street. Keltan House, a former factory, at nos. 89-115, had been adapted by 1970 and Clapton school for girls in Laura Place was used from 1968 until 1988. The administrative headquarters were moved from Dalston Lane to Keltan House in 1974 and to Brooke House, an extensive conversion of the boy's school, in 1990. Chelmer House was converted from a school for joint use with Hackney adult education institute in 1981. Hackney College's eight sites included the original two in Dalston Lane and Cassland Road and two in Stoke Newington and Bow in 1990, when 10,000-12,000 students were enrolled annually for full- or part-time courses.[51]

Clapton and Stamford Hill school of art was established at no. 37 Clapton Common in 1885 and moved in 1888 to no. 81. Both day and evening classes were held in 1910. The school, a noted centre for training art teachers, where Clapton's historian Florence Bagust taught, closed in 1916 after the L.C.C. had withdrawn support.[52]

Ten evening institutes,[53] some of them with branches, met at the L.C.C.'s schools in 1930: 4 were for women, 3 were commercial or junior commercial, 2 were junior commercial and technical, and one was literary. In addition South Hackney day continuation school was held in Homerton High Street. After reorganization in 1948,[54] Clapton and Homerton (formerly Glyn Road) women's institute offered classes to both sexes at Glyn school, with a branch at Lea Marsh school. It was replaced by Clapton and Kingsland institute on the same site, by then an annexe of Clapton Park school, with branches at three primary schools, in 1958. Clapton institute, its successor, was at Upton House by 1967 and at Brooke House school throughout the 1970s. Hackney adult education institute was in Chelmer Road from 1981 and at Woodberry Down school, Stoke Newington, by 1987.

The Cordwainers' technical college, originally in Clerkenwell and incorporated in 1914 to take over the work of the Leather Trades school,[55] moved from war-time accommodation to no. 182 Mare Street (formerly Lady Holles's and the Dalston county school) in 1945.[56] A three-storeyed block with a connecting wing was added in 1956-7. The college was aided by Hackney education authority in 1990 and specialized in courses for the footwear and leather goods industries; a course in rural saddlery, developed in the 1960s, remained the only one in the country. It enrolled 176 full- and 328 part-time students for 1989-90, when numbers were expected shortly to double.[57]

Private schools. Its healthy reputation made Hackney a noted centre of private education for some 200 years, in particular as 'the ladies' university of the female arts'.[58] John Salladine, a French schoolmaster, was resident in 1627[59] and was chosen in 1630 as a vestryman, in which capacity he helped to appoint the parish schoolmaster.[60] Mrs. Winch boarded young ladies in 1637, when a rich City orphan was abducted while walking on Newington common.[61] Samuel Pepys (b. 1633) boarded at Hackney as a little child.[62]

The Presbyterian Mrs. Salmon taught French, housewifery, and polite accomplishments[63] to pupils who included the verse writer Katherine Philips (1631–64), 'matchless Orinda', in 1639[64] and the daughters of the lawyer Sir John Bramston (d. 1670) in 1648.[65] Mrs. Salmon presumably was Elizabeth, wife of Thomas Salmon (d. 1672), a vestryman who in 1671 was allowed to add to his scholars' gallery in the church and who successfully sued for unpaid fees.[66] He occupied a house at Clapton in 1658, presumably that assessed in 1664 at 28 hearths[67] and left with 11 a. to his widow and his son Thomas.[68] The younger Thomas, a clergyman, had moved to Meppershall (Beds.) by 1691.[69] Allocations of the Salmons' pew have led to identification of their school with those of Benjamin Morland and Henry Newcome.[70]

Another fashionable school was established in 1643 by Mary Perwich, whose husband Robert, 'professing schooling and boarding', was licensed to build a gallery in the church in 1649.[71] The school was allegedy associated with the Black and White House south of the churchyard, but in fact that house was enlarged for Sir Thomas Vyner[72] and assessed at only 20 hearths.[73] The Perwichs occupied a larger building: their school took 800 girls during its first 17 years[74] and, after Brooke House, Robert Perwich's was the biggest house in the parish in 1664, when it was assessed at 36 hearths in Church Street, and in 1672, when it had 32.[75] It was probably at the north end of the village,

[49] L.C.C. *Educ. Cttee. Mins.* 3 Dec. 1947.
[50] Inf. from senior librarian, Hackney Coll.
[51] Ibid. For Brooke Ho., above, pub. schs.
[52] H.A.D., D/F/BAG/2, pp. 37–54; *Terrier*, Oct. 1987; L.C.C. *Educ. Svce. Partics.* (1909–10), 259.
[53] Para. based on L.C.C. *Educ. Svce. Partics.* (1930–1 and later edns.); I.L.E.A. *Green Bk.* (1978 and later edns.).
[54] L.C.C. *Educ. Cttee. Mins.* 28 Apr. 1948.
[55] *Cordwainers' Tech. Coll. Prospectus* (1928–9).
[56] L.C.C. *Educ. Cttee. Mins.* 21 June 1939; 7 Feb. 1945.
[57] *Cordwainers' Coll. Prospectus* (1990-1); inf. from vice-principal.
[58] D. Gardiner, *Eng. Girlhood at Sch.* (1929), 211.
[59] *Ret. of Strangers in Metropolis* (Huguenot Soc. of Lond. quarto ser. lvii), 334.
[60] Vestry mins. 18 Apr. 1630; 5 July 1631.

[61] *Cal. S.P. Dom.* 1637, 422.
[62] *Diary of Sam. Pepys*, ed. Latham, v. 132.
[63] *V.C.H. Mdx.* i. 251.   [64] *D.N.B.*
[65] Gardiner, *Eng. Girlhood*, 211; Foster Watson, *Dict. of Educ.* ii (1921), 712.
[66] Vestry mins. 1 Oct. 1671; P.R.O., C 78/719/7.
[67] G.L.R.O., M93/2, p. 121; ibid. MR/TH/4, m. 3.
[68] P.R.O., PROB 11/340, f. 114.
[69] G.L.R.O., M79/G/3, p. 169.
[70] H.A.D., D/F/BAG/8, p. 106; *Lost Hackney*, 64; below, this section.
[71] Vestry mins. 15 July 1649.
[72] Robinson, *Hackney*, i. 96–7, 212 n.; above, Hackney village.   [73] G.L.R.O., MR/TH/3, m. 2; MR/TH/34.
[74] Gardiner, *Eng. Girlhood*, 212.
[75] G.L.R.O., MR/TH/3, m. 2; MR/TH/34.

where 6½ a. held of Grumbolds were conveyed by Ralph Macro in 1653,[76] and presumably was among the copyholds left to Perwich's wife and four surviving daughters in 1676.[77]

The Perwichs offered music and dancing, taught by well known masters, in addition to household skills. A fifth daughter Susanna (d. 1661) played the violin so well that distinguished audiences came from London. In reply to criticism of such accomplishments a memoir stressed Susanna's humility and her regard for William Spurstowe.[78] In the mid 1640s Joseph Lister, a serving man, found that an unidentified Hackney school was merely for 'young gentlewomen to learn to play and dance and sing' and that there were no daily prayers.[79]

Hannah Woolley (d.1677 or later), an early champion of women's education, moved with her husband from Newport (Essex) to Hackney in 1655. There she kept a boarding school and presumably wrote her first works on cookery, published in 1661 and 1664. The school may have closed after her second marriage in 1666.[80]

Other schools included those of Mr. Littelton of Clapton, who was allotted a pew in 1661, George Painter, who had two French boarders in 1668, and Mrs. Freeman and her daughter, who were licensed to build a gallery in 1671.[81] Pepys, who had recently renewed his acquaintance with Hackney, went to church in 1667 chiefly to see the young ladies of the schools, 'whereof there is great store, very pretty'.[82] The prosperous vicar of Earls Colne (Essex) sent his daughters to be educated at Hackney in 1675.[83] The City's court of aldermen in 1682 paid the fees of two orphans to Mrs. Crittenden,[84] who in 1686 had installed her scholars without permission in Thomas Salmon's pew.[85] Mrs. Boardman, another schoolmistress, was threatened in 1685 with the pillory.[86] Samuel Hoadly (d.1705), author of the popular Natural Method of Teaching, moved in 1686 to Hackney, which he left in 1700 to become headmaster at Norwich.[87] Benjamin Morland, son of the ejected Martin Morland, kept a successful private school at Clapton from 1685[88] and took over Mrs. Crittenden's gallery in 1690.[89]

Girls' schools, perhaps influenced by the freer morality of the Restoration, continued to be condemned for frivolity. John Aubrey in 1670 regretted a past when girls had been educated at nunneries, 'not at Hackney schools to learn pride

and wantonness'. At the same time, by catering chiefly for citizens' daughters, they attracted the sneers of court dramatists:[90] snobbery was portrayed in a Hackney educated haberdasher's wife in Thomas Shadwell's The Humourists of 1671[91] and a heroine from Hackney was kept close by her father in Wycherley's The Gentleman Dancing-Master of 1672.[92]

Growing numbers led in 1686 to an order that gentlewomen's schools which had a gallery should use no other pews.[93] Allocations were made for Mr. Sinclair's pupils in 1686 and Mrs. Hopkins's in 1689.[94] Of 13 well known ladies' boarding schools listed in 1694 three, under Mrs. Freeman, Mrs. Beckford, and Mrs. Smith, were at Hackney. Morland's and another grammar school and a writing school were also listed,[95] as later was Hoadly's school.[96] The grammarian James Greenwood (d. 1737) was an usher under Morland before moving to Woodford (Essex) soon after 1711.[97]

By c. 1700 the west side of London was attracting more schools.[98] The lexicographer Robert Ainsworth (d. 1743), who advocated small classes, kept a school in Bethnal Green in 1698 and afterwards, between 1725 and 1729, lived at the Norris family's house in Grove Street.[99] During most of the 18th and early 19th centuries the parish, for all its many schools, was noted chiefly for Newcome's and for nonconformist academies.[1]

Newcome's or Hackney school came to be the largest and most fashionable of all 18th-century private schools.[2] It originally belonged to Benjamin Morland, whose daughter Lydia married Henry, son of the vicar Peter Newcome, in 1714. Henry Newcome (d. 1756), although dismissed as a young preacher of little sense, was long remembered as 'the famous Dr. Newcome of Hackney'. He probably took charge in 1721, when Morland became high master of St. Paul's school.[3] Perhaps an acquaintance begun at Hackney led Samuel Hoadly's son Benjamin (d. 1761), bishop of Winchester, to choose Newcome's school for his own sons Benjamin (1706–57), the royal physician, and John (1711–76), the poet, both of whom wrote plays. John distinguished himself in one of the theatrical performances for which the school became famous.[4] Leading Whig patrons included the Cavendishes, the Fitzroys, and the Yorkes:[5] sons of the third and fourth dukes of Devonshire

76 H.A.D., D/F/TYS/40, p. 209. The land was close to the Templars' ho., which was held of Kingshold.
77 P.R.O., PROB 11/351, f. 104.
78 Gardiner, Eng. Girlhood, 212–14; Robinson, Hackney, i. 212-20; J. Batchiler, The Virgin's Pattern: Life of Susanna Perwich (1661), epistle dedicatory, pp. 2, 7, 21, 34, 41.
79 Autobiog. of Jos. Lister, ed. T. Wright (1842), 32.
80 D.N.B.; Europa Biog. Dict. of Eng. Women (1983), 430.
81 Vestry mins. 8 Apr. 1661; 26 Nov. 1671; Cal. Mdx. Sess. Bks. iv. 61.
82 Diary of Sam. Pepys, ed. Latham, viii. 174; Jnl. of Wm. Schellinks (Camd. 5th ser. i), 59.
83 Diary of Ralph Josselin (Camd. 3rd ser. xv), 167.
84 Gardiner, Eng. Girlhood, 214, 167.
85 Vestry mins. 9 May 1686.
86 Cal. S.P. Dom. 1684–5, 303.   87 D.N.B.
88 M. McDonnell, Reg. of St. Paul's Sch. 1509–1748 (1977), 418; H.A.D., D/F/BAG/8, p. 106; V.C.H. Mdx. i. 243.   89 Vestry mins. 22 Apr. 1690.
90 Gardiner, Eng. Girlhood, 220; V.C.H. Mdx. i. 252; J.
Aubrey, Miscellanies (1857), 219.
91 Complete Works of Thos. Shadwell, ed. M. Summers, i (1927), 247.
92 W. Wycherley, Gentleman Dancing-Master, I. i. 86.
93 Vestry mins. 11 Mar. 1686.
94 Ibid. 28 Dec. 1686; 14 Sept. 1689.
95 J. Houghton, Colln. for Improvement of Husbandry and Trade [weekly newsheet], v, no. 104.
96 Ibid. v, no. 112. Schs. were not listed after vol. v, no. 169 (25 Oct. 1695).
97 McDonnell, Reg. of St. Paul's, 419; D.N.B.
98 V.C.H. Mdx. i. 252.
99 Ibid. i. 246; Watson, Gentlemen, 110; above, manors (Norris). It is not certain that he moved his sch. there, as in D.N.B.   1 Above, prot. nonconf.
2 N. Hans, New Trends in Educ. in 18th Cent. (1951), 70.
3 McDonnell, Reg. of St. Paul's, 362–3; Diary of Dudley Ryder, ed. Matthews, 180.
4 D.N.B.; Lysons, Environs, ii. 477.
5 V.C.H. Mdx. i. 244; below, this section.

attended,[6] as did the second earl of Hardwicke (d. 1790) and his three brothers.[7]

The plays at Newcome's school were produced from 1730 or earlier, perhaps annually in the 1760s[8] but every three years by 1795.[9] Contributors of prologues or epilogues, for both classical and English works, included David Garrick in 1763[10] and later George Keate (d.1797).[11] Actors included the earl of Euston, later first lord of the treasury as duke of Grafton (1735–1811), who was watched by his grandfather in 1751,[12] perhaps the future fifth duke of Devonshire (d. 1811) in the early 1760s,[13] the future earl of Harrington and Lord Robert Cavendish in 1764, when over 100 coaches arrived,[14] and the diarist Thomas Creevey (1768–1838) in 1783.[15] Royalty attended in 1761.[16] Old boys' dinners often took place at the Thatched House tavern, St. James's: stewards included the earl of Hardwicke and Lord Grey in 1768, Lord Ravensworth in 1781, and the duke of Devonshire, Lord Dover, and Lord Henry Fitzroy in 1791.[17] Reunions were still held in 1829.[18]

Henry Newcome died rich,[19] leaving Clapton copyholds to his son Peter, F.R.S., so long as he should carry on the school, and then on the same conditions to Peter's half-brother Henry.[20] Peter (d. 1779) gave up control to Henry,[21] who married a niece of the antiquary William Cole and whose second son Richard[22] had succeeded by 1792. The diplomatist Stratford Canning (1786–1880), a pupil from 1792 to 1794, remembered a priggish potentate who left the boys to a Spartan existence in which the smaller ones were slaves.[23] At the end of 1802 Richard handed over to the Revd. C. T. Heathcote,[24] whose family had long known the Newcomes[25] and under whom speeches replaced the plays.[26] The school closed between 1815, when changes were announced by Heathcote, who also held an Essex living, and 1819, when the property was auctioned.[27] In the 1790s a resident usher kept order in a tall double-gabled brick building large enough for 70–80 boys, while the Newcomes lived next to it in a new house.[28] The two houses, walled grounds, and 8 a. offered a good building site,[29] which was taken for the London Orphan Asylum.[30]

Girls' boarding schools were kept in 1715 by Mrs. Wallis, Mrs. Hammond, and Elizabeth Hutton and in 1726 by Elizabeth Golbourne. Mrs. Hutton's may have been at the Black and White House,[31] occupied as a school by Mary Roberts in 1747[32] and presumably the 'old white boarding school next the church, well known for a century past' whose former headmistress Katharine Thompson died in 1788;[33] the school had ended a long existence by 1795.[34] Mrs. Newton died in 1790, having kept a school for many years. M. and E. Humphries boarded young ladies at Homerton in 1772,[35] the Misses Green kept the Grove boarding school in Church Street in 1782, Mrs. Ranking engaged a Frenchman for her boarders in Tryon's Place in 1784,[36] Mrs. Carter's scholars had lately used a gallery in the church in 1787,[37] and Miss Rogerson boarded girls in the Grove in 1790.[38] Mrs. Larkham, assisted by Mr. Larkham, in 1791 boarded girls at Dalston, where Miss Story was associated with her in 1793.[39]

Boys' boarding schools in the 18th century included one under a Mr. W–, where a pupil stabbed another with a sword in 1727,[40] and one under James Graham, which surrendered a pew in 1738[41] but presumably continued as Graham's school at Dalston, where it staged a play in 1755. An academy in Church Street offered genteel boarding, with emphasis on morals, in 1769.[42] John Bonnycastle (1750?–1821), the mathematical writer, kept an academy at Hackney when young.[43] A French grammar by Isaac Coustell, a teacher at Hackney, was advertised in 1748.[44] John Naudin took boarders in Well Street, where only French was spoken in the family, in 1775 and denied rumours of his retirement in 1785.[45] He may have been succeeded by Paul de la Pierre, a Swiss, and one Gilbert, who advertised their Well Street academy in 1790 and produced French plays in 1791; boys under eight boarded at Miss Gilbert's, Well Street, in 1793.[46] Mr. De Latre kept an academy in the City in 1789[47] but lived in Well Street, where Mrs. De Latre carried on a school, perhaps for girls, in 1790; Mrs. Delavaud and Miss Yeomans were her successors in 1791.[48] Mr. Thurgood, after nine years' experience, moved from Hoxton to

6 Hist. Parl., Commons, 1754–90, ii. 201, 203, 206.
7 Ibid. iii. 675, 678–9, 681; H.A.D., D/F/BAG/8, pp. 116–23 (list of pupils, from programmes and adverts.).
8 H.A.D., D/F/TYS 70/14, p. 13 ('Plays performed at Dr. Newcome's sch.').
9 Lysons, Environs, ii. 477.
10 H.A.D., D/F/TYS 70/14, p. 79.
11 Ibid. H/LD 7/2, pp. 71, 117, 127; 7/3, p. 53.
12 Ibid. 7/2, p. 14; D.N.B. s.v. Fitzroy, Augustus.
13 H.A.D., D/F/TYS 70/14, p. 13.
14 Ibid. H/LD 7/3, p. 41.
15 Ibid. D/F/TYS 70/14, p. 87.
16 Ibid. H/LD 7/2, p. 22.
17 Ibid. pp. 33, 73, 107, passim; H.A.D., 900.2, passim.
18 Ibid. D/F/TYS 70/14, p. 26.
19 Hans, Trends in Educ. 72.
20 G.L.R.O., M79/LH/13, pp. 263–5.
21 Ibid. 15, pp. 22–3; Alum. Cantab. to 1751, iii. 246.
22 Horace Walpole's Corresp. ed. W. S. Lewis (1937), i. 315; ii. 265.
23 S. Lane-Poole, Life of Stratford Canning (1888), i. 9–10; D.N.B.
24 H.A.D., H/LD 7/2, p. 29.
25 Hans, Trends in Educ. 71.
26 Lysons, Environs, Suppl. 168.

27 H.A.D., H/LD 7/2, pp. 171, 186; Hans, Trends in Educ. 75.
28 Lane-Pole, Stratford Canning, i. 10–11; Lost Hackney, 64–5; above, plate 60.
29 H.A.D., H/LD 7/2, p. 186.
30 Above, pub. svces.
31 Diary of Dudley Ryder, 81–2, 84, 102, 151; Stow, Survey (1720), app. i, p. 123; vestry mins. 12 Apr. 1726.
32 H.A.D., M 158(b).
33 Ibid. 900.2, p. 24.
34 Lysons, Environs, ii. 459.
35 H.A.D., 900.2, pp. 21–2.
36 Ibid. H/LD 7/2, pp. 77, 82.
37 Vestry mins. 10 Apr. 1787.
38 H.A.D., H/LD 7/2, p. 103.
39 Ibid. p. 285; ibid. 7/6.
40 Ibid. 7/2, p. 2b.
41 Vestry mins. 27 Feb. 1738.
42 H.A.D., H/LD 7/2, pp. 33, 285.
43 D.N.B.
44 H.A.D., 900.2, p. 14.
45 Ibid. H/LD 7/2, pp. 55, 82.
46 Ibid. pp. 103, 105, 109, 121; Watson, Gentlemen, 110.
47 H.A.D., 900.2, p. 24.
48 Ibid. H/LD 7/2, pp. 103, 107.

open a boarding school in Shore Place in 1791.[49] Barber's Barn was Mr. Worsley's school in the 1790s.[50]

Private schools were most numerous in the 19th century,[51] although many were short lived and some were apparently ill managed. A seller of indecent prints in 1802 had no need to venture farther than Hackney because of his custom from the ladies' schools.[52] Mr. Newham, in charge of a school at Homerton, was sued in 1807 for beating a boy who had been bitten by the master's dog.[53]

In 1826–7 at least 71 establishments were described as private academies. Thirty-five, of which 22 were wholly or partly boarding, were in the old centre and south part of the parish; a further 10 were listed for Clapton, 4 for Homerton, 18 for Kingsland, Dalston, and Shacklewell, and 4 for Stamford Hill.[54] Such schools were often ephemeral; few of the proprietors were still listed in 1832, when some had moved farther north within the parish.[55] In 1838 the total was 75, of which 29 were in Hackney, 16 in Clapton, 27 in Kingsland, Dalston, and Shacklewell, and 3 at Stamford Hill.[56] There were also rival grammar schools, founded in 1830 by subscription.[57] In 1849 at least 68 residents kept schools, while others offered private or specialist tuition.[58]

Longer lived schools included one in 1804 under Richard Barnes, successor to James Pickbourne, in the Cass family's house or in one that had replaced it in Grove Street. As Grove House school, it was kept by Barnes and his son in 1832 and at its height had over 40 boarders.[59] Probably it had been closed by 1848, when a school was established in the nearby Common House.[60] That too was called Grove House by 1849, when, as in 1861, it was under John Willey.[61] By 1869 it was under H. R. Clarke, who prepared boarders and day boys for the universities or commerce in 1872, and by 1879 under E. Watkinson.[62] Clapton House reputedly had both boys and girls[63] before its lease as a classical school in 1830 to Donald Aird, who advertised its grandeur and previously had taught in St. Thomas's Square. Aird may have added some buildings and apparently used Salomon's 'synagogue' as a dining hall.[64] Sutton House contained a boys' school under Dr. Burnet, briefly attended in 1818 by the novelist Edward

Bulwer-Lytton (d.1873), and later Milford House girls' school.[65] The many girls' schools included one near St. Thomas's Square under the Misses Brown, successors to Mrs. and Miss Walker, in 1814;[66] it may have been continued by them in Mare Street in 1826, by Maria Brown in Mare Street, or by Sarah Brown in Cambridge Row in 1838. Hannah Slater's school in Lower Clapton Road near the site of Laura Place, recorded in 1826 and 1838 and perhaps continuing one kept by Mrs. Bell, was highly regarded,[67] as was the school of the Misses Hibbert, in Upper Clapton Road by 1826.[68]

The most distinguished 19th-century school, in the enlightened tradition of Ainsworth, was Madras House,[69] so named by the religious writer John Allen (d. 1839), who adopted the Madras system whereby monitors took responsibility for younger boys.[70] Although it was later claimed that the school dated from 1796,[71] Allen first took pupils in Mare Street in 1817, moving to larger premises on the east side in 1821. The school, visited by Edward Irving (d.1834) and other scholars, had a maximum of nearly 150 boys.[72] They included the lexicographer Sir William Smith (1813–93) and his brother Philip (1817–85), who wrote on ancient history, John Curwen (1816–80), the writer on music, and Sir Charles Reed (1819–81), chairman of the London school board. The missionary Edward Steere (1828–82), bishop of Zanzibar, attended under John Allen's son, the philologist Alexander Allen (d. 1842). On Alexander's death Madras House passed to Thomas Garland,[73] who ran it in 1861, and to Messrs. W. Paine and Wilson, who described it as a grammar school in 1869[74] and took boarders and day boys until 1879 or later.[75] The premises, at no. 208 Mare Street, were used by the Essex Volunteer Regiment in 1892.[76]

Hackney Proprietary grammar school,[77] each of whose proprietors might hold not more than 3 out of 130 shares, was opened in 1830. Its staff was to be well paid and the Madras system was used. Although the headmaster was an Anglican clergyman, the presence of nonconformist teachers led to printed denunciations in 1831.[78] More damaging was a ban on shopkeepers' sons,[79] which stimulated support for a Church of England grammar school (below). Each school had

49 Ibid. p. 109.
50 Clarke, *Hackney*, illus. facing p. 32.
51 *E. Lond. Papers*, iv. 63.   52 H.A.D., 900.2, p. 31.
53 Ibid. H/LD 7/2, p. 161.
54 Pigot, *Com. Dir.* (1826–7).
55 Ibid. (1832–4) listing Hackney, Homerton, Dalston, Kingsland, and Shacklewell under Lond., Clapton and Stoke Newington, inc. Stamford Hill, under Mdx.
56 *Pigot's Lond. Dir.* (1838).
57 Ibid.; below (Hackney Proprietary grammar sch. and Hackney Ch. of Eng. grammar sch.).
58 *Hackney Dir.* (1849); the no. excludes schs. in Stoke Newington, listed under Hackney.
59 H.A.D., H/LD 7/2, p. 148; Watson, *Gentlemen*, 111; Pigot, *Com. Dir.* (1832–4). Pickbourne in 1790 had been a tenant of H. H. Norris: H.A.D., D/F/NOR/2111.
60 Watson, *Gentlemen*, 111; F. S. de Carteret-Bisson, *Our Schs and Colleges.* (1879), 694.
61 *Hackney Dir.* (1849); *Crockford's Scholastic Dir.* (1861).
62 *Green's Hackney Dir.* (1869–70); Bisson, *Schs.* (1872), 261; (1879), 694.
63 H.A.D., D/F/BAG/5, pp. 26–7.

64 Ibid. pp. 50–2; D/F/BAG/ 13A; Pigot, *Com. Dir.* (1826–7); *Pigot's Com. Dir. Lond.* (1832–4); *Pigot's Lond. Dir.* (1838); *E. Lond. Papers*, iv. 69; above, plate 59.
65 *Sutton Ho. Guide*, 3; V. Lytton, *Life of Edw. Bulwer, Ld. Lytton*, i (1913), 49–50; *D.N.B.*
66 H.A.D., H/LD 7/2, p. 171.
67 Pigot, *Com. Dir.* (1826–7); *Pigot's Lond. Dir.* (1938); *Terrier*, July 1987; Clarke, *Hackney*, 195.
68 Depicted on a cup in Vestry Ho. mus., Walthamstow; inf. from Mr. D. Mander.
69 *V.C.H. Mdx.* i. 246.   70 Clarke, *Hackney*, 35.
71 Bisson, *Schs.* (1879), 694.
72 Clarke, *Hackney*, 35.   73 Ibid.; *D.N.B.*
74 *Crockford's Scholastic Dir.* (1861); *Green's Hackney Dir.* (1869–70).   75 Bisson, *Schs.* (1879), 694.
76 Clarke, *Hackney*, 34 n.
77 Following 2 paras. based on *E. Lond. Papers*, iv. 64–7; Clarke, *Hackney*, pp. xiv, 132–4, 205, and n.; *Hackney Photos.* i. 150.
78 S. Curtis, *Strictures on Hackney Grammar Sch.* (1831), answered by S. Roper, *More Words in Defence of Hackney Grammar Sch.* (1831).
79 Attacked in *Hackney Mag.* Feb. 1834, 51.

c. 120 boys in the 1830s, when they formed warring gangs before uniting against the Free school, but the Proprietary school had only 50 by *c.* 1840 and amalgamated with the Church of England grammar school before 1848. The 'dear little building',[80] rendered and with Perpendicular details, was converted to private use as Sutton Lodge, which in turn was replaced in the 1950s by extensions to the Metal Box factory.[81]

Hackney Church of England grammar school sought a headmaster in 1829 and was opened in connexion with King's College, London, with the bishop as patron and the rector J. J. Watson as president.[82] Benjamin Clarke was among the first boys in 1830, when a few boarders were allowed. The composer Alfred Cellier (1844–91) attended and later taught there.[83] The building, on the west side of Back Lane (later Clarence Road) was designed by William MacIntosh Brookes and rendered, with a Doric portico: it was costlier than that of Hackney Proprietary school. The school was rescued from debt *c.* 1880 and continued as King's College or Hackney Collegiate[84] school until 1895. After serving as a soft drinks factory, the building made way in 1903 for flats called Clarence Gardens, which in turn made way for a road on the Pembury estate.[85]

The number of private schools fell only slightly in the mid 19th century. Wick House was turned into a boys' boarding school, entitled Wick Hall collegiate, commercial, and scientific school, in 1841[86] but was again in private occupation in 1861, shortly before its demolition.[87] At least 57 private schools existed in 1861, only 10 of them for boys,[88] and 55, including a Pestalozzian school, in 1869. Many retained genteel descriptions in 1869, when there were also music teachers[89] and, in Dalston, a 20-year old French institute offering art classes.[90] Clapton House was the third home of St. John's Foundation school for the sons of poor clergymen from 1859 until its move to Leatherhead (Surr.) in 1872. As his first school, it was recalled by Sir Anthony Hope Hawkins (1863–1933) (the novelist Anthony Hope), whose father the Revd. E. C. Hawkins was headmaster.[91]

Schools in 1872 included Dalston Congregational or Middle-class training school of 1855, which was often listed with public schools,[92] Kingsland collegiate school of 1865 for 20 boarders and 60 day boys, South Hackney college of 1866 for 40 boarders and 75 day boys, Lonsbury college of 1866 at Hackney Downs, and Dalston

college at Albion hall. Both South Hackney and Lonsbury colleges, offering a commercial education, survived in 1898.[93] Anglican clergymen had charge of St. James's college, called Clapton college by 1879, for boarders and day boys, and Hackney Collegiate school.[94] Priory House school was on the west side of Lower Clapton Road, under Howard Anderton; it had been founded by Samuel Prout Newcome and later continued at Clapton Common under Howard's son Stanley until 1909.[95] Girls' schools in 1884 included the purpose-built Kingsland Birkbeck schools in Ridley Road, founded in 1852 in the old Kingsland Congregational church and originally also for boys, College House, Clapton Square, founded in 1863, and the expensive Grove House at Upper Clapton.[96]

After 1870 a few well known schools were founded, in spite of social changes and better public provision, which were blamed for the closure of Madras House.[97] The Grocers' Co.'s school of 1876 was drawing boys from Clapton college by 1882.[98] The governors of Lady Holles's school in London built a middle-class school at no. 182 Mare Street, which was opened in 1878 and charged fees comparable with those of the Grocers' school; some 300 girls attended by 1884, although numbers fell to 81 in 1895 before reaching 380 in 1921.[99] At Stamford Hill successful schools were founded by the Skinners' Co. in 1890 and the Servite Sisters in 1904.[1] The Church Schools' Co., formed in 1883, had a short lived school in Cazenove Road in 1892.[2] Bodleian House, Upper Clapton, was founded in 1878 and attended by 35 girls, including boarders, in 1884. It may have continued at no. 35 Clapton Common as a music academy, with a kindergarten and preparatory school, in the 1930s.[3] No. 81 Clapton Common, from 1888 the home of Clapton and Stamford Hill school of art, in 1861 had been a girls' boarding school under Miss C. Bush.[4]

Roman Catholic schools were open in Sidney Road by 1887. The boys', next to the church, was called Homerton Catholic grammar school;[5] it had accommodation for 112 and an attendance of 27 in 1890 and closed in 1891.[6] The girls', at no. 21, was a boarding school still managed by Sisters of the Sacred Hearts in 1894.[7]

The Skinners' Co.'s school for girls[8] was opened in 1890, under a Scheme of 1886, following foundations for boys at Tunbridge Wells and Tonbridge (Kent).[9] Purpose-built premises

80 Pevsner, *Lond.* ii. 168.
81 *Lost Hackney*, 68–9; above, plate 44.
82 H.A.D., H/LD 7/2, pp. 215, 221; 7/3, p. 123.
83 *D.N.B.*
84 H.A.D., D/F/TYS/16, p. 326; Stanford, *Map of Lond.* (1862–5 edn.), sheet 7; Bisson, *Schs.* (1879), p. 693.
85 *Lost Hackney*, 72.
86 H.A.D., H/LD 7/11 (prospectus); illus. in H.A.D., P 12047–8.
87 *P.O. Dir. Six Home Counties* (1845); inf. from H.A.D.; above, manors (Wick).
88 *Crockford's Scholastic Dir.* (1861).
89 *Green's Hackney Dir.* (1869–70).
90 Ibid. (advert.).
91 Clarke, *Hackney*, 197 and n.; E. M. P. Williams, *The Quest Goes On* (1951), 3, 6–8; R. Hughes, *St. John's Foundation Sch. 1851–72* (1987), 59–60; *D.N.B.*
92 Above, pub. schs.
93 Bisson, *Schs.* (1872), 260–2; (1879), 693, 695; *P.O. Dir.*

Lond. County Suburbs, North (1898).
94 Bisson, *Schs.* (1872), 260; (1879), 693.
95 Ibid. (1872), 260; H.A.D., D/F/BAG/8, pp. 86–9; *Terrier*, Spring 1993.
96 Bisson, *Schs.* (1884), 533–5; H.A.D., H/LD 7/24; adverts. in *Hackney Gaz.* 10 July 1869 and later edns.
97 Clarke, *Hackney*, 35.
98 F. Geffen, 'Educ. in Hackney 1616 to 1901' (Brentwood trg. coll. thesis, 1963, in H.A.D.), 69–72.
99 Bisson, *Schs.* (1884), 527; *E. Lond. Papers*, iv. 72–3.
1 Below, this section.
2 *Official Year Bk. of Ch. of Eng.* (1892).
3 Bisson, *Schs.* (1884), 527; *P.O. Dir. Lond.* (1934).
4 *Crockford's Scholastic Dir.* (1861); above, tech. educ.
5 *Kelly's Dir. Hackney* (1887).   6 P.R.O., ED 14/8.
7 *Kelly's Dir. Hackney* (1887, 1893–4).
8 Para. based on inf. from the schools clerk, Skinners' Co.
9 A. Fox, *Brief Description of Co. of Skinners* (1968).

at nos. 111 and 113 (later 117) Stamford Hill accommodated 250 pupils aged 8–7, of whom 6 at first held scholarships.[10] Under the Act of 1944, the school was voluntary aided from 1949. Younger girls used the former Mount Pleasant county school[11] from 1972, while older ones remained at Stamford Hill. In 1989 the upper school had 290 pupils aged 14–19 and the lower had 353, aged 11–13.

In 1898 the Girls' Public Day School Co. occupied nos. 1 and 2 Marriott Terrace, Lower Clapton Road, and North Hackney high school for girls had a boys' department and kindergarten at Stamford Hill. Besides those schools, others mentioned above, and a mixed middle-class school in Lauriston Road, there were at least 60 smaller private establishments. A few survived near Victoria Park but most were farther north: 13 were in the Hackney part of Stoke Newington, notably in Brooke or Cazenove roads, 7 in Upper Clapton, including 4 in Clapton Common, and 13 in Lower Clapton, including 3 in Clapton Square.[12]

Ownership in 1898 was more concentrated than the number of schools suggested: H. Anderton's Priory House was at no. 29 Clapton Common and Miss H. A. Anderton's school at no. 57; probably two schools were kept by Miss Bessie Buckley, two by Miss A. Henderson, and two by Miss M. E. Jervis. While most schools were short lived, a few continued in different hands. Stamford Hill and Clapton school for girls, at no. 96 Stamford Hill under Miss Henderson by 1898, moved after c. 1906 to no. 118,[13] where it remained under Miss J. Rothery until 1930 or later.[14] No. 77 Cazenove Road housed a school under Miss E. Plews in 1898 and Wilson college for boys, founded in 1881, under W. A. Warne in 1911 and 1914; a boys' school, under W. Brimicombe by 1930, survived there until the Second World War.[15] Clark's college opened a branch at the Tower House, no. 108 Clapton Common, c. 1909 and soon moved to nos. 147–9 Stamford Hill, where it remained until 1959 or later.[16]

Numbers fell rapidly in the 20th century. Excluding the Grocers', Lady Holles's, and Skinners' schools, 29 private schools were listed in 1905, when 2 were for boarders, 15 in 1914, and 10 in 1930. The Grocers' school passed to the L.C.C. in 1906 and Lady Holles's moved to Hampton in the 1930s. By 1939 there were only denominational schools, apart from the Skinners', Brimicombe's, and Clark's college at Stamford Hill.[17]

A Roman Catholic school whose success may have affected many competitors was opened by the Servite Sisters at no. 14 Amhurst Park in 1904.[18] For girls of all ages and at first also for small boys, it occupied no. 16 by 1914[19] and was described as a high-class day school and kindergarten in 1931, when it also occupied no. 12.[20] As Our Lady's Convent high school, it was voluntary aided from 1944. Nos. 6, 8, and 10 Amhurst Park were acquired in 1966 and all the original buildings were replaced in stages, in 1963, 1966, 1978, and 1986. The school remained in the Servites' trusteeship in 1989, with 575 girls aged 11 to 18 on the roll.

Jewish settlement[21] had led to the opening in 1906 of an industrial school for girls in detention called Montefiore House at no. 69 Stamford Hill, with Claude Montefiore as chairman of the governors.[22] The Jewish Secondary Schools Movement, established by Rabbi V. Schonfield who founded the Union of Orthodox Hebrew Congregations, in 1929 started a boys' school at Avigdor House, no. 96 Amhurst Park, and a girls', with some preparatory classes and boarders, at Northfields, nos. 109 and 111 Stamford Hill.[23] In 1939 the New synagogue also had a preparatory and kindergarten school. All apparently closed during the war, although afterwards Avigdor House reopened in Stoke Newington[24] and the movement had offices at no. 86 Amhurst Park until the 1980s.

Yesodey Hatorah, founded in 1943, was the first and in 1977 the largest of the ultra-orthodox schools.[25] It occupied nos. 2 and 4 Amhurst Park by 1947 and also nos. 5 and 13, as primary and girls' senior schools, by 1964. In 1989 the boys' primary school, kindergarten, and nursery were at no. 2 Amhurst Park, the boys' senior school was at no. 4, and primary and senior girls' schools were at no. 153 Stamford Hill.

The Lubavitch Foundation opened the ultra-orthodox Lubavitch House primary school for girls, with a nursery, at nos. 107 and 109 Stamford Hill in 1959. The Foundation's synagogue moved there from Cazenove Road in 1960, when a boys' school was opened. A senior girls' school started at no. 115 Stamford Hill in 1962 and expanded in 1964 and 1966. Premises for boys were acquired and adapted in 1971 at nos. 133 and 135 Clapton Common, where a senior school was opened in 1983. In 1989 the kindergarten, with 100 children, and 115 senior girls were at no. 107 Stamford Hill, 175 junior girls were at nos. 113–115 Stamford Hill, and 80 senior and 165 junior boys were at Clapton Common.[26]

Yesodey Hatorah girls' and Lubavitch boys' and girls' primary schools unsuccessfully sought voluntary aided status in 1983–4. Although Hackney L.B. later made grants to several Jewish schools, Simon Marks was the only one administered by the I.L.E.A. in 1990 and by Hackney in 1993.[27]

10 Ibid.; *The Times*, 27 Nov. 1890, 3f; *P.O. Dir. Lond. County Suburbs, North* (1898).   11 Above, pub. schs.
12 *P.O. Dir. Lond. County Suburbs, North* (1898).
13 Ibid.; *Hackney Photos.* i. 151.
14 *P.O. Dir. Lond. County Suburbs* (1930).
15 Ibid. *North* (1898); H.A.D., H/LD 7/1 (advert.); *P.O. Dir. Lond. County Suburbs* (1914, 1930); *P.O. Dir. Lond.* (1941, 1942).
16 H.A.D., D/F/BAG/1, p. 69; *Kelly's Dir. Stoke Newington and Clapton* (1909–10 and later edns.); *Hackney Photos.* ii. 55; *P.O. Dir. Lond.* (1959).
17 *P.O. Dirs. Lond.*; above, pub. schs. (Hackney Downs).
18 Para. based on inf. from Sister Mary John, headmistress.   19 *P.O. Dir. Lond. County Suburbs* (1914).
20 *Catholic Dir.* (1931).
21 Two paras. based on *P.O. Dir. Lond.* (1914 and later edns); *Jewish Year Bk.* (1910 and later edns).
22 Bernstein, *Stamford Hill and the Jews*, 20; above, Judaism.   23 Hackney, *Official Guide* [1935], advert.
24 *V.C.H. Mdx.* viii. 218, 223.
25 *Jewish Chron. Colour Mag.* 27 May 1977.
26 Inf. from dir. of educ., Lubavitch Foundation.
27 Alderman, *Lond. Jewry and Lond. Politics*, 127–8, 176 n.; above, pub. schs.

CHARITIES FOR THE POOR

Hackney had many distributive charities from the early 17th century.[19] It was also noted for its large number of refuges, although most of them, including some that were styled almshouses, were not intended for parishioners.[20] A few charities seem to have lapsed, including those founded by of John Matthew in 1568 and Elizabeth, countess of Oxford (d. 1612 or 1613), both of which were still received in 1622,[21] or not to have been put into effect, such as that of Thomas Hawkes in 1657.[22] The other gifts were periodically recorded by the vestry from 1614 and entered in a separate annual account from the early 18th to the early 19th century.[23] In 1789–90 the total income from lands and investments of gifts for the poor was c. £180, of which £75 2s. 6d. was for coals and £22 8s. for bread.[24] In 1799–1800 the income was c. £213, of which only £101 was spent.[25] In consequence of the division of the old parish into three rectories, the Church Building Commissioners apportioned its charities in 1833, when their total income was c. £840.[26]

In 1833 the curtailed parish of St. John, Hackney, was allotted charities with a total income of c. £508, made up of localized distributive charities, two almshouse charities, and half of the large number of charities, together worth £447 13s. 2d., which were divisible among the three parishes. South Hackney was allotted a few localized charities, including an almshouse charity, and a quarter of the divisible charities. West Hackney's share was a quarter of the divisible charities.[27]

Local government changes and the creation of new ecclesiastical parishes raised questions about the right to distribute charities. Claims on South and West Hackney were advanced by the reformed Hackney vestry and from 1855 by its elected successor, which demanded the apportioned lands on behalf of the whole parish. Vestries of householders nonetheless managed the charities in all three parishes in 1894, apportioning the income among the several ecclesiastical districts, whose vicars accounted to the rectors and whose rights to choose recipients had been supported by the Charity Commissioners in 1867.[28]

The incomes were punctually received and applied in 1855.[29] In 1869, however, a newspaper alleged that the parochial authorities were denied information by many of the trustees, some of them City companies: large deductions had

been made from the incomes of several named charities and in 1867 c. £350 had been charged to expenses, whereas only £274 had been distributed among the poor.[30] Soon afterwards many lands and investments were transferred to the official trustees. In 1894 the local application of all the charities was done with great care.[31]

Consolidation began with a Scheme of 1898 establishing the St. John, Hackney, Joint Estates charities, which included all the lands except the almshouse estates, including any not yet vested in the official trustee. Half of the income was to go to the parochial charities of Hackney and a quarter each to those of South and West Hackney. Schemes of the same date, later varied for Hackney and South Hackney, were made for the three sets of parochial charities.

Almshouse charities. Dr. William Spurstowe,[32] the former vicar, had built but not lived to endow six almshouses for widows in 1666. His brother Alderman Henry Spurstowe settled the buildings and c. 8 a. in trust in 1667 and added more land.[33] Trustees were renewed by the vestry, which until 1802 filled vacancies by nominating two almswomen for selection by Dr. Spurstowe's heir and thereafter acted alone. Rents from c. 14 a. were raised in 1771, 1814, and when a 42-year lease permitted the digging of brickearth in 1818. Stock, bought with surplus income between 1757 and 1812, was spent on rebuilding the almshouses in 1819. Each inmate received £6 a quarter from 1667 and 6 guineas from 1753,[34] later augmented by £1 at Christmas under the will of Henry Baker, who left £200 stock by will proved 1775,[35] and 5s. from George Clarke's gift (below). The charity was among those confined to the curtailed parish of Hackney in 1833, whereupon a vacancy was disputed between conservative and reformist vestrymen.[36] A Chancery Scheme of 1835 permitted building on the almshouse estate, where work was in progress in 1855.[37] The consequent rise in revenue was met by a Scheme of 1877 whereby the six almswomen, who must have lived in Hackney for 3 years, received 8s. to 10s. a week besides fuel and Baker's gift; surplus income was to provide £15 a year or less to up to 20 out-pensioners, who might be unmarried or widowed, £16 a year or less to the inmates of Wood's almshouses (below), and fees at convalescent homes or other charitable institutions. By 1893 the total receipts were £2,030, of which

19 Section based on Char. Com. files; *12th Rep. Com. Char.* H.C. 348, pp. 129–44 (1825), x; *Digest of Endowed Chars.* H.C. 433, pp. 20–5 (1867–8), lii(1); *Endowed Chars. Lond. (Hackney)*, H.C. 231, *passim* (1894), lxiii; H.A.D., BW/E/13/15–16 (plans). 20 Walford, *Lond.* v. 514.
21 P.R.O., PROB 11/51 (P.C.C. 21 Sheffelde); vestry mins. 26 Apr. 1614; 16 Aug. 1622.
22 H.A.D., P/J/C/47, f. 28.
23 Ibid., P/J/C/14-40 (1739–41 to 1813–14).
24 Ibid. 26.
25 Ibid. 33.
26 *Endowed Chars. Lond. (Hackney)*, 25–8, reciting apportionment of 1833.

27 Ibid.
28 Ibid. 30, 76; H.A.D., J/V/2, pp. 26–30; J/V/18/1, p.5.
29 H.A.D., J/V/CC/6, p. 7.
30 *Hackney & Kingsland Gaz.* 11 Dec. 1869.
31 *Endowed Chars. Lond. (Hackney)*, 76.
32 H.A.D., D/F/TYS/1 (accts. of Spurstowe's almshos., 1666–1816, at back of vestry min. bk.).
33 Inscription put up over doorway by alderman's son Hen. in 1689: *Lost Hackney*, 50.
34 Ibid. ff. 1v., 19v., 23v.
35 P.R.O., PROB 11/1004, no. 39.
36 *Hackney Mag.* Dec. 1833, 30–2.
37 H.A.D., J/V/CC/6, p. 8.

half came from houses in Graham, Greenwood, and Navarino roads and Wilton Road (later Way) and *c.* £247 from dividends. The largest disbursements were £501 to the trustees' convalescent committee and £300 to out-pensioners. Schemes of 1906 and 1935 placed Wood's almshouses under the Spurstowe trustees. In 1960 the beneficial area of the two charities was redefined as Hackney M.B., whose council was to nominate two of the nine trustees, and the residential qualification was lowered to two years; the buildings of 1666 were to be replaced by at least six new houses, which might be sold.

Spurstowe's almshouses, rebuilt in 1819, formed a single-storeyed range of brick with stone dressings, including shallow pediments over the windows and doorways.[38] They stood on the west side of Sylvester Path, as nos. 1–11 (odd), until 1966[39] and were superseded by a three-storeyed range in pale buff brick, nos. 36 and 38 Navarino Road, which in 1989 contained 16 flats. In 1981 the joint income of Spurstowe's and Wood's almshouse charities was £23,672.

Henry Monger, by will proved 1669,[40] gave land in Well Street and £400 to build six brick almshouses, for men aged 60 or more. He also left a £12 rent charge on lands in Hackney marsh, of which £9 was to provide each inmate with 30*s.* a year and the rest to be invested to pay for repairs. Joanna Martin *c.* 1679 gave two houses immediately west of the almshouses, the rents to supplement each pension by 20*s.* a year and to assist repairs. The Hackney marsh lands were apparently acquired by Sir John Cass (d. 1718), who was said to have paid the £12,[41] as part of the endowment of his school in the parish of St. Botolph, Aldgate (Lond.). Cass's widow was asked in 1732 to substitute men for the women whom she had nominated to the almshouses.[42] In 1819 the trustees of Cass's school paid the rent charge.[43] In 1824 inmates' wives but not their widows were accommodated and coals were provided. The charity was confined to South Hackney in 1833, the rector and churchwardens being free to choose the inmates subject to formal approval by the Cass Foundation. In 1893 the total income was *c.* £146, of which £12 came from the rent charge and £60 from seven houses called Blenheim Cottages, which had been built on Joanna Martin's land and leased from 1847. Three couples and two single men received pensions of £10, beside bread and potatoes under Mrs. De Kewer's gift (below). A Scheme of 1900 included the almshouses in South Hackney Parochial charities (below), whose consolidated income was assigned partly to maintain the almspeople, men or women resident for five years or more who had not received poor relief.

Monger's almshouses stood on the north side of Grove Street (later Lauriston Road), at the edge of Well Street common. In the 1790s they formed a two-storeyed range with small lattice windows and with an inscription beneath a central Dutch gable.[44] With help from the Cass trustees, they were rebuilt in 1847, in a similar style, but with bold stone dressings and the roof hidden by a parapet. They were modernized in 1969 and survived as Monger House in 1990.[45]

Thomas Wood, bishop of Lichfield and Coventry, *c.* 1653 bought land at Clapton where he built almshouses for 10 widows aged 60 or more. By will proved 1692[46] he left a rent charge of £50 a year for the inmates' pensions, besides gowns every second year and £5 for a chaplain to read prayers twice a week. Wood's Clapton estate passed to his nephew Henry Webb (d. 1713), whose heirs sold it to Sir William Chapman, on whose bankruptcy it passed through several hands to James Powell.[47] Almswomen, however, were appointed by the Chapmans until the widow of Sir John Chapman (d. 1781) surrendered her right to the parish in 1798, after which it was vainly claimed by Powell.[48] In 1824 each inmate was chosen by the minister from two nominees of the vestry. The £50 rent charge was paid, with £4 10*s.* every other year in lieu of gowns, and bread and coals, but there was no record of a chaplain. The charity was confined to the curtailed parish of Hackney in 1833. Sir Francis Willes by will dated 1823 gave to the almshouses half of a rent charge of £13 6*s.* 8*d.*, a bequest which was invalid but made effective by the Revd. Edward Willes in 1842. A rent charge for repairing the almshouses was redeemed for £1,110, which was invested in 1869, and £500 stock was bought in 1883 under the will of Anne Ashpitel, who had left money for the repair of tombs, a purpose found to be invalid, and for the almswomen. The total income was *c.* £186 in 1893. Under a Scheme of 1877 the almswomen could receive money from Spurstowe's charity, whose trustees administered Wood's from 1906. Willes's and Anne Ashpitel's endowments still formed part of the charities' combined income in 1960.

Wood's almshouses were restored in 1930. They survive as a single-storeyed red-brick building, with mullioned windows, on the east side of Lower Clapton Road. The central range has six tenements, all originally of one room, and projecting wings each have two tenements. A Gothic chapel in the angle of the north wing, described as 19th-century,[49] had been recently repaired in 1855 by J. C. Powell, the vicar of St. James's, who instituted services.[50] It held ten seats and was described as Britain's smallest chapel after the reopening of the requisitioned almshouses in 1948.[51]

Thomas Cooke of Stoke Newington, the son and grandson of Hackney merchants and a director of the Bank of England, built a house on waste of Stoke Newington common, which he held on a 99-year lease of 1740, for eight poor

38 Hist. Mon. Com. *E. Lond.* 47.
39 H.A.D., 361.1 SPU, p 164; *Lost Hackney*, 50.
40 P.R.O., PROB 11/330, f. 96.
41 *1st Rep. Com. Educ. of Poor*, H.C. 83 (1819), 265.
42 Vestry mins. 13 May 1732; Clarke, *Hackney*, 174.
43 *1st Rep. Com. Educ. of Poor*, 265.
44 H.A.D., 361.2, P 12025; above, plate 65.

45 H.A.D., J/V/CC/6, p. 9; ibid. 361.1, P 10275; *Tower to Tower Block*, no. 37.   46 P.R.O., PROB 11/410, f. 142.
47 Above, manors (Clapton Ho.).
48 Vestry mins. 20 May 1805; 8 Apr. 1806.
49 Hist. Mon. Com. *E. Lond.* 48; Pevsner, *Lond.* ii. 171.
50 H.A.D., J/V/CC/6, p. 9.
51 H.A.D., Bldgs. file [cuttings].

families with small children.[52] By will proved 1752[53] he left property in Eltham (Kent) for its upkeep and payments to the inmates, who were charged nominal rents and were removable by his heirs at will. Although the settlement was found to be invalid, as was a deed by Cooke's heir at law Margaret Fremeaux in 1793, Margaret's daughter and son-in-law Susannah and Thomas Thornton in 1824 still supported eight families, who were usually drawn from the neighbourhood and lived rent free, receiving 4 guineas a year and coals at Christmas. The charity was not recorded in the commissioners' apportionment of 1833, probably because the Thorntons were not obliged to maintain it rather than because they had ceased to do so.[54] The almshouses called Cooke's Rents, whose lease was shortly to revert to the lord, were conveyed in 1837 by W. G. Daniel-Tyssen to the select vestry of West Hackney, which vested the management in a committee of subscribers. Inmates were chosen in 1841, after the building had been repaired and renamed West Hackney almshouses.[55] The site was compulsorily purchased for a school playground in 1885, whereupon new almshouses were opened in 1889[56] on the opposite side of what had become Northwold Road. Under a Scheme of 1890 the eight tenements might be occupied by single people or couples who had lived in West Hackney parish for five years or more, with preference for those reduced from better circumstances; they were to receive 3s. to 5s. a week but must already possess at least 3s. a week. Although no income was derived from the Eltham property, Anna Wilmot augmented the subscriptions by giving £500 stock in 1887. The charity had c. £1,003 stock and total receipts of £270 in 1893. The income was £336 in 1963, when a Scheme slightly altered the inmates' payments, and £2,849 in 1975, when £2,100 was contributed by West Hackney Parochial charities.

The almshouses, on the north side of Northwold Road and called West Hackney House in 1989, form a two-storeyed range of dark brown brick with stone dressings in the Tudor style. Four tenements are on the ground floor and four on the first floor, flanking a central hall beneath a small cupola. A plaque commemorates a fund set up by Commercial Motor Users of Hackney in honour of Charles Fisher Yates (d. 1945), a former mayor, from which annual payments are made to the almspeople.

Subscriptions in memory of the Revd. H. H. Norris, including £300 from his widow, paid for four almshouses which were settled in trust in 1857 by his son Henry, who gave the land.[57] The inmates were to be single women aged 60 or more who were members of the Church of England, preference to be given to widows who

had been obliged to leave Monger's almshouses on their husbands' death. Management was by the rector and churchwardens of South Hackney, who had effective charge in 1894, aided by a committee of subscribers. The income, increased by a purchase out of accumulated subscriptions, was c. £80 in 1893, when the four women received 2s. 6d. a week, bread, coal, and a small discretionary dole from South Hackney Parochial charities. In 1965 the income was c. £75 and in 1967 Hackney L.B. agreed to a loan towards rebuilding, on condition that it should nominate half of the occupants. The restriction to Anglicans was accordingly omitted in a Scheme of 1968, which included the almshouses in South Hackney Parochial charities. A Scheme of 1979 made it possible to require small sums from the inmates towards maintenance.

The Norris almshouses stood in the north-west angle of Victoria Park Road and Handley Road. Designed in red brick with stone dressings in the Tudor style by Charles Parker, they consisted of a two-storeyed entrance section with an inscription beneath the gable, flanked by two single-storeyed tenements to the east and two to the west. They had made way for a flat-roofed block called Norris Court, containing flats for 6 couples, 5 single ladies, and a warden, by 1971.[58]

Pilgrims' Lodge charity[59] was opened in 1863 for members of Trinity Congregational chapel. James Child (d. 1881), a veterinary surgeon, built the almshouses on the north-west side of Lyme Grove, to be supported by rents from Devonshire (later Brenthouse) Road. Later bequests, before the closure of Trinity chapel, probably included two from Child's sisters. The lodge was modernized from 1956 and could accommodate 12 teetotal women aged 60 or more in 1963. It had six one-bedroomed flats for elderly men or women and a warden's flat in 1989. It survives as a two-storeyed building of yellow brick with red-brick dressings, designed by A. R. Pite, with a small walled garden, in the shadow of the Frampton Park estate's ten-storeyed Pitcairn House.

Hackney War Memorial Homes, for married disabled ex-servicemen, were opened in 1923 on land at the west corner of Wattisfield and Fletching roads. Designed by Gunton & Gunton, they consisted of a two-storeyed red-brick range of six cottages, flanked by a pair of two-storeyed buildings each containing two cottages or flats, in 1991.[60]

Other almshouses, not intended for Hackney parishioners, included the Bakers' and the Jews' almshouses, the Goldsmiths' and Jewellers' asylum, and Robinson's Retreat.[61]

Distributive charities.[62] Thomas Heron, painter of London, by will proved 1603 left a rent charge on cottages in Grove Street to provide 12 penny

52 G.L.R.O., M79/LH/126/21. Inclosure of the site was permitted in 1741 (ibid. LH/50), although 1737 was given as the date of foundation in *121st Ann. Rep. of W. Hackney Almshos.* (1962) in Char. Com. files.
53 P.R.O., PROB 11/796, no. 208.
54 Robinson, *Hackney*, ii. 396.
55 H.A.D., 361.1 WES (*W. Hackney Almsho. Reps.* 1842–72), 31 May 1842.
56 H.A.D., Bldgs. file [cutting].
57 Watson, *Gentlemen*, 85.

58 H.A.D., Bldgs. file [correspondence 1967, 1971]; H.A.D., 361.1 NOR, P 4696–7.
59 Para. based on C. E. Moore-Crispin, *Hist. of Pilgrims' Lodge 1863–1963* (booklet in H.A.D.); H.A.D., cuttings.
60 Hackney, *Official Guide* [1925]; H.A.D., D/F/YAT/5/1–4; plaque on bldg.
61 Above, misc. institutions.
62 Details of capital or income after the apportionment between the three parishes in 1833 are for the whole of each char.

loaves every Sunday to the poor of Hackney. The income of £2 12s. was paid into a bread fund (below) in 1824 and still so paid in 1893, by which time it had been slightly reduced following the redemption of the charge for £87 stock in 1866.

Sir Henry Rowe by will proved 1612 left £200 to the Mercers' Co. of London for charitable payments, including £2 12s. a year to Hackney for 12 penny loaves on Sunday and £2 4s. for coals. In 1824 the parish received £2 12s. for its bread fund and, as a result of accumulation of stock, £3 13s. 2d. for its coal fund (below). The total payment had fallen slightly by 1893.

William Swaine by will dated 1613 left £100 for relief of the poor. Some 3½ a. were bought and in 1638 settled in trust. The rent was paid into the coal fund in 1824, when it was £13, and distributed as money in 1863, when it was £50. Most of the land was sold in 1882–3 and £4,905 stock, yielding £135, had been bought by 1893.

Margaret, widow of Thomas Audley, by will proved 1617 left £700 to the Skinners' Co. of London to provide £5 4s. a year for bread, £5 16s. for repair of the church or for fuel, £4 for repairing bridges and fences between Clapton and Shoreditch, and £20 for a schoolmaster.[63] The payments were made in 1824, when the £4 for bridges went to the coal fund, and 1863; they were redeemed in 1894, when £1,400 stock was transferred by the company.

Hugh Johnson, vicar of Hackney, by will proved 1618 left £200 to the Drapers' Co. of London, half of the interest to be distributed among the poor at Christmas; £5 was received in 1824, when it was given in sums of 10s., and 1893.

Valentine Poole of Old Ford, Stepney, by will proved 1624 left the rent of 5 a. called Butfield, in Well Street, for distribution among the poor. A building lease was sought without success in 1824, after the churchwardens had resumed ¾ a. and thereby reduced the rent from £30 to £24. The income was spent on bread in 1824 and on money payments in 1863. Enfranchisement was paid for in 1866 by the sale of stock which had been bought from sales of gravel. A small exchange was agreed with Cass's charity in 1862 and all the land was let on a building lease to John George Bishop in 1867, under which £375 10s. rent was paid and Poole, Valentine, and neighbouring roads were built up. The houses later accounted for most of the large income enjoyed by the St. John, Hackney, Joint Estates charities (below).

Richard Cheney by will proved 1625 gave land at West Ham (Essex) to the churchwardens of St. Mary Woolnoth (Lond.), for charities which included 40s. a year divided among four poor persons of Hackney. The same payment was received in 1824, although the value of the land had risen, and in 1863, after its sale and the purchase of £1,316 stock. An Order of 1893 allotted Hackney £206 stock, yielding £5 13s. 4d.

Henry Bannister by will dated 1625 gave £160 to the Goldsmiths' Co. of London, to pay £8 a year for the parish officers of Hackney to put out four apprentices. The income, being insufficient, had long been spent on coals until £12 a year was added in 1820 from Sir Thomas Vyner's charity (below). The joint sums were not wholly taken up by apprenticing in 1824; half of the £8 was spent on apprenticing and half was distributed in money in 1863. Payments were redeemed in 1886, when £270 stock was transferred by the company.

Sir Thomas Vyner by will dated 1664 left £80 for the purchase of lands, the rents for apprenticing. His younger son Thomas Vyner by will dated 1666[64] left £100 for lands, the rents to provide 12 penny loaves every Sunday and a money distribution at Christmas. The bequests, supplemented by the parish, were spent on buying property in Well Street, which in 1820 yielded £3 for coal, £12 for addition to Bannister's charity, and £10 divided into 20 gifts at Christmas. In 1824 the rents had reached £50, which in 1855 were spent on apprenticing, bread, and many gifts totalling £35 8s. The total income, from eight houses, was c. £346 in 1892.

David Dolben, bishop of Bangor and former vicar, in 1633 gave £30 for land, the rents to repair footpaths from Clapton to Hackney and support six families with the greatest charge of children.[65] George Humble by will dated 1633 gave £50 for land, the rents to provide bread for 12 poor. The bequests, supplemented by the parish, were spent on buying 4 a. in Hackney marsh in 1643. The income was £8 in 1824, divided between six families for Dolben's gift and the bread fund for Humble's, and in 1863; by 1824 nothing was spent on footpaths. The land came to form part of the parish's 27 a. in Hackney marsh (below) which were sold to the L.C.C. in 1893.

George Clarke by will dated 1668 left a rent charge of £6 on his lands in Hackney marsh; £1 was for a sermon and £5 were to be divided equally between the parish clerk, the sexton, the 6 women in Spurstowe's almshouses, and 12 poor housekeepers from Church Street and Mare Street. The money was applied as directed in 1824 and 1863. It was part of the rent paid by the lessee of the parish's lands in Hackney marsh until their sale in 1893.

Sir Stephen White in 1671 settled 3¼ a. at Clapton, the rent to relieve poor people chosen by the vestry at Easter. By will proved 1678 he also left £100 for land, the rent to provide twopenny loaves on Sundays, and 3 a. in Hackney marsh were settled in trust in 1680. The respective rents of £21 and £6 were both added to the bread fund in 1824 but the Clapton rent was distributed in money in 1863. The Clapton land was let on a building lease in 1865 to T. P. Glaskin, under which £138 10s. rent was paid and Winslade (later Stoneham) Road and Wood (later Rossington) Street were built up. Stock was bought with profits from the sale of gravel in the 1830s and the marsh lands were among those sold in 1893.

Anne Wood by will proved 1676 left 4¼ a. in Hackney marsh to provide £1 for a sermon on 5 Nov. and a distribution among 16 widows. The

63 Above, educ.
64 P.R.O., PROB 11/323 (P.C.C. 31 Carr).
65 Vestry mins. 5 May 1634.

income of £8 19s. 6d. was so spent in 1863, after ¼ a. of land had been sold to the River Lee trustees. The remaining 4 a. were among the marsh lands sold in 1893.

Thomas Jeamson, vicar of Hackney, in 1679 gave £100 to the Goldsmiths' Co. of London, to provide £2 for sermons on Good Friday and Ascension Day and a distribution at those times. The company paid £2 to the minister and £3 for bread in 1824 and 1863. It redeemed the payments by transferring £170 stock in 1886.

Thomas Wood (d. 1692), bishop of Lichfield and Coventry, gave £200 stock for the poor. Stock worth £414 8s. 11d. yielded £12 8s. 8d. for the coal fund in 1824 and money payments in 1863.

Esther, widow of Stephen White (Sir Stephen White's cousin), gave £60 for the poor by will proved 1683.[66] Richard South was found to have been the 'young gentleman not willing to discover his name'[67] who in 1691 had given £200. Both bequests, supplemented by the parish, were spent in 1694 on buying c. 3 a. near Grove Street, unspecified land in Hackney marsh, and a further 3 a. in the marsh, yielding in all £47 for the coal fund in 1824. The income was distributed in money in 1863. The marsh lands were sold in 1893, by which time the lands near Grove Street had also been sold.

Joanna Hussey in 1706 left a £4 rent charge on 2¼ a. in Hackney marsh. The sum was spent on coals in 1824 and money payments in 1863.

John Hammond by will dated 1716 gave lottery tickets worth £100 for weekly payments of 3s. to 12 housekeepers, the residue to apprentice a boy every four years. Investment yielded £4 17s., of which £3 12s. was spent on bread and £1 5s., previously spent on coals, was added to Vyner's and Bannister's apprenticing fund in 1824 and 1863.

Jeremiah Marlow by will dated 1764 left 20 a. for sale, the interest to relieve poor housekeepers with 40s. each. Stock worth £1,666 13s. 4d. was bought with accrued rent and the proceeds of the sale, producing £50 a year for 25 recipients chosen by the vestry in 1824 and £56 10s. 4d. in 1863.

Anthony André, father of Maj. John André,[68] by will proved 1769 left £50 stock, which produced £3 a year for the coal fund in 1824 and for money payments in 1863.

James Lance, who died in Jamaica, by will dated 1771 directed that £20 a year be paid for upkeep of the family vault and assisting four families in Hackney. His daughter Mrs. Newell accordingly transferred £978 stock in 1780. Jacob Franco by will dated 1774 left £50. Sarah Albert gave £50 for families to be assisted in the same manner as recipients of Lance's gift in 1785, when the vicar Thomas Cornthwaite added £100 out of accumulated offerings to her gift.[69] In 1824 the four charities together produced £37 3s. 6d. for gifts of £7 to five families, the residue for Lance's tomb or disbursement by the vicar. By 1863 the income was £40 17s. 2d., distributed in money.

Phillis Hindrey by will dated 1794 left £100 stock for repair of tombs, the residue for the poor. After a small addition by the vestry, the income was £5, distributed in money in 1824 and 1863.

Elizabeth Bagshawe by will dated 1797 left £1,000 stock for payments of 20s. a year, half of them to housekeepers of Clapton. The income was £30 in 1824, when 15 of the 30 recipients lived in Clapton, and in 1863, when it was still distributed in money.

Cecil Pitt by will dated 1800 left £100 stock for repairing his tomb and payments of 5s. to 10s. to women aged 60 or more who belonged to the Church of England. After a small addition by the vestry, the income was £5, distributed in money in 1824 and 1863.

Ann Sanford by will dated 1802 left the interest on £200 to buy meat and enough additional stock to produce £25 a year for distribution among five widows; the parish was also to receive the income from a quarter of the residue of her estate for meat. Stock worth c. £2,643 in 1824 yielded £25 for annuitants chosen by the vestry and £54 6s. for meat distributed by the vicar and churchwardens. In 1863 the £25 was distributed in pensions and £58 18s. was spent on bread.

Abraham Lopez Pereira by will dated 1812 gave £200 for coals. Stock worth c. £370 yielded £11 2s. 2d. for coal in 1824 and 1863.

Charles Digby by will dated 1812 gave £300 for the poor. After a small addition by the vestry, stock worth c. £433 yielded £13 for gifts of £1 in 1824 and 1863.

The parochial fund for fuel, to augment the fuel charities, was established from the balance of two local subscriptions, totalling c. £269, supplemented by the vicar. Stock worth £400 yielded £12 in 1824 and 1863.

Mrs. De Kewer's gift was so named by John De Kewer (d. 1818), who in 1816 gave £1,000 stock for coals and potatoes to poor residents around Grove Street and Well Street who regularly attended St. John's chapel. In 1823 the curate H. H. Norris spent £30 on potatoes and 100 sacks of coal and in 1863 £32 7s. was spent on bread and fuel.

William Lewis by will dated 1818 gave a £20 rent charge for repair of his tomb and payments of 40s. to widows. The charity was confined to the curtailed parish of Hackney in 1833 and paid to 10 widows until c. 1845, when it was found to be void under the Mortmain Acts.[70]

John Feild by will proved 1828 and Henry Feild by will proved 1836, both of them collarmakers of Stamford Hill, left respectively £1,000 stock and c. £500 stock for bread and coals. The incomes of £30 and £15 were spent on bread and fuel in 1863.

John Barnes by will proved 1844 left £100 in reversion for three widows of ratepayers. An abated sum was spent on c. £71 stock in 1879, producing dividends whose application was still undecided in 1894.

George Edward Carruthers by will proved

66 P.R.O., PROB 11/373, f. 66.
67 Vestry mins. 19 Jan. 1691.
68 Robinson, *Hackney*, ii. 385; Clarke, *Hackney*, 74;

D.N.B.
69 Vestry mins. 7, 21 Nov. 1785; 25 Nov. 1799.
70 H.A.D., J/V/CC/6, p. 8.

1848 left £100 stock for maintaining his tomb and for bread. The income was £3 in 1863, when it was spent on bread, and was administered with those of Allen's and Sedgwick's charities (below) in 1894.

Laetitia Powell by will proved 1849 left £1,000 for stock to make payments of not more than £10 to poor families. Stock worth c. £936 yielded £25 14s. 8d. in 1894.

Mary Allen in 1853 gave £100 for maintaining her tomb and for bread. The income was £3 in 1863 and was administered with Carruthers's and Sedgwick's charities in 1894.

William Brooks by will proved 1854 left £1,000 stock for maintaining his sister's tomb and payments to 12 families of West Hackney. The income of £27 10s. was distributed in money in 1894.

Marian Sedgwick by will proved 1860 left £50 stock for repair of memorials. The income was applied with Allen's and Carruthers's charities in 1894.

Nehemiah Robson by will proved 1863 left £100 stock to the rector and churchwardens of West Hackney for payment in money or kind on St. Thomas's day.

Robert Poole Barlow by will proved 1892 left £100 to the rector and churchwardens of West Hackney for money payments.

In 1833 the charities of Audley (for the schoolmaster), Clarke, Anne Wood, Jeamson, Lance, Albert, Cornthwaite, Hindrey, Bagshawe, Pitt, and Lewis were confined to the curtailed parish of Hackney, with those for Spurstowe's and Bishop Wood's almshouses, while Mrs. De Kewer's gift was confined to South Hackney, with Monger's almshouses. All the other charities were divided between the three parishes. Later charities were similarly apportioned: those of Carruthers and Allen were for the curtailed parish of Hackney alone, those of Brooks and Barlow were for West Hackney, and the rest were divisible.

St. John, Hackney, Joint Estates charities were established by a Scheme of 1898 for the charities of Swaine, Johnson, Poole, Rowe, South and Esther White, the Vyners, Sir Stephen White, Anne Wood, and Hussey. Six trustees were to be appointed by the trustees of Hackney Parochial charities, 3 by those of South Hackney's charities, and 3 by those of West Hackney's, all three groups of parochial charities being regulated by Schemes of the same date. The trustees were empowered to lease the property and were to divide the income, from rents or dividends, between the parochial charities, Hackney to receive half and South and West Hackney a quarter each. The most profitable land was that of Poole's charity, where the leases were to expire in 1945, followed by that of Sir Stephen White's. The Joint Estates derived rents totalling £27,182 in 1961–2, £55,447 in 1975–6, by which time Vyner Court had been built on White's land in Rossington Street, and £100,865 in 1977–8. By 1983–4 they had reached £196,921, to which rents from Well Street con-

tributed over £71,000, from the neighbouring Valentine Road over £30,000, and from Poole Road c. £29,000. Grants from the Joint Estates then accounted for most of the income of the three groups of parochial charities.

Hackney Parochial charities were regulated by Schemes of 1898 and 1904, vesting their management in the rector and churchwardens of St. John's, three representatives appointed by Hackney metropolitan borough, and five co-optative trustees. In addition to half of the net income of the Joint Estates, they were to receive half of the income of 36 distributive charities, all of which came from dividends and most of which after division yielded under £20; the largest, Swaine's and Ann Sanford's, yielded £61 6s. and £34 19s. respectively. Anne Wood's bequest of £1 for an annual sermon was set aside as an ecclesiastical charity, while that part of the Joint Estates' payment which represented the Vyners' charities might be spent on apprenticing or technical education. Provision was made for annual payments of £300 to the King's Nurses' Home so long as the parochial charities should be represented on its governing body, of £150 for nurses in the parish for five years, and for £200, to be augmented by £150 after five years, in pensions of 5s. to 10s. a week for up to six years, preference to be given to people who had been longest resident. The residue might be spent on loans or gifts of £40 or less, or on subscriptions to homes, hospitals, and benevolent funds. In 1933 Hackney was allotted £450 as its half share in the charity of Thomas Wyles, established by Emma Maria Wyles by will proved 1896. The income was to support childless widows aged 60 or more. A Scheme of 1957 permitted the charities' residual income to be spent on food or other gifts in kind. In 1961–2 the total income was c. £3,826, of which £2,800 came from the Joint Estates; c. £2,462 was spent in grants by the trustees. In 1986–7 the income was c. £28,000, of which £24,000 came from the Joint Estates; £10,466 was dispensed by the rector and £3,161 by a churchwarden, and grants were made to organizations, the largest being £2,075 to Homerton Space Project.

South Hackney Parochial charities, under a Scheme of 1898, were to be managed by the rector and churchwardens of South Hackney and, like Hackney Parochial charities, by three representative and five co-optative trustees. They received a quarter of the income of the Joint Estates and of 30 distributive charities, until a Scheme of 1900 provided for Mrs. De Kewer's gift to be administered separately by the rector and churchwardens. The income, from which payments for apprenticing or education were to be made under the Vyners' charities, was to maintain Monger's almshouses and pay the inmates, any residue to be spent like that of Hackney Parochial charities. The payments for education were transferred to a separate foundation in 1903.[71] South Hackney received £225 stock as its share of Wyles's

71 Above, educ.

charity in 1933. The types of relief that might be given were redefined in 1968. The total income in 1976 was c. £11,609, of which £3,850 came from the Joint Estates and £2,284 from rent from Norris's almshouses; expenditure was mainly on the almshouses.

West Hackney Parochial charities, under a Scheme of 1898, were to be administered by the rector and churchwardens of West Hackney and three representative and nine co-optative trustees. They received a quarter of the income of the Joint Estates and of 30 distributive charities. West Hackney received £225 stock as its share of Wyles's charity in 1933, although it was not formally included among the parochial charities until 1974. The total income in 1977–8 was £5,598, of which £4,000 came from the Joint Estates; expenditure included £1,500 on West Hackney almshouses.

INDEX

NOTE. An italic page number denotes a map or coat of arms on that page. A page number preceded by the letters *pl.* refers to one of the plates between pages 90 and 91.

Buildings and groups of buildings are indexed under their own names, without an indication of their location. Most references to roads, squares, and alleys are to their first occurrence in the text, to subsequent development, or to buildings which do not have individual names. Roads are indexed under their modern names, with cross-references. Proper names which occur only incidentally have not been indexed.

CORRIGENDA TO VOLUMES
IV AND IX

Earlier lists of corrigenda will be found in Volumes I and III–IX

Vol. IV,	page 199*a*,	line 35, *for* 'Typical of the passengers was Thomas Port, a' *read* 'One of its guards was Thomas Port, son of a'
"	" 199,	note 43, *for* 'Robbins, *Middlesex*, 78' *read* '*Greentrees*' (Central Mdx. Fam. Hist. Soc. Jnl.), vii(1), 10.'
Vol. IX,	page ix,	s.v. North End, *for* 'Spaniard's End' *read* 'the Spaniards (later Heath End)'
"	" 4,	map, *under* 'To Finchley' *delete* 'and M1' *and under* 'To Hendon' *add* 'and M1'
"	" 9*b*,	line 29, *for* 'Spaniard's' *read* 'Heath'
"	" 26,	note 4, *add* '; *Recollections of Thos. Graham Jackson* (1950), 19–20.'
"	" 66*b*,	line 4 from end, *for* 'SPANIARD'S END' *read* 'THE SPANIARDS (later HEATH END)'
"	" 67*a*,	line 32, *for* 'Spaniard's' *read* 'Heath'
"	" 70*b*,	line 1, *for* 'Spaniard's' *read* 'Heath'
"	" 71*a*,	line 37, *for* 'Spaniard's' *read* 'Heath'
"	" 146*a*,	line 31, *for* 'The house was sold in 1923.' *read* 'That house was sold in 1875, as was its successor in Redington Road in 1923.'
"	" 146*a*,	line 32, *for* '1924' *read* '1928'
"	" 146,	note 10, *after* 'file 1' *add* '; Ch. of Eng. Record Centre, files CC 51511, E 2015, and K 10059.'
"	" 160*b*,	line 2 from end, *for* '[C.643-I]' *read* '[C.6438-I]'
"	" 208*b*,	line 35, *for* '1901' *read* '1900'
"	" 240*b*,	line 10 from end, *for* 'founder' *read* 'developer'
"	" 273*c*,	s.v. architects, *for* 'Davis & Emmanuel' *read* 'Davis & Emanuel'
"	" 279*a*,	*for* 'Colonades' *read* 'Colonnades'
"	" 279*c*,	*for* 'Davis & Emmanuel' *read* 'Davis & Emanuel'
"	" 281*a*,	*for* 'Emmanuel' *read* 'Emanuel'
"	" 284*c*,	*add new entry* 'Heath End, 9, 66, 67, 70–1; *and see* Spaniards'
"	" 296*b*,	s.v. Simmons, *for* 'John' *read* 'Jacob'
"	" 296*c*,	*for* 'Spaniard's End' *read* 'Spaniards, the (later Heath End)'